Larry Cohen : The Radical Allegories
of an Independent Filmmaker

# Larry Cohen

## The Radical Allegories of an Independent Filmmaker

Tony Williams

McFarland & Company, Inc., Publishers
*Jefferson, North Carolina, and London*

*Frontispiece:* Larry Cohen ponders his next scene.

British Library Cataloguing-in-Publication data are available

Library of Congress Cataloguing-in-Publication Data

Williams, Tony, 1946 Jan. 11–
    Larry Cohen : the radical allegories of an independent filmmaker /
Tony Williams.
        p.   cm.
    Filmography: p.
    Includes bibliographical references and index.
    ISBN 0-7864-0350-0 (library binding : 50# alkaline paper) ∞
    1. Cohen, Larry, 1941–    — Criticism and interpretation.
I. Title.
PN1998.3.C664W56   1991
791.43'0233'092 — dc21                                               97-10731
                                                                     CIP

Manufactured in the United States of America

*McFarland & Company, Inc., Publishers
  Box 611, Jefferson, North Carolina 28640*

To Kathleen Ensor

# Table of Contents

# Acknowledgments

I wish to acknowledge the following for help at various stages of this project: Bryon Kluesner and the staff of Varsity Video, Carbondale, Ill.; Mike Nevins for supplying information about "Branded" credits; Boyd Magers of *Videowest* for video copies of various episodes from "Blue Light" and "Branded"; *Sight and Sound* for permission to reproduce some of my original interview material, which first appeared in the magazine during 1983–84; Mon Ayash of *Forgotten Hollywood* for a much sought-after "Arrest and Trial" episode; WorldVision Enterprises for access to *In Broad Daylight*; WGN Television for a "Rat Patrol" episode; Kevin and Kim Koron for technical assistance and directing my attention to relevant material; Mike Robbins for recording *Man on the Outside*; Daniel Overturf for recording *The American Success Company*; Mike Brosco for obtaining *Scandalous*; Joe Garrett for duplicating some of the stills used in this book; Jerry Ohlinger and his staff at the Movie Material Store, New York; the Humanities librarians of the Morris Library of Southern Illinois University at Carbondale; Vincent Lacey; The Museum of Television and Radio for access to "Coronet Blue"; Janelle Webb Cohen, Michael Moriarty, and James Dixon for interviews given; Larry Cohen himself for his generosity in supplying video copies of his early television work, patience in agreeing to many long hours of interviews, and dedication in checking the record and allowing the facts to speak for themselves; and last, but not least, Kathleen Ensor for good humor, understanding, and support.

# Introduction

Larry Cohen is a director and writer who has broken many Hollywood rules to produce an interesting body of work over the past four decades. This book initially was planned as an examination of the films he directed. But, as the project began, it became obvious that Cohen's significance was not just confined to films. It extended into the areas of live television, New York–based series such as "The Defenders" and "The Nurses," Hollywood television episodes, television movies, screenplays written for other directors, and theatrical plays. Cohen is also a valuable oral source for information about many significant social and cultural movements within American society. He is as insightful about film and television as Samuel Pepys was in relation to the late Stuart Monarchy in England.

In cinema studies, authorship is usually confined to the person who directs a film. If the director has also written and produced the work, critical application of what is commonly known as "the auteur theory" (or the more appropriately original "la politique des auteurs") appears straightforward. That is, unless the critic subscribes to post-structuralist dogmas surrounding Foucault's definition of "the death of the author" or Roland Barthes' notorious axiom of the author being "written" rather than actively writing.

In any case, examining a figure as complex and iconoclastic as Larry Cohen means rejecting the usual critical theories. An author may actively influence a work as well as undergo constraint by social, industrial, and unconscious forces. Definitions surrounding "The Strange Case of Alfred Hitchcock" by critics such as Robin Wood and Tania Modleski similarly unveil a director both antagonistic to, as well as constrained by, the dominant ideology his films attack.[1] Many cultural traditions influence Cohen, such as Hollywood cinema, Hitchcock's progressive vision, and satirical and social justice themes endemic to American Jewish filmmaking. However, these influences are reworked and reinterpreted in the cinema of Larry Cohen.

Authorship is a complicated process eluding precise attempts to define its nature. An author may also exist in areas beyond the director's chair. This is particularly the case with Larry Cohen. He is also a writer who has contributed work for other directors in film and television. In many cases, the screenwriter may have more claims for authorship than the actual director. Thus, the scenarist may be

1

**Larry Cohen (courtesy of Larry Cohen).**

an invisible ghost on the set, acting as an alternative voice in a story or script commenting upon and contradicting the undiscerning minds of those acting, producing, and directing a work intended as harmless entertainment. This definition of authorship is deliberately fluid and indefinable. It is one made less out of perversity than of respect for the subject it covers. Never rigid or dogmatic, this definition intends to be productively iconoclastic. It mirrors the significant role of Larry Cohen whose authorship often exists in areas other than the director's chair.

This book attempts to trace the manifold operations of Larry Cohen's authorship. The flexible definition of Cohen's authorship parallels the many diverse historical encounters with changing industrial factors affecting his work. Larry Cohen's activities, characters, and situations are never static. His work often fictionally and factually reproduces the complex nature of an American society most mainstream representations attempt to deny. The films of Larry Cohen have emerged from different historical eras and respond to varying contemporary issues. Although circumstances may have changed, necessitating the director's movement away from idiosyncratic appropriation of seventies horror to satiric comedy during the next decade, the concerns linking his work are often similar. Fears about parenthood, family conflicts, the alienation and oppression of those designated as "others" in American society, and contradictions between socially expected roles and individual personalities appear in works as diverse as the "My Name is Martin Burnham" episode of "Arrest and Trial" (1963), *It's Alive* (1973), *Perfect Strangers* (1984), and *Island of the Alive: It's Alive III* (1987).

We tend easily to equate a director with the author losing sight of the fact that in many cases the real distinctive authorship of a work may reside in the screenplay and, in certain instances, the story. Tracing the historical development of a future director who wrote pilots for series such as "Branded" and "The Invaders," as well as significantly reworking themes in established series such as "The Fugitive," often leads to revealing insights into the very concept of authorship. The whole production process appears as one of conflict and contradiction. This is particularly so when a number of different texts directed and produced by other names contain insights and ideas later found fully realized in films directed by the same writer many years later.

Larry Cohen's work represents a complex and contradictory entity of achievements, frustrations, and failures. The same is true of any director, including any frequently cited "great" such as Ford, Hawks, Hitchcock, and Lang. However, Larry Cohen's durability, persistence, and accomplishment in an often hostile climate represents one of the most significant and unsung chapters within American cinema and television. Despite his maverick status and supposedly undisciplined techniques lies a talent that has produced several works radically commenting upon American ideological constraints in a manner unthinkable in any mainstream big-budget production. Dealing with themes involving history, gender, and politics, often in a satirical and provocative manner, Cohen's work represents a marginalized, but important, tradition within American cinema. Although his work is often disparaged as "comic strip" or unprofessional, it has far more in common with American cultural traditions than most critics realize. Working in the low-budget world of independent cinema, Larry Cohen has produced a remarkable body of iconoclastic work radically engaging with dominant currents in American society, satirizing outmoded and dangerous conventions in the most subversive manner possible. His achievements deserve both respect and recognition.

# PART ONE:
# A CAREER STUDY

# What Makes Cohen Unique

In American cinema today, Larry Cohen remains unknown to the vast majority of reviewers and audiences. While most people readily recognize names such as Woody Allen, Francis Ford Coppola, Steven Spielberg, Oliver Stone, and Quentin Tarantino as denoting particular films within a less productive, but highly hyped, world of popular Hollywood cinema, Larry Cohen remains marginalized and neglected. Critically misunderstood, his films suffering from limited theatrical distribution, Cohen nonetheless has made distinctive contributions to both film and television. But his reputation and work still await appropriate recognition.

Although some critics such as Fred Camper, J. Hoberman, and Robin Wood have written major articles about Cohen, they remain in the minority. Though featured in mainstream film publications such as *Film Comment, Movie*, and *Sight and Sound*, the director has only received sporadic and inconsistent attention. During the seventies, Cohen became linked with the new wave of American low-budget commercial directors such as John Carpenter, Wes Craven, Brian DePalma, Tobe Hooper, and George Romero, whose early work initially promised a revitalization of a classical Hollywood tradition once producing major figures such as Howard Hawks, Alfred Hitchcock, Douglas Sirk, Anthony Mann, and many others. But while Craven, DePalma, and Hooper gained entry into the system, changing economic and historical circumstances adversely affected their talents. Some (like DePalma) continued directing films lacking the promise of their earlier efforts, while others (like Hooper) became discarded by the system. Furthermore, certain developments within the film industry resulted in the virtual disappearance of the low-budget independent filmmaking world where these talents began their careers. George Romero never gained appropriate recognition nor was welcomed, in eighties Hollywood. The commercial failure of *Day of the Dead* and the dissolution of his partnership with Laurel Entertainment dealt him a professional blow he never fully recovered from. Also, Larry Cohen became stereotyped as a director associated with a family horror genre belonging to the seventies era whose radical potentialities became drowned by the reactionary backlash of "slasher films" in the eighties. The vast majority of viewers usually consider Larry Cohen a seventies director. But Cohen also produced significant work before and after this period. He is a creative artist whose vision transcends any attempts to define it rigidly under generic boundaries or historical eras. This book intends to document the full story of Larry Cohen's contributions to American film and television and argue that his highly important achievements deserve appropriate recognition.

I initially intended to write this book about the films of Larry Cohen beginning with *Bone* in 1972 and concluding with his last work (originally intended for theatrical release), *The Ambulance*. It was to be a book about a film director. However, on closer examination, I discovered a talent defying any form of rigid classification, paralleling the diverse nature of whatever subject he chooses to direct. Cohen's career exhibits no identifiable patterns easily accommodated to the usual interpretations of authorship. He began writing teleplays at a young age, contributing story lines to series he wrote or created, moved on to screenplays, and finally turned to directing after becoming dissatisfied with the way his scripts were treated. Although he began directing films in 1972, he continued to write for both film and television as well as exploring new options for his work in the developing technologies of cable and video.

Usually, the director is regarded as the real author of a work, a definition indisputable in the case of any Larry Cohen film credited as "Written, Produced, and Directed by Larry Cohen." But authorship is a complex process involving other contributions beyond the director, such as cultural circumstances, historical factors and creative input by screenwriters and actors. Since filmmaking is generally a collaborative process, distinctive authorial presences may include other features over and above the individual director. Over 20 years ago Richard Corliss argued for the validity of the screenwriter as auteur, pointing out that in certain cases a work's distinctive qualities may belong to its scenarist.[1] In many cases, particular episodes of "Branded," "The Fugitive," "The Defenders," "Arrest and Trial," and "The Blue Light" rise above the level of formula productions to reveal a particular vision that also characterizes future films directed by the writer of these early teleplays. To dismiss these works from consideration not only ignores their historical and artistic significance, but also denies important evidence of a developing authorial talent attempting to transcend constraining circumstances within television production.

Despite certain unifying consistencies, Cohen's work also represents different responses to changing industrial and social conditions. He began writing during the last years of live television, contributing to acclaimed series such as "The Defenders," creating pilots for Hollywood series such as "Branded" and "The Invaders," and moved on to screenplays before directing his first film. Cohen's work has embraced different styles, ranging from realistic television narrative to independent filmmaking and comic-strip stylization. He has often altered his style to adapt to changing historical and industrial circumstances. Even after directing, he still contributes ideas for television movies and occasional episodes of series such as "N.Y.P.D. Blue." However, Cohen draws a distinction between the works he regards as personal and those that have suffered interference by the system. But rather than adopting a pseudonym and becoming an "Allan Smithee" for the less satisfactory television productions ruined by uncomprehending producers, he honestly allows his name to remain on the credits. Despite changes in his career and the various styles he has chosen to embrace at one point or another, Larry Cohen's work exhibits certain striking continuities in story line and direction, continuities best described by the term "radical allegory."

According to Raymond Williams' investigation of the complex ways definitions change over time, the term "radical" may involve the widely understood general sense of "radical re-examination" of certain aspects of contemporary society. It offers a way of avoiding dogmatic associations "while at the same time reasserting the need for vigorous and fundamental change."[2] An allegory may be understood as a "description, or narrative conveyed by means of another differing from it, but resembling it sufficiently to suggest it,"[3] often stating a particular message of human and social value. In many cases, seemingly harmless and unthreatening genres may become subverted by an interrogative examination both of their very premises and the nature of a society they belong to.

Though these associations appear contradictory, they define the essential nature of Larry Cohen's work. The director never repeats himself but constantly seeks new forms and narrative situations to develop his particular insights. Despite the different forms of his films and screenplays, they all operate in an allegorical manner using standard formulas to express a particular message, implicitly asserting the need for a positive change in human personalities dominated by stifling social conventions. Rather than rigidly belonging to particular generic types, his films operate in loosely allegorical ways. Their special messages often transcend the rigid labels of "blaxploitation" or "horror film" usually applied by reviewers. Cohen's films have general connections with the particular genres he chooses to work in. But more often than not they move far beyond their generic confines. If Larry Cohen rejects categorizing *Black Caesar* as a "blaxploitation" film and *It's Alive* as a "horror film" by arguing for a more complex understanding of the material which transcends simplified formula definitions, he challenges his viewers either to superficially accept his work on the level of mindless entertainment or examine it in detail to discover deeper levels of meaning. Visually and thematically a Larry Cohen film provides challenges to viewers. What may appear raw, unprofessional, unpolished, exhibiting a supposedly infantile comic-strip style, really contains deeper levels of meaning. Cohen's work never fits into any coherent category. It changes from one film to another, exposing audiences to challenging, complex, and fantastic situations never entirely removed from everyday reality. A Larry Cohen film contains far more radical ideas than the average major Hollywood production.

Any attempt to define Larry Cohen's career in a rigid manner faces major problems. As director and screenwriter, his work displays a diverse heterogeneity often making convenient classification impossible. Cohen's work contains recognizable elements of satire, parody, and social justice motifs that are fundamental components of an American Jewish cinematic tradition defined by David

Desser and Lester D. Friedman, a tradition existing alongside the dominant Hollywood cinema.[4] Like Woody Allen, Mel Brooks, and Sidney Lumet, Cohen also began his career in television. In her interesting essay on Jewish humor, Patricia Erens notes that both Allen and Brooks "often deal with difference, especially religious and racial difference — difference between insiders and outsiders, those who belong and those who don't. As descendants of a long line of men and women with a history of persecution in alien communities throughout the world, they are almost genetically aware of the precarious position of those who live on the margins of society."[5] Associations with this tradition certainly appear in Cohen's work. The monster babies in the *It's Alive* films, the alien Messiah of *God Told Me To,* and most of Cohen's characters, from the girl in *Bone* to others in *Perfect Strangers* and *Special Effects,* are all socially marginal. Cohen's fictionally autobiographical play *Washington Heights* presents young Danny slowly becoming aware of the ostracized position the surrounding culture and environment has placed him in. But far more important is the fact that he decides to fight back despite overwhelming odds. Like the rest of Cohen's work, *Washington Heights* breaks generic rules. It is a creative heterogeneous work linking artificially opposed realms of autobiography and fiction.

Humor plays a significant role in the majority of Cohen's films, either indirectly (the pre-delivery scenes and police assault on an innocent baby in *It's Alive;* the fly swatting sequence in *The Private Files of J. Edgar Hoover*) or directly (*Bone, Full Moon High, Wicked Stepmother,* and *The Ambulance*). But it is not "a characteristically Jewish mode of expression" fitting the requirements of an ethnic cinematic definition suggested by Desser and Friedman. Many instances certainly exist of parallels to American Jewish culture in Larry Cohen's films. The movies stress survival, a quality which Sarah Blacher Cohen describes as underlying the essence of Jewish humor. Like Stanley Elkin's writings, a Larry Cohen film also involves qualities of comic detachment and ironic independence, its monsters, maniac cops, and divine aliens containing deliberate qualities of absurdity and grotesqueness. As Mark Shechnar points out, the golden rule of any comedian is to make the familiar even more strange. It would be highly surprising if Larry Cohen totally avoided these significant patterns from his own cultural tradition. Such patterns are definitely present in his work. But Cohen works in a different entertainment world from that once inhabited by Fannie Brice, Eddie Cantor and Al Jolson.[6] If an American Jewish sensibility occurs within Cohen's films, it operates in an indirect, almost indistinct manner. The work of Larry Cohen features a universal critique. Although its origins may emerge from American Jewish roots, no special plea is made for ethnic awareness or special privilege. Socially generated alienation affects gays, women, Chinese, Japanese, and African-Americans as well as Jews. Cohen's films and writings mediate a universal awareness of oppression. Cohen's humor and social justice motifs operate less ethnically, but more on a general level, seeing all human beings, whatever their sex, race, and class, as being entitled to dignity and respect.

While Cohen's films contain traces of a gender role disequilibrium common to Woody Allen, the parodies of Mel Brooks, and social justice concerns found within Sidney Lumet's works, his individual films, screenplays, and television productions transcend their origins from this type of American Jewish cinematic tradition. Like the generic labels critics seek to attach to Cohen's films, these cultural elements become modified in individual works that often move in far more complex directions. For example, Cohen's early awareness of Nazi persecution and genocide may have provided the origins for his understanding of the mutant babies in the *It's Alive* films. However, the overall message of these films is that anybody, at any time, may find himself defined as an "alien" or "freak" in a society that suddenly turns against him. Cohen's outsiders soon find themselves alienated from a social order they once regarded as benevolent and protective of their individual rights. This dilemma affects characters as diverse as Frank Davies, his wife Lenore, Gene and Jody Scott, and Stephen and Ellen Jarvis. But what really counts is their recognition of underlying psychological structures behind such alienation and their refusal to fall into society's convenient scapegoat mechanisms, by either blaming themselves as victims or violently projecting their repressed tensions on to conveniently defined "monsters." Cohen's characters often finally move towards self-identification with those they once denied. The personal solutions reached by all major characters in the *It's Alive* films necessarily lead toward another form of society to replace the old, corrupt order. But in the meantime, Cohen's characters must learn to exist in and come to terms with a life-threatening society before moving on to that ideal goal. A Larry Cohen film often ends in a stalemate situation. The director never offers any false hopes for his characters, only the necessity for continuing struggle.

Larry Cohen's career began well before his debut as a director. Like Martin Scorsese and many of the so-called "movie brat" generation, he grew up on Hollywood cinema, sitting through films as many times as he could. Even before he began college, the fledgling filmmaker began writing and directing his own radio and movie plays. In many ways, Larry Cohen typifies the best of a self-educated principle found in talents such as Jack London and James Jones, learning in a spontaneous, self-aware manner, taking recognizable formulas and molding them according to particular creative needs. Cohen's actual debut began at the age of 17 with the televising of his script for the 1958 Kraft Mystery Theatre presentation of *87th Precinct*. Like his later teleplay, "Night Cry," it appeared during the final years of the "golden age" of live American television. During the early sixties, Cohen contributed several scripts for highly acclaimed series such as "The Defenders" and "The Nurses," filmed in New York by Herbert Brodkin productions. Although no longer live, these series continued an important tradition of serious social drama begun during the previous decade by innovative talents in American television. Moving to Hollywood, Cohen wrote and created pilots for series such as "Branded," "The Invaders," "Coronet Blue," and "Griff." Although most "Branded" episodes are little different than contemporary western series such as "The Rifleman," Cohen intended the whole series to be about a blacklisted cowboy. The episodes he did write, such as "Survival" and "The Vindicator," rise far above mere formula time-fillers and deal with socially relevant issues. As originally conceived, *The Invaders* was meant to be an allegory about the hysteria and paranoia of the McCarthy era, using the science-fiction genre in a manner similar to *Invasion of the Bodysnatchers* (1956). Cohen also wrote teleplays for other series such as "Arrest and Trial" and "Sam Benedict," many of which radically subvert the intentions of the producers. As Richard Corliss argues, the screenwriter (and also any television dramatist) has equal claim to be regarded as an author in certain instances. In many cases, television series crediting Larry Cohen as writer often display distinctive features of a personal authorship also characterizing the works he later directed. On many occasions, a script far transcends direction. Episodes such as "Branded"'s "The Vindicator," "The Fugitive"'s "Escape into Black," and John Flynn's *Best Seller* are recognizably Larry Cohen works. They bear little relationship to other films associated with the actual directors of these works. Larry Cohen has been active for nearly 40 years in television and cinema. Although his films appeal to many audiences, their independent low-budget character often offends mainstream reviewers who castigate them as poverty-row productions. But Cohen's cinema resembles those old Monogram and Eagle-Lion productions that flourished during the heyday of the old studio system. These minor studios often produced far more interesting films than MGM, Paramount, and other "majors." While the Hollywood studio system was once prolific and flexible, allowing for the presence of low-budget films by directors such as Samuel Fuller, Anthony Mann, and Edgar G. Ulmer, contemporary economic factors affecting theatrical distribution (as well as the vast amounts of necessary advertising revenue) make the appearance of minor, yet creatively significant, films on the theatrical circuit far more difficult. It is far more possible to achieve creativity within low-budget cinema than within a contemporary Hollywood now producing wasteful blockbusters. This is something Larry Cohen and John Cassavetes discovered. Although they made different types of films, both preferred working within a low-budget filmmaking system free from Hollywood constraints such as accountants, market-researched, economically safe movies, and box-office stars.

Larry Cohen is a very talented writer. He has made distinctive contributions to both film and television. His recognizable concerns often appear in works he did not direct, such as the "Vindicator" episode of "Branded" and Sydney Lumet's *Guilty as Sin,* which exhibit his own particular claims for authorship. Even if a director never entirely realizes the thematic insights of a Larry Cohen screenplay, certain motifs often appear as recognizably distinctive features. Although most authorship theories elevate director above scenarist, they often ignore highly relevant factors within the film industry itself. Cinema is a collaborative process. It achieves its highest powers of expression when all elements — director, scenarist, photographer, producer, sound person — work in cohesion. While some critics place the director at the center, creatively organizing these various productive forces, other factors are also relevant. Andre Bazin believed any director in Hollywood operated within a particular cultural, industrial, and historical context influencing the final film.[7] Despite his Mercury Theatre achievements, Orson Welles could not have directed *Citizen Kane* without the creative involvement of RKO technicians. He also had the advantage of directing in a studio open to his ideas at that particular time. Larry Cohen has always collaborated with a very close-knit group of colleagues, including Peter Sabiston, Janelle Cohen, Andrew Duggan, Michael Moriarty, and James Dixon, whose names frequently appear in the credits of his films.

Cohen is also aware of Hollywood's cultural tradition. Viewing movies from a very early age, he became aware of the importance of various genres such as westerns, gangster movies, and science-fiction films produced during the golden age of the studio system. In *Black Caesar*, Cohen used *Little Caesar* as a model upon which he developed his own particular vision of an African-American gangster film. *The Private Files of J. Edgar Hoover* uses the propagandist biopic formula of Mervyn LeRoy's *The F.B.I. Story* (1959) to deconstruct the Hoover image. Cohen directed *Black Caesar* in an era that featured a proliferation of ephemeral "blaxploitation" movies such as *Shaft, Slaughter, Cleopatra Jones,* and *Superfly.* These films used traditional Hollywood gangster and private-eye formulas to depict super-cool black heroes. But *Black Caesar* broke all the rules of the "blaxploitation" genre by presenting its hero as both contaminated by false values and destructive to everyone near him. The moral was already present in *Little Caesar.* But Cohen added his own particular interrogative vision to the generic formula and completely undermined it. This is a process characteristic of both his films and uncompromising television dramas. One of the many pleasures of viewing a Larry Cohen film is seeing his use of former actors from the heyday of old Hollywood. Whether Broderick Crawford, Bette Davis, Dan Dailey, Celeste Holm, Sam Levene, June Havoc, Lloyd Nolan or Evelyn Keyes, Cohen uses these actors reverentially as well as self-reflectively. Broderick Crawford's performance in *The Private Files of J. Edgar Hoover* evokes his well-known roles in *All the King's Men* and the long-running television series "Highway Patrol." At the same time, Crawford's role as Hoover is a commentary on the dangerous aspect of the heroic image within American culture. Using journalists, such as Walter Winchell, and the Hollywood studios, the real J. Edgar Hoover used contemporary media mechanisms to promote his image as America's top cop in a starring role. Like a jealous movie star, Crawford's Hoover actively seeks to destroy rivals such as his *alter ego* John Dillinger and "rising stars" like Melvyn Purvis he believes will challenge his position in the system. Hoover also becomes a prisoner of his image, like Norma Desmond in *Sunset Boulevard.* Cohen's films operate on many different levels. His less successful *Wicked Stepmother* arose from the idea of returning from a holiday and finding the witch-like persona of Bette Davis within one's very home. The more interesting features of the film involve satirical attacks on American values such as affluent consumerism and television game shows.

Due to his desire to maintain independence and avoid the interference of major Hollywood studios, Larry Cohen has kept himself free from Hollywood constraints affecting big-budget productions. As a result, his low-budget films are usually dismissed and ignored by mainstream critics. Stereotyped by most reviewers as a B-movie director working in exploitation genres lacking glossy standards of Hollywood professionalism, Cohen has suffered undeserved neglect. But his films contain radical insights into the oppressive and illusionary values of American life that most film and television productions conveniently ignore. Although films such as *It's Alive* (1973) and *A Return to Salem's Lot* (1987) contain monsters and vampires, these generic horror features function as allegorical devices designed to direct audience attention towards human dilemmas within the narratives. These features represent the equivalent of Alfred Hitchcock's "McGuffin," a plot element that is really marginal to the director's real concerns. Although the uranium in *Notorious* (1946) appears to be an important motivating device, it is actually less significant than Hitchcock's interest in the social forces oppressing both Alicia (Ingrid Bergman) and Devlin (Cary Grant). Eventually, like Roger Thornhill in *North By Northwest*, Devlin manages to oppose the "law of the father," whose designs have made Alicia a "guilty woman" in danger of dying for the cause of Western democracy. Similarly, in both *It's Alive* and *A Return to Salem's Lot*, the key moments respectively involve Frank Davis and Joe Weber discovering their true humanity. While Frank briefly identifies with the son his society categorizes as a monster, Joe finally opposes the bloodsucking representatives of a system he once identified with.

Cohen uses satire and comedy as a radical weapon against consumerist and gender manipulations within American society. Ideas in his films often emerge in comic manifestations. The screwball comedy *Full Moon High* (1981) contains devastating assaults against American conformity and rigid gender roles. But Cohen is no theoretician or dogmatic political director. He is a spontaneous cineaste whose ideas flow freely into his films. Like Howard Hawks and Alfred Hitchcock, Cohen often expresses ideas in natural, unpretentious manner. His films continue the radical expression of ideas once characteristic of the best traditions of Hollywood cinema but no longer possible today within contemporary corporate structures. Refusing to compromise, Cohen chooses the territory of low-budget cinema rather than making himself vulnerable to a seductive string of financial successes involving the unavoidable industrial handicaps of constraint and control.

Cohen's major box-office successes were *Black Caesar* and *It's Alive*. Rather than being individual one-shot successes dependent upon fashionable generic movements, both films really deserve to be seen in the context of the director's preceding and succeeding work. Cohen's first film, *Bone*, is a humorous and biting satire of race relations and Beverly Hills lifestyles. The ideas expressed are similar to those within the visually constrained television world of "The Defenders" and "The Nurses" as well as theatrical plays such as *The Nature of the Crime*, *Motive* (aka *Trick*), and *Washington Heights*. Although styles and formulas may differ, the ideas often contain remarkable consistencies.

The cinema of Larry Cohen often appears devoid of visual and thematic personal signatures once thought characteristic of auteur works. Unlike Francis

Coppola, Brian DePalma, and Martin Scorsese, a Larry Cohen film contains little evidence of identifiable visual flamboyance. Defining a Larry Cohen style appears difficult. However, Cohen's films do contain characteristic features. He may best be described as a creator of narrative tension, involving a strong text, historical circumstances, industrial factors, and social formation. His position resembles the final definition of authorship contained in John Caughie's *Theories of Authorship*. Examining several theories, ranging from the director as an ahistorical personal force to post-structuralist "Death of the Author" theories, Caughie concludes that the director still has a significant place within cinema. But rather than understanding the director as a consistent, coherent solitary subject, the figure is really influenced by "other practices and formations," especially social, historical, and psychoanalytic factors affecting the production of a particular work.[8] The supposedly problematic nature of Larry Cohen's work really represents an accurate reflection of a talent affected by many changing contemporary developments affecting the media. Devoid of a studio system that nurtured the distinctive talents of John Ford, Howard Hawks, Alfred Hitchcock, Anthony Mann, and Douglas Sirk, Larry Cohen's cinema has taken a particular distinctive direction.

Cohen's films combine supposedly oppositionally diverse areas of classical and independent cinema. He frequently adopts a "stock company" filmmaking approach characteristic of John Ford and Howard Hawks. But it is one outside the Hollywood system. However, Cohen's tight shooting schedules, rapid improvisation on the set, and editing techniques often lead reviewers to dismiss his work unjustifiably as mediocre and incompetent because it does not reflect acceptable Hollywood professional standards. However, such features also characterize the early work of Woody Allen and the major work of John Cassavetes, both of whom chose to work outside the system, eschewing Hollywood professionalism for their own distinctive cinematic visions. Both these directors applied non–Hollywood independent cinematic techniques to the narratives they chose to film. Cohen does the same thing, but in a different way. Describing his work as "guerrilla filmmaking," he adopts these techniques for the purpose of making his films and releasing them to a wider audience, rather than a limited independent film circuit or isolated groups of fans. In this way, he avoids Hollywood control and interference during all stages of production.

The different cinematic worlds of Woody Allen and John Cassavetes also feature interesting parallels to the films of Larry Cohen. Like Allen, Cohen often brings an American Jewish sensibility to questions of gender and social change. But it occurs in a more indirect manner, having little recourse to specifically Jewish formal devices, such as the *schlemiel* character in Jerry Lewis' films, as well as in Allen's. While Cassavetes often undertook acting assignments to finance his work, Cohen writes television pilots, screenplays, and television movies to gain the initial revenue to begin his films. But while Woody Allen's early films and John Cassavetes's work often exhibited unpolished non–Hollywood, independent film features, critics generally ignored the "flaws" to acclaim the innovative nature of their work. Allen's *Take the Money and Run* and *Bananas* contain the same type of raw shooting techniques, frenetic editing, and satiric humor as Cohen's productions. Cassavetes' *Shadows* and *Faces* are definite products of low-budget cinema. But critics usually turn a blind eye when considering raw stylistic features in "name" directors. They excuse the rough editing and often labored improvisational performances in a Cassavetes film. But they criticize these very "faults" in directors not admitted to an elitist canon. Larry Cohen has not gained the type of critical recognition awarded to his approved independent-minded contemporaries. Yet, in many ways, his films, in attempting to appeal to a much wider audience, are more radical and iconoclastic than the works of these two other directors.

J. Hoberman, Robin Wood, and Fred Camper are three major critics aware of Cohen's work. Reviewing *Q— The Winged Serpent*, Hoberman noted Cohen's work as featuring parallels to the films of independent maverick Samuel Fuller. Fuller's "Written, Produced, and Directed" credits parallel those in a Larry Cohen film. Both directors used a particular type of excessive style generally antithetical to most major reviewers. Hoberman commented on *Q*'s relationship to Fuller's *The Naked Kiss.* He regarded Cohen's work as giving more expression to "the delirious tabloid quality of American life than any film since *The Naked Kiss.*" Later, Hoberman recognized a major Cohen theme in the little-known *Perfect Strangers,* in which a child "becomes the site on which a succession of passively or actively (and sometimes) ludicrously modern adults project their fears."[9] Hoberman was the only critic to speak positively of a particular aspect of Cohen's style having key associations with a comic-strip formula most respectable critics disdain. Noting Cohen's position as screenwriter of the abortive *I, the Jury* (finally directed by Richard Heffron), the critic regretted that Cohen did not direct the film and pointed out that "even as it is, it's filled with the sort of goonish wit fastidious uptown reviewers often think unintentional." Hoberman also recognized the main thrust of Cohen's screenplay and his interpretation of Mickey Spillane's Mike Hammer as "an unwitting pawn of one government agency eager to terminate a sloppy operation run by another — a comment, if you like, on conservative pretensions."[10]

Since his 1977 *Film Comment* article "Gods and Monsters," Robin Wood has been Cohen's most distinguished supporter in the field of film criticism. Reviewing Cohen's career nearly 10 years later, in *Hollywood from Vietnam to Reagan,* Wood associated the director's most consistent and impressive body of work with the congenial climate of a seventies decade that not only saw "a crisis in ideological confidence" but also impressive work within the horror genre. One feature of this movement recognized "not only that the monster is the product of normality but that it is no longer possible to view normality as other than monstrous."[11] Wood sees Cohen as belonging to a group of directors such as George Romero, Tobe Hooper and others who have not survived the changing conditions of more conservative decades.

Certain problems exist in Wood's changed perspective concerning Cohen. Consciously influenced by an F.R. Leavis literary discourse about the Great

Tradition, he draws an arbitrary distinction between major and minor talents struggling for expression, a distinction highly problematic in an economically oppressive era of media representations affecting any type of creative endeavor. If, as Wood recognizes, everyone is in an embattled position "compounded by the commercial nature of cinema and the problems of financing and distribution,"[12] this situation is further complicated by the growth of satellite, cable, and CD-Rom systems almost entirely under the control of new media robber-barons of the late 20th century. Judgments concerning "major" and "minor" talents are not impossible in this particular era, but highly problematic, needing greater redefinition to suit the circumstances of a more complex technological era. Would a Mozart or Beethoven fare better in this time? Better understanding of historical and industrial circumstances is required, as well as a more detailed analysis of formal and cultural circumstances influencing the work of Larry Cohen that reveal a rebellious consistency rather than an artistic decline. Larry Cohen may be a "minor" talent, according to this particular cultural definition. He arguably has yet to direct the great film he has the capacity of making. Ideally, the director needs the economic and creative support of a major studio that will allow him the opportunity of making his films the way he wants to. But Cohen is also the victim of a marketplace situation affecting both free creative expression and independent cinema, one that he has struggled against admirably. Economic and industrial circumstances affect his work and recognition. It is highly unlikely that Cohen will gain studio support, creative freedom, and financial support during this *Waterworld* era. However, Cohen continues to articulate radical concerns in his works, far outshining contemporary Hollywood productions. Possibly, his low-budget guerrilla filmmaking world appropriately allows him to realize his talents in a more creative way. Naturally, his films lack the huge mega-budgets of Lucas and Spielberg productions. But his *It's Alive* trilogy is far more mature and significant than George Lucas' regressively adolescent *Star Wars* films. Also, Cohen's teleplay "Medal for a Turned Coat" is more complex and creative than Spielberg's simplistic vision in *Schindler's List* (1993). Although Cohen's work is certainly problematic, it deserves better understanding, rather than being defined and misunderstood by anachronistic literary and traditional Hollywood studio paradigms.

Wood has not considered the director's television achievements. While providing stimulating readings of the *It's Alive* films, *God Told Me To*, *The Private Files of J. Edgar Hoover*, and other works in *Hollywood*,[13] Wood sees Cohen's significant work as belonging to the seventies era. He is absolutely correct when he points to what he believes is the supposed failure of Cohen to "produce a wholly satisfying, a wholly convincing movie." But whether Larry Cohen wishes to make a work in those terms remains debatable. He may really operate on other levels. However, Wood's discerning definition of certain implications within Cohen's work remains important:

> The "thinking" of the films can lead logically only in one direction, toward a radical and revolutionary position in relation to the dominant ideological norms and

the institutions that embody them, and such a position is incompatible with any definable position within mainstream cinema (or even on its exploitation fringes); it is also incompatible with any degree of comfort or security within the dominant culture. The areas of disturbance expressed in the first minutes of *It's Alive*— disturbance about heterosexual relations, male/female gender roles, the family, the contemporary development of capitalism, its abuse of technology, its indifference to the pollution of the environment, its crass materialism, callousness, and greed — encompass the entire structure of civilization, from the corporation to the individual and the film sees that structure as producing nothing but a monstrosity.[14]

The ideas are certainly in these seventies films. But they are also present in Cohen's earlier and later work. Larry Cohen is no political revolutionary. He works within the system. But he chooses satire as a weapon to subvert it from within. We must not ask more from a Cohen film except what it delivers. But the actual manner in which a Larry Cohen film operates may have more in common with neglected aspects of a cultural tradition whose functions need reading from other perspectives outside both literary discourse and a former Hollywood critical tradition that is now both bankrupt and irrelevant. This is particularly the case with Cohen's stylistic concerns.

The director's particular choice of style often offends certain critics and audiences. However, Fred Camper is one critic who views Cohen's visual style in a sympathetic light. Rather than condemning it as "bad filmmaking," Camper insightfully elucidates its main features. Noting relationships to certain styles and themes found in the films of Samuel Fuller and Alfred Hitchcock, Camper sees an interesting unity between form and content in Cohen's work:

> On a visual level, Cohen's films are always alive with a centrifugal near-chaos. By combining multiple points of view he denies the viewer a single character to identify with. Cohen's scenes, built up from combinations of hand-held with tripod-filmed images, and static shots with moving shots, are alive with multiple tensions and conflicting perspectives. We see things from all sides, and we are encouraged to think and compare without being led toward any easy conclusions.[15]

This style parallels the conflicting and multiple tensions affecting any Cohen character. Samuel Fuller's statement in *Pierrot Le Fou* (1965) concerning cinema's resemblance to a "battleground" also applies to Cohen's world, one involving tensions concerning gender and social meaning. But the stylistic dissonance of a Cohen film is also meant to challenge audiences. Rather than seeing harmless entertainments involving mutant babies, vampires, and killer yogurt, viewers face immersion in a highly complex and challenging world. Larry Cohen once said, "When chaos reigns, I shine." He used this phrase when speaking about the excitement of improvising on the set.[16] But it is a term equally applicable to both the style and content of his films. Camper also notes the relationship Cohen's films have to Hitchcock's work. Both directors avoid morally simplistic conflicts and constantly remind their audiences about the complex nature of human personalities.[17]

Cohen's films are among the most significant in contemporary Hollywood cinema dealing seriously with taboo issues of class, gender, and race. But the style does create a problem for most viewers. This does not necessarily mean we should follow the inaccurate observation of David Cronenberg, who believes Robin Wood claims that we should admire a Larry Cohen film, even though it is "awful," because of its progressive themes.[18] Questions of style and taste are historically bound. They change over generations. Furthermore, the director may be unconsciously employing a particular type of filmmaking that once competed with the classical Hollywood system as an alternative mode of depiction but eventually became obsolete. The rationale governing Larry Cohen's choice of filmic style is important and needs some clarification.

Cohen's cinema operates in a particular mode of raw, unpolished, anti–Hollywood perfectionism described as "guerrilla filmmaking." Critical of the big-budget economic waste of the average Hollywood movie with overpaid stars and directors, as well as front-office interference crippling artistic creativity, Cohen deliberately chooses a certain manner of filmmaking. It is akin to independent cinema in avoiding the classical Hollywood narrative style. Cohen employs a much more freewheeling, heterogenous type of direction, one that features certain parallels to a former pre–Hollywood "cinema of attractions" style. That style was much less polished and professional, having particular associations with a long-lost vaudeville tradition all but vanquished by classical Hollywood narrative. It is a tradition more open to innovation and spontaneity than its Hollywood counterpart, often leading to the best type of on the spot, improvised performance. Cohen manages to obtain excellent performances from some of his actors that far excel their work in mainstream productions. If certain critics balk at D'Urville Martin's excessive delivery in the closing scenes of *Black Caesar,* they often turn a blind eye to certain aspects of Gena Rowlands' unpolished performance in Cassavetes' *A Woman Under the Influence.* Wood also notes how Cohen's supposedly unpolished direction evokes critical disdain:

> Rough and hasty as they may often appear, Cohen's films abound in ideas that are up there on the screen, dramatized in action and dialogue, in a *mise en scene* whose lack of refinement is the corollary of its energy and inventiveness...the roughness and the emphasis on impact tend to conceal effects that are both complex and subtle.[19]

Cohen's films contain features far more important than professional standards of style and content. Sometimes a particular poverty of representation is more of a virtue than a vice. Speaking of theatrical representations of the Vietnam War, Donald Rignalda suggests that a guerrilla genre can be far more effective in moving audiences toward understanding the historical and social consequences of the material than ordinary modes of presentation. He believes that a paucity of scenery can create "a new relationship between author and audience, a new contract with new responsibilities for both parties."[20] If we compare this with a director's refusal of the typical modes of Hollywood representation, we see parallels to Larry Cohen's cinema. This low-budget form of guerrilla cinema may not entirely succeed in gaining audience involvement. It is a strategy as problematic as the supposed progressive claims made for a Brechtian cinema in the pages of *Screen* over 20 years ago.[21] Rignalda also draws attention to Emily Mann's *Still Life* where the use of "tangled, ruptured voices" opposed to the dominant stylistic modes of theatrical performance may enable viewers to see the real theatre of Vietnam in which we are all involved.[22] This, of course, is a possibility depending on many random factors, such as an audience's ability to understand the modes of presentation at work. Having almost 40 years' experience in the industry, Cohen knows what will and what will not work. But he always experiments. Cohen's particular choice of direction results less from bad shooting habits and hasty improvisation, and more from a deliberate strategy to encourage viewers to consider serious ideas within accessible and popular frameworks. He also uses comic-strip or cartoon imagery in several of his films, a device whose significance has not always been properly recognized in film criticism.

Cohen's particular use of the cartoon is not unique. Many directors have used this style in their films.[23] Andrew Horton points to Jean-Luc Godard's *"comic* dimension of his disruptive cinema," a technique dependent upon "a special relationship between creator and viewer/reader, a bond described as a 'state of *conspiratorial* irony.'"[24] Although Cohen and Godard differ tremendously, they both aim at an ideal cinema demanding active viewer participation. Godard's former collaborator Jean-Pierre Gorin now investigates the potentials that popular culture offers to create a new form of cinematic language. One of these potentials is a critically cinematic appropriation of comic strips.[25]

Judging any work according to canonical definitions of artistic integrity and unified development often leads to misunderstanding innovative features. What is important is the nature of the achievement and how it has been realized. Although lacking the technical polish of David Cronenberg, Larry Cohen's work is more progressive and positive. While Cronenberg's films reveal conservative features of nihilistic pessimism and anti-feminism peculiar to the eighties and nineties, Cohen presents characters often struggling against overwhelming forces in difficult situations. If the victory is incomplete and transient, his characters may still actively continue their particular struggles. If Frank Davies dies in attempting to preserve another generation of mutant babies against oppressive institutional forces (after previously admitting guilt and engaging in a poignant temporary reconciliation in *It's Alive*), *It Lives Again* ends by showing his successor, Eugene Scott, continuing the struggle. Furthermore, despite its supposedly non-serious comic-strip style, *It's Alive III: Island of the Alive,* at the climax, moves toward the reconstituted Jarvis couple fleeing society with their mutant grandchild. Despite reduced economic circumstances and a precarious future existence, Stephen and Ellen decide to stay together and fight the hostile ideological forces that attempted to destroy their personal lives and kill mutant children designated as socially alien, as they have been. A Larry Cohen film never ends in the defeatist, pessimistic nihilism characterizing the cinema of David

Cronenberg. Indeed, although differing nationalistically, stylistically, and culturally, Cohen's cinema resembles Cuban filmmaker Julio Garcia Espinosa's rallying cry for a new form of "Imperfect Cinema," a cinema strategically using popular art forms:

> The future lies with folk art. But let us no longer display folk art with demagogic pride, with a celebrative air. Let us exhibit it instead as a cruel denunciation, as a painful testimony to the level at which the peoples of the world have been forced to limit their artistic creativity.[26]

The comic strip is, of course, a peculiarly American form of folk art. Whether consciously or not, it is more than coincidental that "alien" Cubans help Stephen Jarvis to return to his society in *Island of the Alive* and express positive wishes for a humane resolution to his personal and social problems.

American comic strips have influenced Larry Cohen since childhood. His visual style exhibits many parallels to an art form usually misunderstood by American society. Despite the achievements of Andy Warhol, Roy Lichtenstein, and Keith Herrin, the critical establishment is generally reluctant to recognize other approximations of this style. But the comic strip is a valid artistic form within its own right, capable both of progressively innovative and ideological appropriations. While the '80s featured the latter tendency, operating in films such as *Missing in Action* (1984) and *Rambo — First Blood, Part Two* (1985), many artists continue using this medium for artistic and satirical assaults against the dominant order. Cohen became self-educated in cinema, by simultaneously drawing on comic strip influences, seeing films regularly, and developing a unique style transplanted into his films. Cohen respectively used the traditional narrative models of *Little Caesar* (1931) and *The F.B.I. Story* (1959) for *Black Caesar* (1972) and *The Private Files of J. Edgar Hoover* (1977), reworking them both into a comic strip style. He makes explicit concealed ideological premises within his original models prior to deconstructing them. Despite Tommy's black macho masculinity, he will fall in the same way as his predecessor Rico Caesar Bandello. Tommy's black pride is no antidote either to hubris or ideological contamination by the forces he thinks he fights against. He has bought into the American Dream by using the same ruthless violent methods of his white oppressors. Tommy is no aberrant misogynist like Rico. He exhibits a heroic black image for the Harlem community. But it is one easily recoupable within the dangerous nature of the American Dream. The comic strip format of *Black Caesar* depicts Tommy's particular rise and fall in a recognizably abstract moral formula easily discernible from *Superman, Batman*, and *Marvel Comics* contemporaries. But what makes the form significant is Cohen's particular recognition of the dangerous nature of a heroic American Dream — an element usually absent from the average comic strip. He takes the formula and revitalizes it in a particular radical direction, both in style and content, to criticize negative features within the American Dream motivating Tommy's Horatio Alger, upward-mobility aspirations. *The Private Files of J. Edgar Hoover* rejects the rigid ideological pomposity of Mervyn LeRoy's original studio-produced film. It presents characters as comic strip constructions existing within a cinematic framework the FBI director himself used for propaganda purposes. By visually changing the nature of the classical Hollywood narrative formula used complicity by *The F.B.I. Story* for propaganda purposes, Cohen turns it into a stylistic comic-strip morality play for the post–Watergate generation, presenting incidents once accepted as normal as artificial and manufactured, to conceal the dark motives operating within the heart of American politics. *The Stuff* (1985), contains an artificially "born again," reconstructed consumerist family in a film often interrupted by manipulative television advertising. It is perhaps the best example of Cohen's radical usage of the comic-strip form. *The Ambulance* explicitly refers to the world of comics with its hero (Eric Roberts) employed as a graphic artist by Stan Lee of Marvel. While contemporary films such as *Batman* (1989), *Dick Tracy* (1990), *Batman Returns* (1992), *The Crow* and *The Mask* (both 1994) use the comic strip as an overbudgeted, art-designed background for infantile and mediocre depictions, Cohen's lesser-budgeted, but more effective, comic-strip visual style unites form with content by critically assaulting a regressive American society. However, Larry Cohen is never content to borrow devices and plagiarize. He uses his borrowing to explore and develop. The same is true of his use of characters.

Although Cohen's characters initially appear as standard types such as the doctor, the executive, and the father in *It's Alive,* he presents them as well-rounded human beings by means of exceptional acting performances. John Ryan's role as Frank Davies in *It's Alive* and Michael Moriarty's appearances in Cohen's films are major examples. They may appear initially as types but they change and develop throughout the course of the films. Brian Henderson points out that the cartoon status of characters in works by Joseph Heller, Terry Southern, and Stanley Kubrick "reflects those gigantic social forces — determining and stereotyping our lives — that were brought into being by the total mobilization of World War II and that persist in the postwar period."[27] This is particularly the case with a supposedly democratic but ideologically conformist society existing in its most extremist manifestation today. Cohen's characters never accept their conformist slots in an ideologically governed corporation. They usually fight back in one way or another. Cohen's use of comic strips and characters also resembles E. M. Forster's discussion of the ways in which Charles Dickens depicts characters in his fiction:

> Part of the genius of Dickens is that he uses types and caricatures, people whom we recognize the instant they reenter, and yet achieves effects that are not mechanical and a vision of humanity that is not shallow. Those who dislike Dickens have an excellent case. He ought to be bad. He is actually one of our big writers, and his immense success with types suggests that there may be more in flatness than the severer critics admit.[28]

Cohen's films also involve certain parody-pastiche motifs associated with the more critical and ironic interpretations of post-modernism as understood by critics such as Linda Hutcheon in *A Theory of Parody, The Politics of Postmodernism,* and *The Poetics of Postmodernism.* This, of course, ideally explains his cinematically deconstructive use of previous master narratives such as *Little Caesar* and *The F.B.I Story* in *Black Caesar* and *The Private Files of J. Edgar Hoover.* But any claims for Larry Cohen being a closet post-modernist collapse on the grounds of his work having a strongly defined social and historical polemical thrust usually antithetical to post-modernism as it is commonly understood. Cohen's films are not trivial ludic pursuits of referents having little foundation in reality. Their purpose is highly serious and socially relevant, since they function in a more combative and interrogative manner than most operations of post-modernism do. Cohen sees repressive representations in Hollywood cinema, television, and advertising resulting in the production of conformist personalities. By using a comic-strip format usually dismissed as infantile and immature by high-culture critics, Cohen turns it into a radical weapon revealing negative tendencies within American society. The form itself is less important than the use to which it is put. Unfortunately many reviewers never deeply examine the ways in which Cohen uses this particular style. However, the comic-strip technique is not to be exclusively understood from certain operations in escapist comics and films such as *Judge Dredd* (1995). It has other uses.

As Scott McCloud pertinently notes, the comic strip has a long and varied history.[29] It is not just a 20th century creation. Like any art form, it may be used or abused. What really counts is the specific ways in which the form is used in each particular instance. This equally applies to both the comic strip and cinema. Cohen's use of the comic-strip style is far removed from the militaristic "action man" applications seen in *Missing in Action* and *Rambo,* the empty flamboyant nature of *Dick Tracy,* and the boring nature of *The Crow.* As a satiric device, it has antecedents in the work of William Hogarth and Rudolphe Topffer.[30] But the medium, like theatre, cinema, and television, has suffered much from negative appropriations and understandings peculiar to the 20th century. The more popular the device, the more heavily criticized it became. McCloud comments that "comics' low self-esteem is *self-perpetuating*! The historical perspective necessary to *counteract* comics's negative image is obscured *by* that negativity."[31] McCloud's remarks are also applicable to contemporary Hollywood. Students exposed to its present junk food manifestations are often surprised by seeing what the system was once capable of doing.

McCloud comments that the comic-strip style is a form of "amplification though simplification." By abstracting the image through cartooning, the artist does not so much eliminate details, but focus upon specific meanings, amplifying them in a way realistic art can not. In many cases, critics are oblivious to this fact. But the comic-strip nature of a live-action film may denote the *intensity* of a narrative or visual style attempting to focus the audience's idea on particular ideas.[32] Cohen uses similar techniques in delivering the messages contained in films such as *Black Caesar* and *The Private Files of J. Edgar Hoover.* As we have seen, *Black Caesar* subverts the then-popular "blaxploitation" genre by mixing ingredients of the classical gangster movie paradigm in *Little Caesar* to present a modern New York morality play showing that blackness is no antidote to capitalist corruption. Robin Wood acclaims *The Private Files of J. Edgar Hoover* as "perhaps the most intelligent film about American politics ever to come out of Hollywood."[33] However, many reviewers reject this evaluation and attack Cohen's visual style. The comic-strip style has a particular rationale here. Scott McCloud points out that by "de-emphasizing the *appearance* of the *physical* world in favor of the *idea* of form, the cartoon places itself in the world of concepts."[34] Cohen uses the form to mediate conceptual radical allegories within his work. A simple style does not necessitate a simple story. Simple elements may combine in simple ways like an atom and, like an atom, contain great power.[35] Such a principle underlies the nature of *The Stuff*, one of the few radical films that emerged during the Reagan era, attacking the faulty policies of the Food and Drug Administration. Such a critique also occurs in *It's Alive* as one possible explanation for the mutant baby. But *The Stuff* is a frontal assault on the F.D.A., using a more extreme comic-strip style to deliver a simple but powerfully radical message. At the same time, the simplicity of the style resulted in the film not being taken seriously by most reviewers.

Cohen's medium, or particular style, is his message. But it is not readily perceived by most viewers ideologically conditioned to look at comics and movies in a particular way. They are usually regarded as disposable artifacts within consumer culture. As McCloud states in terms of comics, when pictures become abstracted from reality they require greater levels of perception. It is a highly appropriate visual device when integrated with Larry Cohen's specific form of comedy technique. As Steve Neale and Frank Krutnik point out, comedy is ideally suited to a generically fluid form of hybridization. It is similar to the various generic explorations undertaken by Larry Cohen in which he also mixes the two usually distinct forms of parody and satire. Cohen's cinema not only attacks, in the vein of parody, the aesthetic conventions of past Hollywood cinema, but it also aims at a satirical attack on the social realm. Neale and Krutnik also note that both horror and comedy are closely aligned as forms of defensive interpretation. It is another feature applicable to the director of *It's Alive, Full Moon High, Wicked Stepmother*, and the radical satire *Bone*. Finally, Neale and Krutnik note that the cartoon may stretch the laws of narrative motivation to their most impossible levels to transgress the conventions of particular films and thereby highlight the conventional and absurdist elements of both the films and, by implication, the societies to which they belong. However, a Larry Cohen film never breaks rules in such a way that the narrative eventually recoups them. His attacks are so radical that nothing is ever the same afterwards.[36]

Not all of his films explicitly use this comedic cartoon technique. *It's Alive, God Told Me To, It Lives Again, Perfect Strangers*, and *Special Effects* contain little evidence of the style. *Perfect Strangers* combines Hitchcock-influenced thriller with documentary location shooting in Greenwich Village. The comic-strip style is at its height in *Bone, Black Caesar, Hell Up in Harlem, The Private Files of J.*

*Edgar Hoover, The Stuff, Full Moon High, It's Alive III, A Return to Salem's Lot, Wicked Stepmother,* and *The Ambulance.* These films often contain characters and personalities depicted in an abstract manner to create cinematic satire. Cohen's style developed over time. While writing for television, he naturally could not control the visual style used by the director. His television plays from 1958 all use a "realistic" style popular in contemporary productions. The later work combines the same social messages with a developing comic-strip style involving primary colors and types. However, these types are fully rounded characters lacking any form of stereotypical depictions. They represent a complex mixture of positive and negative qualities often formed by the society in which they live. The Lennick family of *Bone* represents a gross and selfish version of the American Dream far more penetrating than the complaisant image Paul Mazursky presents in *Down and Out in Beverly Hills.* Cohen's cast initially appear to be recognizable types but they soon turn out to be complex characters. Yaphet Kotto's Bone seems to be a stereotyped violent black who threatens white security. But later, Bone reveals himself as vulnerable and insecure, his earlier persona due more to white racist paranoid projections than to any natural essence within himself. Cohen's radical allegories either reveal characters as reductive conformist characters in a consumerist world or others (Tommy Ross, Steven Jarvis, J. Edgar Hoover, and Tony Walker) whose differing recognitions of their dilemmas become explicitly related to their awakening awareness of negative aspects within the American Dream. Cohen's use of his form is hybrid in manner. He mixes in several influences, chief of which is one of the major directors within the classical Hollywood system whose films contain the radical ideas Cohen is heir to: Alfred Hitchcock.

*Special Effects* was based on an early Larry Cohen screenplay, "The Cutting Room," filmed 17 years after it was written. The film is a highly significant Hitchcock-influenced self-reflective examination of the fragile boundaries between cinema and reality. It also explores the dehumanizing nature of gendered power relationships within contemporary society. Cohen is a more genuine heir of Alfred Hitchcock than Brian DePalma is. While DePalma emphasizes style over content, Cohen better develops the radical aspects of Hitchcock's work. Robin Wood's observations about the inherent radicalism within the director's works in the revised edition of *Hitchcock's Films* certainly apply better to Cohen than to DePalma.[37]

The first screenplay Cohen ever wrote, *Daddy's Gone A-Hunting,* was for Alfred Hitchcock. Hitchcock's presence invades much of Cohen's work. But the films and screenplays of Larry Cohen are never direct imitations. They often use familiar narrative devices such as surprise plot changes, or the "double twist" where the narrative takes a different direction from what viewers believe will happen. This occurs in one of Cohen's earliest story contributions, the "A Taste of Poison" episode of *Branded,* in which Jason McCord discovers that the poisoned well is not really poisoned at all. The previous part of the narrative plays on a suspense theme involving a besieged group of thirsty characters struggling against temptation to drink from the nearby well. The surprise change in circumstances parallels Hitchcock's own abrupt plot changes, such as Judy's memory sequence halfway through *Vertigo* and the unexpected death of a major star in the middle of *Psycho*. Halfway through "A Taste of Poison," the viewers have to re-orient themselves to a new situation. What will happen when Jason McCord now discovers that the well is not poisoned after all? Unfortunately, television constraints do not allow Cohen to realize the full potential of this situation. Cohen is familiar with this particular Hitchcock tradition, but he innovatively reworks it in different ways. Unlike most contemporary Hollywood productions, he never slavishly borrows from the works of the Master of Suspense. Nor will he engage in over-flamboyant virtuoso stylistic flourishes. Instead, Cohen re-applies in new ways the radical visions of Hitchcock's cinema involving male and female victims of oppressive gender roles within Western society. Cohen's *Special Effects* uses *Vertigo* as a framework to depict the cinematic implications of a director's murderous gaze, placing it as an explicit plot motif within the narrative. *Special Effects* begins by presenting the whole of American society as sexually voyeuristic. It concludes by revealing that the oppressively dominant family relationship depicted at the beginning will continue in a new, pernicious manner. The *It's Alive* films also continue Hitchcock's analysis of perverse family relationships and oppressive social destruction with the aid of Hitchcock's major musical collaborator, Bernard Herrmann.

Cohen's authorship is thus understandable within the broader parameters discussed by Andre Bazin in his influential article "La politique des auteurs." Directors belong to a particular historical era. When circumstances change, their later works may often badly synchronize with a new public mood through no fault of the director. Sometimes a director creatively interacts with changing times. Eisenstein's later films and theoretical interests provide evidence of this. As Bazin shrewdly notes, "the individual transcends society: but society is also and above all *within* him. So there can be no definitive criticism of genius or talent which does not first take into consideration the social determinations, the historical combination of circumstances, and the technical background which to a large extent determine it."[38]

Assuming we do not accept the monolithic and often reductive formulation of Michel Foucault's "Death of the Author" thesis, how does Bazin's still challenging question apply to Larry Cohen? *Auteur*, yes, but what of? The answer lies in the fact of Cohen's role as accomplished screenwriter and director. Whatever form he uses, his better works include a radical allegorical vision taking issue with the dehumanizing aspects of the American experience. This vision operates by using standard formulas within American cinema and television, and attempting to transcend them.

Cohen's first film as a director, *Bone* (aka *Housewife, Beverly Hills Nightmare*, and *Dial Rat for Terror*), began as a self-financed 16mm production before he transferred it to 35mm for eventual theatrical release. *Bone* is a black comedy satirizing a Beverly Hills bourgeois lifestyle the director constantly returns to throughout his career. Its quasi-avant garde, fragmented visual technique supplements the narrative's critical stance towards its subjects. This style paralleled similar radical experiments in mainstream and independent narratives during the '60s and '70s. *Bone* is a low-budget cinematic parallel to theatrical productions such as *Who's Afraid of Virginia Woolf?* George and Martha represent the contemporary decline of a historically revered First Family. Bill and Bernadette Lennick are their Beverly Hills counterparts. *Bone* foreshadowed Cohen's later satirical radical assault upon American society. Cohen's films unveil the dangerous nature of social and personal entrapment within American history and society. His fragmented editing style often opposes the ideological cutting technique present in more highly budgeted and professionally polished Hollywood works. Cohen's horror explorations arose within that creative 70s era of family horror emphasizing the monster, not as a social threat, but as a natural creation of the nuclear family. In both style and content, Cohen aims at an iconoclastic subversion of systems resulting in misery, unhappiness, and oppression. His greatest achievement — *The Private Files of J. Edgar Hoover* — uses the structure of Hollywood's earlier propaganda biopic *The F.B.I. Story* to reveal its original subject (always filmed from behind or in shadow, like American cinema's religious or political figures) as a dangerous monster produced within a political system, whom the *status quo* both fears and needs for its survival. By using a roster of former Hollywood stars and character actors, Cohen indirectly commented on the F.B.I. director's use of the publicity machine during Hoover's lifetime and his influence on past and present media representations, from *G-Men* (1935) to '60s television series, *The F.B.I.*

Cohen's '70s assaults parallel the decade's interrogation of social institutions that occurred within independent, commercial, and European cinema. If Cohen was no Mekas or Godard, he nevertheless belonged to the same historical moment in time. He preferred working on the margins, producing, scripting and directing under his Larco Company.

The '80s witnessed a decline in the horror genre that Cohen appropriated. A decade favoring spectacular gory productions such as the *Friday the 13th, Halloween,* and *Nightmare on Elm Street* series, with their cult hero elevations of serial killer patriarchal avengers was antithetical to Cohen's iconoclastic vision. The '80s included his return to comedy with *Full Moon High*, its theme anticipating the conformity of a younger generation Harlan Ellison earlier warned about in *The Glass Teat*.[39] The era also witnessed other interesting offbeat cinematic explorations such as *Perfect Strangers, Special Effects,* and *The Stuff.* Cohen ended the decade with *The Ambulance,* a film mixing social satire with a devastating attack on an unscrupulous medical industry. Social satire, parody, and the implicit demand for a more just and equitable world characterize all of his work. Cohen's cinema contains radical assaults against the status quo presented in outrageous and innovative ways paralleling the type of guerrilla filmmaking Cohen delights in.

Cohen uses humor in his films, to a greater or lesser degree, with varying success. Whether in *Wicked Stepmother, Full Moon High* or the pre-birth scene in *It's Alive,* humor is a satirical device used to attack the oppressive structure of American society. Even when thrown away, as in the general-store robbery in *Maniac Cop 2,* Cohen presents humor as an absurdist weapon highlighting greed and commercialism in America. The seasickness scene in *Its Alive III—Island of the Alive* depicts socially alienated father Steven Jarvis (Michael Moriarty) singing "Over the Sea to Skye," illustrating not just his momentary revenge upon representatives of a society who use, abuse, then use him again, but also the potential messianic nature of the mutant children who are as used and abused as their father. The scene contains ironic undertones on several levels. Like Mel Brooks, Cohen takes formulas and explodes them from within by using parody and satire. The comic treatment is as much of a political weapon as any serious treatment is. As Mikhail Bakhtin points out in *The Dialogical Imagination,* comedy, irony, and parody are strategic oppositional weapons in any contests against monological texts or oppressive societies. They are not just trivial items but important instruments in any social dialogue.[40] Larry Cohen's comic universe also represents a contemporary radical carnivalesque device paralleling Bakhtin's understanding of the carnival's ironic dislocation of dominating social norms. It is a cinema mingling parody and satire, which makes the two indistinguishable. Larry Cohen is also an heir to Frank Tashlin's "vulgar modernism." As described by J. Hoberman, it is a popular and ironic mode also self-reflectively concerned with the properties of cinema. Many of Cohen's works such as *Bone* deconstruct cinematic narrative. But, unlike Tashlin, the films of Larry Cohen are never "dehumanized" in the way Hoberman describes Tashlin's work. The *It's Alive* films, *A Return to Salem's Lot,* and many others are all concerned with conditions preventing the realization of true humanity and the destruction of human potential. However, Hoberman's description of Tashlin's America also applies to that satirized by Cohen in *The Stuff* and *Wicked Stepmother:* "His America is a nation of robotic image junkies whose minds have been colonized by the media."[41]

Like Woody Allen in *Zelig,* Cohen also proves an heir to "immigrant culture-shock comics" such as Chaplin and the Marx brothers in depicting the dilemmas of "rootlessness and loss of patriarchal constraints (domesticity, monogamy, family loyalty)"[42] within his particular mode of guerilla cinema, often following the conventions of parodic novels by putting the "heroic discourse" of acceptable normality on trial.[43] But, as Linda Hutcheon points out, concerning parody's neglected links with history, subjectivity, and ideology, Cohen's humor is never trivial. Rather, it is as radical as Bakhtin's parodic irony, which is "constructively and deconstructively critical, challenging the monologic dominant discourse with a second voice, a second level of meaning that destabilizes prior authority and unexamined power."[44] Although Cohen's films lack the high cultural seriousness of a Bakhtin text, they operate in similar directions by using fantastic devices such as mutant babies to destabilize the dominant order and cause both fictional characters and audiences to question their adherence to a social order now clearly bankrupt. Social justice predominantly features in Cohen's unique ironic vision.

From his earliest days as a television writer, social justice themes occupied a key role in Cohen's work. Like more acclaimed contemporaries such as Sidney Lumet, Cohen explores the nature of social and political injustices in American life. More often than not, he underscores complexities and contradictions rather than convenient narrative solutions. In his various teleplays for "The Defenders," Cohen usually initiates a situation that appears basic, then reveals some complicating factor questioning the standard American understanding of justice, necessitating careful and complex thought on the nature of the case. His first *Defenders* teleplay, "Kill or Be Killed," presented the case of a condemned but innocent man who kills his guard before he knows his name has been cleared. Faced with a judicial system demanding his execution for the second crime, Lawrence Preston has to convince the accused that his natural desire for freedom resulting in the killing had unconscious motives that could lead to a capital punishment he originally and justifiably attempted to escape from. "Traitor" complicates the issues of treason and guilt in presenting an accused spy whose activities leading to his arrest paradoxically result from a patriotism generally associated with American ideals. Finally, Cohen's "Espionage" teleplay "Medal for a Turned Coat" reveals that a good German rewarded for his anti–Nazi activities is really as guilty as everyone else. The merit of Cohen's teleplay is its applicability to all situations everywhere. His "Branded" pilot "The Vindicator" presents Jason McCord as a complex scapegoat for faults within an American social system that the disgraced hero supports by his complicity in a judicial process that has unjustly condemned him. Cohen's sympathies with outcasts and scapegoats continues in his later films. Although better known as a director, Cohen has excellent claims for being hailed as one of the most radical talents in sixties television.

Robin Wood hails Cohen's work for suggesting potentials for an alternative society devoid of all the oppressive social and gender boundaries affecting human beings today. Larry Cohen's film and television works are critical of the oppressive nature of human relationships. His cinema represents his own critical and interrogative vision of American Jewish cinematic "lifestyle trends" similar to those Desser and Friedman find in the works of Woody Allen, Sidney Lumet and Paul Mazursky. Cohen's treatments range from humorous to serious. Cohen's 1965 "Defenders" teleplay "Unwritten Law" anticipated feminist critiques of rigid gender structures well before the publication of many now well-known writings on the subject. The life-denying aspect of consumer affluence appears in Cohen's first film, *Bone,* and many of his other works, including his unsuccessful satiric treatment in *Wicked Stepmother. The Stuff* represents an ironic elaboration of the old saying "You are what you eat." However, the film's absurd premises really reveal the dangers of American consumerism. Business interests and the Food and Drug Administration collaborate in merchandising a dangerous substance on the market to make a profit. The killer yogurt from outer space destroys people from within. Its victims become mere shells housing a killer substance. Cohen's message can be read literally as well as metaphorically. *The Stuff* is an attack upon a corrupt society that often deliberately disseminates food or drugs without even testing them properly. Also, it represents an allegorical rendering of the death-in-life aspects of American ideology. As *A Return from Salem's Lot* shows, the ancient consumer society of vampires are really all-American. Andrew Duggan's oppressed television salesman in *Bone* exists in an economic and spiritual Beverly Hills wasteland entrapping him as both victim and agent. Denying the display of full personal potentials, the solitary J. Edgar Hoover dominates American society as a monstrous repressive superego in an historical and political environment that encourages his control. Whether conscious or not, Cohen's films and screenplays also deal with the destructive aspect of negative gender roles, particularly the question of monstrous masculinity, as Elayne Chaplin has demonstrated in her excellent doctoral dissertation.[45]

Cohen's work is mixed and varied, ranging from significant achievements in both film and television to highly problematic failures such as *Wicked Stepmother*. However, few directors working within the commercial boundaries of American entertainment have dared so much and produced such significant work deserving attention and respect. The day has gone when we would expect all works to be unified, consistent, and highly realized over a long period of time, but Larry Cohen has done just that. In a contemporary Hollywood system whose climate encourages junk-food, highly budgeted cinematic artifacts, productions bearing Larry Cohen's name represent refreshing and alternative directions that the culturally moribund film and television industry lacks. Although no great master (a title Cohen himself would reject), his films deserve examination and applause for their independent, iconoclastic, and radical nature in a non-progressive era. For that alone, Cohen's place in cinema history is unique.

# Early Work in
# New York Television

On June 25, 1958, "Kraft Mystery Theatre" aired a live transmission of "87th Precinct" written by Larry Cohen and based on characters created by Evan Hunter. This broadcast inspired the 1961 television series starring Robert Lansing as Steve Carella and Gena Rowlands as his wife, Teddy. Cohen wrote this teleplay at the early age of 17, concealing his actual date of birth from the producers. Writers had to be at least 21 for their work to be broadcast. The airing of "87th Precinct" represented an auspicious beginning for Cohen. Produced about the same time he began studying film production at the City College of New York, his teleplay belonged to the last years of what is commonly termed "the golden age of American television." During that time, New York television studios produced live dramas that were transmitted across the country. Although appearing well after famed works such as "Marty" with Rod Steiger and "Requiem for a Heavyweight" starring Jack Palance, "87th Precinct" shared many features with its distinguished predecessors. As well as being shot live in New York prior to American television's dependence upon recorded programs, "87th Precinct" contained stylistic features common to television's early years. These involved black and white, socially realistic dramatic narratives with non-glamorous depictions of the everyday lives of ordinary people. Well before Hollywood sitcoms and the glossy color style of sixties television, New York–produced dramas and comedies often focused on an American landscape far removed from the dream factory's affluent representations. Prior to "I Love Lucy" and "The Burns and Allen Show," early comedies such as "The Honeymooners" showed the cramped living accommodations of working-class families such as the Kramdens, revealing a familiar American way of life that later glossier productions attempted to deny.

Since most of Larry Cohen's early television work is not generally accessible, except in archives such as the Museum of Television and Radio in New York, some content description is necessary in this chapter. Cohen's teleplay "87th Precinct" emphasizes the bleak nature of a New York police department, the impoverished genteel accommodation of an aging woman who loses all her money in the 1929

Wall Street crash, and the unglamorized apartment of the Carella family, who struggle with the demands of everyday life. The plot involves Steve Carella's (Robert Bray) guilt over the death of a caller he regarded as a nuisance. Set in an overpowering New York heat wave before the days of home air conditioning, "87th Precinct" begins with the elderly Mrs. Faye making one of her frequent calls to the precinct about an intruder outside her door. Taking this call while dealing with scared bookie Keetso (Pat Henning), who wants police protection from the mob he owes money to, Steve humors the irritating lady. Due to the hot summer night, he decides not to send a policeman to investigate another of the reclusive Mrs. Faye's crank phone calls. She is rumored to have money hidden in her apartment. Keetso refuses to give the names of mobsters to Carella and decides to try to raise the money. Carella is also unsympathetic to Keetso's pleas for police protection.

A few hours later, Carella learns of Mrs. Faye's murder. Blaming himself for the crime, the psychologically tormented man becomes irritable with his partner, Meyer Meyer (Martin Rudy), and wife, Louise (Joan Copeland), beginning an angst-ridden pursuit for the real killer. Alone in the dead woman's apartment, he repeats Mrs. Faye's final words to him. Sensationalist newspaperman Clavin (Henderson Forsythe) suspects Carella of causing the woman's death. Eventually Carella believes himself guilty and confesses to the sympathetic Meyer Meyer, "This is my fault. You know that, don't you?" "87th Precinct" depicts an early version of Cohen's tormented police officers who appear in *Maniac Cop* and its sequels. Seizing on a lead suggesting that Mrs. Faye's gay artist nephew, Austin Ranny (William Larson), may be the killer, Steve arrests him, hoping for a confession that will remove his guilty feelings over indirectly causing the murder. Like Frank Davies of *It's Alive*, Steve obsessively seeks a scapegoat to relieve guilt over his indirect implication in a criminal act. Eventually, Keetso returns to the precinct after the mob has roughed him up. Carella then reverses his former attitude, offering the bookie protection in jail. Suspicious over Keetso's reluctance, Carella realizes that he was present when Mrs. Faye originally rang and must have overheard the conversation about her hidden money. Keetso confesses to the crime, stating that he accidentally killed her.

The teleplay of "87th Precinct" is tightly constructed, anticipating many of Cohen's later themes. Although directed by Paul Bogart, some of the visual motifs appear to derive from Cohen's teleplay. Before the credits roll, "87th Precinct" begins with a close-up of Mrs. Faye's hand dialing the telephone as she makes one of her frequent calls to Carella. After a shot of the police telephone operator appears, the next scene begins with a close-up of a giant fan. The camera then tracks to the right to show both Carella and Keetso. The giant fan appears in several succeeding scenes, acting as a visual signifier for the heated, non-air conditioned environment in which Carella works, a stifling atmosphere that contributes to the uncomfortable feelings Carella has over the affair. Prior to the end credits, the final scene shows Mrs. Faye's unhooked telephone and a mysterious hand replacing the receiver. This sequence suggests that the unseen intruder acts as an embodiment of Steve's repressed desires to rid himself of an irritating caller on a hot summer night. This mise en scene anticipates the connection of sets and locations to characterizations in Cohen's later screenplays.

Despite Meyer's advice, "Steve. Don't hang around in here. It's not good for you," Carella wanders alone in the victim's apartment. The interior is as stifling as the precinct, since Mrs. Faye's windows have been painted over, preventing ventilation of her room. Her apartment lacks necessary air, due to her fear of outside intruders, a fear similar to that contributing to the deaths of over 500 senior citizens in Chicago during the 1995 heatwave. Carella appears in the background of the shot. The phone looms ominously in the foreground, instilling further guilty feelings in him as he consciously understands his involvement as an accessory in Mrs. Faye's murder. Carella eventually solves the crime when he becomes suspicious over Keetso's reluctance to accept police protection. He feels guilty over his former attitude to Keetso: "I'm sorry, too. Maybe I should have locked you up." As Carella begins to suspect Keetso, the phone rings, jogging the cop's memory about the previous night. The phone also appears prominently in the foreground of the frame.

In "87th Precinct," New York is presented as a physical and emotional wasteland. Although shot at NBC and lacking outside locations, this particular studio-created New York world functions as an additional character, determining human aspirations that anticipate Cohen's later cinematic uses of Manhattan. The world of the 87th Precinct is a bleak environment containing frustrated cops, petty crooks, bored seductive housewives, reclusive senior citizens, and isolated, neurotic gays.

This program is notable for introducing one of Cohen's gay characters who frequently appears in his work. As a gay artist, Austin Ranny appears stereotypical to viewers today, but he functions as a strategic character in the teleplay. Ranny is an outsider lacking friends and family, feeling like an outcast in the New York community. When grilled by Carella and Meyer over possible involvement in his aunt's death, Ranny tells them why he sneaked away from the interrogation: "I didn't want to be seen in that kind of building," suggesting his fear of homophobic victimization. Since Carella fervently seeks a scapegoat to absolve himself from guilt over his complicity in Mrs. Faye's death, Ranny intuitively recognizes his own status as a convenient sacrificial victim.

Although Carella later discovers the actual guilty party, he still feels responsible for the murder. He later tells Meyer, "It doesn't help much. It doesn't bring an old lady back to life." The production concludes with Carella picking up the phone and making a call, via the desk sergeant viewed in the pre-credits sequence. The plot of "87th Precinct" is an early example of Cohen's recognition of the complexity of human nature, particularly the need to ascribe guilt to any convenient scapegoat. Everyone is guilty in one way or another. Carella made an understandable error of judgment in not immediately dealing with Mrs. Faye's call. The victimized Keetso appears in the same frame when Carella originally answers the call. He functions as a "monster" figure carrying out Carella's unconscious desires.

However, "87th Precinct" also reveals that money affects all the major characters in negative ways. Keetso needs money to escape mob vengeance. Mrs. Faye lives alone with memories of her former affluence prior to the Wall Street crash and keeps useless bonds in her apartment. Hiding the worthless paper like desired fetishistic objects, she lives in constant paranoia, fearing attack from intruders. The Carellas live in a cramped apartment and discuss how they will acquire money to send their children to summer camp. Ranney speaks about his deceased aunt in materialistic terms: "If she had not lost all her money, what a beneficiary I'd have today." He lives in an antagonistic relationship with his aunt. His outsider status as a gay artist indirectly depicts the nature of a system affecting all the characters in the teleplay. Ranny has chosen to live outside the system in a lifestyle he feels uncertain with, one open to assault at any time.

Carella's character changes constantly. He moves from being a brusque hard-nosed cop to a guilt-ridden character, a vengeful figure seeking a scapegoat to disavow feelings of responsibility, and finally a human being accepting his character flaws. Carella anticipates later Cohen characters who also react with aberrance to situations they have no real control over, situations confronting how they understand their own personalities.

"The Golden Thirty" is an interesting teleplay in relation to Cohen's other work. Referred to as an "autobiographical play" by its author, "The Golden Thirty" is not a direct representation of an episode in Larry Cohen's life, but a fictional replaying of incidents he viewed when he was a young comedian. In the 1950s, Cohen performed comedy routines in the New York Catskill Mountains region, a vacation resort area catering to exclusively Jewish audiences preferring traditional entertainment. One of the episodes in Woody Allen's *Broadway Danny Rose* presents a humorous treatment of a comic's encounter with this audience. However, Cohen's treatment is less comic and more tragic. "The Golden Thirty" is the term used for every comedian's dream of an ideal routine leading to fame and fortune. Cohen's teleplay depicts encounters between youth and age, inexperience and worldly cynicism, and the lonely world of a standup comedian who is now a loser in the entertainment industry.

Shot as a live television production, "The Golden Thirty" begins with naive law student David March (Keir Dullea) arriving at Willow Lake Hotel to work as a waiter during the summer vacation. Although his father has insisted on his studying law, David harbors dreams of breaking into the entertainment industry as a standup comic performing his own written routines. He meets failed comedian Buddy Parker (Henny Youngman), a composite figure of those sad, failed comedians Cohen encountered during the early years of his career. Despite being warned about Buddy's negative tendencies by singer Fran Loring (Nancy Kovack) and hotel owner Mrs. Ross (Bibi Osterwald), David is sympathetic toward this mediocre talent, looking on Buddy as a father figure who will help him develop a comedy routine to break into the business.

Buddy is a sad, self-destructive talent. Conscious of his own failure, he clearly recognizes that Willow Lake Hotel is his last stop before oblivion. Attempting in vain to persuade Mrs. Ross to allow him to perform elsewhere on Saturday night, he hides in his hotel room taking consolation in a whisky bottle as he admits to David that he has nowhere else to go. His other performances are a lie, since no self-respecting comedian spends Saturday night watching other acts in the hotel where he performs. Heavily intoxicated, he staggers on stage drunk and insults the audience with sarcastic comments. Mrs. Ross decides to fire him, informing agent Harry Brock (Don Di Leo) of her decision and keeping it secret so Buddy will serve his two week notice.

Despite Fran's cautions, David falls under Buddy's spell. He tutors David in performance technique, admires his protege's routine as every comedian's ideal "Golden Thirty," and seems genuinely to wish him success. Buddy tells Harry (who does not have the heart to inform him of his job loss) about this new routine and convinces Fran of his good intentions. He tells her of seeing David as a younger version of himself beginning a career and, possibly, succeeding where he failed. However, once Buddy learns the truth, he begs David to allow him to perform his routine. Although David refuses, Buddy uses his master of ceremonies function to go ahead and perform David's routine. Buddy gains a new contract and an extension of his failing career. David graciously allows him to continue with this deception, having learned many things about the personal costs of being a comedian in the entertainment industry.

"The Golden Thirty" is one of Cohen's most uncharacteristic works as a writer. It does not fit into any definable genre and, like many of his "Defenders" scripts and theatrical plays, reveals a potential direction his later career never took. Like "The Comedian," a contemporary live television production in which Mickey Rooney played an atypical role as a monstrous comedian, "The Golden Thirty" is a morality play dealing with the lonely, unfulfilled life of a comedian. Based upon many failed comedians Cohen knew, and his realization of the dark side of a comic persona, the teleplay is a *bildungsroman* about a naive youth learning from his elderly counterpart what sort of life not to follow. David and Fran have idealistic hopes of breaking into the industry. Heavily made-up and costumed far beyond her actual age, Fran continues in the industry, hoping for the desired golden record that will boost her career, one equivalent to her version of a "Golden Thirty." But she warns David that entertainers face the temptation of trying "just one more time" until they finally realize the years have passed, they are no longer young, and others are surpassing them. If Fran envisages a possible future as a bleached blonde singing romantic songs in the Catskills resorts at the age of 40, Buddy has reached the final humiliating end of his career. Comparing herself to Buddy as "a liar and a failure," she tells David, "It's easy to dream. But it's awfully hard to quit."

Fran also tries to convince David that Buddy is no real friend. "Don't you know, comedians never have friends. Only people they can use." David realizes this after Buddy steals his routine. But the "The Golden Thirty" is not just about a young man learning never to trust an older man again. As David later tells Fran, he realizes that he began to turn into a mirror image of Buddy when he refused the pathetic older man's pleas to use his routine to prevent hitting skid row. Up to this point, David showed qualities of sympathy and understanding toward Buddy far more than he deserved. However, excited by the prospect of stepping out under the footlights for a possible future of fame and fortune, David brutally ignored the old man's dilemma. The formerly nice young man reveals a monstrous side to his personality, one that he recognizes. Although Fran stresses support for him in any future entertainment career, David truthfully answers, "I don't know what I want." He realizes the personal trap he could have fallen into. Buddy represented an older monstrous version of what he could have become. "The Golden Thirty" is an early version of the youth vs. age trajectory Cohen later treats humorously in *Full Moon High*, in which eternally young Tony Walker returns to his old high school and finds that his formerly youthful friends are now aged and monstrous. Like later Cohen protagonists such as Frank Davies, Stephen Jarvis, and Joe Weber, David learns from his experience and does not capitulate to the dark side of his persona.

Before leaving with Harry, Buddy sees David sitting alone outside. Although Buddy puts on an act by bluffing that he believed David's inexperience would never do the routine full justice, David assures him that the stolen routine is no longer his. "I don't have any more need for it. You can keep it." David gains an education far more important than the comedy training Buddy gave him. He sees through the older man and recognizes a lonely figure behind the mask.

BUDDY: "You've got to give up everything and everybody you ever love if you want to succeed."

DAVID: "Is it worth it, Buddy?"

BUDDY: "Yes. It was worth it."

Buddy leaves with Harry. David walks inside the performance area. The stage is now empty except for the ritualistic comic stool upon which Buddy sat to perform his act. David pauses for a brief moment to the left of the frame. He then walks away, leaving the empty stage. The concluding moments of "The Golden Thirty" eloquently express Cohen's views on the empty and unfeeling nature of one side of the entertainment industry.

"Night Cry" is a good example of Cohen's developing powers as a writer. It is not only economically scripted with strong character roles but represents the first appearance of the double theme Cohen uses throughout his career. Continually fascinated by Hitchcock's *Strangers on a Train*, Cohen integrates its duality motifs within a television police drama. "Night Cry" develops themes implicit within his "87th Precinct" teleplay, emphasizing them to Gothic proportions, aided by excellent performances by Jack Klugman and Peter Falk (in an early cameo role).

Mark Deglan (Jack Klugman) is an excessive depiction of Steve Carella's tormented cop. He is a workaholic policeman with character flaws who gradually turns into a violent monster. As Deglan tells Morgan Taylor (Diana Van der Vlis) about the nature of his job and the toll it takes, his language uncannily foreshadows Travis

Bickle's voice-over monologue in *Taxi Driver*'s opening scenes. Emotionally affected by his job, and projecting repressed paranoid feelings onto New York's criminal underworld, Deglan describes the dark world of the evening: "At night, that's when they come out." He anticipates many future Cohen characters.

"Night Cry" begins with Deglan being called into the new precinct captain's office. During the following discussion, we learn that, despite Deglan's excellent record on the force, the authorities regard his methods as too violent. Deglan clearly resents his new superior occupying a position he feels he should hold. Investigating a reported homicide, Deglan and his partner, Riley, believe that former Korean War hero Kenneth Paine may be a possible suspect. Investigating on his own, Deglan discovers that Paine is about to leave town. Provoking him into a fight, Deglan accidentally kills him. He assumes the dead man's identity (anticipating Susan Warfield's situation many years later in *As Good as Dead*) so he can remove the body. Deglan later discovers that Paine was innocent, since another man has confessed. However, since the murderer refuses to sign a confession, the captain orders Deglan to find Paine, who is considered a missing witness. During his investigations, Deglan meets Paine's former sweetheart, Morgan Taylor, and best friend, Redfield (Martin Roberts). They both feel different forms of attraction towards Deglan, since he reminds them of Paine. Avoiding a blackmail attempt by informer Izzy (Peter Falk), who saw him on the night of the crime, Deglan incriminates Redfield. Realizing the depths to which he has sunk, Deglan confesses his guilt to Morgan. Despite recognizing her attraction to him, Deglan decides to accept full responsibility for his actions. He escorts Morgan to the precinct and asks her to turn him in.

Despite attempting in vain to persuade Talent Associates that Hollywood had already used the plot outline for "Night Cry" in *Where the Sidewalk Ends*, Cohen creatively developed his own formula by breaking the rules of the standard television police drama. Whereas, in "87th Precinct," the killer's identity remains a mystery until the final moments, "Night Cry" reveals Deglan's guilt halfway through the drama. The focus thus changes from a standard whodunit formula to an intriguing situation of a cop pursuing himself for a crime he committed. Cohen's twist resembles Hitchcock's method of using innovative direction to creatively engage audience interest in new ideas. In *Vertigo*, Hitchcock reveals the truth during the last third of the film. The director shifts narrative emphasis from the enigma behind the plot to how Scottie (James Stewart) will eventually react. After Marion Crane dies halfway through *Psycho*, audience identification switches from one major figure to another. By creatively changing the standard rules in "Night Cry," Cohen moves the emphasis from a formulaic plot development to building up character dilemma and the duality motif. This results in stronger performances. Jack Klugman delivers a far more dynamic performance than Robert Bray in "87th Precinct." Finally, while the construction of "87th Precinct" indirectly hints at the possibility of Carella wanting the irritating Mrs. Faye silenced during a hot summer evening, with Keetso functioning as his monster from the id, "Night Cry" explicitly develops the duality theme and its social consequences.

Like his cinematic predecessors, such as Robert Ryan in *On Dangerous Ground* (1951), Deglan's 14 years on the force have turned him into a vicious monster. Before his prison sentence, Matt Cordell in *Maniac Cop* also releases his repressed violent energies in "legitimate ways." Morgan recognizes Deglan as a man tormented by violently repressed forces brutally sublimated in his police work. During their brief meeting before Kenneth Paine's death, Deglan recognizes the man as his double. Possibly traumatized by his Korean War service (a fact Cohen suggests indirectly), Kenneth Paine acts violently whenever under the influence of alcohol. Deglan tells Morgan, "I don't dare drink at all." While Deglan legitimately unleashes violence as an institutional officer of the law, Paine is no longer in a military situation officially sanctioning his brutality. The two men are soul brothers. Cohen emphasizes this by having Deglan pause before Paine's door, ominously numbered "2." Redfield later telephones Morgan after finding Paine gone, knowingly reassuring her, "He'll come back. He always comes back."

Paine's former fiancée, Morgan, sees Deglan as another version of Paine. Despite intending to marry the good-natured, non-violent Redfield, she begins to fall for Deglan, admitting her attraction to violent men. However, "Night Cry" avoids any repetition of the past. The anguished Deglan musters enough self-control to feel guilt over setting Redfield up for Paine's murder and implicating Morgan as an accessory. Instead, he accepts responsibility for his actions. As he finally escorts Morgan inside the precinct, Deglan says, "For fourteen years, I'm not a bad cop after all." Although "Night Cry" is a bleak teleplay, it anticipates later Cohen concerns in dealing with character growth and personal redemption.

"False Face" is another variation on Cohen's favorite theme of duality. Written as a short teleplay for NBC's "Way Out" series introduced every week by novelist Roald Dahl, "False Face" not only anticipates later themes in *It's Alive, God Told Me To, The Private Files of J. Edgar Hoover, It Lives Again,* and *Island of the Alive,* but also illustrates Cohen's use of a fantastic plot as an allegorical comment on the human situation. In his previous teleplays, his major characters were all victims of some personal or social problem connected to the world of everyday reality. "False Face" differs in merging elements of reality with fantasy. It is constructed in such a manner that the fantastic motif is important in terms of its function as a commentary on the human predicament. "False Face" anticipates Cohen's later experiments with the generic components of fantasy common to horror and science fiction. The teleplay is of historical interest as an early example of Dick Smith's makeup expertise several years before his work on *The Exorcist.*

"False Face" begins in a darkened flophouse, with egocentric actor Michael Drake (Alfred Ryder) searching for a character whose face he can use in a forthcoming theatrical production of *The Hunchback of Notre Dame.* Successfully finding his object, a man with a hideously deformed face, he offers him $50 to sit in his dressing room as a model for his makeup. Dissatisfied with the phony makeup used in his profession, Drake prowls flophouses every night seeking the most hideously scarred person.

Twenty-year-old Larry Cohen proudly stands between two of his fictional creations for his "False Face" contribution to the 1961 television series "Way Out." Alfred Ryder as arrogant actor Michael Drake is at Cohen's right while the victimized Martin Brooks as the Face stands at his left (courtesy of Larry Cohen).

Plying the Face (Martin Brooks) with drink as he copies his face with makeup, Drake begins to develop an affinity for his subject. When he inquires whether the facial deformity is genetic or the result of an accident, the Face enigmatically replies, "Both," mentioning that he knew Drake was seeking him. Drowning his torment in alcohol while Drake uses him for his selfish ends, the Face rejects the actor's interpretation of Quasimodo as a man who touches Esmeralda with "his underlying humanity." As Drake feigns empathy for his victim's social alienation, the latter begins an anguished monologue expressing internal torment and using gestures that are copied by his abuser.

"I can't live. They won't let me live. You see how a monster looks. You want to know how a monster feels? Ashamed of being a monster. Ashamed of wanting. (He picks up a photo of the actress playing Esmeralda.) Of not being a man. (Drake copies the Face's gesture of clutching the photo to his chest.) Ashamed of hating. I drink to forget. To forget what I am. I drink because I'm afraid of doing terrible things. I drink to forget I'm a man."

These poignant lines reveal Cohen's intuitive sympathy with all those that society categorizes as monsters.

After serving his purpose, Drake throws the unfortunate person out of his dressing room. Now completely resembling the Face, a resemblance his object studies with interest, Drake is now ready to give his greatest performance as Quasimodo. But after the performance, he finds he cannot remove the makeup. "It's grown on me. It's become part of my face. I can't get it off. I'm terrified." As in "87th Precinct" and "Night Cry," a once powerful male figure is placed in a subordinate, victimized position due to factors in his own personality causing emotional instability. In the opening scenes of "False Face," Michael Drake is already a monster in human form. Like Buddy Parker in "The Golden Thirty," he uses and abuses others. But, unlike his more pathetic predecessor, who will at least achieve a temporary respite from his fate by living off his victim's "Golden Thirty" routine, Michael Drake's fall is more sudden.

Living with his victim's face, Drake frenziedly searches for the missing man, hoping their next encounter will restore his own normal features. Returning to the flophouse, he finds that his agonized cry "Give me back my face" will never receive an answer. Drake discovers the Face dead, his features no longer abnormal but now embodying Michael Drake's former appearance.

"False Face" anticipates the type of moral allegories contained in Rod Serling's famous television series "The Twilight Zone." However, while containing a final judgment against its egocentric actor, the play is much more grimmer and realistic than any counterpart in Serling's world. In his agonized speech, the Face utters emotionally touching lines, revealing his disfigured self as embodying a human being suffering extreme internal torments due, not to his inner personality, but to social alienation. He is a victimized figure in a society living according to superficial standards of beauty and normality, a society that rewards handsome and monstrously manipulative figures such as Michael Drake and condemns those who fail to live up to its artificial rules. Arrogant, self-assured, using his girlfriend and manager, living only for the smell of the greasepaint and audience applause, he is more of a monster than the Face is. While the Face's abnormality is only skin-deep, Drake's monstrosity is far more personally internal. At the end of "False Face," he pays the price for his selfish manipulation of a socially unfortunate victim.

Like "Night Cry," "False Face" uses the duality theme that has fascinated Cohen ever since he saw *Strangers on a Train*. However, unlike Hitchcock's slavish imitators, Cohen reworks and reuses the concept in a much more original manner so that it finally appears as a creative motif in its own right. And "False Face" contains another indirect parallel to Hitchcock's cinema. It analyzes the negative features of a human condition resulting from false social values. Handsome and monstrous appearances are only skin-deep. Normality and abnormality coexist and are equally interchangeable, no matter what society may say. By writing "False Face" as a fantastic story, Larry Cohen began a path toward the radical allegorical features that characterize his later work in cinema. "False Face" interestingly anticipates his pattern of merging style and content. It presents a moral judgment, akin to those featured in his later teleplays for "Arrest and Trial," "The Defenders," "The Nurses," and "Sam Benedict."

E. G. Marshall (right) and Robert Reed appear in a publicity pose in their roles as father and son lawyers, Lawrence and Kenneth Preston, in the Emmy award–winning '60s television series "The Defenders."

"Kill or Be Killed" was Larry Cohen's first script for "The Defenders," the CBS Emmy Award–winning series created by Reginald Rose. Televised between 1961 and 1965, the weekly series was produced by the Herbert Brodkin Organization and featured strong scripts often dealing with relevant social issues, putting to shame later empty formulaic television series such as "L.A. Law." Featuring

E. G. Marshall and Robert Reed as father-and-son lawyer team Lawrence and Kenneth Preston, "The Defenders" continued the prominent tradition of socially realistic dramas common to the golden age of television. Although shot in New York by Filmways Studio, the filmed production still remained free from the contaminating glitter and superfluidity of most Hollywood-based productions. Much of the credit for this series goes to activist producer Herbert Brodkin, who continued the ethnic and social dramatic traditions present in live television drama.[1]

Anticipating the premises of Quinn Martin's series "The Fugitive," "Kill or Be Killed" opens with condemned prisoner Bernard Jackman (Gerald S.O'Loughlin) traveling by train to the death house after three trials. Two cops accompany him. Affirming his innocence, Jackman tells his guards about the strain on his domestic life: "I wonder if they know they're killing two people when they pull the switch." Meanwhile, the Prestons learn that the police have discovered the real murderer, proving Jackman innocent of the crime. While the train takes Jackman to Sing Sing, the Prestons tell Jackman's wife, Vera (Joanne Linville), the good news. However, the train crashes and Jackman escapes, pursued by 60-year-old Detective Edward Lundee, who fires warning shots in his direction. The Prestons later contact Jackman and tell the unbelieving fugitive he is an innocent man. However, while escaping, Jackman injured Lundee, placing him in a coma. Lundee dies in the hospital, and Jackman again faces a murder charge.

The Prestons again represent Jackman, who vents his anger at a legal system victimizing him once more: "I was innocent. I had the right to escape... You could not get me acquitted if I was innocent. What are you going to do now that I'm guilty?" Despite arguing about the human consequences of Jackman's dilemma with the district attorney (Simon Oakland), Lawrence Preston finds himself defending his client on another murder charge that also leads to the electric chair.

Angered by his situation, Jackman becomes justifiably paranoid, comparing his situation to that of a friend he saw trapped by a machine many years before: "His sleeve got caught in a machine. But the more he fought the more it chewed him up." Lundee's widow, Elsa (Joanna Roos), mourns for her husband and wishes judicial recompense. While Lundee was still in a coma, Vera Jackman hoped that her husband's arrest would save him from angry police, so she betrayed him by revealing his presence at the Prestons' office. While Elsa suffers the loss of her husband, Vera suffers rejection when her spouse suspects her betrayal. After a heated prison visit, Jackman walks away: "You die by yourself. You might as well live by yourself." The despondent Vera sees little hope, whatever the verdict. As she tells Kenneth, "Get him free so I can leave him." Lawrence Preston hopes the circumstances surrounding Jackman's crime might result in mitigating factors sparing him from the death house.

Agreeing upon a compromise with the district attorney, Preston gains the possibility of pleading guilty to a "manslaughter one" charge giving his client a possible minimum three-year jail sentence. Having already undergone three years in custody, Jackman refuses to spend more time in prison and wishes to gamble on an acquittal verdict on the murder charge. Recognizing his client's irrational attitude and self-deception, Preston rehearses the district attorney's cross-examination techniques with him during the court recess. Breaking Jackman down by provoking him into violence, he makes him realize he really murdered Lundee. Jackman beat him to death after he was unconscious, seeing him as a hated embodiment of all the police who caused his original conviction. Jackman confesses, "Yes. I did want to kill you like I killed Lundee. I wanted to kill him. I did it. I did it. I did! I did!"

Vera runs to comfort her husband. They both decide to face the future together. Although Jackman faces further imprisonment, Preston points out the significance of his confession: "Maybe you'll never be able to forgive yourself for what you've done. But at least you know why you did it. And at least that's more than most of us know about ourselves."

Cohen's teleplay is an excellent contribution to this series, revealing many complex ideas also characterizing his later work, such as the thin boundary dividing guilt from innocence. Beginning with Lawrence Preston's regret over the original guilty verdict, "Kill or Be Killed" encourages the audience initially to sympathize with Bernard Jackman's dilemma. He is an innocent man caught in the judicial machine. But, unlike Dr. Richard Kimble in "The Fugitive," Jackman is a complex figure torn by many contradictions. Gradually he becomes less sympathetic, lashing out angrily at those who wish to help him, exulting in a hurt sense of pride and a false individualism that really conceal destructively negative feelings. Although victimized, and pleading that he acted out of self-defense for a "moral right to live" (in Lawrence Preston's words), he has actually acted out far baser motives unknown even to himself, before he finally understands what actually motivated him. In Cohen's script, the innocent man is really guilty after all.

Rather than following the traditional "Perry Mason" courtroom drama formula, this Emmy-winning series presented more complex issues and socially relevant themes in its day. Hired to write one episode, Cohen could not investigate the personalities of the series' regular characters, the Prestons. But he was able to subvert a common formula, revealing the complexity of a human situation that transcends typical formulas characterizing most courtroom dramas. Forcing Jackman into a rehearsal of the district attorney's interrogation, in case he should gamble on acquittal, Preston challenges him: "I think that you've been lying to yourself." But rather than reproducing the standard arbitrary methodology of a typical "Perry Mason" courtroom confession, Jackman's breakdown represents the sudden self-knowledge of who he really is and what he actually has done. He is a complex character hiding aspects of his real personality both from himself and the world around him. The confession scene is worlds apart from the standard "Perry Mason" "I did it," with its accompanying banal description of the criminal act. It presents us with a figure whose recognition of his real self has individual and social consequences. Jackman realizes the nature of the beast inside him, one admittedly created by social forces but also one he nurtures unknowingly. As Preston tells him, "Maybe we've both won.... Nothing has changed, except for the better." Guilt and innocence are really relative. Like Hitchcock's titular figure, Jackman is also a "wrong man," but in much more complex and subtle terms.

It is often difficult to determine whether Pollack or Cohen is the author of certain scenes in "Kill or Be Killed." Two are particularly noteworthy. As Lawrence Preston suggests a plea bargain to Jackman in the empty courtroom during the closing ten minutes, the camera dollies twice round the back of the jury seats. The invisible jury represents the television audience who will be the only witness to the revelation of Jackman's guilt. Prior to Jackman's arrest outside the Prestons' office, the previous scene shows Vera looking at a phone placed predominantly in the right foreground. The phone figured prominently in certain sequences of "87th Precinct." The scenes may represent Larry Cohen's contributions to this particular dramatization.

Cohen's teleplay "The Traitor" deals with another divided character, suspected traitor Vincent Kayle (Fritz Weaver). This time the division involves personal and political levels. Arrested by federal agents outside Conson Aeronautics, Kayle requests the Prestons to act in his defense. Facing a watertight case on the part of U.S. District Attorney Frank Evans (Tim O'Connor) and the arrogant, aloof nature of his client, Lawrence Preston again has to balance conflicting aims of duty to country and duty to client. Facing various pressure groups represented by television talk-show host Lew Barrett (George Hall), who wishes the Prestons to drop the case, and Communist Front spokesman Malcolm Standish (Howard Weirum), who offers them financial aid, the father and son team find themselves in the same position as their client. Demonstrators brand them "traitors" for defending Kayle, especially when evidence emerges that he is not an American citizen but a foreign agent.

Believing in superior claims of justice and morality, Lawrence Preston is all the more eager to defend Kayle, especially since he is not defending an American traitor, but a man working for his own country as he works for his. Despite Evans' warning that the Prestons are now defending an "enemy agent, a spy," they discover that Kayle informed on himself to the authorities. He tells the Prestons that, by doing this, he "would be free for the first time." Placed in America as a "sleeper" agent eight years before, Kayle lived like an ordinary American citizen for six years. Summoned into service by his country, he lives a John Le Carré espionage existence of "interminable waiting," but chooses not to transmit valuable information. He is now a man of two identities and two countries. Kayle tells the Prestons that David Chernak, his former self who volunteered for espionage, is now dead. "He died of exposure to a free society." Participating in a three-month strike at his former job, he noticed the American government did not ruthlessly suppress it. "We had dignity because we had the right to disagree."

"The Traitor" is one of the best examples of Larry Cohen's talent as a screenwriter. It begins with a standard situation — the arrest of an accused man and his subsequent defense — but Cohen's handling of the material is far superior to the plots of most productions. He complicates the issues and introduces new, refreshing twists. Although aloof and highly intelligent, Vincent Kayle gains the undying trust and friendship of his average American fellow worker, Merv Erwin (Tom Clancy). While most writers would depict Erwin as a dupe, Cohen's characterization presents him as a genuine and trustworthy person far more sincere than the representatives of influential pressure groups who try to seduce the Prestons. Erwin's character represents an embodiment of the American values that influence Kayle. Furthermore, Kayle changes from an American traitor to a foreign agent by being genuinely impressed by the American way of life. But Cohen complicates any expectations of Kayle simply moving from "position A" to "position B" by presenting him as a complex person. Kayle will not simply change suddenly from being a foreign agent to an American patriot. He retains contradictory features within his personality. Although Kayle has the opportunity to accept the U.S. District Attorney's offer of a deal if he reveals everything, he decides to remain true to both his natural and his adopted country by not "naming names." It is hard not to see Cohen's indirect and subtle challenge to McCarthyism here.

Learning of the exchange deal from Evans, Lawrence Preston upholds his system of personal justice. He tells Evans, "Freedom is a real weapon in the war for men's minds," and "We can't let these rights be interfered with for the sake of expediency." Kayle refuses to take the stand and explain his personal conversion. When Preston tells him about the possible exchange, Kayle sees a way in which he can be true to both countries without betraying either one. He has already indirectly helped the United States. But he will not betray his natural home by revealing everything to his adopted country. However, by returning home as a hero in the eyes of his countrymen, he may help his spiritually adopted country by trying to work for change from within his original home. As he tells Preston, "By a devious route, I'm returning home as the hero I always wanted to be." Inwardly, he also thinks about his own family who, knowing of his volunteering for a dangerous mission, would be proud of him. Kayle can now be true both to himself and his two nations.

Although Kenneth Preston knows they will lose the case, his father reassures him that this will not happen "ultimately." Personal and political change is possible in the future. "The Traitor" not only reveals Cohen's mature powers as a writer but anticipates later themes in his films by emphasizing the importance of struggle rather than obtaining false, easy short-term victories.

In "The Colossus," a Nobel prize–winning scientist accidentally kills his wife in a fit of rage after she destroys his experiments in an attempt to gain his attention. Living only for his research into finding a cure for leukemia, the arrogant Dr. Morton Cheyney (Leo Genn) sees himself as a superior being above all human laws. Surrounded by a dedicated research team and regarded as an almost divine figure, Cheyney ignores Lawrence Preston's attempts to defend him satisfactorily. He is supported by various people, including research assistant Dr. Elm (Donald Moffat) who would go to prison on his behalf, a right-wing student (played by young Jon Voight), and ex–Nazi rocket scientist Dr. Ecker (Tonio

Selwart), against whom the American government dropped all war-crimes charges due to his strategic value during the Cold War era.

Cohen's teleplay not only examines the issue of people claiming exemption from the law because of special status but also engages in a comparison of the values of Cheyney and Lawrence Preston. While Cheyney believes that "All men are not created equal," Preston holds that "All men are entitled to equal opportunity and equal treatment before the law." Continuing their debates, Cheyney regards greatness as a "compulsion which drives a man beyond consideration of self," drawing a parallel to Preston's own professional dedication. Reluctant to convict Cheyney of first-degree murder, the district attorney (Joe Mantell) offers the scientist a manslaughter plea bargain in exchange for a confession of guilt. The colossus finally admits his pity for a wife he accidentally killed due to his elevating work above all other responsibilities. But he refuses to believe any ordinary jury will understand the "moral passion" driving him and his enraged feelings over his wife's destruction of valuable research. The two men continue their debate. When Preston states his intention to withdraw, since he puts personal moral feelings above professional conduct, he gains the respect of an adversary who has been testing him continually. Cheyney admits he sees in Preston "a reflection of myself" in the attitude taken by the lawyer. Preston responds, "If so, perhaps you're only human after all." He proceeds with a plea bargain so Cheyney will serve a minimum jail sentence and eventually return to the service of humanity.

"The Colossus" initially presents us with an arrogant, superior scientist who thinks of himself as free from all communal and human ties. However, despite Cheyney's negative characteristics, Cohen presents this monstrous *ubermensch* as not beyond human redemption. He does eventually realize the great personal cost that prestige brought to his married life. Initially regarding Preston as a nuisance, Cheyney, in a manner similar to that of the arrogant, Nietzschean Dr. Von Ecker, examines him under his own intellectual microscope. However, unlike Dr. Von Ecker, Cheyney, seeing in Preston a reflection of what he once was, agrees to compromise. Although still believing in his special status, Cheyney accepts human responsibility and finally decides to face the consequences. The scenario represents an interesting inversion of a future Cohen situation. Whereas *It's Alive* presents the normal figure of Frank Davies coming to terms with abnormality and accepting his son, "The Colossus" depicts its monstrously arrogant superhuman character as recognizing a glimmer of his former humanity in Lawrence Preston. Both Cheyney and Preston parallel each other in particular ways. But in "The Colossus," it is primarily the monster who recognizes his human qualities and the responsibility he has to his own society.

"The Noose" is one of Cohen's minor contributions to "The Defenders." The episode merely reinforces the Preston commitment to justice and equality for all before the law, even if they are suspected lynchers. Arriving in a small town to defend a client for murdering a child, the Prestons find the man hanging dead in his jail cell. Like Governor's Attorney Bennet Fletcher (Bruce Gordon), they believe vigilantes are responsible. When the suspects admit terrorizing the criminal into a confession but not hanging him, Lawrence Preston condemns Fletcher's attempts to make political capital out of the trial, as well as the liberal press' sensationalist reporting, which threatens the accused men's right to a fair trial. Despite the townspeople's opinion that no local jury will convict, Lawrence Preston insists that the law will overrule any local prejudice. He puts the town constable on the stand, who admits that he allowed his prisoner to hang himself after the vigilantes left. Although the charge of murder is dropped, Kenneth Preston accuses the vigilantes of indirectly causing the prisoner's death. They have escaped punishment for murder, but nevertheless bear final responsibility for the crime.

Cohen's next three "Defenders" teleplays — "The Captive," "The Secret," and "Mayday! Mayday!" — concern the relationship of the individual to the state. They form a political trilogy dealing with issues of mirror imagery between Eastern totalitarianism and Western democracy, and freedom and patriotism.

"The Captive" begins with zealously over-patriotic businessman Frank Rawlins (Andrew Duggan) being arrested in the Soviet Union on fabricated charges of espionage and subversion. His wife, Joanne (Mary Pickett), employs Lawrence Preston to gain her husband's release from a 15-year prison sentence. Preston finds the Justice Department unsympathetic to a suggested exchange between Rawlins and convicted Soviet spy Vorchek (Ludwig Donath). Reluctant to exchange a guilty prisoner to free an innocent man, United States officials play a diplomatic game similar to that of their Soviet counterparts. However, Preston makes an eloquent humanitarian plea to the authorities: "I believe in laws that transcend the statutes, universal moral laws... We talk about bringing freedom to the enslaved peoples of the world. This afternoon you have the opportunity to give freedom to one innocent man. I think our laws and our ideals require that we make use of this opportunity."

Meanwhile, Joanne and Kenneth Preston visit Rawlins in the Soviet Union and inform him of the possible exchange. Kenneth meets Rawlins' manipulative Russian lawyer, Lazlov (Robert Ellenstein), whose interest in the deal involves more than freeing an innocent client. Disavowing the Stalinist era, Lazlov speaks of the United States and Soviet Union having different political systems but not "conflicting standards of morality." When the Prestons discover that a post–Stalinist Soviet Union has condemned Vorchek to death in his absence, they find themselves in a moral dilemma. Committed to freeing their client in a deal convenient to both political systems, they face the realization of being accessories to murder after Vorchek returns to the East. As Lazlov notes, the two political systems do not have "conflicting systems of morality" in this ironic turn of events. East and West are both ready to sacrifice morality to political expediency whenever convenient. Although not representing the sinister but cultured, Stalinist Vorchek, the Prestons find themselves pleading his cause not just to unsympathetic Eastern and Western political representatives but also to the equally uncaring Rawlins couple. The drama unfolds in the divided capital of West and East

Berlin, an ideal geographical metaphor for Cohen's borderline motifs in "The Captive."

Cohen's teleplay avoids the manipulative device of making Vorchek a character who gains audience sympathy. He is committed to the Soviet cause, an unreconstructed Stalinist who still hopes for his country's eventual victory in the Cold War. As Lazlov comments, Vorchek is a "victim of changing times." But Vorchek emerges as a full-blooded human personality and not as an easily objectified villain. He is a man with a recognizable (if not positive) code of morality. Vorchek is much more direct and honest in his goals than the opposing political systems using him as a bargaining device. Although Joanna attempts viewing Vorchek as a convenient dehumanized bargaining chip to gain her husband's freedom, Lawrence Preston forces her to confront the real man. Finding herself emotionally affected, Joanna breaks down. She is unable to condemn him. But her response merely evokes Vorchek's sarcastic comments about Western weakness. Although the man has human attributes, he is still a cold-blooded monster solidly adhering to Stalinist beliefs. The formerly unresponsive Frank also listens to Lawrence Preston's humanitarian appeals and refuses the deal. Only Vorchek decides in favor of the deal, despite knowing his country's political rewriting of the past, which redefined heroes and traitors. He is also contemptuous of opportunistic new Soviet men such as Lazlov.

The deal eventually occurs at a German border crossing. Both captives meet each other for the first and last time, equally committed to different political values. Vorchek moves away to an uncertain fate. Although the devious Lazlov asserts his superiority to the old, brutal, Soviet system, and appeals to Preston as a fellow lawyer, Preston counters this equation by noting the inhumane nature of a barrier not only dividing East from West but also serving as a bridge between two systems not so far apart as they believe.

In "The Secret," conscientious scientist Daniel Orren (Martin Landau) discovers the formula for a neutron bomb he decides to destroy. Discovered burning his notes by his superior, Dr. Ladzlaw (George Voskovec), he is arrested under the Atomic Energy Act 226 even though he no longer works in the weapons division. Like J. Robert Oppenheimer, Orren becomes fascinated with nuclear physics. Despite asking for a transfer after finding his former occupation "morally repugnant," he faces a possible sentence as a result of denying his government knowledge of an "ultimate secret." However, Orren continues working out equations on scraps of paper. Unconsciously, he egocentrically works towards producing a weapon of mass destruction while consciously being aware of the dangers. Although less explicitly emotionally driven than Barney Jackman of "Kill or Be Killed" and Leo Rolf of "The Unwritten Law," he is still torn between opposing tendencies.

To prepare "a reasonable defense," the Prestons attempt persuading Orren to reveal his reasons for destroying the formula. Initially reluctant, Orren takes the stand, affirming his right to place "personal beliefs about right and wrong above the law." Drawing a comparison with law-abiding Nazi war criminals who faced justice after World War II, the accused scientist eloquently argues that "a man has to answer to himself first and the letter of the law second." The issue is raised as to whether the defendant's own ideas "belong to himself or his government, particularly those 'he considers harmful to society.'" The U.S. District Attorney (Tim O'Connor) attempts to counter this argument, accusing Orren of engaging in "a compulsive and egocentric need to solve the riddle," contrary to his moral stand. He uses Dr. Ladzlaw as an example of a patriotic scientist. However, Lawrence Preston refers to Ladzlaw's past. Ladzlaw belonged to a group of wartime scientists who failed to persuade the military to give the Japanese prior warning before dropping the Bomb. Asked if he would have acted differently had he known the consequences of August 6, 1945, the older man affirms his "sense of guilt."

"No. I would not have dropped the Bomb if I had known the result, and I would have destroyed the secret."

Cohen draws a parallel between the two scientists breaking down the barriers that formerly divided them. Phyllis Orren (Georgann Johnson) earlier referred to Ladzlaw as being "like a father to Dan," adopting him as his protege, and now wanting to send him to prison. Cohen notes historical similarities between father and son. Although Preston pleads that the jury recognize Orren as a man embodying the highest function of a human being in exercising "collective responsibility" for the fate of mankind, an air raid warning interrupts his speech influencing the final verdict. Despite acting on humanity's behalf, Orren receives a guilty verdict.

Before the trial Orren agrees to deliver his secret over to the government if he is found guilty. Although Orren will only serve a few years in prison, Evans comments that the guilty scientist has engaged in a stand that will end his career: "What did he accomplish?" Preston replies, "He made his point." Orren did. But the personal costs are catastrophic. Orren wishes his wife to make her own decision over his stand. He refers to Thomas Jefferson's remark "I want you to do what you want to do" in leaving her to make her own evaluation. After the jury's decision, she asks Preston, "He was right. Wasn't he?" She now doubts her husband. Ironically, the very people Orren wished to protect and save finally condemn him.

"The Secret" deals with the conflict between the state and human justice. It is a theme also common to the work of Sidney Lumet within the American Jewish cinematic tradition, as well as present in fifties television and the Brodkin Organization's socially conscious television productions.[2] In his later films, Cohen still retains this important theme. But he mediates it allegorically within other generic realms.

"Mayday! Mayday!" emphasizes a problematic father-son family relationship involving political and military issues. The episode opens with the young grandson of famous naval hero Admiral Lucas J. Kiley (Torin Thatcher) playing with a toy nuclear submarine. Significantly named after his esteemed patriarchal grandfather, young Lucas inhabits a room decorated with military items. As Admiral

Kiley attempts to enlist a visitor in his scheme to seize the government and indoctrinate others into the cause, his son Randall (Skip Homeier) listens uneasily. The elder Kiley regards contemporary American society as "anaemic of spirit" and suffering from moral "disease" and a "sapped will" during the Cold War era. Randall stops the conversation and ushers in a U.S. Marshall. To Randall's surprise, his father is arrested on a charge of advocating sedition against the American government. Recognizing his son's involvement in his arrest, Admiral Kiley bids goodbye to his grandson, telling him, "Try very hard to remember this moment." He walks away contemptuous of his son.

Cohen's economically significant introduction depicts this particular family as inseparably connected to society, history, and politics. Young Lucas is already snared by a vicious warrior tradition espoused by his grandfather. He plays with a war toy and is obviously expected to follow family tradition and enlist at Annapolis. Cohen associates him with his grandfather, not his father, in the introductory sequence. Lucas J. Kiley and Randall exist in a state of family antagonism. Although Randall enlisted at Annapolis to please his father, he resents him for the death of his mother, forcing him into a military career, and denying him affection: "What I needed was a father, not a commanding officer ... I was appointed to Annapolis at birth." Although he respects his father and tries to make him avoid a guilty verdict by suggesting insanity, his later courtroom testimony reveals a deep anger built up over several years.

The family emphasis is neither accidental nor marginal. As a strong patriarch wishing to seize power by a military coup and engage in an unprovoked assault against China, Lucas J. Kiley is an early example of Larry Cohen's monster generated within the nuclear family. Excessively patriotic, an esteemed World War II officer mentioned in "the same breath as Nimitz and Eisenhower," and proud of the fathers who dedicated their sons to him as sacrificial offerings during the Pacific campaign, Kiley views himself as a superior being. He bears many similarities to Morton Cheyney in "The Colossus." Lucas Kiley is a major symbol of an insane patriarchy generated by the historical and social forces of the Cold War era, yearning for hallowed nineteenth-century ideals of total warfare and Social Darwinism. Contemptuous both of the United Nations and neutral countries who would object to his doomsday scenario, Kiley believes in the Cold War–era philosophy of "kill or be killed." He is as much of an atavistic monster as Bernard Jackman in "Kill or Be Killed." But unlike Jackman, whose atavistic tendencies are unconscious, Kiley's are conscious and calculated.

Believing it is now time for a soft American nation to pay its sacrificial dues by undergoing the scale of human losses suffered by other nations in World War II ("six million Jews") and Communist China (ten million between 1950 and 1955), he relishes a future Armageddon: "I believe in Darwin's natural selection — the survival of the fittest." Despite the fact that his preemptive nuclear strike will involve human losses exceeding those in previous wars, Kiley believes his illegal military coup and continuing dictatorship guarantee future peace.

Although Randall and the Prestons wish Kiley to be judged insane, neither the old man nor psychological tests allow this. A government psychologist finds Kiley "sane" under standard definitions. Although disagreeing with Kiley's philosophy, Lawrence Preston agrees to defend him, if only to bring about the abolition of a law affecting free speech that caused his client's arrest. Kiley sees the trial as providing a public forum for his views. He hopes to influence a future generation. Wishing to be found guilty under the existing law, he hopes the trial proceedings will supply an accurate record of his beliefs for future supporters.

Anticipating Ronald Reagan's Armageddon speeches of two decades later, Kiley's views are the logical consequences of a society built upon a masculinized death instinct. Faced with defending an all too rational military monster whose destructive goals far exceed any Frankenstein monster, Lawrence Preston achieves a minor victory in getting Kiley to condemn himself by revealing his paranoid, unstable tendencies. He does this by getting Kiley to admit his deep desires, wishing America defeated if it refuses to follow him. Believing that communism will dominate the United States in five years, Kiley concludes, "That will be the final proof that I was a hero after all. *I hope so.*" Preston immediately seizes on the last sentence, emphasizing Kiley's wish to see his beloved country fall just to prove himself right. Confronted with this self-condemnation, Kiley fails to alter the court record. He then paranoically accuses Preston of "being a Communist." But despite Preston's strategy of proving Kiley insane, the jury delivers a guilty verdict, but without the qualification of "by reason of insanity." Kiley gets his wish after all.

Taking compensation in Kiley's damaging admission, the Prestons lose their case but gain a minor victory. The court record will remain to transmit the true facts for those interested in learning them. Cohen's "Mayday! Mayday!" is one of his strongest "Defenders" teleplays. It contains the early appearance of ideas he will develop in *The Private Files of J. Edgar Hoover*. Both Lucas J. Kiley and J. Edgar Hoover are metaphorical embodiments of the dangerous monster figure associated with the patriarchal family and a masculinized society orientated towards death and destruction.

"Go-Between" examines social and psychological pressures that turn a dedicated presidential candidate into a hard-line reactionary. During a political convention, Matthew T. Ryder (Arthur Hill) delivers a speech at the very moment his son, Freddy, is kidnapped. Cohen juxtaposes scenes of the speech with Freddy's being led down a dark corridor. Freddy is last seen as Ryder's lines about America being "the best place to bring up our children" echoes down the passage. In this teleplay, Lawrence Preston acts as a financial advisor to Ryder as well as a "go-between."

Concerned about Freddy's safety, Ryder and his wife, Dolores (Phyllis Thaxter), become victimized by the media, phony well-wishers, and various hoaxers who intrude upon their personal grief. Wishing for his son's return, Ryder offers to pay the $200,000 ransom, wanting his personal family life to take priority over political ambitions. However, after suffering from the intrusions of a manipulative gossip columnist (Sally Gracie), the skepticism of FBI agent Slattery (John Randolph) over his son's survival, crank psychic Riggs (excellently played by

Roberts Blossom), and campaign manager Harrison Alder (Addison Powell) about how submitting to blackmail will affect his presidential hopes, Ryder eventually becomes contaminated. Although he calls a press conference to announce his resignation as presidential candidate, he reacts to journalistic assertions about his son's supposed mental abilities, viewing them as an affront to his personality. Seeing his son less as a person and more as a political liability, Ryder drops his intended resignation speech and continues to run for office. Prior to Lawrence Preston's final "go-between" role, he isolates himself from the proceedings, seeing his son as more useful dead than alive, especially if he gains sympathetic votes from a public he now views contemptuously.

In "Go-Between," Ryder changes from a caring individual into a hard-line reactionary politician as a result of pressures exerted on him by representatives of a sick, callous society. As Dolores comments to Lawrence Preston, "He's (Ryder) not tense anymore. He's risen above it where no one can reach him or hurt him anymore." He has become a "colossus" like Morton Cheyney. After Preston returns Freddy, he sees that Ryder only cares about his own political ambitions. As a monstrous politician intending to "go easy" on civil rights and federal aid for education, he is contemptuous of a public he once wished to appeal to. Like J. Edgar Hoover, he is a monster created by the very system he once thought of sincerely serving. The story ends with Ryder's campaign speech, in which he ironically states, "I hope that someday I repay so many for so much."

"Go-Between" operates on several levels. It criticizes sensationalist aspects of the American press and also anticipates motifs in *It's Alive*. Ryder turns from being a devoted father initially concerned for the safe return of his son into an aloof figure rejecting his son because of allegations aimed at his masculinity. If Ryder does not regard his son as a monster, like Frank Davis does in *It's Alive*, he is still adversely affected by malevolent social influences. Since ten-year-old Freddy is still in third grade, one reporter believes he is "retarded." In Cohen's teleplay, that incident is the final straw leading to Ryder's changing from sympathetic, caring father into inhuman politician. The change has dark consequences for the future if he reaches the White House.

"The Unwritten Law" is one of Cohen's most intelligent teleplays for "The Defenders" series. It examines the dangerous social masks worn by people engaging in civilized role-playing rituals that are extremely harmful both psychologically and socially. "The Unwritten Law" begins with a pre-credits sequence that echoes visual and performance techniques of the golden days of silent cinema. The lack of dialogue also evokes the poignant scene in "87th Precinct," in which Steve Carella wanders alone in Mrs. Faye's apartment, conscious of his responsibility for her death. Apart from Leo's concluding phone call to the police and the sound effects, the scene is virtually silent. Opening with Leo Rolf (David Opatoshu) arriving home unexpectedly, hearing sounds of an adulterous liaison in his bedroom, deciding to leave, then hesitating, and returning to get the handgun he will use to murder Arthur Ruskin, the scene is an excellent example of masterly visual signification. He shoots his wife's lover and then calls the police.

Leo confesses before Lawrence Preston and the police captain. Despite Preston's caution, Leo accepts guilt — "I killed him. I had a perfect right to" — presenting a self-created image of a wronged husband appropriating nineteenth-century codes of patriarchal morality to avenge personal dishonor. He sees his murdered victim as entirely responsible for his wife's adultery: "It had to be done."

Questioning the validity of Leo's confession as evidence in the pending trial, Lawrence Preston confronts a cynical district attorney ( J. D. Cannon) who contests any defense based upon true love and honor: "Most of the time true love has nothing to do with it.... When it comes to something personal like S.E.X., you never believe anything based on what they tell you about themselves." He regards Leo's anachronistic idealism as "a perfect plea for insanity." The district attorney further remarks, "People don't kill for love anymore. They sue for a divorce, like I did."

Leo believes in a "kind of unwritten law" allowing him to avenge personal dishonor. Employed as a statistician, Leo is a fastidious type, adhering to a code of honor — "I have honor. I have pride" — and blaming Ruskin for seducing his wife. Succeeding scenes show Kenneth and Lawrence interviewing the wives of the accused and deceased victim, respectively. Both interviews reveal the social and sexual frustration of two women bound up within differing, but equally oppressive, codes of conduct. Kenneth listens to Eileen Rolf (Kim Hunter). Married to Leo for 17 years, she sublimates her discontented domestic life with alcohol and attempts seducing Kenneth. She describes Leo as an ideal husband always willing to forgive her: "I was never as perfect as Leo. I could never live up to his standards. He's a perfectionist." Eileen Rolf expresses deep dissatisfaction with a husband who places her on a pedestal like a nineteenth-century wife.

While Kenneth interviews Eileen, Lawrence listens to a more sophisticated and swinging example of another generation: Sharon Ruskin ( Jessica Walter). As she talks about her deceased husband, we see a photo of him in the left of the frame. She occupies the right foreground in close-up. Married for nearly half as long as Eileen, she tells Lawrence of her knowledge about her husband's affair. Belonging to a generation that regards extramarital affairs as a norm of everyday life and entertainment, Sharon reveals her frustration with this new code of ethics, which are as oppressive for her as the old moral codes are for Eileen. Wanting to be a good, understanding wife, she expresses deep discontent: "I could have stopped him ... But I didn't want to ask. I wanted him to stop of his own free will." Sharon masochistically blames herself for holding this new attitude, while Eileen turns to drink and sex to escape from Leo's antiquated codes of conduct. Both old and new ideological roles trap these women of different generations.

Lawrence Preston perceives that Leo chose Ruskin as a convenient sacrificial victim to assuage his personal failings and frustrations. The lawyer uncovers the real reasons behind Leo's crime. He makes Leo realize that Eileen's actions represented "a protest against a life which was destroying her identity" and accuses him of self-deception: "You've been lying to yourself. You were lying ever since you pulled that trigger." Leo then realizes that he stifled his wife's potential in a

frustrating marriage, seeing her, not as a person in her own right, but as an ideological object. He changes, viewing Eileen not as an ideal wife, but as an adulterous spouse, casting her in a new role as "cheating bitch," and really wanting
to murder her. It is far easier for Leo to act as a wronged husband rather than
admit to his culpability, oppressing Eileen in a faulty marriage whose very structure he conceived himself. Leo now becomes a spouse avenging his loss of personal honor: "I had to lie. I didn't want anyone to know." Like Bernard Jackman
in "Kill or Be Killed," he is his own worst enemy, operating according to desires
he does not understand.

Although the Rolf marriage deteriorated into personal misery for both partners, Eileen reveals that she loved her husband for the whole 17 years. While Leo
believed she had several lovers, Arthur Ruskin was actually her first and last.
Eileen understands that while she loved Leo, he never really loved her, despite
all the acts of devotion he showed towards her and her ailing father: "It wasn't
love. It was humiliating. The knowledge that it had all been false — that you
really felt nothing." Their whole marriage is based on lies, humiliation, and self-
deceptive role-playing.

Bereft of his illusions, Leo finally hears the guilty verdict in court. Realizing the utter futility of his entire life and adherence to self-deceptive codes of
honor, he can only exclaim, "It's unfair. It's so unfair." By this time, he is stripped
of all illusions and realizes the implications of his criminal acts.

"The Unwritten Law" is an important contribution to "The Defenders."
Strongly critical of devious ideological codes and false social values, it anticipates
later themes in Cohen's work depicted allegorically within fantastic generic frameworks.

Like "The Defenders," "The Nurses" was another Herbert Brodkin production filmed in New York by Plautus Productions. Screened between 1962 and
1965, "The Nurses" focused on two main characters, mature senior nurse Liz
Thorpe (Shirl Conway) and student nurse Gail Lucas (Zina Bethune). Each
episode focused on a serious social issue. Cohen wrote three teleplays for the
series: "Night Sounds," "Party Girl," and "The Gift."

"Night Sounds" deals with a contemporary issue still relevant today. After
escaping an attempted assault by sexually disturbed patient Norman Ruskin
(Donald Davis), Gail Lucas finds not only that very few people believe her but
that she also suffers social blame as an innocent victim.[3] Castigated by impatient
doctor Furst (Noah Keen) for being absent from her post when a patient was
dying, she finds that few people on the hospital staff actually listen to her. Even
the normally sympathetic Mrs. Thorpe initially shares this attitude before she
apologizes, "I'm sorry I wasn't listening to you." It is easy to blame a victim for
being responsible for an unprovoked assault rather than investigate the social circumstances and institutional failures resulting in such acts.

When Ruskin denies the incident happened, Gail faces a detailed interrogation by the hospital lawyer. He is less eager to discover the truth than to protect the institution from scandal and a legal suit. As he later tells the hospital

administrator, Mr. Henry, who believes in the medical profession's ideal of protecting the public from any dangerous disease (sexual or otherwise), a hospital is "also a business" in which unfavorable publicity affects fund raising. Like Frank Davies in *It's Alive*, Ruskin is also in public relations and concerned to avoid any scandal. Since all parties wish to suppress the truth, Gail receives no institutional support to pursue her claim of sexual assault. The authorities request that she temporarily resign until the police resolve the issue. She will lose her reputation and career if no sufficient grounds exist to indict Ruskin.

Meanwhile, Gail becomes hypersensitive, reacting to teasing patients and a young Dr. Kildare figure, John Griffin (Alan Alda), who later believes Gail is a tease responsible for her own dilemma. Gail thinks everyone regards her as "a kind of freak." She finds herself in a position similar to the later dilemmas of the *It's Alive* parents and children. Liz's counsel warns her that she is in personal danger by becoming antagonistic both towards Ruskin and a community she once thought supportive. By overreacting, she also anticipates the overaggressive defensive actions of the mutant babies in *It's Alive* and *It Lives Again*.

Gail finds herself an outcast in her own community, and becomes as much of an outsider as Ruskin. The later *It's Alive* movies often draw parallels between human social outcasts and their monstrous counterparts. But in "Night Sounds," Cohen portrays Ruskin as a pathetic and vulnerable being needing care rather than punishment. Unlike Gail (who does have Mrs. Thorpe as her solitary ally), he is a victim of uncontrollable desires his own wife Edith deliberately ignores. Appealing to Gail in the same utility room which earlier housed his original assault, Ruskin appeals, "If you go to the police, you'll be killing me." Like Martin Burnham in Cohen's "Arrest and Trial" teleplay, he fears future harassment by authorities who will continually suspect him in similar cases. Ruskin fears being labeled as an "other" like Gail. He draws comparisons between Gail's new situation in the hospital and his own: "I lied, and your friends ... Something in them wanted to condemn you. That's a disease too. They need to hate people like me."

Confronted by this frightened victim, Gail no longer hates him. She now understands his dilemma and appeals to him to undergo voluntary treatment. She also feels less hatred for her fellow workers realizing that they act out of fear and vulnerability, and not due to any sort of inherent viciousness. By emphasizing hidden individual and social fear mechanisms leading people to categorize others as monsters, Cohen's dialogue between Gail and Ruskin anticipates later tensions motivating *It's Alive* and other films. Their eventual mutual understanding foreshadows the poignant final reconciliation between Frank Davies and his son inside the Los Angeles storm drains in *It's Alive* and Ellen Jarvis' acceptance of her grandson in *Island of the Alive*.

Mrs. Thorpe eventually stimulates Mrs. Ruskin toward taking final responsibility for her husband's condition. She decides to prolong her husband's stay in the hospital. The episode resolves one individual aspect of a problem occurring again in other Cohen works: the hidden mechanics of social alienation arbitrarily distinguishing normal from abnormal.

Cohen's "Party Girl" poignantly deals with the social exploitation of glamorous working girl Clarissa Robin (Inga Stevens) who ultimately discovers another side of human existence beneath the bleak exploitative materialistic world that dominates her personal life. Brought into the hospital after suffering a heart attack by caring client Mervyn Fowler (Vincent Gardenia) , the glamorous "model" immediately becomes the focus of attention of doctors and nurses until they discover her real profession. Rejected by a hospital community looking on her as an outcast rather than a human being, she also suffers the brutal fate of a call girl rejected by pimp Bert Handell (Tim O'Connor), who has no further use for her. By removing her apartment key and address book, Bert callously casts her aside as a discarded object. Clarissa questions her fate: "Can't an employee get sick for a while?" Bert replies, "We don't have employment compensation on this job."

Cohen sympathetically depicts the desperate plight of a call girl who suddenly finds herself alone and isolated in an uncaring society, suffering the scorn of a community that treats her more as a despised object than as an individual person in need of sympathy. Clarissa finds herself occupying a similar position to Gail in "Night Sounds." Her fate also anticipates the different types of social alienation and rejection suffered by later Cohen characters in more fantastically orientated films. However, "Party Girl" also depicts Clarissa's discovery of another world that is far more sympathetic than the economically affluent and brutal world represented by Bert and her replacement, Ronnie (Arlene Golonka). Visited by the client who originally brought her into the hospital before he disappeared, Clarissa discovers a sympathetic man concerned for her health, respecting her as a human being and not as an object of bodily pleasure. Talking with her on the hospital sunroof, Fowler tells her that he suffered a heart attack in a cinema. As he began to gasp for breath, he found the audience more concerned with the artificial plight of screen characters than with his own deadly real-life situation. Fowler tells her, "My dying was annoying them. They could only understand somebody dying on the screen." Had he died, nobody would have noticed. Fowler evokes Clarissa's long-buried feelings by telling her about the importance of helping suffering human beings.

Fowler's dialogue states key motifs within the work of Larry Cohen. In works as diverse as "The Golden Thirty" and *Wicked Stepmother*, Cohen criticizes the false values of an entertainment world that delivers glamorous, artificial illusions within a world of empty human existence. Buddy Parker's comic in "The Golden Thirty" and Lionel Stander's character in *Wicked Stepmother* are seduced in different ways by a world promising affluence in exchange for real human fulfillment. The college-educated Clarissa becomes trapped in a life-denying existence promising temporary wealth for its victims and ultimate brutal rejection for its useless losers. She lives according to the same false illusionary values that seduce the cinema audience witnessing Fowler's heart attack. Clarissa finally discovers another world of human feelings and understanding during her last days. Criticized by Mrs. Thorpe for objectifying Clarissa after she no longer corresponds to the glamorous ideal in his "little dwelling" ("She let you down, didn't she?"), Dr. Milford learns from his mistake. Encountering Clarissa in her last moments, he touches her by genuinely showing that he wants her to get better. But it is too late. Clarissa suffers her final heart attack, looking at her dying image in an apartment hallway, and realizing the lost potential for an alternative existence she will never realize.

In "The Gift," Cohen introduces a theme that will recur prominently in his family horror films. During a business meeting, Arthur Luskin (Robert Webber) attempts suicide as a protest against efforts by his mother and wife to make company president Phil Granger (Edward Asner) stand down in his favor. It is an act of desperation against a claustrophobic family situation. Arthur Luskin is a victim of a monstrous nuclear family treating him as a child well into adulthood. They ignore the real reasons leading to his attempted suicide. As Phil Granger later tells Arthur's nurse Doris Kelly (Lee Grant), Arthur is the product of a family who did everything for him by making him a "mama's boy." Arthur "never had to make a decision or overcome an obstacle." Now confined to a hospital bed, Phil understands Arthur's new situation: "His mother and Claire must secretly enjoy having him this way. It's always how they wanted him to be — in need of them."

Focusing on Doris Kelly's attempts to give Arthur a reason to live by teaching him to develop without the help of anyone, "The Gift" deals with Arthur's transition from trapped family dependence towards individual independence. Doris recognizes Arthur's dilemma in a family that wishes to deny he attempted suicide. They wish to avoid unpleasant personal realities, as does Edith Ruskin in "Night Sounds." Doris tries an unusual method to help him live. Before his muscles waste away, she prevents Arthur from remaining in a self-induced mental shell by promising to aid him in another suicide attempt: "If you really want to die, you'll have to learn how to live first. I'll help you learn to get the strength." Accompanying Arthur home with his wife and mother who physically and mentally treat him like a little boy, Doris negotiates the dangerous consequences of her bargain, hoping that Arthur will finally make his own decision to live.

Returning to a home where Arthur has lived his whole life (including his marriage), Doris recognizes the suffocating nature of a family situation thwarting her patient's emotional growth. As she tells Claire one evening, "Your husband's learning to walk for the first time. But it's always hard to stand alone when people tell him you don't know how." Eventually, after Arthur realizes suicide is no answer, he decides to move permanently to a private nursing home. Announcing his decision to a resentful mother and wife, he states the necessity of "walking ahead" of his family, leaving them the option of catching up with him or not. "The Gift" ends on a positive note with Arthur acting independently by leaving a family situation that has caused great physical and emotional distress.

"Medal for a Turned Coat" is an appropriate conclusion to this chapter. It formed part of the sixties television series "Espionage" produced by Herbert Brodkin. Like "The Defenders" and "The Nurses," "Espionage" often combined strong dramatic themes with a familiar genre. "Medal for a Turned Coat" is one of the most outstanding episodes in this series, along with "The Incurable One" starring Steven Hill and Ingrid Thulin. Both remain in the memory over 30 years after their original broadcasts.

"Medal for a Turned Coat" is one of Cohen's most accomplished teleplays. It analyzes the character of the "good German" far more intuitively than Steven Spielberg's superficial and meretricious *Schindler's List* (1993). As well as containing Cohen themes of personal self-deception, as in "Kill or Be Killed" and the patriotism element of "The Traitor," the structure anticipates the montage memory techniques Cohen later uses in *Bone*. Although Cohen had no control over casting, the presence of Fritz Weaver as the main character immediately evokes comparison with "The Traitor." "Medal for a Turned Coat" represents an inverse treatment of themes used in the earlier screenplay. It analyzes the character of a man who deliberately distorts his personal and social history by denying his real self and living in a self-deceptive manner. The main character has several parallels with Leo Rolf in "The Unwritten Law." But unlike Vincent Kayle in "The Traitor," Richard Keller achieves agonized self-realization only during his dying hours. Like Barney Jackman in "Kill or Be Killed," he is forced to confront personal tensions and contradictions. This time no Lawrence Preston functions as advocate. Instead, Keller's long repressed, unconscious mind returns to interrogate him in his dying moments. It functions in a manner similar to Kirsch's interrogation of another character practicing similar denial techniques (Ullman) in Cohen's play *Nature of the Crime*.

The pre-credits sequence of "Medal for a Turned Coat" shows Richard Keller (Fritz Weaver) rehearsing his speech in an empty auditorium prior to receiving an award from the West German government for heroism in the anti–Nazi movement. As Keller speaks about a new Germany surviving and rebuilding itself, a young Aryan-looking man in a black leather jacket enters. He seats himself and listens to the speech with contempt showing on his face. Keller looks at him and finds himself facing a revolver. After he finishes the line, "I envy your abilities to live with your own consciences," the young man shoots him.

We next see Keller critically wounded in the hospital. A nurse tells a doctor (Gerard Heinz) that Keller is having "conversations with himself." The doctor comments, "It would help if he wanted to live, but I don't think he does." He describes Keller as a man "who betrayed his country." Keller wrestles with internal forces in his own unconscious, forces he has suppressed for over 20 years, but which now confront him like avenging furies. They take the form of figures from his past and present: sister Ilsa (Rosemary Rogers), deceased Jewish wife Ellen (Sylvia Kay), and former British intelligence officer, now business partner, Harry Forbes (Nigel Stock). As Harry tells Keller in the concluding scenes, "We're only figments of your imagination. You invented us. Why don't you make us disappear?" Although he never appears in the hospital, Keller's assassin, Hans Luber (Richard Carpenter), is really a monster figure from his id, representing final judgment for personal and social betrayal. The appearances of these figures parallel the situation of Keller's mother (Catherine Lacey). Blaming herself for condemning her son at a Nazi show trial, she condemns herself with a self-induced psychosomatic illness.

"Medal for a Turned Coat" eschews conventional television linear narration by mixing past and present temporal levels to depict Keller's mental torment. Cohen's teleplay aims at a psychoanalytical interrogation juxtaposing different levels of memory to reveal the damaging truths that Keller denies. When the drama begins, the audience takes Richard Keller at face value as a returning anti–Nazi hero brutally shot by a neo–Nazi thug. But Cohen's teleplay moves beyond such basic oppositions to engage analytically in excavating disavowed aspects of guilty tensions hidden beneath Keller's individual and political activities. As "Medal for a Turned Coat" unfolds, we learn that the doctor's condemnation of Keller is correct. Keller not only betrayed his country but also himself.

Selected by Field Marshall Von Elm ( Joseph Furst) for a peace mission during 1944, Keller avoids his superior's probing questions about the real reasons for volunteering. When he next encounters the elderly Von Elm, the latter sarcastically categorizes Keller as "an unsuccessful traitor" now being used by the West German government to distract attention away from a forthcoming Nazi war crimes trial. In the flashback sequence, Von Elm criticizes Hitler, oblivious of the fact that another officer not involved in the plot remains in the room. Even in this brief scene, Cohen's teleplay suggests Keller's devious nature. Both Keller and the orderly exchange glances as they listen to Von Elm. After Von Elm realizes his mistake, Keller stands beside the orderly as if he is hedging his bets, wanting to be on a winning side with a possible informant should circumstances change. However, the unfortunate man is led away to his execution.

Von Elm uses Keller in the same way that British intelligence does. Keller is forced to reveal locations of chemical factories near his hometown, thus making the nearby civilian population susceptible to bombing raids. The British also force him to engage in propaganda broadcasts. Keller writes a best-selling book, *The Germans,* condemning his nation for supporting the Nazi regime while promoting himself as an anti–Nazi, a guise both Ilsa and Harry see through. Keller also marries Ellen, a Jewish woman, as a means of further denying guilt for personal complicity in the Nazi regime up to 1944.[4] Like everyone else, he stood by and watched. Confronted with his responsibility, Keller experiences his shooting once again, dying in his hospital bed after pronouncing a guilty verdict on himself.

Formally and thematically, "Medal for a Turned Coat" is one of Larry Cohen's major achievements as a television dramatist. It represents the creative influence of Herbert Brodkin and the type of high-quality work that was possible 30 years ago on television but is absent today. In "Medal for a Turned Coat," Cohen never engages in a simple black and white morality scenario pitting good against evil. He instead engages in a complex dialectical examination of the main issues. Attention is shifted from Frank, the stereotypically bad neo–Nazi seen at the beginning, to focus on Richard Keller's character. As the story develops, Keller condemns himself, finally facing his guilt and stripping away deceiving veils disavowing traumatic personal facts. "Medal for a Turned Coat" is more of a rad-ically constructed psychodrama than a typical television narrative. Its characters are all recognizable individuals with personal flaws. When Richard returns home and talks with Ilsa, she condemns him for also "acquiescing in evil," speaking about a Jewish tailor they allowed the Nazis to take away. The only thing on her mind was the thought that she did not have to pay the 12 marks she owed — a human failing, but one which is shared by anyone in the same situation.

Richard Keller is not a German in the nationalistic sense, but a universal human figure whose dilemma is applicable to everyone. Despite Cohen's emer-gence from an American Jewish background, his work is never solely applicable to isolated characters, ethnic groups, or isolated situations. It has universal dimen-sions. Similarly, although the families in *It's Alive* suffer the unusual fate of hav-ing monster children, the situation affecting them is never entirely fantastic. It has deep social and individual implications inherently associated with the system in which they live. Although "Medal for a Turned Coat" could easily have become a formulaic production pitting a good anti–Nazi hero against guilty Germans, the teleplay engages in a complex analytic interrogation of an all too human sit-uation. Richard Keller could be anyone — a social and psychological victim engag-ing in acts of self-deception concealing his own complicit guilt. As a result, "Medal for a Turned Coat" takes on a universal moral significance, making it one of the most remarkable works Cohen has written.

Larry Cohen's early work represents important achievements during the last years of the golden age of television and beyond. It also reveals themes and motifs that appear consistently in his later film productions. During the next decade, Cohen moved away from the "realistic" formulas of television narrative into other generic realms. But no matter how escapist or fantastic these realms may initially appear, they still contain traces of the same ideas Cohen used in his television dramas of the late fifties and early sixties. However, before Larry Cohen began directing his own work, he moved to Hollywood and made some remarkable contributions by writing television pilots, contributing scripts for established series such as "The Fugitive," and creating some interesting television movies. His work in this area formed important background material for his later role as an independent commercial film director in a fantastic realm supposedly dealing with gods and monsters but actually describing real-life human situations.

# Early Work in
# Hollywood Television

During the mid-sixties, Larry Cohen moved to Hollywood after achieving success in writing for New York television. He became one of the most sought-after television writers of his time. But the Los Angeles–based television industry was a different world from the New York studios where Cohen began his career. Distant, geographically and mentally, from the Eastern landscape of the "golden age of American television" and creative producers such as Herbert Brodkin, Hollywood television tended to be more formulaic and less creatively inclined. However, this did not prevent Cohen from writing some interesting work under more rigid constraints. During this period Larry Cohen contributed distinctive teleplays for series such as "Arrest and Trial," "Sam Benedict," and "The Fugitive," as well as creating popular series such as "Branded" and "The Invaders."

Although it only ran for one season during 1962-63, "Sam Benedict" was an interesting courtroom drama series. Set in San Francisco and based upon the experiences of famous trial lawyer Jacob ("Jake") W. Ehrlich, the series included the television series debut of Edmond O'Brien in the title role. Since Ehrlich acted as technical consultant for the series, "Sam Benedict" featured many complex legal issues as well as outstanding performances from many guest stars. Cohen's contribution, "Accomplice," is a teleplay dealing with the murder indictment of an affluent white man and an African-American. Both are undoubtedly gay. As well as getting this element through censorship groups, Cohen analyzed the destructive nature of power relationships usually associated with the heterosexual domination in Hitchcock's radical tradition. In "Accomplice," Cohen showed that a gay relationship was not immune from contaminations associated with patriarchal society. By supplying no easy solutions for contemporary dilemmas, it revealed a key characteristic of his future works. "Accomplice" is as radical and iconoclastic as *Black Caesar*. It demonstrates that no individual belonging to any race, gender, or sexual orientation is ever immune from society's oppressive psychic mechanisms. Constant vigilance and a movement toward achieving a real definition of humanity represent the only options, no matter how impossible or difficult they initially appear to be.

"Accomplice" opens with Benedict and assistant Henry Tabor (Richard Rust) called to defend Frank Elton (Brock Peters) immediately after the murder of a night watchman during a burglary. Stigmatized by his long criminal record, the hysterical Elton is reluctant to talk about his more affluent white accomplice, Leonard Pitman, due to misguided sense of loyalty. However, the terms in which he describes Pitman indirectly reveal the real nature of their friendship. "He showed me a kind of life I never saw before." Pitman met Elton when he worked at a gas station and immediately dominated the less privileged man by seducing him into an unequal power relationship. The affluent white male became attracted to a poor man of another race whom he could manipulate and tempt into a life of crime to boost his ego. Pitman's attorney, Wiley (Eddie Albert), learns that his client is unmarried at the age of 30, never has had a lasting heterosexual relationship and, at the age of 21, was granted a trust fund by his parents, after agreeing to leave for Europe when he became mysteriously "bored" during his last year at college.

"Accomplice" also operates on another level. The use and abuse element in the Pitman-Elton relationship echoes the one existing between Wiley and Benedict. Initially agreeing on a joint defense to pool talents and save their clients from the gas chamber, Benedict discovers that Wiley has betrayed his friendship in a manner similar to Pitman's deceitful use of Elton. Wiley requests a separate defense motion from the district attorney so he can defend Pitman and place blame for the murder on Elton. By doing this, Wiley becomes Pitman's new "accomplice." Cohen's screenplay juxtaposes an "abnormal" relationship with its supposedly "normal" counterpart (the professional friendship between Wiley and Benedict). Both end in betrayal. After grilling Pitman on the stand, Benedict nearly makes him break down, despite Wiley's attempts to manipulate Pitman in the courtroom. This attempt parallels the more sinister manipulations Pitman practiced on Elton by seducing him into a life of crime. Finally getting the judge to agree on a joint guilty plea, Benedict saves Elton from the death chamber, but only for the equally miserable fate of life imprisonment without parole. The episode ends with both Benedict and Elton realizing the different, but similar, types of manipulations practiced on them by those they once regarded as friends. Pitman manipulates Elton to get his "kicks" and seduces his lower-class ethnic companion into keeping silent about the extent of their involvement, knowing full well that any jury would take the word of an affluent white male against a poor African-American with a criminal record. Wiley once attempted to enter politics in vain. Masquerading as a liberal in a more affirmative sixties era, he uses Benedict as an ally until he opportunistically sees a way in which he can use the law for his own ends. The friendship between Benedict and Wiley ends as the latter faces judicial inquiry into his legal ethics. But while Wiley faces probable disbarment, Elton will serve life in prison and the possibility of a longer term than Pitman.

Cohen's solitary contribution to Universal's "Arrest and Trial" series (whose formula influenced NBC's "Law and Order") is one of his most significant. It anticipates many key themes in his later work, especially those within the less "realistic" realms of *It's Alive* and *God Told Me To.* "My Name Is Martin Burnham" contains many radical themes in its basic story line. Investigating a series of assault cases, Sergeant Nick Anderson (Ben Gazzara) and his partner, Mitchell Harris (Don Galloway), remove riveter Martin Burnham (James Whitmore) from his family to question him as a possible suspect in an attempted rape case. Finding Burnham's name in five-year-old files recording his arrest for sexual assault, the police match his description with the probable suspect. Suspicious about Burnham's guilty behavior, Anderson believes they have found the right person. Neurotically reacting against Anderson and Galloway as persecutors, Burnham breaks down in the police car and undergoes a traumatic collapse after appearing in the dehumanized environment of a police lineup. Although the police release him, Burnham becomes dangerously psychologically disturbed. Blaming himself for the ordeal, Burnham wanders the streets and never returns home. Responding to his partner's comment about Burnham's sensitive nature, the college-educated Anderson replies, "Sometimes it's not what the law accuses a man of. It's what he accuses himself of." Anderson recognizes Burnham's deep-rooted guilt instincts as having negative masochistic overtones.

Enlisting Anderson's help in finding her missing husband, Ellen Burnham (Nina Foch) notes the ironic circumstances of the former persecutor who now feels as guilty as the man he formerly pursued. Fiercely protective of his father, Jerry Burnham (Richard Eyer) demands that Anderson and his mother stop treating his father "as if he was a kid." The arrest opens up deep tensions in the Burnham family relationships. It produces excessive strain on a vulnerable man attempting to be an ideal husband and father, tormented by a past criminal charge he may or may not have been guilty of. As Cohen's teleplay proceeds, the facts of Burnham's past arrest and forthcoming trial become less important than the deep emotions destroying him. These emotions are due more to social than to individual factors.

Anderson and Harris receive a letter from Burnham warning them about some dangerous future action he intends to undertake. Anderson recognizes that the letter reflects Burnham's disturbed mental state, since it reveals a lot about Burnham rather than being a simple warning message intended for the officers. When Harris questions why Burnham sent the letter, Anderson understands that guilt-ridden forces have influenced him. Anderson recognizes that the traumatized former suspect desires punishment by the everyday legal representatives of his guilt-ridden superego. Despite his legal innocence, Burnham masochistically craves for punishment at the hands of symbolic embodiments of the law. Recognizing the nature of Burnham's self-destructive behavior, Anderson comments, "Maybe he thinks we know more about him than anybody else — including himself." The police later find Burnham after he has accidentally thrown his former best friend, Bill Latham (Kenneth Tobey), from the top of a high office building under construction. Arrested in a state of shock and blaming himself for Bill's death, Burnham decides to use the legal apparatus for extreme judicial punishment, desiring his execution in the death chamber without claiming any extenuating circumstances.

Feeling responsible for the whole affair, Anderson persuades his defense attorney friend, John Egan (Chuck Connors), to represent the reluctant Burnham. Refusing to plead guilty to manslaughter, Burnham regards himself as a demonic monster unfit to live in normal society. When Ellen visits him in prison, Burnham refuses her solicitations, rejecting himself as "dirty" and "not clean." Burnham describes himself in terms reminiscent of Nazi attitudes toward the Jews and other "inferior" races. "Men like me should be exterminated." Burnham internalizes his feelings of guilt, seeing himself as a guilty "other" who can never live up to the normal demands of patriarchal society. His descriptions of himself are also reminiscent of a horror-film monster, a Frankenstein creature, seeing itself as a "dirty and unclean" monster from the id after being rejected by its creator and society. Dominated by these feelings, Burnham only sees one logical end to his suffering. He wants an institution, whose psychic and social rules he feels unable to fulfill, to end his life.

But, as the following sequence with psychologist Dr. Fowler (Michael Constantine) reveals, Burnham's guilty feelings and self-destructive desires are not unique to him. His condition is not due to any previous arrest for sexual impropriety nor his present act of accidental manslaughter. It is goes back well before those traumatic events, and has social, rather than individualistic, overtones. Burnham is not just one solitary individual undergoing guilt feelings, but a man feeling different from the rest of society. By attempting to conform to the normal image of father and husband, he is really inflicting great psychic pain on himself. Since Burnham feels at odds with his ideologically proscribed gender roles and cannot even articulate or come to terms with his dilemma, he naturally sees himself as guilty in his inability to be a "regular guy." Burnham's dilemma is not unique, but representative of his entire society. Fowler explains to Egan that Burnham has disliked himself throughout his entire life. The psychologist has no idea what caused these feelings of self-hatred: "Perhaps something in his childhood. Who knows?" Burnham lived his life hating his existence and blaming himself for his inability to conform to the norms of American family life. As Fowler states, "He's spent his life apologizing for mistakes he never made." When we first see Burnham, he performs the role of happy father for Jerry and his friends. But, as we begin to understand him more, a different and tragic figure emerges. Burnham's dilemma is by no means rare. He suffers from self-loathing and undergoes psychic assault by punitive masochistic mechanisms that patriarchal society internally employs against all those questioning its rule. These mechanisms attempt to control and influence individuals from birth into early childhood and beyond. Burnham's condition parallels other fellow unfortunates in his society, such as vulnerable men and women who feel themselves unable to comply with the "law of the father" and its "family values." Whether they be frustrated fathers and mothers, sons and daughters, or gays and lesbians coping with moods of self-loathing and guilt thrust upon them by a society that can never allow them to be openly different, their dilemma is identical. Living within hostile institutional codes and lacking any alternative means of self-definition, these unfortunates see themselves internally and externally as "monsters" whose only path is self-induced extermination, to leave a world in which they do not fit.

Unlike Dr. Richman in *Psycho*, Dr. Fowler is more sympathetic and understanding. He never condemns Burnham nor stereotypes him. Instead, he sees his dilemma as social and not individual. The unfortunate man is not merely a sexual offender with an overdeveloped superego guilt complex: "There are thousands of people with similar problems walking the streets, going to work, making a living, having a family." Fowler understands that Burnham's arrest and lineup appearance ironically triggered off guilty feelings in an innocent man. Fowler's concluding remarks underline Burnham's universal dilemma: "And like most of us, he had suppressed sexual desire which seemed much worse than it really was." Burnham's situation also has Freudian implications. As a vulnerable man attempting to fill the ideologically stipulated role of patriarch in Western society, Burnham is tormented by uncontrollable desires that his society can never acknowledge nor allow means for expression. Lacking an outlet for his feelings, affected by some past childhood trauma, trapped inside a sexually unfulfilling marriage, Burnham undergoes assault by self-destructive guilt-ridden feelings and masochistic desires for punishment by the "law of the father." Ironically, Burnham's psychological and physical odyssey to the gas chamber is generated by an institutional order responsible for his unhappy condition in the first place.

Burnham's earlier arrest as a sexual offender and his later trial as a murderer result in Jerry's alienation from his father. In one sequence beautifully written by Cohen, Jerry watches happy family home movies of himself with his father. As he gazes at these old images, Jerry's expression reveals worry and alienation as he attempts reconciling them with his now-ruined family life. Affected by gossip about his father's sexual crimes, Jerry rejects him as a "fake" who "had us fooled," seeing him as "not a normal man." Ignoring Ellen's pleas to understand Martin as ill and vulnerable, Jerry denies any connection to his father: "I'm nothing like him." He views him in society's terms as a creature who "shouldn't be allowed out on the streets." Jerry also rejected Martin once before. He vocally wished him dead, emotionally wounding an already vulnerable father. Jerry's attitude anticipates the later reactions of Frank Davies, Gene Scott, and Ellen Jarvis, in Cohen's *It's Alive* trilogy, who initially view their children as "monsters."

Reunited with Jerry during a court recess, Martin retreats from a son he can no longer identify with. He confesses something to him, a confession anticipating Frank Davies' admission to his own son in the concluding scenes of *It's Alive*. The vulnerable father admits to his son that he donned a false social mask during the early years: "You didn't know I was afraid of you, did you?" Martin reveals that his fear extended back to even before Jerry was born. It is another parallel to Frank Davies' own fear of his second son before the birth occurs in the hospital.

Martin reveals this fear resulted from his own insecure feelings, since he believed his son would penetrate his mask one day and regard him as an alienated monster. Martin is a sacrificial victim of guilty feelings that are socially generated. Believing himself at fault in his inability to affirm the normal feelings and roles his society expects of him, he naturally assumes that he is abnormal. But Martin mistakenly believes they are unique to him. He cannot see that they are really social mechanisms of a society victimizing him because he feels different. Unable to come to terms with his different nature, Martin fulfills the system's key requirement of "blaming the victim," in this case himself. Despite his efforts, Martin can never be a regular, normal guy, a successful husband and father in the system in which he lives. Denying Jerry's love, Martin warns him, "Don't be a part of me. Be a part of them (the camera briefly cuts to Egan) — the clean people and the normal people. Don't be a part of me. I'm your enemy." He urges his son to adopt the very attitudes that have tormented him throughout his life. His advice also anticipates Frank Davies' disastrous attempts to be part of the system and, until the final moments of *It's Alive*, deny his psychological relationship with a world of abnormality he has created. But despite his plea to Jerry, Martin asks Egan, "Take care of him. He loves me," realizing that the ties between father and son are too strong to be broken by social definitions of normal and abnormal. The sequence ends with the camera panning back to Jerry, showing him disturbed by his father's words.

These scenes represent the emotional core of Cohen's teleplay. Despite belonging to a series formula, the consequences of the dialogue extend far beyond any courtroom drama and Egan's moral judgment over Burnham: "I'm sick of hearing everybody beg you to live." The moralistic attorney shows no real understanding of Burnham's dilemma. Burnham's problem is not individual. He cannot snap out of it in the way Egan expects and become a man in the way society expects. Burnham is really a victim of a society persecuting him because of his difference, a system wishing him to fit into family roles causing him great personal torment, a system whose laws and customs can never really help him. However, the "happy ending" closure of the "Arrest and Trial" series formula disavows any explicit recognition of the nature of Martin Burnham's real predicament. Egan puts Martin on the stand and tells those in the courtroom about his client's guilty feelings and desire for punishment. He represents Martin as an individual client whose dilemma is exclusively personal, not social. Thus the episode ends by attempting to deny the interesting implications raised when Egan successfully pleads for Burnham's life. However, the forced nature of the ending can never entirely erase the dilemma it presents to the audience. The very structure of Cohen's teleplay contradicts any studio attempt at easy resolution, since the issues remain unresolved. Dr. Fowler's testimony recognizing the wider implications of Martin's condition still dominates the drama. The problem will not go away. It constantly occurs in Cohen's other work, where the frameworks are less realistic but more fantastic and satirical.

During 1964, Cohen contributed one teleplay to the popular series created by Roy Huggins — "The Fugitive." Containing an amnesia theme later used by "Coronet Blue" and "A Man Called Shenandoah," Cohen carefully constructed his episode not only to reprise the main plot two years after the series began, but also to provide a rationale for continuing it. In "Escape into Black," Richard Kimble (David Janssen) suffers from amnesia and decides to return home to Stafford, Indiana, and give himself up to pursuing nemesis Lt. Gerard (Barry Morse). Prior to boarding the train, he virtually confesses his guilt, requesting that Gerard "please come and get me." By this device, Cohen provides a reason for Gerard's continuing pursuit over the next few seasons. Rather than being perverse, Gerard's reason for continuing his pursuit has a valid rationale. Gerard hears Kimble make an actual confession over the phone, affirming his feelings about the fugitive's guilt. In writing this episode, Cohen incorporated earlier footage documenting Kimble's first encounter with the mysterious one-armed man (Bill Raisch) outside his home and the discovery of his wife's body. Using newspaper reports of his trial, voice-overs recount lines from the courtroom proceedings. Cohen deals with the theme of an innocent man on the run in "Kill or Be Killed," the opening of which parallels Kimble's escape from a train wreck used in pre-credits footage during "The Fugitive"'s first season. Cohen contributes several interesting ideas in this episode.

Searching for the one-armed man in Decatur, Illinois, Kimble suffers from amnesia after attempting to put out a kitchen fire in a small diner. Although his action of rushing in to help appears understandable, he actually stays too long attempting to put out the fire and unconsciously places himself at great personal risk. His action raises certain questions that the episode explores. Why does he stay too long in the kitchen, especially if it will result in an accident hindering his search? Nothing is accidental in a Larry Cohen screenplay. While in the hospital, Kimble attracts the attention of two antagonistic characters: conservative, self-righteous Dr. Towne (Ivan Dixon) and liberal social worker Margaret Ruskin (Betty Garrett). Discerning that Kimble is a former doctor, the impersonal Dr. Towne looks on him as a test case and begins analyzing him: "I think your mind is hiding something from you. I think you don't want to remember who you are. You don't want to be that person any longer. I think you might even have been subconsciously seeking an accident, a mechanism that might drop a curtain over a memory too horrible for your conscience, a blow on the head, an escape into blackness, actually self-inflicted."

Suspecting Kimble to be a disgrace to the medical profession he reveres, the aloof Dr. Towne regards him as a monster. Offering a chance of recovery under his "control," Towne hopes that Kimble will admit his guilt and confess. Believing in a strict division between good and evil, Towne lives his life according to standards he regards as objective and incapable of any exception. Seeing Kimble as a former professional who has gone bad, he instills guilty feelings in his patient, feelings that already exist: "I think you did kill your wife. You crave the punishment. You're punishing yourself." Interestingly, Cohen depicts Dr. Towne as a social instrument of a system hoping that its victims eventually move toward

A fugitive's constant nightmare. Richard Kimble (David Janssen) fears eventual arrest by his pursuing nemesis Lt. Gerard (Barry Morse) in the '60s television series "The Fugitive."

believing themselves guilty of thoughts and actions they are actually innocent of. This theme is another extension of the issues in "My Name Is Martin Burnham." Dr. Towne represents a physical embodiment of the type of institutional forces tormenting Martin Burnham.

In one sense, Towne is right. Kimble does have internal feelings of guilt. Suffering from the stress of being on the run for over two years, he possibly doubts his own innocence and looks for an excuse to escape into a comforting black world of amnesia. In the "Nightmare at Northoak" episode, broadcast 12 months before "Escape into Black," on November 26, 1963, Lt. Gerard spoke of his guilty quarry as gradually believing a story he fabricated to conceal the murder of his wife. When the confused Kimble later confesses on the phone to Gerard in "Escape into Black," the detective seizes on this as confirming his guilt. Furthermore, Kimble, in a masochistic tone of resignation, says to Gerard, "I understand I may have to accept punishment." When Kimble finally begins to recover on the train returning him to Stafford, he tells Margaret Ruskin, "I can't run anymore," admitting he put himself in personal danger in the diner as a way of escaping from extreme mental pressure. Kimble not only deals with day to day fears as a fugitive but also deep psychic feelings stemming from his own superego suggesting he may actually be guilty of murder. As a former law-abiding citizen now on the run, Kimble succumbs to intense emotional pressure, making him vulnerable to feelings of guilt and punishment originating from social and educational forces that have influenced him since childhood and now are internalized within his own subconscious. Dr. Towne's authoritarian superego figure reinforces such feelings. He is a fellow physician embodying forces of normality that a fugitive fallen from his once-secure world as a doctor feels uncomfortable with. Cohen's "Escape into Black" teleplay stresses internal as well as external forces oppressing Dr. Richard Kimble. It thus forms an interesting companion piece to "My Name Is Martin Burnham."

"Of General Reid and the men who died
He can never speak the truth.
What can you do when you're branded?
Can you live with a lie?"

Cohen also created the Western series "Branded." It combined the well-known plot of the British imperial epic *The Four Feathers* (1929 and 1939) with references to a blacklisting era still fresh in American memory. Each week the series began with Jason McCord (Chuck Connors) being officially disgraced by a guilty verdict at his court-martial. As solitary survivor of the Bitter Creek Massacre (modeled after Custer's Little Big Horn disaster), he decides to keep silent about its real causes, both to preserve the memory of revered commanding officer General Reid and prevent further hostilities against the Indians. These explanations appear in the second episode, "The Vindicator," usually categorized as the official pilot of the series. However, Cohen launched the series without any actual pilot episode being filmed — an unusual occurrence in the television industry. The plot device of a soldier deciding to keep silent and face accusations of cowardice rather than reveal the real story that would clear his name appears in the *Four Feathers*, last filmed under the title *Storm Over the Nile* (1955). In the words of the opening theme song, "He (McCord) can never tell the truth," indicating that he faces condemnation for supposed cowardice. Refusing to "tell the truth" or "name names" (General Reid and his senility) indirectly parallels the McCarthy era. "Branded" is one of the first examples of Cohen's deliberate strategy of using a definable genre — in this case, the Western — to construct a radical allegorical message whose relevance transcends normative generic associations. "Branded" also contains a far darker vision of the family motif characterizing another popular contemporary series — "Bonanza."

Carrying a broken saber as a reminder of his unjust sentence, McCord faced several situations every week as he confronted fresh accusations of his supposed cowardice. Sometimes he convinces a few people of his real heroism. The episodes Cohen wrote for the series involve innovative situations transcending formula plot constructions characterizing other episodes scripted by lesser talents. In other episodes, he only supplied the stories. With the exception of "Taste of Poison," few writers rose to the challenge of matching the quality of Cohen's stories. In "Bounty," McCord finds himself pursued by bounty hunters. Posing as his own killer, he discovers that a jealous fellow officer from his Army days wants him dead. "Coward Step Aside" reunited Connors with Johnny Crawford from the earlier "Rifleman" series. In this episode, McCord tries to help a young deputy (Crawford) stand up to a gang of outlaws. By saving a hostage, he takes on the role of coward again, earning contempt from the townspeople until he is able to redeem himself in everyone's eyes.

The writers often turned interesting story lines of McCord posing as his own murderer and acting the part of a coward, due to circumstances he has no control over, into routine television plots. Of the available "Branded" episodes (the color episodes are those usually in syndication today) Cohen wrote, two are particularly noteworthy: "Survival" and "The Vindicator."

In "Survival," McCord travels on horseback across the desert. He rescues Jim Colbee (Alex Cord) who hopes to be reunited with his wife and young daughter whom he has not seen for five years. Persuading them to travel west after he has struck it rich, he now faces the grim prospect of dying in the desert. Keeping his real identity secret, McCord attempts to keep Colbee's spirits up as they travel across the desert. Colbee regards himself as a better man than McCord (whom he stereotypes as "a real drifter") because of his family responsibilities. He speaks of having a "wife and family, folks who depend on you." But it is clearly evident that Colbee depends on them to give him a comfortable social identity as a normal male in a world dominated by family values. This family man is really insecure, vulnerable, and dangerous to others as well as himself. Colbee's developing hysteria and paranoia about letting his family down reveals that he is a weak and cowardly figure. He is also a "monster" created by the patriarchal family. Like Martin Burnham, Colbee struggles against a status-quo identity he believes easily guarantees him social and personal stability. Learning McCord's real identity, he steals his horse and leaves him in the desert. Family man Colbee regards himself as a better person than the supposed coward of Bitter Creek. He delivers another version of the court-martial verdict by condemning the already stigmatized McCord to virtual death in the desert. Colbee's action replays the opening credit sequence of each "Branded" episode when McCord is left to walk out into the desert after undergoing military disgrace following his court-martial.

Colbee says, "All I can think of is Sally and Jessie. Not being married, you might not see what I mean. But I brought them out here. I made them come. I've got to protect them. You're gambling that we'll both make it. I can't afford that gamble ... I'm going alone. Unless you decide to stop me."

Colbee tosses a gun to McCord, his mind torn between fear and a personal gamble that the Bitter Creek coward will not shoot him. He rides away. Rescued by a Navajo Indian (Robert Carricart), McCord arrives in town to face his adversary. Before McCord reaches Granite Wells, the newly reunited family man appears as a weak and pathetic guilt-ridden figure, certainly no "man" of the family, but a figure dominated by his wife and daughter. Discovering McCord has survived the desert, Colbee puts on his gunbelt to face the consequences of his cowardly act.

Although sketchily developed due to "Branded"'s time limits, the 25-minute episode does contain other interesting elements. McCord's Native American companion clearly represents his vengeful alter ego. However, the Navajo has his own personal reasons for rescuing McCord. Having lost his own family in a massacre years ago, he sees the developing confrontation between the two white men as a surrogate "reprisal" for his own personal loss. He speaks to McCord in vengeful terms. After his tribe's defeat, "the Navajo have never been strong. But he survives in the desert where the white man cannot live. If the desert does not destroy him, he will destroy himself. One man against the other." He clearly sees McCord as a Frankenstein monster he has created. By rescuing McCord from the desert, he hopes the vengeful hero will act as his monster from the id and achieve sublimated revenge against a substitute white man functioning as a scapegoat for those who killed his family.

However, McCord realizes the dangerous nature of his destructive feelings of vengeance: "The desert can burn the reason and morality out of a man and all he's left with is the animal instinct to survive." Seeing Colbee's seven-year-old daughter, Jessy, looking lovingly at her father, McCord exhibits real heroism by refusing to follow his vengeful desires. Wishing Jessy a happy birthday, and recognizing his antagonist's pathetic character ("*Your Daddy* [contemptuous tone] told me about you."), he rides away leaving Colbee alone with his family. In this episode, McCord emerges far superior to a patriarchal monster created by dangerous family values associated with the status quo. He also refuses to be used by another as an instrument to carry out negative desires for revenge.

Directed by film and television veteran Joseph H. Lewis, "The Vindicator" significantly suggests the real subversive implications behind Cohen's original ideas for "Branded." Although designed as the opening episode, it followed "Survival" in the original broadcast schedule. It contains the main ideas motivating the entire series.

"The Vindicator" begins with McCord arriving in a town and meeting Ned Travis (Claude Akins), the reporter responsible for his vilification. Travis is another

deceitful media representative embodying Cohen's distrust of exploitative journalists such as those in "Go-Between," *It's Alive*, and the "Bad News Bears" figures
in *Maniac Cop 3*. McCord refuses to answer questions about the Bitter Creek Massacre. A flashback sequence follows, showing Lt. Pritchett (Harry Carey, Jr.)
appealing to McCord to relieve the aging and senile General Reid (John Litel)
of his command. The Apaches then attack the Seventh Cavalry unit. Appealing
in vain to his general to withdraw, McCord takes over command. By then it is
too late. Hearing his revered commander refer to him as a "coward," McCord loses
consciousness. Cashiered out of the Army, McCord faces the journalist who has
exploited the whole incident by enlarging the number of men killed from 31 to
200. Knowing the truth about 31 men outnumbered by 140 Apaches, McCord
hears the cynical newspaperman reply, "The legend grows with the telling." In
commenting, "Jason McCord is the villain. Every story needs one," Travis reveals
himself to be a version of a vulgar Hollywood producer eager to distort historical and personal complexities to sell his product. McCord decides to keep the
truth of Bitter Creek to himself: "What happened at Bitter Creek is on my conscience."

Travis then visits Pritchett's widow (June Lockhart) whose young son,
Johnny, plays childish games involving demonizing a man he holds responsible
for his father's death. McCord is a scapegoat in the eyes of both children and
adults. Persuading Mrs. Pritchett to let him read her husband's last letters, Travis
discovers the real truth behind Bitter Creek. Several lines in the letter reveal an
interesting side to McCord's character. Pritchett writes that "McCord feels a great
obligation to the general, who is sort of a second father to him. He always covers up for him." This suggests that the heroic Jason McCord resembles a weak
son within a dysfunctional family attempting to conceal its real nature from the
outside world by denying the flawed characters of parental figures. McCord's
desire to remain silent has pathological as well as historically valid reasons. Fearing his revered general's fall from grace, McCord also understands that politicians
will use revelations about the massacre to break a peace treaty with the Indians
and cause a bitter war. Although Travis finally realizes McCord is really a "scapegoat," his motives for revealing the truth are less honorable than McCord's are
in concealing it. Travis opportunistically wishes to rewrite frontier history to
punish the Indians and tarnish the reputation of a general who initiated a peace
treaty between the races: "He kept quiet to protect the general, the man who was
really responsible for the massacre, an incompetent old fool." As Travis tells Mrs.
Pritchett, clearing McCord's name is less important than vilifying the general who
is a "much more tempting target."

Learning of Travis' desire to rewrite history under the banner headline of
"The Villain Wore Stars," McCord rides out to persuade Mrs. Pritchett to destroy
the evidence. At her ranch, he meets a son whose mind is contaminated by ideological forces within his own society. He eagerly seeks a scapegoat to blame for
his father's death. Asking Johnny for the source of his information concerning
the Bitter Creek Massacre, McCord receives the answer, "Nobody told me. I just

know." Mrs. Pritchett arrives before Johnny can respond to McCord's other question, "But *how* do *you* know?

Mrs. Pritchett informs McCord that school playground gossip influences her young son. After revealing his identity, McCord pleads with the reluctant Mrs. Pritchett to destroy the only evidence that would clear his name. Although mentioning the political forces eager to begin another Indian War should the truth emerge, McCord also persuades her in language suggesting masochistic tendencies within his own personality, tendencies linking him to Martin Burnham. McCord blames himself for not acting earlier in relieving a beloved surrogate father of his command: "Maybe I put friendship ahead of duty. Maybe I am responsible, even more than General Reid."

McCord sees the situation in totally individual terms. He blames himself as a guilty son betraying a father oblivious to social and political factors trapping him in an impossible situation. Like young Johnny, McCord accepts one-dimensional, ideologically imposed thought patterns within his society dividing people into stereotypes of heroes and villains, revered fathers and dutiful sons. As Travis pointed out, "Every story needs a villain" and McCord decides to fulfill this arbitrarily imposed social role. Revering a beloved father according to patriarchal customs of military duty rather than recognizing Reid's faults and acting to stop them in time, McCord is in one sense guilty. But others like Pritchett recognize the situation and do not act until it is too late. All are victims of dangerous psychosocial structures determining their behaviors. Before General Reid dies, McCord sees a deranged man changing suddenly from a caring person wishing peace with the Indians into a violent lunatic ordering his men to "take no prisoners." Like Morton Cheyney of "The Colossus" and Matthew Ryder of "Go-Between," Reid's personality reveals dangerous egocentric tendencies. As a psychic victim of his own social structure, McCord never views things in their proper perspective. Although McCord's historical and political reasons for keeping silent are valid, he becomes a victim by consent rather than trying to change the dangerous historical forces in his own society.

"The Vindicator" ends ironically with both McCord and Mrs. Pritchett collaborating to ensure that Travis (like John Ford's newspaper editor in *The Man Who Shot Liberty Valance*) will print the legend rather than the fact. Denying she knew McCord's identity up to that moment, she watches Johnny run after the retreating man, attempting to beat the "Coward of Bitter Creek." As she prevents Johnny from continuing McCord's personal and social purgatory, both she and McCord exchange poignant and knowing glances. The sacrificial victim of an unjust society needing its selected quota of monsters and villains then rides away.

Unfortunately, later writers of "Branded" never realized the potential contained within this opening episode. The series became routine. Cohen contributed the story to a three-part episode, "The Mission," scripted by Jameson Brewer and released in a theatrical version re-titled *Broken Saber*. In this episode, McCord was sent on a "Mission Impossible"–like task by President Grant. While little of Cohen's imaginative qualities exist here, "The Mission" formed a pattern for other episodes in which Grant uses McCord's reputation, sending him on dangerous assignments in the service of the state. While the re-edited version of "The Mission" added a happy ending in which McCord regains his commission and resumes his Army career, other episodes saw Grant sending the always complicit McCord away into dangerous situations, the resolutions of which never guarantee a reversal of the original Bitter Creek court-martial verdict. By June 1965, Cohen had little to do with the series. But in light of "The Vindicator" episode, it is hard not to see McCord's social martyrdom as ironically anticipating other institutional "use and abuse" situations occurring in Cohen's later works.

"If I've got that kind of blood in my veins, what does that make me?" — Brian March, in the "Traitor's Blood" episode of "Blue Light."

Cohen next collaborated with Walter Grauman in developing the idea for a World War II espionage series. Although Grauman suggested the basic idea, the whole conception of "Blue Light" belongs to Larry Cohen. Using the name of an earlier character played by Keir Dullea in "The Golden Thirty," Cohen envisaged a series with several indirect parallels to "Branded." In this case, the victim is an American journalist working for the American government as a traitor in the Nazi regime. Like Jason McCord, David March must keep his real identity a secret, even to members of his own family, like the younger brother he meets in "Traitor's Blood" and secretly helps to escape. Cohen modeled David March on the flamboyant "Scarlet Pimpernel" characters played by Louis Hayward in several classic Hollywood films. March's foppish nature provides an ideal distraction to his Nazi employers. The idea was interesting. Unfortunately, both the casting and formulaic production of "Blue Light" ruined the innovative ideas behind its conception. Robert Goulet was far too stiff an actor to give the part credibility. His costar, Christine Carére, spoke with a distractingly thick French accent and always appeared in fashionable, contemporary sixties costumes (as did all the actresses). Most "Blue Light" episodes looked as if they were processed directly from a factory conveyer belt. The formula allowed little scope for innovative ideas and complex characterization. The series ran for only 17 episodes during a brief season. Cohen's ideas proved ill-suited to the routine nature of television production at the time. "Blue Light" differed enormously from the type of series exemplified by "The Defenders" and "The Nurses," which allowed Cohen adequate scope for displaying his writing talents. Unfortunately, sixties American television never recaptured the idyllic "golden age" of the previous decade. It already foreshadowed the type of unimaginative, conveyer-belt formula production characterizing the medium today.

However, "Blue Light" did contain some interesting ideas. Despite casting problems, David March's character represents another variant on the familiar Cohen theme of a dilemma facing any individual sacrificing himself to the state. Like Jason McCord, March cannot go home again until the system decides to revoke the stigmatic aura surrounding his name. Called into government espionage, he has to keep his real mission a secret from family and friends. The cost is high. His fellow agent, Suzanne Duchard, acts antagonistically toward him. But

Double agent David March (Robert Goulet) matches his wits against S.S. Colonel Richter in the "Target—David March" episode of the television series created by Larry Cohen, "Blue Light" (20th Century–Fox, 1966).

she is another political victim masquerading as a Nazi sympathizer caught in a situation similar to that affecting Alicia Huberman (Ingrid Bergman) in Hitchcock's *Notorious* (1946). Still affected by her treasonable father's execution by the French underground, she forms a female counterpart to March. Unfortunately, Carére's acting abilities and the lack of script development prevent her role attaining its full potential. In "Target—David March," March tells Eddie Fry (Geoffrey Frederick), brother of his British lover who committed suicide on learning he had become a traitor, "I didn't ask for the job. But I had to do it." Although using

March on dangerous missions, the Allies conceal her death from him: "I didn't know she was dead. They didn't want to tell me." Fry replies (with some justification), "So she had to be the first casualty in your Blue Light." No rapprochement occurs between them. Fry departs, hating March as much as he did before he learned his enemy is an Allied agent and on the same side.

In the two-part episodes "The Fortress Below" and "The Weapon Within," March attempts to persuade an apolitical scientist, Gretchen Hoffman (Eva Pflug), about the horrors of a Nazi regime she knows nothing about after working for over three years in an underground submarine missile manufacturing plant in Grossmünchen. Aided by Suzanne, he arranges a meeting with her former professor, Dr. Felix Eckhardt (Peter Capell), whom the Nazis have imprisoned because of his protests against misuse of his scientific expertise. However, in an interesting plot twist, Eckhardt is no longer the type of idealistic scientist represented by Daniel Orren in "The Secret." Revealed as Gretchen's actual father, Eckhardt uncovers himself as a monstrous figure wishing to survive even at the cost of betraying his own daughter to regain favor with the Nazi regime. He urges her to submit and obey as he has. After Eckhardt's accidental death, Gretchen immediately recognizes, "They changed him into a monster." Unlike Daniel Orren who accepts punishment rather than responsibility for countless deaths, Eckhardt believes in his own personal survival. Now disillusioned about Nazi Germany, Gretchen returns to Grossmünchen with David and Suzanne. Questioned about his actions should Gretchen betray them, March replies, "Then I'll have to kill her and do the job alone. She has a chance. I don't." The mission is his only goal, his methods little different from the enemy he fights. Eventually, Gretchen sacrifices herself in the following episode, "The Weapon Within," only revealing March's identity to S.S. security officer Luber (Horst Frank) immediately before the underground plant explodes.

Family tensions characterizing Cohen's later films also appear in one episode of "Blue Light." In "Traitor's Blood," March's younger brother, Brian (David Macklin), has to prove himself more patriotic than his "branded" elder sibling by enlisting at an early age in the Air Force, provoking prison camp guards into assaulting him, and leading a dangerous escape mission. He wishes to prove himself more "normal" than his monster brother, divorcing himself as much as possible from a person he once loved. Brian's attitude resembles Martin Burnham's son in attempting to separate himself mentally from a family member he now hates.

At the request of producer Stan Shpetner, Cohen wrote a teleplay for "The Rat Patrol" series. Based upon the 1953 movie *The Desert Rats*, this 1966-67 television series was little better than a half-hour weekly cowboys and Indians escapade with Americans and Germans substituting for their Western counterparts. Each week, a predominantly American Rat Patrol took on "bad" German Captain Hans Dietrich (Hans Gudegast, later known as soap opera star Eric Braeden, whom Cohen cast years later as the evil genius of *The Ambulance*), who represented the type of villain played by James Mason (as Field Marshall Rommel) in *The Desert Fox* (1950) and *The Desert Rats* (1952). Now syndicated on late-night television, "The Rat Patrol" was a formulaic series that became a notorious "cause célèbre" when shown on BBC television, sparking a storm of protest from former British Desert Rats angry at American appropriation of General Montgomery's North Africa campaign. The opening episode on British television presented a trio of American masculine heroes outnumbering wimpish token "Brit" Sergeant Jack Moffitt (Gary Raymond) who asks his American counterpart, Sergeant Sam Troy (Christopher George), for "permission to brew up." His effete English public school attempts to educate his American ally about the virtues of a British cup of tea provoked a smile from Troy and anger from the British viewing public. The series was withdrawn in Britain after only a few episodes.

Cohen's teleplay "The Blind Man's Bluff Raid" is a minor work affected by formulaic half-hour time constraints and "The Rat Patrol"'s emphasis on the weekly masculine contest between Troy and Dietrich. It is a truncated work containing some interesting ideas but failing to realize its potential. In "The Blind Man's Bluff Raid," Troy becomes separated from his fellow Desert Rats. Suffering from sun-blindness, he awakes in a military hospital. However, both the doctor and nurse are German intelligence agents. They use eyedrops to prolong Troy's blindness. Believing he is safe, Troy reveals the location of his companions to the waiting Captain Dietrich. While Dietrich leaves to trap the patrol, Troy tricks Nurse Patricia Bauer (Salome Jens) by substituting water for his eyedrops. He escapes while under escort to a P.O.W. camp, returns to his men, and causes more frustration to his German nemesis.

Most of "The Blind Man's Bluff Raid" is little better than most half-hour series episodes. Like Cohen's screenplays for *Return of the Seven* and *Deadly Illusion*, only half the ideas were used. Dealing with a German intelligence operation designed to deceive a vulnerable American, the teleplay uses themes from a James Garner World War II movie, *36 Hours* (1965), remade in the early nineties for TNT cable television, starring Corbin Bernson. However, the story has significant parallels with other Cohen teleplays.

Like Richard Kimble in "Escape into Black" and Michael Alden (Frank Converse) in "Coronet Blue," Sam Troy finds himself in a vulnerable situation over which he has no control. While Kimble suffers from amnesia after deliberately placing himself in extreme danger, Troy's blindness causes him to betray his men's position to his deadly enemy, Captain Dietrich. Despite undeveloped potentials, "The Blind Man's Bluff Raid" presents an omnipresent Cohen theme of the hero suddenly thrust into a situation over which he has no control. Learning of his rival's presence, Troy falls into a frustrated rage, cursing his helpless, childlike situation.

The most significant part of this teleplay is the dialogue between Troy and German intelligence agent Patricia Bauer after he discovers she is not an American nurse. Although the sequence ends in Troy distracting Patricia with a stereotypical romantic embrace, the preceding encounter contains several references to

Cohen's treatments of divided loyalties and patriotism found in "Defenders" teleplays such as "Traitor," "The Secret," and "Mayday! Mayday!" Troy learns that
Patricia lived in America and nearly became naturalized before war broke out,
when she returned to her native country. The following dialogue hints at Patricia Bauer as another version of the Fritz Weaver character in "Traitor."

> TROY: "And you decided to double-cross your new country."
> PATRICIA: "Is it a double-cross? I am a German."
> TROY: "And you have to live with yourself."
> PATRICIA: "Don't you think I love my country as you love yours? I do what
> I can to help, to fight the way a woman can to preserve the … (pause) life that I
> grew up with. If I can do that, then yes, I can live with myself."

At this juncture, Patricia Bauer comes alive. She is more than a stereotypical double-crossing female agent, a convenient series formula device. Patricia
emerges as a potentially complex character loyal to her country but perhaps less
so to the political regime in power. However, after she decides not to reveal anything further about herself—"Let's not try to know each other, Sergeant. Let's
say, 'Some other time, some other place'"—the remainder of the episode swiftly
declines and becomes routine. The mass-produced "time filler" formula of "The
Rat Patrol" does not allow development of a sophisticated plot, characteristic of
"The Defenders" and "The Nurses." This situation represented one of several elements leading to Cohen's growing dissatisfaction with television and a desire to
direct his own scripts.

However Cohen's humorous touch is not entirely absent from the disappointing "The Blind Man's Bluff Raid." When Dietrich asks Doctor Keller (James
Philbrook) about Troy's condition, the latter replies that he "tries to enjoy 'being
in poor health!'"

During this period, Cohen also created "The Invaders" for Quinn Martin
Productions. The series merged aspects of "Branded" with Martin's highly successful "The Fugitive." Driving late at night, David Vincent (Roy Thinnes) sees
a flying saucer and witnesses humanoid aliens infiltrating America. Unlike Jason
McCord, who "can never tell the truth," Vincent does. But very few people
believe him. Cohen thus inverted his "Branded" formula, with the hero attempting to inform the American public of the danger in its midst. "The Invaders" also
used a theme familiar to viewers from "The Fugitive." Each week, Vincent would
visit a different part of America, but not in the manner of David Janssen's Dr.
Richard Kimble searching for his mysterious one-armed man. Instead, Vincent
would be actively seeking aliens and attempting to convince Americans about the
danger they face. Like "Branded," "The Invaders" drew upon a Cold War paranoia, one current in fifties science-fiction movies such as *Invasion of the Body
Snatchers*, in which aliens symbolize a communist threat. Cohen focused more
upon the personal dilemma of a man who sees a danger everybody else ignores.
David Vincent's situation anticipates young Jason's plight in *The Stuff* (1985).

Jason accidentally becomes alert to a danger his whole family denies. In several episodes, Vincent often becomes regarded as strange and suffers hostility from uncomprehending individuals. He becomes regarded as alien as the forces he attempts to warn his countrymen about. Though credited as creator, Cohen contributed some story lines but saw none of his actual teleplays used for the series.

A similar fate affected Cohen's project "Coronet Blue." The concept involved an individual, Michael Alden (Frank Converse), suffering from amnesia and having no documented records of his existence in America. Most episodes involved Alden either trying to find his real identity or pursued by some mysterious group of people attempting to kill him. The series ran for only 11 episodes. The latter episodes lost track of the original idea before finishing in September 1967. Despite being produced by Herbert Brodkin, "Coronet Blue" did not last as long as its distinguished predecessors, "The Defenders" and "The Nurses."

Cohen also conceived the idea for the *Custer* television series starring Wayne Maunder, a fact the producers finally acknowledged in subsequent credits. By this time, the television industry had changed drastically from the days when Cohen began as a young writer. It had turned into a factory conveyer belt producing time-filling products with little tolerance for the work of creative talents such as Herbert Brodkin and Larry Cohen. The writing was appearing on the wall, but it was not until Cohen experienced problems affecting his screenplays that he finally turned to directing his own work.

# Screenplays and
# Teleplays of the 1970s

When late sixties television proved unreceptive to creative work, Larry Cohen began writing screenplays. Three were filmed at the time, but their final versions filled the author with so much dissatisfaction that he decided to begin directing his own films. *Return of the Seven* (1966), *Daddy's Gone A-Hunting* (1968), and *El Condor* (1970) all represent highly compromised works. *El Condor* was a journeyman assignment. Cohen wrote scenes for already selected locations, due to the producer's dissatisfaction with the original screenplay. But *Daddy's Gone A-Hunting* and *Return of the Seven* represented more ambitious projects whose eventual realization convinced Cohen that he had to become producer, director, and writer if his creative vision were ever to reach the cinema screen in a satisfactory manner.

*Return of the Seven* was the first sequel to *The Magnificent Seven* (1960) directed by John Sturgis. Despite successfully transplanting Kurosawa's *The Seven Samurai* to the American Western and achieving a huge success in England, *The Magnificent Seven* failed in the American market. Six years later, United Artists attempted a sequel. Unfortunately, Burt Kennedy's poor direction, using only half of Cohen's original screenplay, failed to realize its full potential. Two other sequels, *Guns of the Magnificent Seven* (1969) and *The Magnificent Seven Ride* (1972), followed *Return of the Seven*. But they were no improvement on the original film. *Return of the Seven* is disappointing in terms of direction and casting, with only marginal traces of Cohen's original concept remaining.

Cohen's original screenplay conceived of the Seven rescuing male members of the original village threatened by Eli Wallach in the first film. The villagers are kidnapped by a general to build a church in the desert as a memorial to his deceased sons who died fighting bandits. Angered by their supposed cowardice and lack of involvement during the original battle, General Lorca turns the villagers into slave laborers. The Seven free the villagers halfway through the film. In a surprising double twist, everyone then decides to continue rebuilding the church as a memorial to themselves rather than the general. They now have

Chris (Yul Brynner) and Vin (Robert Fuller) respond to the pleas of Petra (Elisa Montes) to rescue the kidnapped villagers in *Return of the Seven* (United Artists, 1966).

something to live for and identify with. In his original screenplay, Cohen envisages an interesting change of circumstances. General Lorca then returns with his men to destroy a memorial which has now become a sign of his humiliation rather than representing his egocentric desires. A climactic battle follows. Most of the Seven die fighting. Then, the remaining members of the Seven depart and leave the villagers to continue their work.

In its existing version, *Return of the Seven* lacks any trace of vitality and innovation. However, some Cohen themes are still recognizable. The film begins with the Mexican villagers discovering an escaped fugitive. A group of horsemen suddenly attacks them, rounds up all the men, and marches them away into the desert. Many miles away, Chris (Yul Brynner) watches a bullfight. His friend Vin (Robert Fuller) meets him there. They are the only two remaining members of the original Magnificent Seven. (The other survivor, Chico, [Julian Mateos], decided to remain in the village at the end of the earlier film.) He is among the men rounded up in the opening scenes of *Return of the Seven*. His wife, Petra (Elisa Montes), enlists Chris's help to free them. Chris then recruits four other gunfighters and they ride off to the rescue. They discover that General Francisco Lorca (Emilio Fernandez) has forced all the nearby villagers to rebuild a church as a monument to his two sons who died in a battle against marauding bandits. Chris rescues the villagers, but Lorca decides to regain his lost territory and honor by massacring all the defendants. He gains reinforcements from 200 workers he summons away from his hacienda. The Seven appear outnumbered until the villagers rally in their support, using dynamite against the enemy. Chris, Vin, Chico, and Colbee (Warren Oates) survive the battle while Lorca is mortally wounded. Chico decides to rebuild the church to unify all the surrounding villagers while the surviving Seven ride away.

The film includes some significant scenes. In one sequence, Chris and Vin discuss their dissatisfaction with the gunfighter's life, which is now their only option. Ten years after liberating the village in *The Magnificent Seven*, they have nowhere else to go. Chris admires Chico, who put away his guns, married, and adopted a young Mexican boy as his own son. His attraction toward a family and community life he can never share in is a theme adopted from the original film. However, dark alternatives also exist. Although poorly developed, the enigmatic figure of Frank (Claude Akins) functions as a poor option for the family life Chris yearns for. Irritated at Colbee's bragging about his sexual exploits, Frank's reasons for joining Chris are neither mercenary nor altruistic. Not until after the final battle does the mortally wounded gunfighter reveal his real reasons for joining the group. Many years before, Frank lived a family life almost identical to Chico's. But an Indian attack on his ranch traumatically scarred him for life. Left with one bullet to defend himself against a final Indian assault, Frank yielded to his wife's pleas not to be left alive for an envisaged ugly fate as a white female captive. He used his last bullet on her. Contrary to his expectations, the Indians never attacked, but rode away. Frank tracked down his Indian assailants one by one. With no enemy left, Frank has nothing to live for. He now yearns for a final release from personal agony. Frank achieves his death wish after Lorca's final attack.

The unfortunate casting of Claude Akins militates against any real understanding of Frank's significance in the film. At the time, both Akins and Warren Oates were usually known for delivering rudimentary acting performances in television. Oates finally found a director who would realize his potentials: Sam Peckinpah. Unfortunately, Claude Akins never did. He was often typecast in films and television, and never gained the opportunity of delivering more complex performances. Akins and Oates needed better direction in *Return of the Seven*. Frank's role combines two images from a significant American cultural tradition: the Indian hater in Herman Melville's *The Confidence Man* and Nathan Slaughter of *Nick of the Woods* (1853) by Robert Montgomery Bird. The first figure embodies a divided paranoid aggressiveness within a self-denying white culture usually projected against convenient outside scapegoats. This feature appears in America's past and present.[1] Bird wrote the character of Nathan Slaughter as a challenge to the romantic image of the frontiersman presented by James Fenimore Cooper in the Leatherstocking novels. In *Nick of the Woods*, savage Indians force pacifist Quaker Nathan Slaughter to kill his family. He spends the rest of the novel pursuing his Indian antagonists until he has no one left to kill. The novel suggests that, despite external pressure, Nathan actually fulfilled his repressed desires by freeing himself from restrictive domestic confines, allowing him to become an embodiment of the wandering male hero celebrated by Leslie A. Fiedler in *Love and Death in the American Novel.*[2] This explains the hostility he exhibits toward the sexually libidinous Colbee who boasts about his prowess with Mexican females in villages he visits. Interestingly enough, Cohen lets Colbee survive at the end of the film. He becomes free to discharge his libidinous male energies throughout the whole of Mexico, rather than perish in the battle as an ideological punishment for unacceptable desires. But Frank represents a Nathan Slaughter alter ego to Chris's more romanticized Natty Bumppo archetype in *Return of the Seven.*

*Return of the Seven* contains certain parallels between various characters anticipating characteristic motifs occurring in Cohen's later works. The closeness existing between Chris and Vin complements that between Lorca and foreman Lopez (Rudolpho Acosta). Certain scenes between Chris and Vin mirror others between Lorca and Lopez, suggesting significant relationships existing between them all. Chris acts as moral conscience to Vin, stating that he will throw away his guns if he ever takes pleasure in killing. However, Lopez fails in his role as moral conscience to Lorca, since the older man's aggressive desires remain unmodified. Lorca embodies the same type of monstrous patriarchal image that has fascinated Cohen from "Go-Between" onwards. Despite professing love for his dead sons, Lorca is a power-driven figure ruthlessly oppressing everyone both inside and outside his family. Like the Alex Cord character in "Survival," he is a monster driven by power dynamics rooted within the patriarchal family.

Hearing Lorca's desire to build a monument to the 200 men who died fighting bandits, Chris responds, "I won't let you drown your grief in other men's blood, if that's what you mean." Refusing to let him use others to fulfill his goal, Chris drives Lorca and his 60 men away. Later, Lorca tells Lopez about his plans to summon his 200-strong work force to aid him against the Seven, despite dangers of causing the economic collapse of his hacienda. Refusing to listen to reason, Lorca falls into self-destructive feelings of vengeance, and intends to slaughter everyone who causes him personal humiliation over the monument. He cares less about his sons than the insult to his masculine ideas of honor.

The Seven hear Lorca's romanticized images of his dead sons. But Chris reveals the real nature of the Lorca family relationship to Vin. The general's own sons hired him to kill their father. When he discovered this, the general allowed Chris to ride away instead of killing him. Chris cannot explain this. But the general clearly regarded Chris as a surrogate son who stood up to him by exhibiting acceptable codes of masculine behavior not shared by his own sons. Vin understands this when he replies, "Maybe he saw in you what he never saw in his own." Chris then unveils the lies hidden beneath General Lorca's idealized representations of his sons:

> He said they were tall, erect, like finely bred stallions. They were not. They were gentle, like their mother. Lorca thought they were weak. He rode roughshod over

them, trying to make them over in his own image. Their mother tried to stop him, died trying. They hated him, wanted him dead.

Chris also reveals that Lorca "shamed" his sons into dying for his cause along with 200 other men. He tells Vin the real reason for Lorca's passionate desires for building a church as a monument to two sons he knew hated him.

> VIN: Then why is Lorca building this church for them?
> CHRIS: Not for them, but for him. He finally got his chance to do the thing he couldn't do when they were alive — be proud of them.

Dysfunctional family dynamics characteristic of Cohen's later films clearly occur in *Return of the Seven*. But the film never makes them explicit. Chris also shares some features of self-deception with his nemesis Lorca. He idealizes the family and community represented by Chico and his people. But Frank and Lorca are nightmare versions of this family dream. In Cohen's original screenplay, Lorca's final attack represented an assault against a monument taking on the rebellious image of his own dead sons, an image he could no longer deny since it had become a conscious reality. The monument thus embodied a return of Lorca's own family turmoil that he attempted to repress but now haunts him. His attack represents his desire to repress once again contradictory features from the recent past that he cannot come to terms with. For Lorca, the monument and its defenders represent monstrous embodiments challenging his authoritarian patriarchal control as head of a family, capitalist, and military leader. Lorca thus represents a composite embodiment of qualities formerly seen in the figures of Admiral Lucas J. Kiley in "Mayday! Mayday!" and Matthew T. Ryder in "Go-Between." Lorca also acts in the manner Frank Davies will follow in *It's Alive* until he decides to accept the embodiment of his own family contradictions. Had these features been developed from ideas in Cohen's original screenplay, Chris's earlier lines to Petra concerning future hopes for personal and political liberation would not appear as superfluous as they are in the actual film. The attempted liberation by the Seven is also one against negative forces within the patriarchal family. Lorca's assault against the villagers thus has personal and political overtones. Enslaving them to do his will, he attempts to extend the authoritarian practices of his family life. Freedom from an oppressive political figure such as General Lorca also necessitates complementary liberation from an authoritarian patriarchal family situation. Lorca uses 200 workers of his own workers as reinforcements in the final assault. The number mirrors the 200 deceased men Lorca initially sought to immortalize by building his church. Paradoxically, Lorca and his men now embody the type of bandits his own sons originally fought against. By aiding the Seven against Lorca's forces, the villagers change from being passive victims facing slaughter at the hands of a vengeful father to reliving the rebellious spirit embodied by Lorca's own sons many years before. They represent a collective version of a politically progressive return of the repressed fighting against patriarchal oppression.

*Return of the Seven* ends with Chris and Vin riding away after Chico decides to continue building the monument to unify neighboring oppressed villages. Chico intends to inspire the poor Mexican peasants to organize themselves in a strong agrarian collective and defend themselves against future predatory capitalists such as Lorca. Colbee decides to stay and help the villagers, his libidinous energies finding a changed political and personal outlet in a new society. Although Chico and Petra are husband and wife, their family relationship differs from Lorca's. Childless after ten years of marriage, they have adopted a young orphan whom they regard as their own son. Working in a noncapitalist rural cooperative, they represent a different type of family free from the contaminating tensions affecting the Lorcas. Although compromised by poor direction, *Return of the Seven* contains optimistic ideas anticipating utopian directions characterizing Cohen's later films.

Influenced at a young age by Alfred Hitchcock, Larry Cohen worked on two screenplays indebted to the Master of Suspense, but reworking his ideas in an original manner: *The Cutting Room* and *Daddy's Gone A-Hunting*. The first was finally filmed several years later under the title *Special Effects*. Cohen initially had high hopes of interesting Hitchcock in directing one of his screenplays. He temporarily gained his idol's approval until a Universal executive ruled out this potentially interesting collaboration. However, Cohen never intended to write anything in an uninspired pastiche manner. His manner of reworking the Hitchcock tradition is far more complex than the various attempts of contemporary Hitchcock copyists. Cohen's screenplays never aim at simply imitating Hitchcock's style and themes. Instead, he takes many ideas common to Hitchcock and transplants them into a contemporary world far removed from the Britain and America depicted in that director's work, engaging in a highly creative intertexual interplay of ideas.

*Daddy's Gone A-Hunting* and *Special Effects* contain several visual references to Hitchcock's world. They are not plagiaristic appropriations, but intentional utilizations of radical elements in Hitchcock's work concerning the oppressive nature of gendered power structures within society. Cohen has different goals in mind when he reworks Hitchcock motifs and applies them to new situations. *Daddy's Gone A-Hunting* deals with the pre–1973 Roe vs. Wade world of American society, while *Special Effects* mixes Hitchcock with the world of independent cinema in an interrogation of supposedly fixed boundaries concerning fantasy and reality. The first film has clear references to *Shadow of a Doubt, Strangers on a Train,* and *Vertigo,* the San Francisco Top of the Mark location clearly substituting for the bell tower in *Vertigo*'s climactic scene. *Special Effects* is Cohen's metacinematic reworking of *Vertigo,* investigating both its predecessors' themes, as well as the supposedly distinct worlds of independent cinema and documentary to reveal their complicity in a filmic world where the director's murderous gaze hides a creative and physical impotence. (An analysis of *Special Effects* follows later.) Cohen's Hitchcock appropriations thus represent that very "complex dialectic of affinity and difference" Robin Wood sees in the far more derivative borrowings of Brian DePalma.[3] Although Cohen and DePalma represent opposing cinematic styles, *both* (my italics) directors really have "a symbiotic relationship whose basis is a shared complex of psychological/thematic drives" in relation to the Hitchcock text.[4] But while DePalma appropriates the sadistic and voyeuristic elements within Hitchcock's cinema to exploit the female body in films such as *Dressed to Kill, Body Double*, and *Casualties of War*, Cohen subtly concentrates on the complex nature of oppressive male-female roles within Western society by avoiding the seductive nature of a male-oriented camera eye inherent within the flamboyant cinema style of DePalma.[5]

*Daddy's Gone A-Hunting* is a compromised text ruined by poor casting and directing. However, the film also foreshadows certain Cohen motifs that would emerge in later films such as *It's Alive*. Arriving in San Francisco from England, Cathy Palmer (Carol White) encounters likable, boyish-looking Kenneth Daley (Scott Hylands) outside the airport bus terminal. Attracting her attention by throwing a snowball he scoops from a parked car, Kenneth resembles another version of what Robin Wood terms Hitchcock's "murderous gay,"[6] whose key representative is Norman Bates in *Psycho*. Despite Hylands' inability to convey Anthony Perkins' mixed combination of boyishness and menace, Kenneth appears as a vulnerable male attracted by Cathy's inexperience in coping with a New World of impolite San Francisco citizens. As he tells her on their first meeting, Cathy "looks like a little lost kid" reminding him of "when I was a kid." He identifies himself with her vulnerability in a manner anticipating his later symbiotic association with Cathy's kidnapped baby. Like Martin Burnham, Kenneth is a victim of some undefinable past dysfunctional family relationship. Like Norman Bates, and Bruno in *Strangers on a Train*, he has never really entered the oedipal realm. Kenneth's repressed energies can only emerge violently. He lives in an apartment covered with pictures of babies and a nude female implicitly representing that strong pre-oedipal relationship of a child to the mother's body. Kenneth's boyish attractiveness initially appeals to Cathy. They both move into an apartment together. But Kenneth's unrealistic artistic aspirations and unwillingness to find a job adversely affect their relationship. Tired of supporting Kenneth like a surrogate mother, Cathy suggests he either find a job or seek psychological counseling. Insulted by these affronts to his masculinity, he angrily responds, "I do not earn a living ... I am not a man." Kenneth then throws Cathy and her pet cat, Prissy, out of an apartment she is actually paying for.

Discussing her changed circumstances with her friend Meg (Mala Powers), Cathy confesses she is pregnant. She reluctantly considers an abortion and decides to finish her relationship with Kenneth. Meanwhile Kenneth opens a letter revealing the results of Cathy's pregnancy tests. Overjoyed at being an expectant father, he now sees an opportunity to overcompensate for his male insecurities and idealistically construct a family life he never had as a child. As he tells Cathy, "I know how important a strong daddy is to a kid. I never had one myself. I'm going to make up for that." Irritated at Cathy's cool response, he slaps her publicly in a restaurant. Kenneth's reaction resembles Jim Colbee's in the "Survival" episode of "Branded." Defining his entire personality by the supposed benefits family

normality will bestow on
him, Kenneth acts like a violent monster refusing to recognize the vulnerable dilemma
of the person he oppresses.
Fortunately, Cathy is not
trapped alone in a desert like
Jason McCord in "Survival."
She leaves and decides to
undergo an abortion.

Entering Dr. Parking-
ton's (Dennis Patrick) office
with Meg, Cathy exhibits
horror at a cold clinical abortion room containing a
couch, stirrups, and surgical
instruments. Since *Daddy's
Gone A-Hunting* is set in an

An early moment of intimacy between Cathy
Palmer (Carol White) and the seriously disturbed
Kenneth Daley (Scott Hylands) in *Daddy's Gone
A-Hunting* (National General Productions, 1969).

era prior to the 1973 *Rose vs. Wade* Supreme Court judgment, both Cathy and
the doctor are technically guilty of murder. She is "guilty as sin," according to a
future Cohen screenplay. This explains why she later cannot tell her prospective
Republican politician husband about her past. Although the film never mentions
this, Cathy has committed a criminal act as an "alien." She is not even an American citizen at this point, since she has not fulfilled the required number of years
allowing her to apply for green card status. The act also places Cathy in an
extremely vulnerable position, since law enforcement authorities would then arrest
her rather than her demented ex-lover for committing a crime. Since she underwent an illegal abortion while still an "alien," she could be theoretically liable for
deportation if this act was ever discovered in the future. As a result, both doctor
and patient engage in deceptive social masquerades. Cathy has to perform the
dutiful role of untarnished spouse to her husband. Dr. Parkington conceals his
illegal activities under his everyday function as gynecologist to expectant mothers. Cathy is also a woman haunted by a past crime she can tell nobody about
since it affects her later status as an American citizen. She gains it by marrying
an American who could technically divorce her if he proved unsympathetic in
learning about her past. The divorce could lead to her possible deportation.

Cathy later tells the apologetic Kenneth about the operation. Kenneth's
words — "You had no right to do that. He was mine, Cathy. I needed him" —
depicts him as a vulnerable individual seeking an ideologically approved family
status to reassure himself of his normality. Another parallel links him with Jim
Colbee of "Survival." Walking away in desolation, Kenneth abstractly follows a
mother wheeling a pram before he descends an escalator that symbolizes a plunge
into the inferno-like level of his future revenge.

Cathy later meets Jack Byrnes (Paul Burke) at a party. Cohen capsules their first meeting into a wedding by using a clever script montage device. As Jack says, "How do you do?" to Cathy, a swish pan shows Cathy answering, "I do" at their marriage ceremony. The courtship is so swift that it appears due to Cathy's desires for social acceptance, not to any spontaneous feelings on her part. Subsequent scenes show her newly pregnant and shopping for a crib at a store during Christmas. Cathy sees children queuing up to sit on the knee of Santa Claus. The figure is really Kenneth in disguise sublimating his frustrated desires for fatherhood during the holiday season. A series of cuts alternates Cathy's recognition with close-ups of Kenneth. They end with his hostile look at her. The next shot includes a zoom-in to her stomach as she clutches it painfully. Cohen's screenplay emphasizes a hostile male gaze. But it is directed, not just at the offending female, but also at her unborn child. The camera movement reveals the exact nature of Kenneth's planned revenge. Recovering from the shock, Cathy discovers that Kenneth has vanished. As she retreats from the area, the sequence concludes by rapidly cutting to children's toys all mechanically moving in a hostile manner. These shots anticipate the sinister nature of the toys in Chris' kindergarten in *It's Alive*. Like Hitchcock, Cohen gives seemingly harmless objects sinister undertones. It parallels Hitchcock's use of the laughing jester painting in *Blackmail* (1929), which takes on several meanings according to what particular feelings dominate the character concerned. Mise en scene elements in *Daddy's Gone A-Hunting* similarly express hidden tensions within the protagonists, particularly those involving fears of parenthood.

The next sequence builds up such tensions. Recovering from her shock, Cathy lies in bed. But as she gets up, the camera frames her from outside the doorway. It objectifies her in the same way that Kenneth's earlier hostile gaze does. As Cathy enters the bathroom, she believes she sees Kenneth wielding a razor in his Santa Claus outfit. But it is really Jack wearing red pajamas, his foam-covered face resembling Kenneth's Santa Claus whiskers. As directed by Robson and performed by inadequate actors, the scene appears gimmicky. But the original conception shows Cohen's intuitive awareness of the thin line dividing normality from abnormality. It suggests Jack as Kenneth's opposite, similar to Sam Loomis' role as Norman Bates' more normal counterpart in *Psycho*.

The next major scene shows Cathy undergoing a parlor room interrogation by Jack's Republican allies as they attempt to find out whether she has any compromising past secrets. Cathy nervously passes the test, affirming her belief in wholesome American virtues of apple pie and motherhood. But her humorous attempts to conceal her real guilt evoke Kenneth's threatening presence in her life. Kenneth represents the return of Cathy's own repressed feelings of guilt concerning the abortion. Cathy and Kenneth have a symbiotic relationship similar to that of Uncle Charlie and Young Charlie in Hitchcock's *Shadow of a Doubt*. Like Uncle Charlie, Kenneth nearly causes Cathy's death by sawing away at a wooden staircase. He also appears at the top of an underground car park, looking as distant as Bruno Anthony's ominous Washington appearances in *Strangers on a Train*.

Going into labor while pursued by Kenneth, Cathy later finds herself in a hospital and becomes scared seeing Dr. Parkington performing his "legal" medical duties. While Cathy undergoes labor, the two fathers meet each other in the waiting room for the first time. Despite having different reasons for being there, they act identically as expectant fathers. As they nervously await Cathy's delivery, Jack comments, "I guess we're in this together." Kenneth replies ironically, "You couldn't have put it better." Both men later meet outside the hospital incubator room with other expectant fathers. As they view the babies, Kenneth tells Jack, "Mine didn't live." But the shot-reverse shot sequence linking Kenneth's gaze with Jack's baby already suggests a potential identification between the killer and his intended victim.

Kenneth introduces himself as a photographer to infiltrate the family home and ostensibly take pictures of the baby. Now supporting himself as a working photographer, Kenneth's occupation has ominous overtones. Roland Barthes regards working photographers as "agents of death" ironically producing death "while trying to preserve life."[7] A living person becomes frozen within a chemical embalming process reduced at a simple click from life into symbolic death. Photography and cinematography are both methods of freezing time and presenting a dead image as supposedly alive. In *Camera Lucida*, Barthes sees a phenomenological relationship between photography and his dead mother. He regards photography as a prosthetic mother miming, distorting, and usurping the maternal function, seeing the photograph itself as a "tenuous umbilical cord" by which the photographer gives life.[8] However, photographer Kenneth intends death for his former lover's baby. Finding their baby gone, Cathy and Jack discover its photos scattered throughout their apartment, frozen death-like substitutes for the living being Kenneth intends its mother to kill. Kenneth's chosen profession has ironic overtones. As Barthes comments:

> [I]f the photograph then becomes horrible, it is because it certifies, so to speak, that the corpse is alive, as *corpse*: it is the living image of a dead thing. For the photograph's immobility is somehow the result of a perverse confusion between two concepts: the Real and the Live: by attesting that the object has been real, the photograph surreptitiously induces belief that it is alive, because of that delusion which makes us attribute to Reality an absolutely superior, somehow eternal value; but by shifting this reality to the past ("this-has-been"), the photograph suggests that it is already dead.[9]

For Jack and Cathy, the photographs suggest the death Kenneth plans to compensate for the loss of his own baby.

Baby photos also appear in Kenneth's various apartments, suggesting the stunted development caused by his mother's neglect of him when he was young. Kenneth later reveals, "When I was very little, my mother used to give me her cough medicine all the time to put me to sleep while she entertained her boyfriends." He takes on a perverse maternal role, repeating his past history by feeding the kidnapped child codeine to keep it quiet. Kenneth acts as if he identifies with the baby. He talks to it like a caring father as he changes diapers. The former victimized child becomes a dangerous adult victimizer, like Norman Bates. Kenneth's personality conceals a vulnerable persona dominated by harmful memories of an abusive mother and a vengeful aggression against any female reminding him of his past life. Traumatized by his early life, Kenneth exists in a state of perpetual preadolescence, attracting Cathy with his unconventional boyishness until she discovers another dangerous side to his personality. He not only intends to make Cathy atone for aborting his child, but also wishes to punish her as a surrogate image of his own abusive mother. Paradoxically, he repeats his own victimization upon another victim with whom he also identifies: Cathy's own baby. Kenneth also takes a perverse revenge on Dr. Parkington by brutally performing an abortion on him.

Unfortunately, as a result of Mark Robson's inadequate direction and the limited abilities of the leading actress, the film fails to develop suspense and adequately convey the dilemma of a woman pushed toward matricide like Medea in the classical tragedy. (Characteristically, when Cathy escapes from surveillance Cohen features a theater advertising a San Francisco performance by Judith Anderson as Medea.) Although one cop remarks, "I'm no psychologist, but she might crack up. She might just really do it if she got a chance — as a way out," the role needed a much stronger actress to convey this convincingly.

*Daddy's Gone A-Hunting*'s potential never gains appropriate realization.[10] It is a script only Hitchcock at the height of his creative powers could have done full justice to. Robson fails to realize important themes characteristic of both Hitchcock and Cohen's later films. Like *Shadow of a Doubt* and *Psycho*, Cohen's work unveils the perverse nature of family life, contrasting abnormality with normality and blurring the fragile barriers dividing them. Cathy and Kenneth's family relationship in *Daddy's Gone A-Hunting* foreshadows Tobe Hooper's violent Sawyer family of *The Texas Chainsaw Massacre* and Wes Craven's cannibal kin in *The Hills Have Eyes*. They all reveal aggressive tensions lurking beneath the supposedly loving nature of family ties. The final reunion of Cathy and Kenneth appears as a mock parody of nurturing parents. Unknown to her, Kenneth poisons the milk she intends to feed her baby. Rather than preserving and nurturing their baby's life, father and mother will destroy it.

On their first date, Kenneth climbed to the Top of the Mark restaurant watched by Cathy. At that time she feared heights. In an ending deserving better direction, Cathy climbs up to Kenneth on her own, deciding to end the psychological reign of terror he has inflicted on her. The climax has overtones of Hitchcock's *Vertigo*. But, as with Cohen's Hitchcock appropriations, it is never imitative. Instead, it reworks a former narrative plot motif in an innovative manner. This time no demented male like Scottie overcomes his vertigo at a female's expense. Instead, a vulnerable woman conquers her own fears and faces a situation she also bears some responsibility for creating. Kenneth holds up the baby he has hidden in a cat taxi. He has also killed the family cat. He hopes to dominate Cathy for the last time, expecting her to comply with his insane romantic demands. Kenneth dreams of Cathy finally becoming a submissive wife and mother by bowing to his monstrous patriarchal desires and destroying her own child. Kenneth becomes as demented as General Lorca in *Return of the Seven*, demanding the unquestioned submission that only death can guarantee. He wishes Cathy to throw her own baby from the Top of the Mark. Cathy initially persuades Kenneth of her final submission by playing the role of a perversely loving wife and mother who will kill her own baby to prove her loyalty to an insane patriarch. Kenneth sees the baby's death as his own surrogate death, believing both he and Cathy will then be able to begin a new normal family life together. By forcing Cathy's compliance, he will punish her (as well as his own abusive mother) for acts committed against himself. Kenneth sees Cathy as a surrogate image of his mother. He hopes to rewrite the classical tragedy of *Medea* for his own benefit. Whereas Medea killed her own children as an act of vengeance against Jason's patriarchal intentions of abandoning her, Kenneth will make Cathy kill her own baby as punishment for her desertion of him in an era witnessing aggressive demands for female independence. He intends the deed to prove his ultimate powers of masculine control. By climbing to the Top of the Mark, Kenneth creates his murderous theatrical performance on a grandiose stage compulsively viewed by an audience below. His act has several parallels with the murderous thespian egocentricity exhibited by Tony Chappel in *In Broad Daylight*.

Cathy initially performs her subordinate role under Kenneth's demented theatrical direction until she finally tricks him and rescues her baby. Kenneth falls off the Top of the Mark like Frye in the concluding scene of Hitchcock's *Saboteur*. The final shot shows Cathy standing, unafraid of the heights, like Scottie in the concluding scene of *Vertigo*. It contains several potentials never adequately realized, ingeniously reversing the ending of Hitchcock's earlier film. This time the demented patriarch falls to his death, while the guilty, wronged woman survives at the top of the heights after conquering fears of vertigo she exhibited earlier in the film and finally triumphing over her patriarchal oppressor. But as directed by Robson, the ending is shot like a typical Hollywood happy ending, the climax to a poorly acted, mediocre film from a screenplay demanding better direction. If Hitchcock had collaborated with Cohen, it would have been a more superior film.

*El Condor* is the least characteristic screenplay of the three Cohen wrote during this period. It represents a journeyman employment, with Cohen acting in the capacity of script doctor. The screenplay is a joint contribution. Cohen rewrote an earlier draft so that the new version would conveniently suit already chosen Spanish locations that increased the film's budget. However, *El Condor* is not entirely without interest. Cohen based Lee Van Cleef's character on Bogart's Fred C. Dobbs in *The Treasure of Sierra Madre*. He also tightened up the original writing. But production problems involving direction and performance hindered whatever potential the film had. *El Condor* finally emerged as an average Western.

*El Condor* begins in a Northern prison camp during the Civil War. African-American convict Luke (Jim Brown) learns from an old convict (Elisha Cook)

Luke (Jim Brown) and Jaroo (Lee Van Cleef) arouse the suspicions of General Chavez
(Patrick O'Neal) in *El Condor* (National General Productions, 1970).

about the location of an impregnable fortress, El Condor, containing Emperor
Maximilian's gold. Wishing to aid General Sherman's campaigns with his engi-
neering skills, Luke escapes and teams up with the eccentric Jaroo (Lee Van Cleef)
who offers him an army of Apaches to take El Condor. Journeying to the fortress
with Apache chief Santana's braves, Luke and Jaroo unsuccessfully attempt to
infiltrate the fort. Suspicious of the two men and ignoring the pleas of his mistress, Claudine (Mariana Hill), to execute them, El Condor's commandant, General Chavez (Patrick O'Neal), orders them staked out under the sun. The two men
escape, liberate a village from Chavez's men, and launch a surprise attack on El
Condor. During a truce, Chavez successfully bribes Jaroo with some of the gold
ingots concealed in the fort. Claudine decides to join the winning team and distract Chavez's men by undressing in full view so Luke may lead an assault on the
fort. After the battle, Chavez and some men escape, leaving the assailants in possession of the gold. Deciding to keep the gold a secret from the Apaches, Luke
and Jaroo enjoy the spoils of victory. Jaroo kills Santana when he discovers the
gold. Chavez and his men decide to join the Juaristas, while the Apaches leave
the fort after finding Santana's body. When Luke sees Chavez and the Juaristas
approach El Condor, he attempts to fool them, hinting that the Apaches are still
there. Chavez informs Luke that El Condor's entire treasury is fake. He kept the
information secret to persuade his men to continue fighting on Maximilian's side.
After learning of the Emperor's execution, he told his new allies everything. Luke

and Chavez fight to the death. Chavez inflicts several deadly wounds on Luke before he dies. Enraged at the truth and the deceptive tactics used to bring him to El Condor, an angry Jaroo seeks to kill Luke. The wounded Luke kills Jaroo. Luke and Claudine remain alone in El Condor, surrounded by dead bodies and fake gold.

*El Condor* is an interesting treatment with twists and reversals leading to a surprise ending. But, as directed by John Guillermin, the film is leaden and plodding, filled with lackluster characterization and Lee Van Cleef's unconvincing comedy performance. Under a better director, Cohen's parody of *The Treasure of Sierra Madre* could have succeeded. It contains interesting possibilities, teaming changed versions of Humphrey Bogart and Tim Holt from the original film with a femme fatale in revolutionary Mexico. However, the potentials are never realized.

Jim Brown's role is a re-drafted version of the Tim Holt character in *Treasure of Sierra Madre*, with Lee Van Cleef's role combining Bogart's Fred C. Dobbs with Walter Huston's garrulous old prospector. But the final film is formulaic and lacks recognizable Larry Cohen touches.[11] Virtually all the main characters are defined solely in terms of their lust for gold, the only exception being General Chavez who functions with very few complex character dimensions. He easily transfers his allegiance from one political power to another, given little rationale at all. *El Condor* concludes bleakly in a desolate aura of waste and needless destruction, with Luke and Claudine's survival in the deserted fort appearing highly tentative.

Cohen's experience with television adaptations of his work fared little better, as *In Broad Daylight* (1971) and *Man on the Outside* (1975) reveal. However, *In Broad Daylight* is a very ingenious teleplay. But the inappropriate casting of Richard Boone in the leading role hinders plot execution and plausibility. Although Boone's performance is adequate enough for a television movie, his star persona is not one lending itself to character disguise. As a result, Boone's disguise is no better than Robert Mitchum's in John Huston's *The List of Adrian Messenger* (1963). Both actors are immediately recognizable on screen. No amount of makeup can ever conceal their characteristic features.

However, allowing for these problems, *In Broad Daylight* is still one of Cohen's most innovative works. It is a cleverly executed story dealing with a recently blinded actor's revenge on his unfaithful wife. *In Broad Daylight* represents a variation on theatrical elements in Hitchcock's films such as *The Lodger*, *Murder!*, and *Stage Fright*, with an actor as the main character. Although Tony Chappel (Richard Boone) is blind, his gaze is nonetheless as murderous as the one ascribed to Hitchcock by William Rothman in his book *Hitchcock: The Murderous Gaze*. Cohen also engages in playful movie inter-textualism. The name Anthony Chappel clearly evokes the mysterious "Ambrose Chapel" of *The Man Who Knew Too Much* (1956). When deciding which disguise he will wear for his forthcoming murderous performance, Chappel immediately decides to don the makeup for one of his most successful theatrical roles: Sheridan Whiteside in *The*

*Man Who Came to Dinner.* It is also another indirect tribute to Hitchcock's dark sense of humor, since eating and murder often intertwine as motifs in films such as *Suspicion* (1941), *The Birds* (1963) and *Frenzy* (1972). Chappel intends to feast visually upon the theatrical spectacle of his wife's murder. Finally, Chappel decides to speak with a Greek accent so he will appear like an old tourist: "Once I played a Greek. An Anatolian Greek. Not like Zorba. A real Greek." This is an in-joke reference to Richard Boone's previous performance as Kirk Douglas's Anatolian Greek father in Elia Kazan's *The Arrangement* (1969). *In Broad Daylight* is also an actor's film, since Cohen presents Tony Chappel conceiving, rehearsing, and executing his role as if arduously and meticulously preparing for a successful opening night. It is only an unforeseen flaw in his plans and the alert nature of quick-witted detective Lt. Bergman (John Marley) that closes the play after a short run.

*In Broad Daylight* begins with the camera zooming out from a close shot of Chappel's dark glasses to frame his face. The actor appears stone-faced, his inner emotions hidden from the camera eye. He thanks Doctor Grant (Ken Sansom) for everything his rehabilitation center has done. The audience never learns how Chappel became blind. Cohen's teleplay begins with this current situation and emphasizes the bleak nature of an existence Chappel now faces in coping with his loss of livelihood. Dr. Grant's request for an autograph ironically underlines Chappel's loss of stardom. It is possibly the last time anyone may request another autograph. Accompanied by rehabilitation worker Kate Todd (Suzanne Pleshette), Chappel wishes to enter his lawyer's apartment unaided to pick up an anniversary present for his wife. Despite his disability, Chappel attempts to compensate for his loss of sight by using acting techniques of knowing where to walk in a theatrical arena. He tells Kate he knows how to reach Alex Crawford's (Fred Beir) fifth-floor apartment. Entering the apartment, he goes through Crawford's desk drawers, finding a gun with cartridges before the sound of his wife's adulterous liaison stops him in his tracks. Hiding from Elizabeth (Stella Stevens) and Alex, he hears them relishing his now impotent condition. When Alex speaks about getting the books ready for Chappel, Elizabeth replies, "But he can't *see* them, darling." As they leave the kitchen, Chappel retreats downstairs.

These opening scenes are excellently constructed. They not only immediately give the audience an insight into the way Chappel will conceive the method his revenge will take, but also present important information via mise en scene. A photograph of Chappel, Elizabeth, and Alex appears in the apartment, suggesting the actor's blindness to the adulterous relationship that existed even before he lost his sight. Several meanings appear in this photograph. Chappel looks toward the camera while Alex and Elizabeth embrace with eyes only for each other. The nature of Chappel's monstrous egocentricity as an actor already appears. He has eyes only for the camera. However, Chappel looks toward the photographic lens as if heeding instructions from the unseen director, while Alex and Elizabeth continue to look at one another. Although the photograph presents Chappel as breaking the rules of Hollywood direction and looking directly at the camera, it also underlines the fact that Alex and Elizabeth are too involved in themselves to perceive a real threat to their adulterous relationship. Finally, by breaking the rules of not looking directly at the camera, Chappel's image also parallels the creative nature of the activity of a Larry Cohen who often breaks the rules for his own innovative ends.

Arriving downstairs, Chappel slams down his cane in an act of petulant rage. In one sense he puts on an act for his audience of Kate and doorman Charles (Paul Smith) by lying about his failure to reach Alex's apartment. But, on another level, Chappel feels emotionally betrayed and impotent. He transmits the emotion into an artificial performance. Chided by Kate for his behavior, he makes her promise not to tell Elizabeth of his attempt to reach Alex's apartment. Stopping off at a drug store to purchase a two-gun target set, he arrives home. Elizabeth warmly greets him, engaging in her own type of performance. When Kate lets slip the fact that they stopped at Alex's apartment, Chappel then reveals to his wife he had actually entered the apartment and thus puts her on edge.

During the following weeks, Chappel rehearses for his new role, practicing by firing targets at a radio he positions on top of a grandfather clock. He asks Kate to accompany him on bus journeys around Los Angeles, using her as a theatrical prompter so he can time the various stops on the route. They also travel in taxis. Kate believes Chappel is attempting to develop mobility and independence. But his motives are more deadly. They involve an actor's revenge. As he tells Kate, writers hate him for cutting preliminary speeches and unnecessary verbosity from their scripts, since he believes in going to "the heart of the matter." Encouraging Kate to leave him with Elizabeth, he then plans his murderous performance.

Disguised as an old Greek tourist, Chappel manages to enter Alex's apartment. But he breaks his own rules by taunting Elizabeth with an unnecessary preliminary speech rather than getting to the "heart of the matter" and killing her directly. Playing a nineteenth-century romantic opera on a small cassette, he egocentrically begins to applaud his own performance. Chappel believes he has achieved his greatest role. But it is a judgment best left to an audience, not the actor: "I did it. Nobody knew I was really blind. Nobody has played Oedipus who was actually blind. Not Gielgud, Scofield, Olivier, Burton — nobody." Chappel relishes his envisaged lease of life as a theatrical performer. He tells Elizabeth that he will now divorce (rather than murder) her, since juries would obviously be more sympathetic to him. Angered at his selfishness, Elizabeth throws the photo showing the triangular relationship of herself, Chappel, and Alex at the gun, causing him to shoot her accidentally. Affected by this new turn of events, Chappel has to improvise by climbing outside a fire escape window to reach the lift on the fourth floor. He uses a mother and child to aid his escape outside. Since Chappel loses the umbrella he used as a walking stick, he holds the child's push chair, directing himself outside, where he pretends to take a photograph before escaping in a taxi.

Delivering the news of Elizabeth's death to Chappel, Lt. Bergman becomes suspicious of the actor's lack of emotion and his sudden response to Kate when she notices her umbrella is missing. When Chappel learns that the missing umbrella contains Kate's identity, he immediately returns to his former role as the old Greek tourist and successfully discovers it. Chappel achieves another masterly improvised performance. But it his last bow before an audience. Two people observe him. Discovering his makeup kit at home, Kate immediately works out how Chappel committed the crime and drives to Alex's apartment. In the meantime, Lt. Bergman accidentally discovers the identity of the missing suspect by finding a photo of Chappel as Sheridan Whiteside in scrapbooks Alex keeps for his client. The final scenes show Kate watching Chappel enter a vehicle he believes is a taxi. But it is Lt. Bergman's car. *In Broad Daylight* concludes with Bergman driving Chappel away after his last performance.

Despite the casting of Richard Boone, *In Broad Daylight* is an exciting television movie. It uses suspense at key moments in a manner Hitchcock would have acclaimed. Chappel is no superman avenger. He is vulnerable to chance events such as a whistling kettle that threatens to reveal his presence to Alex and Elizabeth on his first blind journey inside the apartment. On his second journey, he presses the wrong lift button and finds himself on a different floor. Escaping down the fire ladder, he loses Kate's umbrella. Only later does he find out it has her name on it. *In Broad Daylight* is not an average television movie. It has several interesting plot movements and deserves reviving.

If *In Broad Daylight* proved a disappointment to Cohen, *Man on the Outside* was even worse. Screened in 1975, several months after the end of the series, "Griff," starring Lorne Greene, this original television pilot again exhibited several Larry Cohen themes poorly realized by T.V.–movie production. Although Cohen's teleplay contains interesting features, Boris Sagal's direction is uninspiring. *Man on the Outside* appears little different from an average television movie. Yet, even here, certain themes appear, anticipating later motifs in less realistic productions.

*Man on the Outside* begins with retired police captain Wade Griffin (Lorne Greene) wandering aimlessly through a Los Angeles park. He passes several senior citizens who have nothing better to do than wile away their remaining years. Griff notices police dragging the lake for a body and attempts to offer advice. Initially dismissed as a nuisance, Griff informs Lt. Matthews (Ken Swofford) that the police operation is a waste of time. He tells them that the aged Mrs. Stella Daniels (Ruth McDevitt) phones police headquarters every year on the anniversary of the death of her husband, who drowned in the lake. Unlike Steve Carella in "89th Precinct" and Mark Deglan of "Night Cry," the 35-year police veteran prides himself on knowing his community and taking a personal interest in former clients such as Mrs. Daniels. Later, Griff comments, "Good police work means knowing your community," thus avoiding wasting time and money by following up crank phone calls.

So far, Griff appears a caring ex-cop condemned to an empty wasteland into which society casts its senior citizens. However, Cohen's teleplay undercuts the viewer's initial assumptions. We learn that, not only has Griff obtained a good

Retired police officer turned private eye Wade Griffin (Lorne Greene), in a publicity shot from the short-lived television series "Griff" (1974).

post-retirement job working as a corporation security officer, but that he had the reputation of being a workaholic while on the force. An older police officer tells Lt. Matthews that Griff was originally known as the "seven day wonder" who even expected his men to work on their days off. He also mentions that another officer awoke from a nightmare, believing that Griff had returned to the force. When Griff has dinner with his son's family, he pontificates to his grandson about police work, causing his son to comment, "Dad, I don't like to talk about my work." Griff obviously lived for the job, like his later demonic counterpart Officer Matt Cordell in *Maniac Cop*. When we later see Griff's apartment, the only items exhibited on his wall are clippings from his heyday as a police officer, official plaques and badges. They parallel the publicity material Matt Cordell delights in showing Sally Noland in *Maniac Cop*. It also suggests an egocentricity linking him with other darker Cohen creations such as Tony Chappel.

However, unlike Matt Cordell, Griff has a family. Although his wife has died, he keeps in touch with his son, Gerald (James Olsen), daughter-in-law, Nora (Lorraine Gary), and grandson, Mark (Lee H. Montgomery). However, with no other close male friends or girlfriends, he constantly intrudes on their privacy, like the grandmother in Cohen's play *Washington Heights*. But his desire for contact stems more from loneliness than from a wish to interfere in their lives. However, tensions exist in the Griffin family.

Antagonisms exist between father and son. Gerry Griffin refused to follow his father into the police force and sought an alternative career as a private detective. He obviously felt uncomfortable living up to his father's image. Griff later discovers that Gerry kept a newspaper clipping of Griff's major exploits in his wallet. The relationship between father and son is clearly one of attraction and repulsion, anticipating those in the later *It's Alive* films. Gerry complains to Nora about being an "only child, and child is the word. Having a super-cop for a father is something like being perpetually a nine-year-old. I always feel I'm up for sentencing." Ironically, his own son, Mark, appears the same age as Gerry's other persona. Griff and Mark's relationship is much closer than the one they have with Gerry. Mark actually annoys his father when he suggests that he work with Griff on his present case. The relationship between Griff and Mark also parallels that between Admiral Kiley and his grandson in "Mayday! Mayday!"—a teleplay also involving a dysfunctional family situation between a grandparent and his actual son.

Gerry leaves to pursue his mysterious assignment. As he leaves, Griff watches him from the window and views the sudden murder of his son. Rushing downstairs, he reaches his son, who utters, "Dad. I'm sorry" before dying. Griff then sets out in pursuit of his son's murderer and tries to help Mark release the grief he has stored up over the death of his father.

From this point, *Man on the Outside* becomes a typical television movie with uninspired direction. The potential in Cohen's teleplay never achieves adequate realization. A duality theme is definitely present. Griff's quarry, Ames (William Watson), is a corporate hit man who works at the San Pedro scrapyards, dismantling former World War II battleships and P.T. boats. By setting the final confrontation between Griff and Ames in this environment, Cohen suggests parallels between Griff as a retired ex-cop removed from active duty and the still-functional battleships doomed for the scrapyard. This location also echoes the graveyard for decommissioned battleships Sam Peckinpah chose for the final battle in *The Killer Elite* (1975). It also complements the park and lake where discarded senior citizens wander at the beginning of *Man on the Outside*. Furthermore, hit man Ames is also a family man with a wife and six-year-old daughter, a darker alter ego of Gerry Griffin. Like Gerry, he conceals from his wife information about his real job.

Parallels also exist between Griff and Mark. Despite their ages, both conceal grief over the death of Gerry. Until the end of the film, Mark never shows any emotion. Gerry's secretary, Ellen (Jean Allison), sees links between Griff and Mark. One conceals hidden violence, the other grief: "I think there's a lot of violence in you and you've got it locked in you too." Griff replies that his personal code of ethics has little to do with New Testament forgiveness, but with Old Testament morals "and [concepts] way before, too." The comments not only evoke Lorne Greene's performance as the Bible-quoting Ben Cartwright in the first season of *Bonanza*, but also anticipate Cohen's later versions of divine justice in *God Told Me To* and *Q*.

In representing his demonic side, Ames also has certain parallels with Griff. Like Griff, Ames loves his job. In punishing his disobedient son, he is seen as a demonic monster from Griff's id. In his final confrontation with Ames' ship, Griff switches his own safety deposit key for the one to the box containing the money Ames accumulated during his career as a hit man. Ames does not realize the switch until Griff points it out. Griff worked for a corporation, while Ames freelances as a corporate hit man. Ames is also an early version of the more-developed Cleve, while Griff anticipates certain attributes of Dennis Meachum in Cohen's later screenplay *Best Seller*. Unfortunately, the direction never realizes these potentials. *Man on the Outside*'s tentative duality between retired cop and corporate hit man will receive far better treatment in *Best Seller*.

Cohen's screenplays for *Return of the Seven*, *Daddy's Gone A-Hunting*, and *El Condor* were all written for mainstream productions under circumstances he never wished to experience again. All three films exhibit hasty construction, poor direction, and a failure to realize the many interesting possibilities contained in their screenplays. Television productions of his work fared little better. Dissatisfied with the results, Cohen turned to directing his own work. About the same time, Clint Eastwood noted the economic waste of the big-budget productions he starred in following his return from Italy, such as *Where Eagles Dare*, *Paint Your Wagon* (both 1969) and *Kelly's Heroes* (1970). He decided to found his own company and gain complete control over his films. But Eastwood was more fortunate than Cohen. Lacking huge Hollywood budgets, Cohen's ensuing films would appear visually impoverished for most critical tastes, in comparison with the multimillion dollar works emerging from the studios. However, Cohen turned to a form of visual style and direction totally different from the type of uninvolved production techniques that marred his screenplays. Far from being unpolished, unprofessional works, Cohen's subsequent films really represent appropriations of a visual style antithetical to contemporary Hollywood, but one highly appropriate in realizing the radical nature of his creative insights.

# First Films as Director, Producer, *and* Writer

Larry Cohen's first film, *Bone*, differs in several ways from his future work. Unlike *Black Caesar* and *It's Alive*, which have some basic connections with recognizable genres such as the gangster movie and horror film, *Bone* is difficult to classify generically. Its formal structure differs from the type of realist narrative characterizing the film and television productions scripted by Cohen. It represents an early example of the director's cinematic appropriation of a comic-strip style that influenced him from a very early age. The characters are all types: an affluent Beverly Hills couple, a threatening African-American intruder, a dizzy young woman, and a devious business executive. In certain ways, they are caricatures. However, Cohen's choice of methodology is neither superficial nor without historical precedent. He is a director constantly using satire as a critical weapon in all his films that challenge many dehumanizing aspects of the American experience. As Donald Crafton has shown, both comic strip and caricature are not entirely trivial artistic devices. They have played instrumental roles in the development of cinema. In his definitive study of film pioneer Emile Cohl and the development of caricature, Crafton points out that caricature played a very important role both in animation and early cinema as a critical ideological weapon against conformist tendencies in bourgeois society.[1] However, Cohen imbues his characters with definable personalities, making them rounded individuals. On one level, they are artificial creations representing average social types. But on a much more deeper level, they are human beings undergoing contradictions and tensions. They are at war both with themselves and a social environment defining their behaviors and desires. In *Bone*, Larry Cohen unconsciously uses caricature techniques that were once familiar features in the work of forgotten pioneers such as animator Emile Cohl and contemporary comic-strip artists. But, as with all his traditions, he develops them cinematically to engage in his first radical, allegorical, satirical assault upon American society.

*Bone* is not easy to classify. At each point, audience definitions of reality and fantasy become constantly undermined. After the opening credit image of the

Larry Cohen begins directing his first feature film, *Bone* (1972) (courtesy of Larry Cohen).

solitary lightbulb, the film begins with what appears to be a car commercial. Then, the audience discovers that the preceding image was a fantasy within the mind of Bill Lennick (Andrew Duggan). Bill discovers a rat in his pool. Suddenly, out of nowhere, the threatening figure of Bone (Yaphet Kotto) appears. Acting out a violent stereotypical role, he demands money from the Lennicks and threatens to rape and kill Bernadette Lennick (Joyce Van Patten) if Bill never returns. At the end of the film, Bone disappears as mysteriously as he appeared, suggesting his creation as a figure of paranoid white fears. However, rapid montage inserts appear intermittently throughout the film, showing a young man (Casey King) in a dark cell laughing silently at the proceedings until he decides to end the narrative (and the film) by breaking the lightbulb seen in the opening shot. By this time, the audience guesses that the young man is the Lennicks' abandoned son rotting away in a Spanish jail. The final image on the screen is a television set showing Bill selling cars, as in the beginning. This screen suddenly goes black as if the plug had been pulled out. *Bone* is a film operating on several levels, mixing reality and fantasy, humor and danger, operating in a manner deliberately at odds with the normal narrative devices present in film and television. It is Larry Cohen's first attempt at an avant-garde movie with a narrative framework — a contradictory mixture for a deliberately contradictory film hoping to awaken audience

awareness in a manner similar to the films of John Cassavetes.[2] Although both
directors differ enormously, their films draw upon a peculiarly American tradition involving a "notion of the film experience itself as essentially affiliated with
the dream experience"[3] and a socially governed "interactional strategy" designed
to present any capitalist model of self-contained and competitively protected
identities as open to disruption and possible change.[4]

The comic-strip style is by no means irrelevant to Cohen's intentions. In a
film deliberately blurring the boundaries between reality and fantasy, the style
actually appropriates a pre–Disney animation technique having many parallels
to surrealism. Crafton points out that "Although the creators of the first animated films were not surrealists or even cognizant to that movement, they inad-
vertently made films that demonstrated a disregard for everyday existence, normal logic, and causality, and a propensity for dreamlike action which Andre
Breton and his followers admired.[5] This description also parallels Cohen's methods behind his first feature films as director. As well as noting the important presence of comedy and satire in a cinematic tradition also involving interrelated elements of animation and the comic strip, Crafton also notes an extremely
important element in his pioneering study of Emile Cohl. Like Cohen, Cohl eventually became relegated to a marginal position by ghettoizing institutional tendencies that were developing in his era, dominated by its version of a classical
Hollywood narrative tradition. However, Crafton points out, "As a caricaturist,
Cohl had chosen to view society from its margins. His adoption of the most
marginalized branch of cinema, animation, was not a departure for him; it was
his characteristic way of doing things."[6] Similarly, Larry Cohen often uses both
comic-strip style and satirical humor in his films as his own characteristic way of
doing things. The prevailing academic blindness concerning this tradition has
resulted in Cohen's unjustified neglect. What could be more natural than his first
feature employing these two motifs that are highly personal aspects of his cinematic style? Crafton also notices an element characteristic of both Cohl and
Cohen: "The humor in Cohl's comic strips is primarily visual. It arises from the
irrational, unexpected magnification of an everyday incident into an unreal, often
oneiric event."[7] This is as equally true of *Bone* as it is of Cohen's other films.
Finally, *Bone* is by no means an incomprehensible film, as it may appear to those
reared exclusively on the classical Hollywood narrative tradition. It is a film uniting many different traditions and following several acknowledged, but alternative, routes. Like the graphic artist Lyonel Feininger, Cohen's cinema productively
links caricature and fantasy as well as political satire.[8] Although the cinematically
polluted, appropriated cartoon form appears frequently in recent atrocities such as
*The Crow* (1994) *Batman Forever*, and *Judge Dredd* (both 1995), it is important to
remember that alternative positive traditions do exist, traditions followed by Cohen
in his films. Cohen's politically committed, cinematic comic-strip usage has many
precedents in the work of artists such as Neal Adams, Dick Briefer, John Buscema.
Mike Kaluta, and Ogden Whitney, all of whom operate within similar filmic and
satirical traditions.[9] *Bone* is not as difficult to understand as it initially appears.

However, due to its very unique and disjunctive nature, *Bone* presented a problem in terms of distribution. It resisted classification within commercially definable terms. Seeking a convenient label to market this difficult product, the distributor launched it as a "blaxploitation" film rather than the sophisticated satirical allegory it actually is. Like Cohen's other films, *Bone* requires several viewings for the spectator to appreciate the deliberate strategies of visual style, performance, plot changes, and pointed meanings. Most distributors misunderstood *Bone*'s thematic complexities and chose to exhibit it under definable categories such as sex film (*Housewife*), horror movie (*Beverly Hills Nightmare*) or Hitchcock copy (*Dial Rat for Terror*). But *Bone* is really a clever cinematic satire not easily classifiable under any particular generic framework. It also mixes other forms — freewheeling independent film style, off–Broadway theatrical performances, and a social parody of affluent lifestyles and attitudes — demanding a sophisticated type of viewer interaction not easily attainable within the envisaged market audiences. Like John Cassavetes, Cohen wanted to make his audiences work at discerning meanings in his first feature. *Bone* is a unique work. Originating from a theatrical script, changed according to the low-budget exigencies of independent film, *Bone* also contains associations with Cohen's previous television dramas. Like many of his "Defenders" scripts ("Unwritten Law," "The Go-Between"), it analyzes the dangerous effects of socially conditioned behavior upon the American psyche. At the same time, it anticipates many themes in Cohen's horror films, where emphasis lies less on actual monsters but more upon a society that produces such creatures and their human parents who are pressured toward civilized aggression. *Bone* intermingles motifs appearing in the early television drama "False Face" with the type of later satiric explorations appearing in *Island of the Alive* and *A Return to Salem's Lot*. It is a radical allegorical examination of the dangers affecting human beings within a psychically damaging American culture.

Bone contains a particular disjunctive style absent from Cohen's later work. It involves a satirical use of intellectual montage revealing real motivations within the minds of various characters. Abrupt montage inserts contradict the lies spoken by various characters. They resemble cinematic experiments undertaken by Alfred Hitchcock in his early British films such as *Murder!* In one scene, Hitchcock undermines Doucebelle Markham's weak attempt at feigning social etiquette with Sir John by revealing that her little "tidbit" is really a bottle of beer and a loaf of bread and cheese. In a later scene, Hitchcock reveals the lavish meal Sir John relinquishes when he reluctantly agrees to Markham's arrangement of spending the night in a policeman's rudimentary accommodation. Sir John appears to accede to the wishes of his working-class hosts. However, Hitchcock shows that his mind is really in the meal he will miss. This technique also resembles Fritz Lang's temporary use of montage techniques in his early years in Hollywood, as *Fury* (1936) demonstrates. Cohen's appropriation of this device is important. The editing inserts display a highly motivated political unconscious that reveals everyday lies conditioning each character's routine existence. Cohen's filmic style in *Bone* is always relevant to certain plot developments.

One scene is particularly insightful. While seduced by the girl (Jeannie Berlin), Bill Lennick's mind is on the automobiles he sells. Rapid shots of automobiles reveal his attitude to sex as equivalent to the mechanical operation of a car on display at a showroom. Bill earlier stated that sex distracts attention away from making money. What is more natural than his mind drawing parallels between an act he regards as mechanical and thinking about a car's seductive performance for the consumer? Seduced and subjected to male rape by a girl he may have molested years ago in a New York cinema, Bill mentally transforms the sexual assault into a car commercial! He fits Herbert Marcuse's definition of a consumerist human being in *One-Dimensional Man*. When accosted by the X-Ray Lady (Brett Somers) in the bar about the deceased dog, Fury, he once used in his car commercials, Lennick lies to her about the pet's actual nature. However, rapid inserts of a not so friendly animal reveal to the audience what lies hidden beneath the explanations he gives her. The Lennick marriage is also based on a lie; so, too, is the economic foundation of their lifestyle.

Bone's (Yaphet Kotto) first appearance occurs when the camera tracks up from his reflection in the pool, where a rat is trapped by the suction, to a close-up of his seemingly threatening face. Throughout the film, tilt up and tilt down camera movements often suggest constantly reversing circumstances affecting the protagonists. The camera tracks up from Bill Lennick driving away to get ransom money to show Bone and Bernadette (Joyce Van Patten) watching him from an upstairs window. Holding Bernadette as hostage, Bone is now in control. Leaving his business manager's office later, Bill's elevator descends to an underground car park, passing Bone and Bernadette waiting for him on the ground floor. Earlier, the camera movement suggested Bone as embodying the Lennicks' repressed tensions, as it tracked up from Bone's reflection in the water. Bill's descent places him in a dark underground environment. It parallels the depths from which Bone originally emerged. The car park is a violent area where Bone attempts to run down Bill with the Lennicks' car. Bone's attempt also parallels the method Bill used to kill Fury.

Economic motivations corrupt all the leading characters in *Bone*. Fury's death results in more ratings and sales for Bill from sympathetic television audiences. While attempting to obtain the ransom money to save Bernadette, Bill remembers her repugnance toward him while they were tied up. Bill hopes that Bone will murder Bernadette so he will make more on television and profit from her death, playing the role of bereaved husband. Bernadette and Bone, hoping to profit from Bill's life insurance, later become allies and plot his murder.

Role reversals and power struggles occur throughout the film. Initially Bone dominates Bernadette. But after she discovers his vulnerability, she dominates him, initiating the sexual act according to Masters and Johnson by lying over him in a masculine "superior" position. Although the act ends with vaseline-lensed images of Bernadette and Bone (a common cinematic method suggesting romance and fantasy), with Bone lying over Bernadette, the visual imagery implicates them as equal partners in a deceptive illusion. Although Bone achieves orgasm in the white man's way, the sequence ends with Bernadette's lines: "Oh Bone! You're everything I imagined you to be!" This not only reinforces Bone's role as a return of the repressed, but also his changed image. Bone is no longer an archetypal dark force conjured up by white racist tradition, the "big black buck doing what's expected of him" (as Bone says), but a subdued black stud used and abused by his white mistress. Bone's transformation is another of Cohen's strategic role reversal themes. The monster is no monster at all. Despite his threatening veneer, Bone is a vulnerable and sensitive being donning an aggressive mask to protect himself from a threatening society. By doing so, he thus conforms to the image expected of him. Similarly, the *It's Alive* babies initially act to protect themselves from a hostile society. But the aggression soon becomes second nature to them, due to social conditioning. They act in the way they are expected to.

Split-second fragmented images of Kenneth Lennick (Casey King) appear at the beginning of the film. They endure longer on the screen during other intermittent appearances and break up *Bone's* narrative diegesis. Kenneth's presence acts as a framing device, initiating the action and concluding the film. The lightbulb imagery is highly suggestive. *Bone* begins with a bulb slowly emerging from darkness until the camera zooms into it, making the screen white, leading to Bill's car-salesman address to the camera. The lightbulb is a diminutive object surrounded by the darkness. But the camera eye zooms into it until the whole screen becomes white. This movement represents an ideal metaphor describing the Lennicks and their affluent Beverly Hills culture. Despite their privileged white lifestyle, they are really vulnerable to a surrounding darkness that will eventually engulf them. *Bone* concludes with Kenneth's destruction of the lightbulb. It not only plunges the cinema screen into darkness but switches off a small television monitor once more showing Bill performing as a salesman. This is a fitting demise for Bill, since he lived his entire life like a character in a television advertisement. Before Bernadette murders him, Bill pleads for his life, using language reminiscent of the car sales pitch featured in previous scenes. *Bone's* whole structure now appears to be the result of vengeful psychodrama created by a son whose existence his parents deny. Kenneth languishes in a Spanish prison cell, convicted of drug-smuggling charges. Bill and Bernadette deny what has happened to Kenneth and abandon him. They construct their own fantasy scenario about Kenneth serving as a helicopter pilot in Vietnam, a scenario they eventually believe to be real. They ignore Kenneth's actual existence in much the same way that they deny the reality of their marriage and financial circumstances. The Lennicks also condescendingly ignore people from other racial and class backgrounds. In the opening scene, Bill complains about Japanese gardeners and garbage men who "take no pride in their job." He refuses to let his departing Hispanic maid receive a phone call from her brother. Bone soon appears as the archetypal image of a working-class black whose presence the Lennicks chose to deny.

In his first film, Cohen already illustrates the disastrous consequence of denials involving family, class, history, and race. Like other families in seventies "family" horror movies such as *The Night Walk* (1972) and *The Hills Have Eyes* (1977), Bill

Larry Cohen's shadowy presence as director oversees the performances of Yaphet Kotto, Joyce Van Patten, and Andrew Duggan on the set of *Bone* (1972) (courtesy of Larry Cohen).

and Bernadette Lennick choose to ignore unpleasant realities in their own society. They live a selfish, affluent lifestyle, totally oblivious of a pernicious class structure oppressing racial minorities. Their denial also operates on a personal and family level, as seen in their refusal to acknowledge Kenneth's plight.

    *Bone* also anticipates Cohen's future tendencies of closely associating fantasy and reality. All the characters live in some form of deceitful illusion. Bone may be a creation of Bernadette's desire to murder her husband, a desire she disavows in the film's conclusion, similar to her rejection of Kenneth. When Bill discovers a rat in his pool, he utters the famous words in *Frankenstein* (1931) (also the title of Cohen's fourth film), "It's Alive," Bernadette denies its presence: "I don't see a rat in the pool." Bill immediately responds, "You don't want to see." After Bill notes that the rat is trapped in the pool — "He can't get out. The suction keeps him down" — Bone immediately appears. Viewing Bone's working-class appearance, and initially repulsed by a dominant black physique clad in a paint-splattered denim shirt and jeans, Bernadette begins to demean her husband: "I don't see anything. Maybe he imagined things." This line leads to an extreme close-up of Bone's face as he looks at Bill, asking him, "You imagine things?" The following shot frames Bone in the left foreground of the screen, with Bernadette opposite him in the background, with the pool separating them. Their cinematic framing suggests undefined associations linking them. Bone kills the rat but brushes it briefly against Bill's robe before throwing it away. The act suggests some link between the men. Bone is Bill's fantasy creation. But Bone also lives the same sort of lie as the Lennicks. He acts out the role of a black man that white society prefers not to see. Bone never realizes that his behavior does not represent his real identity, but rather results from desired objectification by a racist culture preferring to view him as a dangerous "other." At first, Bone plays the role of a violent black threatening to rob the home and rape the white woman. However, he achieves neither goal. After Bone fails to rape Bernadette, he appears as a vulnerable, pathetic being susceptible to further manipulation by white culture. He becomes Bernadette's stud and accomplice. While driving to confront Bill, Bone talks about the racially biased dualities present in American culture from the earliest times, stating that he never knew whether his real identity was as "Wild Bill" or "Fuzzy." Later events educate him. After Bernadette's brutal murder of Bill, he finds out that his white mistress really despises him. When Bone and Bernadette surround Bill as he vainly pleads for his life on the sand dune, she tells Bone, "Come on Fuzzy. Cut him off at the top." When Bone protests that murdering Bill was really his job, she retorts, "Hey You! Leave us alone. This is a family affair." Having undergone the dominant culture's transformation from a violent Magua to a harmless Chingachgook or Tonto, Bone disappears after hearing Bernadette scornfully say, "Fuzzy. I never needed you." *Bone* reveals that all characters, whether white or black, are all victims of a depraved culture, one implicitly needing radical change. It contaminates everyone within its domains, as the entire film reveals. Whatever one's racial group, no one is ever entirely free from the surrounding corruption, a fact *Black Caesar* also emphasizes.[10]

After the opening lightbulb shot in *Bone,* the next sequence features Bill Lennick. At first, it appears realistic. Bill sells cars in a television commercial reminiscent of those All-State Insurance commercials appearing during sixties television shows such as "The Defenders" and "The Nurses."[11] However, as the camera cranes out we see dead bodies in the cars and understand that Bill broadcasts in a used-car lot full of road accident victims. Bill denies what is really present. He becomes increasingly agitated: "Nobody gets turned away… Somebody take the car off my hands." The sequence ends in a close-up of Bill's face as he concludes, "It's a god damn shithouse." A zoom-out camera movement showing Bill in the different environment of his Beverly Hills swimming pool suggests that the previous images represent his own nightmare realization of complicity in a death-dealing culture of car accidents. Bill then complains about the state of his property and a working-class proletariat no longer answering to his bidding. Television commercials featuring Bill appear intermittently throughout *Bone,* depicting him as a latter-day Willy Loman. He lives an American Dream based upon denial and lies, as does his counterpart in Arthur Miller's *Death of a Salesman.* The imagery also reveals that the supposedly affluent lifestyle Lennick leads relies upon deception and violence for its very existence, since he sells cars with a history of high body counts on American highways. The actual number of deaths and injuries parallels the body count then going on in Vietnam, a heroic imaginary battlefield into which the Lennicks banish their son. As a salesman, Bill also incarnates the trickster figure of Herman Melville's *The Confidence Man*, a character whose presence articulates those ideologically denied factors of violence and murder within American culture. Bill's shaky demeanor at the end of his car sales pitch shows a social mask dropping. Bone then appears in answer to the different frustrations within a husband and wife who want to murder each other. All three characters exist in a symbiotic relationship to each other, emphasized by the same letter ("B") that begins their names.

*Bone* also uses motifs from the Hitchcock tradition. But Cohen interweaves them into his own narrative so the appropriations are barely discernible. Bone evokes repressed desires on the part of an American dysfunctional family. He resembles the Uncle Charley figure conjured by Young Charlie in *Shadow of a Doubt*, as well as the demonic alter ego figure of Puritan mythology depicted by Nathaniel Hawthorne in "Young Goodman Brown." Hitchcock also indirectly influences Cohen's choice of mise en scene. Bill Lennick wears a green robe at the pool. Bernadette wears a green bikini. She later dons a yellow robe. In his visit to the bank, Bill wears a light yellow jacket. In *Vertigo* and *The Birds*, green and yellow are symbolic primary colors having deep associations with violence and sexuality.

*Bone* operates on several levels. It resembles an off–Broadway theatrical satire transferred to film, borrowing aspects of screwball comedy, the American Jewish tradition parodying complacent bourgeois lifestyles, and fantasy. It also appropriates modernist and post-modernist styles (especially using irony, satire, and parody). *Bone* may also be described as a cinematic Chinese puzzle box leading the viewer along with the promise of a narratological resolution but finally leaving the enigma open. *Bone* contains all of these features but cannot be reduced to any of them. At the same time, it is not a ludic play of hyper-realistic signifiers with visual and thematic referents dependent on an undefinable reality. Cohen's intention is highly serious.

Like George and Martha in Edward Albee's *Who's Afraid of Virginia Woolf?*, Bill and Bernadette Lennick live a life of psychic prostitution denying any unpleasant realities. The opening shot reveals Bill Lennick totally defined by his job as television car salesman, an occupation based on selling products denying the violent undertones of a corporate American machine culture. When Bone forces Bill and Bernadette into their house, a voice-over accompanies the scene. Although this appears clumsy, since it is superimposed over the action and bears no relationship to lip movements, it is also formally understandable as representing the Lennick's deceptive denial of the threatening situation they find themselves in. It is deliberately unreal and paralleling the false denials they practice in daily life. Despite their affluent image, the Lennicks are actually close to bankruptcy. Bill guides Bone around the house like an estate agent showing a respective buyer a highly sought after property, thus denying another dangerous reality threatening the unreal nature of his existence.

Ransacking Bill's office, throwing books off the shelf (including William Styron's *The Confessions of Nat Turner*), Bone not only discovers the real financial situation of the Lennicks, but Bill's deceitful borrowing of $5,000 on Bernadette's life insurance. As he dominates the Lennicks with his powerful black presence, a modernist painting of a nude black female appears on the wall next to him. It illustrates the reverse nature of the racially biased objectifying process dominating Bone. The painting represents the acceptable form of black female racial depiction — sexually objectified by the white male gaze. Bone represents another, equally pernicious, product of white representation: a dangerous, threatening black male conjured up by white phobia. The nude female painting also complements the abstract image of Theda Bara as vamp later seen in the girl's (Jeannie Berlin) apartment. It embodies Bill's depiction of her dangerous, sexually threatening nature. However, we later learn the girl is no threat. She is as mixed up about her real identity as Bone is.

The girl initially appears to be untouched by the problems affecting the Lennicks, a freewheeling spontaneous spirit ripping off consumerist society. But, she is actually a neurotic victim of the same type of family situation oppressing the Lennicks. She ascribes her condition to sexual molestation by an older man one evening in a New York theater many years earlier. Her mother denied the reality of the event in much the same way the Lennicks deny what has actually happened to their son. As the girl says, "She never really wanted to look at me after that. She really didn't want to hear it."

The girl believes Bill was the molester. Although Bill lies about ever being in a movie theater in his life — "I don't go to the movies. It is a waste of valuable business time" — he does reveal he has attended movie shows. When the girl speaks about her assailant's cold hands being the result of washing under a cold tap, Bill comments, "There's never any hot water in theaters." Bill may be the actual assailant. But even if he is not, he is still a powerful white male with the same type of perversity that logically leads to child assault as a form of patriarchal domination. Bill speaks of sex being a waste of time: "All that energy could be better spent by expanding profits and getting ahead." He began his capitalist career selling used comic books, which he used to keep under his pillow at night. Associations of repressed sexuality and capitalistic acquisitiveness are present in his personality. Even if Bill is innocent, both he and the girl are equal victims of an oppressive system resulting in sexual and economic perversion. When Bill tells the girl about his early days selling comic books, she calls him a "pervert." Although she takes revenge by sexually assaulting him, her victory does not represent a strategic reversal of her condition. It is as meaningless as Bone's "successful" laying of Bernadette that occurs at the same time. Bernadette penetrates Bone's black macho posture and discovers a vulnerable being whom she will use for revenge on Bill. Bill also reaches orgasm by thinking of her body as mechanical parts of cars he sells. As he earlier tells the girl, all that energy should be spent on business. Nothing is really changed. Everybody uses each other. It is "business as usual."

*Bone* constantly demonstrates the inherent futility of trying to reverse power situations under the present system. No matter who gains the upper hand, nothing actually changes. Power will remain and corrupt everyone. Bone first dominates Bill and Bernadette, sending the husband out to get money. Bill becomes dominated by the girl, becoming her accomplice in a supermarket robbery and a victim of female rape. Bernadette dominates Bone sexually, making him her passive accomplice. The girl is a neurotic victim of a traumatic child assault that has conditioned her adult behavior. Perverted by the urban squalor affecting impoverished African-Americans, Bone acts in the way most white people expect — as a dangerous "Menace 2 Society." Bernadette's contempt for Bill leads to a murder. The entire film operates by showing changing power relationships. But no matter what gender or race holds the final card, any real improvement in the situation is negligible. The same system remains in control.

*Bone* illustrates that an American society based upon lies and deception can only logically lead to violence and death. The personal Lennick family dilemma parallels that of the contemporary body politic. Bernadette finally reveals the truth to Bone. Their son, Kenneth, is imprisoned in Spain for smuggling drugs. However, she denies responsibility for his plight, uttering lines duplicating the ones she repeats to the camera at the end of the film when she rehearses her alibi for Bill's murder: "I don't know whose idea it was. It couldn't have been mine. I'd remember. It might have been Bill. I'd remember ... I'd remember, wouldn't I?" As Bill retreats from Bernadette, and Bone makes his last appeal to them — "We're not acting normally" — he states explicitly that Bernadette never replied to any of Kenneth's letters while he was in jail. Bernadette murders Bill. Bone mysteriously disappears in the same way he entered the film. In front of the camera, Bernadette rehearses her alibi for the murder. She blames Bone in stereotypically racist terms, using him as a convenient scapegoat for the murder in a manner similar to a recent court case. Bernadette repeats the lines she initially spoke to Bone about the Lennick denial of Kenneth's existence — "I don't know whose idea it was. It couldn't have been mine ... I'd remember it. Wouldn't I? Wouldn't I?" — long after the image fades to black.

*Bone* is a black comedy revealing a nihilistic underside beneath an affluent American lifestyle. The film is far more radical than *Down and Out in Beverly Hills* (1985) in the nature of its criticism. It reveals a society in which no character wishes to confront reality and change for the better. In his first film, Cohen depicts dangerous flaws within contemporary society still present today for alert audiences to recognize, understand, and move toward changing.

*Black Caesar* opens and concludes with a shot of the New York landscape. The skyscraper image is a device that frames a morality story involving the rise and fall of Black Caesar Tommy Gibbs (Fred Williamson), the "Godfather of Harlem," according to the British release title. These images denote a favorite Cohen theme of using New York as a character in his films. Manhattan's affluent skyscraper area acts as a social force determining a character's destiny. Such images are not superfluous but essential to the film's structure. Tommy Gibbs is not as

Larry Cohen with cast members of his second feature, *Black Caesar* (1973). Cohen holds the distinctive gun used by Fred Williamson in the film (courtesy of Larry Cohen).

free as he believes himself to be. His destiny falls into an ideologically defined upward mobility pattern that appears in the writings of Benjamin Franklin and Horatio Alger. But these definitions of the American Dream contain personal and social traps for the unwary, snares recognized by Jack London in his stimulating writings "What Life Means to Me," "How I Became A Socialist," and *Martin Eden.* Tommy's destiny is less than the sum of its parts, which are defined by Western capitalistic civilization, with its seductive traps for any victim. As a visual signifier of Eastern material affluence, the Manhattan landscape dominates Tommy Gibbs, no matter how much he may think of himself as master of his destiny.

   *Black Caesar* owed its box-office popularity to its marketability as a "blaxploitation" movie, a genre Cohen rightly rejects. Although promoted to reviewers and audiences as such, *Black Caesar* is a much more complex movie. It owes more to a radicalized definition of elements contained in both the classic gangster movie and Robert Warshow's essay "The Gangster as Tragic Hero." The immediate model is less *Shaft, Slaughter,* or *Superfly,* with cocky black heroes and heroines (*Cleopatra Jones*) flaunting superior notions of black ethnicity before subordinate white allies or demonized villains, but more the moralistic dimensions of *Little Caesar.* Like his predecessor Rico Bandello (Edward G. Robinson), Tommy Gibbs (Fred Williamson) aims high and finally falls. Although Cohen borrows a classical formula, he changes it by infusing it with contemporary themes and radical nuances. At the time, critics recognized that the "blaxploitation" formula merely borrowed old Hollywood formulas initially popular with white audiences. It just changed the color of the hero's skin and discarded the form after it served box-office purposes. The black hero often gets the white girl and lives happily ever after, once bad "whitey" (either crooked cop or gangster) is out of the way. Cohen's film is never this opportunistic and superficial, but far more devastating, mature, and radical.

Beginning in September 5, 1953, the pre-credits sequence reveals the influences that will make young Tommy Gibbs into the future Godfather of Harlem, influences resulting from negative aspects of white capitalist culture. Following the Manhattan landscape, an establishing shot shows an economically depressed part of the city rarely seen in most movie representations. An anonymous white male (Andrew Duggan, in an uncredited cameo role) pauses for a shoeshine by young Tommy (Omar Jeffrey). The opening scene economically establishes the racial power relationships structuring the entire film. As Tommy shines the man's shoes, the sequence begins with a high-angle, overhead shot from the man's shoulder, revealing Tommy kneeling in a subordinate position, polishing the man's shoes. A cut follows, showing the shoe being shined. The next image is a low-angle shot of the man seen from Tommy's perspective. This opening sequence, mixing high and low angle shots, also occurs elsewhere in the film. Alternation between high- and low-angle shots recurs in two significant scenes: McKinney's beating young Tommy a few scenes later, and the adult Tommy's final revenge on McKinney many years in the future. A simple introductory sequence of establishing shots is more important than it initially seems. It reveals a cinematic gaze depicting violent power relationships within a white-dominated society seeking to trap members of underprivileged groups within its domain.

As a black-suited white hitman appears, he looks at Tommy. Cohen cuts to a close-up of Tommy. Tommy then holds on to his victim's leg, making him vulnerable to assassination. After the murder, Tommy and the man walk away. The scene reveals Tommy's fascination with violent white power relationships. Although we never see the assassin after these opening scenes, young Tommy clearly considers him a father figure. As they pause in safety, Tommy puts his hand inside the man's jacket. Responding to Tommy's admiring gaze, the man withdraws his murder weapon and shows it to his young protégé. The adult Tommy has the same type of gun in later scenes. These initial scenes stress Tommy's early fascination with the violent, white male, corporate power trajectory he later emulates.

The man takes Tommy up an iron ladder. The next shot shows Tommy descending. He holds an envelope intended for crooked cop McKinney (Art Lund). Although McKinney later accuses Tommy of stealing some money in the envelope, there is no definite evidence that he has actually done this. In fact, although Tommy and McKinney are part of the same corrupt system, Cohen implies that it actually screws both of them: young bagman and corrupt cop.

Tommy enters a dark building in a run-down area of New York. As he ascends and reaches the top of the staircase, he is framed behind the bars of the stairs as he knocks on McKinney's door, intimating his forthcoming physical imprisonment and mental entrapment within a corrupt ideological system. Most scenes in a Larry Cohen movie are never as haphazard as most critics believe. He usually shoots scenes that reinforce his main themes.

McKinney's introductory scenes reveal him as a malevolent racist. He taunts Tommy about his color: "Niggers aren't allowed in this building." However, although McKinney represents a stereotypical character, he is actually more of a victim of circumstances than the powerful authoritarian figure he thinks he is. McKinney lives in a run-down apartment little different from where Tommy resides in Harlem. Both characters are products of an alienating system relegating them to impoverished ghettos. While Tommy sees the white man's way as the only means of escape for him, McKinney takes bribes from the mob to supplement his policeman's wage. Both are victims of the same system. As an Irish cop, McKinney vents racial hatred against someone lower down the ladder than he is. No matter how repugnant his taunts to Tommy are, he is a victim of his environment, seeking a scapegoat upon whom he can vent his frustrations. Like Tommy, he takes the easy way out by accepting bribes. McKinney attempts to demonize Tommy as a monster. But the relationship between them both is much more symbiotic than either realizes. They are equal monsters wearing different skins. Both are contaminated by a system offering them no other escape than a life of violent crime.

The relationship between Tommy and McKinney becomes emphasized in the following scenes. Believing Tommy has stolen $50, and refusing to believe the young boy's explanation — "They wouldn't dare short change *me*! They did it, didn't *they?*" — he acts out frustrations against the system by beating Tommy with his nightstick and injuring his victim's leg. Cohen films this using a hallucinatory series of abrupt montage images, rapidly cutting between high-angle shots of McKinney and low-angle shots of Tommy after he falls down the stairs. This alternation between high angle and low angle had already appeared in *Black Caesar*'s opening sequence, with Tommy and his victim. This recurrence presents a nightmare counterpart for Tommy revealing the dangerous side of the violent gangster life. An adult Tommy, discovering Joe with Helen, throws him down the stairs of his Beverly Hills home. In the final sequences of *Black Caesar*, Cohen returns to this alternating shot pattern when Tommy finally beats McKinney, showing scenes of his earlier brutalization in rapid flashbacks.

The next shot shows Tommy in the hospital, with his broken leg in traction. Following the camera's slow pan along Tommy's bound leg, suggesting castration by a violent, white adult society and the beginning of his emulating the "law of the father," he orders Joe (Michael Jeffrey) to undertake a college education so that his vulnerable friend will be useful to him after he serves his prison sentence. Becoming streetwise after receiving a valuable education from two white father figures, Tommy begins pursuing the path to power in the tradition of his ethnic predecessors (Irish, Jewish, and Italian) to obtain his version of the American Dream, fully identifying with patriarchal values.

Subsequent scenes show the adult Tommy (Fred Williamson) stylishly dressed in the manner of his cinematic predecessors, Enrico Caesar Bandello, Tom Powers, and Tony Camonte, about to begin his rise to power.[12] Entering a barber shop, he listens to a white gangster mouthing racial epithets as a black shaves him. Once Tommy announces his intention of killing him, the black attendant deliberately nicks his obnoxious customer's face, taking the same sort of indirect pleasure in the act as J. Edgar Hoover's black servant does in the fly-swatting sequence in *The Private Files of J. Edgar Hoover*.

Tommy introduces himself to Mafia boss Cardoza (Val Avery) by dropping his victim's ear into a future employee's spaghetti. He unscrupulously uses his race to gain entry into the mob. Since the Mafia is as racist as McKinney, Tommy points out that nobody will associate the killing with Cardoza since his "organization doesn't employ any niggers." A black face is as anonymous as the title character of Ralph Ellison's *Invisible Man* (1952). "They never look at me, because I'm black." Although Tommy impresses Cardoza with his knowledge of Italian and counters the racist question, "I never heard any dinks speak Italian before," with "How many of us do you know?," Tommy really plays the white man's game. He requests a piece of "territory" he can call his own, the Harlem area between 127th Street and Edgecombe Avenue.

Now secure as a gangster boss, Tommy builds up his criminal empire, using Reverend Rufus (D'Urville Martin) and his tax-exempt religious organization as a front to funnel illegal criminal profits into legitimate businesses. He also gains access to mob payroll ledgers listing the names of prominent figures in society. As Tommy recognizes, the ledgers represent "power, political power." While Joe (Phillip Roye) wishes the money to go toward "a fair share for black people in Harlem," his wishes are really futile, since Tommy desires to emulate an oppressive affluent society represented by crooked lawyer Alfred Coleman (William Wellman Jr.) and police captain McKinney.

Throughout his rise to power, Tommy uses and abuses those closest to him. He uses Helen (Gloria Hendry) as an accessory to his murder of mob accountants, gaining control of an incriminating ledger. Tommy keeps Joe bound to him as a criminal accountant by manipulating his naive loyalty. He also destroys his own mother in the process. *Black Caesar* initially attributes Tommy's rise to the fall of others. It depicts him as a self-created monster, emulating the corrupt values of the white social structure while condemning members of his own race to social deprivation. Tommy buys into the system. As a solitary selfish individualist, he does not see himself as a "token" figure whom society will tolerate because he represents no real threat to its institutional survival. The system humors him until the time it has no use for him. When Tommy takes over for Cardoza, he demeans his own race, humorously referring to himself as a "jungle bunny" to Coleman and McKinney. He presents himself as one who knows the Harlem territory of other jungle bunnies, providing "cheap" black Philadelphia bodyguards to Cardoza. Tommy's remark to Cardoza, "Who said Lincoln freed the slaves?" depicts him as no real liberator, but another exploiter of his people. Tommy's relationship with his race is as superficial as the Italian he speaks. Cardoza insightfully remarks, "Each time you speak Sicilian, it's like a dubbed-in movie." After ousting his former boss, Tommy jokes about keeping him on as a "token white." He merely inverts a corrupt system of racial values and never intends changing the system for the better. As Joe recognizes later, Tommy is really a "white nigger." He accuses Tommy of going after "whitey's house and whitey's women," and buying members of his own race, as white America did during the previous century. Tommy accuses Joe of making him "lose respect before my people." But his former friend caustically replies, "I'm not one of your people. Not in cash... You're not one of us." His most devastating words to Tommy are "I never wanted to own anybody."

Throughout the film, Tommy appears little different from his white oppressors. He uses Helen like a body slave on a pre–Civil War plantation and rapes her when she does not respond to his advances. She eventually leaves Tommy and marries the more sensitive Joe. When the mob later turns against Tommy, McKinney threatens to harm her family if she does not help them. Helen again prostitutes herself with the still-arrogant Black Caesar, but this time to bring about his downfall. Even Tommy's fall brings disaster to others. The still-loyal Joe dies after foolishly listening to Tommy's pleas for help. Despite the "blaxploitation" promotion that made *Black Caesar* a box-office success, the film has little relationship to that ephemeral genre. It breaks all of the rules associated with the formula. Fred Williamson's Tommy Gibbs is no super-cool, super-stud hero in the vein of contemporary stars such as Richard Roundtree, Jim Brown, and Jim Kelly. His ethnic identity fails to protect him from contamination by the system. Not only does Tommy corrupt himself, but he succeeds in contaminating all those closest to him before undergoing eventual betrayal and death.

Tommy believes that emulating the white man's capitalist path to success will bring happiness to himself and others. But his family relationships are far from ideal. When Tommy buys Coleman's elaborate apartment and property, he wishes to install his mother into a new racial and class system, providing her with "a couple of white girls to do the housework and a snooty chauffeur to drive you around." However, Mrs. Gibbs (Minnie Gentry) is far more aware of the society in which she lives than her son is. She tries to make Tommy understand that a lifetime of class oppression cannot change her overnight. "I wouldn't know how to talk to them... I'm only a maid. You could never see that." She also recognizes that social, racial, and class factors will never allow Tommy to break the rules: "They'd hang me off the building. Jewish folk aren't even allowed in here."

Tommy's desires to make Mrs. Gibbs share his own values only result in her premature death. Before she dies, she turns to the dubious religious comfort of Reverend Rufus. Mrs. Gibbs asks him to pray for her son. Although Rufus is still exploiting the people of Harlem, her request makes an impression on the crooked clergyman, who later prays for her after her death. Alone with Rufus at Mrs. Gibbs' sparsely attended funeral, Tommy still cannot understand his mother's refusal to share his way of life: "I gave her the best. I never really made her

**Tommy Gibbs (Fred Williamson) rises to the top of the criminal underworld in *Black Caesar* (1973) (courtesy of Larry Cohen).**

happy." Tommy never realizes he has merely paid lip service to false values within the dominant social structure. He believes riches can heal any individual or family problem.

Although *Black Caesar* contains little information about Tommy's early family life, the Godfather of Harlem believes as much in the false ideology of family values as he does in an equally illusionary American Dream of economic success. Meeting his father (Julius W. Harris) many years after he abandoned his wife and child, Tommy is devastated upon learning of his illegitimacy. Initially intending to kill his father for desertion, Tommy learns some relevant historical and social facts that contradict his naive illusions. Mr. Gibbs tells Tommy of his hard life in the Depression and World War II. He enlisted in the service at the age of 20, after finding family life more suffocating than fulfilling: "You've never been trapped." Confronted with information he never knew about, Tommy lets his father go. The sequence ends with Rufus asking Tommy, "What are you going to do now? Kill your mother?" *Black Caesar* implies that Tommy indirectly does this in his pursuit of a false American Dream.

Characteristically, Mr. Gibbs now works as a traveling salesman with no connections to home and family. When Tommy later attempts to reach out to him after his mother's funeral, Mr. Gibbs refuses to take up Tommy's offer to stay with him: "No. I travel a lot." He has obviously no desire to share in Tommy's dreams of a reconstituted family. Mr. Gibbs belongs to those wandering American heroes in both literature and cinema, such as Natty Bumppo, Ishmael, Shane, and Ethan Edwards, all of whom flee from the confining domestic constraints of home and family, a tradition analyzed by Leslie A. Fiedler in *Love and Death in the American Novel.*

After Tommy experiences several betrayals and finds his power slowly receding, the mob moves in to dispose him. Escaping from a failed assassination attempt outside Tiffany's, the wounded Tommy goes to Coleman's office to search for the ledgers now representing the last card he has in his possession.[13] He discovers McKinney there. The police captain has murdered Coleman and intends to set up Tommy for the crime. Before proceeding to kill him, McKinney engages in one last act of racial humiliation by making Tommy replay his former role of shoeshine boy, to educate him to the fact that he is after all just "a nigger." Characteristically, Cohen reveals an American flag prominently displayed before Tommy's old shoeshine box. McKinney's intended revenge is not just an act of individual malice. It is clearly institutionally supported.

Tommy manages to overpower McKinney. But Cohen edits the subsequent shots to reveal an understanding of Tommy's supposed "victory" much more sophisticated than the one characterizing the final revenge sequence of most "blaxploitation" movies. From their very first encounter, Tommy and McKinney appear as symbiotic figures throughout the film. As an Irish-American, McKinney suffers from the same form of racism affecting Tommy. While Tommy emulates the American Dream by becoming a gangster like his ethnic predecessors Arnold Rothstein, Meyer Lansky, Al Capone, and Lucky Luciano, McKinney chooses an alternative path on the side of law and order. However, many traditional gangster films show revealing parallels between the forces of law and disorder, visually and thematically. The police often mirror the gangsters they pursue. Tommy and McKinney choose different, but equal, paths to economic success in the American Dream. One is a gangster. The other a crooked cop. Yet concluding scenes in this sequence contain important implications other than basic ones like a black hero obtaining revenge on a white villain. They are far more significant than cheering black audiences may have realized at the time of the film's original release.

Tommy blackens McKinney's face with the shoe polish he uses on his enemy's shoes. He makes his antagonist black. But he humiliates his enemy by placing him in the same demeaning position as McKinney once did to him many years before. Tommy makes McKinney sing an Al Jolson song, "Mammy," teaching him the words as he bludgeons his face. Cohen mixes past and present in a rapid montage. Rapidly cut shots of McKinney beating young Tommy many years before match shots of the adult Tommy taking his violent revenge against McKinney in the present. Both McKinney and the adult Tommy are shot from a low-angle perspective. Not only is Tommy equated with McKinney, but the audience is also placed in the victim's perspective by experiencing the assault waged by two violent monsters, white and black. Another alternating shot sequence juxtaposes high-angle shots of a battered McKinney with high-angle shots of young Tommy beaten by McKinney's night stick. No simple act of justified revenge occurs here. The film champions neither McKinney's past assault nor Tommy's present revenge. Both are vicious acts sanctified by an American society founded upon an oppressive system of power relationships. Although Tommy thinks he avenges himself on his enemy, the sequence shows that his act differs little from the ugly violence inflicted upon him at the beginning of his career. Nothing has really changed.[14] As *Bone* earlier revealed, it is just another different form of "business as usual."

Fleeing to Harlem with the ledgers, Tommy staggers into a devastated area of rubble. He dies at the hands of black teenage gang members who do not recognize him as the Godfather of Harlem. Ironically, Tommy becomes as victimized as the unknown man whose death he participated in during the pre-credits sequence. The youths move away. The ledgers once symbolizing Tommy's power become buried under the rubble. Another irony emerges from Tommy's death. The youngsters represent those in the black community whom Joe hoped to help in his dream of using criminal profits to create a "fair share for black people in Harlem." The system still remains victorious. The final image on the screen is the Manhattan skyline that opened the film. It concludes the film with the date of Tommy's death, August 20, 1972.

*Black Caesar*'s box-office success resulted in American International's desire for a sequel. Since Cohen re-edited scenes of Tommy's death, making his demise ambiguous (necessitated by negative audience reaction to the original cut), Tommy's return to life became a viable commercial possibility. However, due to his commitment to film *It's Alive* for Warner Bros. in Hollywood, and the weekday unavailability of Fred Williamson, Cohen shot *Black Caesar*'s sequel during the weekends. *Hell Up in Harlem* is one of the two films Larry Cohen expresses deep dissatisfaction with. The film bears obvious signs of a rushed production schedule, and contains far too many ideas crammed into the screenplay. But although *Hell Up in Harlem* may be an incoherent film shot over weekends on a frenzied shooting schedule, it is often fun to watch and more viewable than many large-budget action films emerging from contemporary Hollywood.

After introducing a new character, crooked District Attorney Di Angelo (Gerald Gordon), and showing Helen undergoing a change of heart by warning about Tommy's impending assassination, the film uses previously shot climactic footage from *Black Caesar* behind the credits, editing out all nonessential items (such as McKinney's final appearance and Joe's death) to concentrate on Tommy's survival. However, not all the new material is superfluous.

Cohen's opening shot of *Hell Up in Harlem* shows a high-angle view of the New York Supreme Court. It resembles the opening shot of "The Defenders" series. The ironic undertones are certainly not accidental. Whereas "The Defenders" opened with the Supreme Court, leading to shots of Lawrence and Kenneth Preston, the father and son team who represented an idealistic view of American justice, *Hell Up in Harlem* uses a similar shot to introduce the corrupt figure of Di Angelo. The system is deeply implicated in the subsequent events.

Discovering the ledgers in Coleman's office, Tommy phones Di Angelo, telling him of surviving the attempted assassination outside Tiffany's. He then contacts Mr. Gibbs by appealing to his neglected sense of family duty: "You turned your back on me when I was a kid. Don't do it to me again." As in *Black Caesar*, Tommy involves a parental figure in his criminal affairs, creating dark consequences. Although Tommy is more of a heroic figure in this film, enough evidence remains of his destructive capacities depicted in the earlier work, making parts of *Hell Up in Harlem* interesting. After a deal with Di Angelo, Tommy manages to escape from Harlem Hospital and await exoneration by a judicial system clearly out to get him. Acquiring the ledgers means re-acquisition of the "political power" he had in *Black Caesar*. Following his grand jury acquittal, Tommy speaks to the news media in front of the New York Stock Exchange. Seen prominently with Di Angelo and his associates, he jocularly remarks, "Anything can be fixed in the good old U.S.A."

Prior to this, when Tommy meets his father in the hospital, he greets him with the remark, "Welcome to the club, Pop." Tommy soon involves Mr. Gibbs in his world of violence. Earlier, Mr. Gibbs faced death at the hands of Di Angelo's men. He also killed for the first time in his life. Mr. Gibbs recognizes the consequences of his action: "I shot them. I had to... They went down easy." Tommy then offers his father a partnership: "We're both wanted men now. Father and son." Although Mr. Gibbs proves more malleable than his deceased wife did in dealing with Tommy, he suffers more harm from associating with a monstrous son. Both *Black Caesar* and *Hell Up in Harlem* anticipate key themes in the *It's Alive* films, particularly that of the monster produced by the family who is equally destructive to its parents. The family reunion scene concludes with Cohen's ironically written line for Tommy: "If Momma could just see us now together, she'd be happy."

Tommy's viciousness manifests itself in his attitude toward Helen. Oblivious of the fact of her last minute effort to avert his assassination, Tommy takes away her children, abandoning her to a life of drugs and prostitution. Although Tommy's ambitious henchman, Zack (Tony King), is later responsible for her murder, Tommy is also indirectly culpable. Unjustly blaming his father for Helen's death, Tommy relocates to California, leaving his aging and vulnerable parent in charge of New York operations. Eventually, his father dies at the hands of Zack. *Hell Up in Harlem*'s inherent sketchiness leaves many promising themes and characters undeveloped. Zack's ambitious nature complements Tommy's in *Black Caesar*. By collaborating with Di Angelo, he echoes Tommy's own involvement with the white power structure in *Black Caesar*. In *Hell Up in Harlem*, Tommy remains aloof from the system and only deals with its representatives when he has to. Highly ruthless and sarcastic towards Mr. Gibbs in an earlier scene (an act Tommy forces him to apologize for), Zack represents Tommy's dark monstrous alter ego, perpetuating acts Tommy personally wishes to accomplish. Zack's insolent attitude toward Mr. Gibbs anticipates Tommy's later petulant condemnation of his father for Helen's murder. In an earlier scene, Zack rescues Mr. Gibbs from Di Angelo's men, paralleling Tommy's "rescue" of his father by offering him a partnership in his business. Finally, Zack is responsible for the deaths of two people once close to Tommy: Helen and Mr. Gibbs. In *Hell Up in Harlem*, Tommy is less of a monster than he is in the preceding film. However, this change in character results from Zack becoming Tommy's alter ego in *Hell Up in Harlem*. But, as in *Frankenstein* (1931), boundaries between creator and monster are never clear-cut. Tommy still retains some negative traces of his old *Black Caesar* self.

These elements appear in the final scenes of *Hell Up in Harlem*. Abandoned by his new love, Sister Jennifer (Margaret Avery), who runs away with a "daughter"[15] Tommy cares little about, the repentant Black Caesar turns over his ledgers to the authorities and sets off to retrieve his eight-year-old son that Di Angelo has kidnapped. Paralleling his inverse racist revenge in *Black Caesar*, Tommy hangs his enemy like a black in the deep South. "I'm going to send you to W.A.S.P heaven. I'm going to make you famous — the only whitey to be hung by a nigger." However, Tommy's act of revenge is merely another version of the negative nature of role reversals featured in Cohen's films. Only the roles have changed. Power still remains waiting to corrupt its next victim. Reunited with his son, Tommy tells him, "I'm going to love you like I loved my Pa." In view of the fate of Mr. Gibbs, such a comment is highly ironic. The film concludes in a freeze frame containing a caption about the Gibbs' disappearance from society.

Although far beneath Cohen's other achievements, *Hell Up in Harlem* still contains several moments of appealing cinematic spontaneity. As in *Black Caesar* and *Q — The Winged Serpent*, New York locations serve as commentaries on the action. During a gang war, one victim is shot near a small statue of Lincoln and a young black child. An informer who reveals that Zack murdered Helen is killed near Grant's Tomb. An American flag flies prominently on the balcony of Di Angelo's office near the Supreme Court as he discusses Tommy's removal midway through the film. These historical locations illustrate the corruption of a former era of American idealism by twentieth-century corporate and criminal activities. Tommy pursues Mafia boss Palermo to Coney Island, impaling his victim as he lies upon a Confederate flag blanket. The most striking set-piece of all is Tommy's pursuit of Zack across the continental U.S.A. Failing to catch up with Zack's T.W.A. plane at a New York Airport, Tommy runs through cars to the American Airlines building, purchasing a ticket for a plane that will arrive in Los Angeles at the same time as Zack's does. Arriving in Los Angeles, Tommy runs across to the T.W.A. baggage area, fighting with Zack on the carrel before killing him. The sequence is one of the most ambitious and breathtaking in the entire film.

Reverend Rufus' characterization is as undeveloped as Zack's. After abandoning Tommy for religion at the end of *Black Caesar*, Rufus becomes a televangelist, using his pulpit to condemn Tommy. Tommy criticizes Rufus' hypocrisy: "You weren't so high and mighty when you were pimping for me up Lennox Avenue," denying the charge that he is involved with drugs. Tommy wins over Sister Jennifer by having more social awareness than his former persona did in *Black Caesar*: "We have the names of all the syndicate men who have exploited the black community since we were children." He accuses Rufus of "taking money from whitey, preaching about blacks exploiting blacks." But these interesting features do not add up to any coherent whole. They appear abruptly out of context. Similarly, Rufus' turn from pacifism to aid Tommy in the climax is never developed properly.

*Hell Up in Harlem* is a rushed film with interesting sequences failing to make a coherent whole. However, Cohen's next film represents one of his major achievements in American cinema.

Like *Black Caesar*, *It's Alive*'s association with a particular genre often leads to a neglect of its distinctive features that are not generic, but more indicative of concerns present in Cohen's television and theatrical ventures. Larry Cohen films are never typical generic products. They are idiosyncratic reworkings of themes the director has explored throughout his artistic career. Despite studio tendencies to classify his films as recognizable cinematic types to sell them to audiences, Cohen's movies are far more unclassified and iconoclastic. Cohen rejects any understanding of *Black Caesar* as a "blaxploitation" movie, since it breaks all the "genre rules," and he does not regard *It's Alive* as "more of a horror story than *The Elephant Man*." Although fascinated by the actual story of *It's Alive*, Cohen also notes its inter-textual relationship with two particular Hollywood genres: the horror film and the melodrama: "But it did cross my mind that if I could make a horror movie that made audiences actually shed a tear it would be an accomplishment."[16]

The melodrama is most commonly associated with the family, a theme fascinating Cohen from his earliest days as a television writer. Once disparaged as a "women's weepie," contemporary opinion now regards melodrama's emotional effect as one of its most important characteristics.[17] *It's Alive* is one of the great films of seventies horror. But its roots also lie within Cohen's earlier work. In this particular instance, it is far more important to trace these patterns rather than emphasize connections with family horror.[18]

*It's Alive* begins with individual flashlight beams bouncing back and forth behind the opening credits. Unseen figures search for a yet unidentified quarry. The flashing beams finally coalesce, ending in a blinding flash of light assaulting the viewer's eyes. The film immediately places the audience into the victim's perspective. Subsequent scenes depict the Davies house as the camera, through a series of dissolves, gradually moves into their bedroom. Lenore suddenly begins her labor pains. Although lacking Hitchcock's voyeuristic treatment in *Psycho*, these introductory scenes place the audience in the position of observer-participants emotionally experiencing an abnormal plight in a supposedly typical environment. As *It's Alive* continues, the audience moves further into an empathetic association with the plight of Frank Davies, until that key moment of emotional identification and tears during the penultimate scene as father and son temporarily reconcile in the storm drains of Los Angeles before the police pursue

**John Ryan as father-of-the-monster Frank Davies in** *It's Alive* **(Warner Bros. 1973) (courtesy of Larry Cohen).**

them. *It's Alive* is a major example of Cohen's radical allegorical strategy, presenting the audience with an unusual situation that encourages them to identify with a fictional character's dilemma. At the climax of the film, Cohen evokes memories of an earlier scene as the police confront Frank with revolvers and torches. Unsympathetic police had flashed beams into Frank's face in the schoolroom corridor as he walked toward his normal son's kindergarten room. Once believing himself a normal member of society, Frank suddenly finds himself in the position of an alienated outsider victimized by a civilization he once took for granted. Frank is thus an audience surrogate. The opening credit scenes emphasize the fact that we are as much victims as Frank Davies is. We are not really victims of a supposedly threatening mutant baby, but of a society insisting on a rigid institutional order condemning all those who threaten its boundaries. Security is never certain. Secure citizens may become persecuted victims the next day. Society operates along the lines of blaming the victim no matter how blameless they may actually be.

The situation in *It's Alive* resembles one appearing in many Hitchcock films. An ordinary person, whether Richard Hannay in *The 39 Steps* or Roger Thornhill in *North by Northwest*, suddenly becomes caught in a situation beyond his control. This very situation questions his very relationship to a social order he once felt comfortable within. In *Notorious*, the state uses and abuses Alicia Huberman. Trapped into subordinate roles by the very democracy they hope to serve,

Alicia and Devlin become victims of a personal and political sadomasochistic power relationship threatening to destroy them until Devlin decides to disobey the deathly realm of the "law of the father," anticipating his successor, Roger Thornhill, in *North by Northwest.*[19] If the uranium is a "MacGuffin" for Hitchcock,[20] the mutant baby represents a similar device for Cohen. Both are superficial textual strategies providing viewers with cinematically escapist ingredients of suspense and fear, allowing the radically crucial ideas to pass through unchallenged. Neither uranium nor mutant baby represents the real issues in *Notorious* and *It's Alive.*

In *It's Alive,* no Frankenstein scientist creates a monster in a faraway laboratory somewhere in Europe. Instead, a normal American finds that he has fathered a monster. On one level, it embodies repressed tensions within his own personal and social life as a public relations Hollywood "organization man." But on another level, a corrupt institutional order bears responsibility for the mutant baby, as the various references to manmade pollution and drug-industry abuse suggest. Frank's offspring may represent a new form of human evolution attempting to survive the abuses perpetuated by a profit-driven capitalist society. But the very nature of its violent acts reveals that even a new form of life may be as contaminated by a corrupt social order as its predecessors. The baby's violence against a hospital staff attempting to kill it is justifiable. But the brutal murders of a single woman and a milkman are not. As *Black Caesar* reveals, the legacy of institutional violence corrupts everyone. Whether a potentially rebellious African-American, mutant baby, or superhuman alien, difference is not enough in itself. A new social order erasing the dark legacy of past and present is necessary, one that Cohen leaves to his audience's imagination.

Throughout the film, Frank undergoes various personal dilemmas, oscillating between rejecting his murderous offspring to finally accepting it. In the final scenes, he carries his baby in his arms like a protective mother while the authorities pursue them. Asking forgiveness from his wounded son as tears stream down his cheeks, Frank moves from being a monstrous patriarchal aggressor to a nurturing maternal figure before that final moment of separation. He reconciles the opposites within his own personality. Moving from one gendered extreme to another, discovering repressed qualities of sympathy and compassion, he moves toward being the benevolent calm protector of *It Lives Again.* He becomes a figure at peace with himself, reconciling opposites in his personality, allowing his true self to emerge after casting aside the socially acceptable masks of bland public relations executive and murderous patriarchal killer. He finally refuses to kill his son and engage in society's manipulative version of a regeneration through violence scenario.[21]

In the opening scenes of *It's Alive,* Frank leaves his young son, Chris, with Charley (William Wellman, Jr.), a divorced neighbor who "loves kids," while he takes Lenore to the hospital. But once inside the hospital, they find not the comforting environment they expect, but one hostile to their real needs. Cohen's critical attitudes toward hospitals also appear in films as diverse as *The Ambulance*

(1990), *Maniac Cop 3: Badge of Silence* (1992), and *As Good as Dead* (1995). Prior
to the delivery, Lenore tells Frank about doctors who do not listen to her: "I can't
make them understand. It's different." Their attitude appears due, not to medical speculation over the forthcoming delivery, but to institutional arrogance
denying the female any voice in the birth process. The audience also discovers
previous problems in the Davies relationship:

> LENORE: "I'm glad we decided to have the baby."
>
> FRANK: "We both *want* it."
>
> LENORE: "It's not going to tie you down... You're not going to feel trapped like
> last time."

Despite his bourgeois existence, Frank is really like another potential wandering hero from Leslie A. Fiedler's *Love and Death in the American Novel* attempting escape from domestic constraints. His Walter Brennan imitation to Chris
while taking him to Charley is by no means accidental. It places him in a particular traditional relationship to Western figures such as Brennan's characters
(usually solitary old-timers), Shane, and Ethan Edwards of *The Searchers*, all of
whom experience tensions with family life. Similarly, the LOVE-patterned wallpaper in Chris's bedroom may be there to assure father rather than son about the
appropriate feelings he ought to possess. Frank reluctantly decided to have a second child after feeling "tied down" with the first. Also, Frank and Lenore initially
considered an abortion before deciding to have the second child. Tensions clearly
existed in their marital and family life, resulting in the birth of a monster child.
Although not as emotionally disturbed as Martin Burnham, Frank's attitudes to
marriage and family life are by no means positive. However, *It's Alive* also reveals
that the problems are as much social as individual.

The conversation between expectant fathers in the waiting room suggestively depicts a society on the verge of complete breakdown. One anxious father
nervously hammers at malfunctioning machines. Another speaks about an exter-
minator formula producing a new breed of roach "hard to kill." References to
lead pencils and the polluted environment also feature in the dialogue. This dialogue is less important for possible clues to the mutant's genesis than its emphasis upon an uncaring, malfunctioning, and vicious social order that will eventually turn on Frank. After Frank leaves the waiting room, Cohen creates a sense
of unease in the corridor by shooting the area with a fish-eye lens. The accompanying visual distortion suggests ominous consequences.

In the delivery room, Lenore encounters a similar version of a dysfunctional
social order. A doctor reassures her, "I *think* we've got a really effective anesthetic."
Ignoring the woman's concerns, they decide to use forceps on the baby's "gigantic head." Another doctor tells her, "We just cut you. You didn't feel that, did
you?" These lines suggest reasons for the mutant baby's aggressive reactions. Experiencing violence in its initial seconds of birth, it fights back against the system,
using the same violence it encounters. Later, Lenore tells Frank that she believed

the doctors were "frightened" because the baby was "different": "I think he was afraid they were going to hurt him." Dr. Norton's (Shamus Locke) attitude to the Davieses is skeptical. He asks Frank to submit to tests, implicitly blaming him for the birth.

Angered by this attitude ("Can you imagine those guys trying to blame us?"), Frank finds himself the subject of media attention, and loses his job. His publicity conscious boss (Guy Stockwell) has connections to the hospital where Frank's child is delivered, and fires a conscientious worker whose very presence is now incompatible with public relations. Isolated and treated like a leper, contemptuous of an exploitative news media resembling that depicted in "Go-Between," Frank's character undergoes a change similar to Matthew Ryder's in Cohen's earlier "Defenders" teleplay. He regards his son as a "monstrosity" and is eager to sign a deal donating the body to a university for $100,000. While the professor (Andrew Duggan) calmly speaks about what methods may facilitate the child's destruction (including the use of "some kind of gas"— a line having obvious parallels to a previous regime's extermination of those they categorized as different), Frank denies any sense of fatherhood and describes his offspring as "not my child." However, a drug company executive (Robert Emhardt) wishes the remains totally destroyed. Believing that his company may be responsible for the Davies birth by rushing a product through the Food and Drug Administration, he bribes Norton to see that nothing exists to connect his company with the mutant baby. Frank finds himself oppressed by various branches of the state apparatus— police, medical authorities, and corporate businesses with political connections— eager to destroy him as well as his mutant offspring.

Despite Frank's antagonistic feelings, both Lenore and Chris are willing to accept the baby. She pleads with Frank, recognizing the deep insecurities generating his violent behavior: "You've got to be the one to do it, don't you?" The sympathetic Lt. Perkins also recognizes this. Used as a decoy by the police and Norton to attract the wounded baby out into the open, Frank finally faces his offspring, lays down his weapon, and pleads for forgiveness. He recognizes that his son's aggression derives from the same sources stimulating his own violent reactions: "I was scared, like you."

The moment of reconciliation is only temporary. Father and son run away from the police, fugitives from a vicious system seeking to destroy them both. Dr. Norton earlier regarded Frank as an ideal bait for an angry son, and exhibited little concern for his survival. Emerging from the storm drains, Frank faces a vicious L.A.P.D. eager to open fire. Attempting to protect his son and regain Lenore's respect in the process, Frank assigns the baby to the unscrupulous Dr. Norton. Whether Frank does this out of fear or revenge is uncertain. But the latter interpretation is probably valid under the circumstances. Frank recognizes the real enemy. He cannot save his son, but he can facilitate one last moment of revenge upon the representative of a system responsible for his personal and social dilemma. Both Norton and the baby die in a hail of bullets. It is a fitting death for a member of the medical profession who knowingly prescribed faulty drugs for Lenore's pregnancy.

As Lt. Perkins is about to drive the now-reunited Frank and Lenore home, he receives a message on his car radio. Informing them that "another one's been born in Seattle," he drives away, the police car receding into the darkness.

*It's Alive* is a significant Larry Cohen achievement. It unites the social concerns of his earlier teleplays for "The Defenders" and "The Nurses" with mainstream generic formulas such as those associated with Hollywood series such as "Branded" and "The Invaders." But instead of courtroom drama, Western, and science fiction, Cohen now appropriates features characteristic of horror and melodrama for his own particular concerns. However, he never remains dominated by the forms he chooses to work in, but instead inverts them, reworking their familiar characteristics and turning them into radical allegories. They become works less of harmless entertainment and more of protests against various forms of social oppression, pleading for a more tolerant recognition of difference. Toward the end of *It's Alive*, Frank shows himself capable of change, one already exhibited by his wife and son. However, the social order already contaminates his mutant son, revealing at the moment of birth a world where violence and oppression is the norm. Seeing no other alternatives, the baby strikes out in fear against all those it regards as threatening its existence. Its violent activities echo the very attitudes of a father who rejects it and the medical staff witnessing its birth. In such a world, tragedy is the only result. Paradoxically Frank and Lenore reunite. *It Lives Again* will suggest further alternatives involving different forms of personal existence far removed from a threatening and soulless civilization. The struggle continues in difficult circumstances where the final victory remains open.

# Directorial Achievements in the 1970s

*God Told Me To* (1976), *The Private Files of J. Edgar Hoover* (1977), and *It Lives Again* (1979) represent the pinnacle of Larry Cohen's achievements in the seventies. Although usually classified generically, they are more than mere science-fiction, crime movie-historical biopic, or horror films. Like all Cohen's work, they function as radical allegories transcending their supposed generic frameworks, operating as hybrid, self-reflective, inter-textual constructions. *God Told Me To* mixes themes from the diverse subjects of science-fiction, horror, and religion. *The Private Files of J. Edgar Hoover* treats its historical subject in a comic-strip style akin to thirties and forties B-movies, intuitively recognizing the ways in which its titular subject manipulated contemporary forms of popular culture for propaganda purposes. Rather than examining J. Edgar Hoover in the plodding reverential manner of Mervyn LeRoy's *The F.B.I. Story* (1959), Cohen's treatment eschews any attempt at making a redundant Hollywood biopic. He instead utilizes comic-strip techniques to investigate subversively the dark underside of an agency under the control of one of the most powerful men in America. *It Lives Again* is less a horror sequel to *It's Alive*, but more an extension of implications contained within *God Told Me To* and *The Private Files of J. Edgar Hoover*. All three films form a united trilogy, treating in different ways themes involving individual repression by the social forces of law and religion, and the urgent need for an alternative society guaranteeing human freedom.

Like Alfred Hitchcock, Cohen is both a product of the social system he belongs to and an astute observer of its failings. Avoiding the dangerous path of explicitly suggesting unrealizable alternatives, Cohen presents his audiences with images of an oppressive society. Individuals are both victims and victimizers in a system needing radical change. Cohen's films often end ambiguously but not hopelessly. There is always the potential for change. As an independent director influenced by the Hollywood tradition, Cohen realizes that the medium he

127

chooses to work within is inappropriate for any explicit messages. Instead, Cohen directs his films according to a deliberately chosen policy of interpretative ambiguity, presenting cinematic statements within popular forms and leaving viewers to make their own interpretations. His seventies trilogy presents different facets of historical and social dilemmas affecting not just fictional characters but also audiences who may be as trapped and confused as their fictional counterparts. Cohen's cinematic statements represent a deliberately chosen strategy common to a particular tradition within American literature presenting tensions and contradictions, challenging its readers to recognize the dangers and hopefully work against them.

*God Told Me To* explores the personal and social dilemma of repressed Catholic cop Peter J. Nicholas (Tony Lo Bianco) in a spiritual odyssey affecting not only himself but his relationship to a system he uneasily adheres to. Like Mark Deglan in "Night Cry," Peter Nicholas lives a dissatisfied existence in the New York urban jungle and confronts an alter ego challenging the very foundations of his personal and social existence. Peter's discomfort with a moral code he uneasily adheres to echoes Leo's dilemma in "Unwritten Law." Subconsciously tormented by social codes of masculinity, both men resort to violence in an attempt to repress uncontrollable desires. Most of Cohen's work explores a double theme the director inherits not just from Edgar Allan Poe but from Alfred Hitchcock. It is a tradition he develops in his own particular way.

In *God Told Me To* Cohen again pushes Hitchcock motifs to their very limits. He takes particular situations, merging them with unfamiliar themes in different constructions to explore them in new ways.[1] Mrs. Phillips' charge down the staircase, wielding her knife against Peter, is an obvious nod to *Psycho*. But the moment is a brief episode in the film. The scene reinforces a possession motif structuring the entire film. It is not a gratuitously spectacular moment thrown in to liven up the film and appeal to film buffs. In *Psycho*, we finally learn that Norman's patriarchally constructed mother image dominates him and motivates his sexually violent acts. But Mrs. Phillips is possessed by her alien son, who causes her to attack Peter. Cohen thus reverses Hitchcock's use of the possession motif in *Psycho* by having the son possess the mother as an invisible force. In *God Told Me To*, this short scene functions as a minor unit. However, Cohen extends the possession scenario beyond the limited terrain of the family into the wider ideological domains of state and religion. Although this broader picture also occurs in *Psycho*, it operates implicitly within the text. Hitchcock's film is geared toward revealing the enigma of Norman as its major plot motif. But in *God Told Me To*, Peter's discovery of his origins represents a significant hermeneutical goal. It is indissolubly related to a wider quest involving his ideological adherence to oppressive forces of law, state, family, and religion that are less benevolently natural and more aggressively alien to his well-being. In *God Told Me To*, Cohen performs his own version of Brechtian alienation, making the familiar appear strange, directing his audiences to discern everyday facts in a new, disorientating light.

Viewers familiar with Hitchcock's *Shadow of a Doubt* (1943) immediately recognize the significance of Peter's comment following his knife wound by Mrs. Phillips: "I didn't even get hurt when I was a kid and fell off my bike." In the earlier film, Emmy (Patricia Collinge) mentions that her younger brother was a normal child until he had a bicycle accident — a deceptive metaphor suggesting possible incestuous associations.[2] But what is significant here is not the fact of the statement's direct parallel to circumstances in the earlier film, but its suggestive analogies to dualistically incestuous parallels made between Uncle Charlie (Joseph Cotten) and Young Charlie (Teresa Wright). In *Shadow of a Doubt*, Hitchcock draws incestuous analogies between uncle and niece, both visually (the parallel shots introducing the characters) and verbally ("Not yet, Charlie, let it get a little faster."). In *God Told Me To*, the lines anticipate the incestuous relationship Peter faces by coupling with his sexually androgynous alien brother. Both Uncle Charlie and Bernard Phillips are monsters from the id conjured up by the normal protagonists.

Finally, although Larry Cohen usually avoids Hitchcock's characteristic cameo appearances in his films, he often performs his predecessor's role as "enunciator"[3] within the text, identifying himself with one or even both the main characters. Peter Nicholas' birthdate is the same as Larry Cohen's, while Bernard Phillips resides at Washington Heights, the director's old family address.

Describing *God Told Me To* as a dark version of the Superman story, Cohen understands his alien, supernatural messiah as embodying features associated with two of Alfred Hitchcock's rebellious females: Rebecca and Mrs. Paradine. Although one dies before *Rebecca* begins, and the other is arrested during the opening scenes of *The Paradine Case,* both women function as embodiments of oppositional forces fighting against patriarchal law. But Rebecca and Mrs. Paradine are contaminated by a system they struggle against. Like the mutant babies of the *It's Alive* films, they exhibit dangerous aggressive qualities. As critics note, both Rebecca and Madalena are the real heroines of *Rebecca* and *The Paradine Case*. In *Rebecca*, the invisible presence of a past independent mistress hovers over the narrative, opposing efforts by normal characters to deny her powerful presence beyond the grave. In *The Paradine Case*, Alida Valli's Mrs. Paradine gradually loses acceptable feminine signifiers of attractiveness — hairstyle and fashionable clothes — during her incarceration and trial. She takes on almost supernatural overtones, resembling a matriarchal deity and openly exhibits contempt against the male order. The high-key lighting compares her cold mask-like expression to a sphinx. *Rebecca* and *The Paradine Case* both contain bedroom scenes in which representatives of patriarchal normality encounter the unseen presence of a powerful female dwarfing them into insignificance. Both the nameless heroine of *Rebecca* and Anthony Keane in *The Paradine Case* enter a private sexual realm resembling a holy temple, the domain of a woman asserting independence from the patriarchal order. In *Rebecca*, Mrs. Danvers guards the bedroom like a vestal virgin worshiping her deceased mistress. A huge photograph of Mrs. Paradine dominates the bed as if the actual woman invisibly takes pleasure in her powerful image from many miles away. If Rebecca and Mrs. Paradine are strong but contaminated personalities, the same is true of Cohen's Bernard Phillips. He is a figure who has potential claims to be the real hero of the movie. But like the mutant baby of *It's Alive*, he is corrupted and contaminated by negative institutional forces in the world he inhabits. Rebecca, Mrs. Paradine, and Bernard Phillips are three monster figures designated as evil within a male-dominated society.[4]

*God Told Me To* has received significant readings by Robin Wood and Elayne Chaplin. While Wood sees the figure of Bernard Phillips as embodying "stronger positive connotations than any other manifestation of the return of the repressed in Cohen's work, or indeed in any other contemporary horror film,"[5] Chaplin emphasizes contradictions affecting such a positive reading, particularly those revealing Bernard and his followers as inextricably implicated in the type of violence associated with the patriarchal order.[6] Both critics see *God Told Me To* as a contradictory and confusing film, never entirely following up the implications of the its ideas, but valuable for raising pertinent incoherences. Bernard is a fallen angel existing in a corrupt world that views him as monstrous. Any potential he ever had for positive growth and development has been undermined by his appropriation of patriarchal society's image of a powerful punitive judge, the ideological mainstay of law, religion, and justice.

*God Told Me To* is another Cohen radical allegory. It is both a subversive alternative to the Superman legend and a popular-culture version of Dostoevsky's "The Grand Inquisitor" episode in *The Brothers Karamazov*. Society cannot cope with any returning messiah, whether alien or divine. Cohen merges contradictory opposites into a radical creation uniting high and low cultural motifs within a low-budget format. The Superman motif derives from Cohen's early interest in comic strips. Bernard (Richard Lynch) resembles an androgynous hippie. His sexuality is indefinable. As an alien, Bernard is born into an earthly culture he feels isolated from. Searching for a clue to his otherness, he models his persona upon destructive aspects of the Christian deity. Although his aggressive activities echo the Old Testament Jehovah, he is not so far removed from the New Testament image of Jesus, a figure who is not only savior but also final judge at the end of the world, separating sheep from the goats in bloodcurdling imagery found in *Revelation* and apocryphal imitators. Bernard founds his own dark version of the 12 disciples: affluent W.A.S.P. and Jewish Wall Street capitalists. As the Judas figure of Logan tells the assembled group when they discuss Bernard's divinely ordained random acts of violence, "The last time a living God came to earth, he's the one who got murdered." Like the *It's Alive* babies, Bernard Phillips emerges in a world that would kill him because of his different nature. But ideologically armed with Biblical rationale explaining his very existence, he decides to re-enact arbitrary acts of punitive justice characterizing Old Testament religious fundamentalism and terrorist activities of death squads in Latin American (CIA-aided) countries. As Logan states, "The only way the Lord has ever disciplined us has been through fear. Cure a man and you impress a few people who already believe you anyway, kill a multitude and you can convince a nation."

**Alien progeny Bernard Phillips (Richard Lynch) believes himself to be the anointed messiah terrorizing New York in an unexpected version of the second coming in *God Told Me To* (1976) (courtesy of Larry Cohen).**

As most religions show, any god of love is also a god of judgment. Deities often exhibit contradictory features within their personalities, paralleling the complex nature of their human subjects. As *Q* later shows, a savage messiah, rather than anthropomorphosized gods of love, may be a more accurate image of mankind's original definitions of primitive deities. Bernard Phillips is clearly a mixed being, a Cesarean-born alien with an undetermined sexuality, embodying hippie-culture signifiers. But he does not offer New Yorkers a summer of love like his San Francisco counterparts. He is contaminated and compromised. Nor is he a god of love embodying a healthy brave new world of gods and monsters. Bernard never offers Peter the possibility of a gay sexual relationship at their last meeting. It is really a different form of procreative activity designed to achieve the successful outcome of the many alien experiments inflicted on human females. Although it is impermissible by Biblical standards, Bernard still wishes to fulfill traditional religious commands to be "fruitful and multiply," populating the earth with a "new species." Bernard's offer to mate with Peter never contains any progressive, anti-family institutional elements common to radical branches of gay liberation. His offer is merely a one-time opportunity to his alien twin brother to get the experiment right for a change. Furthermore, this new world of gods and

monsters may be little different from the present regime of violent humans populating the earth. With parents such as Bernard and Peter, their offspring would
probably continue their alien father's Biblical reign of terror on New York. *God
Told Me To* shows human and alien societies operating according to a law based
on violence, fear, and oppression.

At first sight, *God Told Me To* appears to be a nihilistic film. Several critics
believe that it does not satisfactorily develop the contradictions it reveals. But,
far from being a failure or ideologically dominated "incoherent text,"[7] *God Told
Me To* is more of a dark, Hitchcock-influenced satire on personalities motivated
by oppressive mechanisms owing as much to their personal assent as to forces over
which they have no control. If Hitchcock regarded *Psycho* as containing comic
undertones, *God Told Me To* has dark satirical elements. Rather than living an
earthly life in childlike altruism like Wim Wenders' angelic characters in *Wings
of Desire* (1988) and *So Close Yet So Far Away* (1993), Bernard Phillips becomes
as corrupted and contaminated by earthly practices as avenging brother Peter
Nicholas does. *God Told Me To* is not a text implicitly arguing for either gay liberation or bisexuality. It is a much more complex work. The gay males Bernard
uses engage in the same type of manipulation and violence as the 12 disciples he
chooses on Wall Street. Ironically, like Tommy Gibbs, Bernard moves up the
social scale to achieve his desired aims. Like *Black Caesar*, *God Told Me To* also
reveals that no group, no matter how oppositional it may think itself, is ever free
from corruption and contamination.

Although Bernard Phillips occupies the "actant" role stimulating the narrative development of *God Told Me To*, Peter Nicholas is its most important character. The film is really about his development and dilemma. Like Frank Davies
and other Cohen characters in earlier television plays, Peter believes that he
belongs to his society. But he also intuitively feels like an outsider. It is only later,
after committing a murder, that he feels comfortable with his newly accepted role
of being outside the system. Like the mutant baby in *It's Alive*, Bernard Phillips
functions as Cohen's MacGuffin. Despite science-fiction and horror associations,
Larry Cohen films are important because of the human dilemmas they reveal, not
the spectacular monsters. He never indulges in overwhelming assaults of fetishistic special effects common to most contemporary generic counterparts. Even if
Cohen had an appropriate budget, it is highly unlikely that he would ever indulge
in special effects. Cohen prefers to concentrate on the human issues motivating
supposedly monstrous events. The issues he examines in his films also appear in
his live television works, as well as teleplays he wrote for earlier series such as "The
Defenders," "The Nurses," "Sam Benedict," "Arrest and Trial," "The Fugitive,"
and "Branded." Although a Larry Cohen film may present viewers with "gods and
monsters," they are merely marginal units of a more complex narrative. Although
limited by budget, Cohen avoids what Cosimo Urbano defines in another context as mainstream "generic investment in the spectator's masochistic involvement" in a typical horror film that usually attempts to repress radical issues and
keep them "in their ideologically safe and predetermined place." Like Marlene

Gorris, Larry Cohen takes the seductive, spectacular "kick" out of his films in the hope that spectators will consider more important issues.[8]

Peter represents a fallible human character whose reactions we note and sympathize with. They are the confused and contradictory actions of a character attempting to come to terms with challenging events exceeding the realms of everyday understanding. Separated from his wife, Martha (Sandy Dennis), Peter lives in sin with his girlfriend, Casey (Deborah Raffin), whom he promises to marry one day. The audience learns that this is Peter's own personal theatrical performance, one he uses to avoid committing himself to any woman. Peter's personal life represents a bleak counterpoint to the New Testament Messiah he ostensibly worships, a figure who also never commits himself to any women. Peter Nicholas also denies his own personal uniqueness, choosing miserable forms of personal and social existence rather than acting to change his particular situation. If Bernard Phillips never appeared, Peter would have invented him. As the film develops, we learn that Peter is Bernard's alien twin, the result of an unsuccessful experiment in which the human genes became dominant rather than recessive. Yet, throughout the course of *God Told Me To*, Peter appears as much more than a figure struggling with patriarchal ideological and religious burdens he cannot understand and break away from. He is also a figure with undisclosed potential, dimly perceiving a "difference" he seeks to deny and repress. Believing himself "chosen," Peter submerges his difference into an oppressive adherence to ideological norms, causing him deep unhappiness rather than personal joy. Orphaned, adopted by foster parents, and reared in a Bronx Catholic Boys School, he became the sole support of his stepbrothers and stepsisters when his parents died. Peter sacrificed himself for his two stepbrothers, putting them through college (the stepsisters' education significantly is left unmentioned in Casey's testimony to the police) after studying for one year at Fordham University before entering the police force. Peter took on the early burdens of parental support, denying himself at an early age for family reasons, submitting to the "law of the father" in more than one sense. Possibly suffering from this weighty sense of responsibility, he masochistically identifies with the "law of the father" in its institutional manifestations, hoping to find approval for the personal burdens he imposes upon himself. Like Jason McCord in "Branded," he has taken on an impossible task. As Martha notes, "You really believe. But where is all the joy it's supposed to give you?"

Peter lives with his substitute teacher and girlfriend, Casey, whom he deceives by sneaking off to Mass each day and lying to her about Martha's supposed reluctance to divorce him. Using Martha as a substitute mother for personal support and her house as a storage facility for his religious artifacts, Peter's activities echo those use-and-abuse attitudes Bernard exercises on his various disciples. As Elayne Chaplin notes, Peter's attitude toward the two females he uses to support his shaky sense of masculinity differs little either from patriarchal attitudes toward vulnerable female victims of the alien spaceship[9] or from those unseen aliens who use and exploit female bodies for procreative experiments. His very name, Peter

J. Nicholas, embodies his very kinship with religious motifs in the film. Although no "doubting Thomas" nor the "beloved disciple" that Bernard later desires him to be, Peter's name evokes the image of the chief disciple (later to become the rock upon whom the savior would found his church) who betrayed the Lord three times. Ironically, after Peter has been missing for three days, Casey finally meets Martha when he returns to say good-bye to them both. The three days parallel the three days and nights Christ spent in the underworld before his resurrection. Ironically, Peter has just discovered the secret of his true origins from his human mother, Elizabeth Mullin (Sylvia Sydney). He then leaves the two women who resemble Martha and Mary in Christian iconography. Like Tommy Gibbs in *Black Caesar*, Peter causes personal unhappiness to anyone near him. Although Martha also evokes the image of the Virgin Mary in her flowing nightgown, the color is significantly red, not blue. Due to several miscarriages (which we later learn Peter mentally caused), she is now sterile after seeking Church permission for an operation. As a Catholic, she is unable to fulfill her church's requirements of being fruitful and multiplying. The color red also illustrates the hellish nature of Peter's discovery as he tells Martha about feeling close to God all his life but now finding out it was not really the deity at all. Ironically, after descending into a basement for his first meeting with Bernard, he ascends the staircase of an abandoned tenement building for their final deadly encounter. By this time, Peter undergoes his own type of spiritual resurrection.

After saying good-bye to the two women he loves, Peter tests his supernatural powers against Zero (George Patterson) and his gang. By doing so, Peter becomes a mirror image of Bernard Phillips, forcing the psychically dominated Zero to kill two of his men and then commit suicide in a manner similar to Bernard's "execution" of Logan, the Judas among his 12 disciples. Parallels also exist between Peter and Zero. After killing crooked cop Jordan, Zero, by writing "God" on the wall, tries to depict it as part of the current frenzy of religious killings. He "sneaks" into police headquarters and sneaks out again, in a manner similar to Martha's description of Peter's secret activities of sneaking away from Casey every morning. Furthermore, most males in the film use and abuse females. Zero is a pimp, called by that name because he gives his prostitutes "nothing." Peter gives his dependent wife and girlfriend nothing but misery and frustration, exploiting them like Zero does. In Zero's poolroom enclave, the camera shows a sign reading, "Women Not Admitted" before it pans to reveal Zero's black hookers who exist in conditions akin to slavery.

While Bernard kills his earthly subjects by ordering a series of random assassinations and telepathically destroying others, Peter commits the unpardonable crime of murdering his own unborn children. He not only unconsciously reacts against their alien origin but also performs the religiously indefensible crime of abortion. Peter and Bernard both commit crimes that are motivated by displays of male power. As Peter kills Zero, his face lights up. The faint lighting resembles the brighter light surrounding Bernard. During their final meeting, Bernard remarks, "You've tested yourself since we last met and you've experienced it."

Despite Peter's denial that he will never "do it again," his aggressive assault against Bernard follows his brother's invitation to mate. Bernard's invitation has no progressive overtones of a gay liberation that will finally remove Peter from his repressive Catholic upbringing. It belongs to Bernard's final power play as he attempts to control Peter. An optically printed shot shows Bernard's murderous and sexually aggressive eye filling the frame and gazing at Peter. It suggests that Bernard's invitation arises less from wanting his brother to realize bisexual components in his personality, but more from his desire to trap him in a darker, cosmic version of a patriarchal power game contaminating both of their personalities.

Peter refuses for several reasons: obviously repulsed by Bernard's sexual embrace and the revelation of the vagina on his chest, Peter desires to stop his reign of terror in New York. Discovering that his brother never feels pain, Peter ruthlessly assaults him and is about to shoot him before Bernard causes debris to fall on the handgun. While Peter escapes from the tenement building being assaulted by Bernard's supernatural powers, the final image shows Bernard, in a mocking parody of Christ's heavenly ascension, rising amongst the flames commonly associated with him. Whether Bernard survives or is destroyed remains unanswered. The final sequence shows Peter facing reporters before he is incarcerated in a state mental institution, one that releases inmates after only a few years of confinement. The nature of his crime is left unclear. He appears to face trial for Bernard's death. Questioned by an unseen reporter (portrayed by Larry Cohen), Peter plays his own version of the deadly game structuring *God Told Me To*, repeating an explanation for his crimes previously given by Bernard's disciples. The frame freezes as Peter stares at the camera, having uttered, "God told me to." Rather than tell the truth, he decides to remain complicit in a lie as deadly as those surrounding the forces of law, patriarchy, and religion that he uneasily assented to during his life. Peter sees the destruction of all his beliefs and illusions. He could speak out, but chooses not to. Like Jason McCord in "Vindicator," he prefers to live a lie and remain silent. *God Told Me To* ends ironically with Peter's blank stare challenging the audience to affirm or deny his particular choice. Although the film does not conclude with a jeering jester pointing his finger at the audience, as in *Blackmail*, the joke is still played on the audience.

Acclaimed by Robin Wood as "perhaps the most intelligent film about American politics ever to come out of Hollywood,"[10] *The Private Files of J. Edgar Hoover* remains unjustly neglected in most accounts of contemporary American cinema. This is not entirely due to the film's problematic distribution history. Like Cohen's preceding and succeeding works, *The Private Files of J. Edgar Hoover* is an iconoclastic film, stylistically and thematically. It usually offends audiences desiring the polished professionalism of a recognizable Hollywood political film such as *The Best Man* (1964) or *All the President's Men* (1976), as well as those looking for an identifiable heroic character finally redeeming a system corrupted by a few bad men. In *The Private Files of J. Edgar Hoover*, we enter a universe of inescapable contamination where no Henry Fonda is going to restore conclusively some degree of acceptability to the system as he does in *Twelve Angry Men* (1957) and *Fail Safe* (1964). Instead, Cohen's major character is one formerly eulogized in Mervyn LeRoy's propagandist *The F.B.I. Story* (1959). There J. Edgar Hoover appears sporadically, either seen from behind or indirectly via shadow imagery usually associated with reverential depictions of the savior in Hollywood Biblical epics. But Cohen's Hoover is no totally evil figure. He is a complex, tragic figure combining a mixture of unfulfilled positive potentials and monstrous oppressive desires. The audience first sees Hoover as a biased and idealistic young man (James Wainwright). Although hating Reds, Hoover exhibits praiseworthy feelings for justice before his eventual contamination by a system he uneasily exists within. J. Edgar Hoover is both tragic hero and vicious oppressor. He is neither totally good nor totally bad, but a compromised figure within a familiar social and historical world demanding a mature level of audience understanding that eschews typical moralistic judgments. Unlike *All the President's Men*, there are no identifiable clean-cut heroic figures who will set everything right again. Even Dwight Webb, Jr. (Rip Torn) eventually recognizes his personal contamination by a system that will never fulfill his desire for honesty and justice. His final awareness parallels the similar awakening of young Hoover many years before when he finds out that his own boss, Attorney General Palmer, suspended the constitutional right of arrested aliens to obtain legal counsel. As in Cohen's other films, the focus is less on issues of isolated individual dilemmas but more on the influence of a corrupt system upon human potential.

Like Cohen's other films, *The Private Files of J. Edgar Hoover* breaks many standard rules of Hollywood professional direction. It seems to be an uneasy amalgamation of documentary footage, hand-held camera shots (such as those at the beginning that show Hoover's deserted office), rapidly edited footage, and raw guerrilla filmmaking techniques breaching the rules of classical Hollywood invisible editing. However, these features also occur in other Cohen works, operating as devices to jar the viewer into recognizing the manufactured nature of filmic reality and its ideologically manipulated world. *Special Effects* later engages in another form of analytic investigation of cinematic illusion. *The Private Files of J. Edgar Hoover* is an act of cinematic interrogation. Using *The F.B.I. Story* as a loose framework for most of its narrative, *Hoover* engages in a deconstructive investigation of ideological premises in the earlier film. Cohen wanted deliberately to contradict the political, sexual, and illusory positions in LeRoy's film by revealing alternative oppositional directions suppressed within it.

*The Private Files of J. Edgar Hoover* also engages in a polemical parody of *The F.B.I. Story*, criticizing it as the type of compromised work resembling those botched studio versions of Cohen's own screenplays such as *Return of the Seven* (1966), *Daddy's Gone A-Hunting* (1968), and *El Condor* (1970) that resulted in his decision to write and direct his own films. *Hoover* is a parody engaging its predecessor in a manner akin to Mikhail Bakhtin's methodology:

> Parody resembles an approach in which "the author again speaks in someone's else's discourse, but in contrast to stylization parody introduces into that discourse

a semantic intention that is directly opposed to the original one. The second voice, once having made its home in the other's discourse, clashes hostilely with its primordial host and forces him to serve directly opposing aims...Thus in parody the deliberate palpability of the other's discourse must be particularly sharp and clearly marked. Likewise, the author's intentions must be more individualized and filled with specific content."[11]

In *Hoover*, Cohen "clashes hostilely" with the conservative premises of *The F.B.I. Story* that he uses as a model for his own film by presenting his own individualized version of the Hoover story in a more historical and oppositional manner. If Cohen's *Hoover* lays bare the ideological bankruptcy within *The F.B.I. Story*, it also takes issue with traditional constructions within the Hollywood biopic, particularly those operating within political depictions. Nothing is natural. Much is hidden. The individuals depicted — whether Lincoln of John Ford's *Young Mr. Lincoln* (1939), Woodrow Wilson in Henry King's *Wilson* (1944), or Franklin D. Roosevelt in *Sunrise at Campobello* (1960) — are all ideological constructions often presented as flawless and non-contradictory beings. By using a seventies style, independent movie homage to old Warner Bros. gangster movies, many eulogizing the FBI itself (such as the 1935 *G-Men*, which was re-issued during the forties with a prologue filmed in a recreated version of the bureau), Cohen deliberately deconstructs the premises of *The F.B.I. Story*. Since Hoover's FBI used contemporary media for propaganda purposes, Cohen filmed his version of a biopic by using a non-reverential cinematic technique deliberately at odds with the polished studio production style characterizing *G-Men* and *The F.B.I. Story*. Cohen depicts the media manipulations of the bureau's image by publicist Harry Suydam (Henderson Forsythe) and Walter Winchell (Lloyd Gough), and also lays bare many visual devices used in constructing these images.

One example exemplifies this technique. As Robert Kennedy (Michael Parks) delivers his televised funeral oration following the death of Martin Luther King, Jr., his head moves at least twice to reveal a studio light behind him generally used to highlight the back of a person's head in a glamorous star-like manner. Kennedy's movement is jarring to audiences and appears to be an act of bad filmmaking. Why didn't Cohen film the speech again? However, Kennedy's clumsy head movement reveals the artificial nature of cinematic techniques designed to create a false illusion. By revealing studio mechanisms usually concealed in Hollywood invisible editing techniques, Cohen also unveils the false manufactured nature of the speech Kennedy delivers. It sounds sincere. But it is the speech of a man who earlier betrayed the subject he now so eloquently speaks about. It is also the beginning of a presidential campaign by a figure out to bask in the political glory of a deceased brother. Cohen does not include the fact that Kennedy entered the race after he saw the early primaries favoring Eugene McCarthy rather than the incumbent President Johnson. But the implications of Tolson's earlier comment about Robert Kennedy being a "baby-faced bastard" are certainly there, especially when the audience recalls his demeaning treatment of Hoover.

*The Private Files of J. Edgar* Hoover also contains deliberate elliptical devices challenging viewers to fill in the gaps and make their own decisions. Cohen's treatment of Robert Kennedy's assassination is less hurriedly constructed than it initially appears. Although this sequence (as well as several others in the film) may appear to be an example of "bad habits acquired from television"[12] (as Wood terms certain aspects of the Cohen style that irritate professional reviewers and audiences), it does have a particular rationale, whether conscious or not. Kennedy's final speech before his assassination both precedes and follows scenes containing implicit suggestions linking the murder to Hoover. Before the speech, Tolson believes that Kennedy's election will mean the end of Hoover's dominance in the political arena. But Hoover assures his long-standing friend that they are not beaten yet. After the assassination, two abruptly jarring shots reveal Kennedy's solitary stone cross at his Arlington Cemetery grave and then a wooden sign giving the number of Hoover's new Washington residence. The visual associations are arbitrary. They certainly do not belong to any professional Hollywood editing practice. But taken together they represent an independent cinematic use of an Eisenstein type of editorial collision in which two arbitrarily opposing scenes unite to produce a new dialectical meaning. The jarring shot composition radically suggests that Hoover has personally benefitted from the Kennedy assassination. Rather than retiring after Robert Kennedy's victory and moving near a Miami racetrack, as Tolson humorously suggested, Hoover buys a house in Washington. Robert Kennedy has not beaten him. Instead, Hoover is now more powerful than ever. The rough, supposedly clumsy, editing of these separate images contains many metaphorical nuances, outweighing objections to Cohen's lack of professional Hollywood filmmaking polish. By its very incoherence, it draws the viewer's attention away from illusory relationships and toward understanding implicitly radical meanings contained within this particular sequence.

Furthermore, the very aggressively edited nature of this sequence echoes previous masculine power struggles between older and younger man in the political jungle. Robert Kennedy seeks to overthrow a man he once revered. As Hoover tells Tolson after his first successful victory over the younger man, "I was his idol." Hoover's suppressed homosexual attraction toward the young eight-year-old Kennedy emerges in his slip of the tongue to Tolson: "He'd sit on my lap and ask if I was packing a gun," a line emphasizing the very nature of a culture wherein repressed sexuality (of any type) becomes channeled into destructive violent activities. It also anticipates the nature of Robert Kennedy's future assassination by a gun-wielding Sirhan Sirhan who may have been Hoover's actual hit man (a possibility the film chooses not to explore). After enduring further humiliations from Kennedy, Hoover takes a malicious pleasure by personally phoning him twice following news of the Kennedy assassination and after the president dies. Having endured the attempts of a powerful son-figure to castrate his powerful father image, Hoover hears his younger rival break down at the other end of the phone. Seeing his opponent castrated by the loss of political power after his brother's death, Hoover removes the attorney general's phone from his own office. Robert

Kennedy's bid for the presidency may result in the election of a powerful younger rival whom Hoover will be unable to control. Whatever the historical facts of the matter, Hoover benefits from Kennedy's assassination. The old order acts against the threatening avatar of the new. Even if Hoover had nothing to do with the assassination, Cohen's editing suggests that it may result from wish fulfillment similar to that which motivated the death of the FBI director's earlier rival, Melvin Purvis.

*The Private Files of J. Edgar Hoover* has as little to do with the traditional political film as *Bone* does with "blaxploitation." Both films operate independently and transcend definable generic categories. *The Private Files of J. Edgar Hoover* resembles *Bone* in one respect. They reveal directions Larry Cohen could have gone had it not been for problematic audience reception. Like his "Defenders" and "Nurses" teleplays, they are filled with radical social concerns as well as an awareness of the waste of human potential existing within an institutional system oppressing everyone trapped within its boundaries.

*The Private Files of J. Edgar Hoover* is also a study of social pathology and sexual repression existing throughout the entire social body politic. As a victim of sexual repression, Hoover is easily identifiable as a companion to the monster children inhabiting seventies family horror. In this case, the monster exists not just within one particular family but is created by a system that both fears and needs him for its very existence. By suggesting Hoover's nature as possibly due to repressed homosexuality, the film could be read as a text warning of the dangers of social repression and arguing for gay liberation. But like all intuitive artists, Cohen is never dogmatic, choosing instead to reveal complexities and avoid easy answers. The achievement of *The Private Files of J. Edgar Hoover* lies in the fact that it attracts different meanings while also transcending them. It is as unique and iconoclastic as Cohen's other films. Eschewing easy narrative devices and treatments, and engaging in complex characterization, *The Private Files of J. Edgar Hoover* presents a world of oppression and unfulfilled potential as poignant as that depicted in "Party Girl." The film emerges as a story of a tragic hero. Like Leo in "Unwritten Law," Hoover is compromised and destroyed by the very values of a system he adheres to. But he causes more destruction on a national scale than the pathetic figure depicted in Cohen's earlier teleplay for "The Defenders."

Broderick Crawford's casting as Hoover evokes memories not just of the actor's familiar fifties role as America's "top cop" in the long-running fifties television series "Highway Patrol," but also his earlier Oscar-winning performance as the contaminated politician in *All the King's Men* (1949). Robert Rossen's pre–McCarthy era allegory revealed a world in which everyone became corrupted by a disease-ridden system betraying American ideals. Many features in *All the King's Men* anticipate Cohen's world of J. Edgar Hoover. Rossen's film also contains a character (played by John Ireland) whose persona suggests an ideologically motivated redeeming hero. However, like Rip Torn's Dwight Webb, Jr., he also succumbs to corruption and recognizes his complicit involvement in the system. Nevertheless, *All the King's Men* was just one of many influences on *The*

*Private Files of J. Edgar Hoover.* Cohen's Hoover bears many similarities to earlier figures tormented by social codes of restraint in his earlier teleplays for series such as "The Defenders," "The Nurses," "Sam Benedict," and "Arrest and Trial." Like Martin Burnham, Hoover is tormented by feelings he cannot control. He is a victim of sexual repression unable to express feelings of love and affection toward anyone. Believing in Victorian values of placing women upon pedestals, Hoover adheres to the same impossible ideals motivating Leo in "Unwritten Law," leading to murder and self-destruction. Molded by society in ways he does not understand, Hoover unconsciously channels his dissatisfied tensions into violence and aggression against acceptable scapegoats. Ironically, when Wright finally confronts Hoover at the Miami racetrack, the latter accuses the younger man of the very things he also has done. "I know you Webb. You're trying to sabotage the bureau to feed your paranoid delusions." Hoover is a human version of monsters in Cohen's other films. Although no alien messiah like Bernard Phillips in *God Told Me To*, he rules his American, earthly realm, exercising similar strategies of fear and terror that Logan noted as characterizing the androgynous deity. Like the mutant babies in the *It's Alive* series, Hoover violently reacts against any threat to himself, whether actual or accidental. The latter reaction explains the sad death of Frank Davies in *It Lives Again*. Living in a society based on injustice, oppression, and aggressive competitiveness, Hoover rises to the top using (sometimes reluctantly) the very mechanisms he once protested against as a young man. Cohen's J. Edgar Hoover is no good man. Nor is he a metaphysically evil character with no redeeming features. Cohen once more creates a complex character full of positive and negative features, a tragic hero capable of good deeds but ruined by a system he adheres to.

The film begins with the death of Hoover and the destruction of his files. After introducing the audience to retired FBI employee Dwight Webb, Jr., who accedes to a request that he prevent Nixon obtaining the files, the film moves into linear flashback occasionally punctuated by Webb's voice-over commentary. Webb may appear to be the film's token hero, but, like Hoover and Tolson, he is part of a contaminating system and powerless to overturn its premises. Like his predecessor in *The F.B.I. Story*, he is the son of an FBI agent (William Wellman Jr.) whose dying wish was for his son to fulfill his desire to enter the bureau. But, unlike the earlier film, where the relationship between the adoptive FBI father figure (James Stewart) appeared to be one of Eisenhower era patriarchal benevolence, the more distant contact Webb has with Hoover is contradictory and ambivalent. In his first appearance, Webb tells those meeting him about his dismissal by Hoover as a result of his liaison with a female employee at the bureau: "You know how Mr. Hoover was about anything sexual." But well before he confesses his guilt to the audience as a "hypocritical son of a bitch," the film supplies the audience with ample evidence of Webb's close relationship with the Hoover figure. The normal son and monstrous father are not so far apart as they believe themselves to be. Abounding in Cohen's favorite motif of dualistic representation, *The Private Files of J. Edgar Hoover* inherently suggests that the political and social order relies upon oppressive forms of psychic relationships for its survival. Although tensions against this order continually appear, they may never become realized in positive directions unless the oppressive mental structures of a patriarchally ordained society become overthrown in some distant future. Both Hoover and Webb are psychic products trapped in different ways by the same system. Although one is less contaminated than the other, both are implicated in an order needing radical change. While Webb can express his sexuality with Ethel Brunette (Jennifer Lee), he also exhibits signs of Hoover's repressive tendencies. Reluctant to spend the night with his mistress under the same roof as her daughters, he responds to her comment "You're such a prude!" with "I'm a G-Man. It comes natural." Earlier, he remarked about Hoover to the enthusiastic surveillance FBI man, "I kind of admire the old bastard. He reminds me of my father." Although Webb later prevents all the president's men from gaining the files, he really acts to preserve the final legacy of a father figure who will bring down his last presidential opponent from beyond the grave. McCoy (José Ferrer) refers to this perverse relationship in his final remark to Webb: "Still Hoover's man, eh?" The touching last meeting between Webb and the aging Tolson over Hoover's significance is more of a homo-social alliance between two figures out to preserve further abuse of the system rather than bring about its overthrow. As "Deep Throat," Tolson will bring about the fall of Nixon, Agnew, and the rest of the president's men — a positive outcome during the heyday of the immediate post–Watergate era. It is an act of individual revenge. But the system still remains. After Nixon's downfall, the more threatening political figures of Ronald Reagan, George Bush, and a vacillating Bill Clinton wait in the wings for their turn in the Oval Office. Looking at the film in an era when the disgraced president is now restored to honor, Agnew's portrait is again fully on display, and the remaining president's men tour university campuses and earn huge guest lecture fees, the impression remains a legacy still awaiting definitive realization. So far, but no further. The ending of the film is really as bleak as the conclusion of *Black Caesar*. Individual revenge and power reversals are simply not enough. The whole system needs radical alteration.

The parallel existing between Webb and Hoover is one of several involving other characters, including those that appear throughout the film. Considering appointing his brother as Attorney General, John F. Kennedy (William Jordan) initially comments, "Maybe you're too much alike." Both Hoover and Robert Kennedy got their start "hunting Reds" while working for Palmer and Joseph McCarthy, respectively. Each also caught his big criminal: what Dillinger was to Hoover, Hoffa was to Kennedy. Hoover was young Bobby's idol, as he was for Webb. But all the male figures in the film are caught within a vicious cycle of repression and violence, and they are powerless to change. Personal and political aspects are cleverly interwoven in a system devoted to a "law of the father" involving violence and sexual repression, an arena where powerful males struggle for control. It is a world in which J. Edgar Hoover is both winner and loser. In fact, far from being flawed by the psychological family dynamics it employs, *The*

James Wainwright as the young, repressed J. Edgar Hoover with his mother (June Havoc) in a tender family moment from *The Private Files of J. Edgar Hoover* (Larco Productions, 1977) (courtesy of Larry Cohen).

*Private Files of J. Edgar Hoover* actually reveals how much a perversely political realm is actually over-determined by an equally aberrant personal realm of harmful psychological family structures. Far from exhibiting "confusion and haphazardness," as Richard Combs believes, *The Private Files of J. Edgar Hoover* actually gains its richest insights from the family features he notes as being key components of the film. Combs writes that "Hoover's service under eight presidents, and his difficult father-son relationship with most other men (with Hoover moving from one side of the equation to the other at the point where Broderick Crawford takes over the role from young James Wainwright) give the hallucinating impression that the power struggles are all in the family."[13] Although Combs asserts that the film "almost demands to be approached psychoanalytically before it can be approached politically," he is oblivious to the fact that the political and psychoanalytical levels complement each other, especially in regard to his earlier statement that "Hoover's lifelong devotion to his mother seems to put him in some naturally hostile posture towards all president fathers,"[14] including the dangerous usurping figures of Robert Kennedy and Richard Nixon, both of whom undertake actions far beyond what Hoover regards as appropriate for the status quo. The psychoanalytic aspects of the family dynamics are crucial parts of the political drama of *The Private Files of J. Edgar Hoover*.

Introductory sequences depicting the young Hoover reveal what exactly is at stake in the film. Webb narrates scenes in which young Hoover spies on Italian communists, detailing the future FBI director's obsession with communism. But, despite illustrating a paranoia Hoover exhibited throughout the rest of his life, Webb notes that, although Hoover wanted to deport communists, "he wanted to do it legally." Contradictions exist between paranoid mechanisms that society induces in its subjects and the legal apparatus of prescribed justice supposedly holding the former at bay. But the system changes the rules whenever convenient, as young Hoover discovers. Encountering the reactionary Benchley (Art Lund) during an immigrant round-up, Hoover protests about illegal police activities until he finds that his own boss, Attorney General Palmer, has actually suspended the legal right to counsel. This is the first of many instances when Hoover finds that the system breaks constitutional laws when circumstances deem it necessary. Sneered at by Benchley as "Mr. Palmer's man, aren't you?" — a line echoing McCoy's final comment to Webb ("Still Hoover's man, eh?") — the young Hoover faces threats of dismissal. Ironically, Benchley taunts Hoover as "a real bleeding heart," an unusual description of the future FBI director. However, Benchley's comments suggest alternative potentials within Hoover's character that never gain appropriate realization. Nor will Hoover have the possibility of romantic involvements holding his monstrous aggressiveness in check.

His abortive romance with Carrie DeWitt (Ronee Blakely) follows this scene. The sexually repressed Hoover rejects her tender advances, believing he is under surveillance (possibly thinking of Reds under her bed!). He exhibits paranoia on a personal level paralleling hysterical political mechanisms motivating the Red raids. As Hoover leaves her apartment, the door slams. It forms a match-cut to the door opening into the office of Attorney General Stone (Lloyd Nolan), a father figure whose gentle nature anticipates similar features in Hoover's lifelong friend Clyde Tolson. Stone appoints Hoover as Acting Director of the FBI, agreeing to reasonable requests of appointing agents on the grounds of merit from the only reliable pool of candidates available at that historic moment: "lawyers and accountants." Although Stone appoints Hoover, believing him the right man for the job, one door (Carrie's) slams shut, resulting in another door opening to await his entrance in a far more dangerous direction.

Stone appears as the one benevolent father figure in young Hoover's life. A defender of pacifists during World War I, critical of the Palmer Red raids, this aging figure owes his appointment to a president (Coolidge) with whom he had little sympathy. After firing Hoover's corrupt predecessor, William J. Burns, the old man attempts to clean up the system, hoping that his young protégé will fulfill the hopes he has for a just and honest administration. We never see Stone again in the film, his quick exit suggesting that his good intentions and aging persona will end in ultimate futility. He will never change what is already a corrupt system. Also, Stone exhibits a naive blindness in failing to recognize the real nature of the man he has appointed. He appears like a doting father unable to recognize the dangerous nature of a figure he idealizes as a good son. Throughout *The Private Files of J. Edgar Hoover*, father-son relationships appear both dubious and flawed, whether they are between Stone and Hoover or Hoover and Robert Kennedy.

The good son soon finds himself controlled by less benevolent father figures, especially a cynical Franklin Delano Roosevelt (Howard Da Silva). Cohen's treatment of Roosevelt is particularly significant in the film. Roosevelt shares certain similarities with Hoover. Both figures owed their public image to publicity machines that avoided depicting their true personas. Contemporary news media never showed the president in a wheelchair (or carried in the arms of attendants to different destinations), presenting him as a supposedly physically whole leader figure. Later Warner Bros. films often used a Roosevelt look-alike and voice impressionist (Captain Jack Smith), sometimes presenting the president with the same oblique representational strategies used for Hoover in *The F.B.I. Story*. The publicity machine presented Hoover in heroic imagery that recalled his position as "America's Top Cop." Cohen's Roosevelt is deliberately presented in unheroic imagery. Cohen also reveals that the beloved leader was directly responsible for two appalling chapters in America's recent history: the beginning of wiretapping and the incarceration of California's Japanese-American population after Pearl Harbor. As with his earlier attitudes towards the injustice of the Red raids, Hoover expresses reluctance at the president's suggestion of breaches to the constitution. But he is soon coerced into submission. Initially protesting against the future Justice, Earl Warren's plans in 1941 as "arresting the prospective victims," and querying whether the plans also involve Italian-Americans, he submits to Roosevelt's hidden threat of "Be a good soldier and stay silent." Later constitutional abuses by Richard Nixon and Oliver North were nothing new to a system Cohen reveals as corrupt from its very beginning.

Although he is a dangerous and monstrous figure, Hoover owes his power less to the presidents who keep him in office but more to a public allowing him full reign and ascendancy over their lives. Damon Runyon ( Jack Cassidy) comments at the Stork Club about Hoover's parallels to Cardinal Spellman (also the subject of gossip as a closet gay). When a fellow journalist denies any similarities between Spellman ("He's a priest.") and Hoover, Runyon counters, "So is Edgar, and we ordained him."

As head of the bureau, living a celibate, repressed life with his mother ( June Havoc), young Hoover allows himself to be influenced by the publicity-machine manipulations of Harry Suydam and Walter Winchell becoming a prisoner of an apparatus hiding his real personality behind grandiose and false heroic images. Protecting his newfound masculine image as America's "top cop," Hoover becomes jealous of supposed threats, such as FBI agent Melvin Purvis (Michael Sacks) who killed the "Public Enemy Number One" fascinating Hoover throughout his life: John Dillinger. Hoover indirectly causes his rival's suicide, acting behind the scenes in a manner suggesting a similar strategy that later resulted in the death of future rival Robert F. Kennedy.

Florence Hollister (Celeste Holm) recognizes Hoover's lifelong fascination with sexual and legal outlaw John Dillinger. Secretly yearning to become like his rival, but repressed from acting out his desires, Hoover can only become a frustrated simulacrum exhibiting violent aggressive actions against all those he

Broderick Crawford as the older, more powerful, FBI director in *The Private Files of J. Edgar Hoover* (Larco Productions, 1977) (courtesy of Larry Cohen).

feels threatened by. Existing within a system that prevents the positive release of energies, Hoover is more dangerous than the gangsters he hunts: he has institutional power over the people, invades privacy, destroys lives (offending FBI agents), causes executions (the Rosenbergs), lies to criminals who surrender (Louis "Lepke" Buchalter), blackmails opponents (Martin Luther King), and possibly engages in political assassination. Unable to express his repressed sexuality, he becomes little better than a pimp providing titillation and gossip for the jaded Washington establishment. Although Hoover expresses contempt for the audience relishing his pornography, Florence correctly asserts, "You're a purveyor of it. I understand you distribute obscene material all over Washington." Unable to counter these accusations and afraid of her willingness to initiate him sexually, Hoover leaves her home as abruptly as he had departed from Carrie DeWitt's apartment long ago.

Hoover's character and actions are all contradictory. He attempts to live by an impossible ideal and is blind to the damage he inflicts upon the American political landscape. Vainly attempting to reach out to his favorite waiter at the Mayflower Restaurant, he only succeeds in upsetting the man by intruding into his private life. For the waiter, Hoover recites a favorite Kipling poem about the importance of will power — a work he had learned from his mother — but the last shot we see of him in this scene shows his image divided by the mirror behind him, metaphorically illustrating contradictory tensions within his personality, now destroying whatever positive potential he once had as a human being. He is now an impossibly split subject unable to recognize the devastating nature of the forces destroying him internally.

Hoover utters the Kipling verse during his last day as he attempts to counter the Nixon administration's encroachment upon his appointed territory. His firing of McCoy and movement against the presidency represent the last acts of a dying man confronted with the implications of a political system whose explicit criminal activities offend his sensibilities. Despite its depiction as the last example of a bad system, the Nixon administration is no less corrupt than its predecessors (or its successors). Hoover moves against it. But his act is not the last expression of a desire for justice in abeyance since his early protests against the illegal Red raids, but the final act of an old dying king preventing a corrupt son from gaining his throne. Despite Watergate, the system will continue.

*The Private Files of J. Edgar Hoover*'s significance lies in its intelligent recognition of the mechanisms of personal and political entrapment contaminating the lives of everyone within Western society. By focusing on an alternative depiction of J. Edgar Hoover, Larry Cohen reveals the symptoms of a sick society to his audience but leaves the eventual cure to them. He never offers any false utopian solutions, deciding instead to reveal the contradictions and hope for radical remedies outside the theater. *The Private Files of J. Edgar Hoover* offers no remedies, hence its marginal reputation. It is not falsely optimistic. However, no other contemporary American, mainstream political film has ever dared to reveal the dangerous nature of contaminating elements in a system based on a fear of difference and resulting in oppressive and violent forces that affect everyone within its domain. The implicit message is change. But it is up to an alert audience to decide what that change will be.

*It Lives Again* forms an appropriate conclusion to Cohen's work in the seventies. Unlike the unimaginative and manufactured sequels to *Friday the 13th* and *Halloween*, it is not just an attempt to cash in on the success of *It's Alive* (following distribution problems affecting *Hoover*), but an intelligent and highly innovative work. It not only develops themes implicit in the earlier film, but synthesizes *It's Alive*'s motif of the vulnerable family with *Hoover*'s dangerous, oppressive mechanisms of the authoritarian state seeking to destroy any potential threat of difference challenging it. Despite misleading promotion and publicity emphasizing the mutant baby in its pram, *It Lives Again* is less important for monsters and more significant for issues it raises concerning human vulnerability in a dehumanizing and threatening society. The mutant babies are merely metaphorical items borrowed from the horror genre and used as props to develop radical issues within the text. They are again Cohen's version of Hitchcock's MacGuffin. Following *God Told Me To* and *Hoover*, *It Lives Again* further illustrates Cohen's tendency of using different generic structures, as he did in "Branded" and "The Invaders," to express social ideas in unfamiliar allegorical contexts.

*It Lives Again* opens in Tucson, Arizona, as the Scott family hosts a baby shower celebrating the expected delivery. Despite the social context, all is not well with the happy couple, Gene (Frederic Forrest) and Jody (Kathleen Lloyd). Marriage causes inequality in their relationship. Guests comment that "Jody would have become a hell of a lawyer had she not quit law school," ostensibly to support Gene. Tensions are already present in the family, which soon gain unexpected realization.

Also present at the party is Frank Davies (John P. Ryan). Although looking happy amongst the guests, he is actually an isolated gate crasher, a lonely figure unresponsive to a female guest's offer of a lift, and thus designated as "queer." Davies' supposed lack of normality acts as a harbinger of abnormal events awaiting the Scotts, events arbitrarily designating them as dangerous outcasts in the eyes of the state.

Although *It Lives Again* develops implications inherent in *It's Alive*, Cohen's strategic treatment far transcends any associations with the horror genre. Like the young J. Edgar Hoover and Frank and Lenore Davies, Gene and Jody Scott find their former acceptance of a supposedly benevolent and democratic government challenged when they confront the realities of its oppressive operations. Both the Davies and Scott families, like the Bosnian Moslems, find their secure positions within society overturned by arbitrary events suddenly pushing them into the position of selected victims. Initially reluctant to believe Frank Davies' warnings about government surveillance and the threat to their unborn child, Gene and Jody Scott find themselves in a position similar to that of the Jewish population of post–Weimar Germany and the Moslems of the former Yugoslavia, who awoke one night to find an oppressive regime in power and their lives changed for ever. Similarities to historical events occur in *It Lives Again*. These features make *It Lives Again* more than "just a horror film." Although these parallels are definitely present in Cohen's work, they never dogmatically interfere with the complex construction of the narrative. Like all his films, *It Lives Again* operates on more than one level, avoiding the dangerous, moralizing tendencies that ruined the style of authors such as Emile Zola, whose novels following his Rougon-Macquart series provide a good example.

Like the young Hoover, Gene recognizes the difference between legality and a state's actual oppressive practices. Commenting to Jody about the government's murder of the mutant babies — "If this thing were tested in the courts, it would never hold up"— he then begins to understand that the law is no abstract element, but altered to fit the needs of the prevailing social order. Although Gene speaks about India's explicit prohibition of the formerly sanctioned murder of unwanted female children at birth, he begins to understand the ways in which the state continues these practices by indirect methods such as smearing mothers' nipples with opium: "I think today they just starve the little girls to death … and I guess it's easier to kill what you think is inferior."

By noting these relevant factors, *It Lives Again* not only evokes echoes of the intelligent and complex teleplays Cohen wrote for "The Defenders," but also parallels scenes in *Hoover* in which the state decides virtually overnight to designate ordinary citizens as threats to national security — whether Italian immigrants in the 1919 period or Japanese-American citizens after Pearl Harbor. Furthermore, after Jody allows Frank to touch her body to discern any resemblance to his own mutant child, the latter comments that the condition is "going to happen to a lot of people. Thousands, millions, before this century is out." His remarks are double-edged. The statement not only asserts that millions of parents will find themselves bearing mutant children, but that they will also face victimization by a state designating both them and their children as "inferior." Such parallels with history need little emphasis. However, the new designated "inferior species" never passively accept their fate, but fight back with aggressive superhuman powers. Dr. Perry (Andrew Duggan) later comments that the mutant babies Adam, Eve, and Scott represent "the beginning of a new race of humanity which is going to eclipse our own. This way, the human race is going to survive the pollution of the planet." This reference to "pollution" has more than one meaning, extending also to a defunct social order needing abolition. Furthermore, like *God Told Me To*, the very circumstances affecting the characters in *It Lives Again* contain macabre parallels to religious elements usually regarded as having no direct relationship to the human condition. As Robin Wood notes, Frank's initial appearance evokes New Testament imagery of the angel Gabriel announcing the Messiah's birth, an act duplicated by Gene in the closing scenes.[15] However, as in *God Told Me To*, a supposedly spiritual world has definite connections with the contemporary material world. Cohen abruptly juxtaposes Dr. Perry's comments about the mutants representing a new phase of human development with an action shot from Bruce Lee's *The Chinese Connection* (1972) being watched in a cinema by Jody and her mother. By comparing the superhuman exploits of a person who develops his own version of martial arts to combat national adversaries with the mutant babies' use of highly developed claws and teeth against their enemies, Cohen draws interesting parallels. In seventies Shaw Brothers and Golden Harvest films, vastly outnumbered Chinese often face overpowering numbers of occupying Japanese and their allies, and only prevail by using superhuman martial arts techniques. In seventies Hong Kong cinema and its contemporary counterpart, the key issue is survival, not aggression, a survival dependent on either superhuman physical prowess or endurance and inner strength.[16] By using the Bruce Lee clip to complement Perry's comments, Cohen tentatively suggests that the mutants possess a positive quality, not just mere aggressiveness. Like their cinematic Chinese counterparts, they attempt to survive in a hostile world. Predicted as being capable of reproducing at the age of five or six, the babies also break one of society's most strict taboos: infant sexuality. The new era also involves different forms of social organization.

However, the mutant babies are also complex beings. They are equally capable of destructive violence as well as love. When Gene approaches Adam and Eve, they both react aggressively against him. But their reaction does not define the full nature of their personalities. As Perry notes to Gene, "Your fear seems to threaten them." The babies instinctively react to any potential threat, seeing fear as the root cause of any human aggressiveness toward them. As Frank tells Gene and Jody, the state designated his baby as a "monster" because it was "different." Like Bernard Phillips in *God Told Me To*, the babies are affected by whatever forces of human society they initially encounter. Although *Island of the Alive: It's Alive III* concludes on a positive note with the human grandparents fleeing from society with their new "child" after accepting its different nature, this progressive image is impossible in *It's Alive* and *It Lives Again*. But far from being confused by "Cohen's recurrent preoccupation with biological parentage: the babies' demand to be accepted into an impossible nuclear family, the inherent tensions and inequities of which the film has already thoroughly exposed,"[17] *It Lives Again* begins the process whereby "monstrousness" *will be* returned to the normality it really belongs to. In *It Lives Again*, Cohen moves toward defining a new type of world where normality and abnormality become irrelevant. His new society will be less psychically restrictive than the old one. By now, the traditional nuclear family and capitalist society are morally bankrupt. The film suggests not just a new world of gods and monsters, but also a new world of humans (and newly constituted families) aware of ideologically induced mechanisms of fear and paranoia infecting their personalities, and openly changing and developing to accept the monsters. This tentative hope appears at the end of *Island of the Alive*.

In his speech to the Scotts, Frank reveals the real circumstances of events he once failed to comprehend as he tells them about what actually happened in the delivery room in the earlier film. Frank acknowledges the personal struggle he underwent, the outcome of which gives him an inward serenity that makes his later accidental death at the hands of baby "Scott," frightened by a security guard's light, all the more poignant.

At one point, Frank says, "They tried to suffocate my child. But, naturally, he fought back... He found us. He came to me, his father, for protection and I shot him. I wounded my own child. But he forgave me. Is that an animal? Is it? Is that a monster that can forgive?"

At first, they cannot believe the situation they face. Jody's disavowing response "Over here, we run the country" soon faces a severe challenge. Unable to reach Frank when Jody's labor pains begin, the Scotts phone the hospital and find themselves surrounded by hundreds of waiting police. However, Frank's successful rescue attempt frees them from the hospital, allowing the successful (but not incident-free birth) of the Scott baby.

But, as in *It's Alive*, the main emphasis in *It Lives Again* is on personal and emotional strains in the family. The mutant birth results in the emergence of tensions originating within dysfunctional social relationships caused by conformity to an oppressive status quo. In the opening scenes, the viewer learns of inequalities within the Scott relationship, in which the talented Jody has given up a promising legal career to become a nurturing wife and mother. When Jody's mother berates her over recent events, the language she uses equates Gene with the mutant offspring. Like Frank Davies in the opening scenes, Gene becomes the monstrous outsider, his dubious hereditary background explaining every-thing: "You can't feel guilty about this... You only knew Gene for a few years... It has to be him. All I know is you could have made something of yourself if you stayed in school in New York."

When Jody arrives at the secret destination, she is reluctant to embrace her husband whom she unconsciously blames for the mutant birth. Although she asserts, "I just want things to be the way they were," Gene recognizes the cause of her reticence: "because of what we created." After an argument erupts, Gene explodes, "We're not going to be the same people anymore." The scene appears like any domestic breach following the birth of a child. *It Lives Again*'s monstrous element acts as an excessive metaphor for tensions within traditional family rela-tionships, an arena adversely affecting all trapped within its domain. The abnor-mal echoes the normal. When Lt. Perkins (James Dixon) receives a phone call, he is depicted as tired and exhausted due to the oppressive demands of his own family life. Furthermore, although he retains his sympathy and understanding from *It's Alive* in expressing discomfort with his officially ordained role of "baby killer," he is still a social victim. Although he pleads with Mallory (John Mar-ley) for a better understanding of the mutant babies — "We'd be better off finding the cause — pollution, drugs — instead of just killing" — he is forced to follow the dictates of his society.

Mallory embodies the same feelings motivating Frank Davies in most of *It's Alive*. As father of the Seattle baby born during the final minutes of the previous film, Mallory engages in a regeneration-through-violence quest, acting like a twentieth-century version of a psychopathic frontier hero seeking to exterminate other mutant babies. Although he tells Gene about his personal tragedy — arriv-ing home and discovering his wife ripped apart by his baby — the film suggests he has guilty feelings over his use of a service revolver to kill his offspring. A police officer later notes Mallory's trigger-happy propensity in shooting "Eve" before it reveals human qualities when trying to say something to its executioners. When they watch Jody and Gene's hideaway, Lt. Perkins notes Mallory's blood-stained, nail-bitten fingers, which reveal repressed, agonized feelings over his possible guilt in killing his own baby.

Jody's mother not only helps to poison the now-traumatic relationship between her daughter and Gene, but she also places a bug in Jody's grip, allow-ing the police to trace their whereabouts. Parental interference not only damages Jody and Gene's once close relationship, but it also turns their son against them when he believes Jody planted the bug.

Like Lenore in *It's Alive*, Jody is more accepting of her son than Gene is. She has to force her husband to touch and finally hold the child. As the police iso-late the house, Cohen shows Jody and Gene in a touching fireside scene, as proud parents with their newborn baby. The abnormal baby now peacefully coexists with his normal parents. However, aggressive law enforcement officers break into the house and disrupt this temporary harmony. Attempting to defend itself against Mallory, "Scott" jumps on his throat. Before it can tear Mallory to pieces, Jody prevails on the agonized Gene to kill their child, holding the gun as he pulls the trigger. Unable to tolerate the sight of another human being under attack, they rapidly change their attitudes and destroy their abnormal child. Repressive normality prevails. Ironically, the Scotts again embrace each other immediately following the death of their son.

The final ten minutes of *It Lives Again* are among the most complex and contradictory within American cinema. They express irresolvable tensions characterizing the film up to this point. The parents in *It Lives Again* move away from accepting social definitions of normality and toward embracing a monstrous element threatening society. They also become outsiders. Like Frank Davies, the Scotts learn that the mutant baby only reacts aggressively when humans show fear. The babies understand that any human fear results in irrational violence against them. Paradoxically, they often irrationally attack whichever human they fear in particular instances. Fear begets fear and violence causes violence in a vicious circle needing drastic change. The mutant babies are as contradictory as their human counterparts. Contaminated by the society that produced them, they meet aggression with further aggressiveness, even accidentally destroying those wishing to help them (Frank Davies and Dr. Perry), and alienating even the humans closest to them (the Scotts) by their violent activities. *It Lives Again* concludes as it began. This time a prematurely aged Gene warns another prospective family. The wheel has come full circle.

*It Lives Again* honestly chooses to end on this bleak and ambiguous note. By using monsters for allegorical aims, it unveils the dark nature of a destructive society composed of unhappy and self-destructive people torn by contradictions. It implicitly calls out for alternative changes in daily living. Unless such changes occur, the wheel will again come full circle. Formally diverse but unified in presenting radical allegorical treatments of social dilemmas, *God Told Me To, The Private Files of J. Edgar Hoover,* and *It Lives Again* represent important achievements for Larry Cohen. They reveal his intuitive awareness of his cinematic and cultural heritage, his indebtedness to it, and, most importantly, his creative and original reworkings of key issues within that tradition.

# Social 7omedy
# Brings in the 1980s

In *Hollywood: From Vietnam to Reagan*, Robin Wood describes the seventies era of Watergate and Vietnam as revealing a crisis in ideological confidence resulting in the appearance of a remarkable number of talents producing work of "vitality, force, and complexity," none of whom "convincingly survived the retrenchments of the 80s."[1] Although this decade revealed a swing toward conservatism, ending an era characterized by "the great period of the American horror film,"[2] not all the directors Wood lists changed in the same way or were entirely devastated by the new decade. Although Wes Craven, Brian DePalma, and George Romero suffered adverse changes of fortune during the eighties, Larry Cohen still continued directing low-budget films exhibiting his trademark concerns. While these directors made major contributions to seventies family horror films, not all of them were specifically identified with this movement. Cohen's relationship is far more complex. Furthermore, if we evaluate any talent as major or minor according to Wood's definition — involving a congenial climate sustaining nourishment "into vigorous growth from sources within the culture"[3] during a certain period — it tends to limit Larry Cohen's significance to one particular decade. This is definitely not the case. Cohen's obstinate resilience is due less to input from the seventies era but more to motifs already present in his work. The basic ideas remain the same. They merely take on new forms according to changing circumstances.

Although *Full Moon High*, *Q— The Winged Serpent*, and *The Stuff* appear less realized works than their predecessors, they are not entirely bankrupt. They exhibit the explicit appearance of comedic tendencies already present in Cohen's other work such as *Bone*. Although the Reagan era included the hegemonic dominance of mindless Lucas-Spielberg-Stallone blockbusters, it also contained certain particular complexities and contradictions.[4] The decade was not entirely dominated by Rocky and Rambo. If some radical streams within Hollywood cinema dried up, others emerged expressing views antithetical to the dominant mainstream in marginalized areas such as the developing made for video feature film.

During the eighties, the films of Larry Cohen never really changed. Instead, they underwent a particular metamorphosis using different forms to express the same radical ideas as their predecessors. Comedic and satirical elements are never absent from his work. They came to the foreground to continue radical allegorical assaults in a more conservative era. However, Cohen now used humor as a major weapon to attack the same type of dehumanizing social movements as his earlier film and television work did.

Cohen's early teleplay "The Golden Thirty" was based on his experiences as a comedian. His films reveal, in greater or lesser degrees, satirical and parodic devices common to an American Jewish tradition of filmmaking also characterizing the films of Woody Allen and Mel Brooks. Even Cohen's action films contain moments of humor lightening the tone of the narrative. Prior to Tommy's men invading a Mafia swimming-pool party in *Black Caesar*, Cohen includes a low-budget parody of *The Godfather* complete with a sleepy, aging Don and Sicilian music. In *Hell Up in Harlem*, a modern version of the Hattie McDaniel "Mammy" figure takes gleefully sadistic pleasure in feeding her white masters traditional African-American food. She achieves a surrogate revenge for the way her predecessor suffered racial stereotyping in a predominantly WASP-orientated Hollywood cinema. Despite its serious implications, Lenore's birth process contains some humorous moments, as incompetent doctors confront her enormously large child and appear helpless before the baby emerges. While *God Told Me To* is almost uniformly somber, *The Private Files of J. Edgar Hoover* contains several funny scenes, such as the Birdman of Alcatraz conning the gullible young director by giving him a fake-pedigreed bird as a gift, Hoover's black servant relishing swatting an imaginary fly on his hated employee's shoulder, and the angry wife of a criminal turning on the impetuous director after a tear-gas attack. *It Lives Again* contains a humorous scene involving the two "birthday girls" (Cohen's younger daughters) engaged in the hide and seek game of "monster" and Indians! Humor and satire are as much radical weapons as are any serious polemical devices. Working in an increasingly conservative era dominated by huge, wasteful Hollywood blockbusters hostile to the radical motifs of seventies films, Cohen returned to his roots and developed comedy features from elements common to both his life and work. Although his appropriation of comic devices appears trivial and often crude to most viewers, Cohen intuitively returned to a very important tradition of early film narrative that most critics neglected until fairly recently.

In his interesting work *What Made Pistachio Nuts? Early Sound Comedy and the Vaudeville Aesthetic*, Henry Jenkins examines a neglected and misunderstood tradition in film comedy.[5] He argues that the evaluation of certain early comedies according to "classical criteria of thematic significance, character consistency, narrative unity, causal logic, and psychological realism" results in misunderstanding the unique basis of their very operations, especially if their intention involves transgressing classical norms.[6] The real vitality of the film Jenkins chooses as his opening example — *Stand Up and Cheer* (1933) — "lies in the heterogeneity of its material, the virtuosity of its performances, (and) its wild and wonderful violations of the rules of classical storytelling."[7] Such a description parallels many of the satires and comedies directed by Larry Cohen that owe their very composition to a number of diverse sources and stylistic necessities, not the least of which involves improvisation and the constraints of low-budget "guerrilla filmmaking." In excavating this long-forgotten tradition influencing film comedy, Jenkins describes slapstick comedies dominated by the vaudeville tradition as reflecting "alternative film practices responsive to different aesthetic impulses, striving to fulfill different functions within the larger cultural economy."[8] This also parallels the ways Cohen's films often work. Their very nature suggests radical comedic, subversive visions dormant even in his more serious films. However, they explicitly evoke tendencies present in Cohen's first feature *Bone*— but Cohen now uses them in other directions.

Like several critics of film comedy, Jenkins notes the presence of disruptive or disintegrative gags involving antagonistic tensions between the demands of performance and narrative constraint. These former features also appear in *Full Moon High* and *The Stuff*, which often contain exaggerated performances by actors such as Alan Arkin, Michael Moriarty and Paul Sorvino. Furthermore, the infectious yogurt of *The Stuff* appears as a spectacular element equivalent to the old custard pie in comic routines. In this film, rather than receiving the substance in his face like an old-time comedian, Moriarty is nearly engulfed by "the Stuff." Also, victims eat the Stuff like a custard pie from an old silent movie. But like its old vaudeville equivalent, the Stuff takes over the victim's character, obliterating identity in an entirely different way than its comic equivalent.

If Cohen also employs editorially fragmented comic-strip material, in the peculiarly American manner of Frank Tashlin and Jerry Lewis, in some of his films,[9] he attempts using such devices to call the viewer's attention either to the absurdities of social existence or to institutional abuses. For example, the Food and Drug Administration is culpable for the different outbreaks in both *It's Alive* and *The Stuff*. The accusation is the same, but the manner of treatment differs in both films. Also, in *It's Alive*, Frank and Lenore Davies live a bland bourgeois existence as repressed and absurd as their Beverly Hills counterparts, Bill and Bernadette Lennick, in *Bone*. By bearing the mutant child, the Davies find themselves in the absurd and dangerous situation of now being outcasts in a society whose norms they unquestionably adhered to. A callous attitude to now-unfortunate friends or employees typifies the characters played by James Lee and Guy Stockwell in *Bone* and *It's Alive*. *Bone* operates on a more satirical level, while *It's Alive* is more serious in tone. But the same moral judgment operates in both films. Bill and Frank find their lives turned upside down in an absurd manner. They find themselves outcasts in a society that now suddenly and arbitrarily rejects them.

The "Golden Thirty" ideal of a consistently effective comedy routine is a challenging one. It is often difficult to realize, in a comedian's performance as well as in Larry Cohen's comedy films. Many scenes in *Full Moon High*, *Q— The*

*Winged Serpent,* and *The Stuff* exhibit a hit-and-miss routine, with some jokes working, others overworked (the violin player in *Full Moon High,* for example) and the better ones being hilariously funny. Cohen's comic and satirical explorations have many similarities to early sound comedy films involving "fragmentation, heterogeneity, and disunity," often deviating from classical Hollywood stylistic and narrative patterns by emphasizing "gags and comic performance at the expense of story and character development."[10] But a gag itself may contain alternative aspects competing with narrative causality and plot progression. *Full Moon High* contains an interesting inversion of that old done to death, clichéd shower scene, first used in *Psycho* and later revived in *Friday the 13th.* Pleading with Ricky (Joanne Nail) to tie him up on the bed so she can film his transformation into a werewolf, Tony Walker (Adam Arkin) has difficulty convincing her that he has no kinky sexual activity on his mind. Furthermore, after he changes, she chases him into the shower with a knife, and he cringes in terror at his female assailant. Cohen turns the familiar *Psycho* sequence on its head in a manner similar to that used by Brian DePalma in *Phantom of the Paradise* (1974). In both cases, a vulnerable, un-masculine male figure becomes the victim. This is not just an instance when Cohen's comedic spectacle overwhelms the narrative, but one involving aspects of highly relevant characterization. As a token monster in *Full Moon High,* Tony needs as much protection from an aberrant normal order as the mutant babies do in *It Lives Again!* The comedic aspect of the shower sequence becomes understandable when viewed according to a particular operation found within gags and slapstick comedy: "Gags may become devices for characterization, suggesting a problematic relationship between the comedian and the larger social order, or mapping a series of oppositions between comic protagonists and antagonist."[11]

Furthermore, as Mary Douglas notes, gags and jokes contain a potential subversiveness since they often contradict mechanisms governing the existence of everyday normality. As she states, "The joke merely affords the opportunity for realizing that an accepted pattern has no necessity. Its excitement lies in the suggestion that a particular ordering of experience may be arbitrary or subjective."[12] As the final appearance of the laughing jester in Hitchcock's *Blackmail* intuitively asserts, the joke is really on the audience as well as Alice and Frank.

Used in a satirical sense, the comic strip may also contain elements of dysfunction and disequilibrium by taking a commonly recognized unit of meaning and subverting it. One well-known comic-strip artist recently acclaimed Cohen's strategy in *God Told Me To* of reworking the Superman legend and inverting its very premises.[13] Furthermore, both Cohen and his comedy films often operate in the way Frank Krutnik describes the technique of an actual comedian:

> It is as if the comedian — the disruptive element in the smooth functioning of the genre — has been dropped into the fictional world by accident, and like a playful child, proceeds to toy with its rules. The comedian refuses to act "straight" — unlike the other characters in the film — or is incapable of doing so... Thus two sets of expectations come into conflict: the comedian "interferes" with the

ostensible fiction, the fiction "constrains" the comedian. It is the play between the two which is responsible for much of the comedy.[14]

Cohen's comedies (including the highly idiosyncratic *Wicked Stepmother*) actually belong to a forgotten tradition of anarchistic comedy. It is one attempting to deliver a sense of vicarious escape from emotional restraint through stylistic excess and exaggerated performances.[15] The plot elements in this tradition often aim at building "comic disruption upon comic disruption toward a final explosion that rips away the remaining structures of the social order, provokes total chaos, and liberates personal expression...."[16] This description also helps explain the structure and conclusion of *Wicked Stepmother*, in which Miranda (Bette Davis) has the last word over the prevailing social order.

Jenkins' definition of "anarchistic comedy" involves a particular excessiveness also characteristic of Cohen's other films, which act against classical Hollywood narrative patterns:

> The anarchistic comedy provides perhaps the most unstable balance between performance and plot, with each scene transformed into a battleground between these two competing forces. Here, stories exist to be disrupted and overwhelmed by excessive performances, while narrative destabilization is experienced as a liberation of the comic performer's creative potential.[17]

This latter element is particularly appropriate in explaining Alan Arkin's role in *Full Moon High*. He is really a comic performer whose presence destabilizes the narrative and dominates important scenes.

Unlike affirmative comedy, Larry Cohen's movies offer no possibility of integration into the social order nor any movement toward a stylistic or narrative restraint obliterating the radical implications of the narrative. Recognizing this fact helps explain the narrative structure of a seemingly disorganized work such as *Full Moon High*.

If *God Told Me To* is regarded as a rough draft for the major work Robin Wood believes Cohen may make one day, *Full Moon High* represents a first attempt at filming a total comedy that Cohen's other films often move toward. In his analysis of *Full Moon High*, Kim Newman comments on the filmic structure as a diverse work involving very few unifying elements. Noting that Cohen abandons many themes "in search of laughs," Newman comments on the director's abandonment of an expected climax in which the werewolf hero redeems himself by winning the high school game he abandoned 20 years before. Full Moon loses again to Simpson High "while the film switches into another track entirely." Newman concludes that *Full Moon High* resembles "the work of a comedian doing a live act that hasn't had quite enough rehearsal."[18]

Much of *Full Moon High* is hit and miss. It resembles a comic routine including both good and poorly conceived jokes needing further refinement before it attains perfection. Following Cohen's major achievements such as *God Told Me To, The Private Files of J. Edgar Hoover*, and *It Lives Again*, *Full Moon High* superficially appears to be a descent into comic triviality. But, despite several flaws, it is not entirely an aberrant chapter in the director's career. As a fully fledged satirical comedy, *Full Moon High* has several connections with Cohen's other work. Approached in isolation, the film seems unusual and disappointing. But viewed in the light of a particular comedy tradition, *Full Moon High* has its own rationale, even if the results are mixed and contradictory.

*Full Moon High* appears to move toward a positive resolution, with Tony breaking free from his curse by winning the football game for his high school. But it does not happen. Tony appears on the field as a werewolf and scores six points for his team before mayhem breaks loose, leading to his death at the hands of Dr. Jacob Brand (Alan Arkin). But he returns to life a few minutes later, the curse still intact, to pursue Miss Montgomery who also has changed into a werewolf. The film concludes with a family portrait of husband, wife, and several children — all of whom are in various stages of lycanthropy. This final image is not entirely arbitrary. It represents, not just the normal characters accepting their abnormality, but also their embrace of highly diverse and abnormal children. The image recalls themes in *It's Alive* and *It Lives Again*, and anticipates the climax of *Island of the Alive*. *Full Moon High* is not a traditional affirmative comedy. Its roots lie in an alternative style of film comedy that is radically, rather than traditionally, affirmative.

If Tony won the football game and cleared himself of his curse, it would result in a narrative resolution entirely foreign to the director's work. As Robin Wood notes, "There is never a suggestion that things can be put right and solutions found *within the system* (italics mine); the conflicts are presented as inherent in that system — fundamental and unresolvable."[19] The appalling *Teen Wolf* (1985) bears some derivative resemblances to *Full Moon High*, but departs from it by having its werewolf win the high school championship game. But *Full Moon High* radically departs from the traditional formula, satirizing what would have been the melancholy end of its hero in standard generic treatments, before breaking all the rules in a characteristically Cohen manner by bringing its hero back to life. It thus provides an entirely different "happily ever after" ending. Furthermore, after scoring on one try, Tony destroys any chance of winning the game by chewing up the football!

Like *Bone*, tragedy and comedy complement each other. Filmed before *The Howling*, *An American Werewolf in London* (both 1981), and *Teen Wolf*, *Full Moon High* is a comic treatment of many themes appearing in Cohen's serious work. As in *Bone*, *It's Alive*, *The Private Files of J. Edgar Hoover*, and *It Lives Again*, the adult world presents the most serious threat in the film. Forced to accompany his blustering CIA father (Ed McMahon) on a trip to Romania, Tony (Adam Arkin) is bitten by a werewolf. His nocturnal escapades pose no real danger to the 1960 community except bites to victims' rear ends. Tony's werewolf infection results in his transgression of civilized and sexual boundaries. Indeed, after Tony obtains filmed evidence of his transformation "that even Mike Wallace will believe," Ricky comments, "I'm your witness. You're out of the closet now." Since Tony's victims include males (the bearded youth in 1960 and gay cabbie Eddie, whom he first met driving a bus) as well as females, his werewolf condition has overtones of a polymorphous sexuality transcending civilization's rigid gender codes. As a werewolf, Tony is viewed by society as a threat to the dominant order, much as oppressed minority movements are. But Cohen never pursues any politically correct line. He presents humorous portraits of gays, such as Coach Cleveland and Eddie (James Bullock), as equal targets of comic satire in his diversified cinematic world. However, it is only when he goes "all the way" with Miss Montgomery (Elizabeth Hartman) that Tony finds a suitable mate. However, although the final portrait reveals Tony and Miss Montgomery as normal human beings, their children resemble werewolves. The conclusion humorously presents the utopian conclusion that *It's Alive* and *It Lives Again* attempted to move toward: the ultimate union of humans and monsters.

Despite being designated as a traditional horror-film monster, Tony is more sinned against than sinning. Pursued in his pre-werewolf incarnation by pushy girlfriend Jane (Roz Kelly), and eyed by the gay but status quo figure of Coach Cleveland (Kenneth Mars), Tony later finds himself in a position similar to the mutant babies in *It Lives Again*, needing protection from society rather than embodying any real threat to the dominant order. Furthermore, although Cohen treats the father as a comic figure, he is, nevertheless, as dangerous as Frank Davies in *It's Alive* and Mallory in *It Lives Again*. As a pompous right winger yearning for the good old days of Senator Joseph McCarthy, Mr. Walker bullies his son in the opening scenes, exercises emotional blackmail by forcing Tony to accompany him to Rumania, and attempts to shoot his son with a rifle — the very object Frank Davies carried in the tunnel before the final reunion with his mutant child. Ironically, fleeing from his transformed, monstrous son, Mr. Walker accidentally kills himself in his nuclear shelter. Despite his pathetic attempts in aligning himself with discarded right-wing ideas, Mr. Walker also acts in a contradictory manner. When Tony returns after being bitten by a Rumanian werewolf, he finds that his father has hidden some secret microfilm in his rear end. This contradictory act belies Mr. Walker's self-proclaimed patriarchal masculine identity. The narrative significance of the hidden microfilm humorously anticipates Christopher Walken's perverse monologue concerning the hiding place of Butch's family watch in Quentin Tarantino's *Pulp Fiction* (1994). *Full Moon High* is formally a comedy, but it transcends its generic context by using satire as a radical weapon, bringing in motifs from Cohen's other serious film and television works. Indeed, it is less a film in "the spirit of *Mad* magazine's movie satires" as Newman notes,[20] but one having a distinct relationship to the old traditional anarchistic comedy, with added variations by Larry Cohen.

The adult worlds of 1960 and 1980 are characterized by deep absurdities and contradictions undermining any claims to normality. As the credits begin, sounds of a growling wolf appear on the soundtrack against a dark background. It then mixes with the grunts of the Full Moon High football team as they play on the open field. Both sounds finally become indistinguishable, making it impossible

Ed McMahon takes a brief vacation from Johnny Carson and "The Tonight Show" to play the right-wing father of a werewolf in Larry Cohen's satirical comedy, *Full Moon High* (Filmways Pictures, 1981) (courtesy of Larry Cohen).

to separate the human voices from the animal growl. A nuclear drill routine, in which students hide under their desks for protection, complements the absurdity of a communist Rumanian society where hookers ply their trade underneath portraits of Lenin and Stalin. The 1980 world of *Full Moon High* reveals several contradictions: winos lying outside, a violent group of ethnic students, drug smoking, and a student openly masturbating in the corridor. But it is also a world marked by the presence of spontaneous energy capable of negative as well as positive expression, as in the high school dance sequence. Commenting on Miss Montgomery's attractiveness, Tony re-awakens her repressed sexuality, leading her to break rigid social taboos by sleeping with one of her own students before she becomes a werewolf herself.[21]

*Full Moon High* also contains a virtuoso comic performance by Alan Arkin as sadistic psychiatrist Dr. Jacob Brand. At many points in the film, he steals scenes by making asides to the camera in the traditional manner of Groucho Marx in thirties anarchistic comedies. Brand represents the comic performer in this type of film. He frequently destabilizes the narrative by creative use of comic lines. In his first appearance, Brand challenges a potential suicide to jump from a building. His sarcastic comments provoke an outraged fireman (Paul Kandel) to attack him: "You're just like my father. I'll kill you." The suicidal man then intervenes to protect the doctor. Then both rescuer and jumper fall. Modeling his performance on a sadistic version of Groucho Marx, Arkin's Brand wishes to obtain Tony's body for dissection. As he interviews Tony in the jail cell, Brand humorously and sadistically taunts the guard nicknaming him "Narcissus" when he returns with a mirror. He snaps at his intended victim, "Speak up Mowgli. Let's get this down on tape." As Tony begins transforming, Brand attempts to make the guard shoot him. But the guard's bullet penetrates the camera lens, blacking out the screen temporarily as Brand exclaims, "He'll never pull focus again. The best scenes, the best special effects are missing because you shot the camera!" This scene acts as a tribute to the old tradition of self-reflective cinema in earlier comedies such as *Hellzapoppin* (1941). But it also satirizes the problematic and haphazard conditions affecting low-budget non–Hollywood filmmaking. In one scene, Tony's voice-over repeats the Rumanian fortune teller's pronouncement of his destiny. But he ends the monologue with "Did I leave anything out?" expressing an actor's insecurity over blowing lines that could lead to another (and expensive, as far as low-budget filmmaking is concerned) shot. As Tony recovers from the silver bullets Brand has fired into him, he breaches not only one of the laws of the werewolf movie genre, but also a standard Hollywood practice by speaking directly to the camera and commenting that inflation now makes eight silver bullets ineffective! Cohen also uses the old werewolf movie device of background violin music, featuring frequent shots of an unseen player appearing in fantastic and normal situations at different points in the narrative. The violin player first appears in Rumania. When Tony sees the musician in America, he comments, "You get out of here. Find a roof to play on"—an obvious reference to *Fiddler on the Roof*. Encountering the player at a fancy restaurant, Tony refuses to tip: "I gave in Rumania." But, at the concluding football game, Dr. Brand offers a dollar bill as a tip.

*Full Moon High* is a chaotic production exhibiting last-minute changes and a rushed production, as well as spontaneous moments of vitality and energy. Some individual parts are more amusing than the whole, making the film equivalent to a comedy performance needing further rehearsal and refinement—an impossibility for any low-budget feature film. However, Cohen wrote several hilarious scenes and funny gags deserving moments of audience applause. He uses rudimentary low-budget techniques to good effect, achieving better creative realization than most highly budgeted special effects movies can manage. For example, in scenes detailing Tony's 20-year exile, Cohen inserts into the background a series of ticking clocks displayed in a manner suggesting traditional Hollywood dissolves and superimpositions. As newspaper headlines humorously record Tony's werewolf activities ("Jack the Nipper Still At Large." "Australian Tourist Bitten Down Under."), a series of presidential portraits appear on a wall. They begin with Eisenhower and end with America's first black female president. Nixon's face is smashed by a hand, while Gerald Ford's portrait is held up to the wall and suddenly dropped. Also, in depicting Tony's flight to Rumania, Cohen begins with a shot of an actual plane, then shows a model plane buzzing across a map of Europe, accompanied by the sound of a fly until a hand moves into the frame and squashes the plane.

*Full Moon High* contains many funny gags. Enjoying his Rumanian hookers, Mr. Walker comments on the virtues of American democracy. "You would be free to walk the streets at night — and you certainly would." Miss Montgomery confesses to Principal Cleveland that the last of six sexual school assaults she suffered happened at an elementary school for handicapped girls: "They bussed in some very wild pupils." Meeting Tony for the first time, she remarks, "You're new here. You aren't even armed." Suspicious of Tony's past involvement with his wife, Jack (Bill Kirchenbauer) asks Jane, "Did you have sex with anyone else?" and receives the highly ambiguous reply, "No. Only with me." Jack then arrests Tony, reassuring him that his probable fate will involve a flea bath and a book contract.

*Full Moon High* is a mixed work. It is not entirely successful, but does contain some interesting moments. In his next film, *Q — The Winged Serpent*, the comedy would be more low-key but better integrated into the narrative.

Critical commentary of *Q* generally focuses on its ambivalent structure. Engaging in a retrospective look at Cohen's work during the '80s, Wood notes that it "scarcely marks an advance on his earlier work, or adds significantly to its thematic complex, but it is characteristically odd, subversive, inventive, and marvelously acted, if once again confused and unsatisfying."[22] Elayne Chaplin sees *Q* as "a fast-paced, dense and highly ambiguous text which offers neither easy interpretation nor neat resolution."[23] Both critics recognize *Q* as a difficult text defying convenient description. However, *Q* does fit the main parameters of Cohen's work. The director often combines different genres by making them unrecognizable in the final mix, confusing audience and distributor expectations. *Q* is another such work, deliberately relying on ambiguity (as Chaplin recognizes), but not one as "confused and unsatisfying" as it initially appears. Although *Q* defies easy explanation, it is really a black comedy unconsciously echoing developing tensions in the new decade as much as Cohen's seventies films reflected those in their own particular era.

It is the first of a series of collaborations Cohen made with Michael Moriarty. As Jimmy Quinn, Moriarty delivers a show-stopping performance, dominating the narrative with his virtuoso acting style, very much like Alan Arkin in *Full Moon High*. Although *Q* is a hybrid production with serious features, it also contains certain comic elements. If *Bone* combined the comic and the serious, so does *Q*. It represents another Cohen reworking of a Hitchcock cinematic tradition that introduces comic elements into serious works. Comedy dominates *The Trouble with Harry*. Humorous touches appear throughout Hitchcock's work, providing light relief before the suspense begins again. One such moment is Cary Grant's use of Eva Marie Saint's small cosmetic razor as he shaves in front of astonished males in a washroom in *North by Northwest*.

Larry Cohen's cinema uses Hitchcock's tradition in a sophisticated manner by breaking down the barriers between cinematic characters and audiences. If Cohen blurs traditional generic barriers between normal characters and monsters, he also places audiences within the perspective of his monsters. As Fred Camper notes,

> Cohen's camera enlivens his horror films by giving us point-of-view shots through the eyes of the monster-baby in *It's Alive* or the giant bird in *Q* ... they also remind us that the very different and more conventional views of its adult pursuers that make up the bulk of the film are themselves representative of only one particular way of seeing. Similarly, as we sweep down toward apartment building rooftops to attack unsuspecting victims with the Q-bird, the feeling of excitement engendered by flight *incriminates* us into the monster's evil.[24] (italics mine)

Cohen places us within the monster's perspective to emphasize that at any time we may suddenly find ourselves outcasts from a society we once regarded as our own. The nature of this vicious isolation often generates more violence. In *It's Alive*, the audience may initially sympathize with Frank Davies' desire to destroy his monstrous son. But it then becomes implicated in guilt after recognizing the dangerous atavistic nature behind this desire. In *Q*, the audience shares in the liberated aerial perspective of the Q-bird. But at the same time, it becomes implicated in its violent activities. *Q* provides no easy answers for the monster's appearance. The official explanation for the sacrificial killings resembles the deliberately weak science-fiction explanation for the zombies in *Night of the Living Dead*. But, like the zombies, the Q-bird's appearance is associated with tensions in human society, tensions which have no definite identifiable source. In the opening scene, the audience is clearly invited to see the first attack as a wish fulfillment on the part of the saleswoman against a voyeuristic window cleaner. The solution appears supported by the next attack on the female sunbather seen through the binoculars of a male voyeur. However, when the bird attacks, Cohen shows the voyeur disturbed by what he has seen, thus undercutting any direct wish fulfillment associations between what he sees and the attack itself. *Q* also suggests certain tantalizing associations between the giant bird and various characters such as Jimmy Quinn (Michael Moriarty), Shepherd (David Carradine), and Kahsa (Shelly Desai). Kahsa believes his ritual sacrifices with willing victims result in *Q*'s resurrection. However, *Q* never confirms any of these possibilities. Possible links may exist between the winged serpent's cinematic acts of violence and audience demands for voyeuristic special effects. But Cohen's idea of special effects involves making the ordinary extraordinary by implicitly hinting at suggestive connections between human desires and violent manifestations. Viewers wish for violent displays in most action and horror films. Producers supply the demand. But some directors play with the conventions and openly satirize their audience's need for artificial thrills. Hitchcock supplies audience expectations for suspense and thrills. But he often delivers more than they expect in revealing hidden connections between the entertainment and the disguised ideological deals people make in everyday life, deals having threatening associations. As Hitchcock affirms at the climax of *Blackmail*, the joke is really on compliant audiences. *Q* is Cohen's own version of a cinematic Hitchcock joke. It is a dark comedy satirizing audience expectations for violence but revealing hidden connections between entertainment, desire, and masochistic enslavement to the dominant norms of the status quo.

The editorial structure of the opening sequences contains suggestive links relating certain characters to the violent activities of the giant bird. Like the mutant babies in *It's Alive*, the giant bird is really Cohen's MacGuffin, a deceptive device having no other relevance than to make audiences consider other important implications in the film.

A panoramic view of the Manhattan skyline begins the film, recalling the opening and closing shots of *Black Caesar*. It suggests that the subsequent supernatural associations are indirectly rooted in human and social realities. Cohen pans left, revealing a window cleaner working high up the Empire State Building. Although he drools over the attractive female saleswoman inside, his desires are not reciprocated. Irritated by the scraping sounds of his cleaner, she tells someone over the phone, "I wish he'd take a walk." Quetzalcoatl's attack immediately follows, decapitating the source of her irritation. Arriving on the scene and searching for the missing head, detectives Powell (Richard Roundtree) and Shepard debate the probable cause. When Powell speculates, "Maybe his head just fell off," Shepard replies, "What do you want from me?" The scene immediately cuts to show a chicken being sliced by a chef (in the foreground of the frame) while Jimmy Quinn appears seated (in the background), busily consuming cashew chicken. Quinn's associates, Doyle (John Capodice) and Webb (Tony Page), interrupt the discussion, commenting on Quinn's huge appetite and accusing him of being a "nervous eater." Resentful of his proposed percentage in the robbery, Quinn comments, "I might just have another job." The scene concludes with the long shot seen at the beginning of the sequence, but it now shows the chicken being skinned. The next shot shows the maid discovering the sacrificial victim's flayed body. She tells Lt. Murray (James Dixon) that the victim "bought a copy of *Q* Magazine and took off." After Powell comments that "Yesterday we had a window washer whose head just flew away like a balloon," the second shot begins a new sequence, showing a balloon flying over the Manhattan skyline as Quetzalcoatl's claw suddenly enters the frame. The winged serpent then attacks a female sunbather whose half-naked body is watched by an avid male voyeur. Despite temptations to regard this scene as illustrating Raymond Bellour's hypothesis concerning the alternation of the male gaze leading to violence against the female body, Quetzalcoatl's assaults are really arbitrary. It randomly selects its targets. The victims are males of different classes as well as females.[25] Jimmy Quinn's first appearance links these two assaults in the narrative. But, apart from foregrounded visual associations with chickens, no direct evidence initially appears to link him with Quetzalcoatl. However, the bird's appearance coincides with our first view of Jimmy Quinn. He will later sacrifice his oppressors to Quetzalcoatl and, like his winged counterpart, hold the city for ransom.

Having the ability to lay an egg, the phallic-shaped Quetzalcoatl is clearly female, an interpretation later confirmed by Quinn when he tells Shepard, "I've seen the bitch in action." Despite resembling an adult male, Quinn's gender status is also ambivalent. Initially reluctant to cry before Joan (Candy Clark), he tells her, "I haven't cried since I was a little boy. But I'm supposed to be a man... I don't know what I'm supposed to be." Quinn's mixed gender status parallels Quetzalcoatl's. When Powell later sees Quinn during his ransom negotiations, he tells Shepard, "Give me fifteen minutes alone with her and I'll give you any answer you want." As portrayed by Michael Moriarty, Jimmy Quinn belongs to a particular tradition involving early sound comedians with diffuse gender identities who often resist social integration in their films. Both Jerry Lewis and Pee-Wee Herman represent modern examples of this figure. Recent critical work on this tradition contains revealing parallels, both to Jimmy Quinn and the absurdist nature of Q— The Winged Serpent:

> These clowns take pleasure in their ability to play with their identities and to thwart dupes, killjoys, and counterfeits. The films often embrace the "expressive individualism" of the clowns as preferable to the repression, hypocrisy and narrow-mindedness of the dominant order, with exuberant performance linked to this liberation from social constraint.[26]

As in Hitchcock's The Birds, Quetzalcoatl's assault is arbitrary and unpredictable.[27] Little evidence exists to associate the winged serpent with a monstrous return of Quinn's repressed bisexuality. The film chooses to operate on a number of different levels, suggestively linking the serpent's return with decaying cultural and social values. They result in the reappearance of atavistic manifestations conveniently ascribed to primitive societies but now becoming a fundamental part of daily life.

Early scenes link Shepard and Quinn as future participants in a quest involving Quetzalcoatl. Shepard's concluding comment to Powell, "What do you want from me?" suggestively leads to Quinn's association with birds in the restaurant scene and his future involvement with Quetzalcoatl. Although Quinn's comment, "I might just have another job" ostensibly relates to his failed audition as a jazz pianist, it also obliquely refers to his future role in providing Quetzalcoatl with fellow gang members as sacrificial offerings. An allusive web of associations connects the major characters and opening sequences in a deliberately ambiguous strategy. It is somehow mysteriously related to the material circumstances of their lives.

After Quetzalcoatl snatches the female, the scene changes to show a huge humanoid-chicken on a sign advertising a fried chicken take-away restaurant. It leads to scenes of feces randomly dropped from above upon New York citizens. This sequence ends as birds fly leftwards toward a building, the camera panning to follow their movement. Quinn's failed audition follows. The scat rendition he performs is ominously named "Evil Dream," suggesting dark associations between Quinn and Quetzalcoatl. After the failed robbery, Quinn briefly leans against a window containing roasted chickens. When he later ascends the Chrysler Building, Quinn comments, "I'm about afraid of anything. But I've never been afraid of heights." A few scenes later, birds fly into his face. He then discovers a female skeleton that the winged predators later nibble on. This leads to the following sequence showing Quetzalcoatl preying upon his next meal: an unfortunate hard hat whose lunch was stolen by coworkers. When Quinn returns to his apartment, he tells his girlfriend, Joan, of his "Evil Dream" above the Chrysler Building. Shot in close-up, his distorted features faintly resemble those of Cohen's *It's Alive* monster babies.

As a two-time loser framed by a cop for his first offense, an alcoholic, an ex-junkie, and an abusive boyfriend living a socially dysfunctional life in New York City, Jimmy Quinn also resembles a monster. But he is one created by society and cops such as Powell. Provoking Powell in the commissioner's office, Quinn compares him to the cop who, wanting a conviction, framed him at the age of 19. Quinn's outrageous demands for amnesty and ransom parallel more respectable incidents in everyday life. As he points out, Ford pardoned Nixon for "everything and anything," and many murderers and crooked politicians financially benefit from their crimes. Quinn's pleasurable revenge upon a system oppressing him for many years reinforces Shepard's comment about Quetzalcoatl's increasingly bravado raids: "The son of a bitch is getting bold."

The film suggests that one reason for Quetzalcoatl's very presence involves wish-fulfillment desires on the part of the high priest and his victims. Both social orders need victims for their existence. Powell needs a patsy like Quinn, while the high priest worships his carnivorous god with willing victims. The two societies need gods and monsters. Before the scene showing Quinn's ransom demands, a point-of-view aerial shot shows the winged serpent flying over the well-known Manhattan landmarks of a church and Wall Street, revealing deep connections between all three. The winged serpent may be an original version of a deity often depicted in benevolent human form. Similarly, Bernard Phillips in *God Told Me To* represents the Old Testament's version of a violent deity. Quinn's visual associations with chickens and the later sacrifice of his criminal partners to Quetzalcoatl parallel other elements in the film. Although Quinn's partners die unwillingly, he performs a similar function to Kahsa by making sacrificial offerings to the winged serpent god. Quinn later wonders why Quetzalcoatl never pursued him. Shepard replies, "Maybe it's using you," thinking that Quinn intends making a larger offering of the city SWAT team to the winged serpent. Shepard himself is not immune from such associations. He terrifies his girlfriend by imitating a monster and squawking before asking her, "Give me some bird, will you?" He correctly discerns that Quetzalcoatl will return to the nest on the day after they raid the area. "Shepard gloats at Quinn, who lost his reward and amnesty after a first assault in th Chrysler Building, by making chicken sounds." As in Cohen's other movies, even the representatives of normality have characteristics not too different from those they deem monstrous.

Quinn and Quetzalcoatl parallel each other. They both have the same initial letter and are associated with birds. Quinn's "scat" jazz composition "Evil Dream" evokes memories of deceased junkie musician Charles Parker, nicknamed "Bird." Quinn learned the music from a black cop killer, identifying himself with an alienated subculture. Speaking of Joan to Shepard, he comments, "What's a white chick doing with an ex-con like me?" But, like Tommy Gibbs in *Black Caesar,* Quinn identifies himself with the very system responsible for oppressing him. Relishing his sacrifice of Doyle and Webb, Quinn refuses to prevent further deaths unless New York City meets his ransom demands. His very actions disgust Joan, paralleling Helen's revulsion to Tommy in *Black Caesar.* If Quinn, like Quetzalcoatl, relishes his newfound status when he holds New York City to ransom — "All my life I've been a nobody and right now I've got the chance of being somebody important"—his monstrous counterpart returns to exercise power over the earth again. As the winged serpent's high priest Kahsa pronounces over his second victim, "I have fallen. But I will rise again."

The viewer is placed in the position of both monster and victim throughout various scenes. As a black comedy with horror associations, *Q* relies upon our compliance with the narrative and its effects. Like Kahsa's victims, we must all be willing subjects. This applies not just to indulging in vicarious thrills of cinematic spectatorship but also in submitting to dominant social and ideological mechanisms governing our consent to the social order, an order Cohen reveals as thoroughly bankrupt in all his films.

As Shepard learns from the museum curator, the Aztec god's former victims "gave themselves willingly," a habit followed by their contemporary counterparts, all of whom are affluent white middle-class males. Like Jaime Gumb in *The Silence of the Lambs* (1991), the high priest dons the victim's skin, "wearing it like a garment." The action suggests any established order's necessary dependence upon willing, rather than reluctant, victims. *Q— The Winged Serpent* demonstrates intrinsic connections between the old world and new worlds.

Reading books about the plumed serpent, Shepard comments that "It wouldn't be the first time in history that a monster was mistaken for a god." His remark not only anticipates Quinn's later media self-promotion of himself as savior of New York City, wanting acclaim from Rupert Murdoch, but the film's revelation of the thin line dividing deities and monsters — a predominant Cohen theme. Finding the gutted body of the second victim, Powell comments, "All you have to do these days is take the wafer and drink the wine. That's what I call civilized." But the Catholic Eucharist is really a symbolic enactment for literally eating the body and drinking the blood, the very things Quetzalcoatl does.

Visiting a Columbia University professor (Larry Pine), Shepard hears opinions about the recent attacks. The professor believes that even sophisticated New Yorkers would also worship the winged serpent "if they came to fear it enough." His comments echo those of Logan in *God Told Me To*: "The only way the Lord has ever disciplined us has been through fear. Cure a man and you impress a few people who already believe you anyway; kill a multitude and you can convince a nation ... What is God but an invisible force that we fear?"

As Shepard and the professor walk through the grounds of Columbia University, they stop at an open plaza whose square mosaic patterns resemble those found in Mayan society. Similarly, the Chrysler Building contains doors with Aztec designs and bird gargoyles outside. As the professor speaks about the appearance of the winged serpent in many ancient societies, both men stand in front of a university building with Graeco-Roman pillars suggesting further evidence of the past's hold upon the present: "Perhaps at one time, the whole world was covered with these birds and then they became extinct or about extinct." The scene ends with the professor suggesting that the winged serpent is actually a god: "Perhaps God is a much better word." Shepard then attempts to convince his colleagues about the creature's resurrection. "This thing has been prayed back into existence." However, when Shepard attempts to present his findings to the commissioner (Malachy McCourt), the Irish-American (and obviously Catholic) figure ignores him: "I've got to kill this thing and I'd rather think of killing a monster than killing a god, so tear up that report." Like Peter Nichols at the end of *God Told Me To*, he believes in maintaining an already bankrupt social order by remaining silent.

However, the film suggests that everyone (including the serpent god) is implicated in a chain of connections they cannot deny. If Quetzalcoatl preys on victims, law enforcement and criminal types prey on vulnerable figures such as Jimmy Quinn. Jimmy Quinn also abuses his long-suffering girlfriend. The god-monster Quetzalcoatl is really the ultimate expression of a system based on oppression and violence, consuming victims as humans consume fried and cashew chicken. Despite the winged serpent's Mexican origins, its predatory activities resemble features common to the American way of life. If *A Return to Salem's Lot* presents vampires as a fundamental part of America's economic and institutional structure, Quetzalcoatl is by no means as alien as the commissioner would like to think. A silhouette of the American eagle appears behind Kasha after one of his sacrifices. Powell and Lt. Murray find the final sacrifice performed in the Liberty Warehouse. The warehouse not only has the original Statue of Liberty model above its entrance, but also has an eagle statue inside with other ancient artifacts.[28] Finally, Quetzalcoatl not only inhabits the needle of the Chrysler Building located in Manhattan's business district, but dies clinging to a building resembling an Aztec pyramid: the Banker's Trust Building on Wall Street. It flew past the building in an earlier scene also including shots of Manhattan's business district and St. Joseph's Church. The winged serpent has undeniable connections to another type of system preying upon human beings.

Although Quetzalcoatl finally dies, *Q* concludes ambiguously. Jimmy Quinn gains his brief moment of fame as temporary King of New York when he has the city at his feet succumbing to his ransom demand. He loses his fortune when Shepard and the SWAT team kill Quetzalcoatl's serpent child, a fact nullifying Quinn's financial contract, since the parent is not there. Ironically, Shepard refuses Jimmy Quinn's constant pleas to place a canopy over the top of the Chrysler Building to trap the giant bird, a method successfully used by Lt. Perkins and his team in *It Lives Again*. Thrown out of his apartment by Joan, Quinn moves into a seedy hotel where Kahsa waits to avenge the god's death by sacrificing his betrayer. Like Logan in *God Told Me To*, Jimmy Quinn betrayed a dubious divine savior. Refusing to repent and pray for forgiveness under Kasha's avenging knife, Jimmy Quinn is saved from death by Shepard. The cop kills Quetzalcoatl's devotee, and everything appears resolved. Quinn tells Shepard that he is "not afraid anymore," leaving the detective to put a "do not disturb" sign on Quinn's hotel door. Shepard then decides to adhere to the official version, commenting, "Just another old-fashioned monster." However, the final scenes reveal aerial point-of-view shots originally associated with Quetzalcoatl as the camera descends upon a ruined building. Another egg rests on a nest. As it cracks open, the camera zooms in, plunging the audience into the egg's dark interior. Like the climax of *It's Alive*, this ending suggests that the nightmare will continue.

The *Stuff* is the second film Cohen made with Michael Moriarty. Containing "a light toning down of the manic Method-ism"[29] characterizing Moriarty's performance in *Q*, *The Stuff* is a further exploration of the familiar comic-strip satirical surrealism appearing throughout Cohen's work. Including a manic satire of television advertising and mindless consumerism, a critique of the Food and Drug Administration, and inter-textual parodic references to earlier films such as *Invasion of the Bodysnatchers* and *The Blob*, *The Stuff* contains the same type of freewheeling, undisciplined hybrid style also characterizing *Full Moon High*.

Although *The Stuff* appears more frivolous than Cohen's earlier work, a similar dialectical combination of satire and seriousness operates in the film. *The Stuff* was shot during the heyday of the Reagan era. But far from following conservative Hollywood directions inherent within the dimensions of Reaganite entertainment,[30] *The Stuff* iconoclastically operates as a freewheeling comic-strip satire attacking government and big business in a manner inconceivable in contemporary Hollywood. Characteristically, Cohen launches his frontal assault on topics usually sacrosanct in American society and often avoided by Hollywood. If *Q* treats elements of *God Told Me To* in a humorous light, *The Stuff* borrows one theme from *It's Alive*, namely the inefficiency and corruption in the Food and Drug Administration, to assault a supposedly democratic society caring little for the health and well-being of its citizens. Like *Black Caesar* and *Q*, the American flag functions as a prominent part of the mise en scene in several sequences, acting as an indirect signifier to the rationale behind *The Stuff's* success in American society. The director was, of course, aware of the parallels between *It's Alive* and *The Stuff*:

> Basically, what you have there (in *It's Alive*) is the pharmaceutical people who are selling people potentially dangerous products. Obviously, we were ahead of our time because it turns out that there is a famous birth control product that now has been determined causes damage and deformities to children and cancers to mothers. There's another device — a shield, and if you ever used this shield, you should go in and take a medical examination. That proved that the company knew the shield was dangerous for many, many years and still kept silent about it. So there

definitely is a progression between *It's Alive* and *The Stuff*, where people are selling this killer ice cream to the public even though they know it is deadly. If people are buying it, that's their problem isn't it?[31]

*The Stuff* opens on a snowy night in Georgia. An old miner (Harry Bellaver) discovers a milky substance bubbling beneath the snow. Tasting it, he persuades his friend to try it and immediately thinks of making a buck, oblivious of the consequences: "If there's enough of this we might have enough to sell to people." The scene immediately cuts to young Jason (Scott Bloom) discovering the substance moving in his refrigerator at night, his warnings denied by a disbelieving father, and then to a shot of the American flag flying prominently on the boat of ice-cream executive Evans (Alexander Scourby). This rapid editorial sequence is particularly crucial in understanding Cohen's style. Far from denoting a low-budget filmmaker cutting costs by frenziedly moving from one scene to another, the rapid-time transition actually reveals the Stuff's swift ascendancy into the American way of life. The Stuff first appears as an unknown substance bubbling from the ground. Once found to be pleasurable, its discoverer immediately thinks of making money by selling it to the American public without any thought of safety. When David later observes the Stuff's delivery, he comments, "That Stuff came straight out of the earth and straight into our supermarkets." As the workers siphon the Stuff into waiting vehicles, a public address system speaks of a "new order of life" with "no hunger," a scene obviously inspired by *Invasion of the Bodysnatchers*. The audience never sees whatever tests the Food and Drug Administration may have run. As the film reveals, the organization is really redundant, lacking any real power to protect the American people. David later learns that both the Stuff and the Coca Cola company (which once used cocaine ingredients as part of its magic formula) are still protected under the Statute of Identities rule. The committee who supposedly tested it were either "paid off" in the typical "American Way," as David Rutherford (Michael Moriarty) aptly notes, or "left the country." David later finds the surviving committee member, Vickers (Danny Aiello), addicted to the Stuff and frightened of his similarly addicted pet dog who will kill him. As a key member of a supposedly responsible team, Vickers is a mere administrator, not a chemist, awaiting disposable retirement after 19 years on the job. As in many Larry Cohen films, audiences are left to draw their own conclusions.

The American flag features prominently in the film. It appears flying above the battlements of Col. Spears' (Paul Sorvino) castle and inside his private radio station. But its first appearance is on the boat taking David to the ice-cream executives threatened by the Stuff's economic success. Before David arrives, the executives discuss the threat the Stuff poses to their ice-cream empire, noting how a rival concern run by Chocolate Chip Charlie (Garrett Morris) was bought out in 60 days. One executive makes a revealing slip of the tongue, commenting on the Stuff's secret ingredients. "We could copy it. I mean, we could improve on it." They decide to hire ex–FBI agent David "Mo" Rutherford to deliver the secret to them.

While Mo investigates the severely depopulated town of Stader, Virginia, where the Stuff was originally consumer tested, Jason finds his family becoming addicted to the substance. His father (Frank Telfer) and mother (Beth Tegarden) begin to resemble and speak like families from television commercials. These family scenes represent one of the many humorous moments in *The Stuff*. Jason's comment, "Why are you talking as if you're in a commercial?" represents Cohen's reappropriation of themes from *Invasion of the Bodysnatchers*. The family audience become consumerist zombies that television sponsors ideally hope their present-day counterparts will also turn into. After Jason throws the deadly substance against the wall, his mother comments, "Look at it. Low on calories. It doesn't even stain or spot. And he doesn't like it!"

The visual style of *The Stuff* appropriates the high-key, clinically colored lighting of advertising techniques, making distinctions between the real world and television deliberately ambiguous. In several instances, these distinctions are cleverly blurred. Before introducing the ice-cream executives with the shot of the American flag, Cohen shows a Stuff television commercial in which a glamorous model uses sexual suggestiveness to promote the substance. The woman wears a fur coat, like the scantily clad bathing-suit models seen later during the rehearsal that Nicole (Andrea Marcovicci) directs. These interspersed commercials associate violence, sexuality, and death in a satirical manner. The models wear beautiful fur coats taken from the bodies of animals murdered for consumer satisfaction. They offer the Stuff to audiences, a substance whose addictive properties eventually lead to grotesque deaths. David later watches another commercial featuring the elderly lady (Clara Peller) associated with the fast food advertising line "Where's the Beef?" during the early eighties. When Nicole takes responsibility for promoting the Stuff, her direct address to the camera initially appears to violate her role as a character in the film. She begins the narration, "And the people did believe," over shots of the American public destroying the Stuff. However, her subsequent reference to a teleprompter makes it clear that she reads the lines. Until we learn that she is broadcasting on live television to an audience that includes Fletcher (Patrick O'Neal), the executive responsible for the Stuff, normal barriers between screen and audience temporarily appear in abeyance. This is one of several instances in which Cohen's narrative style creates a deliberately ambiguous structure, making it difficult to distinguish reality from artificial representation.

Although David enlists the help of Chocolate Chip in his crusade against the Stuff, he is often on his own. Nicole and Jason prove ineffective allies, so he is reduced to using discredited remnants of an American system ironically responsible for the Stuff to destroy the Georgia processing base. Although Col. Spears appears as a figure of parody in *The Stuff*, he is a paramilitary representative of the same oppressive system responsible for allowing the American public free access to the substance. If Jason's family exercises conformist controls nightmarishly revealing mechanisms inherent within fifties family sitcoms such as *Father Knows Best*, *Leave It to Beaver*, and *The Donna Reed Show*, Spears represents a similar comic mirror image. As a soldier now reduced to leading a private army of inexperienced young male recruits, he exhibits the violent and sexually aggressive features characteristic of the enemy. During his first meeting with David, he threatens to throw the former agent from his castle wall. Spears also adopts Jason as a surrogate son, placing his arms round him in a fatherly gesture when the boy escapes the attack of the Stuff in his recording studio. He also makes sexual overtures to Nicole, paralleling Charlie's later Stuff-directed assault against her. Despite Cohen's burlesque of a figure treated seriously in Reaganite Schwarzenegger and Stallone films such as *Rambo — First Blood Part Two* (1985) and *Commando* (1986), Col. Spears is no joke. The American flag initially associated with big business corruption appears twice in scenes involving Spears. It is a familiar Cohen signifier often used ironically to depict the inherent corruption within the American system. After the chairman of the board's chauffeur picks up Peter Nicholas in *God Told Me To*, the scene ends by showing an advertising logo depicting the American flag on a New York electronic billboard. This represents one of several instances when Cohen significantly inserts important elements into the background of his selected locations.

Although Spears disappears from the film after the successful attack on the Stuff's Georgia base (possibly inspired by the 1957 film version of Nigel Kneale's *Quatermass II*, a.k.a. *Enemy from Space),* Mo discovers the new partnership of Fletcher and Evans about to launch a new product, "The Taste," on the American public, a dairy product containing "twelve and one half percent of the Stuff, just enough to get people to want more," a tactic similar to manufactured ingredients whose secrets are still protected by the FDA's Statute of Identities. Although David and Jason force the executives to consume the Stuff before the police arrive, the substance still exists as an illegal drug on the street.

Larry Cohen began the new decade with humorous subversive films. But before long, he changed direction and tried some innovative approaches that used influences from his early years — the documentary tradition he studied at college and an alternative, Hitchcock-inspired approach blurring boundaries between reality and fantasy, one influencing his major works.

# New 8 York
# Independent Productions

In 1984 Larry Cohen shot *Perfect Strangers* and *Special Effects* almost simultaneously with a small crew in New York. Both films never gained proper theatrical distribution and went straight to video. They are virtually unknown to most Cohen enthusiasts. *Perfect Strangers* and *Special Effects* differ stylistically from more well-known films such as *Black Caesar, It's Alive, The Private Files of J. Edgar Hoover,* and *Q— The Winged Serpent.* They exhibit little evidence of Cohen's comic-strip visual style. Evidently he was exploring different avenues while making these films. *Perfect Strangers* has many affinities with French New Wave documentary filmmaking techniques, using actual Greenwich Village locations and unsuspecting crowds as extras during particular scenes. *Special Effects* is a self-reflective interrogation of Hitchcock's murderous gaze in relation to director, characters, and audience.

However, despite their different stylistic explorations, both films have affinities to Larry Cohen's familiar methods of directing. *Perfect Strangers* and *Special Effects* reveal Cohen's relationship to the independent, low-budget type of filmmaking seen in the works of John Cassavetes. Although thematically different from *Shadows* (1960) and *Faces* (1968), *Perfect Strangers* and *Special Effects* (as well as other Cohen films) exhibit many similarities endemic to the world of independent filmmaking: spontaneous performances, improvisation, and the employment of crude cinematic techniques antithetical to Hollywood's polished professionalism. Ephraim Katz's comments concerning Cassavetes' work as "self-indulgent, unpolished, and erratic but striking and audience-involving" bear an uncanny resemblance to Cohen's own type of cinema.[1] Futher exploration needs to be undertaken on parallels existing in the work of both directors. Although Cohen and Cassavetes employ different styles and techniques they also explore similar cultural and personal dislocation within the American psyche.

Cohen is, of course, influenced by traditional Hollywood cinema, as his various films show. But, operating outside the studios, Cohen realizes the impossibility of even attempting to emulate the style of the classical Hollywood system.

He chooses instead to employ the more economically appropriate techniques of low-budget independent filmmaking. Larry Cohen's films exhibit more of a heterogenous rather than a homogenous quality. They contain many styles, influences, and deliberate references to cultural and cinematic traditions. But, at the same time, production factors determine style and content. The restrained economic circumstances of low-budget filmmaking never restrict Cohen to operating exclusively within any marginalized ghetto arena. Instead, he employs the necessary technology at his disposal to comment inter-textually on contemporary social issues in as accessible a manner as possible, aiming to release his films either through the distribution outlets of large (Warner Bros.) or small (New World) companies. Today, video and cable television markets usually offer access to his work.

*Perfect Strangers* and *Special Effects* are interesting and rewarding films deserving more examination than the cursory reviews they have received so far. The importance of both films lies in their explicit use of low-budget techniques already present in Cohen's other works. Like Cassavetes, Cohen often began his films without necessary financial backing, producing on credit and using friends and associates to compensate for his limited resources, until his eventual distribution contract finally guaranteed settlement of any accumulated debt. Most of his films feature his own home as a location, a practice similar to Cassavetes' use of his own house in *Faces* (1968).

The various credits of Cohen's films reveal familiar names such as James Dixon, William Wellman, Jr., Peter Sabiston, Paul Glickman, Armond Lebowitz, and Bobby Ramsen. Family members often appear. Janelle Webb Cohen is often listed as co-producer, stills photographer, and lyricist. Bob Cohen, Pamela Cohen, Louis Cohen, Jill Cohen, and Melissa Cohen often appear in cameo roles or work behind the camera as production assistants. Their presence parallels Cassavetes' own use of friends and family in his films. Most of them worked on deferred salaries. Coincidentally, Cohen also used two actors mostly associated with Cassavetes' films, Val Avery and Seymour Cassel, in *Black Caesar* and *Wicked Stepmother.*

Like *Black Caesar, Hell Up in Harlem, God Told Me To,* and *Q, Perfect Strangers* and *Special Effects* are New York–based location films using the city as an essential background to character dilemma. *Perfect Strangers* opens with a shot of a New York bridge before diagonally panning left to reveal the desolate wall upon which Johnny Ross (Brad Rijn) leaves his spray-painted shadow imagery. *Special Effects* opens in a New York pornographic photographer's studio designed to resemble the Oval Office. Both films make important use of their various locations. Characters participate in urban allegories resembling those many stories introduced by the opening commentary of the old sixties television series, "Naked City": "There are a million stories in the Naked City and this has been one of them." In *Perfect Strangers* and *Special Effects*, Cohen's particular choice of stories also owes much to his customary radical allegorical appropriation of themes in the work of Alfred Hitchcock.

With the exception of *Special Effects*, these appropriations function as marginal textual references illuminating motifs in specific scenes. *Perfect Strangers* contains two references to *The Birds*, one to *Psycho*, and another to *Spellbound* (1945). Already present in *Q*, shots of a flock of birds flying away from the camera depict elements of tension and danger symbolizing emotions within the protagonists.

In *It Lives Again*, a bird suddenly flies through the window of the hideaway containing Gene and Jody Scott. It not only signifies deep marital antagonisms dividing both partners, but also anticipates the arrival of a mutant baby personifying the very nature of their alienation. During Johnny's knifing of the Wall Street drug courier, Cohen inserts a shot of birds suddenly flying toward the sky. When John beats up Fred (John Woehrle) after Fred attempts to stop him from pushing Matthew (Matthew Stockley) from a swing onto spiked railings nearby, two shots of flying birds interrupt the sequence. The method chosen by Johnny evokes Hitchcock's traumatic flashback sequence showing the accidental death of John Ballantine's brother in *Spellbound*. Finally, when Matthew discovers the body of the private detective (Otto von Wernherr) hired by Fred to follow Johnny, screeching strains from *Psycho* appear on the soundtrack.

These references are far more significant than the gratuitous appropriations of the *Friday the 13th* school of direction. They function as thematic leitmotifs alerting viewers to traumatic undercurrents generating Johnny's violent acts. As a Vietnam veteran conscious of his role in destroying babies, Johnny's perverse professional activities force him to re-employ the violence he once used in his former "legitimate" military occupation. Other authority figures probably forced Johnny to kill babies in Vietnam, using the same type of pressure as the mob now exerts on him. Johnny is torn between two desires. He becomes attracted to his new role as Matthew's surrogate father and feels the necessity of removing a potential witness to his killing. Encountering Fred, he viciously beats him, intending to eliminate a rival to his now half-desired role as Matthew's father. The *Psycho* chords express not just Matthew's shock at discovering another body (after earlier witnessing a murder), but the changed deadly nature of a playful hide and seek game initiated by a father figure who wishes to murder him.

Furthermore, although a realistic thriller, *Perfect Strangers* has affinities to Cohen's other films, especially *It's Alive*. Like Frank Davies, Johnny becomes a reluctant father. He eventually sees the child as a threat to his existence and pursues it in a deadly chase, like Frank in the penultimate scenes of *It's Alive*. John also resembles other divided characters in Cohen's films. As Meletti (Zachary Hains) reprimands John while giving him a haircut, "You dropped a lot of bombs on kids during the war didn't you?" John also feels guilty about his pregnant girlfriend's intention to seek an abortion to reassure him. She notices Johnny talking in his sleep and assumes the references apply to her: "You talked about a baby to get rid of... There's no baby to get rid of. So relax." Although Joanna (Kitty Sumerall) mentions having done it twice, she concludes, "It makes you feel really bad afterwards." Her comments evoke strong feelings of guilt within Johnny's psyche.

Sensitive hit-man Johnny Ross (Brad Rijn) finds himself trapped in an emotional family blind alley in *Perfect Strangers* (Hemdale, 1984) (courtesy of Larry Cohen).

*Perfect Strangers* opens by showing the dark outlines Johnny sprays around his shadow on various walls in New York. His impromptu art work not only denotes attempts at personal therapy, but also recognition of his shadowy, underground existence as a contract killer. As his contact (Steven Pudenz) later tells him in their cemetery rendezvous, Johnny's very anonymity makes him useful to the mob. He describes Johnny's currently lost status as equivalent to the baby he will have to kill: "Up to now, you've been clean as a baby." Johnny is observed by Matthew when he kills his latest victim, and a series of reverse shots makes it apparent that the child has actually seen and understood the killings. But like Jason in *The Stuff*, Matthew finds that the adult world generally ignores the veracity of his perceptions. When Lt. Burns (Stephen Lack) brings a series of mug shots for Sally (Anne Carlisle) to see, Matthew actually recognizes Johnny's photo. But Burns brushes his perceptions aside, regarding him as a nuisance. The mob regards Johnny as a similar nuisance, as long as he desists from removing the only witness to his crime. Both Johnny and Matthew become alienated figures in danger from different forces in society. The once secure, affluent professional hit man is threatened and nearly murdered by a rival seeking to take his place. Matthew's position changes from a harmless two-year-old living a happy life with his mother to a potentially harmful child "who knows too much" plunged abruptly into a dangerous social abyss. His situation parallels other figures in the *It's Alive* films, both human and non-human. The Davies and Scott families in *It's Alive* and *It Lives Again* find themselves suddenly under hostile surveillance in a society whose protection they once took for granted. They also face fear and paranoia, as Frank Davies does in the schoolroom sequence of *It's Alive* when hostile police flash torch beams into his face while making derogatory comments about him.

By focusing on its main character's sudden reversal of fortune, *Perfect Strangers* contains parallels to other Cohen movies. The main difference involves the director's stylistic emphasis upon independent documentary narrative rather than the supernatural features of earlier films. The film also demonstrates that fantasy and reality are never divided opposites in Cohen's work. They are always complementary. *Perfect Strangers* also examines the dilemmas of different characters caught up in what Norman Bates describes as a "private trap" in *Psycho*. But these private traps are never exclusively individual; they are all socially generated. Like other Cohen characters in *Bone, It's Alive, God Told Me To, It Lives Again*, and *The Private Files of J. Edgar Hoover*, the major protagonists of *Perfect Strangers* are all enclosed in a spiritual and physical ghetto crippling any realization of their full potentials as individual human beings. Johnny is a Vietnam veteran now using his talents for the mob. He finds himself, as a matter of professional survival, torn between removing a dangerous witness to his murder and being attracted to the role of surrogate father. Johnny is also a family victim in some undisclosed sense. When he finally introduces himself to Sally and Matthew, Johnny hints that Sally reminds him of his mother, a figure he cinematically associates with Jane Darwell in *The Grapes of Wrath* (1940). Johnny admits he had a father who never exercised a major influence on his life: "He just sat there and he never said things much." When Sally realizes he is following her, she intuitively recognizes his vulnerability: "Are you lost?" Similarly, Fred represents himself as a lost figure to the detective he hires to follow Johnny. Speaking of his estrangement from Sally, he compares himself to movie representations of fathers returned from the dead and viewing their families from a distance.[2]

Sally also seeks an independent identity. Now involved in the feminist movement as a single mother, she formerly existed as a mere appendage to Fred, often conforming to his desires by identifying herself with images in glamor magazines. Speaking of her former status as "furniture" and realizing her non-identity ("I didn't know myself"), she now wishes to be a "good mother" to Matthew and free herself from her former ties to Fred.

Like Frank Davies in *It's Alive*, Fred initially was reluctant to become a father. Discovering Sally's pregnancy, he gave her money for an abortion and went away leaving her with the responsibility. On his return, he found she had left him. Fred's earlier dilemma forms an ironic parallel to Johnny's relationship with Joanna. He is as much a "monster" as Johnny is. While Johnny functions as a hit man, Fred works in an art gallery, producing skeletal artifacts, figures hinting at a sublimation of unwholesome desires.

Sally's radical feminist friend, Maida (Anne Magnuson), has undeniable and contradictory connections to a patriarchal world of male violence she supposedly rejects. Supporting Sally's decision not to volunteer any information to the police, Maida brandishes an automatic weapon in her store and relishes the prospect of using it on any male assailant. She desires a feminist apocalyptic conflict between men and women. Her lines anticipate the ironic conclusion of *Perfect Strangers* when the frantic Sally knifes the man she believes threatens both herself and Matthew: "Men don't realize that the kitchen they've locked us into is full of weapons." Like Lt. Burns, Maida ignores Matthew's perceptive understanding of the world around him, dismissing Sally's concerns ("I wish you wouldn't talk like that in front of Matthew. He understands everything.") by commenting, "He's just a kid." However, Sally's remark, "All this thing about feminist homicide is making me crazy," foreshadows the tragic climax of *Perfect Strangers* when she finally stabs Johnny in an act of madness.

Every major character is trapped in a world of violence, a physical and spiritual "Blind Alley" (the British video release title of *Perfect Strangers*). Wishing to protect Matthew, even identifying himself with E.T., Johnny finds himself murderously enacting the game he imagined earlier when playfully chasing the two-year-old: "I'm going to get you, Matthew, and you know what I'm going to do when I catch up." Johnny enacts Frank Davies' initial goal in *It's Alive*. But, like Davies, he cannot perform his socially ordained act of professional ritual sacrifice. He takes Matthew home. However, this time the father dies, not the son as in *It's Alive*. After Sally stabs Johnny, his body falls to the floor, revealing Matthew directly behind him. Johnny has now identified himself with Matthew rather than shadowy images of himself he once painted on city walls. Matthew begins to cry, traumatically upset at the act of domestic violence he witnesses. In the alleyway below, Maida threatens to shoot his real father. The action complements an earlier reference, when Sally told Maida that she never wanted Matthew to grow up into a world where "some woman would stab or shoot him."

The climax operates ironically, emphasizing the various dualistic patterns developing throughout the film. Following Johnny's murder by Sally, and her discovery that Matthew is still alive, a final image appears on the screen. It reveals the shadowy family of Johnny, Sally, and Matthew that Johnny earlier sprayed on the wall. Previously Johnny only sprayed individual images representing his solitary sense of identity. But the new family image suggests his desire to align himself with others and no longer undergo alienation and isolation. It again states Cohen's utopian goal of the eventual unity between normal and abnormal. Like Jim Colbee in "Survival," Johnny wishes to be part of a normal family. However, the unit he seeks membership in is part of a real world and subject to various forms of contamination. The climax of *Perfect Strangers* ironically inverts certain themes in *It's Alive* and *It Lives Again*. This time the normal family member, not the abnormal monster killer figure represented by Johnny, becomes contaminated by violence. He decides to return Matthew to a supposedly secure world, but his decision proves tragic both to himself and Matthew's future emotional development. Following the traumatic climactic violence, the reappearance of Johnny's spray-painted family image in the final scene poignantly reinforces the destruction of the characters' hopes for a tranquil future.

*Perfect Strangers* is a highly personal and suggestive film. Its only flaw is the irrelevant figure of Lt. Burns. He is superfluous to the plot. Although designed to represent another outsider, a gay detective on the police force whose marginal status enables him to investigate alternative communities, *Perfect Strangers* already contains better treatments of social alienation in the characters of Johnny, Sally, Fred, and Maida. They all are victimizers and victims socially and personally affected by a dysfunctional world perverting their personal growth. As in all Cohen films, any alternative is better.

Although filmed in 1984, *Special Effects* was based on a screenplay titled *The Cutting Room* that Cohen wrote 17 years before. It emerged during a time when he became interested in writing a work for Hitchcock to direct. Like *Perfect Strangers*, *Special Effects* was shot in New York under conditions akin to independent cinema. It features some of the same actors, such as Brad Rijn, John Woehrle, Kitty Sumerall, and Steven Pudenz, with the addition of several talents, including Eric Bogosian and Zoe Tamerlis (later Zoe Lund, scenarist of Abel Ferrara's *The Bad Lieutenant*), associated with the New York avant-garde who would later achieve success in their own fields. Like other Cohen investigations of Hitchcock, the director pushes his mentor's influence to the outer limits. In the case of *Special Effects*, Cohen engages in a self-reflective investigation of the cinematic construction of personal identity. Such features already occur in Hitchcock's work as several critics point out. However, as the original title "The Cutting Room" denotes, it is editing, as well as the cinematic gaze, that constitutes murder. As William Rothman notes, the *Psycho* shower sequence "is a testimonial to the power of montage."[3] He also quotes Hitchcock's one-line speech at the 1976 Lincoln Center tribute, which followed a compilation of his famous murder scenes, including Swann's murder by a pair of scissors in *Dial M for Murder* (1953): "As you can see, scissors are the best way." In *Special Effects*, Chris Neville (Eric Bogosian) attempts to kill Keefe Waterman (Brad Rijn) with a pair of editing scissors. He fails, but Keefe accidentally kills Neville by electrocuting him in his swimming pool with a studio generator light. The death is perfectly cinematic. Neville also directs himself in his own theatrical performance when he kills blackmailing lab technician Wiesenthal (Richard Greene). It is reminiscent of Tony Chappel's murderous theatrical performance in *In Broad Daylight* (1971). *Special Effects* is more than a reworking of Hitchcock's *Vertigo*. Unlike DePalma's *Obsession* (1975), it applies a meta-cinematic self-reflective Hitchcockian analysis, both to its source material and its own particular premises.

*Special Effects* begins with voice-overs of a news interview with Chris Neville concerning his recent failures as a director. When asked about the director most influential on his own work, he cites Abraham Zapruder. It is an ironic reply. Zapruder was no director, but an ordinary home-movie enthusiast who accidentally filmed the Kennedy assassination. However, as Oliver Stone's *J.F.K.* (1992) shows, the 8mm documentary footage became the grounds for different forms of interpretation concerning the nature of the actual events. The documentary reference continues motifs Cohen began in *Perfect Strangers*. It has autobiographical connotations, since Cohen studied cinema at the City College of New York, which specialized in documentary film at the time. The future director enjoyed learning the techniques while his mind was on his own particular cinematic and writing preoccupations far removed from documentary filmmaking. When Cohen began directing, his own particular version of "guerrilla filmmaking" included techniques akin to documentary cinema but he appropriated them for other types of films far removed from the realist aesthetic. As *Special Effects* shows, nothing in cinema is ever realistic. Realism and fantasy blend together, a conception endemic to Larry Cohen's own type of cinema, often allegorically using fantasy elements to express radical ideas relevant to everyday life. As Hitchcock's films show, even documentary realism is not free from the murderous gaze. When Neville mentions the Zapruder footage, Cohen's credits as writer and director immediately appear on the screen announcing his authorship of the film which follows. Like Hitchcock, Cohen challenges audiences and fictional characters by eroding the artificial barriers dividing "pure" reality from cinematic manipulation. This challenge immediately begins after the final credits. The black screen cuts to the image of Andrea Wilcox (Zoe Tamerlis) displaying her seminude body to the camera in what appears to be the Oval Office of the White House.

At first, our impression is that the surroundings are real, an impression reinforced by Neville's earlier off-screen reference to President Kennedy. The reference evokes common knowledge of J.F.K.'s sexual exploits while occupying high office. However, as Andrea revolves on the dais, intercut shots show male photographers voyeuristically capturing her image. Andrea's revolution around the camera initially appears realistic. But it is as manufactured as similar camera movements in both *Vertigo* and *Obsession*, films also designed to unveil the dangerous fetishistic aspect of the male gaze. If we are initially caught mistaking camera manipulation for actual reality, then the joke is on us, as Hitchcock and Cohen would say. But, while Hitchcock and DePalma never reveal the mechanics behind their respective movements, Cohen does. In *Special Effects* we see Andrea revolving in a 360-degree rotation on a crude dais. The mise en scene and Andrea's sexually theatrical performance are all manufactured to trap unwary audiences. Sexual possessiveness underlies the nature of the patriarchal male gaze. The director links the political (the Oval Office) to the personal (voyeuristic desire) showing them as complementary aspects of a dominant power relationship involving entrapment and possession. The initial images are false in the sense of actual reality. They are there to appeal to audience tendencies toward wish fulfillment. As one voyeur comments, "It's great being in the White House." But does the false illusion really matter? Does not the illusion speak for itself?

One exception exists amongst the voyeuristic males in the "Oval Office." Keefe enters and stares at Andrea, making her feel ashamed. As she runs away, he hits the proprietor and kicks him as he lays defenseless on the floor. Attracted by this alternative sensationalist spectacle, a photographer transfers his voyeuristic instincts from sexuality toward violence as he avidly photographs Keefe's victim. Not only does this brief episode reveal atavistic links between aggressive sexuality and violence fostered by patriarchal society, but it also parallels Hitchcock's associations between the camera's fascination with the female body and the appetite for violence seen in his many films, from *The Lodger* (1927) to *Psycho* (1960).[4]

Keefe has followed his errant wife, Marjean, who has run away from Oklahoma. She now resides in Manhattan using the pseudonym Andrea Wilcox. As Keefe desperately searches for his wife, he interrogates a receptionist, above whose desk an American flag prominently appears. As *Black Caesar, Hell Up in Harlem, God Told Me To, The Private Files of J. Edgar Hoover, The Stuff*, and *A Return to Salem's Lot* all show, Old Glory functions as a telling signifier, linking individual dilemmas to the system responsible for them. Associations between sexuality and violence, political and personal concepts, reality and fantasy, documentary realism and cinematic manipulation, camera voyeurism and dark unconscious forces economically appear in the opening scenes of *Special Effects*.

Chasing after Andrea, Keefe encounters her roommate (Kitty Summerall) who challenges his claim that he knows his wife's real identity and his involvement in a patriarchal system of gender exchange whereby one woman may easily substitute for another. This brief encounter foreshadows later events in the film. *Special Effects* is no uninspired copy of *Vertigo*. Like Cohen's other Hitchcock-influenced work, it appropriates a cinematic tradition and pushes it into even more extreme and revealing directions. The dialogue between Keefe and Andrea's roommate is significant:

> GIRL: "My name is Mary Jean. I can be whatever you want me to be."
> KEEFE: "You're not Mary Jean. You're not my wife."
> GIRL: "Are you sure?"

The final scene of *Special Effects* invests this encounter with great irony. Keefe catches up with his wife, forces her into a car, and drives to her apartment, intending to return her to Oklahoma and the child she has abandoned. Forcing her to watch home-movie footage of the boy, Keefe intently gazes at the image while Andrea reluctantly looks on, torn between the guilty feelings her husband wishes to instill in her and the rejection of a life she feels unsuited to. Keefe runs the film on an old 16mm projector. Cohen's choice of technical apparatus is important. Rather than having the images run on an 8mm projector, the director chose the same format that his character, Chris Neville, later chooses to use for his independent feature *Andrea*. Like Chris, Keefe is also a director preferring "non-professionals" for parts in his movies. Although Andrea rejects the role of wife and mother, Keefe wishes her to perform: "It's not me but someone you made up." He sarcastically retorts, "You're supposed to be an actress. Why don't you learn the damn part?" Keefe speaks to his wife like an authoritarian director.

Andrea's chosen method of escape leads her into the world of New York pornography. She flees there as a reaction against Keefe's puritanical attitudes and exchanges one form of exploitation for another. Although Keefe sneers at the imaginary job Chris Neville supposedly offers her as involving work on a "sex film," Andrea responds by commenting that nearly 15 million American women view such films. She also condemns Keefe's repressive tendencies: "I remember you from school, erasing all the dirty words from the john. You were real good about rubbing things out." Ironically, the lines suggestively reinforce Keefe's later indirect participation in "rubbing out" his later alter ego Chris Neville. Without Keefe's interference, Andrea would never have ended up in Neville's apartment. Andrea's recognition of Keefe's repressive nature later appears in the comments of a taxi driver who takes him to Neville's apartment. Perhaps recognizing his passenger's repressed sexual ambivalence, he twice attempts unsuccessfully to interest Keefe into going to a transvestite bar: "You can't tell them from the genuine article," a line emphasizing the main theme of *Special Effects*.

Escaping from Keefe, Andrea arrives outside Neville's Greenwich Village residence and awaits admissions as a surveillance video camera views her from above. Andrea suffers several dominating male gazes throughout the film. Like Marion Crane in *Psycho*, her journey eventually leads her into a cinematic heart of darkness involving sex, violence, and death.

Inside, Andrea finally meets Neville. He looks intensively at footage of Oswald's assassination on a moviola. Neville inhabits an apartment decorated with rose imagery — a motif fascinating him because of its combination of beauty and death. Roses fade away very quickly after they bloom. They also have sharp thorns combining beauty and violence. The roses not only emphasize motifs in *Special Effects* but also recurring themes in Hitchcock's films. In *Shadow of a Doubt* (1943), Uncle Charlie's Philadelphia hotel room has rose-pattern wallpaper. His landlady wears a dress of similar design. Young Charlie's Santa Rosa room has the same wallpaper, a room that her uncle moves into after his arrival. *Psycho* also features rose-pattern wallpaper in Marion Crane's motel bedroom. Finally, rose thorns prick the fingers of both Neville and Keefe at different times in the film, revealing the two characters as symbiotic personalities.

Neville's introduction not only links themes of cinema and death, but also blurs conventional boundaries dividing manipulated entertainment and reality, and questions any individual's self-assured sense of identity. It is a dilemma affecting all the major characters in *Special Effects*. As Andrea expresses shock at the footage showing Oswald's assassination, Neville challenges her mode of perception, a challenge taken up by *Special Effects*:

ANDREA: "Jesus! That's real."

NEVILLE: "*What* made it real?"

ANDREA: "Because I know it happened."

NEVILLE: "Would you have known it if you hadn't seen it in the news?"

ANDREA: "That face. Nobody could fake it."

NEVILLE: "What makes it so different is that we believe it. What if there's no difference between real death and make-believe death?"

Andrea dons another role for Neville by masquerading as an N.Y.U. cinema student wishing to write a paper about his work. Seeing through her disguise, Neville auditions her for a performance in his particular type of theatrical feature. Like Sir John in *Murder!* (1930), Neville has a particular use for her, wishing to confine her within the lens of his imagination.[5] Neville attempts filming Andrea's audition in his bed by using a camera hidden behind a mirror. However, his intended victim hears the camera motor and immediately attacks her seducer's artistic and physical impotence, ironically falling back on her former identity as Mary Jean Waterman: "Jesus! You're just like the others ... I don't go that route. I'm a married woman... Why, you're really losing it. (She looks at his crotch while he looks away.) What happened to your *special effects?*" Enraged at his victim's recognition of his impotence, he scars her back with thorns from the rose on the bed, beats, and strangles her. Looking back on his accomplishment, he equates cinema with murder. "That's a take!"

At this point, the film changes direction. A caption — "Andrea. A film by Chris Neville" — appears on the screen, moving the diegesis from objective narration into a self-reflective, stylistic investigation. Viewers are now privy to Neville's cinematic construction of events. The murder and subsequent events are (what Hitchcock once said to Ingrid Bergman) "only a movie." Reality and imagination now merge.

After cleaning Andrea's body, Neville abandons it in her car amidst the desolate wintry landscape of Coney Island. Coney Island is both an amusement park and a location for *The Little Fugitive*, a narrative film using documentary shots of the actual environment. Cohen begins a shot by showing a sign, "Golden Fried Chicken" (paralleling the "Cold Meat" newspaper advertisement headlining the discovery of Annabella's body, which Richard Hannay reads about in the crofter's cottage in Hitchcock's *The 39 Steps*) before panning right to reveal Andrea's dead body. Her eyes are open like the dead Marion Crane's in *Psycho* while the windshield wipers move back and forth, recalling similar movements of wipers during Marion's rainy odyssey toward the Bates Motel.

Arrested by Detective Lt. Delroy (Kevin Conway) for Andrea's murder, Keefe duplicates his wife's earlier flight by going to Neville's apartment. He fails to meet Neville and is arrested again. Neville films the arrest from the top of his roof. Neville's high-angle camera perspective parallels the earlier image of Andrea shot by the video surveillance camera. Neville then bails Keefe out of jail, intending to use him in a 16mm low-budget recreation of Andrea's life and death. Like Hitchcock, Neville intends blurring boundaries between documentary reality and sadistic-voyeuristic fantasy by using Keefe "like cattle" in his own theatrical venture. However, Neville's practices are not exclusive to him alone. Virtually everyone in the film becomes seduced by the cinematic machine, even those aligned with supposedly secure social institutions such as law and order. Neville enlists high-profile lawyer Thomas Wiesenthal (Steven Pudenz) to facilitate Keefe's release. Mistaken by Keefe for Senator McCarthy's attorney, Roy Cohn, Wiesenthal hopes his involvement with Neville will lead to a future cinematic biography: "I want a movie to be made of my life one day." Nearly every character in *Special Effects* is movie-mad in one way or another, a condition leading to insanity, violence, and death.

Neville prefers to direct non-professionals in his intended movie *Andrea*. He describes his cinematic method as follows: "The idea is to make it real, as totally real as I can get it." After obtaining images of Andrea's murder on 400 feet of reversal film from lab technician Gruskin, he views it through the same moviola on which he earlier ran Oswald's assassination. Switching it off as Delroy arrives, he reveals his cinematic philosophy to the detective, one shared by Hitchcock and Larry Cohen but pursued in different production circumstances by both directors: "People assume special effects means taking models, miniatures, tricking them up, making them look real. I'm taking reality and making it look like make-believe. That's a special effect, too."

Whether fantasy, suspense, Hitchcock thriller, or horror film, all branches of cinema have a material base. While some deny this and plunge their audiences into an illusionary world of escapist entertainment, others suggest (and sometimes make explicit) that the boundaries are not as rigid as they appear.

After an unsuccessful casting session to find Andrea's replacement (one also featuring the dead woman's roommate, who earlier propositioned Keefe), the bereaved husband finds a body double in Elaine Bernstein (Zoe Tamerlis). When Elaine appears reluctant to play the new part, Keefe condescendingly takes over the director's role, using language he earlier used with Marjean/Andrea: "Can't you shut up and nod your head?" Neville completes the process by using his team of cosmeticians to transform her into the dead Andrea: "Don't take it seriously, kid. It's only a movie." As Elaine undergoes the process, Keefe phones his 18-month-old son in Oklahoma, promising eventually to bring back his mother. The camera circles around the phone booth in a 90-degree angle, emphasizing the mixture of self-illusion and deliberate lies contained within Keefe's conversation. Both Keefe and Neville are deeply trapped in an illusory cinematic world of patriarchal fantasy indelibly linked with dominance and violence.

If Keefe wishes the dead Marjean returned to her former role of submissive wife and mother, Neville theatrically pursues the implications of the murderous gaze to their logical conclusions. Like Tony Chappel in *In Broad Daylight* and the hubris-filled Sir John of *Murder!*, he theatrically performs a dual role as director and murderer. If Sir John bears an indirect responsibility for the suicidal execution of Handel Fane, Neville directly murders the gay, blackmailing lab technician Gruskin. Prior to performing his cinematic execution, Neville speaks to the camera. Deciding against using a flick-knife to stab his victim ("No. It's been done."), he chooses to strangle him with 35mm celluloid film while wearing editing gloves. After the performance, he applauds himself, substituting for the audience: "Now. That's fresh!" During another Neville performance in a restaurant overlooking a neon sign advertising *A Chorus Line*, Elaine comments: "You don't talk to people. You do routines." She later tells him, "You don't do things. You rehearse them."

As a dissatisfied Jewish American princess filling her time with "busy" daily routines, Elaine also seeks an identity. She is as bored with her weekly existence as Melanie Daniels is in *The Birds*. As Elaine becomes more identified with the role of Marjean/Andrea, she rebuts Keefe's criticisms concerning the "sick" nature of the process: "For the first time, I want to be somebody when I wake up in the morning." She sleeps with Keefe but then becomes alienated from him, just like the character she plays. Telling Neville that Keefe "wanted me to be like Mary Jean, not like Andrea," she reluctantly accepts Neville's invitation to sleep with him, unwittingly falling into the same trap as Andrea. Elaine has no firm identity: "Who am I? I used to be a number of people, none of whom I particularly liked." Like audiences attending the cinema to experience surrogate fantasies, identifying with the manufactured nature of stars and fabricated adventure, she slowly falls into Neville's trap. After she asks him, "Who are you inviting to bed?" he replies, "I want to mould a new personality. You're perfect raw material."

Unknown to her, Keefe destroyed Neville's original footage of Andrea's murder by running it through the same 16mm projector he used to show Marjean the home movie of their son. Keefe stole the wrong footage. Faced with the destruction of his key footage, Neville decides to recreate the event using Elaine as a literal body double for Marjean/Andrea. As he envisions the scenario, captions will fill the screen for scenes 193–212, which will depict Elaine's murder and Neville's accidental killing of Keefe as the "real" murderer. It resembles Sir John's diary prior to his interrogation of Fane in *Murder!* As in the earlier film, wishes will conflict with the reality of future events. Unlike Alfred Hitchcock, who could only use leading men such as Cary Grant, James Stewart, and Sean Connery as surrogates to realize his cinematic fantasies, Chris Neville intends to play the leading role.[6]

However, Neville fails to achieve his cinematic authorship. Aided by Elaine, Keefe accidentally electrocutes Neville in his indoor swimming pool. Keefe does not know a studio light has fallen into the pool he pushes Neville into. When power returns to the apartment after Elaine puts the fuses back, Neville's performance changes from leading man to deceased villain. Like Hitchcock, Neville plans in advance his own type of storyboards and screenplay. However, changed circumstances and sudden improvisation akin to independent cinema change the supposedly fixed nature of Neville's screenplay, which is constructed according to the classical Hollywood system. Unlike a major studio set, Neville's apartment allows no opportunity for any additional takes.

*Special Effects* concludes ironically and self-reflectively. As a news camera team interviews Detective Lt. Delroy, a caption evokes a documentary image by giving his identity to the audience. Although Delroy earlier became captivated by the filmmaking process, to the extent of drafting scenes, taking associate producer credit, and believing Neville's story about Keefe's supposed guilt, he tells the newsmen (among whom is Larry Cohen in an uncharacteristically Hitch-cockian cameo), "I always had a feeling about Neville." Delroy intends to complete the film Neville began. Unlike Frank in *Blackmail* who avidly views Scotland Yard movies such as "Fingerprints" to see if the director gets the facts wrong, Delroy belies that his "skill and insight and knowledge of police procedures" will make "one hell of a picture."

But, as he speaks to the camera, Keefe and Elaine run to catch their plane to Oklahoma. Keefe tells the attendant, "Our little boy is going to meet us at the airport." Elaine begins to fall into the role Marjean rejected: "I wonder if he'll recognize me. It's been so long." Keefe replies, "Don't worry about it. You look just like your picture." The camera then zooms in to a close-up of his dominating look before cutting to Elaine's face as she realizes her new entrapment. Before they rush to the plane, the attendant tells them that the flight has "a complimentary luncheon and a movie." The final captions roll: "The End." Then "A Philip Delroy Film" precedes the actual director's credit, "A Larry Cohen Production."

*Special Effects* is a remarkable achievement for Larry Cohen, deserving better distribution and critical recognition. By aiming to avoid certain dangerous processes of identification inherent in certain cinematic practices, the film attempts to stimulate viewers into objectively perceiving their operations. Thus, while Richard Combs sees Zoe Tamerlis as little "more than the faintest simulacrum of Novak in *Vertigo*," and recognizes that Cohen does not insist that "we participate in this fantasy like DePalma", he is mistaken in believing that *Special Effects* never analytically reveals how the desire for fantasy operates, as Hitchcock does.[7] The film demands that the audience stand back and analyze, thus avoiding the dangers of voyeuristic seduction inherent in some of DePalma's work, such as *Dressed to Kill* (1980). *Special Effects* is definitely a more analytical work, exposing processes of cinematic identification also present in Hitchcock's films by emphasizing them further, and revealing dangerous mechanisms of dominance present in entertainment and society itself. The malady is revealed. Like Hitchcock, Cohen functions as a critical surgeon. But the remedy is really in the hands of the audience, at least those alert enough to take notice.

# Parody and Satire

During the mid–1980s, Larry Cohen saw fundamental changes affecting the distribution of his films. The development of the new technologies of video, cable, and satellite television meant that his work was no longer limited to sporadic theatrical distribution. However, despite wider audiences gaining access to his films, the consequent lack of effective promotion and the loss of any possibility for guaranteed theatrical release meant further marginalization. Cohen found himself in a similar position affecting low-budget filmmakers during this decade. The growth of video made it possible for Cohen to continue directing small-scale movies that could make a profit on the video circuit. However, due to contemporary Hollywood's huge economic investment in multi-million dollar movies with lavish promotional budgets, corporate forces controlling the studios were less likely to take a chance on the type of work produced by Cohen and others that did not reflect a more standardized type of filmmaking. The 1980s included the virtual obliteration of the type of stimulating work produced by George A. Romero and others a decade before. Similar restraints affected the films of directors who remained working for the studios, including Francis Coppola, Wes Craven, Brian DePalma, and Tobe Hooper. Mind-numbing, spectacular special effects movies appeared, decimating the type of effective characterization and social interrogation characterizing achievements in cinema a decade before. As always, Cohen decided to remain independent, operating on low budgets, and producing several films continuing his satirical observations on American society. *Island of the Alive: It's Alive III* (1986), *A Return to Salem's Lot* (1987), and *Wicked Stepmother* (1988) represent several attempts in this vein. They analyze various facets of eighties American society, using the comic-strip visual style Cohen employed from *Bone* onwards. However, lacking effective theatrical exposure, Cohen's later work ended up in a video ghetto ignored by most critics.

Like Samuel Fuller, Larry Cohen prefers to work on a low budget, with a team of associates he feels at ease with. Looked at purely from the economic standpoint, he is often unfairly designated as a B-movie director. However, despite such elitist nuances associated with the label, cinema history demonstrates the superiority of many low-budget, modest films to their heavily advertised and bankable counterparts. Released theatrically as supporting features

186

during the classical era, audiences had an opportunity to see various alternative films made within the same Hollywood tradition as their A-movie counterparts. The same was true for low-budget films before megabuck studio productions began dominating theaters. But the proliferation of the video market and the lack of interest shown by most critics unwilling to explore its parameters led to a neglect of Cohen's later work. Many established critics are often too lazy to explore the diverse nature of various productions now released to video. Despite the quality of most of this work, certain films contain alternative perspectives absent from their more fortunate theatrical counterparts. If Cohen ever obtained the financing that kept *Waterworld* (1995) afloat, he could have directed some 84 features.

*Island of the Alive* and *A Return to Salem's Lot* were financed by Warner Bros. and intended for direct video distribution. Similarly, MGM saw *Wicked Stepmother*, featuring a star past her peak who no longer appealed to youthful audiences, as an ideal commodity for video stores with a Bette Davis section. Accommodating himself to the video market but shooting on 35mm, Cohen produced three different types of films. He also temporarily worked on *Deadly Illusion*, which did gain a brief theatrical release and the astonishing praise of reviewers normally hostile to his work, such as *New York Times* critic Vincent Canby. Although Cohen worked with his collaborator, director of photography Daniel Pearl, on *Deadly Illusion*, he appears to have intended to shoot a highly polished and professional film on a limited budget.[1] *Deadly Illusion* lacks Cohen's identifiable comic-strip characteristics. It is a private-eye movie with *film noir* undertones representing the director's attempt to change his style and produce a successful movie with the possibility of future sequels. But, like *I, the Jury*, the attempt proved disastrous.

However, the comic-strip style employed in *Island of the Alive*, *A Return to Salem's Lot*, and *Wicked Stepmother* represented a continuation of familiar visual characteristics already seen in *Bone*, *Black Caesar*, *Hell Up in Harlem*, *It's Alive*, *Full Moon High*, *The Private Files of J. Edgar Hoover*, and *Q*. These films also involve a combination of satirical insights and character types containing contradictory mixtures of humanity and complexity. Cohen's use of comic-strip technique owes less to the slavish pastiche formulas employed in self-styled postmodernist productions such as *Batman* (1989), *Batman Returns* (1993), *Batman Forever*, and *Judge Dredd* (both 1995), and more to a critically modernist investigation of social norms and practices. Unlike contemporary Hollywood's plundering of past generic legacies and appropriation of comic books for juvenile audiences, the marginalized cinema of Larry Cohen adopts what are supposedly identifiable formulas (such as black movies or horror films), both to question their conventions and investigate their presupposed ideological assumptions. Thus, like its predecessors, *Island of the Alive* challenges audiences to consider who the real monsters are: the physically normal or alienated physically abnormal. Similarly, *A Return to Salem's Lot* is less of a sequel to Stephen King's '*Salem's Lot* and more of a thematic demystification of ideologically generated Gothic overtones surrounding the work. Like an intuitive cinematic deconstructionist, Cohen tears away mystifying elements. But, unlike conservative deconstructionist schools, he aims, not at showing meaningless signifiers, but to reveal those hidden ideological agendas most works attempt to conceal. In many ways, Cohen's self-reflective investigations and parodic treatments represent the last remaining continuation of a generic revisionism and cultural critique formerly present in "New Hollywood" cinema of the '70s.[2] As Raymond Williams and others point out, the present cultural malaise results less from the death of modernism and the emergence of solipsistic post-modernist practices, but more from the fact that the modernist legacy still awaits further realization.[3] Larry Cohen's films represent one way of continuing this tradition. By adopting and transforming popular formulas, he applies a heterogenous mixture of self-reflective, modernist critical and political devices to his material, aiming to produce radical meanings questioning personal and social definitions of normality. Like an eighteenth-century satirist, he uses the graphic conventions of the comic strip as a means of achieving his particular vision. It is also a device with which Cohen raises certain issues questioning conservative norms within American society, which Hollywood cinema of the Reagan era and beyond conveniently ignores. The comic-strip format is never taken seriously by most censors and reviewers, thus making its use by Cohen all the more important.

  *Island of the Alive* continues exploring tensions raised in the earlier *It's Alive* films. It begins in an alienating New York street at night. A distraught taxi driver (Kevin O'Connor) runs up to a cop (John Woehrle) distributing parking tickets, upset that a vulnerable pregnant woman (Jill Gatsby) is giving birth in his cab. As Elayne Chaplin pertinently notes, neither man shows any real humanity towards her, even before discovering the mutant baby.[4] When the cop discovers it is "one of them," he pulls out his gun. The mother attempts to stop him from firing, a protective gesture anticipating Ellen's (Karen Black) final acceptance of her grandchild. Although the cop's bullets wound the baby and kill the mother, the actions do not save him or the taxi driver from death. Caring for his vehicle rather than a distraught human being, the taxi driver anticipates the character of Ellen's brutal boyfriend who attempts blackmailing her in Cape Vale, Florida. Ellen later throws up in his car. Prior to his justified homicide by one of the fully grown mutant babies, the selfish human screams in fury, "Look what she did to my car. I love my car."

  When Lt. Perkins (James Dixon) arrives, he traces the wounded baby's blood trail to a Catholic church. He discovers that his now-dead quarry has performed an identifiable human action by baptizing itself before death. Realizing this, Perkins crosses himself before the baptismal font. This pre-credits sequence closes with a shot of a stained glass window depicting a baby as a heavenly angel, subtly suggesting the positive human qualities concealed within the mutant child's inhuman body. The film continues to develop parallels between humans and mutants, often to the former's disadvantage. Furthermore, unlike the previous *It's Alive* films, no ambiguity surrounds the violent acts of the babies. They clearly act in self-defense whenever human antagonists act violently toward them or invade their territory.

Defining humanity is a key theme in Larry Cohen's work. Both *Island of the Alive* and *A Return to Salem's Lot* attempt seriously to explore this issue, which most critics choose to ignore, due to prejudices against the visual comic-strip style Cohen employs. But, as with *The Private Files of J. Edgar Hoover*, style is inherently linked to content, particularly one having serious connotations. In the earlier film, social, familial, and political circumstances resulted in the FBI director becoming a monster used and abused in the service of the state. But Cohen's direction of Broderick Crawford as Hoover never became one-dimensional. A frustrated human being always lurked beneath Hoover's oppressive exterior. Hoover's other side often emerged in poignant situations such as the director's awkward attempt to reach out to his favorite waiter at the Stork Club and the ambiguous nature of his relationship with Clyde Tolson. Although the infants of *Island of the Alive* are less human in form than Hoover, they parallel his situation in being victims of an unjust society. Cohen may employ the form of a comic strip to typify or abstract his characters to represent them as creatures of society. But he never dehumanizes them. On the contrary, he makes his types fully human, complex, and capable of generating audience involvement and sympathy.

The post-credits sequence of *Island of the Alive* begins in a courtroom. Attorneys argue over whether the surviving mutant babies have any claim to be regarded as human. The scene introduces us to Stephen Jarvis (Michael Moriarty), a character whose humanity comes under question throughout the course of the film, either by himself or others. Designated as a freak by Florida prostitute Sally (Laurene Landon), rejected by his former wife, Ellen, and exploited by the legal and medical establishment, Stephen's reactions to his alienating, normal society take a defensively bizarre, comedic form. His madcap activities parallel the defensive violence performed by the mutant offspring. Like his son, Stephen soon finds himself used and abused by an uncaring society. While Stephen is forced to become a best-selling author to pay his huge legal bills, the mutant children become similarly exploited by the legal ruling of Judge Watson (McDonald Carey). Although his decision exiling them to an isolated island appears benevolent, we later discover that the environment recently experienced nuclear tests. Furthermore, the government secretly supports the scientific expedition Stephen later accompanies, since it wishes to find out whether the mutants have survived radiation on the island. During the fifties and sixties, both the American and British governments carried out secret radiation tests on unsuspecting human subjects for the same purpose. Even if Judge Watson grants the mutant babies a reprieve from the death sentence the state secretly executes against them[5], the nature of their stay of execution has ironic overtones. Dumped on a radioactive island, the babies find themselves in a situation similar to those other aliens used in Dr. Mengele's infamous medical experiments during World War II, and the unwitting subjects of government radiation experiments in Britain and America during the postwar era. The latter victims were usually members of working-class or ethnic groups conveniently designated as "others."

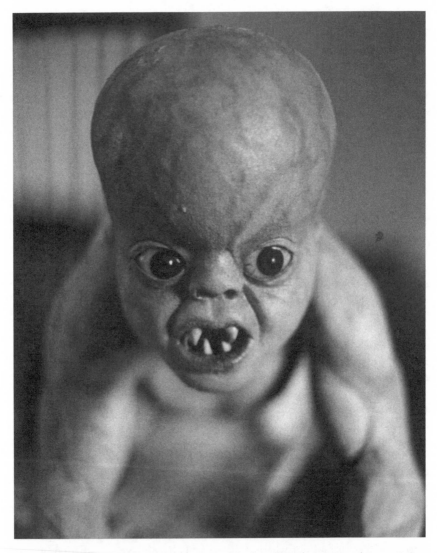

The mutant baby representing a new world of gods and monsters haunts Larry Cohen's trilogy, *It's Alive, It Lives Again*, and *Island of the Alive: It's Alive III* (courtesy of Larry Cohen).

By writing a best seller to pay his legal bills and fulfill contractual obligations to his lawyer, Stephen is exploited by the system. When first faced with this dilemma after hearing that public appeals for funding have failed because he is not a "popular cause," Stephen begins his extremist protective humor. He signs an autograph book as "Father of the Monster" and begins telling tasteless "Baby Jarvis" jokes. The following scenes show Stephen gazing into a bookseller's window, where his autobiographical confession is on sale. He imagines himself talking to his own baby, similar to a happy father looking at his child after delivery. His position resembles those of the expectant fathers in *Daddy's Gone A-Hunting* and *It's Alive*. But, like Dwight Webb, Jr., in *The Private Files of J. Edgar Hoover*, Stephen knows he has compromised himself, and confesses his guilt (off camera) to a son he has exploited for money due to his entrapment by the system. His dilemma resembles the legal system's exploitation of Katie Sullivan in *Maniac Cop 3: Badge of Silence* (1992). Whenever possible, the lawyers in both films eagerly distort the truth to gain residuals for future book, film, and television rights.

The next scene shows Ellen reading Stephen's sensationalist autobiography and tossing it into the fire, commenting, "Lies! Lies!" She also becomes a victim of the system. Leaving Stephen and changing her identity, she finds herself sharing Jody Scott's predicament in *It Lives Again* when she learns her own mother revealed her whereabouts to her former husband. After undergoing sterilization as an extreme reaction to her situation as "Mother of the Monster," she attempts a new surrogate family life with an older man and his children until her identity becomes known. Dropped by her former family, she falls into a relationship with an abusive blackmailing boyfriend until she finally escapes, condemning him as a "ridiculous human being" more concerned about his car than her emotional situation. Isolated from society, like Stephen, she finds the only option she has is low-income employment as a waitress in the increasingly ugly environment of Cape Vale, Florida. While Stephen resorts to bizarre defensive comedy, Ellen's protective device involves a hysterical overreaction against both her former husband and abusive boyfriend.

The supreme example of the system's arbitrary use of alienating labels that separate normal from abnormal in *Island of the Alive* occurs in Stephen's encounter with the Cubans. After he has left the mutants' island environment, Stephen is rescued by inhabitants of another island that his society deems equally monstrous and alien. Suspected of being a CIA agent, Stephen finds himself in Cuban territory on the way to interrogation. Like the pregnant women in the *It's Alive* films, he finds himself strapped to a hospital gurney, accompanied by Cuban soldiers who refuse to believe his protestations of innocence. His situation echoes those of Lenore and Jody, who both face the alienating attentions of an inhumane hospital system in *It's Alive* and *It Lives Again*. However, in Stephen's case, he finds that satellite inhabitants of Reagan's Evil Empire prove far more sympathetic than his fellow Americans. The Cubans actually help Stephen return to Florida. Their final dialogue is particularly revealing:

STEPHEN: "Why are you doing this?"
CUBAN: "Haven't you heard? We're human beings."
STEPHEN: "You know, some people might want to know about that."
SECOND CUBAN: "No, they wouldn't."

A Cuban hands Stephen a Russian-made weapon and jokes about the incongruity of a Cuban arming an American. But his parting words reveal a generosity of spirit far exceeding that of most other Americans in the film: "Good luck with your kid. Maybe you don't have to shoot him." Despite its comic-book style and bizarre plot, *Island of the Alive* is a film containing far more important ideas than most studio-supported, multimillion-dollar counterparts.

An overhead camera shot introduces the post-credits courtroom sequence. The position duplicates overhead camera angles opening *Deadly Illusion, A Return to Salem's Lot, Wicked Stepmother, The Ambulance,* and *As Good as Dead,* dwarfing the mundane world of normality into insignificance. Viewing Judge Watson looking at a photo of mutant babies presented by Ralston (Gerrit Graham), the camera makes a 360-degree overhead movement before craning back to reveal the rest of the courtroom. As Elayne Chaplin notes, *Island of the Alive* differs from its predecessors in depicting the father as defender of the babies and the parent who has to convince the mother to accept them.[6] Unlike Frank Davies and Gene Scott, Stephen belongs to a lower socioeconomic group in American society. As a struggling actor relegated to walk-on roles in commercials for the past 14 years, he lacks the masculine self-assuredness associated with either successful advertising executives or lawyers. Stephen's very career in the acting profession has possibly led him to understand the arbitrary nature of any stereotyped definitions. He finds himself on an unexpected world stage, playing a role he never thought he would perform.

Seeking legal authority to destroy the babies, Ralston attempts to demonstrate to the court that Stephen fears his own son. His lawyer warns him, "If he can show the people you're afraid of your own son, then he's through." Stephen replies, "I don't want him to die, but I'm scared shitless of him." Despite his fears, Stephen goes to the cage containing his son and attempts to comfort him. When Ralston orders the police to drag Stephen away, the baby breaks out of his cage and jumps on to Judge Watson's desk. Stephen appeals to the courtroom: "He's just a baby and he's trying to defend himself... How would you feel if you were born into a world which wants you dead. He's just a baby... There must be a place on earth where they won't hurt him and where he won't hurt them."

Stephen succeeds in his appeal. But the system decides to use the babies as guinea pigs to test the effects of radiation. Meanwhile, Stephen is as socially alienated as the mutant babies. He now becomes regarded as a monster. Ellen rejects him in the Boat House, the Cape Vale nightclub where she works as a waitress. In the background, two nightclub comedians (one of whom singles Stephen out when he arrives) perform comic routines about family alienation and the weird nature of contemporary adolescents. Seeking solace with Florida happy hooker Sally, Stephen finds her rejecting him as a "freak" when she discovers his real identity. As his social alienation and exploitation increase, Stephen begins to act more abnormally, transferring frustration into aggressive humor. On the boat trip to the island, he performs a rousing rendition of "Over the Sea to Skye" for his seasick companions. He takes pleasure in humorously baiting Dr. Brewster (Neal

Israel) and Dr. Morrell (Ann Dane) during the expedition. But, as Elayne Chaplin notes, Stephen's behavior results both from his social alienation and a deep desire to protect the mutant children. As he says on the island, "Kids love clowns." He also attempts warning them about the "assholes" from the courtroom. Stephen's actions also represent an extreme version of the behavior exhibited by the unhappy comedian in Cohen's earlier teleplay "The Golden Thirty," who also uses humor as a form of aggression. By picking out Stephen as he enters the Boat House, one comedian performs the type of aggressive humor used by British comedians Bernard Manning, Foo Foo Lamarr, and their American counterparts who seek unfortunate victims to subject to offensive comic routines.

When Stephen returns to Cape Vale, he finds it a much more violent place than before. In many ways, it is little different from the mutant island, with one major exception. The mutants violently react against hostile invaders. When Sally first attempted to pick up Stephen, she remarked, "The kids are taking over this place." On his return, Stephen finds the kids have grown up into violent counterparts of the mutant children. However, they are far more dangerous, engaging in aggressive activities and gang rape on vulnerable humans. The Boat House has now turned into a violent punk-rock playground. Ironically, a mutant saves a girl from gang rape and attempts to comfort her. The police arrive and kill it, only to find that they will have to undergo a quarantine similar to other main characters in the film. Whether mutant children or human parent, society forces those infected with any dangerous virus (biological or ideological) to undergo isolation from normal society.

However, even isolation is not enough for society. Earlier, the mutants' island sanctuary underwent assault by pharmaceutical executives. Led by Cabot (William Watson), a figure paralleling the unnamed executive played by Robert Emhardt in *It's Alive*, the group wishes to eliminate any incriminating evidence linking their pregnancy drug to the mutant babies. Like Fletcher (Patrick O'Neal) and Evans (Alexander Scourby) in *The Stuff*, Cabot wishes to launch the drug back onto the market under a new name. But the babies wipe out the invaders. The later scientific expedition led by Dr. Swenson (Art Lund) tricks Stephen and Lt. Perkins into accompanying them on the understanding that they only intend obtaining blood samples and fluid from a drugged baby. However, Stephen discovers that Swenson wishes to capture a live baby for dissection so that the government may learn whether humans can survive nuclear explosions.

Like the babies, both Stephen and Lt. Perkins find themselves used and abused by the system. Perkins attempts using Cabot's expensive suntan lotion on the trip, only to find it ineffective and possibly dangerous to his skin. The scientific expedition really represents the legitimate realm of government violence complementing the "illegitimate" assault attempted by Cabot. Stephen eventually realizes this and attempts warning the mutants. Challenged by one of Swenson's team, "Are you siding with them against the human race?" he responds, "We should never have come here." The babies deal with their aggressors, meeting violence with violence, leaving Stephen and Lt. Perkins as sole survivors of the expedition. They take over the boat and travel to Cape Vale for some mysterious purpose. While Stephen's son throws him overboard to save him from the other mutants, Lt. Perkins finds himself a human castaway on the island reserved as a quarantine area for the inhuman mutants.

*Island of the Alive* moves toward a positive conclusion by breaking down ideological barriers separating normal from abnormal. This time, the mother has to accept her offspring. If Stephen copes with his personal dilemma by displaying bizarre forms of behavior, Ellen subjects herself to a fall into patriarchal exploitation and abuse by older and younger men. Both Stephen and Ellen eventually realize that normal society will never accept them. While Stephen eventually understands the illusory nature of any line dividing normality from abnormality, a line finally destroyed by his experiences in Cuba, Ellen moves toward her own form of self-discovery by undergoing a nightmare version of her original birth trauma. Awakening from this frightening dream after escaping from her abusive boyfriend, Ellen again confronts the implications of a situation she has refused to face. Captured by the mutants, she is challenged to accept her child and her grandchild. When Stephen finally reaches her on the motel roof, she hesitates about accepting something she rejected as alien and abnormal. Stephen tells her that the mutants traveled to Cape Vale personally to deliver their child to her. Realizing the implications, she reaches the stage of acceptance formerly attained by Frank Davies and Gene Scott in *It's Alive* and *It Lives Again*: "I hurt you... But I'll love him, I promise."

The surviving mutants are dying from measles, perhaps brought to the island by one of the many aggressive human visitors they faced during their five-year exile. Realizing that society has no place for them, the newly reconstituted Jarvis family steals a car and light out for some undefined territory. Although alienated from normality, like the mutants, Stephen and Ellen arrive at a closer form of understanding. Lacking money and suitable clothing, they drive away in darkness toward some unknown future. Like the climax of *Washington Heights*, *Island of the Alive* ends positively, with the characters fully aware of the precarious nature of any future awaiting them. As Stephen and Ellen laugh about this uncertainty, their grandchild releases a contented burp. Normal and abnormal now have the potential of defining themselves as a new family unit outside the aggressive boundaries of a corrupt and decaying social order.

*A Return to Salem's Lot* also explores the theme of becoming a real human being. Co-written by Larry Cohen and James Dixon, the screenplay satirically reworks ideas present in Stephen King's *'Salem's Lot*. Before executives decided to make it as a television movie directed by Tobe Hooper, Cohen wrote one of the many screenplays for a proposed theatrical feature. The only idea from his original screenplay to survive in the television version is Barlow's resemblance to Murnau's vampire in *Nosferatu* (1922). It also survives in Judge Axel's actual vampire persona during several scenes in *A Return to Salem's Lot*. As with *Island of the Alive*, Warner Bros. offered Cohen another opportunity to direct a film designed for the video market, which he immediately seized. *A Return to Salem's Lot* was

Cohen's last film with Michael Moriarty, since both decided they had reached the end of their creative collaboration after four films together. However, the film also features a key figure who embodied the type of radical, iconoclastic, low-budget cinema that indirectly influenced Larry Cohen: director Samuel Fuller, in the role of Dutch-Rumanian Jewish Nazi hunter Dr. Van Meer. Fuller often steals the film from Moriarty, his character resembling those feisty old men portrayed by actors such as Sam Levene in *God Told Me To* and Red Buttons in *The Ambulance.*

Like *Island of the Alive, A Return to Salem's Lot* was filmed in a simple comic-strip style that belies the satirical thrust of its ideas. The film represents Cohen's version of Thornton Wilder's *Our Town*, a reference made explicit when a vampire threatens a group of youngsters: "Are you making fun of *our* town?" Coincidentally, Thornton Wilder also collaborated with Alfred Hitchcock on *Shadow of a Doubt* (1943), a film whose opening scenes depict Joseph Cotten's Uncle Charlie with shadow imagery reminiscent of a vampire film. Like *Shadow of a Doubt*, Cohen's *A Return to Salem's Lot* represents an exploration of the dark side of the American Dream, one involving the oppressive effects of business, consumerism, and family restraint on individual expression. Although the title appears to be a sequel to Stephen King's '*Salem's Lot*, the only connection is the location. While King's novel and the television version stressed Gothic imagery, Cohen's film subordinates the monstrous elements and emphasizes the material nature of a society affecting vampires and human beings.

*A Return to Salem's Lot* opens with a deceptively tranquil scene. The camera reveals a river surrounded by luxuriant palm trees in some unknown South American jungle. But violence lurks beneath this beautiful landscape. The camera moves toward the right, ascending to an overhead position revealing a grotesque sacrificial ritual. As the camera moves away from the river, the sounds of the ceremony occur on the soundtrack. This initially deceptive appearance concealing violent activities anticipates the viewer's introduction to a seemingly calm New England landscape that later hides bloodthirsty activities.

A high priest paints religious symbols on the victim's chest prior to carving out the heart. The camera then cranes to reveal Joe Weber (Michael Moriarty) dispassionately filming the ritual with his movie camera. His assistant expresses apprehension about the bloody ritual. Preventing him from interfering in the ceremony, Joe coolly explains that the ceremony is not a fertility rite, but the socially sanctioned execution of a sexual offender. The ritual is "their society, their rules. How would they feel looking at our gas chambers in San Quentin?" Like cold-blooded news reporter Wallace Barrows in *Motive,* Joe shows no emotion as he views the bloody ritual. As Joe continues filming, his partner exclaims, "You're a cold-blooded son of a bitch. You're not even human." When a police boat arrives and disrupts the ceremony, Joe harangues the unwelcome visitors for ruining his anthropological research until he learns they have news of an emergency involving his son in America. Noting the change in Joe's attitude, his partner comments sarcastically, "Well, well. The son of a bitch is human after all."

This opening sequence economically introduces the major theme of *A Return to Salem's Lot*. Rather than being a typical vampire movie, the film is really about Joe's personal odyssey toward human involvement and his movement away from a cold, inhumane, "organization man" attitude toward people. Like other Cohen characters, he soon confronts the real forces in his society that motivate his behavior, forces allegorically represented as vampires but undeniably civilized in their motivations and behavior. Initially articulating glib cultural relativist, discursive arguments to his alienated partner, Joe soon discovers the value of taking sides and arrives at a true understanding of humanity, overruling artificial cultural barriers and the ideological values of his own society. *A Return to Salem's Lot* again reveals the universal dimensions of Cohen's vision, a vision transcending the stylistic, generic, and cultural patterns of his own tradition. Again, he uses comic-strip imagery to deliver another radical attack on dehumanized aspects of the American Dream championed in Reagan's America, where people feed off each other in more ways than one. Larry Cohen's vampires in *A Return to Salem's Lot* are equivalent to the zombies in George Romero's trilogy, *Night of the Living Dead* (1968), *Dawn of the Dead* (1979), and *Day of the Dead* (1985). These monsters are recognizably the products of a symbolically cannibalistic, capitalist society.

Joe later discovers that the personal realm is actually political, and intervention is necessary against any form of oppression. He intuitively recognizes this when he reacts to his partner's jibe about his son ("I hope he's nothing like you, Jack") by punching him in the eye. Although he has abandoned his son to his ex-wife and concentrated on his career, he still feels some concern. When Joe arrives in New York, he discovers that his divorced wife, Sally (Ronee Blakely), cannot handle their maladjusted 12-year-old son, Jeremy (Ricky Addison Reed), and has decided to dump the responsibility on him. Confronting Joe with a choice between parental custody or Jeremy's commitment to a mental hospital, she leaves father and son together after an absence of several years. Joe decides to take his streetwise, uncommonly mature son to the only place where he ever experienced a brief moment of happiness when he was 14 years old: the New England town of Salem's Lot. At this juncture, Joe and Jeremy exist in a state of mutual antagonism very similar to that shared by the parents and children in the *It's Alive* films. However, like *Island of the Alive*, *A Return to Salem's Lot* also moves toward reuniting the family unit in a new form of relationship beyond socially acceptable ideological norms.

As they drive toward Salem's Lot, Joe tells Jeremy about his brief liaison with 17-year-old Cathy before his Aunt Clara discovered the relationship and sent him away. They find Salem's Lot deserted by day, except for the slow-witted Clarence (Brad Rijn) and his wife, Sarah (Georgia Janelle Webb). Clarence operates a run-down garage above which hangs a sign advertising "Worms and Crawlers." It announces the status of these people whom the hierarchical Salem's Lot vampire community designate as "drones," paralleling the Old Testament designation of conquered races as "hewers of wood and drawers of water"—a Biblical term also used to justify slavery in the pre–Civil War era. An American flag conspicuously appears in the background. Although briefly appearing in the film, its presence is no less ominous than its other significantly brief, but pertinent, appearances in other Cohen films such as *Black Caesar, Hell Up in Harlem, God Told Me To*, and *The Stuff.* "Old Glory" represents the emblem of a system used to oppress others. The "Worms and Crawlers" sign also articulates the "death in life" existence Clarence occupies as a human "drone" bred by the vampire community to serve its needs. During these early scenes, Cohen inserts several shots of cattle and sheep, hinting at the ways in which the vampires regard their human servants. As Hitchcock once described actors as cattle, the Salem's Lot drones find themselves viewed in similar ways by their masters. The vampire community breed cattle and feed on their blood to avoid human diseases such as alcoholism, hepatitis, and AIDS.

Although Salem's Lot is in New England, the town resembles a pre–Civil War, rural Southern community organized along strict class, gender and racial lines. The drones resemble pre–Civil War African-American slaves. Clarence's very name is more appropriate for an African-American than for a white man. During the later classroom scene, a vampire child articulates the status of drones in their society: "We breed them for service like we breed cattle for blood." Like another drone, Constable Rains (James Dixon), Clarence passively submits to any form of aggression exercised upon him by his masters. When Joe knocks Clarence to the ground, the latter passively replies, "It's O.K. to hit us drones. That's what we're here for." Although Rains is the grandson of Judge Axel (Andrew Duggan), he tells Joe that Axel treats him "like shit." Both Clarence and Rains resemble plantation slaves fathered and abused by their white masters.

Joe later discovers the strict hierarchical nature of the Salem's Lot vampire community. As subjects of Judge Axel, the predominantly rural community follows traditional family values. The men rule the women and children who dress in traditionally acceptable clothing. Women wear unattractive print dresses like their counterparts in patriarchally governed fundamentalist cults. Boys wear white shirts, ties, and long trousers, and the girls wear demurely feminine short dresses. Whether vampires or drones, the Salem's Lot women wear unattractive, printed cotton dresses resembling the one worn by the rural wife in the well-known "American Gothic" painting by Grant Wood, the most reproduced artifact in American culture. When Jeremy becomes infected by the community, he ceases to wear the casual clothes Joe bought for him and accommodates himself to the Salem's Lot dress code, one resembling the inappropriate, adult-like designer suit Sally made him wear. On their first date, Amanda (Tara Reid) takes him to a wedding ceremony. The prepubescent bride and groom eagerly accommodate themselves to traditional patriarchal values of religion and monogamy. During the evening school sessions, the vampire children begin class by citing the pledge of allegiance to the American flag, an unconstitutional custom that conservatives again wish to make mandatory in the United States. The Salem's Lot schoolchildren receive a one-sided education inversely resembling the type of learning that right-wing groups are attempting to introduce into American schools. It is an education dividing society up into opposing groups of humans and vampires. As Joe humorously remarks to Jeremy while they listen to the historically biased lesson about the Spanish Inquisition, "Three hundred years of this! Guess they don't have sex education?" Salem's Lot is an idyllic conservative community dominated by the type of traditional family values espoused during the Reagan era and beyond.

Salem's Lot wants to represent itself to the outside world as a civilized community wishing to disavow bad publicity originating from its vampire image. Judge Axel attempts to persuade Joe that the community prefers dining on animal blood, with cattle often resembling humans during blood transfusion sessions. Cohen's satirical digs against hospitals again appear, as in *It's Alive, It Lives Again, Maniac Cop 3: Badge of Silence*, and *As Good as Dead*. The cattle are never slaughtered, but kept alive to build up their blood. Humans are supposedly reserved for special occasions "in memory of past events." However, Mrs. Axel (Evelyn Keyes) conceals her grin from Joe during her husband's explanation, recognizing the lie beneath his propaganda. The brutal deaths of adolescent punks, sole survivor Sherry (Jill Gatsby), the tramps, and occupants of the bus diverted into Salem's Lot show that the vampire community is as violent as its normal counterpart.

Axel attempts to seduce Joe into writing propaganda for Salem's Lot, using the same type of relativist arguments Joe used at the beginning of the film: "You've seen more than most people. You've traveled through a world of starvation, war, and killing for profit. Do you think that world is any better than ours?" He wants Joe to become the community's official historian by writing a Bible about them. Joe's qualifications as a "professional anthropologist" and "true chronicler of information" impartially documenting the customs of other cultures make him an appropriate choice. However, although Judge Axel initially wants Joe to write a "history," he then changes the project to a "Bible," an object representing a work of faith, whether true or not. Joe's proposed "Bible" will obviously be as biased as the Spanish Inquisition lesson Joe listened to in the classroom, one using facts selectively to demonstrate the "brutality of man," a lesson he dismisses as "bullshit" and "anti-human propaganda." Judge Axel intends this "Bible" to appear 500 years later, when the mists of time veil the true nature of Salem's Lot. As he tells Joe, "You could change the way outsiders feel about us — for ever." Judge Axel has the same goals as his fellow conservatives in the Reagan era and beyond who attempted to demonize the sixties, changing the traumatic event of the Vietnam War into a "noble crusade" and converting Richard Nixon's Watergate persona into a revered "great statesman." Joe's role in the community is resident revisionist historian. He is to perform the same type of whitewashing function as right-wing historians and teachers undertake when they deny the violent nature of American society throughout the ages.

Axel attempts seducing both Joe and Jeremy ideologically and sexually. While Axel uses Amanda as Jeremy's playmate, he employs Joe's former 17-year-old sweetheart, Cathy (Katja Crosby), as a vampire seductress, leading Joe back into a macabre version of the family life he sought escape from. Cathy represents another version of Alicia Huberman in Hitchcock's *Notorious*, with Judge Axel performing the function of Prestcott (Louis Calhern). But, unlike her earlier counterpart, she performs her service for the Salem's Lot community willingly. When Cathy later announces her pregnancy, Joe becomes trapped by the sexual and ideological world of Salem's Lot. Characteristically, Cathy now appears less seductive and more conservatively maternal after performing her socially sanctioned sexual role. Her hair is drawn back and she wears the traditional drab female costume of Salem's Lot. In one scene, she appears together with Amanda, silently instructing her younger counterpart to seduce Jeremy.

Jeremy sees his future role in Salem's Lot as seductively using a child's body containing a cunning and mature vampire mind to trap future human victims. He is in danger of becoming a deadly substance like the Stuff, an artifact combining an external normal appearance with hidden, deadly internal qualities. His comments to Joe reveal that he is becoming a slavish clone like Clarence. Jeremy's remarks also anticipate the Salem's Lot future for Joe's drone son: "I'll *serve* better in the image of a child." Father and son eventually understand how Salem's Lot has seduced them in different ways. However, by agreeing to write their Bible, Joe regards himself as more blameworthy: "I'm the ultimate asshole writing their Bible."

Joe discovers that the vampire community is as American as Old Glory in Clarence's garage. Axel tells Joe that "the oldest and most despised race" now exists in America and not in any "Slavic, distant country." He also tells his intended victim that the community fulfills conservative ideals of the American way of life: "We're very wealthy people. Can you imagine how rich you'd be if you got to live three hundred years? Real estate. Property in Maine and New Hampshire. Vampire life and financial security go together."

Despite Axel's benevolent appearance, Joe discovers that the patriarch has a "real face" that emerges whenever he is angry. Although Axel hopes that Joe will sell out, love the vampire community, give his soul willingly, and become his successor, he also tells his wife, "If not, I'll send his soul straight to hell." He is the archetypal business executive concealing violence beneath a smiling face. Axel's real persona finally appears when he confronts Joe in the stable after his chosen successor has set Salem's Lot on fire. The audience now realizes that the enigmatic, grotesque vampire figure appearing intermittently throughout the film is actually Axel. Angered at Joe's attack on the community, he utters, "You angered me. You made me show my true face," which applies to contemporary America as well as himself. It is an America responsible for the deaths of millions throughout its entire history, whether Native Americans, Blacks, dissenters, and innocent Iraqi civilians and conscripts in a Gulf War that occurred a few years after this film was released. Joe and Jeremy initially prove powerless against Axel's physical strength until Joe uses an American flagpole to impale him. As Axel expires and decays, he clutches at Old Glory, the symbol of all the values he espoused throughout his centuries-long reign over Salem's Lot. This meaning emerges during a climactic action sequence whose significance Cohen understates. This represents another example of his implicit, non-flamboyant style aimed at stimulating audience members to discern the implications of the material.

Unlike the original novel and television version, *A Return to Salem's Lot* reveals the vampire community as recognizably American, a community whose values reflect those of their adopted country. As Joe learns in the classroom, the vampires are alter egos of the Pilgrim fathers who fled in the Mayflower to escape persecution. However, the vampire ship *Speedwell* did not perish at sea, but arrived safely at their New England destination in 1620. A vampire child tells the teacher, "We lit out on our own, like Roger Williams did for Rhode Island," the verb paralleling Mark Twain's final description of Huck Finn's desire to "light out for the territory." Like their fictional and real-life American counterparts, the vampire community achieves the American Dream of financial security. But it is one dependent upon exploitation bleeding dry humans as well as animals.

Recognizing this, becoming involved, and fighting back against supernatural and capitalist forces of darkness, Joe becomes fully reunited with Jeremy. The father enters into a new relationship with a son in danger of becoming a monster. But, formerly, Joe was a dehumanized social monster functioning as an ideal unit in the world he belonged to. *A Return to Salem's Lot* thus develops several motifs seen in *It's Alive*. Joe achieves a newfound unity with his monster son that Frank Davies only temporarily realized. Like Frank, Joe acted like a monster in his own civilized world. But in Joe's case, the outcome is much more positive. He also turns into a real "human being" and survives. Aided by Van Meer, Joe impales vampires by day. They set Salem's Lot aflame, making the vampire's traditional escape to their coffins impossible. The dawn's "early light" incinerates any surviving vampires. Rescued by Van Meer, Joe and Jeremy leave Salem's Lot. Van Meer helps Joe become a father.[8] He educates Jeremy to understand the real nature of the vampire community he sought to join by making him look directly at the vampire attack on helpless bus passengers. Like the trio at the end of *Island of the Alive*, Joe, Jeremy, and Van Meer represent an alternative family whose relationship is based upon equality and respect, and not any hierarchical servility characterizing the patriarchal structure of Salem's Lot. Admiring Van Meer's resourcefulness, Jeremy comments, "Maybe growing old is not so bad." Van Meer sees a change in Joe's character: "I think you're becoming a human being." However, Cohen reserves the last two scenes for other former victims of Salem's Lot. As the bus drives past, the audience sees a herd of cattle grazing peacefully for the first time in the film. The scene then cuts to a medium shot of cows in a meadow before the film ends with one cow uttering a contented "moo" on the soundtrack. This parallels the peaceful "burp" of Steven and Ellen's grandchild concluding *Island of the Alive*. It is a very positive note on which to end the film. Cohen emphasizes that liberation from oppression involves animals as well as humans. Both are victims of a vicious system preying upon their lifeblood. Larry Cohen has intuitively made a film arguing for animal, as well as human, liberation.

*Deadly Illusion* (1987) is an interesting example of a film whose final realization betrayed the original ideas behind its conception. In traditional authorship studies, a film is regarded as totally the result of the director's personal vision. Despite attempts to remove the director completely from the film process by academics influenced by the "death of the author" theory, personal authorship is still viable, assuming that collaborative involvement, industrial factors, generic changes, historical situations and ideological issues are also relevant. The same is true of a compromised work ruined by producer interference. But it is often valuable to examine how compromises alter meanings in a completed film.

Today, it is rare for any major film to remain unaffected by corporate and economic forces determining its production. The same is true for "bad decisions" affecting a film's final version. *Deadly Illusion* is one example. Although Cohen left the project following disagreements with producers who then hired William Tannen to direct the remaining sequences from an altered screenplay, *Deadly Illusion* is worth examining. It is a typical example of what directors face in a world where producers, market researchers, and accountants believe that they are the real authors.

Although he regards the film as disappointing, *Deadly Illusion* does contain several Cohen features. The director's trademark appears in certain scenes and dialogue. An overhead camera cranes over people in a license bureau (including the film's hero) during the film's opening shot. It dwarfs them all into insignificance. This movement parallels the overhead courtroom shot following the credit sequences in *Island of the Alive*. A shot tracking to the right then follows. It features the various frustrated customers. They all deliver various lines giving us immediate, sometimes humorous, insights into their characters. A gay male comments, "Just because I'm gay doesn't mean I can't shoot straight." It is a characteristically humorous Larry Cohen line. After Hamberger (Billy Dee Williams) shoots a violent and demented customer (played by the late, great Joe Spinell), credit sequences appear, showing him warmly greeting and shaking hands with several New Yorkers (shot from a hidden camera). These scenes form a vivacious and lively contrast to the rest of the film. Significantly, Cohen's writer credit appears on the screen as Hamberger walks in front of a poster reading, "I Love New York." Cohen did not shoot the Shea Stadium battle, nor the clumsy ending and the first meeting between Hamberger and Sharon Burton (Morgan Fairchild). *Deadly Illusions* exhibits several dead spots and script flaws uncharacteristic of Cohen. Although his fascination with the double theme is long-standing, the final version's inclusion of Morgan Fairchild as both Sharon Burton and Jane Mallory not only gives away the plot too early in the film, but also destroys interesting nuances in the original screenplay.

Like *I, the Jury*, *Deadly Illusion* appears to have been an attempt to create a series of films about a black private eye modeled on Dashiell Hammett's Nick Charles in *The Thin Man*.[9] The film also uses the voice-over characteristic of the private-eye tradition in *film noir*. Admired by his sophisticated girlfriend, Rina (Vanity), Hamberger uses a coffee shop as his office. A wealthy businessman

**Larry Cohen on the set of *Deadly Illusion* (1987) discussing a future scene with Billy Dee Williams and Morgan Fairchild (courtesy of Larry Cohen).**

named Burton (Dennis Hallahan) employs him to murder his wife. Hamberger takes the $25,000 down payment and travels out of town to warn the woman (Morgan Fairchild). She seduces him and he drives her to the airport. However, on returning to New York, he discovers that he is suspected of the woman's murder. At the morgue, Hamberger learns that he has been set up, since the murdered woman is unknown to him. He begins a pursuit of the real killers, to clear his name and find connections between beauty cosmetician Jane Mallory (Morgan Fairchild) and the murdered woman's husband, Alex (John Beck). Working for the business corporation owned by Alex, Jane uses her models to smuggle raw heroin into America. The guilty partners die in the final scene and Hamberger clears himself.

The above synopsis describes a very badly written and directed crime movie. *Deadly Illusion* lacks Cohen's iconoclastic comic-book style. Operating on a low budget, it attempts (successfully) to resemble a highly budgeted contemporary *film noir*. However, Cohen's ventures outside his usual style are not generally successful, and producer problems affected *Deadly Illusion*. Hamberger's final off-screen voice-over appears to have nothing to do with the actual film: "It's amazing how greed and growing old can make people act strange. By the way, what was in those green bottles?"

Greed certainly explains the alliance of Jane Mallory and Alex Burton. Beginning as a six-year-old child model, Jane moves up the ladder and achieves a successful corporate career by managing models. Her lover, Alex, runs a small segment of corporate America now turning to raw heroin, a more stable commodity than gold or silver, which are affected by fluctuating market conditions. When Hamberger confronts Alex and his executives in their boardroom, he accuses them of investing in raw heroin, since the value always rises. Inflation or currency changes never affect profit margins in this area. Ahead of his time as usual, Larry Cohen wrote the screenplay and filmed this section in December 1986 — several months before the Wall Street crisis.

Although greed motivates the villains, "growing old" is never satisfactorily explained in *Deadly Illusion*. Although Jane later appears in the dark wig she wore in her first scene, making her look a few years older, she is still recognizable as Morgan Fairchild. Her Jane and Sharon personas are identical. This makes Hamberger's failure to recognize Jane on their first meeting really incredible! A wig creates the only distinction between them. The discrepancy is not Larry Cohen's fault, but resulted from producer interference. It eliminated an important plot motif from the final version.

Earlier in the film, Hamberger and Rina investigate a mask factory run by a man who got his start developing prosthetics for disfigured war veterans. They discover a mask with Jane Mallory's features beside some mysterious green bottles left unexplained in the film. (But in Cohen's original screenplay, Jane Mallory was a much older woman who hid her features behind an artificial mask.) The green bottles contain liquid that holds the mask in place. When Hamberger meets Jane for the first time (masquerading as Sharon), he sees her real face, which is completely different from her glamorous false face. Jane Mallory is really the "Deadly Illusion" of the film's title. This plot device reworks Cohen's original "False Face" teleplay. Furthermore, if the producers had left Cohen's work alone, *Deadly Illusion* could have become an interesting companion piece to *The Stuff*. In the earlier film, the Stuff uses false bodies to pass as normal citizens while destroying American society from within. In *Deadly Illusion*, Jane Mallory conceals her real face behind a glamorous facade. Like the vampire children in *A Return to Salem's Lot*, she hides behind an American illusion of deceptive youthfulness to exploit others and feed off their misery. In both *The Stuff* and *Deadly Illusion*, the corporate business world is eager to make profits and exploit others. By linking the artificiality of the cosmetic industry to the dangerous nature of American business, Cohen's original *Deadly Illusion* screenplay represented another radical cinematic assault on American social practices.

However, the final film is as mangled as *I, the Jury*. But *Deadly Illusion* still retains other interesting features such as the antagonistic relationship between Hamberger and his Irish-American cop buddy Detective Lafferty (Joe Cortese). Their association resembles the eternal triangle existing between Mickey Spillane's Mike Hammer, Captain Pat Chambers, and Hammer's secretary, Velda. Irritated at Hamberger's exploitation of Rina, Lafferty becomes frustrated at her willingness to do anything for the detective. Handcuffing Hamberger, Lafferty beats up his helpless prisoner. After the assault, Hamberger comments, "I'm glad you got that out of your system." Lafferty replies, "So am I." Hamberger ironically responds, "I'm not." He notes that Lafferty has been "beating the shit out of me since I was twelve years old" and asks whether he will ever get a chance. Lafferty curtly replies, "Never." The African-American and the Irish-American exist in a morbidly symbiotic relationship where underlying sexual tensions are expressed via sadism and violence. When Hamberger later gatecrashes a New York fashion show, Jane attempts undercutting his macho attitude by suggesting that he knows the male attendants are no threat to him:

> JANE: "Are you one of those guys who likes to beat up on homosexuals?"
> HAMBERGER: "I tried that once. He was a five times heavyweight champion of the Marines. I only lasted five rounds."

Hamberger also denies he is sports star Reggie Jackson, choosing to identify himself as Jessie Jackson, the presidential candidate. However, these pleasurable moments are not enough to save *Deadly Illusion* from being a highly compromised film.

*Wicked Stepmother* is the most problematic film Cohen ever directed. The production difficulties surrounding it are already well known and fully documented elsewhere. Any further details are unnecessary.[10] Bette Davis's ill health affected the entire project. Her abrupt departure left Cohen in a dilemma. His silence while Davis made negative comments about him on talk shows such as *The Tonight Show with Johnny Carson* revealed a generous spirit few critics ever acknowledge. *Wicked Stepmother* emerged from a screenplay Cohen wrote specially for Bette Davis. Saddened at her lack of employment and neglect by an industry whose prestige she once contributed to, Cohen conceived one of his typically unusual situations for a film designed to give the neglected actress a comedy role. What would happen if you arrived home and found the notoriously difficult star living in your home? The screenplay contained imaginative potential. Playing twentieth-century witch Miranda, Davis' proposed role combined *The Man Who Came to Dinner* (1942) with the "Unruly Woman" figure of American film and television comedy.[11] On this occasion, Davis would play the Monty Woolley role. She also appeared as the heroine in the earlier film.

Davis' abrupt departure from the set and the necessary rewriting of the original screenplay presented a huge challenge, even for anyone working under the most favorable circumstances. Rather than wasting the 15 minutes of Davis footage, Cohen decided to continue the film by modifying the screenplay and improvising accordingly. Barbara Carrera's role as Miranda's daughter, Priscilla, became enlarged and changed. She now appears as a younger version of Miranda. The original screenplay began with Steve and Jenny Miller arriving at the airport after a Hawaiian vacation.[12] But the final film opens with a highly amusing pre-credits sequence revealing Cohen at his most idiosyncratic and inventive. Police officers McIntosh (Tom Bosley) and Flynn (James Dixon) arrive at a deserted Beverly Hills home. The black maid tells them about a chain-smoking old lady

**Larry Cohen aims at ensuring the comfort of Bette Davis on the set of *Wicked Stepmother* (1988) (courtesy of Larry Cohen).**

who had wormed her way into the Clinton family and been employed by them for 20 years until she was fired. Upstairs they discover a miniaturized family inhabiting a shoebox. After the credits, the audience sees a police lineup of cantankerous old ladies reminiscent of those Bill Lennick encounters on the bus in *Bone*. McIntosh attempts to find the old lady, who moved out after financially cleaning out the family, who had won the lottery. The police find themselves unable to deal with the lineup, which resembles "Hell's Grannies" from a well-known Monty Python sketch. Also, the high-pitched squeaky voices prevent the reduced family from recognizing any of them. The scene ends with Flynn asking McIntosh about the eventual charge should they apprehend the real culprit: "What do we charge her with? Grand Theft and Shrinkage?" Totaling 10 minutes, these scenes represent Cohen's bizarre comic genius at its best. Unfortunately, they do not save the rest of the film. Many comedy scenes appear forced and labored, making the entire film highly uneven and often difficult to view. *Wicked Stepmother* has some interesting scenes, but there are few pleasurable moments.

As originally written, Miranda Pierpoint was a former mistress of Aaron Burr, "once the richest woman in New York City, married and widowed four times under suspicious circumstances." Although becoming wealthy over the centuries by marrying victims, one of whom "rises to become one of the founders of the

New York Stock Exchange *and dies*", she lost her wealth due to the silver market's collapse in 1981.[13] Like the greedy executives of *Deadly Illusion,* she schemes at regaining her lost finances. Miranda moves in with affluent families, practices her spells on them so they win at game shows, and then disposes of them, moving on to other victims. Both the original screenplay and final film involve a nightmarish scenario of a yuppie Beverly Hills family confronted with a chain-smoking Bette Davis now married to their widowed father and overturning their comfortable lifestyle.

It is difficult to imagine what *Wicked Stepmother* might have become had Davis remained under more favorable circumstances. It might have resembled *Bone,* with Davis' role resembling Yaphet Kotto's as the "return of the repressed" forces within the Miller family. Miranda completely overturns the family's clean and comfortable lifestyle, causing the most drastic forms of chaos imaginable in Beverly Hills. As in *Bone,* addiction to television forms a significant part of the satire. Like the vampire community in *A Return to Salem's Lot,* Miranda is another perverse example of the American Dream. She is also a fundamental part of the country's historical tradition, one deeply implicated in economic exploitation and violence.

However, certain pleasurable moments do exist in *Wicked Stepmother.* Cohen caustically satirizes the American addiction to television and trivial game shows. Miranda coaches Jenny's father, Sam (Lionel Stander), into watching game shows so he will eventually become a competitor and earn millions of dollars. Sam eventually appears on a show resembling "Wheel of Fortune," with Laurene Landon's greedy blonde "Vanilla" character satirizing Vanna White. Miranda puts a spell on Sam's bald head, enabling hair to return so he will become acceptably photogenic for television audiences. In the original screenplay, Sam and Jenny (Colleen Camp) talk about the excellent television reception they have had since Miranda's arrival. They even receive cable stations without paying for them. Sam leaves Jenny in front of the set. She comments, "It's like having a dish." Other comments in the original screenplay are highly suggestive: "She's almost mesmerized herself. The reflected colors dancing across her face. Then she snaps out of it and quickly turns the TV off, but it almost got her."[14] Unfortunately, the scene was never filmed.

Neither McIntosh nor Flynn appears in the original screenplay. McIntosh's suspension from the police department, his lone pursuit of Miranda, enrollment in a witch college run by the witch mistress (Evelyn Keyes), and eventual reduction in size were all additions to the screenplay made after Davis' departure. Tom Bosley's performance is far more amusing than Richard Moll's detective character Nat Pringle.[15] But amusing moments are rare and not enough to save *Wicked Stepmother* from being one of the few major disasters in Cohen's career. Fortunately, he immediately returned to form with *The Ambulance.* But before examining this more interesting film, other examples of Cohen's authorship as screenwriter and playwright deserve some attention.

# Screenplays of
# the 1980s and 1990s

Most studies of a director's work usually do not include detailed consider-
ations of his or her screenplays, especially those filmed by other directors. Critics usually focus on definitions of authorship stressing the director as sole creative force behind the film. However, as earlier chapters show, Larry Cohen motifs
appear in several television works he did not direct. His work necessitates a more
fluid definition of authorship extending beyond those exclusively concerned with
the director's role. In many cases, a film is only as good as its screenplay. Although
the author's vision may not be fully achieved unless he or she occupies the director's chair, sometimes an innovative screenplay influences positive choices a director makes during filming. The screenplay, as much as the complete film, often
has a significant claim to be included in definitions of authorship.

Although cases exist in which an entire screenplay has been directly transferred to the cinema screen, other instances occur of a conflict between two
authors—writer and director—a conflict in which the text takes on a productive
hegemonic clash of personalities and ideas. Sometimes the results are problematic, as *I, the Jury* (1981), *Maniac Cop 3: Badge of Silence* (1992) and *Guilty as Sin*
(1993) all show. *Maniac Cop 3* includes ideas that do not gain appropriate realization. Other films reveal the scenarist's vision as being far more significant than
that of the person directing the film. *Best Seller* (1985), *Maniac Cop* (1988) and
*Maniac Cop 2* (1990) support this. They appear more identifiable as Larry Cohen
products, rather than films with a John Flynn or William Lustig personal vision.
In such cases, Cohen's signature operates like an invisible "ghost in the machine"
indirectly influencing the film. This suggestion is by no means detrimental to the
role played by the actual director. Film is really a collaborative process. A director deserves respect for realizing the creative vision of another individual. Examining the author as scenarist does not mean displacing and ignoring the director
as the person who has full responsibility for the final film. It involves gathering
significant evidence to establish the scenarist as an important collaborator in the
filmic process.

*I, the Jury* furnishes one example of a screenplay that is more important than the work of its director. The abysmal nature of the finished project represents an absolute travesty of Cohen's original vision. He was removed from the film after working one week as director. Poorly realized, perfunctorily acted, hastily edited, and resembling a bad television movie, *I, the Jury* initially appears as a work deserving quick oblivion. However, certain components of Cohen's original screenplay remain. They contain interesting parallels to radical visions charac-terizing his own films as director. Although *I, the Jury* deserves critical condem-nation, it is an important case study in understanding the work of Larry Cohen and how it is often drastically altered by lesser talents.

Cohen wrote the screenplay and cast all the actors. Although one-third of the screenplay does not appear on the screen, it sheds fascinating light on the entire film. Had success resulted, *I, the Jury* would have been the first in a series of Mike Hammer films similar to the James Bond series. However, Richard T. Heffron replaced Cohen as director and changed much of the screenplay. None of Cohen's original footage survives in the current version, which is crudely directed and never realizes Cohen's radical insights into the Mike Hammer char-acter. The feature was rushed into production before the screen actor's strike (1981). But, as Paul Taylor notes, "most of the smaller-scale mayhem exhibits a comic strip insolence so totally at odds with current genre expectations that it has a kind of perverse charm."[1]

Cohen envisioned Mike Hammer's character as containing a mass of com-plex and contradictory elements. Although he still superficially resembles Mickey Spillane's "macho" original, Armand Assante's Hammer is a repressed homosex-ual venting his frustrations on others by violent assault, a figure with a death wish, attending Alcoholic Anonymous meetings, and chewing on candy bars as a sub-stitute for liquor, like Orson Welles' Hank Quinlan in *Touch of Evil* (1958). The exasperated Pat Chambers (Paul Sorvino) tells Mike, "Why don't you join the mercenaries and go to goddamn Africa, or maybe the I.R.A.? Any place where there's plenty of killing." Confronted by Dr. Bennett (Barbara Carrera) with evi-dence of his dead friend's desires for him, Mike becomes devastated. When he later undergoes torture by members of Romero's illegal CIA group, he faces the recovering alcoholic's nightmare of booze being poured down his throat. Finally confronting Romero, Mike bludgeons him to death with his deceased friend's artificial arm, a brilliant metaphor for Hammer transforming his attraction for the phallic symbol into a deadly weapon.[2] This particular scene would have been the key image around which the entire film centered. In the current version, Mike presents Dr. Bennett with his deceased friend's artificial arm before he kills her. A sexual connotation exists in this scene, but it is not as strong as its origi-nal version.

Cohen's Mike Hammer is an alcoholic Vietnam veteran grieving over the death of his buddy, Jack Williams (Frederick Downs). Although Mike believes his quest for vengeance is self-motivated, he is actually used by the CIA to "search and destroy" a black operations unit begun in Vietnam that has grown increasingly out of control. As CIA official Goodwin (F. J. O'Neil) tells Detective Pat Chambers, Hammer is "the perfect killing machine" for company purposes. As in Cohen's other films, the threat resides less in actual monsters (and Hammer is clearly one) and more from the system creating them, a system based on law and religion. As Goodwin tells Pat, "Your Mr. Hammer has done us another good service. His point of view is so refreshingly Biblical. A dozen eyes for an eye." Part of the irony of *I, the Jury* lies in the fact that Mike's friend Pat is forced to betray him. Like Mike, he is being used and abused by the system. Pat has also committed "past indiscretions." Goodwin uses these against him, as J. Edgar Hoover, in Cohen's earlier film, uses similar evidence to dominate American society for nearly 50 years.

Both in screenplay and direction, *I, the Jury* contains abundant evidence of the duality motif that has fascinated Cohen since his first viewing of Hitchcock's *Strangers on a Train* (1952). The pre-credits sequence shows Mike being hired by a suspicious husband, Kyle (Mike Miller), to shadow his wife. Mike promptly seduces her and cuckolds Kyle. He tells his client on the phone, "I'll stay right on top of it." Although played for laughs in a James Bond manner, this sequence establishes the theme of *I, the Jury*. Indeed, as originally written by Cohen, the credit sequences would have used animated images of Mike drawn in the style of comic-strip artist Jim Steranko, a figure used by Clint Eastwood to design deliberately self-reflective, excessive images for the poster promoting *The Gauntlet* (1977).[3] Mike believes he is a solitary individual who beats the system by screwing his client. However, he is also unknowingly used and abused by the same system he thinks he is "on top of." Mike believes in his deadly individualistic persona. But beneath it is a shadowy side he attempts to repress. This becomes manifest in the surnames of other characters in the film, which begin with "K," *two letters* away from "M" in the alphabet. They all represent various dark sides of the Mike Hammer character.

Mobster Kalecki (Alan King) scornfully refers to a government that is afraid to let him engage in covert activities such as assassinating Fidel Castro. Kalecki caustically condemns "faggot politicians" who are "nervous about being caught in bed with their Uncle George." This reference combines the political and personal realms. It refers to a government using sexual therapy to brainwash its victims, concealing political assassinations under the guise of sex crimes as well as indirectly denoting the nature of Mike's own personal demons. Mike is "nervous" about confronting his real desires to be in bed with a best friend who loves him: the deceased Jack Williams.

The original screenplay also depicted a Mrs. Klawson from Ohio looking for her missing son whom Mike discovers working as a "male go-go dancer in a gay bar on Christopher Street." Mike decides to deceive the woman, passing her son off as a Marine stationed at NATO headquarters in Belgium.[4] This scene reveals Mike denying an unwholesome reality for the sake of an imaginary family image. It reveals him as a complicit partner in society's ideologically governed version of an "official story" disavowing actual evidence in the same way as young

Mike Hammer (Armand Assante) considers pleasurable options offered by the twins (Lee Ann Harris and Annette Harris) in *I, the Jury* (American Cinema, 1981).

Jason's parents deny the dangerous reality of the Stuff. However, the film drops this reference to focus on another aberrant son figure: programmed assassin Kendricks (Judson Scott). Romero's renegade operations use Dr. Bennett's sexual therapy clinic to program this disturbed mother-fixated figure to eliminate threats to national security. These include not only left-wing politicians and activists but incriminating witnesses such as female twins used in sexual therapy. Raging against his mother, Kendricks, creating surrogates for his hated parent, puts wigs and heavy makeup on his female victims, making them act like suffocatingly possessive, loving mothers before killing them. Kendricks' activities are a dark version of government approved sex-and-violence strategies used against selected enemies. Visiting Kendricks' mother, Hilda (Jessica James), as she watches a soap opera in which the leading man unconvincingly tells his girlfriend, "I want to have our baby as much as you do," Velda (Laurene Landon) encounters a figure who bears as much responsibility for her son's activities as the U.S. government does. Judson Scott's Kendricks bears a surprising resemblance to Richard Lynch's Bernard Phillips in Cohen's *God Told Me To*. Like Mike, Kendricks releases tensions by acts of brutal violence that conceal his real feelings. As one twin tells Mike, "You're like your friend. He loved to act tough, too, only he was afraid."

Confronting Hammer at their first meeting, Dr. Bennett comments, "I would very much like to treat you to find out what makes you hate so deeply. To find out what allows you to do the things you do." When Mike sees Jack's widow, Myrna (Mary Margaret Amato), after viewing his friend's body, she intimates he did not know Jack as well as he thought, stating, "There are things only his wife could know about him." In the original screenplay, Myrna notes Mike's masochistic reactions to the hot coffee she brings him — "You want it to hurt"— understanding the links between violent masculinity and repressed homosexual feelings common to both him and Jack.[5] Had Cohen directed *I, the Jury*, the scene showing Mike reading Jack's file and learning of the implications behind their friendship would have received better realization.[6]

However, Mike Hammer is merely a minor pawn in a corrupt game organized by his own government. Fellow veteran Joe Butler (Geoffrey Lewis) tells him that Jack discovered a CIA mind control operation first organized in Vietnam and now operating in America. After psychologically programming captured Viet Cong prisoners, former Green Beret Captain Romero uses the same techniques for political assassinations in America. As left-wing newspaper editor Danny (Daniel Faraldo) tells Mike, "Maybe the streets are not safe for well-known leftists" whose political murders are covered up as sex crimes. Mike initially encounters Kendricks' first victim, Cynthia Gonzales, in Central Park. Her body (and face made-up to resemble Mrs. Kendricks) lies beneath Jose De Creeft's "Alice in Wonderland" statue.

Although many Cohen themes from the original screenplay remain in the final film, the hasty direction never realizes their potential. Sexual therapy scenes in Dr. Bennett's Northridge clinic are merely exploitative and voyeuristic, lacking implications. Cohen initially understood them metaphorically as belonging to a film whose characters deceive themselves as much as other people. The screenplay significantly comments, "This, like Sandstone and other retreats, is a place of sexual awakening where all rules are set aside and persons are suddenly able to 'be themselves' or are they simply putting on a sexual performance to fool themselves?" (61). Similar types of self-deception appear in "The Unwritten Law" episode of "The Defenders." Cohen presented both Eileen Rolf and Sharon Ruskin as equally unhappy victims of the sexual ideologies in their different generations. As in the original novel, Mike finally kills Dr. Bennett. But she is a figure equally used and abused by the same system pulling Mike Hammer's strings. The final film version unfortunately omits the interesting manner in which Mike finally discovers who actually killed his friend. Rather than Mike learning the information from Romero's computer files, the screenplay depicts Mike looking at hidden police photographs of the crime showing the dead Jack touching the wrist of his artificial arm with his fingers — standard sign language for the word "doctor."

The final version of *I, the Jury* is a disaster, ruining a promising screenplay. But despite minor flaws, John Flynn's *Best Seller* (1987) is a far more accomplished work fully realizing ideas in Cohen's screenplay.

*Best Seller* gains from having two accomplished actors in leading roles: Brian Dennehy and James Woods. It is another Cohen screenplay influenced by Hitchcock and written many years before its cinematic realization. *Best Seller* develops the duality motif of *Strangers on a Train* and takes it in a new direction. In this version, a retired cop now working as a famous novelist (modeled on Joseph Wambaugh) meets his alter ego, corporate hit man Cleve. Like Bruno Walter in *Strangers on a Train*, Cleve conceals his dangerous nature beneath a seductive personality, a trait common not only to Hitchcock figures such as Johnny Aysgarth in *Suspicion* (1941), Uncle Charlie in *Shadow of a Doubt*, Vandamm in *North by Northwest*, and Norman Bates in *Psycho*, but also Cohen's rogues gallery of dangerous and likable young men in *Daddy's Gone A-Hunting* (1968), *Guilty as Sin* (1993) and *As Good as Dead* (1995). Like Kendricks in *I, the Jury*, all these characters have suffered from some form of maternal child abuse.

*Best Seller* opens with a point-of-view shot as the credits roll. The script and direction already place the audience within Cleve's perspective as a van drives toward the Los Angeles Police Depository Building in 1972. Ironically, the criminal gang masquerades as campaigners for Richard Nixon's Republican nomination for a second term as president. The van shows Nixon's head appearing next to the logo "Now more than ever." The occupants wear Richard Nixon rubber masks as they make their way into the building, shooting any cop who tries to prevent them.[7] One cop, Dennis Meachum (Brian Dennehy), manages to stab a robber, who has cigarette burns on his wrist, before receiving further bullet wounds. After undergoing surgery, Meachum survives to write a best-selling book based on his experiences — *Inside Job* — referring to a crooked cop's involvement in the robbery. The title also ironically foreshadows the psychologically symbiotic nature of his future relationship with Cleve.

The experience is significant on more than one level. Meachum decides to remain on the force and continue to write. He thus has his feet in two camps: the creative world of authorship and the working environment of law enforcement. But this situation has perverse overtones. By shooting Dennis, Cleve creates the cop's new role as a policeman-writer. Like a director, he manufactures a new performing role for his subject. Cleve resembles Hitchcock's theatrical author figures such as Sir John in *Murder!* and Bruno in *Strangers on a Train* who dissolve the barriers separating life from art by authoring performances for chosen victims.[8]

Saving Meachum's life on at least two occasions, Cleve reveals his designs to the disbelieving cop. Identifying himself as a corporate hit man for Kappa International, Cleve wishes Dennis to write a "best seller" about himself and his former employer, David Madlock (Paul Shenar). Recognizing Dennis' financial difficulties over paying his dead wife's medical bills and a creative block preventing him from repeating the success of his first book, Cleve decides to author Dennis' new book. On one level, Cleve desires to get even with David for abandoning him, an abandonment having more than one meaning. On another level, Cleve's interaction with Dennis breaks down barriers until both men finally become mirror images of each other. While Guy rejects Bruno in *Strangers on a Train*, Dennis eventually forms an appreciative kinship with his murderous alter ego in a manner he never envisioned.

At first, Dennis attempts to arrest Cleve, but he eventually becomes involved in the latter's revenge. Cleve confesses his role as a corporate hit man for Kappa International, claiming authorship of its head: "I helped make David Madlock." By enlisting Dennis in his quest to write a best seller, Cleve intends not just to unmake the friend whose position he once created, but also to help *make* Dennis the author of a "best seller," a goal he achieves in the final scenes when his posthumous voice accompanies images of Dennis succeeding in that goal: "You can't let things get by you, Dennis. Best Seller."

Ironically, Cleve's robbery at the Los Angeles Police Depository not only authored David's rise to corporate success, but Dennis' initial start as a best selling author. The two are identical in a film full of dualities. Cleve saves Dennis from death twice in their early encounters. He and Dennis eventually become twins. The robbery results in the beginning of Kappa International and David's rise to corporate power. Business and crime are identical activities within the American system. Cleve educates Dennis in the real nature of the system he strives to defend as a cop. When Dennis protests that "Corporations don't have people killed," Cleve refutes his argument.

> Corporations deal in two things — assets and liabilities. I removed the liabilities and provided some of the assets. I was a corporate executive in charge of just those very things. And you were in on it from the very beginning. We both were. It's all a question of Capital, Dennis. How does an ambitious man get started? Capital. And David was an unusual man. He got unusual financing. And you wrote about this in your first book.

Like Frank Davies, Peter Nicholas, and Eugene Scott, Dennis Meachum finds himself inextricably caught up within a dark world he never thought applicable to his own personal situation. He sees the dark fabric of a society whose phony benevolence he once took for granted. In a later conversation, Cleve refers to himself as being "the dirty part" in Dennis' life, as opposed to his deceased wife who represented "the clean part." Subsequent events in *Best Seller* undermine such arbitrary divisions.

Cleve educates Dennis in the harsh realities of his society: "Money. It's the American way, seed money. Kappa International was formed six months later on Venture Capital." Like Al Capone, David engages in charitable activities to foster a public image that fools everyone except Cleve. He refers to his former partner as a "modern robber baron" who belongs to a specially privileged group who "built this country," and in whose service he operated as a professional hit man.

Covering the territory of his previous murders for Dennis' benefit, Cleve gains access to the apartment of his first victim, an old man who discovered patents for David but committed a cardinal sin in the American dream of economic success: "His only sin was he did not want to be rich. He liked this street, this house. A man can be dangerous when he doesn't care about money." As Cleve describes the murder to Dennis, the camera represents his point-of-view reminiscence tracing the events in a manner similar to Maxim's confession of

Rebecca's "accident" in Hitchcock's *Rebecca* (1941). Although saddened by his first murder, Cleve exhibits no guilt over his next victims, a couple he killed in bed. The husband was an accountant, but the wife "knew more about business than her husband." She was "greedy, always wanting more. They deserved what they got, believe me."

The following bar sequence further depicts Cleve's pathological nature, placing him firmly in the realm of Larry Cohen's dangerous young men manufactured by the normal American family. Cleve plays and sings "Au Clair de la Lune," his voice explicitly out of tune. Showing off his prowess as a pickup artist to Dennis, Cleve provokes a situation with the woman's male companion from which Dennis "rescues" him. Dennis recognizes that Cleve could really have injured the man. Cleve speaks about the importance of a will power that "distinguishes the amateur from the professional." In this scene, Cohen unveils the pathologically aggressive nature of Cleve's seduction technique, which is as much a performance as other routines he uses to charm those he wants something from. Cleve exhibits his prowess to Dennis, burning his arm with a cigarette butt. His activity parallels Mike Hammer's consumption of boiling hot coffee in front of Myrna Williams in the original screenplay of *I, the Jury*. Cleve admits to Dennis that he uses this masochistic technique to impress girls. Dennis then remembers that the masked assailant of the 1972 robbery had cigarette burns on his arm. He assaults Cleve, but his murderous double manages to calm him down.

At Cleve's luxurious apartment (which he acknowledges as his due reward in the American Dream), Cleve attempts to interest Dennis in his bar pickup: "She wants you. She likes the way you fight. She thinks you're cool. She wants you to hurt her. There are some pretty sick people in the world. Come on Dennis. Haven't you ever shared a girl with a friend?" His gestures towards Dennis are by no means altruistic. He uses the female as a symbol of exchange between men, as a form of homo-social bonding between himself and Dennis that paradoxically also has homosexual overtones.[9] Cleve obviously performs on Dennis the same routine he once used with David.

Refusing the offer, Dennis goes on the offensive against Cleve and expresses a desire to visit his partner's Oregon home. Unknown to him, Cleve has planned the visit but acts insecurely as a means of trapping his author-subject in a murderous scheme. Dennis taunts him: "I bet your Mom and Dad still live in the home where you were born. Am I right, Cleve? A little farm somewhere with the smell of leaves burning in the fall. We're going to make that place famous, Cleve. The place where a vicious, amoral killer was spawned and set loose in the world. We're going to Oregon, Cleve. We're going home."

Although one scene, revealing that Cleve's mother knows about her son's activities, was eliminated from the film, Dennis' visit to Cleve's Norman Rockwell–esque family hearth suggestively reveals the dangerous murderous killer as a product of the average American family. At the dinner table, Dennis observes Cleve's father, who is clearly an irrelevant figure in a family dominated by his more powerful wife. When Father tells Dennis that he "could not kill a living thing," his wife retorts, "That's right, Harold. You eat the chicken but leave the killing to someone else"—a clear reference to her knowledge of who the actual bread-winner in the family is and exactly what he does. Wearing a down-home, checked shirt during the visit, Cleve asserts that, by practicing denial techniques, his family would protect his name after the book appears. "They'll deny it. Defend me. It'll give them a reason to live. It'll add ten years to their lives." He wishes Dennis to depict him as a "lovable son" to his parents in a book he is actually writing. Despite Dennis' aversion to him, Cleve recognizes certain things: "You don't have to like me. But I think you do in spite of yourself," a feeling Dennis admits later in the film.

Eventually the barriers between Cleve and Dennis dissolve, allowing them finally to function as one personality. Cleve rescues Dennis' daughter, Holly (Allison Balson), from David's men, until she is kidnapped by the very Los Angeles Police force Dennis works for. Before they assault David's home, Cleve tells Dennis about his idea for a perfect ending for the book: the death of David Madlock. Although Dennis objects, Cleve answers, "Anybody can kill anybody, even the president, remember," a sentence Dennis repeats verbatim in his later encounter with David. Despite Cleve's successful infiltration and execution of his hit man successors, David manages to use Holly as a shield against Cleve's bullets. While Cleve maneuvers himself into a position whereby he can kill David, he finally decides to acquiesce to Dennis' plea, "Don't do it. Give it up." Cleve puts down his gun, leaving himself open to David's bullets. Despite his anger at Cleve's fate and his violent assault on David (viewed apprehensively by Holly), Dennis decides to be the final author of his book and write his own ending, not Cleve's. The dying Cleve criticizes Dennis for the last time: "You should have killed him. Always a good cop. It would have been the perfect ending. You should have killed him." Dennis thanks him for saving Holly, a gesture Cleve affirms as an all–American, heroic status: "Put it in the book. Remember ... I'm the hero."

The film concludes with a book display showing Dennis reborn as a best-selling author, with Cleve's off-screen voice approving his partner's newfound status in a project he authored. *Best Seller* is one of the most accomplished Larry Cohen screenplays transferred to the screen with relatively little alteration. It is a film directed by John Flynn, but owing more to Larry Cohen's ideas. This transference parallels the influence of Cleve on Dennis in the fictional world of *Best Seller*. Influenced by Alfred Hitchcock, particularly the developing implications in *Strangers on a Train*, *Best Seller* relates them to the wider realm of political corruption from the Nixon era to the Reaganite world of crooked robber barons. They are inherently as much a part of the American way as Old Glory. As Cleve says to Dennis in his lavish apartment paid for by numerous murders, "Only in America."

Cohen wrote the *Maniac Cop* screenplay under the original title of "Cordell" in 1987 and offered it to William Lustig, who directed it the following year. The promotion used the ingenious phrase printed on the screenplay's title page: "You have the right to remain silent ... forever."[10] Perhaps recognizing Lustig's involvement in directing *Maniac* (1980), the title was changed to *Maniac Cop*. In the original screenplay, Teresa Mallory refers to Cordell as the cop upon whom Clint Eastwood's "Dirty Harry" was modeled. But this was cut from the final version, modifying Cohen's playful self-reflectivity and making Cordell a more threatening figure. Since Cohen originally offered the role of Mike Hammer to Eastwood, the latter's reluctance to appear in *I, the Jury* may have stimulated this "in-joke" reference, since Eastwood's involvement in a Cohen project would have avoided many problems besetting the ill-fated American Cinema venture.

Although William Lustig acted as director on the *Maniac Cop* films, the underlying ideas are Larry Cohen's. Unfortunately, he chose not to direct. *Maniac Cop* is competent enough. But, as Paul Taylor notes, it lacks "Cohen's quick-witted improvisational flair"[11] to draw the viewer away from the many holes in the plot and the leaden performances of Bruce Campbell and Laurene Landon as the two heroic leads. *Maniac Cop* lacks the necessary vitality characterizing a Larry Cohen film. Although it contains several significant scenes, such as revealing New York's loss of tourist revenue due to the killings and a murder victim's face grotesquely drilled out from the cement Cordell pushed him into the previous night, the direction is mostly pedestrian.

However, one problem in the film was contributed by the original screenplay. No explicit reason is given for Matt Cordell's attainment of superhuman powers after his return from the dead. Although Cohen mentions elsewhere the influence of religious myths involving the resurrection of divine beings with exceptional powers, the actual screenplay and film contain little support for such ideas. The viewer is left to guess at the reasons for Cordell's return. Furthermore, as Cohen himself admits, Matt Cordell lacks the horrific charisma of either Karloff's Frankenstein monster or Freddy Krueger, who fascinated viewers so they forget searching for rational explanations.

However, clues appear in both the screenplay and the film. Cohen has never been a director to spell things out. He leaves certain suggestions for viewers to entertain at will, particularly those familiar with his films. *Maniac Cop* contains several parallels to Cohen's other religious investigations in *God Told Me To* and *Q*, particularly those involving the murderous salvations of divine beings. If Bernard Phillips takes on the persona of an Old Testament god of judgment contradicting the benevolent features associated with the New Testament god he resembles, Matt Cordell (Robert Z'Dar) returns from the dead like Quetzalcoatl to exact deadly revenge upon a city and inhabitants he once swore to protect. As a Catholic cop, Matt Cordell exercised swift retribution upon New York's criminal underworld until city and police authorities railroaded him into certain death at the hands of Sing Sing's prison population. In his former existence, Cordell obsessively lived only for his religion and law enforcement activities. His only pleasure was a narcissistic enjoyment in reading police scrapbooks detailing his exploits. Betrayed by an establishment whose ideological claims he once fully affirmed, this New York street savior is resurrected as a monstrous demonic counterpart of his former self. Now reincarnated as the Maniac Cop, Matt Cordell

"You have the right to remain silent—forever!" Publicity handout for *Maniac Cop* (1988) (courtesy of Larry Cohen).

walks the New York streets exercising a last judgment over guilty and innocent alike. He performs a travesty of his former occupation as one of New York's finest. Rejected by his institutional family, the law enforcer returns as a monstrous figure created by a corrupt system and acts as a punitive Old Testament savior undertaking an obsessive, deadly re-enactment of his former role as protective cop. Parallels to the *It's Alive* films and *The Private Files of J. Edgar Hoover* are certainly present.

Matt Cordell also represents an excessive example of a character acting out the role of his personal monster from the id. Until his unexpected demise halfway through the film,[12] alcoholic, suicidal cop Frank McCrae (Tom Atkins) barely restrains himself from following Cordell's destructive patterns by masochistically engaging in his own particular damnation. Like Lt. Spencer in *The Ambulance*, he has attempted suicide due to work pressures. While Cordell embodies a "return of the repressed," changing from honest, puritanical cop into superhuman killer, Frank McCrae is more passively affected by his law enforcement role. He shows many of the strains exhibited by his counterpart, Mark Deglan, in "Night Cry." Like Matt Cordell, Jack Forrest (Bruce Campbell) is railroaded by the police on suspicion of his wife's murder. Similarities between Forrest and Cordell appear in their introductory scenes. In dressing for night duty, Forrest's actions resemble those of Matt Cordell in the opening credits scene. Forrest is designated a marked man by two people responsible for Cordell's railroading and death: Police Commissioner Pike (Richard Roundtree) and Captain Ripley (William Smith). If Matt Cordell commits the sin of pride by admiring his press coverage, Jack commits a mortal sin through his adulterous liaison with Teresa Mallory. Like Cordell's aging sweetheart, Sally Noland (Sheree North), Teresa is both a Catholic and one of New York's finest. The relationship between Jack and Teresa parallels the darker one between Cordell and Sally. As police archivist Casey ( James Dixon) tells McCrae, Sally is "of course, a cop." While Teresa sins in her adulterous relationship with Jack, Sally attempted the unforgivable act of suicide by jumping out of a window after learning of Cordell's death at Sing Sing. Her action also parallels Frank McCrae's failed suicide; as Clancy notes, a "terrible thing for a Catholic girl to do." Another parallel between the two couples appears in the disturbed mental condition of Jack's wife, Ellen (Victoria Caitlin). Trapped in an unfulfilled marriage, as Cordell and Sally are within the laws of their church, Ellen follows Jack to his rendezvous with Teresa. Although spurred on by the equally disturbed Sally, Ellen's attempted shooting of Jack and Sally clearly reveals dangerous tendencies paralleling the deadly activities of Matt Cordell. Like all Cohen's works, *Maniac Cop* reveals that everyone is guilty in one form or another. No one is ever innocent. They all exist in a hellish environment that soon adversely affects them. The system they live in becomes increasingly out of control producing different types of monsters and victims.

Eventually Cordell achieves his revenge by killing Pike and Ripley during the St. Patrick's Day Parade, a ceremony he once loved. But, as Teresa notes, "Whatever he loved, he hates now." Although Cordell achieves his goal, he is now an out of control monster murdering the innocent as well as the guilty, including the pathetic Sally, who still loves him. Capturing the police van in which Jack is held prisoner, Cordell attempts further sacrificial revenge until Teresa's intervention aids Jack's escape. Although Cordell supposedly dies by being impaled on a pole like a vampire, he returns from the dead in the final shot. As the police authorities lift the empty van from the harbor, a huge, powerful hand emerges from the depths to grasp one of the pier's timbers. The image goes into freeze frame. Cordell's final appearance resembles the Frankenstein monster's opening movement in *The Bride of Frankenstein* as Karloff emerges from an underground cistern. Although obviously motivated by thoughts of a sequel, the scene contains an important meaning. Like the Frankenstein monster, Cordell can never really die. He lives off the thoughts and emotions of human beings trapped within a corrupt urban society. As Nancy (Heather Langencamp) recognizes in *A Nightmare on Elm Street* (1984), any monster lives off the fears of others, especially those caught within a dangerous life-denying and debilitating society.

*Maniac Cop 2* opens with a point-of-view shot placing the audience in Matt Cordell's position. As the camera moves around a police car junkyard, the soundtrack features contrasting sounds. A children's chorus sings a nursery rhyme, "Two Dead Boys." Operating in a manner akin to the revealing use of nursery rhymes in Hitchcock's *The Birds* and *Marnie*, the song emphasizes the death-in-life imagery surrounding Matt Cordell, as well as a duality suggestively linking Cordell to two other figures: emotionally and physically scarred Detective Sean McKinney (Robert Davi) and deranged serial killer Turkell (Leo Rossi). The "Two Dead Boys" theme occurs later when Turkell offers Cordell sanctuary in his morbidly furnished apartment. While McKinney's pock-marked facial features parallel Cordell's more disfigured appearance, Turkell's Catholic-inspired altar to the women he murders is a blasphemous inversion of Cordell's religion. Like Cordell, McKinney is an Irish-American, Catholic cop experiencing personal problems similar to those that affected his predecessor, Frank McCrae, in the earlier film. In *Maniac Cop 2*, McKinney takes over Jack Forrest's role. Jack literally becomes one "dead boy." McKinney becomes his successor as Cordell's walking-dead counterpart in New York's mean streets. Cordell, McKinney, and Turkell all embody a death-in-life existence in different ways. The second musical leitmotif in this scene is a religious chant underscoring Cordell's physical resurrection in a car junkyard, a consumerist wasteland paralleling the used car lot Marion Crane encounters in *Psycho*. Prior to their eventual destruction, these police cars remain in a graveyard after serving their useful function. This automobile wasteland echoes Cordell's own situation as a once-honest cop who came too close to revealing city hall corruption and ended up abandoned and dead in Sing Sing.

After the credits, *Maniac Cop 2* opens with a holdup sequence revealing Cohen's innovative black humor. A hood robs a store and forces the owner to play a game of lucky chance with competition scratch cards. Ironically, the hood gets lucky and wins $5,000. But Cordell appears and overpowers him. However, believing in divine providence, the storekeeper looks forward to winning the prize as he utters, "Goodness is its own reward." But Cordell's appearance is not due to providence. And the storekeeper's prospective economic gain is the result, not of goodness, but of greed. As if recognizing this, Cordell kills the storekeeper with the hood's shotgun. He then sets up the unfortunate robber by returning his shotgun so he will face police bullets outside. The Maniac Cop returns to resume his reign of terror.

Despite their experiences, Jack and Teresa find police authorities unwilling to believe their story about Cordell's return. Pike's successor, Police Commissioner Doyle (Michael Lerner), prefers the official version of Cordell's death in Sing Sing. He sends Jack and Teresa to police psychologist Susan Riley (Claudia Christian). Like young Jason in *The Stuff*, they find themselves regarded as naughty children by an institution choosing to deny uncomfortable facts and realities. While Jack wishes to return to active duty and complies with the official version, Teresa adamantly affirms the truthful nature of their experiences. Jack eventually falls victim to Matt Cordell after ironically repeating the narcissistic patterns the latter developed in his previous life. Gloating over newspaper coverage concerning his heroic reinstatement, Jack comments, "That's not a bad picture. I'll buy a dozen of them. How often do you get a celebrity round here?" Cordell's attack ensures that Jack does not live to enjoy his glory.

Teresa dies before she can appear on television and denounce police suppression of Cordell's return. The police intend to prevent Teresa from speaking out, a policy that leads to her martyrdom at the hands of Cordell. As McKinney recognizes, the authorities care little for Teresa and show no sympathy for her personal grief over Jack's murder. He recognizes that keeping Teresa under control by preventing her from going to the newspapers is merely for "the good of the department." It is a strategy similar to that constraining Shepard in *Q— The Winged Serpent*. Society demands the maintenance of deceitful status quo principles no matter how dangerous they are to the general public.

Susan earlier informed Jack of Teresa's suspension from duty: "Jack, I'm afraid I'll have to give her a negative evaluation. I cannot let anyone out on the street with a gun who has emotional problems." This line immediately leads to McKinney's introduction. The following sequence shows him shooting down a criminal. As part of police routine demanding that any officer who kills a suspect must undergo counseling, it leads to his obligatory interview with Susan. As a lapsed–Catholic cop with "emotional problems" and a failed marriage, suffering from the devastating experience of his former partner's suicide, McKinney's personal dilemma uncannily echoes Frank McCrae, Jack Forrest, and Matt Cordell. Like Cordell, McKinney lives for his job. His pock-marked features designate him as a normal version of the walking dead Maniac Cop.

The most bizarre relationship in the film is the one between Cordell and Turkell. Cordell saves Turkell from the police before he can kill another female victim. In gratitude, Turkell offers the Maniac Cop sanctuary in an apartment he has turned into a perverse religious shrine. He shows Cordell his collection of female victims, dead strippers whose photographs are on display in a candle-lit altar. Turkell regards Cordell as a "fellow crusader." While Cordell's repressed sexuality operates in a paranoid crusade against innocent and guilty alike, Turkell murders strippers so their bodies belong to him in death. As he tells Cordell, "These are my girls. They aren't going to dance for anyone but me again." Like Hitchcock's dark figures, possessiveness motivates the nature of his destructive activities. Appealing to Cordell as a potential blood brother—"Maybe you see the possibilities in me?"— he draws out his knife. Cordell automatically displays his own deadly phallic nightstick. As Turkell ironically states, "You got a big one, too." Both figures exhibit similar traits involving morbid relationships with sexuality, possessiveness, death, and violence. They are both dualistically aberrant products of the same system.

Unfortunately, *Maniac Cop 2* does not develop these suggestive implications into a more coherent narrative. The film moves on into typical action territory, with Cordell leading Turkell and a death-row inmate into a last-stand battle at Sing Sing before Doyle officially admits institutional guilt for Cordell's unjust conviction. Avenging himself on the prisoners who murdered him, Cordell finally dies a fiery death after being set aflame in Sing Sing.

The final scene shows Cordell's funeral. Now officially exonerated, McKinney and Susan hope the Maniac Cop will now finally rest in peace. Underscoring the dualistic motifs in Cohen's screenplay, McKinney recognizes Cordell's deadly relationship to any police officer who takes pleasure in killing: "There is a piece of Cordell in every cop." As McKinney and Susan leave the cemetery, Cordell's white-gloved hand smashes through the coffin to seize his police badge placed there by McKinney. The danger is not over.

*Maniac Cop 3: Badge of Silence* (1992) suffers from disastrous interference making it almost unwatchable.[13] Producer Joel Soisson shot several additional scenes after both Cohen and Lustig left the film. These probably represent the last 20 minutes of the movie, replaying again the already tedious display of Matt Cordell's spectacular incineration in *Maniac Cop 2*. But although *Maniac Cop 3* is highly compromised, certain features do hint at interesting ideas in Larry Cohen's original screenplay. Perhaps having *The Bride of Frankenstein* in mind, Cohen conceived of *Maniac Cop 3* along the lines of a modern-day "Beauty and the Beast." Although Kate Sullivan's brain-dead condition appears in both the screenplay and the film, Cohen originally envisioned her becoming pregnant with Cordell's child. This would have added a further dark overtone to the question of terminating her life-support, involving the additional issue of abortion. Unfortunately, the current *Maniac Cop 3* bears no relation to what could have been an interesting amalgamation of themes common to *Maniac Cop* and *It's Alive.*

The film contains a few brief, interesting ideas. A voodoo "houngan" (Julius Harris) performs a ceremony raising Cordell from the dead at the very moment a Catholic funeral service designed to give peace to his wandering soul concludes. Later that evening, McKinney practices at the police firing range before attending a political dinner he has no interest in. Although no longer pock-marked as in *Maniac Cop 2*, and appearing in a more heroic light, McKinney still exhibits revealing psychological traits. He uses the firing range to express anger at the continuing city hall corruption that railroaded Matt Cordell. At the same time, female officer Kate Sullivan releases her tensions in a similar manner. She tells McKinney (who often acts as her protector-mentor on the force) about her anger against "establishment figures" in the mayor's office. Kate faces charges due to the "unnecessary violence" she used against an assailant's attempted rape. McKinney sympathizes with her dilemma. Like Matt Cordell, both are outsiders existing in a corrupt establishment dedicated to enforcing a law no longer supported by those in control. Any infringement leads to "railroading" on judicial charges by a system interested more in its own power than in protecting the public. Cordell, McKinney, and Sullivan express various degrees of psychic maladjustment, according to the respective circumstances affecting them. Commenting on Kate spending her birthday night by shooting at her imaginary "bad guys," McKinney gives her a present. Ironically, Kate's birthday night ends in a death-in-life situation paralleling that of Matt Cordell, a figure wishing to replace McKinney as her father-figure protector.

Arriving at the scene of a crime, McKinney views a headless body with a chicken feather inside its severed neck. Educating his partner, Hank (Paul Gleason), with the supernatural information he has acquired since his involvement with Matt Cordell, he tells him that the feather is a symbol allowing "the soul to take flight" after death. He conceals the body from two independent newsmen (based on the Los Angeles "Bad News Bears") who drive around seeking sensational stories. The two drive away, illegally listening to police radio bulletins while seeking lurid items they can sell to the networks. Like Matt Cordell and the corrupt city forces, they are products of a system debasing human values for economic gain. Noting that the networks never consider any crime story unless it involves "three confirmed deaths," they drive around in search of the next deadly incident. Tribble (Frank Pesce) prays "to the news gods to grant us just one good misfortune."

Their prayers are granted. Listening to a police report of a drugstore robbery, they arrive in time to film Kate Sullivan shooting drug-addicted psychotic Jessup (Jackie Earle Haley) before the latter's pharmacist partner, Terry (Vanessa Marquez), pumps the unsuspecting cop full of bullets. Although they film the whole scene, they re-edit footage so the already exploited "Maniac Kate" gets the blame for wounding Jessup and killing Terry.

Although Kate becomes railroaded like Matt Cordell, the film also reveals parallels between Jessup and Katie. While Jessup helps himself to drugstore pills like a child in a candy store, he drops several of them on the floor. Upstairs, Kate drops several bullets as she loads her gun. Although acting in the name of the law, she is clearly "high" on violence, a trait linking her both with Matt Cordell and the drug-addicted Jessup.

Following Kate into the hospital, McKinney encounters her mother. Despite her Catholicism, she appeals to him as her daughter's "protector": "If the Lord calls her, make sure she goes right away." Although Mrs. Sullivan's humanitarian feelings outweigh the rules of her religion, her request to McKinney has ironic overtones. The city authorities later work on her, gaining written consent to terminate Kate's life-support system. Since Kate used an illegal weapon against Jessup, the city faces a $1 million damage suit. But as McKinney points out, Kate needed to utilize the weapons of the street against the criminals using them. Less concerned with finding out the truth and more worried about financial liability, the authorities make a deal with Jessup's lawyer to drop criminal charges in exchange for a six-month suspended sentence should the plaintiff drop the suit. When McKinney learns of this from a city hall informant, he caustically remarks, "How bad is the stench in the Hall of Justice these days?" Prior to their poetically justified murder at the hands of Jessup and two escaping convicts, a city-authority lawyer bargains with Jessup's attorney over dropping all reference to homicide and manslaughter so the psychotic killer can collect all royalties resulting from "standard commercial exploitation of the story." Their deaths at the hand of their collective beneficiary parallel Cordell's avenging execution of the newsmen — especially after one ruthlessly exploits the feelings of a black teenager grieving over his murdered sister. Cordell's murder of uncaring city doctors such as Myerson (Doug Savant) and Powell (Robert Forster) appears justified by their callous attitude toward patients and those desperately in need of attention who wait for long periods. Irritated by Myerson's selfish nature, McKinney points toward a desperately ill, aged couple ignored by everyone in the hospital, telling him, "Help these people." Powell acts in a manner similar to Dr. Jacob Brand in *Full Moon High*, making banal jokes and laughing at his injured patients. In contrast to the first and second *Maniac Cop* films, Cordell's deadly activities are now justified. The character is changing and moving toward embodying the type of positive features characterizing the mutant babies in *Island of the Alive*. Unfortunately, he becomes a stereotypical monster in the climax.

Cordell's attraction to Kate Sullivan is obvious. Like Cordell, she suffers sacrificial martyrdom at the hands of a corrupt establishment. Like Cordell, Kate is Irish-American and Catholic. His feelings toward her parallel those he once had for Sally Noland, which echoed those existing between their normal counterparts, Jack Forrest and Teresa Mallory. In this respect, the "houngan's" remark to Cordell — "I could not have brought you back unless you wanted it, and your spirit will never be at rest, will it, Officer Cordell?" — is relevant, both about Cordell's tormented nature (one he shares with McKinney and Kate) and his awakening sexual desires. The screenplay moves from emphasizing links between McKinney and Kate to those between male and female "maniac cops."

As in *Maniac Cop 2*, Cordell and McKinney have certain associations. When McKinney first confronts the "houngan" in the abandoned Catholic Church linked to the hospital, the dialogue has interesting overtones. The "houngan" comments, "I have a way of attracting restless souls who find no comfort in conventional wisdom," a remark also applicable to Cordell. McKinney is also Kate's protector, a role Cordell aspires to. *Maniac Cop 3* contains parallel scenes showing Cordell and McKinney experiencing different reactions to news reports about Kate's supposed illegal activities. Cordell listens to it on a radio. McKinney watches it on television. While McKinney expresses anger at the obviously reedited footage, his less-repressed counterpart, Cordell, picks up the radio and smashes it. McKinney tells Dr. Susan Fowler (Caitlin Dulaney), "Katie is like a kid sister to me." However, the dream sequence involving Kate's wedding in the abandoned Catholic church contains significant parallels between all the main characters. While Susan gradually becomes the focus of McKinney's attentions, Kate finds herself attracting Cordell's desires. While Kate continues in a coma, Sean sits by her bed, protectively holding her hand as he falls asleep. She then experiences a dream. Dressed as a bride, she walks down an aisle toward a Catholic altar. Kate passes several elderly and middle-aged male and female cops who apprehensively look at her. These figures represent either those who died in the line of duty (like herself and Cordell) or aged embodiments of a death-in-life aura affecting the institutions she and Cordell belong to: law and religion. As she nears the altar, her groom waits. Wearing a tuxedo (similar to McKinney's in the opening scenes of the film) and having her protector's dark hair, the unseen person mentions Kate's unconscious desires for her father-protector, McKinney. But, as she arrives at the altar, she sees Cordell's skeletal, scarred features. He grasps her hand. The dream sequence ends with McKinney grabbing Kate's hand during her traumatic seizure. However, he tells Susan, "She grabbed my hand — like this." The "houngan" later recognizes that even the brain-damaged Kate realizes what her resurrection as bride of the monster means: "I cannot revive her soul. She will not allow it."

The "houngan" acknowledges a bond between Cordell and McKinney, "because you both walk in the same path." Both men live in a world that often leaves the "cry for justice" unanswered. Yet despite their conscious desires for justice, both men act in aberrant ways. While McKinney and Kate become affected by the adrenaline of violence inherent in their jobs, Cordell represents the monstrously realized expression of such perversely over-determined desires. He becomes a monster created by the system he once maintained. Cordell turns against everyone with the legally sanctioned violence he once performed in the name of law and order. It derives from a system causing him (and others such as McCrae and McKinney) intense psychological damage. As before, Cordell embodies the monstrous consequences of a system that is no longer honest and necessary, but corrupt and unredeemable. It causes everyone trapped within it either neurotic frustration or violent psychic disturbance.

Similar features also appear in Cohen's *Guilty as Sin* screenplay directed by Sidney Lumet. The completed film represents another example of a disjunction between Cohen's intentions and the particular style used by the director. As Phillip Strick notes, *Guilty as Sin* (1993) is evocative of a Hitchcock thriller, but one trapped within the confines of an average Hollywood production by a director unsympathetic to vibrant potentials contained in the screenplay.[14] Although the film lacks Cohen's subversive tendencies toward excess and absurdity, it nevertheless has several associations with the director's familiar ideas. Originally titled *Beyond Innocence*, *Guilty as Sin* utilizes, in another interesting manner, Cohen's favorite device of the double.

*Guilty as Sin* parallels two seemingly contradictory but symbiotic figures: upwardly mobile Chicago defense attorney Jennifer Haines (Rebecca DeMornay) and murderous psychopath David Greenhill (Don Johnson), depicting them as monstrous products of the same social situation. Unfortunately, Sidney Lumet's

In a scene from *Guilty as Sin*, master of control, Greenhill (Don Johnson) traps his attorney Jennifer Haines (Rebecca DeMornay) in a web of maneuvers and intrigue from which there is no legal escape (©Hollywood Pictures Company. All Rights Reserved).

direction fails to recognize the intuitive sense of radical absurdity that Cohen uses throughout the screenplay. Although Don Johnson captures the appealing, child-like nature of a monstrous threat, such as that typified by Cary Grant in Hitchcock's *Suspicion*, Rebecca DeMornay's inadequate performance fails to evoke sympathy for either her dilemma or her eventual understanding of the symbiotic kinship she has with her pursuer.

The screenplay contains several ingenious themes. Jennifer Haines makes a successful career defending clients both she and her prestigious law firm know are actually guilty. She encounters a charming killer she initially believes innocent but whom she discovers is really guilty of his wife's murder. Wishing to get her client convicted, Jennifer breaks the law by planting faked evidence until she finally faces the consequences of technically manipulating evidence to free dangerous criminals. Jennifer is also a performer playing to the gallery, like Tony Chappel in *In Broad Daylight*. When she was a little girl, Jennifer was taken to criminal trials by her "courtroom groupie" mother as a cheap substitute for going to the movies. But her law career actually began when a judge brought her back to his chambers after she interrupted courtroom proceedings with "I object." Fourteen at the time, Jennifer became his assistant a decade later. The full implications of this incident are left subtly open. But clear parallels exist between Jennifer's early career and David's occupation as a paid gigolo performing his charms on older women. Both Jennifer and David began their careers in undisclosed ways.

Like the deranged young men in the works of Alfred Hitchcock and Larry Cohen (from *Daddy's Gone A-Hunting* onwards), David suffered from some undisclosed childish trauma similar to Uncle Charlie's bicycle accident in *Shadow of a Doubt*. He tells Jennifer of his life as the only child of a military officer who died in Vietnam. David's mother took money out of his father's pocket to give to him for reasons the screenplay does not disclose. But it is obviously relevant to his later career as a gigolo. David informs Jennifer that he hardly dated in high school and never went out until after the death of his mother and "then mostly with older women." In a later scene, David launches into a tirade against women resembling Uncle Charlie's diatribe in *Shadow of a Doubt*:

> I've been described as such an exploiter of women, but now you can see for yourself, they use me and they drop me whenever they fucking please. Talk about women as a sex object, what about me? And I'm supposed to be some kind of a low-life because I take money when it's offered to me. Women do the same thing every day of their lives and it's perfectly fine!

Although David appears to criticize a particular type of sexual inequality, his lines really represent the type of performance Jennifer uses in the courtroom. As Jennifer later recognizes, David represents the "monster-client syndrome lawyers all dread." He is also the monster created within the dangerous confines of the family. Although we and the audience suspect David to be guilty throughout most of the film, the suspicion never gains confirmation until after Jennifer's attempt to fake evidence and set up her client on a murder charge. Alone in the courtroom, David thinks back to how he actually committed the murder, to assure himself that the newly discovered incriminating evidence does not belong to him. As in *Vertigo*, the audience enters into the mind of a "guilty" partner during a flashback. However, although Cohen borrows a technique from Hitchcock, his use is by no means derivative. In *Vertigo*, Scottie appears vulnerable and insecure when he first meets Judy. Only later does he become the monstrous patriarchal avenger unable to gain any audience sympathy. In *Guilty as Sin*, David's flashback represents his response to Jennifer's planted evidence. One guilty act actually follows another. Unlike *Suspicion*, in which Lina's suspicions concerning Johnny may result from a paranoid delusion, *Guilty as Sin* reveals both its doubles as equally guilty. Both are products of dysfunctional families. They equally use the system for their own gain. While David, like Uncle Charlie, lives off and murders wealthy "merry widows," Jennifer enjoys a successful career defending racketeers and murderers who can afford her prestigious law firm's huge fees. As an unequivocal and conscious guilty woman, she eventually encounters her satanic counterpart who will exercise deserved punishment on her. Unlike Marion Crane in *Psycho*, Jennifer is upwardly mobile and affluent and does not transgress in a moment of weakness. Unfortunately, both Lumet's direction and Rebecca DeMornay's performance fail to realize tantalizing implications contained in Cohen's screenplay. Seeing Jennifer for the first time at her junior-partnership celebration, David decides to cast her in his own perverse drama. Like Sir John in *Murder!*, he uses the woman for his own egotistical gratification. But, unlike *Murder!*, in which class and gender barriers separate Sir John and Diana Baring, Cohen's screenplay presents both Jennifer and David as guilty alter egos. As Strick notes, after the hung jury verdict, David "has already rewritten her past and infected her future."[15] Jennifer is more guilty than Cathy of *Daddy's Gone A-Hunting*, since her transgression is not a momentary one resulting from a temporary personal dilemma. It arises from her conscious egotistical involvement in a system delivering guilty parties from justice — as long as they can pay! Forced into an assisted suicide, like David's murdered wife, Jennifer finally becomes a victim of the type of dangerous criminal she successfully defended. The screenplay's ending logically necessitated her death, along with David's, as both fell from the balcony. However, the generic "happy ending" that was filmed denies the audience this appropriate satisfaction.

*Guilty as Sin* is another compromised product, the work of a director unsympathetic to nuances in Cohen's screenplay, and a film diluted by disavowing tendencies in contemporary Hollywood. The "happy ending" restores Jennifer to life and lets the audience off the hook. *Guilty as Sin* again illustrates the tendencies that led Cohen to begin directing his own work, following his similar experiences writing screenplays during the late sixties. As a creative person, Larry Cohen has many options, not the least of which is the stage. By showing what he has accomplished in the theater, the following chapter will reveal a neglected feature of Cohen's innovative talents.

# Theatrical Work

*Nature of the Crime, Motive* (a.k.a. *Trick*), and *Washington Heights* are plays that provide illuminating insights into the work of Larry Cohen.[1] They either rework or expand particular motifs from his television plays or films and antici-pate future projects. Usually performed off Broadway or outside London, Cohen's theatrical work reveals a multifaceted creative talent who could easily have suc-ceeded as a dramatist had his career not taken other directions. All three plays contain parallels to his earlier dramatic work in the final years of the "golden age" of live television. Rarely (if ever) performed since their initial stagings, Cohen's plays deserve to be better known, since they shed important light on a director usually neglected by most cinema scholars.

*Nature of the Crime* (originally titled "A Clear and Present Danger") was first performed in New York's Bowerie Lane Theater. Directed by actor Lonny Chap-man[2], the play featured an actor Cohen would later cast in *God Told Me To*— Tony Lo Bianco — in the role of accused scientist Daniel Aronoff. *Nature of the Crime* was a fusion of ideas Cohen had already used in series such as "The Defend-ers" and "Espionage." As in "The Secret," a scientist is accused of destroying a formula the American government needs for its research on the neutron bomb. Cohen uses the play to investigate the motives of the scientist in a far more pen-etrating and thorough manner than television allowed. Plot motifs also appear from two other episodes of "The Defenders": "Traitor" and "Colossus." Like "Traitor," *Nature of the Crime* examines the motif of betrayal, but at a far deeper level, merging the political with the personal. District Attorney Garrett's open-ing prosecution address in Act One, on page 14, touches on the theme of the superman used in "Colossus," but in a sarcastic manner:

> Certainly if we make exceptions for the insane...the mentally deficient, ... why shouldn't we make similar provisions for the superior intellect — the *super sane?*
> (Another pause)
> After all, look what they've done for us. They got us out of one war — ushered us into a new age of scientific development. We fought the war to destroy one "Master race." And out of it another master race arose. A gifted minority who apparently hold our survival in their grasp. That's why this case holds a very dan-gerous precedent. There's never been one like it. That's why we have to be so careful about what we decide here.

228

*Nature of the Crime* is a three-act play comparing and contrasting the two betrayals of Daniel Aronoff and his former mentor, Samuel Ullman (played by television actor Robert F. Simon). The first act, titled "The Crime," begins with Aronoff burning papers, his arrest, and the beginning of his trial. But the focus is equally upon the guilt felt by Samuel Ullman for the manner of his escape from Nazi Germany and complicity in the atomic bomb project. It is a complicity paralleling the involvement of his unseen tormentor, Kirsch, in the "final solution." In the play, Kirsch's presence is known only to Ullman and the audience. As the prosecutor questions Ullman on the stand, Kirsch asks the latter even more penetrating questions. Both Aronoff and Ullman are on trial. From the play's script, it appears Cohen envisioned the drama as articulating an almost cinematic "collision" structure resembling the theories of Sergei Eisenstein, especially those involving intellectual montage. This approach anticipates later developments in Cohen's work, especially those characterizing his first feature as director. His teleplays became adapted for broadcast within the normative "realist" practices generally adopted by the media. Cohen's live television dramas and scripts for "The Defenders" and "The Nurses" contain several radical ideas. But their effectiveness is often diluted by the formulaic nature of television production. Written before his first film as a director, *Nature of the Crime* already reveals his intuitive search for a style necessary to articulate fully the nature of his work. The stage directions reveal this, as we shall see. *Nature of the Crime* develops the self-deceptive nature of the human condition seen in the "Espionage" episode "Medal for a Turned Coat," a motif that appears in most of his films. In *Nature of the Crime,* the second and third acts are respectively titled "The Trials" and "The Secrets," revealing that more than one character is on trial. As in Cohen's later films, there are no heroes. Everyone is guilty in one way or another, sharing some secret that they deny both to themselves and the outside world. The play investigates both Aronoff and Ullman and ends with the former being brain-dead after taking a suicidal dose of lysergic acid and the latter's defiant refusal to admit his own particular guilt.

In an average television production, Aronoff's liberal defense lawyer, Theodore Benjamin, would have finally emerged as the hero who would save the day, like Perry Mason or Lawrence and Kenneth Preston of "The Defenders." However, even Benjamin is finally revealed as unheroic and guilty of the same self-deceptive egotism motivating Aronoff and Ullmann. In the final act, he discovers Daniel's suicide attempt and realizes that it is the hypocritical ploy of a "goddamn cop-out artist" pleading for sympathy. Instead of saving his client, he leaves him to die and decides to engage in a mission that is by no means as heroic as he believes: "I'll keep this case alive for ten years. I'll change the law of the land — because I believe in something — and I go all the way." (3-40) However, Benjamin is clearly deceiving himself. But unlike Dwight Webb, Jr., in *The Private Files of J. Edgar Hoover,* he lacks the necessary self-awareness to recognize this.

Aronoff, Ullman, and Benjamin are all Jewish. But, despite the play's important references to Jewish history, identity, and guilt, the issues extend into the wider world — a characteristic Cohen concern. Even his little-known theatrical ventures reveal these motifs as less ethnic, but more universal and relevant to other times and places.

Cohen's stage directions are extremely significant. He required "simplified sets" of a "suggestive" nature, features anticipating his later cinematic style. He describes *Nature of the Crime* as a "play of lighting rather than scenery, and the quick changes in time and space must be accomplished without stage waits." Cohen's strategy is more cinematic than theatrical, since it emphasizes filmic lighting technique and spatial-temporal changes that cinematic montage easily facilitates. His directions for the Aronoff home exhibit an intuitive sense of meanings suggested by mise en scene: "The furniture is that of an average middle-class family without children... There are twin beds." Something is clearly lacking in the Aronoff family.

The courtroom set is equally sparse, since Cohen decided that the "jury box will not be seen, since the audience is the jury," a feature anticipated in the final scene of "The Defenders" episode "Kill or Be Killed," when the camera pans left from behind the empty jury box, as an invisible observer of a debate between Lawrence Preston and his client. The dialogue focuses on whether the latter concealed his real feelings when he murdered the cop who pursued him. Similar revelations concerning self-deception feature prominently in *Nature of the Crime*.

Cohen's instructions concerning scene changes reveal an intuitive sense of cinematic construction. Short sequences are played in limbo: "Since they are taking place in the mind of the characters it is necessary only to focus attention with the lighting." Furthermore, since "during the set changes characters will be on stage performing scenes which bridge these changes," Cohen's economic techniques in this play parallel the cinematic use of lap-dissolves.

The author envisioned his play "in tones of black and white" limiting the "usual range of colors" for costumes and furniture. *Nature of the Crime*'s visual style contains undeniable overtones of Gothic expressionism akin to horror film technique, focusing on internal mental crises and dilemmas — features characterizing Cohen's later explorations within the realm of fantasy.

Act One opens with nuclear scientist Aronoff burning papers and his discovery by Ullman, who informs security about possible espionage. As District Attorney Garrett begins his address to the jury, the stage lights diminish, leaving an overhead spotlight over Ullman who faces his own internal demons personified by a military figure, Kirsch. Although he is the S.S. officer who allowed Ullman to escape in 1938 from certain death in a concentration camp, Cohen's descriptions reveal that the figure is to be taken, not as a historically specific character, but a more universal one: "We cannot quite make out the details of the uniform." Later, we see that, although Kirsch wears a German officer's uniform, he includes no Nazi arm band.

The next scene involves dialogue between Aronoff and Benjamin. As they discuss the implications of the charge, the audience discovers the isolated nature of Aronoff. It anticipates the outsider status of later Cohen characters. Lacking a real father, Aronoff made a fool of himself during Ullman's lecture many years before, demanding attention from a surrogate figure. Aronoff's description of himself also resembles Cohen's future character of David Greenway in *Guilty as Sin*:

> I was sixteen years old. I had never shaved or been out with a girl or really had a friend. I had graduated from high school when I was thirteen. I was still a child, but I had never been a child. [1-13]

As the play continues, we also learn about a personal problem affecting the Aronoff marriage similar to that affecting the married couple in Basil Dearden's *Victim* (1961). Both couples are significantly childless. The more experienced Ruth Aronoff married a man who was "a twenty-five-year-old virgin" whose early childhood experiences at the hands of a punitive mother resulted in masochistic tendencies. As the conversation continues, the audience learns that Daniel Aronoff's stand as a martyr for world peace and freedom of thought may be less heroically inclined and due more to hidden desires for punishment. Ruth comments, "You're strong enough to defy the whole system. I thought maybe you were strong enough to face up to..." It clearly has something to do with her husband's repressed homosexuality, a factor linking him to future Cohen characters. Despite Ruth's desires to help her tormented spouse, Daniel prefers to wallow in the depths of a guilty secret.

In a revealing speech, Daniel regards himself as a monster, his only youthful contact being with a retarded child he looked at every day before it was taken away to a home to die. He sees an affinity with the world of the abnormal, as do his later successors in Cohen's films. Like Frank Davies in *It's Alive*, his attempts to fit into the system cause him traumatic misery.

Benjamin then arrives with Ullman. The older man makes a final plea to Daniel to consider the ethnic implications of his forthcoming trial. A refugee from the Nazi era, he cites historical figures such as the Rosenbergs, appealing to the younger man not to feed the fires of hate:

> I went through this once. I didn't think it could happen either. But bit by bit they alienated us from gentile society until everyone believed we were the enemy. [1-24]

Despite Ullman's appeals to racial solidarity, Daniel condemns the older man's hypocrisy and prejudice, contradicting his proclaimed sense of ethnic patriotism. Daniel refuses to participate in the nuclear arms race, preferring capital punishment or life imprisonment under the amended Violation of the Atomic Energy Act indictment. He condemns Ullman's participation in the arms race.

As Daniel leaves, Ullman is left alone to face his own personal demons personified by Kirsch. The audience learns how Kirsch rescued Ullman, making an obligatory gesture of saving him by giving him the identity of a Düsseldorf merchant. He tells Ullman of the Nazi state benefiting from a financial deal with insurance companies by gaining 15 percent of the face value of death benefits on non–Aryans. Despite initially refusing Kirsch's offer and failing to convince him to escape with him, Ullman breaks down and accepts the false identity.

The act closes with Garrett's significant concluding address: "Well, you're aware of the charges — you understand the nature of the crime. You've seen the principals, you know the facts — now, the trial."

The second act's title, "The Trials," makes evident the fact that more than one defendant is involved. As prosecuting and defense attorneys verbally spar in the courtroom, the drama moves toward Ullman's cross-examination undertaken by both Garrett and Kirsch. Unseen by all except Ullman and the audience, Kirsch wanders around the courtroom performing actions that are sometimes comic in nature. As Cohen's stage directions state, "HE may sit on the edge of the prosecution's table or even move to the JUDGE'S bench to pour a glass of water for himself from the pitcher." When Benjamin begins his cross-examination of Ullman over participation in the Los Alamos Project, Kirsch drives the interrogation even further by asking more penetrating questions about the older scientist's obeying orders from the state. Despite Ullman's participation in scientific protests against the use of the Bomb, Kirsch accuses him of hypocrisy: "You wanted that bomb — but you wanted someone else to carry the responsibility." Both Benjamin and Kirsch unveil Ullman's guilt feelings over the Bomb's effect upon Hiroshima's inhabitants. Despite Benjamin's attempts to compare Ullman's dilemma with that of the defendant, the older scientist attempts to make an arbitrary division between government ownership of his scientific research and his personal individual freedom. It is a division questioned by Benjamin, who shows that Ullman's supposed personal freedom did not prevent his complicity in naming names during the McCarthy era. The judge disallows further interrogation into Ullman's many submissions to the state apparatus of (in Benjamin's words) "A country set up to protect your individual rights — not to *own* you body and soul."

As the court adjourns, Ullman faces Kirsch. Kirsch's comments are clearly designed to compare the challenges both men enjoyed when respectively working for their own particular states, challenges devoid of any human concerns:

> There was a great challenge to face. A tremendous problem in organization and logistics. To transport so many millions of families — in relative secrecy — some of them halfway across Europe. Without panic — without undue violence. To keep accurate records — to feed — to clothe. [2-21]

He unveils the "organization man" mentality linking them both, and reveals to Ullman his execution by the Gestapo in 1943, an act we later learn resulted from his informing on himself. In Act Three, Kirsch admits that the other side of his personality performed the deed, a monstrous organization-man superego affronted by the one act of humanity the S.S. man performed to disrupt the operations of his own system: "Someone else had to stop me. I was so good at it." (3-24)

Kirsch (Adam Keefe) acts as an avenging conscience from beyond the grave questioning nuclear scientist Samuel Ullman (Robert F. Simon) in Larry Cohen's theatrical play *Nature of the Crime* (1970) (courtesy of Larry Cohen).

Affected by Benjamin's interrogation of Ullman, Daniel decides to change his plea to guilty, perhaps fearing a similar disclosure of what really motivates him. As the play continues, Benjamin learns the perverse sexual dynamics motivating the marital life of both Daniel and Ruth. Accepting an unfulfilling sexual relationship with Daniel, Ruth masochistically indulged "that wonderful warm feeling that she was *giving up something, something* for someone else" in her involvement with a man who refused to admit his bisexuality to her. By paralleling Daniel's personal guilt with the political guilt felt by Ullman, Cohen links both characters as mirror images in a highly revealing manner. Like the Fritz Weaver character in "Medal for a Turned Coat," Daniel Aronoff is no real hero. His supposedly heroic actions veil damning flaws in his character. Daniel's desire for punishment is not politically motivated but masochistic, a flaw having an indirect connection with both his early family life and his present difficulties in living up to masculine definitions in a patriarchal society. His actions are sublimations of sexual and personal insecurity. As Benjamin comments:

> Daniel, some men assert their masculinity by climbing mountains. Others are satisfied to climb on top of the first woman that comes along. You had to fuck the entire United States government.

However, Benjamin himself also wants to fuck the United States government. At the end of the play, he leaves Daniel to die, seeing him as an abstract object to use in his fight against the system rather than a human being needing help. His final action reveals that he is little better than Ullman and Kirsch.

The third act begins with Benjamin's opening defense address as he questions modern developments in surveillance techniques and the right a person has to ownership of his own thought processes. But issues raised by *Nature of the Crime* extend far beyond the tidy resolutions of courtroom dramas such as "The Defenders." This final act is, after all, appropriately titled "The Secrets."

Daniel now takes the stand and testifies to the destruction of his "private research" to prevent it from falling into government hands. However, as in "The Secret," Daniel's problem-solving activities are more than a harmless game. They really represent a cold, superhuman, soulless egotism paralleling the activities of both Kirsch and the title figure in "The Colossus." Daniel's compulsion to solve problems while working on the neutron bomb formula, months after he requested release from the project, represents an addiction motivated by a monstrous ego he refuses to acknowledge. In language paralleling the motivations of Kirsch and Ullman, Daniel states, "I was only doing a job, the only way I know how. The best I could."

After Kirsch shows the scars of his execution to Ullman, the scene changes to the Aronoff home. In a long monologue, Daniel tells Ruth about his father's ritual Sunday morning drives when he vented his repressed anger at other motorists after six days of selling haberdashery. Sunday was no day of rest for his father, but an opportunity to exercise pent-up aggression against the outside world during a long-distance drive to no particular destination. Daniel's dysfunctional family experiences contribute to his later personal dilemmas. Confronting Garrett's accusation of being a cheat, he can no longer face himself and attempts suicide.

As Garrett and Ullman talk about Daniel after the event, Cohen places Daniel on the stage behind them, swallowing pills in a cleverly executed theatrical montage of attractions linking the past consequences of his act with present implications for the two men. After a blackout representing the final destruction of Daniel's mind by lysergic acid, Benjamin enters and then leaves, deciding to use him as a pawn in his own practical problem game against the state apparatus.

The play ends with Ullman confronting the brain-dead Daniel who has regressed into a pre-adult condition to escape from his own personal demons. He burns the last letter Daniel sent him before his suicide attempt in an act recalling the one opening the play. The letter contains a selection of poetry and essays written by Daniel's young radical supporters, which he felt approached an understanding of what he did. However, it is not enough to prevent Daniel's final descent into the masochistic tendencies dominating him since early childhood. He "dies" a victim of family and state, refusing them admission to his mind by committing an extreme act that guarantees no entry. Ullman attempts asserting his lack of guilt to Kirsch, who is no longer present. The stage lights dim out as the paper in Ullman's hand blackens into ashes: "The play ends as it began on a solitary flame in the immense blackness of the theatre." (3-43)

*Nature of the Crime* is an extremely revealing play developing ideas in Cohen's earlier teleplays and anticipating the themes of his future films, such as the guilt-ridden, frustrated individual at odds with his society, the "monster" created by a society paradoxically needing it for its inhuman operations, the trauma of a sexually and politically divided subject moving toward self-destruction, and the implicit necessity for individual and social change as the only way to avoid chaos.

The two-part play *Motive* opened in Guildford, England, in 1976, with Honor Blackman (later replaced by Carroll Baker) as Paula, George Cole as Creed, and Ian Hendry as Barrows. Four years later, *Motive* opened in New York under a different title, *Trick,* with Tammy Grimes in the role of Paula, Lee Richardson as Creed, and Donald Madden as Barrows. Cohen later sold the property to a film company who drastically ruined the story and released it as *Scandalous* (1983). Despite featuring Pamela Stephenson (then well-known in England for her *Not the Nine O'Clock News* comedy series) and John Gielgud, *Scandalous* is only worthy of mention as the most disastrous, altered version of a Cohen story ever filmed. *Motive* is far more interesting.

The original play features three characters: news commentator Wallace Barrows, dangerous, murderous blackmailer Paula Cramer, and sexually ambiguous police detective Andrew Creed. *Motive* is a highly innovative twentieth-century comedy of manners including typical Larry Cohen themes concerning masculine insecurity and gender ambivalence.

In one version of the script, Cohen set the entire action in the theatrically limited confines of Barrows' cooperative apartment in the affluent vicinity of the United Nations Plaza in New York. But both the London and New York theatrical versions set the events in England, with Barrows depicted as a BBC newscaster. The play differs from *Nature of the Crime*, since it involves few internal psychological investigations aided by expressionistic lighting and more combative dialogue between three different characters who reveal their real natures through

Distinguished 30s Group Theater veteran and critic Harold Clurman meets Robert F. Simon and Larry Cohen backstage during the off–Broadway production of *Nature of the Crime* (courtesy of Larry Cohen).

significant lines and actions. *Motive* does not resort to hidden characters such as Kirsch to reveal the split subjectivities of its leading characters. It is a clever comedy resembling *Sleuth*, but concentrates more on internal charades and deceptions that characters employ in a mental chess game involving changing deadly power relationships akin to a Hitchcock thriller.

The play opens in darkness. A woman's scream pierces the auditorium. A thud follows, leading to silence before the curtain lifts. Barrows' large cooperative duplex appears, containing traditional furniture, "plenty of masculine items in leather but with a decided woman's touch." Like Jeff's apartment in *Rear Window* (1954), we learn the nature of the occupant's life from the mise en scene. One corner contains awards, plaques, statuettes, and handsomely framed photographs including several noteworthy figures such as De Gaulle, Eisenhower, and Truman all posing with Barrows. Although "Everything is compact, neatly arranged," the juxtaposition of scattered art work by Klee, Moore, and Miro, "with blowup photographs of some of the great tragedies of our decade, a flood, an assassination, a funeral of a head of state, a race riot"[3] denote an uneasy balance of chaos and control suggestive of Barrows' own personality. Barrows constructs his particular image as a news reporter, giving himself an assumed importance through his association with the famous men in the photographs. Significantly, no women appear in these photographs. Furthermore, he plays a role in front of the camera when presenting the news to a hidden audience during his broadcasts. One of the most significant descriptions in Cohen's stage directions involves the world outside:

> Most important is the vast courtyard visible through the huge windows now that the drapes are open. There are hundreds of windows out there. Thousands of eyes may be peering across, hidden by Venetian blinds. Eyes watching as we. [1-1-1]

Like other Cohen characters such as advertising executive Frank Davies in *It's Alive*, Barrows plays a role for particular audiences. But the stage directions suggest a fear of revelation, a fear that a sudden turn of events may bring out hidden characteristics repressed during everyday existence.

Barrows rises from behind a couch and speaks as if to an invisible audience, describing the discovery of his wife's body. Since nobody else appears, Barrows looks like a performer rehearsing his role. The stage directions are suggestive:

> (There is no one else in the scene. Either BARROWS is talking to himself or perhaps testing his "alibi" out loud, after having just committed murder.) [1-1-2]

Although several answers may explain Barrows' stage entry, the initial impression tends to suggest his kinship with those dangerous performers or stage managers in Cohen's other work, such as Tony in *In Broad Daylight* and Cleve in *Best Seller*. However, we then see Creed rise from a chair. He is Barrows' immediate audience.

During the subsequent dialogue, we learn that Barrows' wife appears to be the latest victim of the "Strangler Killings" affecting New York. Creed continues interrogating Barrows and suggestively probing his media mask. At this point in the play, we do not know if Barrows has actually murdered his wife, but his dialogue reveals a man who is clearly manipulative and who could have performed the act. Like all major Cohen characters, Barrows has another side, one perhaps as dark as that revealed by the presidential candidate in "The Defenders" episode "Go-Between":

> CREED: "My God, for ten years I've seen the world go to hell through your eyes.... They gave it to you all by yourself with the hot lights burning each casualty report into your grain, but I saw it, times when you slipped. I thought I did. Times when one eyelid would twitch when your throat ran dry in mid-sentence ... and at the very end of the half-hour — when you'd try to convey some hope and you'd fail at it — and only show the pain you felt at having to tell us all these awful facts of life.
> (Beat)
> Was I wrong then? Was I reading all that into you?"
> BARROWS: "I assure you I was never trying to create that impression."
> CREED: "At any rate, you're a most effective actor."

Unlike his more prestigious (and humanitarian) contemporaries such as Ed Murrow, William Shirer, and Eric Severaid, Barrows succeeds as a newscaster by maintaining a spurious tone of neutrality. He admits to Creed that his rise to fame began during the fifties — an era characterized by the revealing historical forces of McCarthyism and the Cold War significantly left unmentioned in his conversation. Barrows is a successful organization man confident about his chosen masculine self-definition and successful career, a character ripe for the necessary fall awaiting similar self-satisfied males in Cohen's work. Two characters are instrumental in threatening Barrows — gay detective Creed and independent blackmailing hit woman Paula Cramer — characters whom Cohen describes as representing two of the worst nightmares confronting traditional males.

Creed suggests taking Barrows on a date with him, offering two tickets to the Philharmonic. As the first scene ends, Cohen describes Creed as having an "implied threat" in the smile he offers Barrows, an action whose significance the audience will later understand.

The second scene features Barrows confronting Paula Cramer. Paula initially passes herself off as a friend of his deceased wife but, soon revealing that she is the real murderer, blackmails him. If he refuses her demands, she will set him up for the police by reporting that they are accomplices. Paula advertises her perverse profession as another example of the American way of life:

> Women are breaking through into all the professions! Taking the initiative. Getting out there and developing new markets. Isn't this the American way? Don't wait for a demand — create one. That's how our gross national product has risen to its current heights. American business anticipates the public needs and supplies the services. Sell them the dreams and desires they never knew they had. Don't you watch your own commercials?

She represents the darker side of the same system employing Barrows. As a newscaster using neutral tones and language to sell bad news to his audiences in the manner his station expects, he encounters Paula as a monstrous embodiment of the disasters he sanitizes in his news reporting. Like Creed, Paula also observes his performance:

> I've watched you reeling off the casualty figures every evening at six, documenting the deaths in some hotel fire with utter detachment. Earthquakes, floods, riots, bombings. You've never lost your cool. I thought that a man so unmoved by the realities of life ... would be approachable. [1-2-45]

Paula gives him Elizabeth's engagement ring, which she stole during the murder as "incriminating evidence" should he not agree to her plan. The second act continues the power struggle, with Barrows becoming further overpowered by the combined gender assaults of Creed and Paula. Unlike Elizabeth, Creed manages to get Barrows into the kitchen to perform the "female" role of cooking that he previously spurned. The actual killer has now been caught and shot by the police. But Creed notes the differences between Elizabeth's death and the other victims as well as one particular parallel: "He was a big fellow like you, he didn't require an edge."

The detective seductively invites Barrows to join him on holiday, despite the latter's involvement in a new form of reporting political conventions that will not affect television time. Like Bill Lennick in *Bone*, Barrows does not wish to waste any valuable time:

> We're going to use an entirely different technique this go — around. Our computer will pick the winner forty-five minutes after the nominations — and we'll return to normally scheduled programs. We're on an economy kick. [2-1-7]

When Creed becomes jealous over Paula's presence, Barrows agrees to accompany him on holiday. The second act shows Creed and Paula together in Barrows' apartment. They watch their victim on television neutrally recounting the latest toll of death and disaster. As she listens, Paula becomes "honestly concerned"[4] about the families of the victims, significantly adding that the media has made everyone "helpless listeners." Creed begins interrogating her and uncovers her long history of fraudulent activities. Paula then tells Creed a different story about her involvement in the affair. She tells him she heard Barrows murder Elizabeth. Creed then enlists her in his plot to trap Barrows. The intended victim arrives to find Paula in his apartment. Creed listens to the proceedings upstairs.

Barrows admits that he is terrified of them both. Finally, Paula provokes Barrows into delivering incriminating dialogue for Creed's benefit. He gives Elizabeth's wedding ring to Paula as partial payment. After she leaves, Creed reveals himself as Elizabeth's lover and intends booking him for murder. But Barrows appears less upset at this new change of events. He is more affected by the fact that Creed's friendship was only a pretense. It was as much a performance as his nightly television show. Affected by feelings he cannot deal with, Barrows bludgeons Creed to death. Paula returns and admits seeing Creed with Elizabeth. Barrows places money beneath the murder weapon so her prints appear on it. After she leaves, he calls the police, informing them that she is Creed's murderer. However, the final lines reveal the real agony Barrows faces.

Tearing Creed's notebook containing the incriminating notes he wrote upstairs, he trembles in "frustrated rage." His final words are highly revealing — "You never liked me. You never liked me at all" — as he looks at Creed's dead body and attempts propping up the shaky foundations of a masculinity now radically undermined. The conclusion has several ironic overtones. As Terry Curtis Fox noticed, Barrows discovers he is now the "Other," a designation he has applied to outsiders such as Creed and Paula.[5] If Barrows did not actually kill his wife, he discovers he has the potential for murder, one linking him to Paula. Furthermore, throughout the course of the play, the self-assured newscaster is attracted by Creed's seductiveness while he attempts repressing its implications. Although the play ends with the probable arrest of Paula, and Barrows' escape from suspicion, his self-certainty has already been internally undermined. *Motive* is a chamber play exploring gender tensions and the unveiling of monstrous masculinity within everyday life. It illuminates several issues raised in Elayne Chaplin's fine doctoral thesis *Monstrous Masculinity*.

Originally titled "Churches Nearby," *Washington Heights* is the most recent play written by Larry Cohen. It is a fictionalized semi-autobiographical representation of major influences appearing in his film and television ventures. Like "The Golden Thirty," *Washington Heights* is not a factual representation of events in Cohen's early life. The play begins in 1939, two years before Larry Cohen's birth and America's entry into World War II. Dealing with four characters — Al Greenwald, his wife Marcia, their young son Daniel, and his Irish-American grandmother — *Washington Heights* continues Cohen's theatrical psychological chamber dramas, but concentrates more on family tensions. It also depicts the uneasy Jewish American relationship with the world. Despite a sad ending, *Washington Heights* contains an affirmative note. But it is one tempered by the recognition that any victory is really provisional in view of the continuing threats affecting everyday existence.

The play opens in the nicely furnished Greenwald apartment situated in the Jewish area of New York's Washington Heights. Twelve-year-old Daniel, his 30-year-old parents, Al and Marcia, and Daniel's 68-year-old grandmother sit at the dinner table. Although not as oppressive as in Cohen's other films, family tensions affect the Greenwalds. A generation gap exists between Al and Daniel. Al works as a radio salesman in a New York store, as well as collecting rent from poor black tenants who live in his father's apartments in Harlem. He also conceals his Jewish identity by using a false surname in the anti–Semitic world of Depression America. Grandma constantly interferes in the Greenwald's family life, intruding into the home every day, and constantly speaking about her deceased Irish-American brothers who all worked on the police force. Every evening, the phone rings with messages from tenants wishing repairs to their apartments. As a result, Al's social, economic, and family pressures cause him to develop ulcers.

Like Chris Davies in *It's Alive* and Jason in *The Stuff*, Daniel senses tensions within family relationships. But his family often refuses to acknowledge them, resulting in Daniel's feelings of alienation. He retreats into an imaginary world of comic books, believing that he is an unwanted child isolated from a father who cannot understand him. Although *Washington Heights* initially appears to suggest the presence of Cohen's favorite theme of the monster created by the family, it moves in other directions. The play is more of a positive *bildungsroman* in which Daniel eventually gains important insights into the nature of his personal and social world, as well as finally achieving reconciliation with his father. This latter aspect represents a direction *It's Alive* only realized temporarily — a utopian unity between a father and son who manage to overcome negative influences originating from both the family and the outside world. Before Al leaves for military service in 1941, he and Daniel finally unite and realize a new form of relationship based upon respect and friendship. This conclusion also echoes the final moments in *Island of the Alive*.

The opening scenes reveal the tensions affecting the Greenwalds. Daniel irritates Al by making wise-guy suggestions. Grandma appropriates Marcia's role as wife and mother. At this point, Daniel does not really understand the realities of the external social, cultural, and economic tensions affecting his family. He feels guilty about his father's role as rent collector: "I don't ever want anything to do with those buildings. I don't like taking advantage of poor people." (1-1-6)

Al believes comic books adversely affect Daniel, while Marcia blames the movies. But Daniel's reply to his mother reveals the real cause: "I only blink when I'm home. I don't blink at school. I don't blink at the movies. Something around here makes me blink." (1-1-7)

Overburdened by family responsibilities, Al yearns to be drafted into the military. Like Frank Davies in *It's Alive*, he lives a lie in a job he feels unhappy about. While Al's Jewishness results in his loss of employment, Frank Davies later finds himself in a position resembling that of a German Jew in 1933. His "guilty by association" status as father of the monster baby results in his social and economic alienation. Al Greenwald loses his job when Danny accidentally reveals his identity to anti–Semitic employers at Dunlap's.

When Marcia tells Danny the reasons behind his father's WASP masquerade as "Al Stevens," the young boy gains his first insight into the threatening forces surrounding his world. During this moment, the lighting ominously changes. The apartment becomes slowly darker, "almost frightening. Lightness has been replaced with shadow and uncertainty":

> MARCIA: "Don't you know when we read the ads for schools and summer cottages in the *Times* when it says in the ad 'churches nearby' that means no Jews allowed? That's how they put it so that it's nice and polite. So that nobody will get embarrassed. Look at the ads next week, next Sunday. All the hotels that put that in, and the camps...This part of Washington Heights is predominantly a Jewish neighborhood. Didn't that ever dawn on you? But outside of here a lot of people don't like us. Some of them even blame us for what's going on in Europe. They think their sons may have to fight to protect the Jews from Nazis." [1-2-3]

She explains to Danny that, like Al, his favorite entertainers, Jack Benny and Eddie Cantor, also compromise by changing their names to succeed in an anti–Semitic world in which "a Negro has a better chance of being considered for the White House." Marcia also comments ironically upon a "business as usual" philosophy featured in Cohen's film and television work: "There are some companies that just will not hire Jewish help. And that's their business. They're allowed. This is America. It's a free country." (1-2-4)

Danny also understands the role playing his family performs as a means of disavowing the traumatic circumstances of Al losing his job. It is a family ritual paralleling the findings of Erving Goffman in *The Presentation of Self in Everyday Life*:

> MARCIA: "I don't listen to what he says. I look at the man. He's lost his job and he doesn't want to scare us. So he puts on this act and you're going to have to learn to put on an act, too.
> (she crosses to him and puts her hands on him, speaking softly)
> He's going to keep pretending that he's going to work and we're going to let him

keep pretending. We're not going to do anything to show him that we know
different. He wants to protect us and we're going to let him because we love him."
[1-2-7]

The scene ends with Danny reading the Sunday paper, a scene ending with
the light fading and a church bell chiming in the distance:

DANNY: "Campbell's Dude Ranch. Trail riding trained instructors. Heated pool.
Churches nearby.
  (he looks out at the audience)
All of a sudden our street and the whole neighborhood seemed lonelier and darker
and I didn't like traveling too far away from our building anymore.
  (he reads again from the paper)
Grover's Cottages. Tennis, boating...churches nearby.
  (to audience)
The terrible things that were happening in Europe seemed closer now. I felt
different — and I didn't like being different.
  (The shadows on the stage deepen and Danny seems very isolated in the midst
of darkness)
I started noticing all the movie actors and singers who had changed their names.
Because maybe no one would like them if they used their own name. And I wondered if the whole world out there wasn't a lot like Dunlap's." [1-2-14]

Act two, scene one is the longest in the entire play. It contains the deepest
conflicts affecting the Greenwald family. Danny finds out his parents once considered an abortion, becoming seriously affected by this revelation. He wishes to
find out if it is true. But his family attempts ignoring the issue, as they avoid
Danny's questions about their fate should the Germans invade America. Danny
reacts to this evasiveness by getting his father fired a second time, after Dunlap's
rehires him because he sells the most goods. On one level, Danny's act is petulant. But, on another level, it represents the act of a son who wishes his father to
drop all pretense and become a real hero like his comic strip idols:

Always the heroes in my comic books were weaklings and cowards — to everybody
else — but secretly inside they were brave and gallant and true. And they never
hesitated to fight injustice once they had their masks on. I tried to figure out why
they could never be strong as themselves? Why they had to keep their courage
hidden.
  (a pause)
And it bothered me that nobody in comic books was ever Jewish. [2-1-24]

By getting his father fired, Danny duplicates the actions of the monster baby
in *It's Alive*. He acts aggressively in an attempt to force his father to recognize circumstances affecting their real lives in a hostile world. Al responds by destroying
most of his son's precious comic collection, an action paralleling Frank Davies
shooting his son in *It's Alive*. Though different in nature, both actions have traumatic consequences for the victims. As the second scene shows, Danny really acts
as his father's "return of the repressed," but in a less violent manner than the *It's*

*Alive* babies. Danny's act is a provocative gesture meant to force his father to fight back against threatening forces in his society, as the monster babies react against their aggressors in the *It's Alive* films. His actions also parallel those of Lee Grant's Doris Kelly in "The Gift," whose provocative methods return her patient to life and the exercise of responsibility.

Danny's lines about dressing up as a girl so that any Germans would not look for the revealing mark of identity cause Al anxiety about his son's gender identification. Although the masquerade is treated humorously in the play, it does represent a radical Cohen insight. The director recognizes a common identity between all those individuals whom society labels as "monstrous" during any historical period — whether Jew, African-American, female, or "queer."

Act two, scene one serves as a catalyst for the remaining scenes, which move *Washington Heights* toward a rapid conclusion. Scene two includes a touching reconciliation between Al and Danny. Now wearing a buck private's uniform, Al enlists a year before Pearl Harbor. He gains the admiration of his son who proudly wears his father's military cap and studies his reflection in a mirror. Danny now asks his father the "unwanted child" question, which dominates his mind. Avoiding any clichéd "happy ending," Cohen has Al answer ambiguously, "What kind of question is that? You were a wonderful baby. It wasn't till you were seven that you started getting on my nerves." (2-2-3) The question remains unresolved. Father and son then walk proudly together through Manhattan.

In scene three, Al finally exercises control over his family. Like the Robert Webber character in "The Gift," he asserts his independence and gets Marcia to demand from Grandmother the keys to their home. Al presents Danny with a special Captain Marvel "Whiz" comic as an apology for the ones he destroyed. But Danny begins to realize a significant difference between his imaginative world of comics and the real world outside. As his concluding lines note, "But unlike my favorite comic-book characters, Daddy wasn't made of steel." (2-3-7)

The final scene depicts the family mourning for Al, who has died at Anzio. Although Marcia, in a momentary fit of grief, initially blames Danny for Al's death, she soon understands the real reasons motivating her husband and attempts an apology: "Danny, look at me. I was wrong. The reason he joined up wasn't what you did. It was what *they* do. It was things like 'Churches nearby.' Do you understand that?" (2-2-4)

*Washington Heights* ends with Danny's final address to the audience. He speaks of changes in the family relationships, his burning the comic books (except one) the day the wire announcing his father's death arrived, the posthumous union with Al, and the ominous realization that the threatening nature of the world outside also awaits him:

> DANNY places that one solitary comic book back under his pillow from where he picks up a SOLDIER'S CAP. He puts it on and goes to stand beside his uniformed father, AL, who has materialized on stage. They stand together again, admiring their reflections in the mirror — as on that day — so long ago. That precious and endless moment — gradually the stage goes to black.

In the distance we HEAR the faint chiming of CHURCH BELLS — as the CUR-
TAIN FALLS. [2-4-4]


Co-written by Larry Cohen and Janelle Webb Cohen,[6] with music and lyrics
by Richard and Robert Sherman, *Levi!* is a satirical musical-comedy with serious
overtones. It represents the same type of heterogenous mixture appearing in
Cohen's other generic interventions. Still unproduced, this work forms an appropriate conclusion for this chapter. Written by founder members of Larco, it is far
superior to the over-acclaimed, glossy, trivialized productions of Andrew Lloyd-
Webber and reactionary works such as *Miss Saigon*. Like *Black Caesar*, *It's Alive*,
and *The Private Files of J. Edgar Hoover*, *Levi!* transcends any generic definitions
and resists convenient categorization. It is as much a musical as *Black Caesar* is
blaxploitation and *It's Alive* a horror film. Instead, it is another of Cohen's radical heterogenous mixtures.
    The performance begins with the arrival in New York of a group of Jewish
immigrants during the early 1840s. Prior to their arrival, three musical themes in
an opening medley function as a montage of ideological collisions characterizing
various forces that Levi Straus confronts in America. Two rapacious businessmen,
Stafford and Howard, sing "Business Is Business," a number that occurs throughout the musical, stressing economic advancement as the real goal of the American way of life in which profits are more important than people. Levi's Aunt
Frieda sings "The Streets Are Paved with Gold," a paean to another version of
the American Dream, stressing the idealistic aspect of immigrant desires. The final
number, "Welcome to the U.S.A.," is sung by a cynical group of immigration
officials who regard the newcomers as "taking our country away." These medleys
serve to introduce the competing ideologies influencing Levi throughout the
musical, forces that compete for his very soul.
    The young Levi has left a Bavaria where Jews can only marry by special
license. He hopes he will obtain both wealth and a family in the New World, and
coaches his fellow immigrants into getting past the officials by posing as readily
exploitable cheap laborers. As the immigrants disembark, their idealistic medley
clashes with the cynical "Welcome to the U.S.A." song of the officials. Once the
contrasting medleys conclude, steel bars drop down from above, incarcerating the
immigrants in a series of cages. While Levi's consumptive friend, August, fails to
pass the medical examination, Levi and others get through to pursue the American Dream.
    Levi soon finds that his rich family members are really poor peddlers living
in a New York Sixth Ward ghetto area. They soon set him to work selling clothes
in a city that is still infested by wild pigs. As his uncle says, "They were supposed
to be New York's garbage collectors, but it got out of hand. Now there's hundreds. And they bite." (1-2-15) Like Samuel Fuller, Cohen often inserts neglected
historical features into the most unlikely of contexts.
    On the streets of New York, Levi sings about his desires for bourgeois domes-
ticity and a family of seven children. After some disappointments (including an

encounter with a prostitute who sings her version of the "Business Is Business" medley), he learns about the California Gold Rush and travels to San Francisco. While on the boat, he meets his first love, Sarah Zimmermann, who is traveling there for a marriage as part of a business deal arranged by her father. Although she loves Levi and feels uneasy about her role in the business transaction, Sarah expresses some uncertainty about his eager desires for a marriage and family in which she also would be a conveniently calculated asset. She decides to follow her father's wishes. Refusing her plea of just being friends, Levi rushes off to make a deal with Howard and Stafford, who financially exploit him.

Levi arrives in San Francisco with a group of Chinese who are all dressed alike. Apart from one male, Han Chow, they are all females masquerading as males to gain entry into an America exploiting male immigrants but refusing entry to females on racist grounds. The Chinese parallel Levi's situation in Bavaria where similar racist fears resulted in the strict regulation of marriages in the Jewish community. In act one, scene six, the Chinese group perform an amusing musical number, "Like a Man," in which the females perform a male masquerade satirizing traditional gender roles.

Bidding farewell to Sarah after she meets her future husband, Mr. Goodman, Levi heads for the gold mines, carrying "two dozen rolls of very fine sail cloth that the two speculators did not want because of its blue color." In the gold fields, Levi becomes the inventor of the famous Levi Strauss blue jeans. He uses the material to replace the torn pants of the Chinese girls and makes his fortune. He also discovers the Chinese masquerade. Deciding to protect them, Levi receives acclaim in a musical number, "Great American Friend," as well as the love of Su Lin.

Act two, scene four opens showing Levi's San Francisco jeans factory run by outcasts from the white community—Chinese laborers and prostitutes who worked in the mining camps. Although Levi's factory represents a partial realization of the American Dream, its founder's appearance changes. He is not only older, but begins to resemble physically the businessmen who exploited him on the boat.

Waiting at the docks in San Francisco, Levi learns of the death of his friend, August, whose passage he paid from Bavaria. Before he has had time to get over his grief, Howard and Stafford attempt to influence Levi not to employ Chinese laborers in his factory. Here there are parallels between the practices in Bavaria and the Chinese exclusion act Congress will pass to keep the immigrants in their place:

> Yes, I know it too. I can smell it in the air. Back home they used to scream "hep hep." That was the chant of the Bavarian anti–Semites, and it wasn't wise to be on the streets if you didn't want to be beaten or even killed. "Hep hep." I grew up with that in my ears. I grew up in a world where they said we couldn't vote or own property and raise children. Maybe that was good business over there.

Stafford replies, "Stop talking as a Hebrew and start thinking as an American and you'll know the right thing to do." (2-5-29) Before this exchange, Stafford and Howard reprise the "Business Is Business" medley, emphasizing the fact that their "kind of business" is "the *white* kind of business." Toward the end of the scene, Han Chow takes up the medley, acting as Levi's conscience. Levi concludes the scene by singing, "I'm gonna do business as usual" in opposition to "the *white* kind of business."

The following scene presents the ugly spectacle of a race riot in San Francisco, concluding with the silhouette of an unfortunate Chinese hanging from a lamp post. After meeting Sarah again, Levi finds she is also childless. Both regret the lost opportunities they once had. Levi then returns to his factory, now wrecked by a rioting mob. Generous to his workers and knowing Han Chow's love for Su Lin, Levi sends them both to safety in Chicago. However, he admits his capitulation to the reactionary forces represented by Stafford and Howard: "They won. I let the bullies win." He receives an honorary reward from the community, one heralded by the Levi Straus mural, which includes an addition to the old label, "Made by All White Labor." As the spotlight focuses on these words, Levi sings a touching soliloquy, "Look How it Adds Up," in which he condemns himself as a failure. But unlike Dwight Webb, Jr., in *The Private Files of J. Edgar Hoover*, the confession is not hypocritical. Levi has tried to work the system for his own ends. But it has been too powerful for him to fight on his own. Among the poignant lines are "I played it wise by closing my eyes and just look what I've won! ... Look how it adds up. All that I've got. What a fortune I'm worth." (2-8-40)

Sarah and Levi decide to return to New York to see the people they are bringing over from the Old World to substitute for the family they never had. Among the new immigrants is a little boy whom Levi picks up: "There is another chance — and we don't have to make the same mistakes every time, do we?" He finds August's grandson and counts seven children representing those he never had. Sarah encourages Levi to help them: "Because it all begins again — teach them, Levi. Help them to do better than we did." (2-9-45)

*Levi!* ends on a positive note of optimism and hope for the future. Although both Levi and Sarah have made certain compromises and suffered personal defeats, their struggles will be continued by the new generation. Levi's final number merges the familiar strains of the youthful idealism of "Opportunity" and the more cynical "Look How it All Adds Up" into a new dialectically oriented synthesis emphasizing future struggle. After telling the children to avoid his mistakes — "Gold in the streets — Forget that! You can't have your *hand out*. You've got to have your *fist clenched*."— Levi launches into a musical version of a Vertov *kino fist* encouraged by Sarah. They both affirm the validity of their idealistic and negative experiences ("They're out to get you to tear you apart"), with everyone joining in the concluding lines, "Now we've got the right to fight the good fight and who knows, we might win." (2-9-46)

The musical ends with Levi speaking, "Next time..." followed by everyone singing, "We might win." Now closer than they have ever been and united in true friendship, Sarah watches Levi embrace the child, "symbol of the dream that still might come true..." (2-9-47)

Whether it is performed or not, *Levi!* represents an important testimony to Larry Cohen's personal vision. Conscious of the dangerous nature of the system and its continuing power, Cohen never delivers an easy, over-optimistic conclusion. Despite the reverses, he offers hope and the necessity of a continuing struggle for whatever future may emerge. Although Jewish cultural overtones are definitely present, Cohen's *Levi!* represents no exclusive "Next year, Jerusalem" vision. Articulating the common plight of oppressed groups, whether immigrant Jew, exploited Chinese coolie, or enslaved American in a musical set before the Civil War, and envisioning a future conflict, *Levi!* represents an important synthesis of the best features of Larry Cohen's creative vision.

# Film and Television
# Work in the 1990s

Although directed in 1990 and available in Japan soon after, *The Ambulance* was not released in the United States until 1993. Despite Cohen's attempts to release the film theatrically, it went straight to video shelves, both in America and Britain. This was unfortunate since *The Ambulance* represented Cohen's return to form after problems surrounding *Wicked Stepmother*. However, Cohen's unusual film style differed from most mediocre and homogenous features then being released theatrically. As a result, distributors became unwilling to gamble on the film's box-office potential. Despite favorable reviews in magazines covering video releases, *The Ambulance* has remained critically neglected by those reviewers who regard films released on video as beneath consideration. However, as Franco Mingati has recognized, video and cable television have now become the "great equalizers," relating to theatrical features as paperbacks once did to hardback novels. These new distribution outlets are particularly appropriate for a director whose films are innovative, fluid, and often indefinable in terms of the generic descriptions used to market films today.[1] Cohen is very optimistic about these new outlets for his films:

> You don't have to worry about whether your films will be booked in a theater for a few days here and there... On video, they are always available. Those who want to have a Larry Cohen film festival can go down to the video store and create their own.[2]

If Larry Cohen had never directed another film after *The Ambulance*, this project would form a fitting conclusion to his highly idiosyncratic career. After making the film, he decided to relax and concentrate on writing screenplays before returning to directing *As Good as Dead* for cable television in 1994. *The Ambulance* is another creative low-budget Larry Cohen film whose inventive style and creative intelligence puts to shame many contemporary mega-buck productions. Its modest B-movie nature is far superior to inflated and pedestrian movies such as *Waterworld*. *The Ambulance* is a satirical comedy shot in the director's characteristic comic-strip style, reworking the premises of Hitchcock's suspense formulas, but also containing an element of seriousness never totally absent from Cohen's films. Instead of a main character such as Robert Donat's Richard Hannay in *The 39 Steps* or Roger Thornhill in *North by Northwest*, who find themselves suddenly thrust into a world of excitement and danger, Cohen uses the figure of average New Yorker Josh Baker (Eric Roberts), who (more than coincidentally) happens to be a Marvel comic-strip artist immersed in a dangerous world paralleling the imaginative storyboards he creates. But, despite this imaginative situation, the world of *The Ambulance* has undeniable connections to reality as well as fantasy, a dangerously real world always aiming to exploit people in the name of profit. Like his other '80s films, *The Ambulance* is another radical comic-strip allegory using a supposedly escapist visual style to critique features of the contemporary market economy that few mainstream Hollywood productions dare to face explicitly.

Cohen based the screenplay on personal experiences. Like his character Zacharias (Red Buttons), the director fell ill after eating black and red Cajun crawfish. After he summoned an ambulance, he became powerless. The attendants strapped him to the gurney and drove him quickly to the hospital. Ironically, Cohen experienced the type of fictional scenario befalling his characters in *It's Alive, It Lives Again,* and *Island of the Alive* who are victimized by dehumanizing situations in environments they previously thought were caring and benevolent. Musing over this traumatic event after his release from the hospital, Cohen imaginatively weaved together several plot components — a Hitchcock-style comedy-thriller, New York locations, comic-strip motifs, and an institutional critique of a ruthless threatening society, into a fictionalized recreation of this real-life situation.

Like in *Black Caesar, Hell Up in Harlem, Q, Perfect Strangers, Special Effects,* and *Deadly Illusion,* New York functions as both location and an actual character in *The Ambulance.* It is used to its fullest potential in the quasi-cinema verité opening sequence when Josh propositions Cheryl (Janine Turner) on a crowded New York street during lunchtime. This is one of the most accomplished and imaginative dramatic "re-creations" Cohen has achieved in his career. It parallels the Manhattan scenes in *Q* and his use of Greenwich Village in *Perfect Strangers,* and surpasses the New York locations in *Black Caesar* and *Hell Up in Harlem.*

Josh Baker is a character modeled on certain components of Larry Cohen's personality. In fact, Cohen has admitted that Eric Roberts based the performance on his personality. It makes *The Ambulance* an interesting self-reflective movie. Larry Cohen also appears in more brief cameos in *The Ambulance* than in his other films. Josh works as an artist for Marvel Comics, having realized a youthful ambition he had as an avid comic-book collector. In one scene, Josh leaves the Marvel Comics office and greets Larry Cohen as he makes a brief walk-on appearance. Furthermore, Marvel Comics creator Stan Lee appears in a cameo role as an editor whom the young Larry Cohen would undoubtedly have loved to work for. As it is, the older Cohen inserts himself into the narrative, thus achieving his desire, if only on the level of fantasy.[3]

Josh is also a comic-strip figure plunged into a Hitchcock world of menace and suspense after briefly seeing the girl of his dreams, whom he envisions as "Veronica" from *Archie* comics, mysteriously whisked away in an old-fashioned ambulance and disappearing from the face of the earth. During the film, Josh ignores the interest that the "Betty" figure, Officer Sandy Malloy (Megan Gallagher), shows in him. "Jughead" appears in the character of Detective Ryan (James Dixon). Cohen directs Ryan as an older version of the comic-strip adolescent. The situation represents another aspect of Cohen's wild imagination. What would have happened if "Jughead" ended up as one of New York's Finest? Although having no direct resemblance to Archie's rival in the comic strip, Eric Braeden's sinister doctor acts as a "Reggie" substitute in the film. *The Ambulance* is another gourmet work of a cinematic chef mixing ingredients from different sources into a new creation and presenting the finished delicacy to his audience.

Like *North by Northwest*, *The Ambulance* begins on a crowded New York street. But this time Manhattan functions in a more strategic background role than it does in Hitchcock's film. An overhead camera shoots the actors as they perform in the midst of crowds oblivious to the fact that they, too, are also performers in a film. Josh breaks a lunch appointment with his friend to pursue a girl he has often seen on the streets. Like an actor auditioning for a role, Josh goes through several verbally seductive routines in an attempt to woo a desired member of his particular audience. However, before he succeeds, Cheryl collapses in the street. Josh discovers she is diabetic. Before he can learn anything further, an ambulance suddenly appears and removes Cheryl.

Vainly attempting to find Cheryl in various New York City hospitals, Josh encounters several instances of rudeness and inhumanity in what really should be a caring profession. His initial contacts with an institutionalized medical world represent the first stages toward his discovery of a nightmarishly repressed underside personified by the sinister doctor (Eric Braeden) and his business operations. They are sides of the same coin. Josh also fears that Cheryl may represent a product of his own imagination since the drawings he shows Detective Spencer (James Earl Jones) bear an uncanny resemblance to "Veronica" of *Archie* comics. Reared on the old, culturally esteemed *Classics Illustrated* comics, Spencer has little sympathy with contemporary productions. Looking at Josh's drawing of Cheryl, he comments, "You just made her up." This supposedly imaginary nature of Josh's quest is something the doctor later attempts using as a "bargaining chip" when he offers Zacharias (Red Buttons) his life on the condition that he persuade Josh to tell the police that the artist's story is only a comic-book fantasy. Although suggested implicitly in *The Ambulance*, Josh fears that his encounter with Cheryl was a product of his imagination resulting from overactive desires stimulated by his work as a comic-strip artist. Prior to his suspension from Marvel Comics, Josh sees his "brief encounter" affecting his work: "Every female character I draw looks like her." His editor comments, "Your drawings all look very much alike."

Josh is a character with personal problems. *The Ambulance* contains suggestions that he has difficulty separating fantasy from reality even before his encounter with Cheryl. Josh's apartment reproduces features of his work environment that have no identity as objects usually found in a private home space. A Captain America poster hangs on the wall, suggesting Josh's escapist nature as well as his deep desires to become a great American comic-strip hero rescuing heroines from danger, like Danny Greenwald in *Washington Heights*. The job is actually his life. As stewardess Patty (Laurene Landon) notes when Josh later staggers around after drinking his drugged milk, the artist is really a "loner" with few friends who has difficulties relating to the opposite sex. Josh once took Patty to a "lousy concert" and dropped her soon afterwards. When Josh recovers from the overdose later in the hospital, Spencer remarks, "A lot of people think you're odd, Josh. They call you, 'a loner' who keeps to himself, a strange fellow." However, as Cohen's other works reveal, boundaries between reality and fantasy are not as rigid as they are commonly supposed to be.

Josh has several affinities with Scottie Ferguson in *Vertigo*. Both men desire an imaginary female rather than an actual woman. However, unlike *Vertigo*, *The Ambulance* ends positively. Although Josh's romantic desires as a knight in shining armor rescuing Cheryl end abruptly when he discovers she has a boyfriend, he does form a better relationship with the more mature and streetwise Sandy Malloy. We never learn Cheryl's occupation. But Sandy is a police officer. She has entered the profession to survive in a New York she understands much better than Josh. Unlike the tormented male cops in the *Maniac Cop* films, Sandy has survived occupational stress. Like Midge in *Vertigo*, she is a down-to-earth working woman. Although more attractive than her Hitchcock predecessor, Sandy keeps a maternal eye on the vulnerable, suicidally inclined Spencer. Both play-act antagonistically in a relationship whose premises they understand but never consciously admit. Unlike Midge, Sandy never attempts to destroy Josh's fascination with his dream woman. When Josh attempts kissing her in his apartment, Sandy comments, "Don't do that, because you're thinking of Cheryl. Close your eyes and you see her there." She also counters his male tendencies toward seductive flattery, telling Josh she does not like to be called "Beautiful." Despite her feelings for Josh, she decides to remain in the background and never interfere until he escapes from his romantic illusions involving Cheryl. Unlike Hitchcock in *Vertigo*, Cohen rewards the Midge figure of Sandy for her positive qualities when, toward the end of the film, she attracts Josh's attentions after dealing diplomatically with his disappointment over losing Cheryl.

Like Danny in *Washington Heights*, Josh turns to comic books as an escape from reality. He secretly desires to be a Captain America by fighting dark forces and winning Cheryl. However, as Danny destroys all but one of his comic books at the end of *Washington Heights* and moves further toward understanding a dark world of reality, so does Josh in *The Ambulance*. At the beginning, Josh has much in common with Detective Spencer who functions as his alter ego. Like Josh, Spencer is a "loner." Both men have no home life and live for their respective

Larry Cohen (right) rehearses Eric Roberts (left) for a scene in *The Ambulance* (1990) (courtesy of Larry Cohen).

jobs. They share a common bond, having interests in comic books. Spencer remembers his youthful interests: "Comic books? You make up comic books. I used to love the old joke books years ago, especially the classics. They got me through college. But the stuff today! It's too bizarre, too weird, and gets the kids whacked out of their fucking minds. Comics scare me these days."

Like certain officers in the *Maniac Cop* films, Spencer has already attempted suicide and is under surveillance in his own department. Sandy knows this and attempts to look after him. However, Spencer never really reciprocates Sandy's support and acts as a loner toward the end. Compulsively chewing candy bars (perhaps as a substitute for alcohol), he recklessly chases after the ambulance without calling for the back-up Josh suggests. When Josh accompanies Zacharias to the *New York Post* building after they leave the hospital, he tells Spencer that the mysterious ambulance is outside the building. He pleads in vain with Spencer not to act alone: "For once in your life, listen to somebody." Spencer does not take Josh's advice and dies. In his last moments of life, he compulsively chews at a candy bar before expiring, his action revealing the childish streak in his personality that eventually kills him. By contrast, Josh begins as a loner but moves toward accepting the help of others such as Sandy and Zacharias. Unlike Spencer, he lives by cooperating with others and does not end up as a dead loner.

Josh discovers a dark world where premises are far more deadly than any work of comic-book imagination. It is a world having far more associations with everyday reality than fantasy, since it is an extension of market-economy philosophies endemic to the Reagan and Thatcher eras. Several associations exist between the doctor's particular form of exploitation in *The Ambulance* and the other business practices revealed in *It's Alive, God Told Me To, The Stuff, Island of the Alive,* and *Deadly Illusion.* The doctor is supplying a demand and operates according to this business axiom, no matter how harmful his directions are for his helpless victims. He runs a racket organized by businessmen who sell live diabetic patients to private hospitals for medical experiments. His mysterious ambulance picks up vulnerable people in the streets who collapse due to faulty insulin injections. Although this premise is currently fictional, it represents the logical extension of inhumane institutional medical procedures affecting both Josh and Zacharias in the film. Both men are relegated to the role of passive "patients" with no claims for human status once they are inside a New York City hospital. The medical authorities intend keeping Zacharias in a hospital ward so they can reap the financial benefits of his medical insurance. As he says, "But as long as I got insurance those sons of bitches don't want to let me go." Recovering from a drug overdose attempt by the sinister doctor, Josh finds himself verbally threatened by Nurse Feinstein (Deborah Headwell) and a burly intern who offers him the choice of being a model patient or undergoing an enema. As in "Night Sounds," the American hospital is an institution organized on business lines, seeing its patients, not as human beings, but as objects having a particular use value within the capitalist economy. Like the vulnerable insulin patients preyed upon by the ambulance, both Josh and Zacharias find themselves "unreliable" and totally disposable objects within the hospital. They are both loners. Zacharias is a 73-year-old reporter now relegated to the obituary page by his newspaper editor who hopes the older man gets the message: "He hopes I'd write my own."

But the doctor who runs the operation is no loner. He is the logical extension of a system viewing people as exploitable commodities. He tells Cheryl of his plans to cure her diabetes by transplanting pig membranes into her body. Cheryl finds herself facing the fate the scientific expedition plans for the mutant babies in *Island of the Alive.* She is no longer a human being, but a laboratory animal designed for live medical experiments and vivisection. Like the parents and children in the *It's Alive* movies, she wakes up to find herself an alienated "other" in a society she thought she belonged to. As Jews in Nazi Germany found themselves regarded as disposable and usable commodities virtually overnight, Cheryl and her fellow diabetic victims find themselves the objects of an insane East Coast Dr. Mengele who is merely the logical extension of the capitalist system in which they exist. Nobody is safe in such an environment. The doctor puts on a surgical glove and touches her body in a fetishistic manner: "But I promise you, you'll be in perfect health before you die." When Zacharias later wakes up in the same hellish environment, he encounters a mad doctor he would like to believe is a solitary figure. However, the doctor tells him, "I'm not alone in my madness." He supplies products for a particular form of market demand by delivering live human bodies to private research hospitals along the Eastern seaboard. Since humans are better than animals for medical research, the doctor operates in a logical manner for a late capitalist world regarding the market economy as the supreme arbiter of human fate. Zacharias recognizes that the kidnappings and eventual merchandising of live insulin patients is a nightmare version of an all too familiar American Dream: "You mean, *sell*? You mean, this is a money-making profession?"

The doctor's secret hospital is situated above a fashionable New York nightclub significantly named "Vintage," suggesting a dark continuity between the traditional and modern features of American life. Furthermore, the live patients represent a form of vintage product. They are equivalent to rare wine supplied to connoisseurs. But in their particular cases, the disposable diabetics have their own envisioned destinations — private medical centers preferring live humans rather than animals for their experiments. When Josh meets Cheryl again, in a makeshift hospital ward pierced by agonized cries and containing tortured bodies of the doctor's preliminary experiments now destined for the police "meat wagon," he encounters a world far more threatening than the ones he drew for Marvel Comics. He inquires about the identities of the kidnappers:

> JOSH: "Were they doctors?"
>
> CHERYL: "No. Some of them sounded like salesmen… They were trying to sell me like an animal."

Like other Cohen heroes, Josh finds that a world he formerly took for granted as unthreatening really exists on a ruthless "business as usual" ethic. Josh and Sandy destroy the doctor's base, but he makes one final attempt to kill them. Although they survive, they find themselves ironically strapped on ambulance gurneys on the way to the hospital. On one level, hero and heroine reunite after the threat from the chaotic world has finally gone. On another, darker level, despite their romantic union, they are on their way to an institution that has shown little concern for humanity, one having close associations with a nightmare world they have temporarily destroyed.

During 1994, Cohen wrote, produced, and directed *As Good as Dead* for the USA cable network. Since his recent movies frequently appeared on cable stations, at least one company offered him the opportunity of directing a movie specifically for television release. Unlike his former activities in independent low-budget cinema, Cohen found certain restrictions affecting his freedom to direct in the way he preferred. In one instance, USA insisted he direct an airport sequence, not outside the San Diego airport, but outside a hotel specifically modeled to look like an airport taxi stand! Cohen would have preferred using the actual location but had to bow to producer demands. Any attempts at unusual camera angles and iconoclastic ideas ran up against the formulaic restrictions that dominate television productions. Finally, Cohen could not insert many features of his comic-strip style into this made-for-television movie. As a result, the visual look is not as innovative as that of *The Ambulance* and his other major works. Thus, *As Good as Dead* did not entirely escape television constraints. But it has an interesting plot worthy of a big-budget movie. Had Cohen gained more time and freedom, he could have developed the premises in his screenplay to their fullest potentials.

The acting is competent but never entirely stimulating. Judge Reinhold fails to capture the interesting nuances of his role, nuances that Don Johnson succeeded in delivering in *Guilty as Sin*. However, as a television movie written, directed, and produced by Larry Cohen, it often transcends its production limitations. The screenplay is both highly ingenious and socially relevant, giving a fresh treatment to the often-used change of identities scenario. Furthermore, Cohen attempted to direct the work in as cinematic a manner as possible, avoiding the usual television movie techniques of static camera, extreme close-ups, and shot-reverse shot sequences. He moves the camera as much as possible, either craning above characters or following them whenever the dialogue suggests their vulnerability to some form of personal and psychological entrapment. For example, Cohen uses the same overhead camera shot to introduce Susan Warfield (Crystal Bernard) and Nicole Grace (Traci Lords) in their introductory appearances before they actually meet each other. The camera movement anticipates the developing nature of their future relationship. This introductory use of the overhead camera is a common feature of Cohen's recent work, as *Island of the Alive, A Return to Salem's Lot,* and *The Ambulance* all demonstrate. When Susan later looks for medical technician Eddie Garcia (Carlos Carrosco), the camera frames her from high above, through apartment balcony railings. It then moves over the railings to view Susan below as she walks toward the entrance. At this point, Susan is still seeking to discover who murdered the woman she changed identities with to gain swift access to medical treatment. The real Susan does not exist. She has become an insignificant non-person, and no longer exists as an identifiable human being. During earlier scenes, the camera tracks and frames both Susan and Nicole as the latter introduces her new friend into the supposedly free world of glamor and parties. But Nicole's world is as trapped as the office surroundings in which we see Susan. When Susan answers a phone call from Nicole, the camera tracks right across Susan's fellow workers until it finally stops at the cramped work space of her desk.

In *As Good as Dead*, Susan exchanges identities with Nicole at a hospital so her sick friend can use her medical insurance. When Susan returns from holiday, she finds that Nicole has died in the hospital under her own name. Susan loses all traces of her identity: apartment, occupation, credit card, and everything that designates her as a real human being in American society. As a result, she takes on Nicole's identity, dying her hair blonde and wearing the dead woman's clothes. Before Nicole dies, Cohen makes significant use of mirror imagery to anticipate the transfer of personality theme in his screenplay. During their first meeting inside a Hollywood night club, Susan and Nicole pause before a mirror reflecting their bodies. Nicole is a makeup artist working on rock videos and commercials, a self-employed person contributing to an industrial Hollywood world of artificial glamor. The first thing she does is to introduce her newfound friend to the appropriate way of wearing eye shadow to fit Hollywood standards of female beauty. After Nicole's death, the distraught and isolated Susan ends up in her friend's apartment. She sits in front of a large mirror as she begins changing her physical appearance to resemble Nicole as much as possible. While the huge mirror reflects her image, two smaller mirrors (one circular, the other square) also contain her face in close-up. The scene contributes to the sense that Susan has lost her former identity, and the clash of identities she will now have to deal with. Unlike her previous existence, she now has circumscribed and limited choices. When Ron (Judge Reinhold) takes Susan to a Japanese restaurant, their table faces a mirror reflecting them both. Both characters perform roles. Susan continues her performance as Nicole, while Ron speaks of his musical performance interests. As the audience learns later, Ron is also performing another kind of role during this scene. The deceptive and deadly nature of masquerade is a key theme in Cohen's work, appearing prominently in *In Broad Daylight*.

Despite television's preference for using the more mundane stylistic aspects of naturalistic and realistic depictions, Cohen does manage to insert briefly a significant montage segment in one scene of *As Good as Dead*. When Susan first meets her long-lost father, Edgar (George Dickerson), Cohen inserts two shots of the wedding photograph showing Susan's parents. Earlier, Susan showed Nicole the same photograph when she spoke about her father's desertion many years before. Although Susan blames her father, Nicole pertinently comments that her retention of the photograph really reveals her true feelings. The photograph features the same actress playing her mother, and suggests certain unresolved Oedipal tensions in the broken family relationship. When Susan looks at her aged father, Cohen uses montage inserts to depict her reactions. The first shot reveals mother and father together in the frame, while the second only shows a close-up of her father. On one level, the inserts have the purpose of suggesting the older man's identity to the audience. On another level, they significantly reveal the repressed nature of a deep emotional bond existing between the daughter and her long-lost father. Masquerading as Nicole, Susan listens to Edgar as he speaks about the daughter he last saw as a two-year-old being clearly upset over his desertion. Cohen significantly shows Susan in close-up, emotionally reacting to her father's words as she realizes that he actually loved her years ago. A deep family bond exists between father and daughter, a counterpoint to the undisclosed relationship she has with a stepbrother she never actually knew. Her unknown stepbrother, Aaron, was the product of Edgar's former marriage. The threat Susan later realizes and faces suggests that it represents the return of repressed desires she has for her father, arising from a past dysfunctional family relationship. Aaron represents the monstrous son produced by the family who reacts to his particular abandonment by his father in a different way than Susan does. While Susan clearly loves her father, Aaron hates him. Obviously jealous of the second family his father chose after leaving him, he exists in an antagonistic relationship with his father and stepsister. Aaron is jealous of the male nurse who helped his father get over a stroke (whom Edgar regarded as a substitute son), and aggressive toward the various girlfriends he regards as surrogate objects for a sister he has never seen. When Susan eventually realizes the real nature of the feelings she has for her own stepbrother, she finally understands those she has for her own father. These themes are never emphasized in *As Good as Dead*, but remain evident in the hidden motivations of certain characters.

However, *As Good as Dead* is not another recapitulation of Cohen's favorite "monster in the family" theme. It forms part of a plot in which the emphasis again falls on the plight of a vulnerable human being suddenly discovering that a life once took for granted by society is no longer there. An arbitrary set of circumstances places an innocent woman in the position of a socially alienated figure.

Susan and Nicole accidentally meet outside a fashionable Hollywood disco. Before introducing them, Cohen opens the film with night scenes showing the Los Angeles landscape before dissolving to the "Hollywood" sign. The movie capital stands as a symbol for an artificial world of illusion and glamour concealing the harsh realities of society. Such realities appear in the opening scenes. The unglamorous Susan learns the cost of not accommodating herself to Hollywood's acceptable image of female glamor. Plain looking, demurely dressed, with mousy hair, she attempts to enter the disco to meet her friends who are supposedly inside. The bouncer comments rudely, "If they look like you, they're not inside." When Nicole arrives a few seconds later, she immediately gets to the head of the queue and gains free admission due to her glamorous image.

However, Nicole's freewheeling lifestyle really conceals deep insecurities. She suffers from ulcer attacks, has a history of petty crime, and is not permanently employed. The glamorous woman has no job but plenty of invitations to fashionable Hollywood parties. Nicole's attacks and recklessness suggest masochistic undercurrents in her personality representing unconscious reactions against the glamorous artificial image Hollywood expects of her. After telling Susan about being arrested for shoplifting and then running away, she comments, "Why do I do this to myself?" Although Nicole believes she has control over her own life, her words of advice to the less-assertive Susan are really ironic: "If you want things to be different you've got to be in control instead of heading for the nearest exit."

However, Nicole's lifestyle catches up with her. Falling ill from an ulcer attack during a Hollywood party, she is taken by Susan to a nearby hospital. Realizing Nicole has no medical insurance, and reluctant to take her to a hospital for poor people, she changes identities, giving Nicole her medical insurance so she can receive professional attention. Susan goes to Scottsdale, Arizona, for a week, taking a leave of absence from her job on the grounds of needing an operation for "female problems." Learning of Nicole's death from a botched blood transfusion, Susan returns home to find herself "as good as dead" and having to take on Nicole's identity. When she returns to her former apartment, the young son of a neighbor sees her and tells his mother, "The lady that died. I just saw her." Like Jason's parents in *The Stuff*, his mother ignores the reality of his observation and ironically sends him to the twentieth-century "opium of the masses," as in *Wicked Stepmother*: "Go watch television."

Although Susan technically broke the law for humanitarian purposes, she now becomes the guilty woman, like those in Hitchcock's movies. As Robin Wood shows, a Hitchcock guilty female is no criminal but one arbitrarily designated as guilty by oppressive forces in society. Susan now finds herself occupying Nicole's former role as a guilty woman. She does not face parking fines or parole violation, but a more serious guilt involving insurance fraud and five years' imprisonment. *As Good as Dead* reveals that an inhumane system is really responsible for Susan's dilemma. When Susan accompanied Nicole to the hospital, she saw the receptionist turn away an impoverished Hispanic woman with a sick child. The woman faced taking her child to a poor hospital full of homeless people, drug addicts, and huge waiting lists. On hearing this, Susan decided to help her friend obtain proper medical treatment.

When Susan later learns of the probable sentence she might face, she finds herself facing victimization by a society she once took for granted. Like Hitchcock's Alicia Huberman, Marion Crane, Melanie Daniels, and Margaret Edgar, Susan now becomes a "guilty woman." Cohen underscores the Hitchcock implications in a scene showing Susan phoning from outside the San Diego airport. Realizing that she has descended into a chaotic world, she finds herself temporarily trapped in the glass telephone booth before she opens the door. Her position evokes Tippi Hedren's similar entrapment in a telephone booth in *The Birds*, as the winged avatars of patriarchal vengeance attack the helpless woman. However, in *As Good as Dead*, there is no need for any monsters to veil the social consequences of Susan's "good deed." Like the families in the *It's Alive* films, she has suddenly fallen from her former secure position of normal citizen into that of alienated outlaw.

Susan is guilty of a criminal act. The law will not bother to understand the humanitarian reasons for her actions. It is only concerned with technicalities and finding convenient scapegoats, preferably those of different races. As Susan investigates the $10 million suit her unknown stepbrother has filed against the hospital, she finds that the law is less concerned about finding out how the wrong blood type entered Susan's body than conveniently blaming a Hispanic medical technician for the "error." By developing Hitchcock's "guilty woman" tradition in his own creative way, Cohen now brings in the equivalent of Norman Bates, Uncle Charlie, or the winged avengers from *The Birds* to symbolize the aggressive forces of a patriarchal world seeking to punish Susan for her "sin." In *As Good as Dead*, Aaron Warfield symbolizes this force.

If Marion Crane violates the "law of the father" in *Psycho* by stealing, Susan Warfield commits a lesser, but definitely punishable, offense, breaching the legal and medical norms of her society by helping a sick friend. While Marion recognizes

Larry Cohen poses for a publicity shot with Crystal Bernard and Judge Reinhold on the set of *As Good as Dead* (1994) (courtesy of Larry Cohen).

Norman as a shadowy self caught within a "private trap," Susan builds up a similarly dangerous symbiotic relationship with Ron, a young man who aids her quest. When Ron rescues Susan from the police, he drives her away in his hired car. Susan notices the untidy mess inside the car. When she later invites Ron into Nicole's apartment, he tells Susan about his former girlfriends who were all "neat freaks." Admiring the untidy state of the apartment, he comments, "I was an amateur. You're a professional." While Nicole confides in Susan after knowing her for only a brief amount of time, Susan feels at ease with Ron. But she only tells him Nicole's story, not her own. By admitting Nicole's criminal past to Ron, he reassures her, "I'm on your side. We're two of a kind." The duality existing between Susan and Nicole in the first part of *As Good as Dead* now continues between Susan/Nicole and Ron. Another affinity exists between the dead Nicole and Ron. Nicole worked on rock videos, while Ron tells Susan he is a musician. Gradually, the relationship between Ron and Susan develops. Both become attracted to each other. However, Susan is shocked when she later discovers that Ron is actually her long-lost stepbrother, Aaron Warfield.

Aaron arrived at the hospital, attempting to borrow money from Susan, when he learned that she acquired cash from the sale of her deceased mother's house before moving to California. When Nicole refused and kept her identity secret, Aaron changed the computer records of her blood type so she would die on the operating table. He could then sue the hospital for negligence. After learning of the $10 million settlement, Aaron enlists Susan as an ally in his plan to murder his father, as he reveals his real identity to her. He states, "Sharing a murder will bind us closer than sex ever will." Aaron also looks forward to an affluent future when neither he nor Nicole/Susan will ever have to tidy up after themselves again. Like Uncle Charlie in *Shadow of a Doubt* and *Psycho*'s Norman Bates, Aaron Warfield is Cohen's version of the monstrous, anal-retentive, aggressive son produced by a dysfunctional family. Like Susan, Aaron was deserted by his father. But unlike Susan, Aaron harbors deep feelings of resentment toward him. He followed Edgar to the Florida oil rig he worked on and sponged off him financially to compensate for the love he sought and never received. He now intends venting the hatred for his father he has held since he was the age of ten by throwing him over the cliff. Edgar is there, mourning over his daughter's supposed ashes prior to casting them into the ocean. Susan hits him with a rock and attempts to warn her father.

The now fully aware Aaron shouts, "No wonder I felt so close to you. You're my flesh and blood. That's why you didn't want me to touch you. You felt it, too." Although Susan prevents Aaron from carrying out his envisioned "family reunion" by murdering his surviving relatives, she will always live with the implications of her stepbrother's realization. She prevents him from throwing her father over the cliff by casting Nicole's ashes in his face. The blinded Aaron then falls to his death.

Although the final scene shows Edgar and Susan finally reunited as father and daughter, it contains ironic undertones subverting any sense of a resolved "happy ending." A lawyer believes that Susan will receive a light sentence. But she will lose her job and become like Nicole, a guilty woman with a criminal record. Although Edgar attempts comforting her — "From now on, you don't have to be anything but yourself" — the last shot is highly ambiguous. Susan hugs her father and initially appears happy. Then her expression changes as she realizes the implication of his words. She will no longer be her former self. As a guilty woman, conscious of her past and the incestuous desires evoked by Aaron, her future is highly problematic.

*As Good as Dead* is an interesting television movie containing many Cohen themes implicitly woven into the text. Although bearing evidence of a less flamboyant visual style and an accommodation to television practices, it is best described as a work in tension with its production base. Nonetheless, despite certain compromises, it is definitely an interesting and radical achievement for the world of television that Cohen initially sought escape from to direct his own films.

On February 18, 1996, NBC broadcast the television movie *Ed McBain's 87th Precinct—Ice*, adapted by Larry Cohen. This represented a return to the director's original roots in television where he began his career nearly 40 years earlier by writing the live version of *87th Precinct*, a fact Cohen hid from executives who may have queried the presence of an "old guy" on a new production. *Ice* was not entirely a lighthearted deja vu adventure. Although following much of the original novel's structure, Cohen's teleplay added some interesting changes.

Cohen followed the basic plot of Ed McBain's novel, but added more suspense to the original material. He also inserted some characteristic Cohen features. Although Dale Midkiff's Steve Carella is less anguished than his 1958 counterpart, he has some revealing dark features. When Carella arrives at the scene of Sally's murder, he speaks to her corpse in a manner similar to Vincent Parry's imaginary conversation with his murdered friend in David Goodis' novel *Dark Passage* (1946). Carella's understanding partner, Meyer Meyer (Joe Pantoliano), notices this and remarks, "You know, one day, one of those stiffs is going to get up and answer you." Cohen also develops the relationship between Carella and his mute wife, Teddy, emphasizing the sign language they use to communicate. As Carella later tells Meyer, they have a better relationship than most married couples. Another new addition to the novel is the threat Teddy faces from the sadistic Emma Forbes, the mistress of Brother Anthony. While waiting for Steve at a theater, Teddy accidentally reads the lips of Emma and Brother Anthony as they discuss their plans, and places herself in immediate danger. Not realizing Teddy is mute, Emma pursues her with a razor. This is one of the best sequences in *Ice*. As Teddy flees from Emma, she passes a phone that she naturally cannot use. Although Emma finally corners her in an alley, Teddy uses a mace spray to escape. At the climax of *Ice*, Carella confronts his wife's assailant and nearly murders her. For a brief moment, boundaries between cop and criminal dissolve.

Cohen also uses the incident of the pregnant hooker giving birth at the precinct station, but adds some significant features. In contrast to the novel, he introduces the tormented Detective Kling, who suffers from a traumatic divorce. While married, Kling's masculinity suffered from the fact that his wife, as a successful model, earned more than he did. When Kling sees the image of his ex-wife on a magazine, he angrily tears it up, his violent act immediately leading to the trauma of Angie's (Lenore Zann) delivery, suggesting the birth as the result of Kling's repressed, surrogate violence. However, the whole precinct (including Kling) then crowds around the kindly father figure of Meyer in a gesture of solidarity as he delivers the baby. Immediately after the successful delivery, the cop who intended to book Angie rips up the charge sheet, realizing the impossibility and redundancy of his official position. Cohen succinctly changes the mood of this sequence from violence to concern and, then, to humor. *Ice* is a minor work but nevertheless contains some interesting features, despite the restraints placed on Cohen whenever he writes for television.

Like *Ice*, *Original Gangstas* did not result from Cohen's own initiative. He undertook directing the film as a favor to Fred Williamson, thus enabling a project from the actor's Po' Boy Productions to achieve widespread theatrical distribution by Orion Pictures on May 10, 1996. Cohen did not direct from his own screenplay, but from a script originating from Williamson's associate Aubrey Rattan. However, he still manage to adapt the screenplay to include aspects occurring in his own work.

*Original Gangstas* represents a reworking of features within Cohen's early career, especially the black representation peculiar to *Bone*, *Black Caesar*, and *Hell Up in Harlem*. The film reunited him with Fred Williamson, an actor-director who founded a production company stimulated by Larco's independent, free-wheeling structure. Also featuring other stars associated with the '70s era of black action cinema, such as Jim Brown, Pam Grier, Richard Roundtree, and Ron O'Neal, *Original Gangstas* contained certain features that would appeal to the innovative mind of Larry Cohen. What would happen if the now middle-aged stars of black action cinema returned to their original home territory and discovered that they were responsible for creating far more monstrous progeny 30 years later? The brutal Rebels gang are the descendants of the original gang founded by John Bookman (Fred Williamson) and his friends Jake Trevor (Jim Brown), Laurie Thompson (Pam Grier), Slick (Richard Roundtree) and Bubba (Ron O'Neal) years before. But while John and Jake have taken the traditional route out of the ghetto to fame and fortune by becoming sports professionals, Laurie, Slick, and Bubba remain behind in Gary to face a growing problem they unknowingly created in their youth. The original gangstas are responsible for a situation now increasingly out of control in which the gang structure they created has become as monstrous as the mutant babies in the *It's Alive* films. The middle-aged former gang members bear the same type of blame as the government authorities and the parents in the earlier films. But unlike the *It's Alive* trilogy, there can be no reconciliation. Outside the domain of horror, grim social reality is far too powerful. Unlike the mutant children, the Rebels are beyond redemption. However, like all Cohen films, *Original Gangstas* does not end on a totally optimistic note. Although John and Jake eventually destroy the Rebels, the Diablo gang still remains as a possible threat to the security of Gary. Despite the "Safety First" sign displayed on the ruined industrial battleground in the closing images, any future for Gary is bound to be precarious.

Although Fred Williamson's initiative in envisioning the project as a response to the decline of his original hometown is important, Larry Cohen's contribution is also significant. If *Black Caesar* and *Hell Up in Harlem* parallel features in the *It's Alive* series, *Original Gangstas* contains elements from two major fields Cohen has worked in, those loosely defined as black action and horror. However, *Original Gangstas* contains key social meanings never entirely absent from any Larry Cohen film.

Shot mostly on location in Gary Indiana, *Original Gangstas* eschews Cohen's familiar comic-strip style for the documentary realistic approach of *Perfect Strangers*. The grim reality conditioning the violent events in *Original Gangstas* is overpowering, and no distracting formal representations are needed. To his credit, Cohen recognizes this and introduces the audience to the impoverished circumstances resulting in the violent landscape depicted in the film. It is implicitly linked with an industrial deprivation accelerated by the Reagan era and continuing to the present day. *Original Gangstas* opens with the characteristic helicopter shot often introducing the affluent city landscapes of Manhattan, San

Francisco, or Los Angeles in Hollywood films. However, *Original Gangstas'* introductory shots emphasize images of industrial and social decay. A voice-over
commentary describes Gary as having the "highest murder rate in the United
States, if not the entire world." But the commentator also notes other significant
features such as the closure of a steel mill, once the major economic support of
the community, and *Star Wars* being the last movie seen in Gary's cinema. These
remarks highlight relevant social forces that began during the Carter era and
reached their destructive culmination under Reagan. The once-thriving steel mill
and train depot are now, ironically, the respective headquarters of the Diablo and
Rebel gangs who dominate the community. As the camera reveals run-down,
once-thriving business areas and deserted homes that resemble desolate city areas
after bombing raids, the environment appears more like a war zone (the original
title for the film) rather than a habitable community. Cohen uses the location of
Gary as a character in its own right, similar to his use of New York in *Black Caesar, Hell Up in Harlem, Q, Perfect Strangers,* and *Special Effects.*

After his father, Marvin (Oscar Brown, Jr.), is nearly killed by the Rebels
for implicating them in the murder of Kenny Thompson (Tim Lewis) over a
minor basketball hustle, L.A. football coach John Bookman returns home to confront a situation he and his friend, Jake, created many years before. Although both
men left their hometown to find fame and fortune, the gang they originally
founded has grown into a dangerous force after many decades.

But neither of the two founding Rebel members have found fulfillment outside Gary. Bubba recognizes John's guilt over a community he has abandoned and
rarely revisits, a charge Cohen emphasizes in camera movement framing both
men as they speak. The shot begins when John walks across the road and accidentally encounters his old friend. Both walk toward the camera until Bubba
leaves John in disgust after condemning his friend's lack of concern for Gary. Former professional boxer Jake has retired from the ring after accidentally killing an
opponent. He returns home to mourn for a son he has never known. Many years
earlier, the young Laurie rejected him after they conceived Kenny, wishing Jake
to succeed in his ambitions without any restraining family commitment. Although
Laurie told her son about his father, the intervening tragedy and Kenny's desire
that Jake know him as an adult and friend outside the traditional family relationship add a deep poignancy to his return. Cohen conveys this with a significant
sequence in which he dissolves from an overhead crane shot of Kenny's funeral
to his basketball hoop before tracking down to Jake silently grieving over a son
he will never know. The world of sports represented the only exit for father and
son from Gary, Indiana. Years before, Jake entered the world of professional boxing. Prior to his murder, Kenny was going to U.C.L.A. on a basketball scholarship. Thirty years later, a competitive sports situation indirectly leads to Kenny's
final exit from his hometown.

Although the opportunistic Mayor Ritter (Charles Napier) accuses John of
responsibility for Kenny's death — "You used to be a gang member yourself ...
the founding member of the Rebels... You started something and it's still out of

control" — the charge is still valid, even though it comes from the mouth of a character who, later in the film, decides to drop all responsibility for controlling the gang violence. Both John and Jake recognize their guilt. Ritter also emphasizes that he came back to Gary after law school and the death of his father. Despite his manipulative nature, the mayor (played by an actor best known for his portrayal of the scheming bureaucrat in *Rambo*) did voluntarily return to his home community. Although John visually returns to Gary as a redeeming hero, Cohen undercuts his stature with the Chi-Lite's song "For God's sake. Why don't you give power to the people," making his first appearance deliberately excessive, and punctuating his egotistical nature. The words of the song also anticipate that any future individual heroism will not be enough, only group effort on the part of the besieged community. When John reunites with his family in the hospital, they criticize his domineering attempts to make them leave Gary, commenting on his repressed kinship with the Rebels: "You're just like them, telling us what to do." Cohen subverts any sense of John's heroic return in his opening scene by using music as a dialectical intellectual montage to undermine any idea of John as a redeeming hero. As in his other films, Cohen subtly breaks down rigid distinctions between hero and villain. Both old and new gangstas echo each other. Spyro (Christopher B. Duncan) and Damien (Eddie Bo Smith, Jr.) now occupy the positions formerly held by John and Jake in the original Rebels. This dualism recapitulates familiar mirror imagery between heroes and antagonists in Cohen's work. The John-Spyro and Jake-Damien relationship parallels the Chris-Lorca and Vin-Lopez bonding in Cohen's *Return of the Seven* screenplay. The original rebels and their successors are different but parallel responses to a failing social system. Community figures such as Marvin Bookman and Reverend Dorsey (Paul Winfield) attempt various reconciliations that are all doomed to failure. Despite economic success, John and Jake never appear fulfilled or satisfied. Bubba criticizes John for neglecting his hometown over the years, sensing his friend's guilty feelings for having done nothing. Slick initially exhibits coolness toward Jake in their first meeting at the bar and appears suspicious of any future moves his old friend may make. Jake bears a deep guilt for killing his opponent in the ring and mourns for his lost years with Laurie. Those who remained in Gary, such as Laurie, Slick, and Bubba, exhibit feelings of frustrated resignation at the hopeless state of affairs. Since Mayor Ritter abandons all sense of responsibility, it is left to John, Jake, and Laurie to terminate the effects of what they started many years before. They teach the community self-defense tactics similar to Chris and Vin's strategy in *Return of the Seven*.

However, the final result leads to a stalemate situation with fathers and mothers killing their symbolic children after a bloody confrontation. It only ends in a temporary peace left to the discretion of the Diablos, which may be broken at any time. While Laurie kills Kayo (Dru Brown), the murderer of her son, Jake exercises patriarchal justice on Spyro by snapping his neck in the same way Damien disposed of young Dink (Shyheim Franklin). Earlier in the film, a bond of sympathy existed between John and Dink, the former looking on the young hustler as a surrogate son. Jake's killing of Spyro represents John's repressed vengeance for the murder of a symbolic son killed by Damien. It also replays the original killing that led to Jake abandoning his professional boxing career many years before. Damien now occupies Jake's position in the original gangstas. An implicit antagonistic family relationship unites all the major characters. It is one that becomes explicit in the final scenes. Before his death, Spyro compares Jake to his own father and justifiably accuses him of abandoning his son Kenny. His other accusation — "I'm your son. You made me what I am... You created me and now you want to kill me" — is also true. Although John fights Damien, he does not kill him. Blood (Tim Rhoze), the leader of the Diablos, performs the execution. He performs an act similar to the one Jake performs for John. Unlike Spyro, he is polite to both men, addressing them as "Mister" like a dutiful son toward the older generation. A parallel relationship also exists between Blood and John. Blood sees himself as an "acceptable" alternative to the random violence of the Rebels. Yet despite Blood's admiration for two older men, John and Jake refuse to acknowledge another member of a younger generation who may become another threatening son. Having learned from their past mistakes, they refuse to create another monster.

As this book goes to press, three other films written by Larry Cohen are scheduled to appear: *Invasion of Privacy, The Ex*, based on the novel by John Lutz, and *Uncle Sam*. All three contain recognizable Larry Cohen features. If *Original Gangstas* bears comparison with *Black Caesar* and *Hell Up in Harlem*, Cohen's next three projects reveal his further exploration and development of Hitchcock's radical social traditions involving the patriarchal nightmare contained within the American Dream.

*Invasion of Privacy* updates Hitchcock and Cohen themes into the conservative world of the 1990s. Again, another likable but dangerous young man cast in the mold of Hitchcock's Norman Bates and Cohen's David Greenhill of *Guilty as Sin* entices a young woman with his charms. After the pregnant victim discovers a family-created monster behind the charming exterior, she attempts an abortion. But her patriarchal oppressor wants her baby, whom he can then dominate as a controlling father. He kidnaps her so she will pass beyond the legally proscribed period for an abortion. Like Frank Davies in *It's Alive, Invasion of Privacy* involves a parental figure moving from rejecting a child toward wishing to protect it. Similar to Jody's predicament in *It Lives Again*, the heroine also has to deal with her over-protective mother as well as a deranged ex-boyfriend. According to the screenplay, *Invasion of Privacy* is set in St. Louis and uses individual locations as key mise en scene elements. The final version was disappointing.

In *The Ex*, Cohen combines Hitchcock's insights about the negative, sadomasochistic tendencies in monogamous relationships with the character of a dangerous, aggressive female used as a plot motif in his contribution to the March 22, 1995, episode of "N.Y.P.D. Blue." In this story, Det. Simone (Jimmy Smits) has to deal with a dangerously disturbed female witness, Joyce Novak (Susanna Thompson), who pursues him with a vengeance. Although this situation appears in *Fatal Attraction*, it is also a key element in the social explorations of Alfred Hitchcock, as his various dangerous females reveal. Furthermore, the deadly heroine motif also appears in another Hitchcock-inspired reworking, Jonathan Demme's *Last Embrace* (1979), as well as Clint Eastwood's directorial debut, *Play Misty for Me* (1971). In *The Ex*, an ex-wife pursues her former husband, provoking him to achieve the deadly climax of their earlier sadomasochistic marital games. Characteristically, Cohen depicts the hero (now re-married, with a five-year-old child) as equally responsible for a situation he was complicit in creating. Wishing to parallel Hitchcock's famous use of the shower as a deadly environment in *Psycho*, Cohen ironically uses the bath as a murder weapon in his screenplay.

*Uncle Sam* is Cohen's fourth collaboration with William Lustig. Indebted in many ways to ideas in *Maniac Cop*, *Uncle Sam*'s plot involves the return to life of a Gulf War veteran on Independence Day to avenge all those who discredit the American way of life. During his lifetime, Uncle Sam was a patriarchal oppressor as well as a victim of a dysfunctional family situation. Inspired by the World War II stories of Jed, Sam passes on the patriotic tradition to his nephew, Jody, before he ironically dies in a friendly-fire accident. The screenplay hints at Sam's resurrection by depicting the wish-fulfillment desires of his young nephew. However, Uncle Sam is also a monster created by a community having deep associations with traditional patterns of the American way of life. His July 4 "Uncle Sam" carnival disguise is not the only indication of his symbiotic "return of the repressed" bond with the community. Both Jody's desires and the burning of the American flag bring the monster to life. Finally Jed, Jody, and the town survivors destroy something they all bear some guilt for creating in the first place. Like the mutant babies, Quetzalcoatl, and Matt Cordell, the monstrous "other" is undeniably a part of the American way of life.

Although Larry Cohen is in his fifties, he is still capable of making the big-budget, mainstream movie he has always dreamed about. But it will have to be a film of his own choosing, a film that the controlling forces in Hollywood allow him freedom to make in his own particular way. At the present time, this seems unlikely. However, anything is possible as in a Larry Cohen film, and the system may allow him the opportunity he has always desired. He has the relevant experience and undisputed record in film and television writing and directing. In the meantime, Cohen will continue making whatever projects he chooses.

However, Larry Cohen's career is not one of wasted opportunities or marginal significance. As an outsider from the Hollywood system, he has directed several significant works that deserve greater recognition than they have received. They are works featuring radical allegories, filmed on low budgets, having several points of contact with independent cinema, indebted to the classical Hollywood tradition and the influence of Alfred Hitchcock, in particular, and commenting on social patterns in a satirical and accessible, entertaining manner. Perhaps they represent the real essence of Larry Cohen, achievements he need not be ashamed of.

Cohen may be easily associated with the American Jewish tradition of cinema. His varied works indirectly reveal an ethnic awareness of marginalization common to one community's experience of prewar America and the devastating revelations after 1945. It is possible to read Cohen's monster babies and alienated parental figures in this light. Both *Washington Heights* and the yet to be produced musical *Levi!* explicitly suggest such associations. But Cohen is a director with a broader canvas. His critiques are universal and humanitarian. They seek the possibility of a better world and a new social order sometime in the future, a world including everyone in both genders and different racial groups. His vision is all-inclusive. Although operating within the domains of popular culture and low-budget filmmaking, it deserves both respect and attention.

In many cases, important work is ignored whenever it does not fit into standard definitions of mainstream Hollywood or academic fashions. Larry Cohen's work has suffered this fate. But it is still there, in theatrical screenings, cable, and video, allowing retrospectives of a substantial body of work that will continue in the future.

The first part of this work has covered Larry Cohen's film and television productions. Part Two contains information provided by members of Larco, a company involving key figures such as James Dixon, Michael Moriarty, Janelle Webb Cohen, and Larry Cohen himself.

# PART TWO:
# INTERVIEWS WITH
# AND ABOUT COHEN

# Cohen on Cohen

This interview is based on sessions conducted in Chicago during 1993 and 1994. It comprises Cohen's personal history of his early involvement with film and television, his contributions to the last years of the "Golden Age of Live TV" and his later career in the Hollywood film and television industry. Larry Cohen is an important source of information concerning the history of film and television over the last few decades and this chapter attempts at a comprehensive approach related from his own particular perspective. I'm grateful to Larry Cohen for checking the material and adding corrections. The responsibility for the presentation is mine.

## Early Years

TW: Various sources often have different birthdates for you ranging from 1938 to 1941. Which is correct?

LC: 1941.

TW: Then you began writing for television at a comparatively early age?

LC: I was not allowed to sell any scripts unless I was twenty-one. So I said I was twenty-one and not seventeen. You lie about your age to get jobs. I was going through college at the time.

TW: What influenced you towards working in television and film?

LC: I always loved motion pictures since I was a child. Going to the pictures was a big event for me. I drew my own comic books as a hobby. They were all intricately worked out stories with characters, surprise endings — quite adult in terms of content — rather than being silly or frivolous. My comic style was really more dramatic than what you'd call comedic. It was just like doing storyboards for movies. I also made my own radio programs when I got a tape recorder, a WEBCOR recorder, as a present. Then I started directing and acting out original radio programs. I'd make my own radio show up. My parents would say, "What's he doing in his room, talking to himself all afternoon?" In making up these programs I also added background music. I must have been twelve years old when I was making these movies up in my head.

271

TW: So you are really self-educated in the medium?

LC: When I went to the movies and liked any film, I'd sit through it for the second or third time until they finally threw me out. I was into it from the beginning and wanted to make films. So it wasn't something that came up late in life. It was an early obsession.

TW: When did you attend the City College of New York?

LC: In the very late '50s. I think I graduated during 1962-1963.

TW: That's about the time you started contributing to the final years of the "golden age of television."

LC: I was writing the "Kraft" episodes at the time, but not making a great deal of money from them. When I went to school, I worked part-time as an NBC page. I was down at the studios all the time, watching rehearsals, trying to meet people and make contacts. Several years before that, I'd sneaked into NBC. I trespassed so often that everybody finally believed I worked there and didn't bother me. Every week NBC would rehearse the "Philco Television Playhouse" on Saturdays and Sundays on the fifth floor. I'd follow the directors around, watching these great television productions. In fact, I got my training from watching rehearsals such as the "Kraft Television Playhouse" on Wednesday and the "Hallmark Hall of Fame" (with Sarah Churchill), which they'd do down on the third floor. Their rehearsals would take place on Friday and Saturday afternoons. The telecasts would air live on Sunday afternoons without interruption or retakes.

Truthfully, the college work was secondary to everything else. The City College Film Institute was a school specializing in documentary film. It wasn't a theatrical filmmaking school. But it was actually good training. I learned to edit and how to load a camera in the black bag. I edited 16mm film on a moviola. So I learned some of the basic skills I never use now. Later, I always hired the best technical people to do the jobs for me. But it was enjoyable doing the basics then.

At college we made films as part of a project. But I'd been making films ever since I borrowed my father's 8mm camera.

I'd make little suspense movies and shoot them around my neighborhood in Washington Heights around Fort Tryon Park. It was a great location for movies. The Cloisters were there, a medieval monastery the Rockefellers built as a museum. It was a great place to shoot chases. I'd go up there with my friends from school. But the only problem was in not having editing facilities. So I had to edit the whole thing in the camera. I'd do a master shot, then go in for a close-up, another master shot, an over-the-shoulder shot, cutting everything in the camera, shooting just the amount of frames needed for the shots. So when the film picture came back from processing it was completely finished. There were some mistakes, here and there, but there was nothing I could do about them. That's how I began making pictures. I had to bribe kids with ten-cent comic books to appear in these movies. My very first film was a spy picture. I shot it on the day Stalin died. It was about spies hiding a microfilm in Fort Tryon Park, Manhattan. So I was already doing movies long before college. Coincidentally, the FBI later discovered that Russian spies actually used Fort Tryon Park as a meeting place to drop off and pick up microfilm.

TW: Since you wrote at the end of the "golden age of live television," did you ever meet Woody Allen or Mel Brooks who wrote for Sid Caesar's "Your Show of Shows"?

LC: That show appeared long before I wrote. When it was on, I was in high school. I watched it on television when I was a child. I remember the show very well. I didn't know Allen or Brooks personally. But I did start out doing a stand-up comedy act when I was in college. I performed in one club called the Duplex in Greenwich Village. Woody Allen was usually there. He was breaking in his nightclub act, too. At the time he was a writer. But his manager made him agree that he'd appear for six months, trying to be a stand-up comic although he hated it. You could see he hated it. He was just miserable being there. But he would do his fifteen–twenty minutes and sit down looking like the unhappiest guy in the world. I remember him. I thought, "If I could get that guy with the glasses to laugh it would be such an achievement." But he sat through my act looking so unhappy. So I did know Woody Allen slightly. When I see him today there's some recognition. He looks at me as if he knows me but he's not quite sure from where. I knew Dick Cavett when I was a page boy at NBC. He was a writer on the "Jack Paar Show." We sometimes used to go out for dinner at a cheap steak place and talk about the future. I did meet Mel Brooks when I was trying to sell *Bone*. A producer, Sidney Glazier, had a small motion picture company. He loved the script of *Bone*. One day when I was in his office, Mel Brooks was there. Glazier had produced *The Producers* for Mel Brooks. So I did meet Mel Brooks and have run into him a few times over the years.

## Television Scripts

TW: When did your other teleplay, "The Golden Thirty," appear?

LC: Before I went into the Army.

TW: You mentioned it is based on events in your actual life. Did a down-at-heel comedian steal your routine once?

LC: Oh, no! The only reality behind it was my work experience. When I was in school I worked a few summers in the Catskills, seeing shows, putting them on, and doing an act. It was about the same time I used to perform at the Duplex. I didn't like the life of a comedian. I didn't like working at night, getting up and doing the same material every night. My basic problem was I never had a set act. I'd make up a routine, do it, then the next time I'd want to get up and do something else. Other acts used the same material for ten years. If I did something once or twice, I wouldn't want to do it anymore. I thought of it like having my own TV show. Every evening I had to get up and do a brand new show, doing new material as if I was being telecast somewhere. I'd write new material every week, and perform it.

When I was in City College, I put on shows. There used to be a free period from twelve to two on Thursdays. People would go to school clubs. I presented a weekly show in the Townsend Harris Auditorium, a variety show with sketches. I had a couple of singers, an opening monologue, satires on the latest movies. I thought I was doing my own "Sid Caesar Show." But when I went up to the hotels in the resort area, they didn't want this kind of smart material. They wanted ethnic family humor and didn't understand my kind of material. They didn't get the political stuff.

TW: In "87th Precinct," the guilt-ridden Steve Carella appears an early version of your tormented cops such as Jack Klugman in *Night Cry*, and Tom Atkins of *Maniac Cop*. Robert Z'Dar's Matt Cordell is the most extreme version.

LC: I think police work is a really high-pressure job, full of anxiety, and you always make mistakes. In any kind of business or stress-related job, this happens. They're things you have to live with.

TW: Are there any features in the American Jewish culture, such as comedy, which influenced your work?

LC: I don't think so. I didn't do the traditional Jewish Catskill routines. That's why I didn't do well up there. I did audition for Max Gordon at the Blue Angel, which was a hip New York club where Mike Nichols and Elaine May, Peter Paul and Mary, and the Smothers Brothers played. But I guess I wasn't ready for the Blue Angel and too sophisticated for the Catskills. I was somewhere in between. But then, I really didn't like the personality of a performer. I tended to find that you don't focus on people. Everybody is just an audience! You're playing to people and you don't deal with them as individuals. You don't care about anybody. All you want to do is make them laugh. You want the constant affirmation that you are funny all the time. Also you begin to say things without any sensitivity to people just for a laugh. You hurt their feelings. I didn't like being that kind of person.

TW: So is the Henny Youngman character in "The Golden Thirty" a personification of all this?

LC: He's a personification of the failure aspect, of trying to be a funny man and not making it. It's a particularly sad profession for those who don't make it. I've known performers who've been doing the same thirty minutes of material for nearly twenty years, watching everybody pass them by. They're still knocking around in the business, living just in the slow lane, watching everybody in the fast lane go by. I felt sorry for them.

When I wrote the script I didn't write it with any intention of Henny Youngman being in it. I was hoping we'd get Jack Carson. He was a very gifted actor (as well as a good comedian) who could have given the role some depth. Henny was a non-actor. But he was certainly right for the part. There was something very poignant about him. This makes this production a collector's item because it's the only dramatic role Henny Youngman ever played in his life. Nancy Kovack was also in it. She made some movies afterwards but later married Zubin Mehta. She really didn't want to be an actress.

TW: Desser and Friedman's *American Jewish Filmmakers* notes several motifs in this cultural tradition such as satire and social justice. Your work seems to contain the social justice themes of a Sidney Lumet as well as the type of parody found in Mel Brooks. That's what I had in mind when I asked you about the American Jewish cultural influence.

LC: I really don't know (pause). You don't know why you write what you do. I was certainly aware of Sidney Lumet's work. When I was a kid I went on the set of a few of his pictures and followed him around when he was shooting in New York. Then I was enamored of the whole process of making movies. Sidney Lumet doesn't usually write scripts. He's an interpretative artist, interpreting what someone else has written and choosing what he wants to make. Mel Brooks is different. He's a seminal figure who creates the whole picture from the idea onwards. That's what I wanted to do.

TW: Were you in college before or after the Army?

LC: I was in the Reserves after college. I was in the Army just before I started writing for "The Defenders." I wrote my first couple of "Defenders" when I was down in Virginia, near Williamsburg on a military base. I had access to a typewriter and would sneak away during the day. Instead of stevedore duties, I'd be writing teleplays. I'd then mail them to the producers. Then I would go AWOL on Fridays for meetings in New York. So I wrote my first three "Defenders" in the Army.

TW: Janelle said you met Jim Dixon and David Carradine in the service.

LC: I met Jim Dixon at Fort Dix during basic training. David Carradine was in Virginia. We appeared in a show together, a musical called "Once Upon a Mattress"—anything to keep from performing normal military duties. It wasn't like there was any war on. This was a period of peace and absolute boredom. We put the show together and toured it around all the military bases in the South. He played a prince and I was the king. In those days his name was John Carradine, Jr.

TW: How did you originally break into television writing?

LC: This began before my military service. It was just a matter of submitting scripts to people with such a degree of consistency that when they didn't buy anything you gave them something else — and then something else, until you wore them down and they finally bought a script. I never got discouraged! I would be back the following week with a new teleplay. If it wasn't satisfactory for their needs I'd write another one and return five or six days later. They couldn't believe I could write them so quickly. Eventually, they gave me an assignment. It was encouraging to finally get paid five hundred dollars. This was a script for a series which never went on the air. It was a teenage situation comedy (not really something I wanted to write, but it paid money). It was "Too Young to Go Steady" with Don Ameche, Tuesday Weld, and Joan Bennett. They made a pilot, ordered some scripts, then shelved it. But they produced it four or five years later with Donald Cook and Joan Bennett. It only ran for a few weeks. So, I wrote my first paying script but it never went on the air.

Talents Associates then asked me to do an adaptation of "87th Precinct" from one of Evan Hunter's books. At the time he'd only written a few of them. I was hired to write an original screenplay based on the characters. It was a live television show and the first work of mine that was produced. It was in color, one of the early NBC television color shows.

Next, they requested I adapt a book, *Night Cry* by William L. Stuart, for television. When I read the book I told them it had been made before. They kept telling me, "No! It's never been made before. You're wrong!" I knew the actual movie — *Where the Sidewalk Ends* with Dana Andrews and Gene Tierney. They denied it. It turned out I was right. When I saw the feature again I noticed the screenplay was based on William L. Stuart's novel. As far as Talents Associates was concerned, they didn't know the novel had ever been bought and made into a movie. I was surprised the rights were available. But I wasn't going to make a noise about it, because I wanted the job.

However, I changed it a lot. That was the first show Peter Falk ever appeared in. It really made his career. He might have been in a daytime soap in a bit part but "Night Cry" was his first prime-time television appearance. He had one great five-minute scene. When the show went off the air (it was live), all the phone calls started coming into the control room. Jack O'Brien of *The Journal American* called and asked, "Who's that new guy? What's his name?" O'Brien wrote his entire column about Peter Falk, which got him loads of attention. The actual star of the show, Jack Klugman, always laughs each time I see him and Jack says, "*We* created Peter Falk." A few years ago, I made a couple of video copies of the show, giving them to both Peter and Jack as a memento.

Right after the show Peter rang me up and said he wanted to do the scene as his audition for the Actor's Studio. He asked to see the actual show, so I got a 16mm copy and ran it at Talent Associates especially for him. Peter came down with a pad and wrote down all his dialogue as well as any improvised lines. He did this as his audition at the Actor's Studio. A week later he called me and said, "They turned me down." In those days the Actor's Studio turned a lot of people down at the first try. You had to go back and do two (or even three) auditions before they accepted you. They were trying to maintain their exclusivity. Thanks to being seen on "Night Cry," Peter got called to do a role in *Murder Incorporated* (1960). So he got the same suit, tie, and hat, and played the same character again in the movie for which he got an Academy Award nomination as Best Supporting Actor. After that he was a star. Jackie Gleason had seen "Night Cry" and hired both Klugman and Peter Falk to play kidnappers in a CBS TV special, as hoods who kidnap him. So many people got work out of that teleplay. But not me.

After my first two shows I finally made my first sojourn to Los Angeles and found, to my surprise, that nobody was interested in someone who had written live television shows. I survived in Los Angeles for some months on unemployment insurance. I sold one half-hour storyline to the Dick Powell "Zane Grey Theatre" which was filmed with Wendell Corey — "A Member of the Posse." They wouldn't let me write the script. They just wanted to buy the story for three hundred and fifty dollars — which looked good when you'd been in unemployment. Everybody I knew was asking, "When's your next show going to be on?" Once you sell a show and you're not on the NBC staff as a page boy anymore, you run into friends who all ask about your next show. And you think, "Oh God! I had my one big chance and I blew it." It was really very embarrassing. I kept avoiding people because I didn't want to answer the question of what's next.

Finally, I returned to the East Coast. I think my good fortune was that my reserve unit got called into active duty and I went into the Army. That got me off the hook. In the meantime I'd written a "U.S. Steel Hour" show and an episode of the "Way Out" series, "False Face." So I did have a few more jobs but, mercifully, I got called into the Army and I didn't have to explain why I wasn't working much. I'd sent an outline to "The Defenders" with an idea for a show. Then they contacted me while I was in the military. My mother called me up saying, "They're trying to reach you from 'The Defenders.'" I was down in Virginia at the time and got them on the phone. They said they wanted to develop the story. I didn't want to tell them I was in the Army so as not to scare them off. I sneaked back to New York from Virginia periodically, without a pass, to attend meetings with Reginald Rose and David Shaw. Finally, after I gave them the first draft, they decided to film it. It was called "Kill or Be Killed." Sydney Pollack directed it. When I finally told them the truth that I was in the Army, they were very sympathetic. They gave me a few more chances to write for the show. By the time I got out of the service I was writing for them regularly. I also contributed teleplays to a couple of shows made by the same producer, Herbert Brodkin — "The Nurses" and "Espionage." So I had a rush of work, working like mad turning out scripts every month. After the service, everything opened up for me.

TW: Did you write pilots for "Peace Corps" and "House of Bryson"?

LC: I did a thing called "Peace Corps," which was one of many unproduced pilots. I'm not sure about "House of Bryson." It may be a title I gave to something I wrote but I don't remember what it was. My basement is full of scripts I've forgotten I ever wrote.

TW: One of my favorites from the shows you sent me is "Night Sounds" from "The Nurses." A patient attempts assaulting Gail. When she reports the incident, everybody blames her. It's a classic example of "blame the victim" and so relevant today. Later, there is a brilliant scene when Gail and her pursuer appear almost mirror image victims of each other.

LC: It's pertinent — a terrific show as relevant today as it was when it was written. That's the interesting thing. Like *Bone*, they're shows written so long ago they seem to be ahead of their time even today.

TW: I remember seeing your "Espionage" teleplay "Medal for a Turned Coat" when it was first broadcast in the sixties. It always remained fresh in my mind.

LC: When I went to see *Schindler's List*, I thought that I wrote on this very theme about the good German who's being honored so many years ago. *Schindler's*

*List* was filmed in stark black and white and is very similar in its style. *Medal for a Turned Coat* is an interesting companion piece to *Schindler's List.*

TW: I think it's much better than *Schindler's List.* Turning to the next question, I see that mirror imagery occurs very frequently in your work, especially in early teleplays such as "Night Sounds" and "False Face." What attracts you towards that theme?

LC: I don't know how to put it into words. I very often do stories in which two sides of a person conflict. In *Daddy's Gone A-Hunting*, the guy identifies with his aborted baby and they merge. In *Best Seller*, the killer and the cop merge. That theme's also in Hitchcock's *Strangers on a Train.* I don't know why it keeps recurring but it does. It's part of a thematic pattern. You mentioned that in "Night Sounds" the sexual deviant and the abused nurse have something in common as mirror images of each other. Victim and perpetrator become somehow united. It appears in so many of the scripts I write.

TW: There's a similar motif in "Party Girl." There's a scene where Inga Stevens looks at her image through a mirror in an apartment hallway just before she dies. Was this originally in your teleplay?

LC: I think Stuart Rosenberg put that in. Another interesting scene involved two different women. Inga Swenson played the wife who's just had her breast removed. But they wouldn't let me do it in those days. Also the show was originally titled "Call Girl." But they said, "Oh No! You can't have a show called "Call Girl!" So they renamed it "Party Girl" and refused to deal with a wife having her breast removed. So she had to have her leg amputated. Actually, removing the character's breast would have been much relevant because it's a sexual organ. You understand a woman who fears her husband won't look at her again because she's sexually scarred. She sees the husband talking to a hooker in the hospital room across the hall and her anxiety overtakes her. She verbally abuses the call girl.

We also had another big fight over "Night Sounds," over the guy molesting the nurse in the utility closet. He follows her in there and tries to rape her. In the script it all happens in the hospital room where she's fixing his bed. That was better because it was ambiguous. He didn't follow her anywhere. The incident happened at his bedside. So you could say that perhaps she misconstrued his advances. But when he drags her into another room and tries to attack her, it's an entirely different thing. Let's face it, somebody in a hospital bed might squeeze the nurse's ass or breast. It could be a stupid momentary lapse. But when somebody follows you down the hall and tries to corner you, they're a far more dangerous character. It might have been better to leave it at the hospital bed. But the director insisted on doing it his way. There was a big fight about it, but that's the way it was shot. It didn't really damage the play. It was a good show and I'm reasonably satisfied with it.

You forget a lot about these shows. Alan Alda appeared in it, but I never remembered this. It was only recently when I looked at it again that I recognized him. Alan Alda was at a party with me and he remembered it. But I hadn't. Jon Voight was in another teleplay, "Colossus," on "The Defenders."

TW: Did you know Herbert Brodkin personally?

LC: He was a former art director who later became a producer. He was very budget orientated and wanted to make a large profit on each show. He'd come up to me and say, "Larry, why do they have to have a meeting in a restaurant or luncheonette? Why can't they have it in the empty courtroom during the recess?" I'd reply, "I don't know why. But I thought you'd like to have some production values." He answered, "I don't want any production values. Shoot it at the back of an empty courtroom!" He didn't want to build another set because he was more interested in saving money. He believed that if the writing and dialogue were strong all you had to do was put the camera in the actor's face and you'd have what they'd call "A Brodkin." This was a real tight close-up where they cut off the top of the person's head and the bottom of their chin. So "A Brodkin" was an extreme close-up of somebody talking to the camera. It was very uncinematic, popping these heads back and forth. But that's what he liked. He'd hire good writers like Reginald Rose and would leave them alone. Brodkin did inspire a better quality of television writing. He also produced "Holocaust" and other fine shows. So he does deserve credit. But my experience with him was only on budgetary matters. He was kind of a dour fellow. If he ever said anything complimentary it stood out because he said so little. If he ever stopped you and said, "That was a good script," you felt great. He liked to go fishing. That was his favorite pastime. I don't remember any extensive creative conversations with him. But I'm sure glad he was around. Those shows were a big push for me.

TW: Many of your teleplays such as "Traitor," "Medal for a Turned Coat," and "Unwritten Law" exhibit some really interesting social issues. Did the nature of '60s television allow you to write these themes at the time?

LC: I don't know. Everything had to be a little bit masked in those days. As I mentioned, I couldn't do the breast thing in "Night Sounds," only cutting off the leg which I thought was a little bit ridiculous. It had to be some type of mutilation but they wouldn't allow a breast. So we danced around it a little. "My Name Is Martin Burnham" for NBC TV's "Arrest and Trial" was about a guy who'd once been arrested for a sex crime. Each time one was committed, cops would come to pick him up and question him. So he was being hounded for something he'd done years before. James Whitmore played this character. We managed to get that through although there were not many shows about sexual psychopaths and deviants in those days.

The "Accomplice" episode of NBC's "Sam Benedict" is about two homosexuals who are put on trial together for a murder they committed. That show was aired at seven-thirty on a Saturday night. Maybe NBC was so naive that they didn't understand what it was all about, but it was pretty clear. They cast one of the guys with a black actor. I went to the producer and said, "Does the network realize what this is all about? Not only is it about homosexuals but a mixed gay relationship." I asked a district attorney with whom I was working on another project, and he said that it was common for someone who's a wealthy middle-class homosexual to have an affair with a black male from an entirely different strata of life. The concept was totally valid. So then I thought, "Well Larry ... you've done it again."

But they ruined the entire show by casting the black actor's wife with a woman who had a very light skin and so odd looking that every time she came on the screen you were wondering whether she was black or white. Every time she appears the focus is not on the story but on her. There was also considerable monkeying around with the script. So it's not entirely what I wrote. It wasn't as good as it should have been. The sequences with Eddie Albert and Edmond O'Brien were fine. The guy who played the black man was fine. The only thing I didn't like was the wife.

In "Kill or Be Killed," the actress who played the wife was so draggy and whiny. You wanted to give her a kick in the ass. Each time she came on, she played the scene in the exact same way. She was married to Mark Rydell who was the director's (Sydney Pollack) best friend. Rydell was on the set the whole time we were shooting. The unfortunate actress who played the leading lady in this episode was Joanne Linville. She could have done a lot better if she'd been directed with some restraint. She just whined and cried throughout. To tell the truth, I had my doubts about Sydney Pollack. I thought he did not add much to the show as far as directing goes.

TW: But when you are directing don't you have control over casting?

LC: Yes, to some degree. But you can be pressurized into taking somebody you're not exactly crazy about. When I did *The Ambulance* I would never have cast Eric Roberts in that part. But I directed him into playing that part in a sympathetic way that he's not usually prone to do. He usually plays everything a little on the crazy side. I was trying to make him accessible, a nice guy, a vulnerable person whom you can identify with and care about, because in that kind of Hitchcock-type story you've got to identify with the leading man. Most people who saw the film said Eric was much softer and warmer than usual. But I didn't choose him. They came to me and said, "You're going to get Eric Roberts because we think he's financeable in the picture and that's the reason he's going to be in it." So you have to make the best of who you get. If it's a good actor, you should be able to direct a performance out of them and get what you want rather than leaving them alone to do their usual number. Joanne Linville's usual routine in every part she played is to start crying early and weep throughout the whole show. If you see that type of thing coming you must stop them immediately. Most actors just want to be told what to do. If you ask for something *specifically*, they usually do it for you. If you have an idea they usually respond to it. Actors like to be given some hint as to what pleases you. But most directors don't tell them anything. They just stand there and move the camera around. They're afraid of too much contact with them, so the actors are pretty well left to their own devices.

I think you have to be a very good actor to be in movies, because all this confusion is going on around you. You've got to maintain your concentration and remember where you are in the story and which scene came before the other.

Larry Cohen (left) and Eric Roberts on the set of *The Ambulance* (courtesy of Larry Cohen).

When acting in a play, it's in sequence. But in movies, on a Tuesday, you're doing a scene and next Thursday you're going to shoot the scene that came *before* that one. So you have to know where you are in the story every day. It's much harder acting in movies. You've got technicians warming around you, booms hanging down, cameras in front of your face, lights, smoke in the room, and you've got to get right into the action, picking up where you left off before. It's much harder getting a good acting performance in a movie. I've directed a couple of plays, and directing a play is easy. The only tough day in a play is the technical rehearsal when you do all the lighting and scenery cues. That awful day, rehearsing a two-hour play usually takes ten hours. You stop and you go, you stop and you go. That's what a movie is like *every day*— thirty days of technical rehearsal. Each day of a movie represents the worst day of a play magnified thirty times. Other than that, on that one day doing a play is great because you just get a bunch of actors in the room together, read the script, and go from there.

TW: I think "Medal for a Turned Coat" is one of your best works from the '60s era.

LC: For some reason, I became fascinated with the good German who returns home twenty years later and gets rewarded for being one of the few decent Germans during the Nazi period. I wrote it in a linear fashion and broke it up into flashbacks later. There was a good lengthy scene with Fritz Weaver's mother when she tells him about seeing the neighborhood tailor being arrested and thinking that now they wouldn't have to pay their cleaning bill. I think that's probably the most accurate human reaction people had in that period. They saw those Jews being taken away and wondered who was going to rent their apartment. Even if people felt some sorrow, it was gone in five minutes. The practicality of life took over. "Oh, yes. There's going to be a nice apartment available across the street." It's more of a comment on human nature than on Germans.

I don't know what would happen in America under similar circumstances. If we had identical economic problems and defeat in a war how would we respond to minorities if we were put in the same position as the German people were in the 1930s? You also balance that against the fact that anti–Semitism was not something the Germans created. It was prevalent in Europe for centuries. Ghettos weren't built by the Germans. They were built by the Poles and Ukrainians who were far more anti–Semitic than the Germans were before the war. Prior to Hitler, there was no country in Europe where Jews were treated better. They made marvelous inroads into art, medicine, and law in Germany. It was a haven for Jews and they flocked there for that reason. In America, Jews faced college quotas for law and medicine. In Germany, over seventy per cent of law and medical students were Jews. In America, the number was carefully restricted to around fifteen per cent. So before Hitler, Germany was less anti–Semitic than the United States. Then came the terrible backlash of depression, fear, and unemployment. The Nazis emerged. So, what can you say? Any of this is possible. Look what's going on in Africa and Bosnia.

TW: Even today, some university student newspapers are accepting paid neo–Nazi, holocaust revisionist ads.

LC: I can't understand the logic of that.

TW: They're trying to say the holocaust never happened.

LC: They can't deny it. There is photographic evidence proving it. They can argue the statistics and say, "A few thousand more, a few thousand less, a million more or a million less." But eleven million people died in the camps and, of these, six million were Jews. Skeptics may argue about the statistics but they can't argue it never happened at all.

TW: They're trying to do it in some student newspapers.

LC: There's always some madman around looking to create trouble.

TW: What do you regard as your best teleplay from this period?

LC: I always liked "Unwritten Law" because it's still applicable today. The one that did the most for me in the business was "Traitor." It got the most attention and was the second "Defenders" I scripted. It solidified my position in the Brodkin organization. But the question is difficult. It's like asking a parent which kid do you like best. There were certain scenes in shows which I liked for some particular reason rather than the whole play itself. Also, there were some particular choices of castings I liked.

What I *didn't like* was the casting in "Mayday! Mayday!" Torin Thatcher was completely wrong to play an American admiral. The character was supposed to be played by Lee Tracy who'd gained fame in the original stage production of *The Front Page*. Tracy had just played the president in *The Best Man* on Broadway and in the film version. Unfortunately, he had some denture problems a week before the "Defenders" show so they had to get a replacement. Franchot Tone, or any number of character actors, would have been fine. Then suddenly, they cast this American admiral with an actor with a Scottish accent. It really didn't make a lot of sense. Torin Thatcher was a decent enough supporting player but he didn't have sufficient variety in his line readings for three full acts on camera with all the talking he had to do. Melvyn Douglas would have been great. I was very disappointed. But, it's always easier to pick out the ones you didn't like than the ones you did.

## *California: Pilots and Teleplays*

TW: What made you move to Hollywood?

LC: I returned to California with some degree of fame resulting from this Emmy award–winning television show. "The Defenders" received all the honors and awards that year. I figured that everything would have changed and I'd be welcomed with open arms. But when I got back, the William Morris Agency (with whom I signed) told me I'd returned at a very bad time and there was no work for me. I couldn't believe that I was back in Hollywood and again unemployed after even having had so much success in New York. Then I had a call from a fellow who said he was an agent, Peter Sabiston. He'd heard of me from James Lee, a very good screenwriter and playwright who wrote *Career*, one of the very first successful off–Broadway plays. (It was made into a movie with Dean Martin.) I'd met Jim Lee in New York when I was working for Talent Associates. He recommended me to Peter Sabiston who was a lone-wolf agent. He didn't have an office but operated from his Bentley. Peter was the number-two tennis player in Hollywood's amateur division and knew all the moguls since he played tennis with them. He looked like Ray Milland, a very glamorous guy, and seemed to know his way around. Peter promised, "I can get you jobs." He came back a couple of days later with some assignments. Many of them were for shows which were actually packaged by the William Morris Agency. So I went to the Morris Agency and asked for a job on each of these shows. They said they were all fully booked up. I replied, "Well, I just got assignments on all of them. So you're fired!" I've still been with Peter Sabiston since — for nearly twenty-seven years now.

Once that happened, I broke the ice so other work kept coming in — pilots, scripts, episodes of "Sam Benedict" (such as the one with Eddie Albert). I did one "Arrest and Trial" for Universal. It was the first episode actually aired. James Whitmore was the guest star and it was an interesting script. "Arrest and Trial" was a ninety-minute show. It was really an early version of "Law and Order." "Law and Order" is based on "Arrest and Trial" because Universal owns both shows.

They just revived the format. Actually, the casting didn't work on the original show. It was so eccentric. They had Ben Gazzara and Chuck Connors. Logically, Chuck Connors would have played the rugged cop and Ben Gazzara the brilliant prosecutor. But they reversed it. Chuck Connors didn't look very comfortable with a suit on in a courtroom. So the formula didn't work.

TW: Joseph H. Lewis recently told me that Connors did not want to continue doing "The Rifleman" and wished to appear in a modern-day series wearing a suit.

LC: I must have written "Branded" by then. I quickly got into the pilot business, creating my own show. I went to a meeting with Harve Bennett of ABC. The television business used to be more personal then. You could deal with one executive and actually sell him a show. Today you have to deal with over twenty people! The programming departments have become huge and deal in committee decisions. Harve Bennett later became producer of all the *Star Trek* movies. He was the head of ABC Development on the West Coast. I was in the outer office and was supposed to pitch him a format for a show. Peter asked me, "What are you going to tell him?" I said, "I have no idea." Then I saw a list of old movies on the table from a 16mm catalogue. I opened it and started looking at the titles. Then I saw *The Four Feathers*. I thought, "That's a great idea. A coward. How do we switch that to a Western?" So I went in and made up off the top of my head a Western about a guy who had been court-martialed as a coward. Then it occurred to me that it was much like being blacklisted. Everywhere you went you had a reputation that followed you. You had to live it down. If you're accused of something you didn't do, how can you survive? Well, Harve liked it. But ABC didn't act quickly enough. The next day we had a meeting at Goodson Todman Productions. They were famous for quiz shows. They had a commitment with Procter & Gamble to put something on at eight-thirty on Sunday nights on NBC following "The Wonderful World of Disney" and preceding "Bonanza." I pitched the same idea to Harris Kattleman, who was the head of their company. (He later became head of Fox Television Division.) He said, "This would be great for Chuck Connors. He's so hot!" Connors had done "The Rifleman" for years. Procter and Gamble immediately made an on the air commitment if we could sign Chuck Connors. So based on a little five-page outline they got Chuck to agree to do it. At that time certain companies owned time periods. This was a holdover from the early days of radio and television when advertising agencies controlled programming. Procter & Gamble owned the eight-thirty time period and they agreed to schedule "Branded." So we went to NBC and it was a *fait accompli*. Sunday nights at eight-thirty was one of the best time periods available. And we had gotten the show on with only a five-page outline!

Then I began writing. I wrote the first six or seven episodes. The first one was directed by Joseph H. Lewis. Chuck wanted Joe to direct the show, so we went to his house for a meeting. He was a tough little guy, just like Sam Fuller. I didn't know Sam at the time, but when I met him I thought he was cut from the same cloth. Joe said, "The first script you wrote was terrific. The second one's a piece of shit." Those were the first words he spoke. So I said, "Let's sit down and fix it." So we got along fine. We incorporated his notes into the screenplay and the show was made.

I did go up to Kanab, Utah, to see the shooting of the show's signature title sequence — the court-martial scene. They filmed there because they wanted a lot of extras. If they traveled a certain distance from Hollywood, they wouldn't have to use the Screen Actors Guild people. They could hire non-union extras and they wouldn't have to pay residuals every week. They wisely shot the sequence in color because television was transferring to color at the time. Otherwise, they would have had to go back and shoot it all over again. I got a kick out of it because John Litel played General Reid. He was an old character actor who had been in many classic films I'd seen since I was a kid. I flew up there with Dominic Frontiere who did the music. (He also did the music for "The Invaders") He said, "I'm flying up to the location, so you can fly with me." So I went to the airport in Santa Monica and got on the plane with him, only to find out that he'd never flown that kind of plane before. He was fiddling around with the controls, just him and me and the plane, and he really didn't know how to pilot it. We finally got to Utah. There wasn't even an airport — just a landing field with a torn windsock on a pole. He made four or five passes and finally he landed the thing. I was glad to get out of that plane alive! So we went and watched the shooting.

At the outset time, Connors was very friendly to me until I mentioned, later, that the show was about a blacklisted cowboy. As soon as he heard it, he had a terrible reaction. I guess he was very conservative politically. He felt he'd suddenly fallen into the hands of a left-winger and that I was manipulating him into some nefarious cause. I remember I went to the location on the Paramount lot. It was a big, beautiful Western street which they'd used for "Bonanza" and all kinds of cowboy movies such as *The Paleface*. I was walking up the street and saw Connors on his horse. He saw me, recognized me, turned his horse, and galloped straight towards me. I was standing in the center of the Western street, just looking at him. At full speed, came this horse with this huge guy on it galloping directly at me. I guess I was too dumbfounded to move. He reined up the horse, just inches away, and grinned at me. He said he couldn't believe that I didn't bolt out of the way.

Ten or twelve years later, we were at a dinner on the backlot of the old Republic Studios honoring all the old cowboy stars. Gene Autry, Tex Ritter, and virtually everybody who had done cowboy movies were there. I ended up seated at a table with Chuck Connors. I hadn't seen him for years. All of a sudden he said to me, "You know, I was always amazed about that day when I galloped that horse up the street at you at Paramount and you didn't run. I never could get over that." That had stuck in his memory.

Obviously he had a bug in his head about my involvement with the show because after a few more shows they told me it wasn't necessary for me to write any more episodes. They'd send my money every week and I didn't have to come in any more. It was OK with me. I was gone but Connors' behavior became

**Chuck Connors possibly charging toward Larry Cohen on the set of "Branded," a '60s television series created by Larry Cohen.**

impossible. He finally alienated the sponsors, which was the worst thing you can do. Procter & Gamble would ask him to appear at a luncheon and he would give them a hard time. So, even though the show was among the top ten or twelve shows, it ended up getting canceled after a few seasons because the sponsors were furious at him. Otherwise, I think "Branded" could have run for five years. But what could you do? We talked about it years later when I ran into him again. As

Chuck's career waned he became more friendly. After a while he was just another actor looking for a job. He commiserated with me. "Well, if I had just treated the sponsor a little better I might have had a few more seasons."

TW: Strong family motifs run through most of your work. Even "The Vindicator" episode of "Branded" transcends the Western series formula. In many ways, Jason McCord resembles a son covering up for a dysfunctional father (General Reid). Instead of revealing the truth about Bitter Creek, McCord takes on guilt to continue a false myth of family unity.

LC: That's exactly what it is. There's a little bit of that in "Mayday! Mayday!" but there the son sees his father breaking down and betrays him. So, the motif is definitely there. "Branded" had a nice emotional center which could have been exploited better as the episodes went on, but it just got lost. It was unfortunate. But, by then I wasn't doing the shows.

TW: Was that the time Chuck Connors wouldn't allow you to even suggest stories?

LC: I don't know about that. I submitted a selection of stories before I left. But they brought in a producer, Andrew J. Fennady, a kind of routine television producer, who just went from one show to another and did a workman-like job of grinding them out to fill up half an hour. That's not the way I like to work. I just don't want to fill up time. I like a show to have somewhere to go, taking the characters on a kind of trip, developing the series format a little bit further, because, if I get bored with it, how can I expect audiences not to get bored? Most television is just filling up time.

TW: "Survival" is a really interesting "Branded" episode. The Alex Cord character becomes a monster because he wishes to return to his family at all costs. He abandons Connors in the desert. When we next see Cord, he appears more of a pathetic figure dominated by the family he sought so desperately to return to. Connors recognizes this and decides not to seek revenge.

LC: I liked that kind of story because it was simple and I always wanted to do it again as a low-budget feature. The Cord character decided that his life was worth more than Connors, the Bitter Creek coward. When they have only one horse in the desert and death appears imminent, Cord decides that somebody else has to die: "I've got a family." The story was really about people valuing themselves against somebody else's worth. I enjoyed that particular story. That was the one Joe Lewis liked.

TW: In other "Branded" episodes such as "Coward Step Aside," "The Bounty" and the three-part "Mission" episode, you've only supplied the story. When others write the teleplays it is often difficult to see your original ideas and how they could have been better developed.

LC: Yes. That's absolutely true. But the unfortunate part about it was that I can't stay around continually fighting other people, because I wear myself out. If I find myself in a situation where fifty percent of the day is spent fighting over details and having to live with bad decisions, I depart. It's awful enough having your child raped without being forced to hold her arms. Making you participate in the destruction of your own work can be thoroughly demoralizing. So I say, "Look, if you are going to ruin it, then go ahead. But I won't be around to participate." I'll go on and write something else. Now there's a percentage of people in the business who believe you should stick around and put yourself into an early grave fighting people you don't respect. You can expend all your energy fighting and have nothing left for your own work. In that kind of situation, writers make themselves emotionally sick. They drink, take drugs, and can't sleep at night. Their marriages crack up. I just wanted to write and get pleasure from doing it. I've always said I write for free but get paid for going to the meetings.

At least when I'm making my own movies, I'm truly happy. I love to be writer, producer, director, head of editing, making all the decisions with sole creative control. By the time you finish the picture and hand it over to the distributors, there's not much they can do about it. If they want another close-up in a scene I've already shot, what can they do? If you say you've never shot the close-up, they've got to take your word for it. They don't have time to view ten thousand feet of unedited film, looking for something you've decided not to use. You're really in the driver's seat. But it's a different story if you're directing a picture and executives are looking over your shoulder every day, constantly putting their two cents in. I've never worked too well under those conditions. I was fired from a couple of pictures because I wasn't going to make someone else's picture. If I couldn't make *my* picture, I'd rather not make *their* picture.

TW: So you were very successful with your pilots and teleplays at this time?

LC: "Branded" was a huge break for me. I had sold a television show without even shooting a pilot. What usually happens in television is they spend a fortune shooting pilots. They shoot forty pilots, then usually buy three shows so they end up throwing away thirty-eight pilots and a fortune in money. But I stroll in and get a show on the air without even shooting a foot of film. I approached ABC television on the strength of having "Branded" on the air. Ed Scherick was the head of ABC and Doug Kramer was his assistant. Barry Diller and Michael Eisner were on the staff at the time. I just went directly to the top guys and told them my idea for "The Invaders" and sold them the series based on one meeting. That show also got a commitment to go on the air without shooting a pilot, which was truly amazing. They ended up giving it to Quinn Martin to produce. So now I had the unique accomplishment of having two series scheduled without pilots ever being filmed, making me the hottest series creator on Hollywood. I was the guy who could get a show on the air on the basis of the script, without having to shoot any film. So I would just go to the Beverly Hills Hotel in the late afternoon with Peter Sabiston and wait for people to come over to my corner table at the Polo Lounge and give me jobs. I'd arrive there about six p.m. every day and people would come in and give me an on the spot commitment to do something. I didn't have to go and see them. Almost anyone who bumped into me wanted to hire me. For a while I guess I was the number-one pilot writer in Hollywood. You might also say I was seduced by Hollywood. I bought an estate in

David Vincent (Roy Thinnes) runs to warn a disbelieving world about the presence of aliens in their midst in "The Invaders," a '60s television series created by Larry Cohen.

Beverly Hills, several acres of land, and a mansion the Hearst family originally built back in 1929, the same year they built San Simeon.

TW: Did you write any of "The Invaders" episodes?

LC: I wrote a couple. But they didn't use them. I did write thirty storylines and they used some of them. But, again, it was political. Quinn Martin wanted the show to be *his*, not Larry Cohen's show. So "The Invaders" did not really reflect my intention of depicting paranoia in America and parodying the Cold War years. The stories became rudimentary. The aliens became stock heavies and David Vincent's character became repetitious.

The deal I had made was so out of line for the time, because of the royalties and percentages that I'd negotiated. I got fifteen percent of the gross profits of the show without any losses carried forward, except for the overages on the pilot. It was unheard of then. Television shows usually operate on a deficit. If they got a million dollars, they'd spend a million-five shooting the show. So there'd be a five hundred thousand dollar deficit every week deducted from whatever profits emerged. That wipes out profits. But my contract called for me to get gross revenues without any deductions or overages except from the pilot. The pilot wasn't all that expensive anyway. After the show had earned some two hundred thousand dollars in revenue, they'd have to start paying me my profits. Few had ever had a deal that good. In addition, there was an agency called General Artists Corporation (G.A.C.) who'd asked to represent me. So when I went in and told them that I already had an arrangement with ABC to do "The Invaders" they said, "Well, why don't you let us finalize the deal for you?"

Then I found out that they were asking ABC for a packaging fee, which was a percentage of the gross moneys from the show. In those days you could get a two- to six-percent packaging fee. So I went back to them and said, "Hey, you guys have no right to take a packaging fee. I just found out that you guys are getting more than I am. How can I be creator of the show and you make more than me?" They said, "What do you want?" I replied, "Let's split the packaging fee." So they gave me half. Now I was not only getting paid by ABC and Quinn Martin, I was also getting paid by the talent agency. When Quinn Martin heard of this, he had a fit. As far as he was concerned, I was making way too much money. He couldn't stand it. He couldn't stand seeing me around. Quinn Martin ended up making over sixty episodes of "The Invaders."

I first met Quinn Martin when I had written the "Kill or Be Killed" episode of "The Fugitive." He'd seen the show on CBS and contacted me. "How did you know what we did in our pilot?" I said, "I don't know what you're talking about." He said, "We just made a pilot called "The Fugitive" and your first sequence is the same as the one in our pilot." I said, "I didn't know anything about your pilot." Martin continued, "It starts off when a guy is being taken to the death house. He's on a train. There's a train wreck and he escapes. Not only do you have the same scene but it was shot exactly the same way as ours. The camera angles were exactly the same." I replied, "It's truly a coincidence." Martin said, "I can't believe it." Later on, through no connection at all, ABC asked him to be the producer of "The Invaders" because he was the number-one producer at the time, having done both "The Untouchables" and "The Fugitive."

TW: I sense you eventually became disillusioned with working in television. But you also had some good experiences, too?

LC: You face another situation peculiar to television. If you're on a television series as a writer, they want to own you completely. They want to have you six to seven days a week on call. They also want you to *rewrite* everybody's script. Pretty soon all you're doing is rewriting other people. I told them that I didn't want to become their rewrite man. I'm happy to create new scripts but I don't want to come in and rehash other people's work. It's not my idea of a career fixing up other people's material to prove that I'm a better writer than they are. Even to this day, if you go and sell a series, they want you to be the show runner and stay with the show. Constantly throughout my career they asked me, "Will you stay with the show?" I'd say, "Well, I'll write the first ten episodes. I'll write most of the first season. But I can't write the same show for five years". Unfortunately, when they don't own you they get very frustrated. But if I had stayed in television I wouldn't be as good a writer as I am today.

One show I wrote nearly all the episodes for was "Blue Light." It was a half-hour show for ABC. They had an agency, CMA (which later became ICM). It was looking for material to package. Freddie Fields asked if I could come up with something for Robert Goulet who had development money to pay for scripts. So I came up with a series in which Goulet played something like what Louis Hayward used to play in those old Count of Monte Cristo movies. The guy was a bit of a fop, a Scarlet Pimpernel type. But I put him in Nazi Germany. I thought it fit Goulet because he was so glossy looking. Maybe you could overcome that by making a joke about the narcissistic act he put on to fool those Nazis. ABC again bought the show without a pilot. We did shoot a pilot, but by the time it was actually filming at Fox, the show was locked on the schedule.

I think I wrote eight of the sixteen shows. The producers used three of the episodes in a feature film release, *I Deal in Danger*. I hope Fox will re-release it on video someday. One day I saw the film in the New Amsterdam Theatre on 42nd Street. The man sitting next to me became angry and exclaimed, "I saw this on television!" I didn't want to let him know of my connection with the series. He was boiling mad and ready to kill because he'd paid for something he'd already watched for free on television.

TW: The credits list both you and Walter Grauman as creator of "Blue Light."

LC: Grauman had the idea of doing a World War II series called "Blue Light." But I came up with the rest, creating character, framework, and plot. Grauman had connections with the agency who wanted him to come up with a script. So he ended up getting co-credit. But I had no problem with this since I was quite happy to give it to him. We had a nice working relationship. The show began suddenly and ended just as quickly. For some reason audiences did not take to Robert Goulet.

TW: Seeing the episodes now, I recognize your Scarlet Pimpernel idea for David March, but Goulet is so stiff in the role.

LC: I agree. If you threw Goulet off a truck he'd still get up and look as if he'd just walked out of a tonsorial parlor. You could not mess this guy up. If we had signed up David Janssen or anybody else, it would have been different. The stories were good. But I tried to counter the casting problem we had with a stiff leading man such as Goulet by making him this slick and over-dressed foppish Scarlet Pimpernel type. That would explain his character. But we could not overcome audience resistance to Robert Goulet's personal image.

TW: I understand you had a nice time doing the series.

LC: It was a good time to be at Fox. They were making *Dr. Dolittle* and *Planet of the Apes* at the time. Each time I went for lunch at the commissary, I saw everybody in costume. I particularly remember seeing Burgess Meredith there dressed as the Penguin in the "Batman" TV series. They gave me lovely offices at Fox, left me completely alone, gave me a bunch of secretaries, and treated me so well for a change that I wanted to stick around. Instead of putting me in an adversarial position, they treated me with respect. After meeting with other writers for a few days and finding out that none of them had any fresh ideas, I then decided I'd make up the stories and give them to the writers. I'd tell them the story and say, "Go, write the script." But certain scripts people sent in were quite poor. By the time I told them how to fix them, I realized I could have written the whole thing myself in half the time. After that I would dictate act one in the morning, and in the afternoon I would dictate act two. Every day I would switch secretaries so I wouldn't wear them out. So I was writing four episodes a week and getting quite a kick out of it. I realized that I could dictate scripts the same way I used to make up those radio shows in my room when I was a kid. I was acting the shows out and playing all of the parts. The secretaries gave me an audience to perform for.

Also, at the time I had to have a minor operation on my hand. I got a staple stuck in my finger and, for some reason, the damn thing wouldn't heal. Eventually, they had to graft some skin from my arm and put my hand in a cast. So I was forced into dictating. When I saw how fast it was going, I thought, "Wow! It's not even work anymore. I can stand there, make a complete fool of myself and play all these parts." The pay was very good, especially when you could write a show in a day. Since I was head writer I didn't have anybody telling me they didn't like the scripts. The director was happy. The studio was happy.

Then a friend of mine called me and told me he was producing a series called "The Rat Patrol" and would I be interested in doing an episode for him as a favor? So I said, "Get me a secretary who can take dictation and I'll come over and write the thing tomorrow for you. So I went over to Goldwyn Studios and dictated act one, then act two. It was only a half-hour show, so I was out of there after four or five hours. A couple of days later I received the script but it wasn't quite what I had dictated. It was similar. But this secretary had re-written the script herself. She changed the dialogue, altered some of the scenes, and it was pretty damn good. So I told her, "You really improved this." And that's the way it was submitted. I wonder who that girl turned out to be, because she did a fine job and made it better than what I actually wrote.

TW: Was this "The Blind Man's Buff Raid"?

LC: Yes. It was a cute idea for the show. This was the same producer who had once given me an acting job to do. I don't know if I ever told you about that.

TW: No.

LC: The producer was Stanley Shpetner. He'd come to my house for dinner. He mentioned he was doing a pilot at Fox for CBS. It was a William Dozier production. (He later produced the "Batman" series.) This was supposed to star Ethel Waters and Ed Wynn, called "You're Only Young Twice." It was about an old inventor, played by Ed Wynn, who invents this youth pill. Every week he gives it to different people and they get to be young again for twenty-four hours and relive their youth. So immediately I launched into my imitation of Ed Wynn. I do a pretty good Ed Wynn. He couldn't believe it because he'd been all over Hollywood looking for somebody to play Ed Wynn, because, in the pilot, Ed Wynn takes the pill himself and becomes young. He said, "You've got to come out and do this for Bill Dozier." So I auditioned at Fox Studios and Dozier said, "It's amazing! Now you've got to go down to the rehearsal stage and do it for Ed Wynn himself." I did the imitation for Ed Wynn and got the job. It was a sizable part. I was in about four scenes and I also got to work with Ethel Waters. I was so good that when the show was finally finished, people who walked out of the screening room were certain that Ed had looped me so that it wasn't my voice. Everyone thought that he dubbed me.

TW: In your "Fugitive" episode, "Escape into Black," you have a really interesting plot when Kimble suffers from amnesia and decides to give himself up to Lt. Gerard.

LC: I think I thought of the idea as a kind of joke and suggested it to the producer. My idea involved turning the whole formula of the show inside out by writing the scene when Kimble phones Gerard to confess and give himself up. This scene reinforces the series for the rest of its run because now, no matter what anybody says, Lt. Gerard is now convinced of Kimble's guilt because of his full confession on the phone. So if anybody questions why Gerard continues to chase Kimble for the next three years of the show, the producers can point to this show when any doubts Gerard may have had concerning Kimble's guilt collapse. The scene confirms Gerard's feelings about Kimble's guilt. By reinforcing the whole formula of "The Fugitive" series, "Escape into Black" becomes an integral special episode rather than just a run of the mill product. That's the real reason I wrote the "Escape into Black." I never did any more episodes for the series.

TW: I note you also wrote a pilot in 1967 for a series called "Coronet Blue" involving amnesia.

LC: That was for Herb Brodkin. The series lasted seventeen weeks. It starred Frank Converse as a guy with amnesia. He's found shot, floating in the Hudson River. All he says during surgery is "coronet blue." Then he's released and nobody is able to trace his identity. They can't identify his fingerprints. All he knows is that a character who tried to kill him comes back occasionally and tries to finish him off. Converse does not know why. Nor does he know what "coronet blue" means. So he searches for clues to his identity and gets involved in people's lives. He travels to places trying to find out who he is, followed by the person who is still trying to eliminate him. When the Brodkin Organization took it over, they wanted to turn it into an anthology. So they played down the amnesia aspect until eventually there was nothing about it at all in the show. It was just Frank Converse wandering from one story to the next with no connective format at all. Anyway, the show ended after seventeen weeks and nobody ever found out what "coronet blue" meant. The actual secret is that Converse was not really an American at all. He was a Russian who had been trained to appear like an American and was sent to the United States as a spy. He belonged to a spy unit named "Coronet Blue." He decided to defect so the Russians tried to kill him. Nobody can really identify him because he doesn't really exist as an American. "Coronet Blue" was really an outgrowth of the "Traitor" episode of "The Defenders." After getting amnesia, the Russians try to finish Converse off before he can remember what "coronet blue" really means and give away the identities of the rest of the Soviet agents. I took the "Traitor" episode and made it into a television series. But nobody ever knew, because CBS never revealed the ending of the show.

TW: It's interesting because it anticipates *No Way Out* (1986) with Kevin Costner and Gene Hackman.

LC: Yes — and also Robert Ludlum's *The Bourne Identity*, which was written ten to fifteen years later with the same plot. Again, "Coronet Blue" made me money but it was not a happy experience. Brodkin didn't want to do a popular thriller series like "The Fugitive." He wanted to turn it into a serious anthology drama series. But it didn't work. Perhaps the Museum of Broadcasting has an episode or two. Most of them were awful.

TW: I liked the opening scenes in your pilot for "Griff" with Lorne Greene as the retired cop wandering in the park seeing other discarded senior citizens.

LC: I wrote many pilots, including one for the Lorne Greene series "Griff." The idea for the show was clever and ABC bought the show based on the script and the availability of Lorne Greene. We had to wait six months for him *not* to be picked up by "Bonanza" for another season so it was certain he would be free. I suggested other actors, like Jimmy Stewart, but they were set on Lorne Greene. So by the time he agreed to do the show, another series appeared on CBS called "Barnaby Jones" which had the exact same format. Our first episode and the pilot of "Barnaby Jones" were identical. An old man's son gets killed. He's a private detective. Barnaby Jones and Griff are both former elderly police captains who have no respect for their son because he chose to be a private detective. Both have a daughter-in-law. Everything was identical. I had told the idea for the "Griff" show to some very close friends of mine. Later one became involved in the "Barnaby Jones" show. I wouldn't say he stole my idea, but since then, the former friend avoids me when we meet in public and looks rather guilty. People said to me, "Why don't you sue them? The show's been a hit for years. They obviously stole it from you." But I didn't have any actual proof. Also Universal should have sued them. They were damaged, not me, because "Barnaby Jones" came on first and therefore we had to change the format of "Griff." Also, there was no question that Buddy Ebsen was better than Lorne Greene. Oddly enough, when my pilot "Man on the Outside" finally aired as an "ABC Movie of the Week," *T.V.*

*Guide* wrote in the listings, "This was the TV pilot for the 'Barnaby Jones' series"!
I was getting tired of TV. I was making a lot of money but it was not artistically rewarding. Also I wrote a lot of scripts which never saw the light of day, such as pilots that never got made. Even the series which did get on the air were not done as I had imagined them. Since I didn't want to devote my entire waking life to series, I couldn't get really angry at other people who would revise or alter my concept, because I wasn't willing to sacrifice everything to supervise these shows on a daily basis. I thought that this is not really a rewarding way of working, and if you keep up this kind of work you'll become a worse writer as years go by. You'll become what they call a hack. The only way you're going to be able to do anything with your life is by making your own pictures, which is what I should have done in the beginning. If I hadn't had success with writing "Branded" and "The Invaders," I probably would have got around to making my own pictures sooner instead of later. By that time I'd also written *Return of the Magnificent Seven*. I didn't like the picture they made of it. They only shot half the script and left out all the clever twists in the original screenplay. Even the producer, Walter Mirisch, admitted, "Oh, your script was much better than the movie"!

## Early Screenplays

Then I wrote *Daddy's Gone A-Hunting* with my friend Lorenzo Semple, Jr. It was a perfect Hitchcock script. That came about after a meeting I had with Universal with the head of the story department who said, "That's a wonderful story for Alfred Hitchcock." I said, "I'd love to do it with Hitchcock." He replied that Hitchcock was desperate to find a property and was currently in New York. Since I was traveling to New York, he arranged a meeting for me. I had a three and a half hour meeting with Hitchcock at the St. Regis hotel. He told me stories and anecdotes and plots for movies he never made, and finally I told him my yarn. He jumped up and he said, "Let's do it! When can you be in Hollywood?" So I returned to Hollywood and told everybody I was working with Hitchcock. Then somebody at Universal, Ed Henry — one of the executives nicknamed "Dr. No" because he nixed every project — talked Hitch out of it. I became extremely frustrated. Then Lorenzo Semple said, "Let's write it together. We can probably write it in ten days. You'll have a script and give it directly to Hitchcock." So we wrote the script and sent it back. Hitchcock promptly returned it, stating: "Well, you've left nothing for me to do. You've written every shot and angle." Then Joan Harrison came into the picture. She was Hitchcock's former secretary and writer. She also produced his TV series. She took me to lunch at the Brown Derby, told me she read the script, and wanted to produce it herself. Unfortunately, she did not have financing. I then heard that a company called National General wanted to buy the script for a lot of money. In those days two hundred thousand dollars was a lot of money, so Lorenzo and I sold the script for Mark Robson to direct.

I had great respect for Mark Robson. He'd directed *Von Ryan's Express, Home of the Brave, Champion, The Bridges of Toko-Ri*, and *The Inn of the Sixth Happiness*, which I felt were good movies, so I thought that he would be a better director than he was. I was really surprised to find how uninventive he was. He was more interested in the clothes and hairstyles. I was originally contracted to be co-producer with him, so I worked closely with Robson on the project. I found him a very sweet man, but every nuance in my script had to be explained to him. Lorenzo didn't want to work on the film, but I thought I'd stick with the project for a change. I traveled with Robson to San Francisco, found the "Top of the Mark" (a rooftop restaurant on top of the Mark Hopkins Hotel), and rewrote the ending so the chase would end up there.

TW: Was Judith Anderson appearing theatrically in *Medea* then?

LC: Oh no. I just made it up.

TW: It was a really good touch.

LC: There were a lot of clever things in the script. It could have been a really fine movie. But Robson began casting these actors who were just terrible for the parts. He turned down many good people who were available at the time and instead signed Scott Hylands, a newcomer. Of course, the head of the company had a girlfriend, Carol White, who was a decent actress but certainly no star, and certainly not right for the part. When they cast those two people in the leads, I said to Janelle — my ex-wife — "I don't mind writing this thing, but to sit there now and watch what they're going to do with it — it's too painful!" I told Mark, "I don't think I can stay on as co-producer." I went to Alaska on vacation to get as far away from it as possible. I thought it was going to be such a great movie and they ruined it. *Daddy's Gone A-Hunting* was as perfect a script I'd ever written and I wish I'd been allowed to direct it myself. (By the way, John Williams wrote the musical score but that could not save the picture.)

TW: How did your original screenplay for *Return of the Seven* differ from the final film?

LC: The director only shot half of the screenplay. In the original story, scores of Mexicans were kidnapped from a small village and herded into the desert. A Mexican general forced them to build a church as a monument to his sons who had died defending the country. The Magnificent Seven rode to their rescue. In the original script, the Mexicans were slaves building the church until the Seven freed them and drove the general away. The people were free to return to their own villages. But they decided to stay on in the desert and finish the church because they'd become so enamored of what they'd done. They said, "Each time we plant our crops, they die, wither away, or we eat them as food. And then we have nothing. If we build this church it will last for the rest of our lives. It will live for generations." So they decide to do as free men what they were being forced to do as slaves. Even the Magnificent Seven put their guns aside and, for the first time in their lives, they *build* rather than destroy. So they join the Mexicans in raising the church so there will be something there in life for them more than just killing. In the meantime, the general goes home, gets reinforcements, and returns. He is horrified to find the church has been completed. Once the symbol of his son's loss, it is now the symbol of his defeat. So now he fires cannons, blows up the new church, and then we have the big battle scene. My screenplay had a double twist. That's a trademark of everything I write. But the producers took out the whole twist of the people deciding to stay and build the church themselves. They truncated the whole story. In addition, there were casting problems. *Return of the Seven* was an American-Spanish co-production, which meant they had to cast a number of Spanish actors in leading parts. So, instead of seven great actors in the picture (I'd recommended Peter Falk, Telly Savalas, and some other young character actors), they cast these Spanish actors who didn't have much personality.

TW: Viewing *Return of the Seven*, I remember an interesting dissolve from Brynner and Fuller to the Mexican general and his second-in-command. Was this in your original script?

LC: I don't remember that shot. I reject that movie every time I look at it and very seldom watch it all the way through. It appears on television but I get upset and turn it off. It could have been a great movie and resulted in a series of Magnificent Seven films. United Artists could have developed something like the James Bond series out of that. Instead, they made each sequel cheaper than its predecessor. They didn't get Yul Brynner but George Kennedy and Lee Van Cleef for the later sequels. The films became increasingly shoddy. If they made *Return of the Seven* as a quality film, they could have had a gold mine. The first Magnificent Seven picture was unsuccessful at the American box office. It was a big success abroad, but a disaster in the U.S.A. Then Walter Mirisch wanted to turn it into a television series. I suggested, "Why turn it into a television series when you can make another movie out of it? That's better than giving it away as a television series. You can always sell it to television after the second picture." So I persuaded him to hire me and write a feature film. Then Walter said, "We can't use the music because it's been used for automobile commercials on television." I replied, "If you can't use the music you might as well not make the picture. *The Magnificent Seven* is not *The Magnificent Seven* without that theme. So he finally used the music and Elmer Bernstein got nominated for an Academy Award for the *second film!* He never got nominated for the original one. Instead, he got nominated for the same music used in the sequel the second time around! Bernstein didn't win, but it's the first time somebody got an Academy Award nomination for the music from a revised score. The original *Magnificent Seven* had never gained much critical respect. It opened in New York's Brooklyn Metropolitan Theater on a double feature and later played on the Loew's Circuit for five days before it disappeared. It did no business whatsoever in America. But, as people in the first picture became stars — Steve McQueen, James Coburn, Charles Bronson — it gained a cult following. Actually, *Return of the Seven* probably did better at the box office. Neither film compares with Kurosawa's *Seven Samurai*.

I remember meeting Yul Brynner at the Beverly Hills Hotel on only one occasion. He tried to get me drunk. Brynner asked me what I wanted to drink. I requested a vodka. He brought in an entire water glass and filled it to the brim with vodka so I'd drink it and agree to changes he wanted in the script.

TW: I remember you mentioned having some initial problems with Lee Van Cleef over your *El Condor* screenplay.

LC: After I returned from scripting the picture in Almeria, Spain, the company told me Van Cleef would not get on the plane to go to Spain because he felt that people would laugh at him in *El Condor*. He thought my script would ruin his career. So I met Van Cleef and his agent at a coffee shop in Beverly Hills. There was a great deal of hostility in the air. Van Cleef began by saying he'd make a fool of himself if he played the part as written. I replied, "People are supposed to laugh at you in this part. It's *supposed* to be funny. Your role resembles Bogart's in *The African Queen*. It's an exaggerated character, an unshaven, drunken bum." He replied, "You mean it's supposed to be funny?" I said, "Sure, it's supposed to be funny. It's your chance to do comedy." Van Cleef then replied, "Well, why didn't somebody tell me that?" I said, "I'm telling you now." Then he began to get excited—"I'll play it without my toupee. I'll play it bald." I began to encourage him—"That's a great idea. From then on, after that one meeting, he was as happy as a clam. That incident was one of those things that convinced me I could be a director. Other people were unable to deal with him. I had him doing exactly what I wanted him to do.

*El Condor* was produced by the same company who did *Daddy's Gone-A Hunting*—National General. They had asked me to work on the film because they planned to shoot it in Spain and had already constructed sets such as the fort used in the final battle. Then they decided they hated the original script and had second thoughts about the whole project. Then they called me up and said, "If we fly you to Spain, could you look at the sets we built and write another script that would fit these sets?" So they took my wife and I to Spain and treated us like royalty. I've never been treated so well in my life before. People drove us everywhere and brought us meals. We could never spend our per diem. I came up with a script to fit the locations and sets. It took me about three weeks and I saved everybody's job. When we left, you would have thought that royalty was going home. They even had a fireworks celebration. Then I returned to the States and talked Lee Van Cleef into doing the role. So it was a very rewarding experience.

But *El Condor* was not a good film. I don't think John Guillermin was a very good director. He and producer Andre De Toth had some awful fights over the picture. Personally, I don't think Lee Van Cleef captured the part in the way I'd written it. But the film was successful. This was when I realized I could talk to actors. Actors are not blessed with some kind of mystical power. They're just people who are often confused and need guidance. I knew I could do that. I was completely disillusioned about what other people did to my scripts, as with *Daddy's Gone A-Hunting*. So, that's when I made the decision to go ahead and make my own films.

TW: So *El Condor* was basically a reworking job.

LC: Yes, a reworking job from somebody else's script. So after those experiences and television I thought, "I'm earning a lot of money but I'm just making myself generally unhappy. I've got nothing to show for it except for the plays I wrote for "The Defenders," "Espionage," and a few other television shows I wrote in my early New York period. All the work I've done in California is stuff I don't even want to show people. I'd bought myself a beautiful house in Beverly Hills with a swimming pool and a couple of acres. I was successful. But it was unfulfilling. So one day Janelle bought me a director's viewfinder. I said, "What's this?" She said, "It's what you really want to do so why don't you do it." I said, "Thanks. I will."

## Written, Produced and Directed by Larry Cohen

With a little bit of encouragement I wrote a script called *The Cutting Room*, which later became *Special Effects*. I took that around and had a bunch of "almosts." It didn't quite happen. Then I wrote *Bone*. It was originally called *Unreal*. I wrote it about the same time I wrote my first stage play, *The Nature of the Crime*. *Unreal* was also based on a story I'd written when I was thirteen called *Three Hours to Kill*. But instead of doing it straight, I thought I'd make it as a black comedy. Since *Bone* only had four leading actors I figured I could handle it as my first picture.

One day I happened upon a group of people who were making a low-budget independent picture. There was a director named Jack Starrett who was a great big, gruff kind of a guy. He played the brutal sheriff in the original Rambo picture, *First Blood*. He was a heavy drinker but he was a goodhearted guy, a good actor who also directed a number of pictures such as *Cleopatra Jones* and *Race with the Devil*. He was making a horror picture in an old Hollywood house. I went over, spending the day watching him and his crew. Then all of a sudden it became evident that eight or ten crew people could actually make a picture. They were all really nice guys, too, helping each other out. There was a camaraderie about it. So I asked several of these guys whether they would be interested in helping me make a picture. They agreed. So I grabbed this crew after Jack was finished with them and started making *Bone* on 16mm. I shot for two or three days. Then I looked at it and didn't think it was good enough. I had cast Andrew Duggan, Yaphet Kotto, and Pippa Scott. Neva Patterson had the part later played by Brett Somers (the woman with the X-rays). She was James Lee's wife. James Lee introduced me to Andrew Duggan and also to my agent, Peter Sabiston. So James Lee did me a lot of good over the years. I figured I had to make the picture over in 35mm with a larger crew. For that I needed money. So I happened upon someone who had, at least, *part* of the necessary money to shoot the picture. This was Nick Vanoff. He had produced "The Hollywood Palace," and "The Steve Allen Show." Vanoff was then in what we used to call variety television. He'd just begun doing a syndicated show, "Hee-Haw," which eventually made him so much money that he ended up buying the old Columbia Studios on Gower Street, the entire lot, which he turned into a video producing facility. "Hee-Haw" was in syndication for ten years and made him hundreds of millions of dollars. He eventually died after open-heart surgery a few years ago. Nick put up the seed money to make the picture. About that time I went to a screening of a film called *Glass Houses*, a low-budget picture made with an independent crew. George Folsey, Jr., was one of the producers. It looked like a professional Hollywood movie. So I spoke to George. His father was a great cameraman from the old MGM days who had shot *Meet Me in St. Louis, The Great Ziegfeld, Green Dolphin Street*, and many Fred Astaire and Gene Kelly movies. George Folsey, Sr., had sixteen Oscar nominations but never got the award. He'd been retired for a number of years after he left MGM but was tired of playing golf every day. He wanted to go back to work. So George, Jr., said to me, "My Dad will shoot the movie and I'll operate and edit the picture because I'm a cutter, and I'll find you the crew." So thanks to George Folsey, Jr., I got the picture going. George later became a partner with John Landis and produced pictures like *Animal House, The Three Amigos* and the tragic *Twilight Zone*. He was indicted along with Landis over the three deaths on that film. He was acquitted but I think the stress broke up the partnership. George was a fine technician. Maybe he thought I was a little crazy. I think the father thought so, too. But they all came to work and did a good job for me. We shot the picture in three weeks in my house.

After that, I had to get completion money from somebody else in order to add music, make an answer print, and pay for the costs of editing and the lab bill. I'd gotten credit from MGM's lab and sound department, but I had to pay the bills. A man named Jack H. Harris finally came to my rescue. A lot of people had liked the picture. I'd been around the circuit for months, showing it. I had to carry ten cans of film and ten cans of sound on a push wagon — you know, the kind of wagon you push the refuse out in — into the office of every major studio distributor. At the entrance, guards would tell me, "You can't bring that in here. You have to go around to the service entrance." So Janelle and I would go up the service elevator with all those cans of film, dragging it up and down the halls and thinking, "We've got a big house in Beverly Hills and suddenly we're like delivery men. We're not even allowed in the front of the building!" If an executive said, "Leave the picture. We'll look at it sometime," we'd say, "No! You can't see the picture unless *we're present* in the room. We can't leave the picture. It's the only copy we have, except for a black and white dupe and we won't leave it." When they replied that their policy was "We don't look at the picture while the director is in the room," we answered, "Well in that case, don't look at it!" Invariably, they looked at it with us there.

One day we showed it to Columbia Pictures in New York. The man in charge of screening the pictures was Bosley Crowther. It was a thrill for me. Crowther was the noted critic whose reviews I'd always read in the *New York Times*. He was the definitive motion picture critic of his generation. He kind of

Black intruder Bone (Yaphet Kotto) threatens Beverly Hills housewife Bernadette
Lennick (Joyce Van Patten) like a monster from the id in *Bone* (1972) (courtesy of
Larry Cohen).

liked my picture, but Columbia didn't buy it. At Warner Bros. I ran it for David
Brown. He said to me, "I have a meeting and I may not be able to stay for the
whole picture." That means if they don't like it they're free to walk out. There's
one scene in the beginning when Yaphet Kotto is terrorizing the family. He's
dumping a lot of books off their shelves and he happens to pick up one book and
glance at it. It's *The Confessions of Nat Turner* by William Styron. It's a little
inside joke almost nobody gets. But Brown said, "I bought the rights to that book
when I was over at Fox. I'm staying for the whole picture." So he stayed, but he
felt the movie was good but problematic and didn't buy it.

Then I dragged the twenty reels back to New York and showed it to Joseph
E. Levine. He said, "Come back tomorrow. I want to see it again." We did so.
He's the only guy who sat through it twice. After seeing it again, he said, "You
know, you're another Mike Nichols. If you'd come in a year ago, I'd have tied you
to the chair. But right now I'm having problems with financing. So I don't have
the money to buy the picture, let alone the prints and the advertising. But you're
a very talented man." I said, "Why didn't you tell us this yesterday?" By this time
it was about seven or eight in the evening and we had to get out of the building
with the film. The security guards in the lobby said, "Hey! You can't take this

film out of here." I replied, "What are you talking about? I brought it in." The guard countered, "You can't leave with that film without a pass." So I replied, "Where am I going to get a pass from? Everybody's gone home!" Anyway, it was a nightmarish experience to finally get the film out of Joseph E. Levine's building.

So we had all these showings with heavy hitters about buying it, coming close each time, but "no cigars" as they say. Finally, we ran it for Jack Harris who, as soon as the lights came up, said, "I'll buy this picture." This was Jack (*The Blob*) Harris. I thought to myself, "Well, I've really run through the whole gamut of the business, from David Brown, Bosley Crowther and now Jack (*The Blob*) Harris. But who am I to turn down his money?" So he gave me funds to complete the picture and make a small profit on it, and I gave him the picture.

Harris arranged a preview of the film at the World Theater on Hollywood Boulevard. It was one of the worst schlock houses, a third-run double feature theater. It's not there anymore, but it was below Vine Street. The picture regularly playing there was *The Legend of Nigger Charley*. I said, "Jack. That's not the audience for this picture. There's only one black man in our picture!" But he replied, "Let's have the preview and see what happens." So we went down to the preview and it was almost an all-black audience. But, to my surprise, they ate it up. They laughed at every joke and understood every nuance. They had a great time. The picture played beautifully. I couldn't believe it. Then Jack arranged another preview at the Pickwood Theater in trendy Westwood and sent out fancy invitations. The place was packed. Every seat in the balcony and auditorium was filled. The picture again went over well, this time with a totally white audience. So I thought we had something going. Then we had still another preview at the AVCO Theater in Westwood. Michael Douglas came up to me after the screening and complimented me. "You write like John Guare," he said. Then Jack presented the ad copy to me. It was like an ad for a black action thriller like *Shaft* or *Superfly*. I said, "But Jack, this is the wrong kind of advertising for this picture. It's not a crime movie. It's a comedy. A black comedy. You can't advertise it like this!" He replied, "Well, nobody wants to see a black comedy." I replied, "Well, that's what it is!" He countered, "They want action adventure pictures." I said, "That may be what they want. But this is not an action-adventure picture. If you advertise it that way people won't know what they're looking at. They won't realize it's a comedy. They'll be confused." Jack replied, "Am I going to stand there and tell them *not to laugh*?" I said, "You're not dealing with reality. If you tell people they're going to see a certain kind of movie and they don't get the movie they paid for, they're going to be unhappy. You can make the best chocolate ice cream in the world. But if people order vanilla and you give them chocolate, they're going to be unhappy because they didn't want chocolate." Jack responded, "Well, let's see what happens."

Some audiences understood what the film was about. But in most cases, we got reviews like "The Most *Unintentionally* Funny Movie of the Year"—unintentionally! I couldn't believe it. To compound this, a British company bought the rights to show it in England. I went over to meet them and explain what had happened with Jack. The British executive was a perfectly intelligent man. I thought, "This man is a bright man. He sympathizes with everything I'm telling him." I emphasized, "This picture is a comedy and it should be sold as a comedy emphasizing its satire of American racial conflicts." He agreed wholeheartedly. A month later I get a package in the mail, opened it up, and saw the poster for something called *Dial Rat for Terror*! I was mystified. It was the worst, most embarrassing art work I'd ever seen. They'd done what Jack Harris did, only ten times worse! I guess because the man seemed so cultured and intelligent I felt the film was finally in the right hands. Maybe the British accent fooled me.

TW: You've got to see beyond all that.

LC: I thought I was dealing with Alexander Korda. When *Dial Rat for Terror* appeared, I couldn't believe it. I wanted to hide the posters or bury them somewhere. To this day I can't understand how any intelligent person could do such a thing.

Then Jack came around and told me he'd changed the title of the picture to *Housewife*. I said, "It sounds like a porno movie! What has this got to do with my film?" He replied, "Well, there is a housewife in it." I said, "Jack, you're still not selling the picture. Now you're trying to promote it as a sex film. You're going to have the same disaster as you had before." I started to believe I was in better shape when I was just writing and taking the studio money, because I had my heart and soul in this picture. Janelle and I were killing ourselves carrying this film around and look what happens when it finally gets released!

Actually, I think *Bone* is a very good movie twenty years ahead of its time. I've often thought of adding a little prologue saying, "In 1970, the United States was engaged in a war against one of the smallest nations in the world and, in America, there was once a little village called Beverly Hills..." then reissuing it as if it was made *today*. They'll think, "Gee! Look how they re-created the '70s. Look at the old cars and clothes!" They'll think it is a new picture about the seventies. Nobody ever saw the picture. I think the film really does address the racial issue in America as well as anything that's ever been made on the subject. It also deals with white fantasies. For example, Yaphet Kotto never identifies himself as "Bone." Joyce Van Patten names him that. In the script, she says, "Oh Bone! You're just the way I imagined you'd be." He could be something she conjured up. Her version of a black man.

TW: It's a good satire about the Beverly Hills lifestyle, also.

LC: In one recent movie, *The Ref*, a crook breaks into a house (I don't know if it is Beverly Hills or not) and finds the family members hate each other (*The Ref*). *Ruthless People* had Bette Midler kidnapped and her husband, Danny DeVito, doesn't want her back. So I think *Bone* has a chance if I could find a new distributor. I think the Miramax people might like it. Maybe I can assure them that an audience is out there who've never seen the picture. Almost everyone hasn't seen the picture

TW: Many critics have commented on the opening scene's similarity to

*Weekend.* Having seen your television work with commercials I now believe it is modeled on old '60s car insurance ads.

LC: I've never had the opportunity to see *Weekend*, so any similarity is purely coincidental. I'm not even aware of the plot of *Weekend*.

TW: Did you consciously aim for an off–Broadway theatrical, satirical style in directing *Bone*?

LC: I basically think of *Bone* as a filmed stageplay because it is an intimate performance piece involving three major characters. I directed *Bone* as it was written. My initial creative thrust emerged from writing it, then casting it. It then came to life. All that's left to do is take pictures and edit the print. If the script and casting are faulty, there's nothing more you can do to save the movie. I did shoot too many close ups on this picture. I wanted to control the performances in the cutting room and I did. But there's too much cutting.

## Theatrical Work

TW: You also began writing a play at this time — *Nature of the Crime* (1970), which appears to mix ideas from "Traitor" and "Medal for a Turned Coat" into a good critique of American politics.

LC: It's really based on the play *The Secret*, which I did for "The Defenders," featuring Martin Landau. It was about a scientist who burns his documents and refuses to reveal his nuclear research. The character was a young and brilliant physicist who went to college at the age of thirteen. He was a freak to others as well as himself. I bought the rights back from Brodkin and reworked it into a stage play. We did it off–Broadway. The director was Lonny Chapman. After the opening, Lonny deserted the company but I stayed around to redirect many of the scenes during our six-week run. This was my first opportunity to work with stage actors. The set designer, William Rittman, had done *Who's Afraid of Virginia Woolf?* and other Albee plays. It was my first theatrical experience and I really enjoyed it. I love working with actors. Although other directors say they hate actors, I have a great affection for them. The better the actor, the more questions they ask and the more questions asked, the better the performance.

TW: You followed that with *Motive* (aka *Trick*), a really interesting play in terms of its treatment of murder, power relationships, especially the detective, Creed, who gains control over the leading character.

LC: Yes. That was fun, too. It was originally performed in the Playhouse on the Park in Philadelphia with Craig Stevens, John Randolph, and Elizabeth Allen. We took it up to upstate New York and Maine on tour. It was like summer stock. A few years later, it was performed in London with Honor Blackman, George Cole, and Ian Hendry. We had a nice run of seven to eight months in regional theaters. Then we did another tour of England and Ireland with Carroll Baker. I spent some time in England. We originally opened it in Guildford under Val May's direction. I took over as director when we went on the road. Val May managed the Guildford Playhouse and couldn't travel with the show. So, once we were on the road, I took over and it got much better. I finally hit it off with the actors. The director at Guildford had done his best to keep me as far away from the cast as possible. It was his protective device. But I later developed close rapport with the cast and found I could really direct a play.

I directed the same play in New York, as *Trick* with Tammy Grimes, Lee Richardson, and Donald Madden. It was a great experience. Tammy Grimes was a tough cookie. On the first day of rehearsals, each time she read a line of dialogue she'd stop and ask for an explanation. This went on all day. She'd ask a question about every speech. Each time she did, I gave her an answer. By the end of the day, that was it. She never asked me another question for the balance of the production. Tammy did everything I told her to and was a perfect angel. But the first day was a test. If I didn't know an answer to her question, I'd make one up. She knew what I was doing. That amused her. The play had a nice little run in New York and eventually I sold it to the movies. It became a horrible film called *Scandalous* with John Gielgud, Jim Dale, and Robert Hayes. It was a disastrous picture. But they bought the movie rights. So at least I made some money out of it. But that's another picture I can't watch. It's painful to sit through it. Like *The American Success Company*, *Scandalous* represented material I sold without any form of control. I've never been satisfied with either picture.

TW: I recently saw *The American Success Company*. It was such a disappointment on so many levels, particularly the acting and direction.

LC: Only half of the screenplay was actually shot. They never even bothered to film the second half. So the twist in the story is not even in the film. In my original screenplay, the wife fell in love with Jeff Bridges' criminal alter ego. Bridges created that character to deceive everyone, rob the bank he works in, and blame his "double." His *real* self reappears after his criminal look-alike has vanished with all the money. However, the wife is still in love with Bridges' "double" self and plans to knock off her husband so that his missing twin can return and they can live happily ever after. She does not realize they are the same person. That extra twist comprised the second half of my screenplay. This was not shot, and the film had a flat ending. The entire movie was an embarrassment. The director, William Richert, inserted repetitive business with the clock device serving as a timer during the sex scenes between Bridges and Bianca Jagger as he becomes better in bed. I found it tasteless.

I originally had Peter Sellars in mind for the main role and had traveled to England to meet him. He read the screenplay and agreed to do it. At the time, Sellars was not "hot." He'd made a number of box-office failures and no studio in America wanted him for a film. His agent, Dennis Selinger of I.C.M., offered him for a fee of $100,000 and I made a firm deal. Sellars and I had a wonderful afternoon together. He was known to be a difficult actor, but I think we would have gotten along. I've worked with a lot of actors who are alleged to be difficult, but usually manage to reach a good rapport with them. But when I tried to sell the picture in America, I found that nobody was interested in Peter Sellars. Sid

Scheinberg of MCA-Universal stated he wouldn't make a film with Sellars even if he got him for free. So I finally reported all this to Dennis. I was concerned about the $100,000 I now owed Sellars. But Dennis let me out of the contract. He's a very decent man, a real gentleman.

At the time, Blake Edwards was living in London and he became interested in the script. But he could not get a picture made then, either. He, too, was persona non grata back in Hollywood. His only possibility of getting back in favor was doing another *Pink Panther* movie with Sellars. I don't think he relished the prospect of working with Peter Sellars again. Even though they did great work together, they really didn't get along. But, out of desperation, they made the *Pink Panther* sequel. It was a big success and put them back on top again. So after six months, Peter Sellars was earning $750,000 a film from Universal, a studio which originally would not take him for nothing. They put him in *The Prisoner of Zenda*. But I could have had him for $100,000. So, it was one of those golden chances that slipped by. I eventually got disappointed and tired of lugging the script around, so I sold it for $300,000. I think Bianca Jagger was good and wondered why she never made another film. The other actress, Belinda Bauer, was the director's girlfriend. The director, William Richert, didn't direct again for ten years. But he played the Falstaff character in *My Private Idaho* and was really great. I never laid eyes on him before seeing him in that film. He was fantastic in the part and should have got an Oscar.

TW: What do you most remember about *Trick*?

LC: The most amusing thing about the play was the night Lee Richardson fell sick. Tammy Grimes came to me and said, "We've got a full house tonight. Why don't you play the role?" I replied, "Tammy, you're not serious? You really don't want to be on stage with me?" She replied, "Yes. You can do it just fine." So I went on. That one night was my Broadway debut and also my farewell. I got through the whole play and earned a few more laughs than Lee Richardson. Before the curtain, it was explained to the audience that the author and director was playing the role so they would make allowances. It was a remarkable experience, going on stage and playing that huge role without any preparations. Those are the kind of things you cannot think about. You just jump up and do it.

TW: You went on reading from the script?

LC: I performed with the script in my hand, but because I knew it thoroughly I didn't have to look at it often. However, it was good to have it there for security, particularly for the other actors who knew I couldn't forget the lines. But at the end, Donald Madden kills me and I dropped the script. He's supposed to drag my dead body behind the couch so Tammy Grimes won't see it. As he did this, I whispered, "Now go back and get the script." So he went back, picked up the script, hid it behind the couch, and the audience went absolutely bananas and roared with laughter. It was the highlight of the whole evening. Those moments are unforgettable. You look back and think, "That's a great night in your life."

TW: I believe Robert DeNiro and Al Pacino later applauded your performance.

LC: They were at a party right after the show, but not in the audience. Janelle and I were invited to a sit-down dinner for six people by Janet Villela, the ex-wife of ballet dancer Edward Villela. DeNiro and Pacino were also guests. I knew DeNiro from the time Bernard Herrmann scored *Taxi Driver*. DeNiro came to my house after the funeral. Naturally I told them, "You're not going to believe this, but I just made my Broadway debut." So here were the two best young actors in America asking me about what it was like and how could I dare get up and do the play without preparation. And I'm explaining and telling them my acting technique! That just made the night even tastier. A really memorable night.

## On Joshua Logan

I must mention that Joshua Logan worked with me as producer of *Trick*. If I had to pick the most gifted person I'd ever worked with, I suppose it would have to be Logan. When Josh worked with me on rewriting the play, we'd meet at his Riverhouse Apartment in Manhattan and we'd use a Dictaphone. It was an old-fashioned model with little plastic ribbons that Josh would periodically take out of the machine and toss on the carpet. His secretary, Joe, would come in and retrieve these ribbons. About six o'clock, Josh would offer me a martini and we'd relax for a few minutes. Joe would then appear, usually carrying thirty-five pages of newly scripted material, which we'd written that day. It was hard for me to believe we were turning out this volume of material. I would take my copy home to go over it and immediately climb into bed and go to sleep. I was so exhausted trying to keep up with Joshua Logan's complex mind. It was like trying to keep pace with a long-distance runner.

Josh was a manic-depressive and he was on lithium. Some days he'd be a bit slower than others. I can imagine what he would have been like in his manic state because his mind was quick and agile. Even when he slowed down, his mind worked in intricate patterns. He would always approach a scene from a tangential point of view. I didn't know what he was looking for or where he was going. Then, finally, all the pieces fit together marvelously. Josh had gone through the same process with Thomas Heggen collaborating with him on *Mr. Roberts*. It became a sensational stage success starring Henry Fonda. Heggen became totally dependent on Josh during the writing process after the play had opened. Josh went on to other things. But Heggen fell into a terrible depression and eventually took his own life.

I have to admit it was thrilling working with a man who had collaborated with Rodgers and Hammerstein on *South Pacific* and who had the Pulitzer Prize hung up over the toilet in his guest bathroom. Josh had directed Marilyn Monroe in *Bus Stop* and Marlon Brando in *Sayonara*. He'd also worked with Ethel Merman and Irving Berlin, as well as with my good friend José Ferrer. My manuscript for *Trick* had been originally read by Josh's wife, Nedda, who called it to his attention. Nedda had been an actress on stage and played in such hits as

*Charley's Aunt*, which Josh also directed. I liked Nedda so much and I wanted to give her a job in one of my pictures. When I directed *See China and Die* (which was originally made as a television pilot), I asked Nedda to play the role of a sophisticated rich woman forced to take a bus when her limousine fails to show up. Nedda proved to be a terrific trouper. When the portable bathroom in the trailer wasn't working, all the younger actors were complaining. Nedda Logan simply went into Central Park, relieved herself behind some bushes and laughed about it. This was a woman who was one of New York's most prominent socialites. She said that when she was in summer stock over the years, she often improvised when it came to bathroom facilities. She was such a terrific person, putting the younger actors to shame with all their bitching and moaning. When I began *A Return to Salem's Lot*, I wanted to give Josh and Nedda acting roles. Josh had complained that all the good acting parts were going to Lee Strasberg and John Houseman. Nobody ever asked him to perform. So I phoned and asked if he and Nedda would like to be in the film. Josh replied, "There's only one problem. I can't get up or sit down in a scene. I have to be either seated or standing all the time. Nedda can only be photographed from the left side because something is wrong with her right eye." I couldn't figure out how to accommodate this. So, unfortunately, they didn't make their appearance in that film.

I also remember that when I directed *Trick*, Josh told me he'd better stay away from the actors. Since he was a renowned director, he didn't want anyone to think he was directing the play. So he took on an out of town engagement staging an old Rodgers and Hammerstein hit at some college in the Southwest. After watching one early rehearsal, he was never seen by my cast again until one night following a preview. He stepped into Tammy Grimes' dressing room long enough to tell her he'd been to a party and met someone who told him, "I never liked Tammy Grimes, but the other night I saw her in *Trick* and she was wonderful." He then walked out of the dressing room, leaving Tammy and I staring at one another. Infuriated, she threw a fit and said, "I guess my whole career is shit! That's what he just told me. Except for this goddamn play!" I didn't know how Josh could have been so tactless to say such things to an actress. But that night Tammy Grimes went out and gave one of her best performances.

When Janelle and I visited England, Josh always took us antique shopping. Sometimes we had to get up early on Saturday mornings to go to Bermondsey Market with him. He was a great pal and I miss him very much.

## Television Scripts

TW: During this period, you also scripted some television movies. *In Broad Daylight* (1971) has a really interesting theme about a blind man seeking revenge.

LC: The central character is a blind actor who finds out that his wife and her lover plan to kill him. So he decides to kill her first. But in order to do that, he has to make it appear that a man with sight has committed the crime. He has to act the role of a man with normal vision so eyewitnesses will testify that she was killed by a man who can see. He creates a disguise. He visits the murder location several times so he can rehearse the killing and remember things, like how many steps there are. Then, finally, he commits the perfect murder. But what was wrong with the show was that they cast Richard Boone in the main role. Now Richard Boone was a very fine actor. But he had a face you could never mistake for anybody else's. Then put this awful disguise on him. It became ridiculous because, despite the disguise, it was obviously Richard Boone's face looking at you. *You* had to be blind yourself not to recognize him. So that particular flaw negated the story's premise. It would have been so easy to fix. It was a nice idea, though. As a show, it's passable but far from good.

TW: You also wrote the pilot of "Cool Million" (1972) for the series starring James Farentino.

LC: The series ran for a couple of years. It was a ninety-minute series that rotated on what they called "The Wheel," with "Columbo," "McCloud," and "McMillan and Wife," and appeared every fourth week. It wasn't anything special. It certainly wasn't right for James Farentino. The series was supposed to be about a detective who only takes cases for a million-dollar fee. James Farentino was obviously not the proper actor. Cary Grant embodied the right type. Maybe Robert Wagner could have been acceptable in the Cary Grant image. But Farentino had no style. He was a typical twenty-five-dollar a day gumshoe. It was another case of wrong casting. I wrote the original two-hour pilot. It was another feather in my cap, since I had launched another series.

TW: What do you remember about *Shoot Out in a One Dog Town* (1974)?

LC: Not much except that Richard Crenna and a lot of great character actors like Jack Elam appeared in it. They cast a lot of good Western types and I got a kick of seeing those faces in something I wrote. But, aside from that, it was an undistinguished show which was also rewritten by somebody else, so I didn't receive sole credit. Again, it was the same thing — making money but not getting any artistic gratification. But at the time, I was already making my own pictures and I only did this work as a subsidy for my bank balance. At least if I did some television work, I'd be able to live comfortably. It's like John Cassavetes taking all those acting jobs so he'd have the money to make his own pictures. I guess I could have put other names or pseudonyms on those scripts, as others have done. But I always felt that if I take the producer's money, they're entitled to use my name even on shows I don't have all that much of a high regard for.

## Black Caesar

TW: What led you to make *Black Caesar*?

LC: It evolved out of the *Bone* episode. I'd taken *Bone* to American International and showed it to Sam Arkoff, who was a partner of James Nicholson. They almost bought it but decided at the last moment to back off. Subsequently,

I had a call from Arkoff: "You direct black actors, don't you? (There's one black actor in *Bone*. So suddenly I'm a director of black actors.) Do you have anything we could make into a black movie?" The black exploitation field had become popular — *Shaft*, *Superfly*, etc. As a matter of fact, I did have something. Sammy Davis, Jr.'s manager had come to me some months before and said, "Sammy wants to be a dramatic actor and he'll pay you ten thousand dollars to develop an idea for him." So I wrote a treatment about a tough little guy. I remembered Edward G. Robinson in *Little Caesar*, so I thought about doing *Little Caesar* as a black movie, calling it *Black Caesar*. I sent a twenty-page treatment to Sammy Davis' manager. Then, lo and behold, no ten thousand dollars appeared and I began trying to collect my money. He was avoiding me and wasn't going to pay. Peter Sabiston had the outline in the trunk of his car. So, when Arkoff brought up the subject, we ran down, got it, and in five minutes we had a deal to make a picture for A.I.P. I wrote, produced and directed it. Who do we end up with as a star? Fred Williamson, who had been the star of *The Legend of Nigger Charley*— the picture we previewed *Bone* with that night at the World Theatre!

Fortunately for me, *Black Caesar* was a hit. It opened in New York during February and there were lines along the block. It was five to ten degrees freezing. Ushers had to put barricades to contain the crowds. They started shows at nine A.M., running eight or nine performances a day up to two A.M. They raised the price by a dollar after the first couple of days and eliminated children's admission prices. And still the people were coming in. It quickly rose to the top of the *Variety* charts and made a lot of money. I also think we made a good film. The odd thing about that situation was that, in the original cut, Tommy Gibbs dies in the end. This remains in the video version, since they went back to the original negative to make the video. In it, Tommy gets killed by a gang of black teenagers. We held a preview at the Pantages Theater in Hollywood only a few days before the scheduled opening in New York. Everything was going fine until Black Caesar died. Then we heard all kinds of noise from the audience. In the lobby outside, many black people (especially women) screamed at me: "How could you do such a thing? Black people wouldn't do that to one another." They were really angry. Some even tried to attack me. The next morning, Arkoff phoned and asked me how the preview went. I said, "It went great until the end. Then they went nuts." He answered, "I told you not to kill him." I replied, "Okay, I made a mistake. Do you mind if I fix it?" He said, "Do whatever you want." So I flew to New York, arriving at the Cinerama Theater first thing in the morning. I went to the projection booth and *cut off the last two or three minutes of the film*, spliced the rest on to the end titles, went up to the RKO Theater on 59th Street and did exactly the same thing. The music track only suffered a hardly detectable sound bump in the process. Then I went to the RKO 86th Street Theater and made the cut. It was the first time these projectionists ever had seen a director showing up on the opening day, and re-editing the picture before their eyes.

It made all the difference in the world because it turned the picture into a hit when it could have been a disaster. It also enabled us to make a sequel. But, somehow, I think it's a better movie with him dying. It was like something out of Luis Bunuel's *Los Olvidados*. But the audience who came to see *Black Caesar* didn't want to see their hero die. *Black Caesar* became my first success. Suddenly it was easier to make other pictures.

TW: I understand you reject any interpretation of *Black Caesar* as a "blaxploitation" movie.

LC: Yes. That's correct. *Black Caesar* is not a black exploitation film like *Shaft* or *Superfly* with superheroes. All the genre rules are violated in the film. Tommy Gibbs loses everything, his money, his power, his girl, his friends. He tries to live like the white man he despises and his world collapses.

## It's Alive *and Bernard Herrmann*

TW: Similarly, you don't regard *It's Alive* as a generic horror film?

LC: I don't think *It's Alive* is more of a horror story than *The Elephant Man*. But it did cross my mind that if I could make a horror film that made audiences actually shed a tear, it would be an accomplishment. During the credit sequences, audiences are intentionally placed in the position of the hunted mutant when the flashlights all merge in a blinding light. I'm amused when I see this same concept appear in other films. Spielberg used the flashlight sequence to similar effect later in *E.T.*

The idea of the stomach opening up in *God Told Me To* appears later in David Cronenberg's *Videodrome*. In fact, Cronenberg actually features a poster from my film in *Videodrome*. Perhaps it's a coincidence, or maybe he's saying, "Thank You!" These things never bother me. I'm pleased when I see an idea of mine turn up in somebody else's picture.

TW: You have some really revealing scenes showing tensions in the Davies family.

LC: Frank Davies wishes to be a success in the public relations field. His family comes second. But when he's fired, what else does he have except his family? When going into labor, Lenore anxiously asks Frank about any feelings of resentment he may have towards a second child. They even considered abortion. Problems occurred in the marriage after the birth of his first son. Also, Lt. Perkins has a harassed home life. We slipped that in the background, hoping the audience would pick it up. Many aspects of *It's Alive* link up with everyday concerns of family life. How often have you heard parents express comments such as "Where has this kid come from?" "How could we have had a kid like this?" Their kid may look normal, but the parents believe he/she behaves abnormally, whether sexually or otherwise.

TW: What was it like working with Bernard Herrmann on *It's Alive*?

LC: He was always my favorite composer. He'd quit *The Exorcist* in anger and returned to England, where he lived after his quarrel with Hitchcock over *Torn Curtain*. A former music cutter at Warner Bros. made arrangements over

**Janelle Cohen, Larry Cohen, and Bernard Herrmann endure cold temperatures in London's Cripplegate Church while working on the musical soundtrack for *God Told Me To* (courtesy of Larry Cohen).**

the telephone for Benny to talk to me about *It's Alive*. After a respectful phone call, I sent him a black and white print of the film. Benny had the reputation of being a very difficult man. We worked long distance by phone. At one point I thought he was going to quit because he didn't want to compose music to go with a cartoon playing on the television screen in a scene. Benny said he didn't write music for cartoons and would walk off the picture. This was just a bit of cantankerousness. Once he said he was going to resign, I immediately replied, "All right. Don't do that piece of music. We'll just put funny sound effects over the cartoon. Other than that, we had no other disagreements. He conducted the music in London's Cripplegate Church because Benny wanted the resonance of the great organ there. This happened during the power shortage of 1973. He brought in his own generator but had no way to heat the church, so all the musicians played with overcoats on. It was quite a sight. Janelle and I arrived the day after Christmas at Benny's explicit invitation. He wanted me there. Everyone in the church had scarves wrapped around their necks and you could see their breath oxidizing. They'd installed a projector so everyone could see the picture as they played. Years later I prevailed upon Frank Cordell to record his score for *God Told Me To* there. He also did a very fine job. Frank Cordell was an underrated composer who has since passed away. I think his score for *God Told Me To* was exceptional.

But Bernard Herrmann had the tendency to alienate people and scare them off. He always came on very strong at the beginning of a relationship, so you always had to get past that initial outburst. If you laughed, became amused at what he said, and didn't pay any attention to his insults or needled him back, he quickly became cordial and quite friendly. Benny became a part of our family. When we eventually moved to England, he'd phone us two or three times a week to ask about the children. If we didn't call him up for a few days, he'd phone and ask if anything was the matter. He became a grandpa, a very doting grandpa.

He'd been very hurt by Hollywood and said he'd never come back. He particularly held a grudge against MCA-Universal, who he felt had alienated Hitchcock against him. But, strangely enough, he returned to do *Taxi Driver* and stayed at the Universal Sheraton on the back lot of the studio he despised. It was there that he died.

Mrs. Herrmann stayed at our house during the time of the funeral. Many of the great directors in the business came to our house and expressed their condolences to her. I was surprised how few people really understood and knew him. But then, I knew Benny in his old age and he had already mellowed. As a young man he might have been even more vitriolic and difficult. He could be a devil, but there was always a twinkle in his eye.

I wanted to use Benny and Miklos Rosza for my films because of the sound they created and also the tradition they represented. There are few composers around today who have such an identity. John Williams, who was Benny's dear friend, works in the Herrmann tradition. I love music with a star quality you can identify with a particular composer. That's why I was so thrilled to have the friendship and collaboration of Herrmann and Rosza on my films.

## God Told Me To

TW: Did *God Told Me To* measure up to your expectations?

LC: I must admit I did have more than the usual level of interference on the film. The producer, Edgar Scherick, interfered after the first cut. So I had to omit scenes which explained why Peter Nicholas had such an aversion to children. Scherick held that these scenes slowed the film down. But Warner Bros. and American International never bothered me on any of my other films to the extent he did. But I was pleased with ninety percent of this film.

TW: You have an amazing use of religious motifs in *God Told Me To.*

LC: *God Told Me To* has a plentiful amount of religious imagery because that's what the picture's about: an alien posing as a god using religion to cloud his true identity. He's able to control people by making them believe that he's God. But he controls them for his own ends because he's on a power trip. I've often thought, though, that the alien actually believes he *is* God. Imagine a creature from another planet born and brought up here, not knowing his origins, realizing that he has supernatural powers enabling him to control people. This alien

Larry Cohen and Hollywood composer Miklos Rozsa work together on the sound-track for *The Private Files of J. Edgar Hoover* (courtesy of Larry Cohen).

might soon begin to believe that he is God, particularly in a Christian society like ours where it is preached that God came to earth in human form with unique powers. When he makes other people accept him as God, he believes this to be the truth. My screenplay isn't so far from being the dark side of the Superman legend. Superman comes to earth. He has superhuman powers. He decides to do good. Ours is the reverse. Superman comes to earth, sees himself as superior, believes himself to be God, and inflicts this image on people and forces them to do his will.

Many people think ancient gods were actually astronauts or aliens who came here, procreated with some inferior race, and brought about the birth of human-ity. So there is plenty to think about in regard to *God Told Me To*.

TW: I see you use a lot of actors with Irish names in your films?

LC: Almost all of my actors are Irish. We call them Cohen's Irish Players. I seem to have a preference for hiring Irish actors, which is possibly subconscious. Michael Moriarty is also Irish. My grandmother on my mother's side was Irish and I loved her with all my heart.

## The Private Files of J. Edgar Hoover

TW: Michael Moriarty told me you often take risks during shooting. Is it true that you once shot on the FBI premises, without asking permission, during *The Private Files of J. Edgar Hoover*?

LC: We shot a lot in Quantico, Virginia; the FBI Office in the Justice Department Building; Hoover's office; and the Attorney General's Office. We shot all over the Justice Department building. It was Labor Day weekend. Nobody was around. We just took over the entire Justice Department and filmed anywhere we wanted to. When they came back on Tuesday and found out that we'd filmed all over the place, they had a fit. But we were gone by then. The Attorney General wrote me a letter warning me against using any of that footage shot in his office. Then he sent a second letter relenting and granting permission. I received the *second* letter first, so it took the edge out of the first one. I don't know why he changed his mind. I guess he thought that it probably wasn't worth the hoopla, giving the film more publicity if word got out that the Attorney General refused to allow us to use the footage. So we shot all over Washington D.C. I led a charmed life on that particular film because I had no expectation of getting into all those places. We would not have gained access except for a phone call from the White House. Betty Ford, who was a big fan of musicals, heard that Dan Dailey was in town. She wanted to invite he and Crawford to lunch at the White House. So they asked my permission. I'd have to close the picture down for a whole day, but I knew that if I didn't let these guys go they would be miserable throughout the entire production and take it out on me. I closed the picture down and tried to wangle an invitation for myself, but they wouldn't invite me! I also tried to get permission to shoot on the White House portico so we'd have footage of Hoover and Tolson entering. They wouldn't let me do that, either. So then I did the next best thing. I started calling people up. I phoned the FBI Public Relations Office, asking permission to film at Quantico: "We can't shoot tomorrow because the two stars are having lunch with the president," etc. They would put me on hold. Five minutes later they'd reply, "What day do you want to film here?" I got permission to go wherever I wanted. Washington was suddenly ours. That one lunch at the White House opened all the doors.

TW: Why did you want to make the film?

LC: I'd always been influenced by those old Warner Bros. and Twentieth Century–Fox crime films. I loved FBI movies. I wanted to direct the definitive FBI saga the way it really was.

TW: Was Broderick Crawford the actor you always had in mind to play Hoover?

LC: Some people tried to push us into casting Rod Steiger. We could have had him if he hadn't chosen to play W.C. Fields instead. Personally, I'm glad we got Crawford. He had more humor and a wonderful, gruff speaking voice.

TW: Did you use the old 1959 film *The F.B.I. Story* as a model to undermine and subvert?

Larry Cohen and veteran Hollywood actor Broderick Crawford (left) on the set of *The Private Files of J. Edgar Hoover* (courtesy of Larry Cohen).

LC: There was a similarity in following the life of an FBI agent in various stages of his career. But we also had to follow Hoover's career through the same period. However, *The FBI Story* was pure public relations pap. I used a lot of stock, footage from the film for certain scenes. We got the material from Warner Bros. stock footage library. I didn't have a lot of money to re-create some of the period stuff. So there must be a dozen shots from *The F.B.I. Story* in the final film. In the Dillinger scene, you see a shadow on the wall, but you don't realize it's Jimmy Stewart's shadow. We could have billed the film as follows — Broderick Crawford, Dan Dailey, and Jimmy Stewart's shadow, followed by the rest of the cast. It would have been a nice touch.

Another amusing thing about the film was that we had to get a toupee for Broderick Crawford to wear in the early part of the film. Our makeup girl worked part-time at Universal. She said she could get us Ernest Borgnine's toupee, which he wore in the TV series "McHale's Navy." So we rented Borgnine's toupee and put it on Broderick Crawford. Think of it! An Academy Award–winning toupee appearing on top of an Academy Award–winning actor.

*Hoover* was made on a shoestring budget and I didn't have all the money when I started shooting. Each time I'd hire another actor, I'd phone Sam Arkoff and say, "We've got another Academy Award actor in the picture — José Ferrer!"

or "Celeste Holm. Now we've got seven Academy Award winners in this picture!" In that way I managed to eke out one hundred thousand dollars from Arkoff every week to keep shooting the picture.

TW: *Hoover* was certainly ahead of its time, particularly with recent revelations concerning Hoover and his relationship with Clyde Tolson.

LC: There's nothing that's appeared recently that we didn't have in the film in some form or other. However, I don't believe those alleged stories of Hoover running around wearing women's clothes. No person as discrete and sensitive to security as Hoover was would ever put himself into such a vulnerable position. Besides, I toured his house, went through all his closets, and never found any dresses! I was one of the few people allowed access and examined the whole place from top to bottom. It was amazing that I ever got in. I gained permission from the Boys' Clubs of America, who inherited the house and estate. When Tolson died, he left everything to them. They let us look over the place, allegedly so we could re-create it on screen. Actually I was searching to see if I could find anything. But it was just the house of an old man who could have been anybody's grandfather. If you picked up the doilies from the couch you'd find cracks in the leather. It was the home of an old person who seldom bought anything new. You looked at this guy's belongings and were surprised by the humbleness of it all. He headed the FBI for forty-eight years and could have made himself a fortune if he was really crooked. But he really didn't have anything. The furniture was old. Somebody gave him a blanket and a rug with the FBI seal woven into them. People usually sent him gifts which had something remotely to do with the FBI They were all around the house. What I saw made me realize that Hoover was nothing like you'd imagine, considering he'd been one of the most powerful men in the country for half a century. It made me feel kind of sorry for him. The house humanized him. It had a musty smell, but you could still detect the aroma of his after shave on some of the clothes, a barber shop smell. Tolson didn't live there. He had an apartment some twenty minutes away. Hoover and Tolson never lived together. They were just a pair of old bachelors who liked to watch prize fights, football, and horseraces together. I doubt if there was ever anything overtly sexual between them. But we explored those innuendoes in the picture. I think had he been openly homosexual, Hoover would have been a better person. He lived with such total repression that it made him an unhappy man and he made everyone around him more unhappy. If he had any outlets for expression, he would have been a warmer person. The most sad thing about him was that he was unable to express love openly. That was the tragedy of the man. Anyway, *The Private Files of J. Edgar Hoover* was certainly a worthwhile picture. Actually, I've got enough material from the outtakes to make another J. Edgar Hoover movie if I wanted to.

TW: One of the pleasures in viewing the film is seeing all those old Hollywood actors back on the screen again.

LC: I'm sorry I didn't have more of them. I could have had Pat O'Brien and George Raft. But I didn't do it. I didn't want the film to become ludicrous in having every old-time Hollywood star in it. But when I look back, I could have found parts for those two and, maybe, a couple of others. We nearly had Henry Fonda in the picture. It was close. But he backed out at the last moment. I would have loved to have him and Cagney. I might have got Cagney. But I didn't realize at the time that Cagney and Broderick Crawford had been roommates in New York. If I'd realized that, I could have written to Cagney and he might have done a day for us. But the picture was still great fun.

TW: You had a lot of problems when the film was finally released.

LC: *The Washington Post* was offended that we didn't give them credit for the Watergate expose. We indicated that the FBI itself leaked the information to *The Post*, an opinion Dan Rather and CBS verified in their twenty-year anniversary special on Watergate. *The Post* employed a special reviewer to do a political analysis of the film and destroy it. Then *The Washington Post* movie reviewer hated it, comparing it to the *Tora! Tora! Tora!* syndrome of movies. They tried to nitpick the movie to death and not deal with any of the broader issues raised by it. The last thing newspapers want is for anyone else to use movies as a form of journalism. In fact, *The Private Files of J. Edgar Hoover* has everything in it that was publicized years later by Senator Frank Church's Select Senate Subcommittee. They spent five million dollars of the American people's money to run an investigation. They came up with nothing that was not already in my movie years before. All they needed to do was run *The Private Files of J. Edgar Hoover* and they could've saved the public money. If I, an amateur, can research this material and come up with all these facts, then why can't government investigators and newsmen do a better job?

We uncovered all sorts of evidence undermining the official Hoover legend. A German spy landed from a submarine off Long Island immediately revealed important information to the FBI, resulting in the arrest of a huge spy ring within seventy-two hours. This was publicized as Hoover's great achievement. Hoover had the informant, Fritz Dasch, locked up for years and took all the credit. The FBI never even rewarded this guy or gave him the citizenship he wanted. Hoover felt that if the truth were known, the FBI would look less effective. Then he was deported back to Germany during the Truman administration. The poor man went into hiding, fearing for his life. This was one of the many stories we had no time to show in the film.

We opened the film in Washington D.C. at the Kennedy Center. Of course, both the Democrats and the Republicans hated it. The Democrats didn't like the things we said about Bobby Kennedy and J.F.K., while the Republicans took offense at how we depicted Nixon. American International had put up most of the money. Later on, the film was bought by a tax shelter company, which had to release it quickly before the end of the year. There was no time for any advance publicity campaign. The film played a few dates and was eventually pulled out of distribution. But it played extensively in England after a successful showing at the National Film Theatre and was screened several times by BBC television. In America, we had a wide play on cable. Thank God for cable! I hope *Hoover* will be revived someday soon. When it finally played in New York at the New York Shakespeare Festival, it got some great reviews.

# It Lives Again

TW: In *It Lives Again*, the two mutant babies are named Adam and Eve. Did you mean to suggest they represent the beginning of a new society?

LC: Adam and Eve are not meant to be taken seriously. That was Andrew Duggan's little inside joke. But, nonetheless, the parallels are there.

TW: It's a real shame the mutant baby kills Frank Davies in this film.

LC: The killing of Frank Davies was not because the monster child was evil. It was frightened by the night watchman's flashlight and felt trapped. So it was a tragic accident. *It Lives Again* reverses many themes in *It's Alive*. Here, the parents protect the monster child from the authorities. But when it attacks the John Marley character, they have to kill it. I knew, when I had two parents killing their baby in what was supposed to be a commercial picture, that I was taking a chance. It would have been easy to have the police come in and shoot it. We could have gotten off the spot that way. But I decided to take the chance. But it was too much for most audiences. They didn't want to see that, just as audiences don't want to see Black Caesar die.

TW: *It Lives Again* really develops the marital tension themes already present in *It's Alive*.

LC: Remember, for a while, the husband can't bear to touch his wife because she's given birth to this "thing." So I tried to explore some other nuances in the sequel and it was worth making, much more than the *Black Caesar* sequel. Some people have interpreted *It's Alive* as an argument for abortion. But I regard it as an argument against abortion. No matter how distorted and twisted the mutant babies are, the parents eventually feel love for them. If my own family had access to abortion, I might not have been born, due to the difficult financial problems in the family at that time. But back then it was not a choice,

The Davies family have a lot of marital problems and tensions. Remember when Lenore asks Frank, "You won't be jealous this time, will you? You think this baby's going to push us apart?" The last time Frank and Lenore had a child it almost broke up their marriage. Similarly, the relationship between Eugene and Jody in *It Lives Again* is also strained due to his intense ambition and the inequality in their relationship. She gave up a very promising law career when they got married. After they kill their child, they touch each other again, seeking solace in each other's arms. The anger at each other has been exorcised through the terrible experience they suffered together. Killing their baby has pulled them back together in a tragic way. As you can see, I take this all very seriously.

Lt. Perkins is also definitely exhausted by his family responsibilities. We deliberately put the sound effect of his baby crying in the background to show the type of harassment he faces at home. Lt. Perkins is a typical long-suffering family man. No monster has entered his life to give him release. He must suffer through the ordinary, pedestrian pains of parenthood from which there seems to be no escape.

## Full Moon High

TW: What gave you the idea for *Full Moon High*?

LC: People tell me there is so much humor in my movies that I needed to make a comedy. So I said to Sam Arkoff, "Let's do a comedy version of *I Was a Teenage Werewolf.*" Arkoff put up the money to make it. The film was made long before *Back to the Future.* It deals with somebody who remains young while everybody around him turns old. The boy turns into a werewolf, leaves town, and returns twenty years later, pretending to be his own son. His high school classmates are now all middle-aged. When our hero changes into being a werewolf, he actually changes *less* than those around him have. They've all changed into their own form of monster. *They got old.* Age is a form of monstrousness in itself. They're bald and bloated, and gray, and are far from what they dreamed they'd be when they were young. But the most fun for me was having Alan Arkin in the picture.

TW: Did Arkin model his performance on anyone in particular?

LC: He may have had Groucho Marx in mind. It was a part Groucho could have played. There was a little bit of Groucho in Arkin's character, an insulting psychiatrist who insults his patients back to health. Alan didn't want to be paid money for the film. He wanted two Mercedes. He's still got them. I ran into Adam Arkin recently. He was playing Nathan Detroit in *Guys and Dolls* on Broadway. I asked him how his dad was and he said he still had the cars. If I gave him money he would have spent it. But now, each time he gets into the car, he remembers Larry Cohen. So gifts are better than pay, especially a gift like a Mercedes.

TW: In the film, you have a succession of presidents' portraits to show the passing of time. They end with one of a black female president.

LC: That was my housekeeper. I put her picture in it. She never forgave me for that. "Mr. Cohen, don't you ever show me that picture again!"

TW: Was it your anti–Reagan joke?

LC: No. The point there was that we finally had a black female president. When that picture was made, Reagan wasn't president yet. It was Jimmy Carter. *Full Moon High* wasn't one of my most successful pictures, but we had a good time making it and I have fond memories of it. I especially remember Elizabeth Hartman. Her agent called me and asked if I could do a good deed and give her a job. She'd left the hospital after recovering from a nervous breakdown and hadn't worked in years. I remembered she'd been very good in pictures like *The Beguiled*, so I hired her. She was fine, except for the fact that she couldn't get to work on her own every day. Somebody had to go to her house, drive her to locations, and take her home at night. During the filming she was extremely professional but quite fragile. You had to be gentle with her. I was very distressed when I recently read that she'd killed herself. She jumped out of a window. She hadn't worked much since the time I hired her. I think she could've been saved if she'd had work to do. She was so talented and so nice. It's a great loss. *Full Moon High* also had excellent people in small parts. Desmond Wilson of *Sanford and Son* played the guy who drove his own cab. Bob Saget later became the host of "Funniest Home Videos," and Jim Bullock later became a TV star. Jay Leno was going to play the lead if I hadn't given it to Adam Arkin. Ed McMahon played his father.

TW: Returning briefly to *God Told Me To*, was Sandy Dennis also going through a bad time when you were shooting?

LC: Yes. She had tax problems and needed the money. Her career wasn't going well. But she wasn't in the kind of shape Elizabeth Hartman was. Sandy Dennis' career went on for ten years after *God Told Me To*. Actors' careers are so tough when they are not working and they've once been stars. Sometimes it's tougher than if you never made it. You get used to audience acceptance and when you lose it, it's not easy.

## More Television Work

TW: About this time, did you make two television pilots — "See China and Die" and "Momma the Detective"?

LC: That's the same show. NBC asked me to do a pilot with a very fine black actress, Esther Rolle. I agreed to do it if I could also make a feature version to distribute myself. So I made the TV pilot and a ninety-minute feature-length version. It predated "Murder She Wrote" in that it concerned an older woman who solves crimes, with many guest stars as suspects. Unfortunately, we had complaints from black organizations who didn't like the idea of the leading black character being a maid or a housekeeper. I tried to explain that she was a cook, a gourmet chef highly paid and respected. But it didn't matter, because once NBC gets five or six letters from a pressure group, the chances of scheduling a series are virtually negligible. NBC only ordered three new series that year after making thirty or forty pilots. But I sold the movie into syndication and it plays on cable occasionally. It's no worse or better than any other TV movie around. It was just an enjoyable little exercise. I also enjoyed working with the actors. But it's not a Larry Cohen movie although there are some subversive elements such as a maid getting the goods on the rich people she works for. I liked one scene where a suspect riding in the elevator with the maid says to her, "You people know everything about us. But we don't know anything about you." That was interesting. People live in a house with the help for twenty years but don't know anything about their maid. But the maid knows all their secrets. There was also a very funny scene with Fritz Weaver as a tax expert, in which the maid asks him for assistance with her income tax and proves that she is smarter than he is.

# I, the Jury *and* Q

TW: You mentioned earlier you were fired from two pictures. Was *I, the Jury* one of them?

LC: Sure. I directed it for only a week. Then I left and immediately made *Q*. American Cinema had terrible financial problems on *I, the Jury* and couldn't pay their bills. The company was run by amateurs. Most of the eventual eleven million dollars poured into the film disappeared or was misspent. All I saw was tremendous waste and incompetence. Everything was becoming chaotic and vendors in New York who'd always advanced *me* credit for labs, cameras, and equipment were not getting paid on time. Knowing the economic problems, I called them up and said, "Look, guys. I'm not responsible for these bills. You're not renting the equipment to me, but American Cinema. You'd better collect your money from them quick because I think they're going to go out of business and I don't want you to blame me." I warned my friends and American Cinema didn't like that. It became a very unpleasant situation. I left willingly and they finished the film and went bankrupt. The picture went four million dollars over budget and didn't look it. For the budget they spent, I could have made four good movies with more production value than they achieved.

American Cinema didn't want a Larry Cohen film. They wanted a picture that they themselves could control and manipulate. I was not the right filmmaker for them. They had one hundred people on the crew — most of them loitering outside on the street all day because the location was too small to accommodate them. None of the money spent showed up on the screen. I was well out of there.

I immediately went on to make *Q* for $1,200,000. I began shooting it a week after they fired me. I still stayed at the same Mayflower hotel in New York. So every morning when the actors were waiting to be picked up to go on location, *I, the Jury* would be heading off in one direction and I'd be going in another with my new crew. American Cinema couldn't believe I could be making another movie a week after they fired me. They figured this guy's going to slink off into the woods. But I was shooting with a better cast than they had. We wrapped both pictures up at the same time. Oddly enough, as luck would have it, six months later both pictures opened on the same day, down the street from one another. *I, the Jury* opened at the National while *Q* opened at the Rivoli. But we did four times more business than they did.

TW: Does much remain of your original screenplay in *I, the Jury*?

LC: A great deal of the material remains, but it was overwhelmed by the excessive violence. My concept was to subvert the character of Mike Hammer. The CIA manipulate him so that he becomes a walking weapon pointed in various directions. Hammer never really solves the crime. He's simply moved from point to point by the government specialists who want him to kill on their behalf. This parallels the tragic psychopath who has been programmed by government psychiatrists to perform assassinations made to look like sex crimes. Mike Hammer is not much different from the psychopath performing sex crimes on command. Mike himself is killing the very people the CIA want him to kill. The screenplay underlined parallels between the two. And, of course, Mike Hammer has always been completely psychopathic, a man who is motivated by primal levels of violence.

Mike Hammer is also known as a lady's man. But I introduced the innuendo of a possible homosexual relationship between Mike and his best friend who is killed at the beginning of the picture. He only learns his friend was homosexual when a female psychiatrist hands him a medical file. Up to that point he never realized his best buddy was gay and that he was the focus of his friend's love. It could have been a very powerful scene when a man suddenly realizes that the guy he considered to be his best pal was in love with him. When the character is someone like Mike Hammer, a macho character, this type of information can be devastating. But the bulk of this was omitted from the final picture. They cut the scene in such a way that you didn't really know what was in the report the psychiatrist handed to Mike. Some might understand what was inferred. But it was left to your imagination and the overall impact was lost. This whole idea is consistent with the Hoover-Tolson relationship where I believe the sexual side was never overtly expressed.

The relationship between Mike and Lt. Pat Chambers was ruined. Pat was an alcoholic like Mike, with whom he had attended A.A. meetings. In my original screenplay, Mike is an ex-alcoholic trying to survive on the candy bars he always carries with him. He has a pocketful of them and munches them throughout the film. All this was cut out. There are still some references to candy bars and Mike drinking honey out of a bottle. But the final film never really dwelled on his alcoholism. My script has his CIA captors pouring a bottle of Scotch down his throat. But it was later altered to Mike undergoing electric shocks. This was too impersonal, whereas the whisky was more devastating. Mike had managed to maintain his willpower and not drink. But now, as a helpless victim, he was being *forced to drink*. But somehow we know that at the back of his mind he really wants that drink and his defiance is a way of getting it. So maybe, he's put himself into this position allowing himself to be made helpless and vulnerable so he can get alcohol without guilt.

A good deal of my work remains in the final film but some wonderful parts are missing. The picture is not the one I wanted to make when I optioned the Spillane novel and wrote the original screenplay. I don't see it as a tragic experience because I was well compensated both for the material and for the settlement on the directing contract. This enabled me to go on and make *Q*, which was successful on all levels. When *I, the Jury* was released, many critics commented that it would have been a better picture if I had been allowed to direct it myself.

TW: Did you do all the casting for *I, the Jury*?

LC: Yes.

TW: In a letter written to *Psychotronic*, David Carradine claims he was supposed to work with you on *I, the Jury*.

LC: I tried to get David for the role of Mike Hammer, but American Cinema wouldn't have him. David then left for Cannes to show his film *Americana* at the film festival and I began work on *I, the Jury* with Armand Assante in the leading role. I also had to begin casting the villain. One actor arrived to read for the part, but I asked him to read Mike Hammer's lines. He was so good that I told him he was much better than Armand Assante, who was already signed. I said, "If you were playing the part, I'd be much better off. But don't worry, you're going to be a star anyway. I know it's going to happen for you." Then I forgot about him completely. Years later a man came up to me and tapped me on the shoulder at a Golden Globes Award ceremony in Hollywood. He wanted to thank me for the encouragement I gave him back in New York City. I said, "Thank you. I hope everything is going well for you now." He replied, "Yes. It is," and walked away. My sister seated next to me asked me if I knew who he was. I said I didn't. She then volunteered that he was the hottest young star in television. I had not watched much television that season. He was Bruce Willis, who was then starring in "Moonlighting." He definitely would have been a fine Mike Hammer if *I, the Jury* had been successful. I'd already optioned the rights to *My Gun Is Quick* and *Kiss Me Deadly* as sequels. With Bruce Willis, we would've had a series of films.

But I originally wanted David Carradine to play Mike Hammer. He was still in Cannes when I was fired from *I, the Jury*, and I asked him if he could quickly return and act in something else for me. I wanted to begin another film right away. Without another word he immediately agreed. I asked him to bring a suit. So David soon showed up in a suit at the Greenwich Village location where we were shooting Michael Moriarty playing the piano. He'd never even seen a script. David generously helped me out because I'd been fired. Sadly, eight years later, I had to fire David for drinking on the set of *The Heavy* after two days. I wanted to help him get a decent picture after all the bad ones he'd been making. So I wrote the part especially for him and planned to shoot in Santa Fe. David showed up drunk, stayed that way for two days, and was abusive to everybody, so I had to close down the production and let him go. It was very sad that something like that happened between friends. But he later wrote me a letter of apology and wanted to do anything possible to make amends, even asking if I'd be willing to go to Canada and direct an episode of *Kung Fu*. I suppose if I ever see him again, we'll be on good terms. But not until recently did I reflect on the irony of David helping me when I was fired and me firing him years later.

TW: One thing I noticed on last viewing *I, the Jury* was the assassin's resemblance to Richard Lynch's Bernard Phillips in *God Told Me To*. You also have a really suggestive scene showing his mother.

LC: The mother also harkens back to the mom in *Gold Told Me To* and the mom in my later *Best Seller*. Barbara Carrera was good, as was Armand Assante as Mike Hammer except he was hard to understand at times. But it was a shame. Most Mike Hammer movies were bad, cheap, and shoddy, and made for a price. The only one that was any good was *Kiss Me Deadly*. But even that succumbed to being a bit on the artsy side in blowing up the world, hardly what Mickey

Spillane wanted. That's the only interesting Mike Hammer movie because it was directed by Robert Aldrich. I think we had a chance to resurrect the character and do something really original and make a whole series of movies. But, if it hadn't been for that fiasco, I would never have made *Q*. It all worked out for the best. It put me in the position where I just *had* to make another picture right away to prove to myself that I could still do it. Because if you fall off a horse, you have to get back on it right away and I wasn't going to give them the satisfaction of moving out of the New York hotel and sneaking back to Los Angeles.

Fortunately, I met Michael Moriarty at a sidewalk cafe, sitting with his wife at the next table. I noticed him and explained to the girl I was with who he was. When I looked back over, he was smiling at me, so I guess he'd overheard what I said. We got into a conversation, I sent him a script the same day, and he absolutely loved the part of Jimmy Quinn. It was an offbeat choice for him to play that part.

TW: He thinks it's one of his best roles.

LC: He's great in the part. He's so loose and into the character. One day when we were shooting, he walked on to the set, listening to something on a walkman. I asked him what it was, and he replied it was some music he wrote.

TW: Was it "Evil Dream"?

LC: Yes. I listened to it and said, "That's great! Can we use it in the movie?" He asked how we would put it in. I suggested we change his character to a guy who wants to be a jazz musician. He wants to sing and play the piano in clubs. "We'll find a nightclub or bar with a piano and we'll shoot the scene." We found a bar in the Village, the Bitter End, where Woody Allen used to appear years ago — and we improvised the scene at the piano. In the meantime, David Carradine returned from the Cannes Film Festival. He arrived at the bar without knowing what the picture was all about. I said, "I'll tell you later. Just sit at the bar and listen to this guy playing. Then when he walks past, you say, "I think you're pretty good," and he'll say, "Well, what the fuck do you know about it?" and that's it. Carradine didn't even know what picture he was in. He did it because we were friends in the Army together and he knew I was in trouble.

Once I put Moriarty's song into the movie and let him sing, I was his God after that! He relaxed into the part and felt an affinity towards me, knowing that I only wanted the best for him. He can be a mistrusting kind of a guy, wary of people. Gaining his confidence is crucial. He's the kind of actor who, if he does not give one hundred percent, will clam up and give you a cold "walk through" performance. I got him interested in the part. I got him to swing with me. I got him to relax and have fun. He would do anything I wanted if I'd perform my Ed Wynn impersonation for him. Sometimes, when I asked him to do something he was doubtful about, he'd say, "I won't do it unless you do your Ed Wynn first." So I did it and that made him laugh. He'd turn red in the face and then go out and do a great scene. We got along fine on this particular picture and on all the others to some degree. But we were never able to get the level of magic in the other pictures we did in *Q*. He was good in the other films. They had their

**Michael Moriarty, David Carradine, and Larry Cohen work on improvising a scene on the set of** *Q— The Winged Serpent* **(1982) (courtesy of Larry Cohen).**

moments. But *Q* had a certain rhythm going on in a couple of scenes that were as good as anything I'd ever seen in the movies. You remember the sequence when he was in the coffee shop telling Carradine where the bird was? It's so beautiful. It's almost like watching a ballet. The timing — is so great. Everything cooks like it's really happening in life.

TW: When I spoke with him, he said he loves *Q* and would like to do a sequel with you again.

LC: If I had the rights to do the *Q* sequel, I'd do it. But, unfortunately, everything is tied up with the people who distributed, financed, and got the foreign rights for the picture. Before you know it, you're dealing with three or four different companies. Michael had a nice run of four years on NBC's "Law and Order." As Ben Stone, he influenced all the other actors. They acted *up* to his level, and his performance keyed the entire series. He really raised the level of television acting and they all had to keep up with him. He's one of the best actors around.

TW: *Q* works on so many levels, both as a comedy and in relation to your other films.

LC: It has a god worshiped by people who perform unspeakable acts in its name. Again, characters and human relationships are more important than special effects. The film is full of little sight gags and inside jokes. Jimmy Quinn is a jailbird. His surname begins with the same letter as Quetzalcoatl. Jimmy's music is reminiscent of Charlie Parker, known as "Bird." An Aztec priest performs human sacrifices. Quinn also does so when he sends a couple of live criminals to be eaten by the bird, which is waiting in its nest on top of the Chrysler Building. Everything in that picture has one parallel or another.

## The Stuff, Perfect Strangers *and* Special Effects

TW: *The Stuff* is a really interesting satire about addiction, and highly critical of the collusion between FDA corruption and big business that also features in *It's Alive.*

LC: Yes. That's what I intended. I think that in its absurdity it also revealed many important truths about people and addiction. Even at the end of the film, the company is still selling the same product but they distribute it under a new name. This is similar to the Coca Cola company diluting the amount of cocaine in the drink after it became known they were selling a drug to the general public.

TW: As with several of your films, the visual style resembles a comic strip. I guess this influence goes back to your younger days. You make the references explicit in *The Ambulance* with Eric Roberts working as a cartoonist in Marvel Comics, the cameo role of Stan Lee, and Jim Dixon's resemblance to "Jughead."

LC: I enjoyed comic books when I was a kid. My biggest thrill was in getting a new comic book. It was always kept under my pillow on the first night. I guess that came from going to summer camp. If you didn't stash your comic book under your pillow somebody would steal it. So I always tucked any new comic books under my pillow at night, thinking that, otherwise, they'd be gone in the morning when I woke up. In those days, the biggest event of the week was buying a new comic.

TW: I love the scene of the addicted parents turning into TV ad characters in *The Stuff.*

LC: Yes, that's my favorite scene. This has actually happened to the American public! The actors were perfect for the parts. Both little boys are now stars in their own right. The older boy (played by Brian Bloom) has his own series, playing Smokey in *Smokey and the Bandit.* I haven't seen the younger boy (Scott Bloom) for a while, but I've heard he's grown tall and handsome. I ran into them years later and they were both thrilled with the film and proud of being in it.

TW: I gather you wrote *Perfect Strangers* at the same time you were shooting.

LC: Yes. This was one of the few times I obtained backing without any shooting script. I improvised and made up the film based on the locations I discovered, such as the silhouette drawings on walls of city buildings. Suddenly, that dictated where we would shoot, who the Brad Rijn character would be, and what he was doing. I paid the graffiti artist to use his images in the film. Going through a process of discovery as you work is always exciting. You don't know exactly what the film is all about. You find out as you go along. That happened with Coppola when he was on location in the Philippines shooting *Apocalypse Now*. He didn't know what he was making, but improvised as he went along and went fantastically over budget. But it was worth it.

TW: *Perfect Strangers* is really an interesting film. What attracted you into making it?

LC: The challenge of directing a baby. It was like making a Hitchcock picture. The principal character is a non-speaking two-year-old who appears on the screen in very complex scenes. To direct this kid to move around the set and give the impression it knows what is going on fascinated me. Whether the kid knows what he's doing or not doesn't matter. It's whether the audience believes he does. So it's like a magic trick. I've got to deceive the audience. If that kid moves, turns, smiles or cries, it looks like he's reacting to what the other actors say and it becomes a cinematic experience. It's just like the old Kuleshov-Pudovkin device of juxtaposing scenes with a facial expression. The face looks the same. But the audience believes the expression changes in reaction to the montage cutting. *Perfect Strangers* is a film where the director and editor do everything. We're creating scenes which don't even exist out of clips of film, taking an actor's face and juxtaposing it with action from another scene in which the actor wasn't even there and making it appear that something happened when it never did. For me, that's the epitome of making a film — to create in the editing room something that never really happened in real life by juxtaposing little fragments of film. I've done that in many pictures and get a kick out of doing it. I also liked the story of a non-speaking kid witnessing a murder. Then the killer becoming obsessed about whether the child can identify him and then falling in love with the kid's mother. When we cast Anne Carlisle — who is an androgynous woman I'd seen in *Liquid Sky*— I came up with the idea of making her into a feminist and playing the whole story against the background of the feminist movement. Her involvement with this guy, her estrangement from her feminist friends, build up to the final killing when she stabs him for no reason. I wanted to make the whole film just for that one shot when she stabs him and he falls down and the kid is standing directly behind him. It works perfectly. The kid stayed completely still and didn't stray into view. I was afraid he'd move over a few inches and you'd see him behind the guy. But he behaved perfectly. She stabbed the guy. He fell down and directly behind him was the kid who started to cry right on cue. Perfection on take number one. It wasn't a fancy shot. It economically told the whole story in one cut. The guy has not harmed the child — but the woman has killed him because she thought he had. Then the girl takes the child in her arms, while outside her husband is held at bay at gunpoint in the alley by her feminist friend. I had a tremendous urge to put a gunshot on the soundtrack and end the film so the audience would think, "Oh God! did the feminist kill the poor son of a bitch in the alley?" But I didn't know if that might go too far. So I didn't do it. I also liked the scene on the swing and the scene where the killer talked to his ex-girlfriend who'd had an abortion. It kind of paralleled the idea of killing the child. The fact of killing the baby reverts to ideas I first explored in *It's Alive!*

Anne Rice wrote about *It's Alive!* in *The Witching Hour.* She mentioned a number of movies where babies get even with their parents as a possible reaction (or revenge) for abortion. I think *It's Alive* is first on the list. Watching *Alien* the other night, I noticed that the creature who pops out of John Hurt's chest has a strong resemblance to the *It's Alive* baby. In *A Nightmare on Elm Street: The Dream Child*, I noticed that the birth of Freddy Krueger as a baby also had *It's Alive* parallels. In *Batman Returns*, the Penguin as an infant has a little cage around the crib. Obviously, the Penguin is an adult incarnation of the *It's Alive* baby. I know that Tim Burton likes *It's Alive*. So I have a feeling that the imagery keeps popping up in other pictures as a sort of tribute.

Anyway, I enjoyed making *Perfect Strangers*. It used all kinds of New York people who'd worked in underground movies. They were all non-union. None of them were even in the Screen Actors Guild. They were all very willing to work hard. We made *Special Effects* back-to-back with the same crew and other non-union people. Eric Bogosian was doing off–Broadway at the time. He's since done *Talk Radio* and three Broadway shows. Zoe Tamerlis later wrote the screenplay for *The Bad Lieutenant*. They were all highly interesting offbeat people. It was different from Hollywood pictures where you're dealing with movie stars. Here were these people who lived in strange basements, had no money, but were highly talented. The budgets were very, very low. I'd like to do more films like these.

*Perfect Strangers* and *Special Effects* were cinematic. They had interesting images. I liked one scene in *Special Effects* where I covered an entire floor with 8 × 10 glossies as far as the eye could see. Eric Bogosian walks into the shot over the faces of all the would-be actresses. I also liked the detective who wanted to be in show business.

TW: Did you appear at the end of the film, interviewing him?

LC: Yes. I'm actually in a lot of my pictures. Usually, I end up as a newsman interviewing somebody at the last moment and pushing a microphone into the actor's face. I appear at the end of *God Told Me To*, asking, "Why did you kill the guy?" Sometimes my voice keeps popping into the picture here and there, dubbing somebody's dialogue. Hitchcock did walk-ons. I do "voice-overs!"

TW: Like many of your films, *Special Effects* also contains some historical references, such as the mention of Senator McCarthy's lawyer, Roy Cohn. In *Q*, we see the small-scale model used in constructing the Statue of Liberty. As viewers, we learn interesting details about American history. It's very similar to the historical details we learn watching Samuel Fuller films.

LC: Again, I just incorporate into my films anything that's around. As soon as I saw the Statue of Liberty model on top of the Liberty warehouse, I knew I had to put it into *Q*. I also like linking reality to fantasy by using real-life historical references in my films.

## Island of the Alive *and* A Return to Salem's Lot

TW: In *Island of the Alive*, you return again to your theme of monsters in the family. The film has some very poignant scenes with Michael Moriarty.

LC: The *It's Alive* films are not really about monsters. They are about people who are different and how they face annihilation because they do not fit into the normal scheme of things. The parent-child theme is also a recurring feature in the *It's Alive* films and my other films as well.

TW: I remember you mentioned that you had some problems in depicting the adult versions of the mutant babies.

LC: If I had the opportunity of remaking the film, I would design them differently. Their feet were too large and certain body dimensions were not ideal. We tried not to show them too much, but we probably revealed too much detail. The most effective *It's Alive* movie was the first one, where you see very little of the babies. But when I directed *It Lives Again*, I felt that if I'm asking people to pay and see a sequel, I've got to show them more. In *Island of the Alive*, the babies have grown up. As adults they had to walk upright and I had to put them in clothes for censorship reasons. But, logically, they would have wanted to wear clothes because they also wanted to embrace normality in their own way. They would want to imitate humans by wearing clothes. When they put monkeys on in television shows they often dress them up in little outfits to resemble human beings.

The best parts of the *It's Alive* films do not involve monsters, but so-called normal people acting in an aberrant manner because of the unreal situation they find themselves in. I love the party scene in *Island of the Alive* when Moriarty introduces himself as the "father of the monster" and signs autographs that way. At the beginning of the film, he's a rather serious fellow but he then develops this bizarre sense of humor about it all. In order to live with his dilemma, he resembles a paraplegic or amputee trying to come to terms with their condition by joking about it. Moriarty's Stephen Jarvis has become a freak himself, because he is father of the monster. So instead of running away from it, he turns it into a sick joke. Even when he goes to the island, he never takes the expedition seriously. He's razzing everybody, playing practical jokes, and clowning all the time. I think his performance was great and I would not have done the film had it not been for Moriarty. We improvised all the monologues and singing. As soon as I signed him for the part, I knew he could handle all that eccentric stuff. Another actor would have looked at me and asked why he was supposed to be singing during that particular scene if he was supposed to be the father of a monster about to explore a very dangerous island. But Moriarty's character has to have a certain wacky kind of humor helping him both to adapt to his new situation and keep his sanity at the same time. He's right on the edge of madness.

TW: I like the scene where Moriarty arrives in Cuba. He finds himself in one of the satellite states of Reagan's "Evil Empire." But the Cubans help him to return to America and he finds Miami in an absolute mess.

LC: Yes. His whole world had turned absolutely mad when he gets back. The music is crazy. People dress in a bizarre way. I wanted to show that when the monster arrives it sees a society even more uncivilized than they supposedly are. Humans act like lunatics. A gang viciously fight on a pier and rape a girl. So the humans are really monsters.

TW: Actually, the monster attempts to save the girl from the humans.

LC: Yes. And the police shoot him. I tried to interweave many themes in this film. But I still think *Island of the Alive* and the other *It's Alive* films are not really appreciated. They all need very careful viewing.

TW: I've read you had Thornton Wilder's *Our Town* in mind when you began *A Return to Salem's Lot*. This version also differed from your original *Salem's Lot* screenplay, which generally followed Stephen King's novel.

LC: Thornton Wilder's play was certainly my model. One character even says, "Are you making fun of *our town?*" Years before, when *It's Alive* was a box-office success, Warner Bros. wanted to reward me by offering me a nice high-paying job writing the *Salem's Lot* screenplay. But they didn't like my version. So they paid me and shelved the project. Then, they decided to make a four-hour television version, and Paul Monash wrote the teleplay. It had nothing to do with my script. Later on, Warner Bros. wanted to make some low-budget movies for the video market and offered to let me do another *It's Alive* film. I asked them if I also could do *Return to the House of Wax*. But they wouldn't agree to this. I suggested my doing a sequel to *Salem's Lot*. This time I thought I'd write my own version of *Salem's Lot* without depending upon Stephen King's original novel. But it was ironic that this was the same studio offering me the same basic material all over again. I felt that the television version of *Salem's Lot* was a fair production having some good, as well as poor, moments. All that remained from my original screenplay was my idea of modeling the vampire upon Max Schreck's original in *Nosferatu*.

TW: How did you entice Samuel Fuller into appearing in *A Return to Salem's Lot?*

LC: I met Sam at a Beverly Hills French Film Institute party for *Cousin Cousine*. I mentioned that I thought he originally owned the house I now lived in at Coldwater Canyon. Sam got really excited and wanted his wife Christa to see it. So I invited them over one evening and we became friends. Later, I visited Sam in France several times and asked if he'd like to act in one of my movies since I'd seen him perform minor roles in films such as *The American Friend*. When I sent Sam the script, he saw a difference between the small, cameo roles he usually performed and the forty pages of dialogue he had to learn for my film. But I persuaded him by stressing it was a good part, which would earn him $40,000. That rang the bell because Sam could use the money and he agreed to do it. Sam arrived on the set, knew his lines, and it was delightful to have him around. But for a man who'd directed so many films, he knew surprisingly little about acting before the camera. If I said, "Move camera right," he'd move left. Eventually, I even hid on the ground, physically moving his feet from position to position because after five or six takes he couldn't hit his marks properly. Sam even blocked other actors from the camera during certain takes. So I'd have to be hiding behind furniture, physically guiding him like a puppet.

TW: Janelle has already told me about the cellophane wrappers around Sam's cigars causing sound problems during filming.

LC: Sam was afraid of leaving them in his hotel room in case the maid might steal them. I fired two sound people, blaming them for poor recording quality and static until I found out the real reason. Then I thought, "Here's a man who has directed some twenty-two films, who should know about every technical problem occurring on the set, and it never even dawns upon him that cellophane-wrapped cigars in his jacket pocket were causing all the crackling on the soundtrack!"

TW: I think Michael Moriarty felt Samuel Fuller upstaged him by stealing the film.

LC: Moriarty's annoyed about being upstaged by anybody. But Sam really did not upstage him. Moriarty was a straight leading man in the film. He was not as eccentric as he was in the other films and he did not like playing a traditional leading man. It made him realize how difficult such a role was without any hooks to hang on to. Actually Sam had the eccentric character role Moriarty liked to play. So Moriarty felt that Sam was stealing all the scenes from him by playing the goofy, off the wall character he usually liked to do. Sam's part resembled the Red Buttons role in *The Ambulance*, the feisty, eccentric old man who enters the picture at the halfway point, helps the leading man, and gives the movie a little zest. In *God Told Me To*, Sam Levene's role was in a similar mold. I was always sorry I didn't bring Sam back at the climax of *God Told Me To*, because he was such a good actor whom I enjoyed working with.

But both Samuel Fuller and José Ferrer were directors *and* very cooperative actors. They knew what any director had to deal with and went out of their way to make everything easy for me. They never interfered in the direction or complained about long hours and late meals. Sam and José were super people to work with.

## Deadly Illusion

TW: I understand that *Deadly Illusion* only contains half the material you actually shot. The opening credit sequence with Billy Dee Williams walking through New York and the bank robbery must be your work.

LC: Yes. I shot all of that but not the climax. The stadium chase is a complete mess. I never directed that sequence. My original climax, which I shot, involved a chase on the Staten Island Ferry. We filmed for two days in one-degree temperatures around Christmas. While we were filming, the ferry ran aground on a sandbar in the middle of New York Harbor. We were marooned there for fourteen hours, surrounded by tug boats, the Coast Guard, harbor patrol, and

Larry Cohen keeps veteran director Samuel Fuller in step while directing him during a scene in *A Return to Salem's Lot* (1987) (courtesy of Larry Cohen).

helicopters. Every news station had helicopters flying around and taking pictures, so we appeared on all the news broadcasts. The next day we made the front
pages — "Billy Dee Williams and Vanity trapped in New York Harbor." When
we returned to shore, all the local newspapermen took photographs of us arriving on the pier. I think they put too many dressing rooms, equipment trucks,
and trailers on the boat. I even argued that there were too many vehicles on the
ferry, leaving me no room to shoot the chase. Everywhere I looked, I saw our camera equipment and vehicles intruding into the location. There were so many
items placed on one side of the ferry that it finally got stuck on a sandbar. Whenever I read about all those ferries capsizing and drowning thousands of people (it
happened recently in Finland), I think about my experience on the Staten Island
Ferry several years ago. If we had capsized with all those people and equipment
on board, none of us would have lasted a minute in the freezing cold waters of
New York Harbor. A friend of mine happened to have a video camera aboard on
that day. He covered the entire disaster, edited it for me, and even got the "Saturday Night Live" announcer, Don Pardoe, to narrate it! The Staten Island Ferry
chase I originally planned would have been a great sequence. But the producers
finally chose a cheap location to conclude the film.

The villain was played by Elizabeth Taylor's son, Michael Wilding, Jr. He
was great in the part. However, the finished film made no sense. The producers

never attempted to provide solutions to several elements in the plot, such as explaining the significance of the little green bottles and their relationship to Morgan Fairchild's character. When Billy Dee Williams first meets her at the Southhampton house, he makes love to her. But when he meets her ten minutes later in the film, he doesn't even recognize her. Seeing the finished film, I thought, "This guy must be the dumbest black man in America. How could he *not* recognize her? She only had a brunette wig on when he made love to her. Now she's a blonde, so he doesn't even notice it's her? He just slept with her! How come he's so stupid?" The final cut of the film made absolutely no sense. But when it opened in New York, Vincent Canby of the *New York Times* wrote the best review I've ever had for any of my films from him! I could not figure that out, because *Deadly Illusion* is an absolute mess! In my original screenplay (which we actually shot), when Williams meets the woman in the Hamptons, she's a middle-aged brunette who's seen better days. When he sees her later, she looks like Morgan Fairchild. But she's wearing an artificial face. Fairchild's character was once a famous model. She has aged badly and gone through various terrible operations, which have either failed or backfired, making her look old and unattractive. So by day she wears an artificial face made specially for her. Nobody suspects this. The green stuff in the jars is the lubricant she puts on so her artificial face can suitably adhere to her own. This was a very interesting examination of a woman who was once a great beauty. In trying to maintain this beauty, she turns into a monster hiding behind an artificial face. However, the producers removed this entire subplot and put nothing in its place, making *Deadly Illusion* an absolutely unbelievable mess.

They premiered it at Grauman's Chinese Theatre, the great movie showcase in Hollywood, which has footprints of famous stars in cement outside its entrance. I couldn't believe it. But I went there and took some photographs, since none of my films had ever played there before. I thought, "This is the classiest opening I've ever had for the worst picture I've been involved with, which had the best review I've ever received from the *New York Times*. It was one of the most bizarre experiences I've ever been through! *Deadly Illusions* only played at Grauman's because they'd booked a Whoopi Goldberg film called *The Telephone*, which did such poor business that Grauman's did not run a ten o'clock show at night. They closed the theater early because no audience showed up. Grauman's Chinese was desperate to find a quick replacement for a two-week engagement. So they booked *Deadly Illusion*. But hardly anybody went to see it. I can only marvel at the nerve these producers had to release a film which made absolutely no sense. The leading actress, Vanity, disappears halfway through the film. I built her up as a sidekick to Billy Dee Williams and then she suddenly vanishes. Just before I left the film, I found out that the producers sent Vanity back to Los Angeles. I had two more scenes to shoot with her. But they didn't want to pay her any more money. I'd talked to Vanity the night before and she had agreed to work for scale to complete her part in the film. It was a very generous gesture on her part. But the producers insisted they didn't need her. I then responded that they had better get another director! It took them a few days before they found somebody else to finish *Deadly Illusions*.

## Maniac Cop

TW: What gave you the idea for *Maniac Cop*?

LC: I'd done so many films about things that are supposed to be benevolent but which turn out to be threatening, like ambulances, ice cream, and even babies. So I thought, "How about a cop symbolizing law and order and turning into a monster?" I imagined a victim being pursued by muggers, running to a cop for help. The cop then murders the victim as the muggers look on in amazement. That scene gave me the idea for the whole series. When I attended a film festival in New York, I met William Lustig who introduced himself as a fan of my films. He had made a few films but had not directed anything for almost six years. I felt some sympathy for him. So we had lunch and I told him my idea for *Maniac Cop*. Lustig once directed a film called *Maniac*, which I've never seen. So I suggested we call this new film *Maniac Cop*. I'd write the screenplay and he could direct it. I forgot about my offer for a while. Then Lustig appeared one day, with money to make the film. So now I *had* to write the screenplay. *Maniac Cop* could have been better. Matt Cordell's makeup needed improvement. Some of the stunts were quite good. Then, before we knew it, the producers wanted a sequel, and then another one. I've recently heard that there will be a fourth *Maniac Cop* film soon. It represents more work for Bill Lustig than me. I spend a couple of weeks writing it and he does everything else. I get a kick out of writing them, although I don't think the filmmakers created an interesting look for the maniac cop. The series would have been more successful if Cordell had a face the audience could identify with, such as Freddy Krueger. Then they could have merchandised something which was grotesque but also had an attractive personality. Matt Cordell has no personality. He's just a shadowy figure lacking any charm. Every monster should have charm. Just think of Boris Karloff as the Frankenstein monster. But Matt Cordell's Maniac Cop is just a big lump walking around. I keep telling the producers, "Please, fellows, let's get some good makeup people in and create a memorable character". But they never succeeded. I think the first picture was the best because of its superior characterization.

TW: Matt Cordell returns from the dead to avenge his betrayal on New York. There is no reason given for his superhuman powers in either screenplay or film. Are we to assume that his resurrection makes him a demonic deity? He is, after all, Catholic?

LC: I assumed anybody returning from the dead immediately gains supernatural powers. Every religion and mythology has a figure strengthened by his resurrection. Cordell survives fire and gunshots. It's hard to kill something that's already dead.

TW: One of the funniest scenes in *Maniac Cop 2* is the holdup where the robber wins a prize from one of those giveaway competitions before Cordell arrives and kills him.

LC: Yes. What could be more ironic than winning a lottery during a holdup and then immediately dying?

TW: You wrote and mentioned a really amazing idea behind *Maniac Cop 3*, which never appeared in the film.

LC: In the original script, the authorities discover that the catatonic policewoman is pregnant. She's going to have Cordell's child. Cordell impregnated her while she slept. I had the original Sleeping Beauty legend in mind here. So I merged themes from *It's Alive* with *Maniac Cop*. This brought up the issue of whether the authorities had the right to terminate the pregnancy because she was on life support. But the producers argued that these issues had nothing to do with the basic *Maniac Cop* formula and wanted to get back to the killings. So they eliminated these ideas from the final script.

TW: I read that both you and William Lustig were disappointed about the final film.

LC: Yes. Lustig did not get along with the producers. They wanted to do everything their way. So he left the picture before the end, and the line producer shot the concluding sequences. Happily, we should have better luck on the next *Maniac Cop* film. We lost control over the third one because Bill failed to maintain a united position with me. He didn't like the pregnancy part of the story. So he aligned himself with the producers in eliminating it from the script. By doing so, he broke up our united front as well as the degree of power we had over the production. Once he did that, the producers took away the picture from him. By breaking up our partnership, Bill weakened our position and suffered for it himself at the end. As far as I was concerned, it was much less painful. If they wanted to remove any of my scenes from the film, I could always use them for another of my own movies. I did not have to suffer any of the indignities Bill did. But hopefully, on the next *Maniac Cop* film, we'll both be more supportive of each other and exercise more control over the finished version.

## Wicked Stepmother

TW: When Bette Davis left *Wicked Stepmother*, did you ever consider the possibility of not finishing the film?

LC: Certainly. Since the picture was covered by the insurance, I'd have received my director's fee even if it was not completed. The easiest thing I could have done would have been to agree to closing down the entire production. But I had fifteen minutes of Bette Davis on film, which I didn't want to throw in the trash can. *Wicked Stepmother* is Bette Davis' last film and might be viewed as a cinema curiosity some twenty years in the future. In that respect, it will perhaps have more long-term interest than the vast majority of current movies. It might end up having a life of its own. So I thought about preserving this footage and approached MGM about continuing the film. I argued that we all realized that nobody was interested in seeing a theatrically released Bette Davis movie anyway, since her box-office appeal was nonexistent. But she did have a huge video market appeal, since most video stores had a Bette Davis section. If every video store in the country bought a couple of copies, the production would be profitable. *Wicked Stepmother* would make money by marketing it solely as a video. If we made the film with Lucille Ball or Carol Burnett, there was no guarantee that anyone would want to buy or rent the video. I felt we were much better off finishing *Wicked Stepmother* keeping the Bette Davis footage, and promoting it as her last film. We did try to see if Lucille Ball was available. But she was in the hospital and died shortly afterwards. Everybody else the producers contacted were either unavailable or ill. So MGM decided to retain the Davis material, and I rewrote my screenplay with Barbara Carrera taking over the scenes we never shot with Bette.

The MGM executives liked what we'd shot. About the only thing they disliked about it was Bette Davis herself. They thought she looked so poorly on the screen. She also had problems with broken dentures that affected her ability to speak. Everybody went into shock when they compared how she looked now with her former appearance. They couldn't laugh because it was so depressing. Later on, Bette's associate, Katherine Sermak, said that Bette was willing to return to the film and I'd pulled the rug from under her by filming this altered version. That's not true. Bette Davis' weight had gone down to seventy-two pounds while she underwent dental surgery. She could never have possibly appeared in front of the camera at the time. Sermak's assertion is nonsense because Bette could never have returned to the set nor did she ever intend to. I believe Bette was surprised that we used her existing footage. She commented about me on "Entertainment Tonight"—"I don't know what he's planning to do. But he's a very inventive fellow." I never exchanged unpleasant words with her at any time. We were always on a very friendly basis. The last time I met her, she kissed me good-bye. Even when she later spoke to me on the phone, her conversation was always friendly and I was sorry I never saw her again or had the opportunity to take her out to dinner. Bette Davis was all right. She was selfish and willful but you wouldn't want Bette Davis to be any different. In meeting any star, you want them to embody something of their screen image. With Bette Davis you were not disappointed. You got a little bit of *Jezebel* and something of *The Little Foxes*. But I wasn't ready to play the Herbert Marshall role!

TW: The prologue is really funny, especially your use of the senior citizens who resemble the ones Andrew Duggan encounters in *Bone.*

LC: We shot some cute scenes, and many of the actors were really good. Barbara Carrera, David Rasche, Lionel Stander were excellent. I liked the satire on the quiz show. *Wicked Stepmother* appears regularly on television. MGM did make a profit on it. In fact, it was the only film of theirs that did go into profit that year. The insurance company received a check for $460,000 for their share of the profits. That's a sizable amount of money, considering most MGM films

**Larry Cohen and Bette Davis on the set of *Wicked Stepmother* (courtesy of Larry Cohen).**

at the time under Alan Ladd's regime went deeply into the red. *Wicked Stepmother* was unique in that respect. It's perceived as a failure, but it wasn't.

## The Ambulance

TW: What gave you the idea for *The Ambulance*?

LC: I celebrated my birthday at a Pacific Coast restaurant with blackened Cajun redfish along with a lot of Polynesian drinks. Later that night I had chest pains. It was obviously indigestion, but I didn't know that at the time. The ambulance ride to the hospital was really terrifying. Nobody wants to be strapped up in the trolley. It's one of the most frightening experiences of your life. But I thought this would be a good subject for a film. Imagine if the ambulance was kidnapping you.

TW: The opening location scene is really amazing.

LC: Everybody said it was impossible, but I told the cameraman he could do it. I argued that there is always so much confusion going on in New York that people don't notice anything. All we had to do was build a twenty-foot tower in the middle of 57th Street, put the camera and crew up there, and shoot the actors doing a scene in a crowded street with a longer lens. For the next scene, we'd move the tower across the street. We shot the scenes during lunch hour when there were thousands of people on the street, doing the direct opposite of shooting at the least crowded time of day. I wanted the busiest corner of New York that I could find. So I constructed the tower, camouflaged it (so nobody would notice the camera crew), and made the actors perform in the middle of a jammed New York street during lunch hour. In New York City, I always try to capture the essence on film — the people, the energy of the city. The dialogue was all live. It was never looped. Viewing the final footage, I was really pleased that I'd brought it off.

## For the Record

TW: You are often confused with Lawrence D. Cohen, Lawrence J. Cohen and Laurence Robert Cohen.

LC: Lawrence J. Cohen wrote *Start the Revolution Without Me* and *The Big Bus*. Lawrence D. Cohen wrote *Carrie, If* and *The Tommy Knockers*. I'm often mistaken for them.

TW: A Larry Cohen also appears credited with Mardik Martin on the treatment of Scorsese's *Italian-American*.

LC: That's not me.

TW: During 1965 you were executive producer of the television soap opera "Never Too Young."

LC: ABC gave me this as a reward. My company produced the show but I never did any work on it.

TW: In a 1971 film, *The Manipulator*, directed by Yabo Yablonsky, a "Larry Cohen" is listed as art director and set designer. A recent filmography on directors lists you as having written the screenplay for a 1964 film, *One Shocking Moment*. Are these references correct?

LC: No.

TW: Was the report true about you going to the Soviet Union to direct a new version of *Crime and Punishment*?

LC: That was just something out of a publicity campaign. I was going to the Soviet Union and it sounded like something interesting to say. I went to enjoy the trip as a tourist. But you get treated better if they think you're going to film there. They roll out the red carpet. The story appeared in the trade papers but never had any basis in fact.

TW: In 1977 you co-created and wrote the pilot for *Sparrow*. Do you regard this as a Larry Cohen work?

LC: No. It was a script I wrote. The final version was badly cast and the pilot wasn't bought.

TW: David Carradine claims you wanted him to star in a film version of *The Invisible Man*, not *The Man Who Wasn't There*, so he would not even have to show up on the set!

LC: We did discuss this but not exclusively with Carradine in mind. In fact,

I talked about a new film version with other actors and a producer, Elliot Kastner, who was a close friend of Marlon Brando. Marlon likes to make a lot of money for the least amount of work. So I suggested Marlon playing the Invisible Man. He'd only have to appear in the final scene of the film as Claude Rains did in the original James Whale version. Marlon's voice would be heard throughout the film. But he wouldn't have to show up for most of the shooting. I later sold the "idea" of an Invisible Man film in 3D to Jeffrey Katzenberg at Paramount. I went in with Mace Newfeld (who later produced *A Clear and Present Danger*) to pitch the story. A 3D Invisible Man would provide a good justification for the usual 3D special effects, which traditionally floated objects out into the audiences' faces without any particular reason. I also had the idea for a great promotion campaign — "Now you *can't* see him in 3D!" So I told all this to Katzenberg. Later Newfeld phoned me and said, "They liked the idea but don't want to make the picture with us. They wanted Frank Mancuso, Jr. (who made all the *Friday the 13th* movies) for the film. So they paid us off with several hundred thousand dollars. I earned a huge amount of money from a ten-minute meeting! They actually made the film and called it *The Man Who Wasn't There* starring Steve Guttenberg. It was an absolute disaster. They blew a very good idea.

TW: Did you ever make the statement (reported in *Village Voice*), "Where chaos reigns, I shine."

LC: Yes. I think I did say that. I always work best in a tense situation. When things go wrong, my mind comes up with something better. If I travel to one location and circumstances don't allow me to shoot, I invariably find a better location nearby. It just works out that way. Every time some adversity arises, it turns into an advantage in some way. I've never had to abandon shooting on a particular day and just go home. Something great always turns up down the street or just around the corner. If I select a location to shoot and find permission refused or the sidewalk unexpectedly being dug up, I magically discover some better place as if it was meant to be. When I suddenly had to change my original location for *Special Effects*, it worked in my favor. Had I used the original location, I would never have had access to that beautiful townhouse with all the plants and the indoor swimming pool you see in the finished film. We tailored the story to fit the new location. Sometimes things work out wonderfully when plans do not go so smoothly.

In the last film I shot in San Diego, everything was so perfectly and routinely organized that all excitement was lacking. I much prefer a situation when a crisis on the set communicates itself to the actors and manifests itself on screen. The final movie then carries a feeling that something exciting was actually happening during filming. It's nerve-wracking but I always feel in control. I often say, "God is my production manager."

TW: Recently, Sidney Lumet directed one of your screenplays.

LC: I was hoping that someday I'd get Sidney Lumet to direct a film of mine, and I was thrilled when he chose *Guilty as Sin*. But I don't think he did a very good job. His direction was perfunctory and tedious. The camera angles had no dynamism and the set decoration was lousy. Even the furnishings had no thought in terms of what people like those characters would have in their homes. Don Johnson's married to this rich woman. He's living in her huge apartment. She's "old money," as they call it. But the apartment seemed as if it was furnished from some yard sale! The lamps looked like they came out of a hotel room at Howard Johnson's. There was also the window the victim supposedly jumped out of. It should have been a particularly interesting window but it wasn't. The bedroom looked like a hotel room. The sets did not show any evidence of careful thought. It was just like they threw it all together. If I'd made the picture for a million and a half dollars I could have given it more production value. *Guilty as Sin* was a $14-million film, which is considered a cheap movie by major studio standards. But movies of the week on television have a better look. Rebecca De Mornay was passable but disappointing. Don was good. I must say that, in that particular picture, all the credit must go to Don Johnson and the script. Everything else was substandard.

TW: I noted many things in your screenplay for *Guilty Like Sin* which had great potential.

LC: I thought that Lumet, who always was a master at casting all the little parts, would make them very rich. But the actors he hired, such as the district attorney and the witnesses, were extremely dull. It was just amazing how flat everything was. There's no reason for that. And yet the picture did surprisingly good business. It's the most successful picture Lumet's had in the past ten years. It was very well received at the box office. The video release has done astonishingly well. In fact, it was listed in the *Video Box Office Magazine* as the most profitable picture for video store owners. They made a seventy-nine percent profit on their investment. So Disney will make money on the film, more than any Lumet picture has done since *The Verdict*.

Even though *Q & A* was a great movie, it didn't do any business at all. Most of the other pictures he's worked on have been poor — *Strangers Among Us, Family Business*. But I had hopes because I was a big Lumet fan. We had a very good trailer and television promo, which attracted audiences. I think people generally enjoyed the picture. They didn't know what it could have been. They accepted it for what it was. They had a good time. The film had some surprises. It was a major disappointment for me similar to my experience with Mark Robson.

*Daddy's Gone A-Hunting* had the potential of being one of the best thrillers ever made. Strangely enough, the subject matter is as potent today as it was twenty years ago. Abortion is a hotter subject today than it ever was. Think of all the shows I wrote, such as "Kill or Be Killed" for "The Defenders." They're arguing about killing John Wayne Gacey next week. "Kill or Be Killed" was written twenty-seven years ago and the issue's still as strong as it was then. It's amazing that all this time has passed and the damn thing is more pertinent than it was then. That really amazes me. You'd think those stories would become dated like Stanley Kramer's fifties movies. They were great movies then. But if you look at them now, they're so didactic and boring. They're arguing issues that were settled and generally accepted twenty years ago. These pictures argue tired issues like should whites and blacks ever intermarry?. Sadly, Kramer's movies have not stood the test of time.

I've written some television shows thirty years ago which are more controversial now, as they were then. The major problem is that the public is not aware of these films. You'd think that PBS, which is always looking for artistic stuff to put on, would re-run "The Defenders."

Speaking of contemporary issues, consider the current wave of murders at abortion clinics and then look back at *Daddy's Gone A-Hunting* in which the protagonist murders the doctor who aborted his child. Or examine the irony of the mother who recently accused a nameless black man of kidnapping her children — when she had really drowned them herself. Exactly what Joyce Van Patten tries to do in *Bone* by creating a black scapegoat.

TW: I see you wrote the original story for Abel Ferrara's *Bodysnatchers*. But others rewrote it. Taking a wild guess, did you contribute the plot motifs involving the teenage girl's suspicions about her new mother and the military camp as a pod person?

LC: Only the military base material remains from my original story. Originally, the little boy was my principal character. He discovers that his mother has turned into an alien. After I'd written my original script, the producers showed it to Warner Bros. But they wanted the film to resemble *The Lost Boys*. So other writers added the teenagers to the story. I wanted to do something different. I wanted *Bodysnatchers* to represent the point of view of a child who realizes that his parents have become pod people. The parents take him to nursery school. During the rest period, all the kids are supposed to take their nap — the boy awakes and realizes the pods have turned all the other kids into aliens. He escapes and runs into somebody on the base who helps him blow the whole area up. In Ferrara's film version, the climactic destruction of the camp came from my original ideas. But all my dialogue was rewritten. Warner Bros. liked and retained my idea of setting the action on a military camp. In that environment you really can't distinguish pod people from military types. I came up with the basic concept, which resulted in the film's development. The producers did use some of my scenes and gags. But *Bodysnatchers* isn't a Larry Cohen film.

I remember seeing the original version years ago. It played as the second half of an obscure double feature in an RKO Theatre. I sat through it several times and thought it was a great movie. So to participate in a new version — no matter how small my role was — is something of a thrill for me.

## Hitchcock

TW: Hitchcock appears to be a major influence on your work, especially *Special Effects* and *Daddy's Gone A-Hunting*. Your films also continue Hitchcock's serious themes of male and female social entrapment. You've been trying to direct

*The Man Who Loved Hitchcock* for some years, and your description of *The Heavy* has much in common with *North by Northwest*.

LC: Yes. There's no question about it. One of the seminal works I read was *Hitchcock's Films* by Robin Wood. I just love the book. The first film I ever wrote for myself to direct was *Special Effects*, which is obviously a Hitchcock film. *Daddy's Gone A-Hunting* was written especially for Hitchcock. When he was in New York doing *North by Northwest*, I had followed him around from location to location. I was there the day he filmed Cary Grant being abducted at the Plaza Hotel. The day Hitchcock filled Grand Central station with extras, I was also there. A friend and I started paging Hitchcock characters over the loudspeakers, hoping to arouse his attention. I heard he was a practical joker and thought he would enjoy hearing, "Mr. John Robey. Please pick up the nearest phone." No! Not a flicker of recognition. We tried, "Mr. Huntley Havistock. Please pick up the phone." Not a blink out of him, no recognition, as if he didn't hear it. We went through all those characters from his movies and never got a nod or head turn out of him. I realize now, after directing movies, that sometimes you're so deep in concentration that you don't hear anything extraneous. So, probably, he didn't hear it.

Years later, I had several nice meetings with him. One day, when we were having lunch, I told him about the Grand Central Station joke. He had a bemused smile on his face but he didn't remember anything about it. I was a big Hitchcock fan and always had to see a Hitchcock picture the first day it played. I got considerably disappointed when he went to Universal and made a number of pictures that were substandard. I asked him about *Torn Curtain*, which I thought was deficient in many ways, and he said to me, "Never again, Julie Andrews!" "Julie Andrews?" I replied. "Is she to blame for all that?" "Never again Julie Andrews. They made me take her." I couldn't figure out how Julie Andrews could be responsible for that picture failing, because there was so much wrong with it and it wasn't all Julie Andrews. That was the picture in which he had a big falling out with Benny over the music. When I met Hitch he was trying to complete a script for a film called *Frenzy*. But it was not the *Frenzy* he eventually made. This version had a different story and different characters. It involved a noted stage actress who suspects her son is a serial killer. That premise was abandoned.

TW: Your films differ considerably from those of Brian DePalma. Whereas he concentrates more on stylistic features, emphasizing visual sadism and voyeurism, your films capture more of Hitchcock's penetrating insights into human relationships.

LC: Brian is a technical wizard. If Brian sees a Hitchcock movie with Hitchcock dollying the camera around the actors three times, then Brian will do a similar camera movement nine times. Anything Hitchcock does, Brian wants to do it better. This has nothing to do with the scene's emotional content. It means that "I can dolly the camera longer without cutting" or "I can do a crane and turn it into a dolly shot, and if Hitchcock did it, I can do it better technically than he did." Brian's best pictures, such as *Carrie* and *The Untouchables*, are the ones where other people have written the script. He's a fine director. If he directs what somebody else wrote and he sticks to the material, a very good picture emerges. The most questionable pictures in my mind are the ones based on his own ideas. Some of them don't make much sense. *Raising Cain* was disappointing. I always tell him I enjoyed *Sisters*. But whenever I express my appreciation for *Greetings* and *Hi Mom*, he looks away and never talks about it. It's as if somebody else wrote those pictures and he didn't have as much to do with them as people think. I like *Obsession* although it is obviously a variation of *Vertigo*. It was even better than I thought it would be. Both those pictures had Benny's music in them. This added a great emotional content.

Brian never met Hitchcock. As a matter of fact, at Benny's funeral, Peggy Robertson represented Hitchcock, who was abroad at the time. Peggy was Hitchcock's secretary for many years. I introduced her to Brian and he got a great kick out of meeting her.

TW: So Hitchcock is definitely a major influence on you?

LC: There's no question about it. I liked *Strangers on a Train*, with its duality. There's a lot of *Strangers on a Train* in *Best Seller*. But, as I said, apart from *Frenzy* (which was shot in England), the last six or seven of his films were very disappointing, both to me and to Hitchcock himself. He was very unhappy working in Universal. They made Hitch a very rich man, but very creatively unsatisfied.

TW: Didn't you like *The Birds* or *Marnie*?

LC: I loved the second half of *The Birds*. The first half was very labored in getting there. *Marnie* had very interesting scenes but also hokey sequences that seemed old-fashioned and technically poor. But I'm really talking about the films from *Torn Curtain* onwards, once Benny left. Benny told me that Universal wanted him out. They didn't like the fact that he was the only friend Hitchcock had, his only close association other than with the Universal people. Hitchcock rarely saw anybody outside that circle. He saw Taft Schreiber, who was a Universal executive, and Ed Henry. One night he would go out to Lew Wasserman's house. Then another night Wasserman would come to his. Hitchcock was totally cocooned by Universal people and they didn't like him having any other friends or going outside the studio. Benny Herrmann was one of the few thorns in their side, and they decided to get rid of him. They preferred a composer such as Henry Mancini who could write a pop song. So instead of a mere score from *Vertigo* they'd have a hit song about *Vertigo*. In those days, movies had to have a hit song, containing the title of the picture, at the beginning or end, sung by somebody like Johnny Mathis. Universal kept telling Hitchcock, "That's the kind of music you need in your films." So, from *Torn Curtain* onwards, Hitchcock's films were weak except, of course, *Frenzy*. They called Benny in London to work on the score. But he turned them down. Benny told me he had a phone call while he was in London, informing him that Hitchcock was there and interested in talking to him about doing a new movie. Benny responded, "Well, why doesn't he call me? Tell him to call me himself if he wants to talk about it." But Hitchcock never called. *Topaz* is a pretty bad picture. *Family Plot* is routine and nowhere near what it could have been. As you know, I hoped to do a picture with Hitchcock. Even after *Daddy's Gone A-Hunting*, I still wanted to. I kept meeting him at various functions. He was always very polite and introduced me to his wife as "Mr. Cohen." Then, I'd call him and we'd have lunch in his bungalow at the studio. It'd be a three and a half hour lunch. I was always hoping we'd try again to do a picture together. But it never got that far.

Historically, Hitchcock was very unkind to writers. He would begin by being extremely friendly and invite the writer to his home for dinner and send him a case of wine. Then, one day, all of a sudden, you wouldn't be able to get him on the phone anymore. He'd cut you off completely without any explanations or good-byes. Novelist Leon Uris, who worked on *Topaz*, told me that suddenly it was as if he didn't exist anymore. Other people told me that Hitchcock had a terrible fear of confrontations. He would never get into an argument with anybody, never wanted to fire anyone face to face, never wanted to tell them that he was dissatisfied with their work or anything negative. If he didn't like the work, he'd become unavailable. It was left to studio executives to tell you to leave your office because you were no longer on the picture.

I once worked on a script with a top producer for six months. It was finally in really good shape. Then the director was hired and demanded his own writer be put on. He didn't want to deal with me. He didn't want a confrontation. If he brought in his own writer, he could tell him what he wanted and the writer would simply do it. The director assumed that I'd defend my material and it would be an adversarial situation. But it might very well be that if he had told me his ideas, I'd have said, "Gee. It's a great suggestion. I can do that," or, at least, we could discuss it. If we didn't get along, then he could always hire another writer. But studios seldom give you the chance to sit in a room and discuss. They just cut you off and bring in somebody else. I always feel that's a terrible way of doing business. The best approach to working with a writer would be similar to dealing with actors. If you want something, then just sit down, tell them exactly what you want, work it out together and discuss the scenes. That's the artistic approach. That's what work is supposed to be about — working together openly. There are certain directors who always bring in another writer, no matter how good the original script is. I hope the Writer's Guild can come up with some rules and regulations guaranteeing that the original writer should have, at least, one session with the director to talk about his script rather than being severed from the project. After all, the script was good enough to get the director's attention. It's never fun to be kicked off a movie you initiated just before it's shot.

So, as you can see, that's why I so enjoy writing, producing, and directing my own movies. I don't have much money to do it, but at least it's my picture and nobody interferes from beginning to end. That gives me satisfaction. John Cassavetes did it. Woody Allen does it. There's only a handful of people who do it. For a number of years I was part of that group. I know many far more successful directors who've said to me, "Gee! If only I could do what you're doing." This comes from people who make thirty million dollar pictures. I reply, "What are you talking about? Why can't you? You won't get your two million dollar directing fee, but you have enough of a name and power that if you want to make a low-budget picture like the one I'm making you can do it in a second." But they can't bring themselves to do it. That would be a step down career wise, despite the artistic freedom it would allow. They'd rather go through the torment of the Hollywood system. But they give lip service to the idea — "Oh I wish I could do that." But they don't have the guts to try it.

TW: *Daddy's Gone A-Hunting* has so many interesting ideas. The young man feeds the kidnapped baby cough syrup to keep it quiet. He repeats what was done to him years before as a child.

LC: That character also appears in *Best Seller*.

TW: There's a really beautiful scene when Woods takes Dennehy to visit his Norman Rockwell–like home to meet his family.

LC: They cut out one story point that appeared in the script. They shot it but edited it out. You may remember Woods has sent his mother postcards from all the places he'd committed murders, so Dennehy can check the dates. But there's another scene they omitted from the picture. Woods goes to his mother's room and talks about all the money he's sent her. In that scene it becomes absolutely clear that she knows what exactly he does. His mother is just as nuts as he is. She knows he kills people for a living. That scene added an additional dimension to the character and his bizarre family relationships. But the producers felt it wasn't necessary to the story and too weird. As far as I'm concerned, nothing is ever too weird! We also shot an additional scene with his sister. She was played by a decent actress, Kathleen Lloyd, whom I had used in *It Lives Again*. But in the present cut of the picture, she has no dialogue whatsoever. In the missing scene, Dennehy asks her what Woods was like as a child and she recalls how she's always feared her brother. It added depth to the story. These are the type of goodies we'd expect to see in those videos advertising the original director's cut. I'd like to see how the film would play with those missing scenes restored. It might be even more interesting. Even getting them shot was an achievement. But they ended up on the cutting room floor.

TW: What else did you dislike about the final version?

LC: One particular scene where Dennehy's daughter runs downstairs *right into* the villain's arms — even though he's shooting at her!

TW: The robbery scene with the Nixon masks also appears in *Point Break* but there the director has the hoods also wearing Jimmy Carter and Ronald Reagan disguises.

LC: Sure. But I thought of it *first*.

## Thoughts on the Family

TW: Why are you so fascinated by the family theme in most of your films?
LC: Everything develops out of our home life. Every problem people have

Julius Harris as "Big Poppa" suffers from a fatal heart attack during a fight scene in *Hell Up in Harlem* (1973) (courtesy of Larry Cohen).

and every quirk originates from what they see and experience growing up. At one time I suggested an advertising campaign, "Killers are not Born. They are Home Made." Isn't that a good campaign? That expresses the theme in a nutshell. Even in *Bone*, the couple have a son who they lie about when he's actually doing time for smuggling drugs in Spain. They've spawned a kid who is a monster in their minds. In the sixties and seventies, people saw their kids behaving in a manner they couldn't account for. Kids had long hair, wore weird clothes, and took drugs. Suddenly, parents felt they had a stranger in their home who wouldn't accept discipline and who they couldn't relate to. There was more than one case of a father shooting his kid during this period. I think that was where I got the idea for *It's Alive!* Suddenly, you find a monster living in your home. I think this theme occurs in quite a lot of these pictures. Even in *Black Caesar*, the maid cannot understand why her son grew up to be this killer. The same is true of Black Caesar's father. The family motif definitely keeps cropping up in most of my pictures.

TW: I'm wondering whether the stereotyped image of Jewish family life influenced you. A film such as *Where's Poppa?* has Ruth Gordon as a domineering mother ruling the life of her son, played by George Segal.

LC: It was never like that in my family at all. My father was the undisputed boss of the family. My mother was generally passive. They had their troubles. But it wasn't a broken home. They stayed together. But they fought about money quite a bit. But that's probably the subject of most fights in most families. Aside from that, it was a pretty decent family with no scandals. My father never ran off with another woman. He was never vicious nor drunk. When I hear of other people's family lives, I have to say that ours was decidedly normal. I have to say that my marriage to Janelle and our five children also fell into the category of what's generally considered normal. So I don't know where all this monster in the family stuff comes from.

However, I do recall one interesting feature from my family life. My father made a living as a landlord from property in Harlem. He would collect rents from black neighborhoods. I always felt we were exploiting these people and felt badly about it. But he never made any money. When he died in 1960, he must have made ten thousand dollars a year from his property. Even then, that was not much money. His tenants used to pay a monthly rent of forty to fifty dollars. New York City had a rent control law, which began during World War II. It is still in effect today, even though coal, oil, and the costs of maintaining a building have risen. The authorities have not allowed landlords to increase rents, so the owners finally abandon the buildings. Now we have people living on the street because they have nowhere to go. Previously, there was low-cost housing subsidized by landlords who were unable to raise rents and thus eked out a small living from their property. So rather than being an exploiter, my father was actually a victim. Once landlords found it impossible to maintain property, the city took them over and eventually closed them down. Many tenants finally ended up on the street. Experiencing all this may have stimulated me into eventually writing *Bone* and *Black Caesar*. I had some empathy towards the plight of black people. When I was in City College (which was based in central Harlem), I used to collect rents. My father gave me a list of his tenants and sent me around on certain occasions. Although I only collected rents a few times, it was a traumatic experience for me going to these poor people, seeing how they lived, and taking their money. In those days, the buildings were not as dilapidated as they later became. The situation became worse when gangs took over and graffiti became common. Even when I was making *Black Caesar*, Harlem was much safer than it is now. Although drugs were around when I was in college, they were not as prevalent as they are now. You couldn't buy drugs on street corners. The whole city was different then. There were never any junkies on street corners waiting to rob and kill you. Harlem was a different world and safer place in my grandparents' day. Both my grandfather and mother came from Harlem, grew up in the neighborhood, and went to school there long before whites abandoned the area to the black community. Many Harlem buildings reveal beautiful architectural designs. But all the original mansions and townhouses eventually fell into disrepair. It's a tragedy and I wanted to write about it. Even today, I still think *Bone* is an interesting analysis of black-white relationships. Blacks have traditionally been designated as a dangerous species. Bone embodies this negative stereotype of the black buck who is going to break into your home in the middle of the night, rape your wife, and steal your money. But, actually, the white race has perpetuated most of the violence in history, not the black race. Whites have made blacks scapegoats for violence. That's what I pointed out in *Bone*. Yaphet Kotto was perfect for the role, since he embodied a white person's fantasy image of a black male. Unfortunately, many black people choose to play the stereotypical roles whites have chosen for them. As Bone says, "I'm just a big bad buck doing what's expected of me." Black people do not have to play these roles and should avoid them. There is no biological or genetic factor making them act negatively. Such roles are projections by those wishing to categorize and oppress them. If you demoralize people and make them think they can only be criminals, then you will create more generations of criminals.

    *Bone* was a really important movie for me. However, I think the unfortunate aspect of my career lies in the fact that it was never recognized for what it was. Had it, it would have changed the pattern of all my future films. I believe I would have directed films involving sociological relationships, rather than works categorized as horror movies, thus making me more of an "A" rather than a "B" film director. Although *Black Caesar* was successful, it was also detrimental because it was an American International "B" movie. I could have gone in any direction if the right studio executives had seen *Bone* and recognized my talent in directing actors and my potential for making quality movies. Had that happened it would have changed everything. But I directed a successful "B" film which led to further "B" movies. Then *It's Alive* became a success. I tried to change things by doing *The Private Files of J. Edgar Hoover*. It would have been different if a major distributor had released it. But this never happened. That's how it was meant to be. But, in the last analysis, my films are Larry Cohen movies precisely because of the way things worked out. Had I been hired by a major studio, I might have directed somebody else's script in high-budget productions lacking any sense of originality or personal identity. Like Cassavetes, I created my own show business. Others used their films as passports to get into the system. But once the system adopted them, they never made the same type of individualistic films they made as independents. Once they began making mainstream products, they only became interested in attracting mainstream stars and distributors. So they did make bigger pictures. But they were not their own pictures any longer.

## Spontaneity and the Unconscious

One time I went with Robin Wood to a college up in Canada. He was going to speak, so he asked me to go along and answer questions. There was one student at the back of the room who must have seen a lot of my pictures. He said, "What I see in all your films is a tremendous sense of Jewishness. In the milkman's murder in *It's Alive* you have the mixing of blood and milk, which is taboo in Judaism. (You're not supposed to consume meat and dairy at the same meal.) He made analogies in all my pictures to something deeply embedded in Jewish experience. I replied, "Jesus! These are very interesting ideas. But they never consciously crossed my mind." But it was amazing how he'd make a logical analysis of all these things in my films, which never occurred to me. I had to say, "Well. It's interesting. But I really don't know how these things take shape in your unconscious." Living up at the very end of World War II, being just a little kid at the end of that period and hearing about the concentration camps and attempts to murder Jews might have had some effect on me. After all, you're young and it comes into your mind that a certain powerful group of people want to murder you...I wonder if that doesn't put you into the same sort of position as the *It's Alive* baby? Suddenly, the authorities and the system want to kill you because you're different. You're not the same as anybody else. Maybe that has something to do with it, Jewishness and collective guilt? When I was young, some kids on the street used to say, "You Jews! You killed Christ." I'd go home and ask, "Is that true?" Stupid things like that can affect any child. You begin to think you are part of a group that killed God. In many of my movies, you have people who are basically Judas characters like those in *God Told Me To* and *Q*. In both those films the protagonists kill the "god creature." I notice that theme reappearing and try to analyze whether being Jewish has anything to do with it. So many of my movie characters turn out to be gods or demigods in some way. There's always somebody who betrays the god figure or brings them down. I wonder if that's a reaction to that early fear that, somehow, you are responsible for killing God. So it's a strange burden for a child to carry. I really don't want to go too much into self-analysis, because then you start imitating yourself and trying to do things deliberately.

Robin Wood saw some things in *God Told Me To*. He noted that the people who respond to the god creature are all gay. It's true, but I never consciously planned that. When I cast the first part — the guy who was up on the water tower — I chose Sammy Williams, who had won the Tony Award for *A Chorus*

*Line.* I'd hired him because he was a good actor and a "name." But later, after casting a couple of other gay people, I realized that somebody was going to say that all these characters are gay for a reason. I said to myself, "So what? Maybe that's a good idea." It just kind of happened. A similar thing happened with Richard Lynch who played the god figure. Richard had been horribly burned when he immolated himself while on a drug trip and protesting the Vietnam War. We were in a dressing room and he took off his shirt. His whole body was burned and scarred. He had this opening in his chest where scar tissue had formed. I said, "Well. We don't have to do a makeup job. This is it. It's there! Do you mind if I show you as you really are?" He agreed. That gap in his chest was like a sexual organ in the middle of his body. I didn't know if we could get away with it. But we did it. I imagine some people ran out of the theater, repelled. Tony Lo Bianco called me up and said, "How could you do that? My mother was at the screening...!" I didn't know what to say. Also, the idea of Lynch attempting to seduce Lo Bianco evolved during the making of the film. I knew something was going to happen at that point, but I hadn't decided what. In my play *Trick*, I wrote about a poor straight protagonist besieged by the two great threats to any modern man — the aggressive woman and the gay male. I think coming to terms with one's sexuality is one of the problems of this generation.

*God Told Me To* is another of my films that could stand a revival. I think it would do very well at one of those midnight movies on weekends that used to show *The Rocky Horror Show*. Now *Reservoir Dogs* is playing that circuit. Somebody should try a revival of *God Told Me To*. But I'm too busy with new movies now to investigate the distribution possibilities of old ones.

TW: Many motifs appear throughout your work, particularly those involving gay characters. Your first gay character is the artist in *87th Precinct*. Many others appear — the two gays in the "Sam Benedict" "Accomplice" episode, Creed in *Motive/Trick*, Bernard Phillips in *God Told Me To*, Lt. Burns in *Perfect Strangers*. Have you ever thought about why this theme constantly occurs?

LC: Yes, because it's a part of life. It's always been there, but people chose not to examine it because it was once unacceptable subject material for mainstream films and television. I treat it because it is a part of life, rather than ignore or censor out its presence in human relationships. I've mentioned the accidental aspects involved in casting *God Told Me To* and my decision — "Let's make them gay and see what happens." In *The Private Files of J. Edgar Hoover*, it was part of the actual story. I don't know if it had anything to do with me wanting to make the film. I'm always interested in people who are outside the system, with lifestyles unacceptable to the vast majority of the population. Even thirty years ago, I couldn't believe that the producers of my "Sam Benedict" teleplay were so naive that they didn't recognize what they were putting on. The television play credited with making a breakthrough in depicting two homosexuals was "That Uncertain Summer" starring Hal Holbrook and Martin Sheen. It caused quite a lot of controversy at the time. But I had explored this theme many years before. I also featured a sexually deviant character in my "Arrest and Trial" episode "My Name

Is Martin Burnham." In *Special Effects*, the film laboratory technician is a gay character. I've always been interested in anyone who lives on the edge of what is, supposedly, accepted normality.

Anne Carlisle, who appears in *Perfect Strangers*, is bisexual. She has no problem with her identity, nor in playing the character in the film. However, at the time, Anne had a relationship with the woman who plays the cigarette-smoking feminist, and had to get drunk to perform the love scene with Brad Rijn. She was very upset because her current girlfriend objected to her filming a romantic scene with a man. This is very similar to how any actress might feel about doing a love scene with another woman or how an actor might have reservations over his wife's attitude to him filming a love scene with another man.

Sexually deviant characters also appear in "Night Sounds" and *Deadly Illusions*. Andrew Duggan in *Bone* is also a deviant. He makes love to the girl but he thinks about car parts at the same time. The *It's Alive* baby is a symbol of anyone born with some abnormality whether emotionally or sexually. My film actually anticipated one recent debate. Experts currently argue issues arising out of the ability to genetically predict an unborn child's future personality by examining the DNA. So, if the child shows evidence of any form of abnormality such as being gay, the medical profession can actually prevent this by aborting the fetus. Last week, a news story stated that gay men have specific differences in their fingerprint patterns. If so, this could be noted in an infant. The *It's Alive* situation is now becoming a reality rather than fantasy. In *It Lives Again*, the authorities know in advance from blood samples taken from the mother's body about possible monster births, so they can now terminate them either before or during birth. When I look at my films and television plays, I see that they reveal the same fears and anxieties affecting us today.

## Final Comments

TW: How much improvisation do you generally allow in your films?

LC: Usually, an unlimited amount if we can get something cooking. But it's usually me that's improvising. Generally, I give the actors an idea to work on. Then, very often, during a scene I shout out a couple of lines and they pick up on that. Later, I cut my voice out of the soundtrack and leave their response there. In the dailies, I'm in the film talking along with the actors, feeding them ideas and dialogue. If I have an actor like Moriarty, he can function that way. But other actors just dry up completely and look back at me in silence since I've broken their concentration. In *The Ambulance*, Eric Roberts responded to the challenge, but Judge Reinhold could not do this during the shooting of my recent cable movie *As Good as Dead*. He'd get rattled if I talked during a take. Judge probably could have done it under different circumstances but not under those affecting us during that production. I directed this USA cable movie, *As Good as Dead*, under more controlled circumstances than I'm accustomed to. But I gave Judge tapes of my movies. He would run them at night, and returned in the morning very excited about how good Moriarty was in *Q*. Reinhold also ran *The Ambulance* twice one evening. But when I tried to coax Judge into adding some eccentric bits to his performance, he wouldn't extend himself. Unfortunately, we didn't have the time to really improvise on that kind of production. I couldn't just run the camera to let the actor experiment and develop a particular style. This only happens on the films over which I have total control over.

TW: There is a really beautiful moment in *It's Alive* when John Ryan talks to the nurse about Gaelic outside the hospital delivery room.

LC: That all happened because the nurse was really Scottish. So I told them to put it into the film. "Don't talk about it anymore. Let me run the camera and then you can talk about it." So we ran the camera, listened to their extemporaneous conversation, and captured a bit of reality. I always like to find out if my actors possess some special skills. They may even have something they've never done on camera before, especially if it's a particular hobby. That's how I found out Moriarty wrote songs and Jeannie Berlin could juggle. Anything I find out about them I put into the films.

TW: I remember Jeannie Berlin doing that juggling routine in *Bone*. She also speaks of being thrown out of a movie theater when she was young. Did that come from your own experience?

LC: Absolutely! I was always being thrown out because I often sat through films for two to three performances until the ushers came down the aisle and saw me still there during the evening performances. I'd change seats but they'd catch me and send me home.

TW: The mutant baby in *It's Alive* is threatened by society but is also really aggressive. I'm thinking here about the single woman and milkman it attacks. Will we ever see any positive monsters in your films?

LC: I don't know. I suppose E.T. is a positive monster, the flip side of the *It's Alive* baby. Actually, I'd been trying to sell a television series, *Space Pet*, for about fifteen years. It was turned down each season by every network. Disney turned it down time and time again. *Space Pet* had exactly the same plot as *E.T.* The last rejections came from Disney and ABC Television seven months before *E.T.* was released. If anybody had agreed to go along with the project, we certainly could have made a television movie and you would have had all kinds of positive monsters.

TW: Do you ever intend making another historical film like *Hoover*?

LC: I've written a new script on Charles Lindbergh I'd like to film. But it's hard to make these kinds of pictures because they encompass re-creating a period of some forty years in American life requiring expensive costumes, scenery, and cars. I don't know if I still have the craziness to go out and attempt to do it the same way I did with *Hoover*. When I realize how much trouble I could have gotten into on that film, had things not worked out, I was lucky to get what I managed to get. But it was very dangerous to undertake making a picture of that scope. So I'm out looking for the money to make the project. If I get it, or even a portion of it, I might do the picture. But it's also difficult to find somebody who'd like to play Lindbergh. Kevin Costner could, but he's out of my league. I gave the script to Oliver Stone and he liked it. We discussed it for two weeks and it looked like he would make the picture based on my script. Then I heard he was going to do a picture on J. Edgar Hoover. That's off and now he's doing something on Noriega. Personally, I think that the Lindbergh story is much more worthy than Noriega. Now that's off. But, basically, it may be that Oliver has to make something that Oliver himself has written. He might not be comfortable in the long run making a script that is not his. Oliver is a complete filmmaker and I don't think he'd be happy knowing Larry Cohen wrote his film.

I'm happier directing something I wrote, too. It's certainly a worthwhile project carrying Lindbergh all the way to the end of his life, through his neo–Nazi period and on to his eventual redemption. It's much more interesting than the mere story of his transatlantic flight, which Billy Wilder covered in *The Spirit of St. Louis* with Jimmy Stewart. It's really hard to dramatize a flight. But the most fascinating part of Lindbergh's life was what happened afterwards when he changed from being the most loved man in America to being one of the most hated. It will involve tracing the same era as the J. Edgar Hoover period covered. I don't know if anyone will remake the J. Edgar Hoover story. Coppola was talking about doing it with Oliver Stone and working with him on the script. Coppola would have produced and Stone directed — a couple of heavyweights! But it seems to have fallen by the wayside.

TW: It will be hard to beat your version. They did an awful TV movie of his life, with Treat Williams.

LC: He was so wrong for the part. It was a dreadful picture. They did another TV movie with J. Edgar Hoover in it, about Bobby Kennedy. Hoover was played, of all people, by Ernest Borgnine wearing his own hairpiece! One of the scenes between him and Bobby Kennedy was taken verbatim from my own film. It had the exact same dialogue. I ran into the producer at a party. I said to him, "I guess you saw my picture on J. Edgar Hoover?" He admitted that he had, but claimed that what he used in his movie were actually the words Hoover and Kennedy spoke. I countered, "But no one was there. That was all fabricated by me. There was no transcript of the meeting. I created it for the picture. You took that as true and copied it verbatim." He replied, "Well, that's what they *must've* said." I didn't know whether I should be flattered or insulted!

TW: What happened to *The Apparatus* that you were supposed to direct in 1992?

LC: I never did it. It had been in preparation in France. We went over to do it, but there was a major problem discovered regarding the rights to the screenplay. I had written it for another company, which had gone bankrupt. But before that, they mortgaged the video rights to Vestron Video, another company that had also gone bankrupt. So now, you're dealing with two bankruptcies to clear title. The French producers finally just threw up their hands and said, "It's too complicated. It's going to take too much time. We can't keep a whole crew of people waiting in Paris. We have to shut down production." Even now there's talk of making it some place else. But I had a four-month trip to Paris. I made some money. My new wife, Cynthia, and I had a fine time but I never got to make the picture. There's always tomorrow, right?

TW: What's happened to your screenplay for a Western originally designed for John Wayne and Clint Eastwood?

LC: I keep trying to make it. Eastwood is still interested. At one time, Elliot Kastner attempted to interest Marlon Brando into playing the role originally written for John Wayne. But nothing came of it. Marlon and Kastner are no longer on friendly terms. Eastwood still loves the script. I recently ran into him at the Los Angeles Film Critics lunch. But getting a commitment out of a major star is difficult. He usually has projects lined up for the next two to three years. Another problem involves who the costar may be. If it were Sean Connery *and* Eastwood, that might be a winning combination in terms of casting.

TW: You mentioned once that *God Told Me To, The Private Files of J. Edgar Hoover*, and *Q* are the films you are most proud of.

LC: The question is like asking me which of my five kids do I like best. I don't really know. There's something nice in almost everything I've worked on. I enjoyed *The Ambulance* because of the opportunity of working with James Earl Jones. I got on well with Eric Roberts, and Red Buttons is now one of my best friends. There are certain sequences in *Special Effects* which are among the best camera angles I've ever done, such as the one of Bogosian walking over the photos of the actresses' faces. I have to like *It's Alive* because it made the most money and hit number one in the box-office charts. *Black Caesar* also generated immense box-office popularity, so I'm also grateful for those two films. But there are so many moments in the making of any film that bring back fond memories.

TW: You said once that *Hell Up in Harlem* contained several scenes you should have removed. What were they?

LC: I think I put too many action sequences into the film, such as the attack on the island and the assault on Tommy and his girlfriend in California. There were just too many confusing plot developments. I don't think the later scenes with the Reverend (D'Urville Martin) really worked. However, looking back at the film now, it's not as bad as I once felt it was. By the way, the Chicago newspapers only last week profiled a black minister who was a former pimp. The very character Martin played.

TW: At least, *Hell Up in Harlem* does have some elements of excitement in it and does not look like a tired, opportunistic work just made to make money at the box-office.

LC: We also needed more time, so it ended up being the most erratic picture I ever directed. Our star, Fred Williamson, was only available two days a week. At the time, he was making *That Man Bolt* for Universal. But American International wanted a sequel to *Black Caesar* shot right away so they could rush it into release. Fred had several other films lined up after completing *That Man Bolt*, so he could only work with us on Saturdays and Sundays. So I shot *Hell Up in Harlem* on weekends and *It's Alive* on weekdays. Doing two movies at the same time is an absurdity. We often shot scenes with a double when Fred was unavailable. It's almost identical to the problem facing the director of *Saratoga* when Jean Harlow died before the end of filming. But I had a leading actor involved in chase scenes when he was not actually on the set. After inserting an occasional close-up, I'd try to match this with the rest of the action. On one level, it's ludicrous, but it also presents a challenge making the filming much more interesting. We could never make a film like that with a major studio or production company. They'd say we were insane and refuse to believe we could do it. However, when I exhibited the film, no American International executive knew whether Fred Williamson was really in the scenes or not. I had a similar problem with Tony Lo Bianco in *God Told Me To.* At the time, he was starring in a Broadway play and had to leave the set at six. Once Tony left, I'd begin directing all the reverse shots over what was supposedly his shoulder or back. So, in the final film, it was actually Tony's double going into a building or walking up some stairs. Then I'd cut Tony walking into the shot from the front. In some locations Tony was never present. I shot his close-ups in advance and later patched them together. Years later, Tony swore he was actually present at the location and refuses to believe that he was not. For me, that is the essence of making a film, creating something which does not exist. If you have all the money in the world, there's nothing to it. You can build any set you want, use any number of extras, have all the costumes, second-unit directors you require, and edit it all together. It's easy to shoot ten thousand people walking down a street because all you have to do is hire them and put them in costume. But with low-budget filmmaking, there is a challenge. Look what Orson Welles did in *Chimes at Midnight.* He took one hundred people and made them look like a thousand when he filmed a battle scene. Orson also shot in the rain, which made it much more of a cinematic challenge. When he made *Citizen Kane*, he used a lot of stock footage from other movies and edited it together so it became part of *his* film. That's much more of an achievement than having huge financial resources enabling you to buy as many extras as you want and just film them. I always try to make something more out of my limited resources. The St. Patrick's Day Parade in *God Told Me To* is one such example. I shot half the scene featuring the actual parade in New York City. Then I recreated the parade all over again in downtown Los Angeles, using Irish-American marching bands and organizations, which were only too happy to show up at their own expense and participate in a St. Patrick's Day Parade re-enactment. Usually, they only marched once a year, but now they got the chance to do it again! So I created absolute chaos in downtown Los Angeles with hundreds of volunteers I never had to pay, and later matched the shots with the New York St. Patrick's Day footage I had originally filmed. The editing was extraordinarily good, so the whole sequence cuts together beautifully. For me, that's real cinema, taking two scenes shot in different locations at different times and, seamlessly, putting them together to make them look like the same scene.

Andy Kaufman's dying words in New York City are not really spoken by him.

Deborah Raffin, Larry Cohen, and Tony Lo Bianco ponder the religious implications of the director's highly subversive ideas in *God Told Me To* (courtesy of Larry Cohen).

It's my voice you hear on the soundtrack. We didn't have any sound crew around at the time we filmed him. Years later, Andy said, "I don't know how you did it, because you didn't have a microphone near me and, yet, I spoke these lines." I told him it was my voice. But he refused to believe me and always insisted that it was his voice in the film. This is one of the most amusing things that happens. After participating in these deceptions, the very same actors return and swear to me that they were actually present in a particular location or said something on camera when I actually know they did not. I not only convince the audience but fool my own actors. I don't know whether that's an even greater achievement than fooling the audience.

TW: You've got a great ability in directing black actors. Yaphet Kotto, Fred Williamson, and Richard Roundtree have delivered good performances in your films. But you've said color is not really relevant and that actors are actors.

LC: I never really think about this when I'm directing. But whenever I write about black characters, I think more about the black sensibility and the way they might speak. In terms of directing, color does not really count. An actor is either talented or not. What really counts is how the actor becomes attuned to the role. If the lines are written in such a way so that they can be spoken easily, then a good performance usually results. But, sometimes, an actor may struggle with the way particular lines are written. If this happens, I just change the script because often the actor is right for the part and the lines might sound awkward. Changing just a word or two helps the actors perform better.

TW: Do you see any possibility of change in the present Hollywood system allowing you both support and the freedom of directing films in the way you wish?

LC: There's so many new avenues opening out in Hollywood. Cable stations such as HBO, Showtime, and USA are making movies there now. So I never know if one of these executives at these companies might turn out to be a fan of mine and offer me an opportunity to make a picture. It isn't essential for me to make films exclusively for theatrical distribution. Millions of people watch cable and that's where many of my pictures get their audiences anyway. It never matters to me where my films are shown as long as somebody sees them.

If a cable executive sees *The Ambulance* on Showtime and thinks he'd like to hire me to direct some thrillers, I'd be happy to do so. Over the past five years, I've not made many films, largely because of a very comfortable lifestyle allowing me to travel. I recently remarried and been relatively happy writing screenplays and generating more income in that field than from directing my own movies. It's an easier life and I've written much better material than I've done before, despite the fact that its not been produced. Studios have bought the scripts but not made them into films. It's frustrating when that happens. But some, like *Guilty as Sin*, do get made. It led to four more highly paid screenwriting assignments for Disney, but none of them have been produced. I usually spend some six weeks writing a screenplay. After I deliver it to the producers, I wait another three weeks for them to read it and then attend a one- or two-day meeting doing a rewrite. It's the best possible work situation you can imagine. You can work at home or on a beach in Hawaii. But if you want a *body of work*, which people can see, appreciate, and write about, then you have to direct your own films.

TW: You've recently directed a movie for cable television, *As Good as Dead*.

LC: Several USA cable executives were fans of mine and asked me to direct a film. *As Good as Dead* is not really innovative. It's just a routine thriller. Any innovations I created were removed by the producers, who favor the traditional television style. If I ever tried some interesting camera angles or editing techniques, they eventually remove them so the film resembles every other television movie. I might get a director's cut in the early stages. Then the executives recut that, removing everything innovative. *As Good as Dead* involves a girl who lends her medical ID card to her best friend so she can go to the hospital emergency room. Her friend dies during surgery. So, having loaned her identity, the first girl is for all intents and purposes officially dead. She returns after a weekend away and finds herself without a job, apartment, or bank account. Then she discovers that the dead girl was accidentally murdered. The story resembles a Cornell Woolrich thriller. Crystal Bernard from *Wings* plays the main character. Since the USA channel runs *Wings* three times nightly, they're hoping for huge ratings. I also hired Traci Lords since I thought these actresses would make an interesting combination. Crystal Bernard plays an all–American girl on *Wings*. Her father is a minister. Traci Lords has appeared in a great number of adult films. Judge Reinhold adds a film luster to this television production. It's an unusual role for him, since he turns out to be a psychopathic killer. However, I had no opportunity to make *As Good as Dead* as a true Larry Cohen movie, since I had very little control due to the rigid nature of a television production schedule. But I think it is a tight and competent film with something going on every moment. Once again, it's ultimately about the perversion of family relationships. *As Good as Dead* has a number of twists and turns in it, so it's kind of fun. I found it enjoyable getting back into action again. I had a huge crew — fourteen trucks and seventy-five people — much larger than I usually need. That made it somewhat unwieldy. There were also some absurd things going on. Normally, I'd shoot an airport scene at the actual airport. But instead of allowing me to shoot at San Diego Airport, the producers insisted I shoot the scene at a convention center and dress it up like an airport! What a waste of time and money. The budget was over two million and six hundred thousand dollars. But if they'd allowed me to shoot the film my way, they could have saved a million dollars and had a picture with better production values. But I can't fight the system! In one way, that made it easy. A limousine drove me to the set in the mornings and delivered me back to my hotel in the evenings. But I never had the feeling of being really inspired. Remember, "Where chaos reigns, I shine!" But *As Good as Dead* had no chaos. Everything was routine and pedestrian. I found it difficult to get an extra "zing" out of the performances. Unlike Moriarty, Judge Reinhold became disorientated when I improvised. I didn't have the time to train him. If he had worked on one of my own pictures with a crew of fifteen people and a less rigid time schedule, I believe he could have done better. Despite these problems, I'm interested in doing other cable movies. You have to go where the action is.

TW: I feel you really enjoyed making films such as *Perfect Strangers* and *Special Effects*.

LC: *Perfect Strangers* and *Special Effects* were fun pictures, very inexpensive, and a pleasure to make. There was no pressure at all, just the sheer enjoyment doing it. Why can't we make pictures one after another like that and not worry about dealing with the studio system? It's hard work involving very long hours. It's tough. But when you've finished with it, you have something that's really yours. You don't have to commiserate about how something was ruined.

At least, I can say that, out of the seventeen films I've directed myself, I'm really proud of fourteen or fifteen of them. They're really *my* pictures. I'm only sorry I didn't direct more. However, you do have a more enjoyable and pleasant life just writing. When you're directing pictures, it's totally time consuming. You have no time for anything else or anybody else. It's totally draining. On the other hand, I enjoy screenwriting. It's pleasurable because I do it alone. Just me and the characters playing together. You send it in, get a lot of money, and often that's the last you see of it. The chances are that it will never even be made and if a film does appear, it most probably won't be the picture you wanted to make. If you don't want that and decide to direct, you have to give up a major portion of your life. After *The Ambulance*, I decided to relax and try to have a happy, well-balanced life, and wait and see if a major picture finally would come along. Sometimes I get an inferiority complex and think, "Why am I making movies for a million and a half or two million dollars while others get budgets of forty million?" So, I decided to hold out for a bigger budget. I believe now that this was a mistake.

The cancellation of *The Apparatus* in Paris and the unfortunate need to fire David Carradine and close down *The Heavy* robbed me of two more pictures I would've completed as writer-director. Losing *The Heavy* was an emotional blow because I really cared about Carradine. I did the honorable thing with the backers. I gave them back all their money and ate the losses myself. Closing down that film cost me over two hundred thousand dollars. But I had to do it. In retrospect it all worked out to my benefit. Upon shutting down we checked into a hotel in Santa Fe where a criminal lawyer's convention was in progress. By coincidence, one of Cynthia's friends from Chicago, Lorraine Gore, was one of the attorneys present. We hung out with these defense lawyers for three days and that's how I got the storyline for *Guilty as Sin*—which led to a profitable year working at Disney Studios. And *The Heavy* may someday be produced *elsewhere*.

On a personal level, I'm perfectly happy. I have a wonderful wife named Cynthia Costas who I've been with for six years. I have a very good life. When I'm not making a picture, I'm always looking forward to making one. On the other hand, when I'm directing one, I'm always looking forward to being finished with it. So, I guess I'm never satisfied. I write every day so I feel I'm accomplishing something. I feel better if I've done some work. But, even doing that, I sometimes say at the end of the month, "You know, I could have made a movie instead of writing these pages." It just requires the will power to go out and make the picture. In the past, I never asked for anybody's permission to make my films. All the pictures you're inquiring about were the product of sheer will power. I was determined that I would make the movies and nobody would stop me. I'd always get the picture made somehow. If I didn't have the money, I'd start shooting anyway. I'd shoot a couple of key scenes. Somehow, along the way, I would find the rest of the money. That's what Coppola says. Even if he didn't have the money, he'd start the picture and the money would come. I'm sure one day soon I'll just pick up the phone and hire a crew and camera and go to work again — without asking anyone's permission. That's the essence of outlaw filmmaking: not asking permission. In every art form — writing, composing, painting — you go to work when it pleases you. Only in movies or theater do you need approval of dozens of others. I've tried to avoid playing by those rules.

# Janelle Webb Cohen
## on Cohen

While married to Larry Cohen, Janelle Webb Cohen worked with him consistently from *Bone* to *Full Moon High*. Her interview material contains several valuable perspectives on Larry Cohen films. (This interview was conducted in 1994.) His early production methods definitely parallel those used in independent cinema. Although Cohen's films, as narrative features, are aimed at a broad audience, their components are common to independent filmmaking: rawness, vitality, the sheer exuberance in working long hours, and a desire to produce meanings often antithetical to mainstream Hollywood productions. Like the films of John Ford and Howard Hawks, Cohen's films are often family productions, both literally and symbolically. His use of family and friends in many of these productions reveals a direct connection with his early days as an amateur filmmaker when he used his sister in short movie narratives. Also, his tendency to use his family in home movies and devise impromptu scripts foreshadowed the working methods common to later features that he directed. Now living and working in New York, Janelle Webb Cohen provides some interesting perspectives on the early beginnings of Larco, Inc.

TW: What factors led to you being co-producer on Larry Cohen's films?

JC: Dissatisfaction was the motivating force that thrust Larry Cohen (my ex-husband) and I into independent filmmaking. He was a television writer of note. His dissatisfaction peaked on a chilly, damp December evening during the winter of 1968. We were leaving a preview of his latest screening, *Daddy's Gone A-Hunting*, which had been directed by Mark Robson. He directed Kirk Douglas in *Champion* Larry was angry. We walked through the palm-lined trees of Westwood Village. He felt that his screenplay had been inadequately directed and overproduced. Millions of dollars had been spent on this film. He claimed he could have done a better job on a much smaller budget. Waste always irritated Larry. I challenged him to direct his next screenplay. "What producer would want me?" was his question. "I would!" I replied. We both laughed. The thought haunted me.

Larry's mother, Carolyn, Larry, Tony Lo Bianco, and Janelle Cohen all enjoy the humorous side of the director's work.

I had been around Hollywood now for some six years. I had read and commented on mountains of scripts, seen and evaluated storyboards, lunched with top producers, directors, and actors. I sat in on story conferences and observed how a producer operated to get what he or she wanted. I'd been on the set of many major motion picture and television productions. Realizing that we knew what was required to make a feature film and were acquainted with the right people to ask if we needed help, we tended to believe we could do it.

An additional incentive was a screening we attended of the low-budget movie *Glass Houses*, produced by George Folsey, Jr. Both Larry and I were impressed by the high quality of the production. Obviously, the producer had obtained first-class technicians on this low-budget film. If it could be done once, it could be done again. The next week, I presented Larry with a director's viewfinder, an apparatus resembling a small telescopic camera lens. I attached a card that read, "Let's Do It!" We became partners in a small corporation called Larco Productions, Inc. The purpose of this company was to produce low-budget films. Since we had no credentials as filmmakers, in the beginning we had to use our own funds, which were limited.

TW: What attracted Larry to doing *Bone* as his first film?

JC: He wrote it for himself to shoot and direct. After he got his viewfinder and started looking through it, he sat down and wrote the script. When he wrote it, he had every intention of directing it himself. So we talked about it. It was scary. The finances were a little frightening. But we both decided that was the best way to spend our money. It was what we wanted to do.

Originally, *Bone* was a self-financed 16mm film. We used 16mm because it was much cheaper than 35mm. We planned to blow it up to 35mm later, once we raised enough money. We made a deal with three competent Hollywood actors for the leading roles. They agreed to defer their salaries, which were above SAG (Screen Actor's Guild) scale. In addition, they were to receive an addition of the gross or net profit. We made a similar deal for the non-union cameraman and crew.

Larry knew the original actress, Pippa Scott, through her husband, Lee Rich. Larry didn't enjoy working with her because he did not think she was funny enough and he really needed someone better. Neva Patterson introduced us to Jimmy Lee, an ex-boyfriend of Elaine Stritch. We knew Elaine from London. Jimmy introduced us to Andy Duggan. It happened that we were going to Chasen's one night for dinner and couldn't find it. So we ended up at Frascati's on Wilshire. We met Andy, and Larry wanted to do something with Andy. So it was a perfect thing. It was really quite a vehicle for Andy Duggan. Then Yaphet Kotto inspired the character he wrote as Bone. Larry hoped to get Yaphet and he did. In the 35mm version, we got Brett Somers who was Jack Klugman's wife. Larry knew Jack from television work he had done. A whole series of events happened. I forget how we got Joyce Van Patten. She was friends with Elaine May who got us Jeannie Berlin, her daughter. Joyce Van Patten's son played the boy. If you remember the film, you see him in the beginning. At the end he crushes the light bulb. So one thing led to another for the whole thing to come together.

Larry had written a script that could easily utilize our estate home in Coldwater Canyon as a major location. I set about converting our home into a motion picture studio. I set up dressing rooms and rooms for wardrobe, makeup, and props. We could not afford a set decorator, so I got the job. I also won the responsibility for wardrobe coordination. To save money, I used my credit card at the various department stores to purchase props and set dressings. After receiving a guarantee that my purchases were returnable if the sales tags were intact, I would load my car with merchandise, bring it to the house, and dress the set. We used them, turning them away from the camera so the sales tag would not show. After we shot the scene, I either returned the merchandise to the stores or had them come and pick it up, and credited it back to my account. That saved us a lot of money! This was a Mom and Pop way of making movies.

We learned that certain rooms were not conducive to shooting with sound. Our small breakfast room had high ceilings and a linoleum covered floor. The sound bounced off the ceilings and walls. We had to cover the floor with rugs. We padded the ceiling and walls with part of my expensive quilt collection. Our old blankets were wrapped around the equipment to muffle the sound. Another trick we learned was using a wheelchair for tracking shots. We certainly were not the first to do that, but those are the sorts of problems and solutions you learn as you go along. We did not use a storyboard. We did get a script breakdown though. It located each scene in relation to its length, with information designated according to time and cost, whether interior, exterior, day or night, first or second unit shot.

TW: So you really worked on other aspects of the film over and above the role of co-producer?

JC: Yes. Larry was the writer, director, and producer. What I did as co-producer on this film was just about everything. I was involved in casting, props, scenery coordinating and wardrobe. I also helped to raise money. I was involved in so many ordinary aspects of the production, right down to daily meal services for cast and crew. I was literally making the meals because we couldn't afford a caterer. So I would run out, get the stuff and bring it back. There were difficult logistics involved. We were shooting from the hip, as it were. I was active in all the areas from production to post-production — editing, sound effects, additional music, etc. It was hard! I don't know how we got through it. I was also writing the checks for the crew and actors. We did have an accountant to oversee this. But on the set, I wrote the checks, made the payroll, and did all that stuff. I just remember going from six A.M. to two or three A.M. for four to five days during the week.

Larry would tell me a shooting schedule for the week. We used this schedule very loosely and seldom stuck to a prearranged plan in those early days. What we shot depended on what the weather was like and how long we worked the day before. If we shot too much overtime, it would throw us off daytime shooting and into nighttime shooting, which would drastically alter our scheduled shots. After we shot several drama-packed scenes in 16mm, we rented a screening room and set up a screening of those scenes for potential backers. We were able to raise eighty-five thousand dollars. I believe it all came from Nick Vanoff, producer of "Hollywood Palace" and "Hee-Haw." For us, this was a fortune. We immediately changed to 35mm.

Our leading lady, Pippa Scott, decided to drop out of the film. Had she stayed, we would have tried to save some of the 16mm film by blowing it up to 35mm to save money. But it would have hurt the production. Fortunately, we were forced to scrap the footage. Our new leading lady, Joyce Van Patten, was perfect for the role of the bored Beverly Hills housewife who comes to life after she discovers her husband has left her to die at the hands of a killer-rapist. She now played opposite Yaphet Kotto and Andrew Duggan. We were now legitimate independent filmmakers.

Now we needed a legitimate 35mm cinematographer. Larry found out that retired cameraman George Folsey, Sr., who had been nominated for sixteen Academy Awards, was anxious to work again. He had been director of photography on films such as *Meet Me in St. Louis* (1944), *The Clock* (1945), *State of the Union* (1948), *Adam's Rib* (1949), *Seven Brides for Seven Brothers* (1954), *Forbidden Planet* (1956) and *Glass Houses*. His son, George Folsey, Jr., who produced *Glass Houses*, was breaking into films as a camera operator and editor. George was eager to get his son started. George, Jr., went on to produce a lot of the John Landis films, such as *Coming to America*. We made a deal for the two of them, with George, Sr., as our director of photography and George, Jr., as camera operator and editor. They pulled together an extraordinary crew. Fenton Hamilton, who had

Larry Cohen wears the director's viewfinder Janelle Cohen gave him to direct his first film, *Bone* (courtesy of Larry Cohen).

been head of MGM's lighting department for 30 years, lighting such stars as Garbo, became our lighting supervisor. It was quite an impressive group for a low-budget film with a first-time director.

Although he was a novice director, Larry desperately wanted to appear professional. He thought that the director's viewfinder, which I bought for him and which he actually wore around his neck and peered through to size up a shot, gave him a professional image. One night we had dinner with a couple of veteran television directors and Larry was talking about his new toy. His director friends laughed at him and told him that only amateurs or student directors would use them. The next day he worked on the set without the viewfinder. I have never seen it again. However, it turns out that highly respectable directors — John Huston for one — do use a viewfinder. Larry is no longer among the ranks of those who do.

When he was directing, I helped supervise additional casting and aided him in having extras when needed, scouted and acquired locations. I also assembled props. We now had a crew of approximately ten members. Film studios mostly use sixty or more people as crew and back-up personnel in shooting a feature film. We were still a very low-budget production.

Our day began at five A.M. Larry and I would go over the day's shooting schedule. I would consult my checklist of things to be done and items needed for the day's filming. We had no script coordinator, so I would check the wardrobe against the scenes being shot to be certain they matched the previous day's footage. Actually, Larry had an excellent memory for that sort of thing. He could spot an inconsistency immediately. I would lay on the props, plug in the coffee pot and then drive over to the Canyon Deli for bagels and doughnuts for cast and crew. By seven A.M., we were dressing the first set. Once everything was arranged, we left to view the dailies from the previous day's shooting. We were usually joined by the Folseys and Fenton Hamilton.

We shot a lot of footage for *Bone*. On subsequent ones, we shot less. But, by and large, Larry's philosophy is that one of the least expensive items in the total budget of filmmaking is film. Whether you go for high or low coverage, the sooner you spot problems the better off you are. So we were really into viewing the dailies and seeing if we needed additional shots to improve what could be done while we still had the cast and crew intact.

We were so paranoid about making our first film that we personally delivered it to the MGM laboratories each night when we shut down production. Often, it was three in the morning when we dropped the film off. Our day still began at five A.M. (Once, while shooting *The Private Files of J. Edgar Hoover*, we actually shot a twenty-eight-hour day without a break. We had a day in which Murphy's Law was in full effect. Larry refused to let anything stop him until he had the scene.) The actors went into overtime — time and a half after eight hours, double time after ten hours, and golden time after sixteen hours. We had established a good relationship with the actors. They chose not to demand golden time, which earns the actors the rate of a full day's pay for every hour worked after sixteen hours. They were very sympathetic. Larry was in a bind and they came to his aid. Golden time would have killed our limited budget. By SAG rules, actors have what is known as a twelve-hour turnaround. They must have twelve hours off after every twelve hours of work.

It was my responsibility to see that we avoided violating the turnaround. The cast could be rotated to get around this occasionally. The crew was another matter. Larry and I spent most of the turnaround time either scouting locations, viewing footage, or dealing with production problems. Sleep and filmmaking do not go together — at least on a Larry Cohen production!

After viewing the dailies, we would begin preparations for the next day's shooting schedule. Often I had to cancel arrangements for a location I had arranged, because either Larry was not ready to use it or had changed his mind about what he wanted to shoot. In that case I would need to secure another location suitable for what he did want to shoot. By one P.M., I had to take lunch to the crew. Since I was a health nut, I could not stand giving them pizza, fried chicken, or cold cuts every day. So I prepared fresh fruit and fresh veggie salads to accompany the usual low-budget fare. Larry and I often locked horns over this. I argued the dollar difference in the budget was offset by the good public relations. I also maintained that nutritious food would give his crew energy instead of tiring them out. It took a couple of films on which we continually fought over this issue before he came to see the wisdom of my strategy.

I was also the liaison between the crew and the director. It was up to me to handle the petty arguments that often occur between the various personalities involved in making films. Part of my responsibility was to keep the actors happy. This is a top priority for director Larry Cohen. Really dedicated actors are a breed to themselves. My experience is that, the more secure actors feel about themselves and their talents, the easier they are to work with. Do not misunderstand this statement. There are some talented actors who are extremely difficult to work with. What matters is not their talents or achievements (or lack thereof), but the way they perceive themselves as people. Secure actors exude an attitude of helpfulness, flexibility, humility, and patience. Insecure actors prove to be demanding, complaining, arrogant, and disruptive. As a producer, it was my job to help prevent crises by anticipating them. Having an awareness of actor insecurity helped me avoid many pitfalls. Tactfulness and assertiveness are indispensable qualities for any producer.

On *Bone*, I also did still photography. Fenton Hamilton, the Folseys, and the crew were all helpful. I was new at it then.

Sometimes my role as producer and Larry's wife were in conflict. For instance, we needed a couple of stunts performed in *Bone*. One involved driving a car the wrong way over exit spikes and hitting the brakes hard. The other involved standing in for Andy Duggan when his head was being shoved into the sand. My oldest son, Bobby, had been helping out as part of the crew. He was thrilled to be working on a film and loved earning the money. We were looking for someone to be stand-in when Bobby asked for the job. He had learned to drive that summer and was mature. Even so, I had reservations about him doing this. Because of my conflicting roles as Bobby's mother and co-producer, I found myself at odds with both Bobby and Larry. In the end I acquiesced. Bobby performed the stunts skillfully. *Bone* was indeed a family affair! For future films, we used two stunt coordinators — Paul Stader on the West Coast and Peter Hawk on the East Coast.

We also used our dog, Mickey. She was a German shepherd, and I was concerned about her. But Mickey did very well. She was a wonderful sweet dog, but we made her look ferocious in the film.

TW: *Bone* has definite satirical nuances.

JC: Absolutely! It was really funny when one of the early reviews did not recognize this. The reviewer regarded it as a drama accidentally getting laughs. Hell, of course, it was getting laughs. It was supposed to, and the laughter happened in the right places.

TW: What other things do you remember about *Bone?*

JC: One of the things I remember most about the filming concerned Peter Vizier. He was my hairdresser and an old New York friend of Larry's who wanted to get into the film business. He worked with us on the film. He ended up putting the dead rat Yaphet Kotto gets out of the pool into our freezer. Larry saw it and was furious. He made me throw out everything in the freezer.

TW: How did *Bone* get released?

JC: Jack Harris made the deal for *Bone*'s distribution. Unfortunately, *Bone* was never properly released. He tried to capitalize on it as a violent black film and later as a sex exploitation film, releasing it under the title of *Beverly Hills Housewife* and using sex-orientated copy to sell it. Jack never understood *Bone*. It is neither a sex film nor black action movie, but a social commentary in the form of black comedy about upper-class mores and prejudice. Because an audience feels deceived when it's expecting one thing and getting another, they were disappointed. So were we. However, despite our disappointment over its lack of proper distribution, *Bone* served a good purpose as far as Larry's career as director was concerned. We screened it for Sam Arkoff of American International, other distributors, and studio heads. From it, Larry negotiated a package deal with Arkoff, with himself directing his own script and next film, *Black Caesar*.

TW: What circumstances led to *Black Caesar*?

JC: As I remember it, Larry wrote a treatment for Sammy Davis, Jr., and he never received payment. So Sam Arkoff and his wife, Hilda, accepted the script after seeing *Bone*. They wanted to get involved in it and they did.

TW: What do you remember about *Black Caesar*?

JC: I get *Black Caesar* and *Hell Up in Harlem* confused because we shot them both at the house and New York. But I remember stunts, such as the guys coming over the roof, falling off, and hitting the hedge in either *Black Caesar* or *Hell Up in Harlem*. It scared me half to death, since I felt a couple of them were really going to get hurt. We also had a scene down at the pool in *Black Caesar* with gangsters feasting at a large banquet. Fred Williamson's men kill everyone at the pool and shoot up the whole buffet. I'd made a special turkey for that and they blew it to bits! We found turkey fragments over our lawn for quite a while! When they exploded the turkey, they blew a hole in the table I'd rented so we had to buy it. However, it served us well. We kept it for years and used it for numerous parties. We also had to fill the pool with fake blood. After filming, the pool had to be drained and scrubbed. It was quite a mess, but we did get the film made.

TW: Larry often uses a lot of New York scenes in his films. He really conveys a knowledge and love of the area.

JC: Of course. It's his hometown. It's where he grew up. He loved going to theaters and movies there. He loves New York and knows it very well. It's very ironic that it turned out that he ended up keeping the house in Los Angeles and becoming a real Californian when we divorced. I ended up with the New York apartment and became a New Yorker. He doesn't seem to have the love for New York that he used to. But, hopefully, he will regain that love and make some more independent films here, because I think there's something very special about the way he sees New York. He views it like a character in his films so the city becomes a personality in itself. I had such a fear of New York. But now I absolutely love it. That's the way life goes. But I'd like to see him shoot a real Larry Cohen film here again.

When he was a kid, he used to make movies. He'd get a little camera. I remember stories he'd tell of making little home movies with his sister. She was ten years younger than he was, a little girl. He was already then making home movies with plots. He did that with our own kids. This was before he started making real movies. He would devise a script, the kids would act in it, and he would put together a thirty- to forty-minute short-story piece. I remember one involved a monkey our son Louis owned.

TW: *Hell Up in Harlem* appears a very rough production in comparison to *Black Caesar.*

JC: That's true. *It's Alive* was shot five days during the week. I believe *Hell Up in Harlem* was shot during weekends because Fred Williamson was only available then. So it was very ragged and rough to do. We were shooting those two back to back. Under those conditions it was rough for Larry and all of us. But it was fun. Looking back at it, all of it was a lot of fun — most all of it.

I have a very funny story about when we were shooting *Hell Up in Harlem.* We had to go into Harlem. While Larry was filming, this guy kept coming over and wanting coffee, cakes, bagels, or whatever we had out for the crew. I started to give some to the guy, but Larry said, "No!" I'd already given him coffee and a bagel, so he took off with that. Then he came back an hour later and wanted something else. This time Larry saw him and, before I had a chance to do anything, started yelling, "Get out of here!" "Get him the f--- out of here!" I thought Larry had really lost it. He was nuts running this guy off. We could have had a riot right there in the middle of Harlem. Our crew and cast were mostly black on this location. But there were a handful of us who were not. This guy was clearly of Afro-American descent. Larry kept yelling and would not give this guy an inch. He began to threaten Larry. Larry responded by threatening to call the cops. I thought, "Oh my God! Give the guy some food and let it go!" The man had also been drinking and was a little inebriated. He finally left when some of his buddies took him away. After that, the guys on the set treated Larry with such respect. It was amazing. After we returned home that night, I told Larry that his actions were really dangerous and could have caused a riot. He said, "Why? The guy was just a bum. He was causing trouble." I said, "You were in a black community." Larry replied, "This guy was a white guy!" I responded, "The guy wasn't white, Larry. He was an albino!" Larry said, "Oh, my God!" Then he realized that what he had done could have been a disaster. But, as it turned out, all of the crew and everyone looked at him in awe because they realized they were working with someone who was either totally insane or totally fearless! Either way, they did not want to mess with him.

TW: Larco appears very much like an extended family. Your daughters worked on his films. I note Melissa Cohen was production assistant on *It's Alive III.*

JC: Yes. By that time, Larry and I were separated and I was not involved in the film. I know they shot it in Hawaii and Los Angeles. I saw the work Melissa did on that film as a stills photographer. She's fabulous. She continued working as a stills photographer as well as production assistant on several of his films. In

*It Lives Again*, she and our youngest daughter, Jill, appear as the birthday girls at the party. Our youngest son, Louie, plays a cop masquerading as a clown in *Q*. Bobby was also in *Q*. In *Hell Up in Harlem*, Bobby and Mario Puzo's son, Eugene, get killed. Melissa and Jill also appear in *The Private Files of J. Edgar Hoover*. Larry's Mom, Carolyn, appears in the Stork Club scene, dancing. My dad played an FBI agent, and my cousin Doyle Toliver was also in it. There were lots of family members involved and it was fun. It was long, hard work for the eighteen or twenty-eight days we were in the film. We were working double days. Then we did the editing and went on vacation. I must say Larry worked harder than anyone and that's always the truth. He was always on his feet and always right there in charge.

Several friends of Larry's also worked on the films, such as Jim Dixon. If you see every Larco production, you'll see Jimmy Dixon in there. He's always got a part. I think he collaborated on a script with Larry. I believe they first met in the Army. He also met David Carradine there. I won't tell any David Carradine stories. I'll leave that to others.

TW: What attracted you both towards doing *It's Alive*?

JC: I know what attracted Larry towards writing the script. Nineteen seventy-two was the time when parents and kids were having lots of problems with drugs. *It's Alive* is about the alienation that develops between child and parents.

TW: The film contains a lot of other interesting features, such as fear of fatherhood and problems concerning marital relationships, which transcend the horror genre framework.

JC: I would definitely agree with that. I remember, too, when we were viewing the dailies when John Ryan was holding the wounded baby and crying, that I sat there with tears streaming down my eyes. That was just in the dailies and the rough cut. It was really quite moving. We shot that scene in a Hispanic area of Los Angeles. I went out to get food for the crew and nothing was open in that area. A lot of the places were closed to celebrate a significant day in the community. Anyhow, I did manage to get some food together to feed the crew. I remember setting up a makeshift place. We had to make our own wash basin for everyone to wash their hands and themselves, because they were working in the area where the drainpipes under the city were. So, as they came out, everyone had to scrub up. We had no running water, so we had to bring water in and rig up a little shower.

I also remember outfitting Sharon Farrell in my wardrobe. Fortunately, we were the same size at that time.

TW: How did Bernard Herrmann become attracted to the project?

JC: As I recall it, Larry sent him a black and white dupe and Benny liked it. So they talked and Larry just gave Benny full reign. On December twenty-seventh, we went to Cripplegate Church in London to record the music after meeting Benny and his wife, Norma. We hit it off with them just great. At first, I was taken aback by people calling the renowned and famous Bernard Herrmann "Benny." But, as I came to know him and be with him, that's what I did call him, like everyone who knew and loved him. And that's what he preferred. So he was, in fact, Benny Herrmann. Benny, Larry and I spent lots of evenings together going to "Goodies," a kosher restaurant, and dined there often. There were so many wonderful moments with him. Scorsese joined us one day with his girlfriend, Julia Cameron.

TW: What do you particularly recall about him?

JC: He was wonderful, loving, sensitive, cantankerous, aggressive, difficult, and, of course, a brilliantly talented artist. He was all of these things. He was funny, but he could also be very cutting and terribly cantankerous. If he didn't like something or somebody didn't please him, he would pound his cane on the floor and stomp hard, especially if music was involved. He could not stand bad music. I remember when we went to L'Ambassadors, a private club in London, for dinner one night. They had a band playing and he just couldn't stand it. He started pounding his cane on the restaurant floor, saying, "Stop It! Make them stop that racket!" So we got the bill and left there as fast as we could. We learned that if we were treating him to dinner, to take him somewhere which did not have music, particularly popular music.

We were staying at the Savoy Hotel in London until we could rent a townhouse. While there we became good friends of Elaine Stritch and her (now deceased) husband, John Bay. Through Elaine we met Hal Prince and Stephen Sondheim. Sondheim was one of Benny's biggest fans and had sent him lots of fan mail. So we told Sondheim that we'd introduce Benny and they could have dinner together. He said, "No way!" He did not want to meet him, he said, and ruin his image or fantasy.

While we were at the Savoy, Larry also introduced Rock Hudson to Burt Lancaster. The two stars had apparently never met. We were totally surprised by that.

TW: According to *Monthly Film Bulletin*, you also worked as co-producer on *God Told Me To*. Did you work in any other capacity on that film?

JC: Yes. I was also involved in post-production. I remember going out to meet Frank Cordell once. Frank was the composer on that film. I also worked on some of the locations with Sylvia Sidney and Tony Lo Bianco, but not to the extent I did on some of the other films. I also co-wrote a song for that film.

TW: I believe Larry also wrote some plays and appeared in one of them?

JC: He did some off–Broadway shows like *Nature of the Crime* and *Motive* or *Trick*. I worked on them both. I remember something very special about *Trick*. After the performance, we attended a dinner party and met Al Pacino, Robert DeNiro, and Andy Warhol, who'd seen the play that evening. Pacino and DeNiro ended up talking with Larry all evening about his stage debut. Lee Richardson was unable to perform that night, so Larry took his place and played Creed. It was a three-character play with David Madden, Tammy Grimes, and Lee Richardson. Larry performed by holding the script and reading it. He did quite a good job. These two actors at the party were so amazed and excited at how he pulled it off. They quizzed him about his experience during the performance.

**Veteran actress Sylvia Sidney and Larry Cohen discuss the next scene in *God Told Me To* (courtesy of Larry Cohen).**

TW: During 1977, you worked on *The Private Files of J. Edgar Hoover*, which appears very much ahead of its time. Did Larry use *The F.B.I. Story* (1959) as a model?

JC: Yes. That's true.

TW: Larry once told me that Broderick Crawford was the ideal choice for Hoover since he was America's top cop in the old "Highway Patrol" series. He also played a gay officer, Hank, in *Between Heaven and Hell* (1956). Had either of you seen this film?

JC: No. I hadn't and I don't think Larry had, either. What I most remember about the film was that we had Hoover dying in our bed. That location was in our house. Dan Dailey died soon afterwards. I remember we visited him in the Cedars Hospital. He wanted a hamburger. So I went out and brought it back. He was very, very happy to have his hamburger. That's totally ironic because I'm a vegetarian today. It would have been a more difficult chore for me at this time.

I also remember problems over Rip Torn's pants in the street on location. You couldn't get him to sit still to take the measurements. He was just antsy and said he didn't have the time to let the tailor take his measurements. We actually got him out on the street just before the scene and I had to go get a tailor out on the street to measure his pants! Rip also had this thing about his toupee. He always hid it! Rip wouldn't give it to the prop person. He'd hidden it once again! We were shooting at Pimlico race track, so we had to send a driver to get it since Rip didn't have it with him.

We also ended up with H. L. Murphy, owner of Murphy Oil, appearing in the film. We needed a couple of extras to be FBI guys. Larry's mom, Carolyn, and I were in the Hotel Jefferson in Washington, D.C. This guy walks in with a couple of other guys. So I go up and asked, "Would you like to be in a movie?" He felt we were teasing him, but we told him who was in it and asked again. He said, "Sure!" Then we told him how much we would pay, and he agreed. We got him out and found out who he was! So it was quite a scene. The next thing, they were powdering his bald head. It was a riot. But he absolutely loved it.

As I've previously mentioned, tact and assertiveness are indispensable qualities for anyone undertaking production work. One example involved Broderick Crawford. All during the shooting of *The Private Files of J. Edgar Hoover*, he abused alcohol. Often, he would show up on the set so hung over that he could not get his lines straight. We would send someone back to read lines with him, and Crawford would kick the person out and accuse Larry of trying to humiliate him. Once, Larry sent me in to go over lines with him. As soon as I suggested we do a read-through, he flew into a rage. He cursed, yelling that Larry had sent me over, and that it was an affront to him and his talent. "Broderick!" I said, "We all have our off days."—He had told me never to call him "Brod," as practically everyone did, because of my Texan accent. He said it would come out as "Broad." To this day, I cannot make a verbal distinction between those words. I continued, "You are having an off day. What can I do to help you get through it?" He looked at me with those beefy, bloodshot eyes. "Give me a couple of beers." I drew myself to attention, clicked my heels, and replied, "Ten-four, Chief!" When I came back with the beers, he had calmed down somewhat. I set the beers in front of him. He pulled the tab on one and gulped it down. I took out my script and started reading lines. He shot me a threatening look, shook his great jowls, made a couple of grunting sounds, and then fell into his role as the FBI chief. From then on, whenever he was having difficulty with his lines, he would call for me. I was the only one on the set with whom he would read lines.

Yes, we had some problems with Broderick Crawford's drinking. One night when we were taking him home, he insisted that I take him to this bar. Carolyn and I had to go in with him. However, I had to pick up José Ferrer and Larry. After some time, I said, "I have to leave." He didn't want us to leave. Carolyn agreed to stay and he allowed me to leave. I got back and saw José and Larry sitting on the curb. They had finished shooting. Everyone had gone home and they were waiting for me to return in the limo to pick them up. Oh, boy! What a mess that was. But I must say that José Ferrer was very understanding. Larry was less understanding.

TW: Larry cast a lot of old Hollywood stars in the film — Dan Dailey, Lloyd Nolan, Celeste Holm, and June Havoc. He has a fascination with using actors from this era.

JC: Larry's a film buff. He wanted to see these actors work and work with them. I think it was like a childhood fantasy for him. A lot of them were his idols. He watched them when he was growing up and adored them as part of his world.

Larry Cohen and Broderick Crawford prepare for the next take in *The Private Files of J. Edgar Hoover* (courtesy of Larry Cohen).

To have them in his film was just like a dream coming true. He also wanted to see those actors get work.

TW: I notice Howard Da Silva appears in long shot as FDR.

JC: I really don't remember the reason for that. I do remember that we shot it at the Pathé Studios on 106th Manhattan. During the shoot, one truck broke down. We got the equipment out, but had to leave the truck parked on the street. When we returned, a gang had entirely stripped our truck, absolutely plucked it like a chicken. There was nothing left but the frame of this van. Everything was gone. It was an incredible thing to see. I had my hands full, away from the set. As a result, I missed some of the shooting.

TW: What other things did you do on this film?

JC: I also did still photography. My work appeared in the *Washington Post,* the *New York Times,* the *L.A. Times,* and *Newsweek.* It also formed a part of the actual press kit, as did my work on the other films.

I also acted in the film. Actually, my backside, hands, feet, and other parts of me are seen in a lot of the movies. If Larry needed an extra body or body part, he would grab me if I were in sight. That's how I broke into acting!

One of the toughest decisions I ever had to make in the cutting of a film was on *Hoover.* Larry thought it would be more effective to show Bobby Kennedy's secretary telling Hoover Bobby was dead and then showing Hoover's reaction. It was a spur of the moment decision to shoot such a scene. It was not in the script. Larry cast me as Bobby Kennedy's secretary. I rehearsed the scene for about an hour. The makeup artist worked on me and I looked good. My stomach tightened into knots in front of the camera. I was scared. It was my first speaking part in a film. I managed to cry through three takes. I was very proud of myself. I was going to join SAG. This was my big break. Weeks later, we were assembling the footage. Everyone who saw it raved over my acting ability. "A Pearl!" "A Jewel of a Performance!" I was told. Finally, we were down to a final cut. The film was running long. Something had to go. Larry, Sam Arkoff, and I were viewing the film, looking for places to cut. We had found a couple of spots but not enough. I knew it from the beginning but did not want to say it. My scene was dispensable. I knew it. They knew it, too. Finally, I turned to Sam and Larry and told them that Kennedy's secretary had to go. Larry protested, saying it was a great scene and I was great in it. Sam agreed. "The scene isn't necessary," I said, looking Sam in the eye. "You both know it. It's got to go." Sam Arkoff put his hand on my shoulder and sealed my decision with his words. "You're a good actress, but you're an even better producer." His remark was a balm. But I still felt the ache of being the face on the cutting room floor. I did get another chance later. I played Sarah in *A Return to Salem's Lot*. This time my part stayed intact and I did join SAG.

TW: What circumstances led to a sequel to *It's Alive*?

JC: *It's Alive* was successful and success begets sequels. What stands out most for me was that my then brother-in-law, Eddie Constantine, was in it. He also had the same kind of love for booze that Crawford did. There were some problems with that. But Eddie was a pretty wonderful guy. When he was drinking, he was a little difficult. It was a little hard for Larry. I wasn't around to see much of it because I did not go on location with them in Arizona. My cousin, Glenda Young, did a lot of work in setting them up there. Her husband was the Supervisor of Old Tucson. So she had a lot of connections and was able to get many locations for Larry. She appeared in a small part in the film. She is an actress and still does a lot of work in regional theater.

TW: You are also credited as a songwriter in certain films. In *God Told Me To*, you co-wrote "Sweet Momma, Sweetlove" with Robert O. Ragland.

JC: That was a very typical Larry Cohen maneuver. I was busy doing a lot of other things, and he realized he needed a song. He didn't have one and needed it right away. He didn't want to go through the normal channels, so he said, "Write me a song." So I called a composer friend of mine and wrote the song that very day. I did that on a couple of movies for Larry. I also wrote a couple of songs with Gary William Friedman who composed the music for *Full Moon High*. The first song I ever wrote was the love theme for *C.C. and Company* (1970), a film starring Ann-Margret and Joe Namath. It was produced by Alan Carr and Roger Smith. Lenny Stack was the composer. I had two songs in that movie. After that, I just wrote a lot of songs for Larry and others. Bob Ragland and I also worked together on other movies no one has ever heard of. There's one called *Where's*

*Willy?* It made its debut in a small town in Texas and that was the last that's ever been heard of it.

I also wrote "Big Poppa" for *Hell Up in Harlem*. Lenny Stack and I did it in one day. Larry needed it and it was performed the next day by Edwin Starr. Buddy Kaye and I also wrote the lyrics, "We Came So Close to Love," for Miklos Rozsa's music in *The Private Files of J. Edgar Hoover*. It was performed by Elaine Stritch in the film and published. But at the last moment it ended up being cut from the film. I also wrote a song with Robin Batteau called "Ride the Bull" and performed by him for the pilot, "Momma the Detective" (1981) written and directed by Larry Cohen. Andy Goldmark and I wrote a song for *Q— The Winged Serpent* called "Let's Fall Apart Together Tonight." That was a source music cue Larry needed. He called me and said, "What can you do for me?" So, that's how I wrote the song. We were separated at that time.

TW: *Full Moon High* was your last collaboration with Larry for some time. What professional reasons were responsible?

JC: Both personal and professional reasons entered in at the time. By the end of *Hoover* we had some serious problems with our personalities working together. It had become very difficult for me to coordinate all the many professional roles I was supposed to maintain, as well as being married to Larry. Larry did not have the reputation of being the sweetest guy to get along with on the set. God bless him! And he was right! He wanted to get things done and believed in absolutely no excuses. "It doesn't matter. Just get it done. I don't want to hear about why you can't do it. Just do it!" There is a lot of justification for that attitude. But the point is, it can be very difficult to live with. And, as I pointed out at the time, he had problems with a lot of the crew (Larry seemed to get along with the cast for the most part). They would go home and complain to their spouses about that "S.O.B. Larry Cohen" and I went home with that S.O.B. Larry Cohen! That made it a little difficult. But there was more to it. We had moved to New York at the time. I was getting work with my songwriting. So we had a conflict in each of our professions. I did work for Larry on *Full Moon High* as a songwriter with Gary William Friedman. Gary and I wrote "Full Moon Anthem" and "When the Sun Goes Down." My other collaborators on that film were Robin Batteau and David Buskin. We did "Meet Me in the Moonlight," which was performed in three different ways. We also did another called "Tony, My Pet." When Larry returned to Los Angeles for re-shooting, I chose not to go. That was one of the reasons it was our last collaboration.

TW: You then returned to work with Larry as co-producer (with Barry Shils) on *A Return to Salem's Lot*. What led to this?

JC: Larry and I had been separated for quite a while. He had done a few other projects he had written. Some he directed, others he did not. But this was a return for him to our original way of working. So he and I managed to work out our differences and we became friends. (We're very good friends, now.) He was shooting in Vermont and called me to see if I'd like to be involved. I'd liked working with Barry before, so I agreed.

TW: What do you remember most about the film?

JC: We met some wonderful people in the small towns, who were so glad we came. They were just terrific. When we put out a call for kids, they came out and were all over the place. It was great fun getting the locations. Samuel Fuller was great. So was Andy Duggan who was an old, dear friend. So some exciting things went on. But I must say that, as glad as the town was to see us come, they were equally glad to see us leave! It was like World War II (or III!). Sam Fuller is such a character. He was very cooperative and didn't complain. He's a director himself and knew all the problems involved.

There's one interesting story — I don't know if Larry told you of this already — about Sam's cigars. One day we were having a problem with the sound, and Larry fired the sound man. He was just furious about the sound. Barry and I got another sound man sent out from New York. Larry fired him, too, because the sound was just terrible. He fired two more sound men before we realized what was going wrong. Sam had cigars wrapped in cellophane and he was carrying them in his pocket. That created all the sound static!

We did a twenty-eight-hour shoot. That's a tough one, my friend, but we did it. I'm sure Michael might have mentioned that, too. I don't remember if the actors did the twenty-eight-hour day, but the crew and production people certainly did because we had to get things set up, pulled down, and looking for the next location before we could go to bed. I remember the long days very well.

There was also one amazing difference from the other films I worked on with Larry. *A Return to Salem's Lot* was a Director's Guild of America coordinated film. To date, it was the most expensive one I'd ever worked on. I had eight production assistants working for me. Larry had several assistant directors working for him. There was a number of other people involved in the filming, doing tasks I had done before on my own. We had a wardrobe supervisor, set designer, prop manager, script supervisor, transportation coordinator, stunt coordinator, title designer, publicist, two associate producers, production manager, two still photographers — a fully staffed production office headed by a production coordinator and — glory be — a catering service! I wondered how Larry and I had ever done those other films the way we did them and lived to tell about it.

TW: Michael Moriarty has also mentioned that he believes Larry's strongest qualities lie in his satirical approach.

JC: I would agree. I love the way he satirized Beverly Hills lifestyles in *Bone*. I thought it was terrific. I love the way he can see both things at the same time and see humor in the most incongruous and unfunny situations. If he can find humor in it, he'll put it there. I think that's part of the charm and brilliance of his work.

TW: Does Larry have certain links to New York Jewish humor? He subverts genres, like Mel Brooks, and questions masculine roles, like Woody Allen. But his films appear to have more depth in their critiques than the other two.

JC: I would have to agree. I think he does. He is a New Yorker. He is Jewish. He's a maverick filmmaker not unlike the other two. That's the way they started. Larry says, "I'm a young guy still trying to get into show business." That's the way he sees himself— as a maverick filmmaker. But he also sees himself more on the lines of John Cassavetes or Henry Jaglom. I had trouble with Henry for a long time. I just didn't find him the nicest of people so I avoided him like the plague. But now I understand he's a pretty nice guy. So who knows what he was going through then?

I also know that Larry has always admired Mel Brooks and Woody Allen. Mel Brooks also admires Larry. He once told people that he was a big fan of Larry's, so you might talk to Mel Brooks. I understand he used to run his movies at his house. But I would agree with you that Larry's films are more serious, ironic, and very different. He definitely has a very different way of looking at some of the same issues and questions. He approaches them from a different perspective.

TW: Would you work with him again?

JC: Yes. But I would not stop something I was doing on my own in order to work with him. If he were to do something and I was between projects, of course, I would work with him again.

TW: How would you define his position in American cinema?

JC: Larry has been called a B-rate filmmaker, the King of the Bs, and a filmmaker who's ahead of his time. He has a big following in Europe. I don't think he has quite the same following here. But, maybe I'm wrong about that. I think that Larry has something in his film statements here that is very true. He's a guy who loves filmmaking and writing. He's a fascinating, talented writer. For me, his best work is *Bone*. It was absolutely brilliant, way ahead of its time. It had a lot to say and it said it well. *Bone* revealed different aspects of Larry's creativity, his comedy, his drama, his flair for the unexpected — all of these things but especially the love of just filmmaking. You see so many things in *Bone*, pieces of all the influences over the years, put together in his own unique way. I really don't know how to answer this question. You told me that someone did her doctoral dissertation in England on Larry's work. You're doing this book. So he does have his place in American cinema. I think he's underrated. I don't think he is as appreciated as he deserves to be. I would love to see him do more films like *Bone* and *It's Alive.*

# Michael Moriarty
# on Cohen

Michael Moriarty needs little introduction. As one of America's most gifted actors, his credits encompass many appearances in stage, film, and television. Perhaps most recently well-known for his role of Assistant District Attorney Ben Stone in NBC's *Law and Order*, Michael Moriarty is also a playwright and gifted jazz pianist. It is not surprising that two creative and versatile talents collaborated on four films during the eighties. This interview was conducted in 1993.

TW: After *Holocaust*, you were quoted as saying that you wanted to take roles that were "part of the solution rather than part of the problem." So you turned away from some juicy high-paying roles to act in "B" films offering stronger characters, as in the work you did with Albert DeMartino (*Blood Link*) and Larry Cohen. As one of America's most distinguished character actors, what attracted you towards working with Larry Cohen?

MM: I think it was the success of our first collaboration, *Q*. The film didn't get the great reviews that he'd hoped. It even got bad reviews. But I was pleased with what I'd achieved with him in this role. I had a good time. In fact, when they did a retrospective of my work in Colorado I demanded that they include *Q*. They didn't want to. But I said it's one of my best performances. So they did. I still stand by it. The three following films were done in the hope that we could recapture some of that excitement. I don't think we ever quite equaled it. By the end of the fourth film, I figured that we had sapped our collaborative juices and we'd both better move on.

TW: What was his manner of directing? Were there any particular differences you noted between his style and people you'd previously worked with?

MM: Yes! Entirely different. His sense of humor kept me with him. Larry's an easy man to get angry at. But if you keep with him, it's impossible to stay angry because his sense of humor places everything in perspective. So you're aware that it's only a movie. It's not life or death. And he also puts other things in perspective. If I were in a foxhole in a disastrous situation and had to go out into combat, I'd want him in the hole because I'd want to go out laughing.

379

My bewilderment with Larry is that with his sense of humor he has never wanted to do a straightforward comedy. I think he's insecure with his humor on a public level. He's hilarious privately and he really needs to run the risk of saying, "I'm going to make you laugh." So he creates comedy in a form such as the horror genre, putting his humor in on the side, and, of course, it's *perhaps* funnier. I just wish he'd write a straight comedy, with the character we created in *Q*, that's not a horror film but a plain old film about New York called "Jimmy Quinn." In fact, I may call him up and suggest that we make a low-budget film called "Jimmy Quinn" and pick up where we left off on the last film.

TW: His love of New York really comes out in the locations he chooses.

MM: Yes, it does. He's impatient, though. He's too impatient to be a master. I've worked with neo-masters and so-called masters, and with Larry. But Larry's already thinking about his next film when he's shooting the one he's doing. He always has wonderful scenes, in my mind. But when you put them all together they're less than the sum of their parts. And that's the problem. If he were a little different he might make a better film. Ironically, if he were different he wouldn't be Larry Cohen. So you have to take the bad with the good. He's an original. He's quintessentially American. His films have that quality that could only be found in America, that kind of healthy, snotty resilience that thumbs its nose at almost everybody. And yet you're charmed by it. Some are not!

I think the most interesting experience with the reverse snobbery involved in a Larry Cohen film is Janet Maslin's reviewing *Q* as if she saw the entire thing. And then, on *The David Susskind Show*, she stated that she walked out of the film. That kind of snobbery indicates not only questionable moral character but a dereliction of duty. It's wrong! It's allowed because the *New York Times* is up there and Larry's is down here. It reveals a real low in the depth of a writer to do that.

TW: How many takes does he generally shoot?

MM: Not many. He came from television, so he moves very quick because he has to. He's always working on a low budget. In many cases, it's guerrilla filmmaking. His tradition is television, so he shoots quickly. I like that. Clint Eastwood shoots quick. He came out of television and he also knows how much the material deserves. I prefer quick shooting. If the material wants the time taken and you have a major script.... But even then, if the script was a Merchant-Ivory script, which in many cases deserves the utmost care, Merchant-Ivory finds a way to shoot it very quickly on a low budget. They pick professionals who can do it, and you have a wonderful film. So Larry shoots quickly, and I like that.

TW: I gather he allows a great deal of improvisation. Can you cite any examples from the characters you've played.

MM: I improvised a lot of Jimmy Quinn. In fact, I think I wrote one whole speech. He heard my recording of a tune called "Evil Dream" and threw it into the movie. So it became part of the movie and his character. I wrote the speech about learning the piano in the slammer. So he said, "It's great!" and put it in. Then he added the great thing about Quinn's idea of how they were going to stop the bird. It's insane. But it's human. The interesting thing about that character is that someone described it best as a cross between Frankie Machine from *The Man with the Golden Arm* and Huntz Hall of the Bowery Boys.

If you really want to describe part of Larry Cohen's nature, it has that combination. There's an ingenuous American buffoonery that's in your face. It's honest. There's a kind of naked honesty about who he is and what he does that makes him important on that level. He says, "I am who I am, and I don't think we should get our head in the sand and wail about this or that." Couple that with a real appetite for the absurd, the bizarre, and the comic. The other thing I discovered was that I played Larry Cohen. My idea was, no matter what the role I was playing in the films was, because I was one of the principal characters, I was going to play Larry and Larry's relationship to the world. And, in every one, it worked out to be basically Larry's problems with the world and Larry's happiness with the world.

TW: I have the impression that Eric Bogosian did the same thing in *Special Effects*. What other aspects of the Jimmy Quinn character appealed to you?

MM: He was archetypically American, a symbolic American. He's larger than life because he symbolizes so many people in the street who are racing and running away from the law and from themselves. It's a part of their nature that you're drawn to because of its abandon. When they make the mistakes, they make the big ones. It's the appeal Richard III has when he says, "Richard is himself again." He leaps back into battle and is willing to face his fate. That abandon is a very American thing. The hesitancy of most normal civilized human beings is a cover for what we'd all like to do, which is just *leap* into life.

Larry's essentially American because of his addiction, his verbal music, his humor, and his dreams. They are the dreams of Barnum and Bailey. P. T. Barnum's "There's a sucker born every minute and I'm going to take him." There's a big thing I want. I want a million dollars. It's *not* too far from people who are a little more luckier, and they run movie studios. There's a lot of Jimmy Quinn in the heads of movie studios. Robert Evans is a kind of Jimmy Quinn. Did you see the recent interview in the *New York Times* about *Sliver*? It was pure Jimmy Quinn when he bragged about lying to Sharon Stone to get her to do the film.

TW: Do you remember much about the location work in *Q*, especially the Chrysler Building scenes? I remember reading that Larry quickly shot action scenes there before the New York authorities found out.

MM: We hit the headlines then. They had a helicopter round the Chrysler Building, shooting bullets at the bird. The shell cases fell down into the street and horrified everyone. So they called the police. The news headlines read, "Hollywood Terrorizes New York." That's Larry! I remember being at the very top of the Chrysler Building, filming in that wind tunnel up there, because the wind was pretty fierce so the scene was a hit-and-run operation. You had to get in and out quick.

He used to call us Cohen's Traveling Irish Players because he had a few Irish actors. We were like a band of gypsies. We moved in very quickly and moved out. People don't want to admit how much of the vagabond there is in the player. But it is a good reminder that we are gypsies — rich gypsies!. That's Dustin Hoffman's description.

TW: Why did *The Stuff* appeal to you?

MM: I didn't know what to do with my character except when we decided to give him a little Southern thing — my joke about Mo. That was my hook on him. It was a further exploration of Larry Cohen. Mo Rutherford is quintessentially a Larry Cohen character. And it taught me about leading men. This is where I learned how to explore leading men. They are the moral focus on the piece. I thought the satire was accurate. I still think it's a good metaphor for the present hypocrisy of the war on drugs. *The Stuff* is about drug addiction. Some drugs are allowed and others are not. They criminalize people who are already punished enough by their own addiction. It worsens the situation by calling them criminals. Let's get them into treatment. The inner satire of his films always intrigue me because he's always there like a good satirist pointing out what's ridiculous with the laws and mores of a nation that is in a perpetual state of contradiction with itself. And that appealed to me.

I think the deepest experience of the Cohen character was in *Island of the Alive* in regard to his own children, the child as monster. I don't think there's ever been any parent in the world who hasn't worried about giving birth to a monster in some way or another, raising a monster, not being the right kind of father, doing the wrong thing in creating this monster, or spoiling it. Since there are no set rules to raising children that you can follow easily, it's closer to home than most people are willing to admit. So, of all the four characters, he was probably the most everyday Joe that existed. The rest were theatrical devices or symbols like Jimmy Quinn. In the scenes with Karen Black, there was a level of reality to that plight that was not typical of a Larry Cohen film, when you are usually into such a science fiction scenario that you have to suspend disbelief from the first moment. You have to know that you're into a shock movie and you go along with the game and the conventions. There's something about this guy that seemed more real than most. And I think there were some poignant moments in it — I really do — with the children and the father's plight. There were some good things there.

The least satisfactory thing for me was the vampire movie. That's where we kind of parted ways. It was shot in such a way that…I'm an earnest person and in order to make that film work I had to be as earnest as possible. And it's hard to be earnest around Larry. He is not an earnest human being. That was our last picture together. It had a lot to do with the character I was playing and the world he was creating.

The satire in that film was quite insightful. When you deal with what it is to be a vampire and you start to look at the metaphor of bloodsuckers that exist, you realize it's a part of our everyday world. It's money, or another kind of blood. It becomes interesting. But on the personal level…at the end, I knew that we couldn't do another film together, certainly not a science fiction film.

TW: What was it like working with Samuel Fuller?

MM: Well, infuriating at times. He was a total amateur as an actor. And yet, you knew that he'd be incredibly charming and because, when you behave like a child — which he did as an actor — the audience is drawn to you because, indeed, you're honest. He was very honest with the whole performance. But it creates chaos around you. He stole the film in the way that children do. He's not a professional actor. He behaves like a child and he did steal the film. He's the most charming thing in the film. It's a terrible price when you carry the whole plot, then somebody runs off with the scenes and makes your job twice as hard as it has to be. I'm not into film very deeply. Meeting Samuel Fuller was a nice experience. But I'm not someone who went down to the Film Forum to see every new film. If I had that kind of relationship I would have let Samuel Fuller do anything and not be a bit ruffled. But it was hard. He clearly stole the film.

TW: Had you seen any Fuller films and did you notice any parallels between Cohen and Fuller?

MM: The one I remember seeing was *White Dog*. No. They're not at all alike. Fuller's much more serious. I don't see any similarities between them. I think that their bond was that they are two cult figures who got together, joined forces, and created an interesting character.

TW: I remember reading an interview quoting Larry as saying, "Where chaos rules, I shine."

MM: That's Larry! Where chaos rules he does shine. In *Island of the Alive*, we were shooting on a boat in stormy weather. The boat was not well balanced so it bounced along on the waves. Except for Larry and myself, the entire crew was vomiting. But Larry gets happier and happier. He'd get out and about, singing. When the spray came over, the film broke down because the cameraman couldn't shoot. He and everybody else were vomiting over the side. So, I'm standing there and I was impressed because Larry *was* singing. It was the apotheosis of my experience with Larry, seeing him singing joyously and ecstatically in a boat that, maybe, was in danger, with his leading actor sitting there in a mixture of awe and disbelief. It's true. In chaos, he does shine. He loves chaos. He adores chaos.

TW: Was it his idea to have you singing "Over the Sea to Skye" on the boat?

MM: That went back to my days at the Guthrie Theatre. A very fine actor named Dougie Campbell, who I saw two years ago, used to warm up the entire company with songs and his favorite was "Over the Sea to Skye." If you want to know a real film-buff note about the interrelationship between films, this is a great story. I learned it from Dougie when he warmed up the crew, and I put it in the movie. You know who else put that same song just for the same reason in a movie? Alec Guinness in *Tunes of Glory*. Alec Guinness played Richard III at Stratford before he did *Tunes of Glory*. Dougie was in the company and did the warm-ups. And he *based* that character on Dougie Campbell. I knew that Guinness based his entire characterization of that pugilistic officer on Dougie Campbell. And at one point in the film, he sings, "speed bonnie boat." For me, that has religious implications. But they were actually referring to Bonnie Prince Charles, I believe.

Michael Moriarty (with beard), Christopher Walken (left of Moriarty), David Carradine (right of Moriarty), Larry Cohen (right, plaid shirt), and others together at a party (courtesy of Larry Cohen).

I always thought it was Christ who was "born to be king over the sea to Skye." So my own personal skit on it was Christian. But, literally, it referred to Bonnie Prince Charles. So I picked that song and Larry liked it and we went with it. That's interesting, isn't it?

TW: Yes. Because there are links with the other *It's Alive* movies, especially the second, where the two mutant babies are named Adam and Eve. There's a Messianic theme in the original *It's Alive*, as well as *God Told Me To*.

MM: There's no question about it. *Q* had a religious fanatic in it.

Larry understands that religious fanaticism, because there's a fanaticism to Larry. But it's so erratic and uncontrolled that it's harmless. The best place for any fanatic is in the arts. If *only* the Art Society of Vienna had accepted Hitler, we'd never have had a second World War. There's no doubt about that.

TW: Does Larry's comic-strip cinematic style bother you? The comic-strip style is usually criticized in high art circles.

MM: Never having seen a Larry Cohen film before I did *Q*, all I see as an actor is the role and where I can center on it. And I knew Jimmy Quinn. Some part of my soul immediately answered to Jimmy Quinn. The fact that Larry put a cartoon world around me meant nothing to me. Jimmy Quinn's very real to me on a big level. Holding up the city for a million dollars is part of the American nature — the Fast Buck, the Big Dream, and Las Vegas. So I never considered Jimmy Quinn, my first Larry Cohen role, as a cartoon figure. I considered him a bigger than life symbol of a certain street creature. And, ironically, I still get street people in this city stop me and tell me how much they love *Q* and Jimmy Quinn. I saw that film in a 42nd Street movie theater with friends. I've never been in a movie theater where they treated it as a live performance and cheered and screamed. They cheered Jimmy Quinn when he held up the city for a million dollars. There were people like Jimmy Quinn applauding Jimmy Quinn as a hero! It was my first experience of playing an antihero where I had a visceral relationship with that audience on the screen! After that, and seeing the film, I knew it was a cartoon world. But I could accept it, having been in the theater. Everything is imaginary in the theater. And when you do blue-screen work in science fiction, with the monster not actually there, it's fun because you are acting the way you would in the theater. You are creating the entire thing out of your own imagination. So, to see that was magic. I didn't consider it cartoonish. The appeal was magic. You see magic in an actor because he makes that real, even though when he shot it, it wasn't even there. That's an art in itself.

The real thing that bothers me about Larry is that he moves at too fast a pace. He'll throw everything together. Then in the editing process, he'll get desperately insecure and cut scenes and concentrate on the action. And it seems to get worse with each film. He would get more and more insecure in his editing. And I saw that he wouldn't just tell a story, because he felt he'd lose his audience. Actually, he drove some of his audience out the door because of his insecurities. It's the kind of thing that happened in *Lethal Weapon 2*. And Spielberg. Look at those fantasy-adventure things. He had an accident about every three seconds, and after a while, I said, "I don't care. I've lost track and what are we here for? I don't hear a story. I just see another effect". Then we go to another scene where there's another effect. It's not unlike Larry's personality. He will start to tell a joke, will get on a role, and he'll take it for another forty minutes. And after a while, you're exhausted and tired of the comedy. And you're still laughing because he's funny. But you say, "Enough! I've got to move on with my life. I've got to stop laughing." But he'll keep on going. He's the comedian who can't get off, and you're looking for the hook. The problem is that you're in the middle of the man's deepest insecurities and he keeps dancing and dancing and dancing. And you say, "Wait a minute. No! No! You don't have to do that to live your life. You don't have to do that to entertain me. I have to get out of this room."

I don't mind a cartoon if it's done well. *Terminator 2* is a cartoon. But it's so well done, just at the right tempo. You're still caught in the human situation. You don't lose track of that. There's a scene where you can breathe. There's enough action. There's structure. Have you read the article about *The Last Action Hero*? Schwarzenegger had five writers come in because he knew the film resembled a cartoon. But you've got to have humanity. So you bring William Goldman in. "I can't do the film as it is now. It's an action satire. And I want some humor." Schwarzenegger agrees to do it if they bring Goldman in. *Smart, smart* man! He knows his goal is the biggest audience *possible*. And the biggest audience possible is created by as wide a view of the entertainment possible. Smart man! Smart man! He earned every bit of his success. I don't mind a cartoon if it's well done. I had fun in *Twins*. I'll sit and watch a good cartoon. *Dave's* a good cartoon. That's a well-structured cartoon. A bad cartoon is *Bob Roberts*. That's a "I know more about politics than you and talk down to you cartoon." I politically agree with him. But I don't think you should take cheap shots. *Hoffa* turned into a cartoon.

There's so much insecurity in the world of the arts. You don't want to be around when it's infectious. You get insecure and it's you who suffer. It's a very virulent emotion and it shows itself in strange ways. I pick it up and I get insecure. My best work comes out of a very peaceful setting. I know all the forms, styles of acting, and different types of films. I love variety.

Actually, working with Larry Cohen inspired me to do my first and only film, which I've just completed with my students, called *Chamber Music*. He did his first film all by himself. He and his wife raised the money. He even encouraged me to go ahead. I'm not apologizing any more for my Larry Cohen films.

TW: You don't have to.

MM: Jay Leno wanted me to on his show! He started dragging them up. But I didn't have the presence of mind to remind him of his commercials or that awful film he did in Detroit. He loves making actors feel uncomfortable. The irony is that he sits there and accuses me of doing them for that extra house and car. But I was doing them to put food on the table. That's why I did them at that point in my career. I didn't do them to throw my voice away in a commercial.

I did four films with Larry Cohen. But after them, I feel *strong* the way Jack Nicholson was made strong by working with Roger Corman. You learn from a really earthy fly by night to find your center in weird circumstances of shooting. So I owe him for that. I owe him for one of my best performances — Q. Spielberg sees everything in Florida. He said, "There ought to be a sequel to Jimmy Quinn." So, when you called, I had no qualms about talking about Larry Cohen, because he is an artist. He has his own identity. If the first rule of honesty is being nakedly who you are, then he fulfills it.

TW: *A Return to Salem's Lot* stresses the theme of becoming a human being.

MM: There is a moral world in *A Return to Salem's Lot* and beneath it is Larry. And that's why Larry is a human being on the positive side. Because, despite the craftsmanship, the soul within the man is worth a serious look and can be trusted despite all the erratic elements of his life. I've seen him do foolish things and foolhardy things. But I've never seen him be really petty, ever.

We were shooting in the teamsters' office in New Jersey. We found teamsters there. Larry didn't even talk to the teamsters to get in there. He tried to avoid them as much as possible so that he wouldn't have to use them, and he's making *jokes* and insulting jibes in front of them. And he's really pressing the button. Horrible-looking guys stand there and watch him cracking jokes at them. It's amazing to watch how far he'd push their patience. It's foolhardy. But at the same time it has this kind of American bravado, the kind of way Bogart talks to the Nazis in *Casablanca.*

TW: Did Clint Eastwood see your Larry Cohen films before casting you in *Pale Rider*?

MM: No. Actually, it was a TV hockey movie called *Deadly Season.*

TW: Larry likes using a number of vintage Hollywood actors, as in *A Return to Salem's Lot.*

MM: That was another positive experience, meeting with all those actors who I'd never have met otherwise. We have a short history in American theater and film. It's not a long one. The list of important actors is not long, and to meet some of them is exciting. It's exciting to know that I've met them and worked with them. I've met and chatted with them. They're a part of my *soul.*

TW: Have you seen *Wicked Stepmother*?

MM: I've heard so many horror stories about it. Larry wanted me to do it. I said, "No." I knew the film was headed for disaster. There was no way Bette Davis and Larry would have gotten along. The chemistry was untenable. But, ironically, the fact that she fell prey to him. You do sense there's something beneath it. He's a seducer. But there's something authentic and that's what's seductive. There's an authentic artist there in the midst of the chaos.

TW: In *Blood Link*, you played identical twins.

MM: And the hardest one was the good guy.

TW: Yes.

MM: It always is. That's why I find myself, at this point in my career, trying to define what goodness is. It's the hardest thing to define, but I found it in Ben Stone of *Law and Order*. He makes a lot of mistakes. In fact, mistakes are part of goodness. Making mistakes and apologizing for them is a part of human goodness. We're not gods, but humans. I've learned that with Stone. But I hadn't when I did *Blood Link* or I would have asked that my character make more mistakes in his effort to find out, rather than be so cunning. I'd have made him reach and leap, even hurt someone, then apologize, thrusting to find out this awful thing. I'd have made him more upset. But the essence of his thrust would have been goodness in being part of the solution, not part of the problem.

This is an interesting replay of memories for me, as I haven't thought of any of this *for years.* I haven't seen Larry since 1987.

I'm going to give you a plug. We should really have put it at the beginning of the interview. It's important that the book be written about Larry for a lot of reasons, because of what he has achieved. Despite my reservations, he's extraordinary and very special. The satire and insights in his films are worth looking at again, and again, and again.

# James 16 Dixon
# on Cohen

A Larry Cohen film is often not just identifiable by style and theme, but also by the presence of certain key actors. James Dixon is one such figure. He has collaborated with Larry Cohen since *Black Caesar* in various capacities as actor, co-producer, and co-scenarist. Their friendship extends over 30 years. As an actor, Dixon is most immediately recognizable as the sympathetic Lt. Perkins in *It's Alive*, a role he repeated in the two other sequels. This interview was conducted in 1994.

TW: When did you first meet Larry Cohen?

JD: I first met Larry Cohen in the Army in 1960. I'd been working for the Dramatist Guild in New York City. Every week I'd receive a copy of the weekly *Variety*. In those days, the Army had an official mail call and everybody had to wait around for the mail clerk, just as in *Stalag 17*. When Larry Cohen saw me getting *Variety* every week, he'd come around me: "Where's the *Variety*? Has *Variety* arrived yet?" Anyway, we both went through the service. Before that, Larry had worked in television. I met him again in Hollywood later in the '60s, and he began casting me in several shows. The first television show was "Blue Light" starring Robert Goulet. Larry was the writer and script supervisor on the show. I'd often see him around Hollywood. We used to hang out together until the early seventies. One day I got a phone call from him in New York — I was out in California at the time — and Larry was about to start a picture the next day with Fred Williamson. He wanted me to come to New York and play a cop. He said, "And, oh, by the way, before you come, go over to Western Costumes and pick out six cop uniforms. Make sure one fits you." So, the next day, I'm in New York City, in front of Tiffanys on Fifty-Seventh and Fifth Avenue in my police uniform directing traffic in the middle of the street. I hadn't read the script at that time. I was simply posing as a New York policeman directing traffic. So Fred Williamson came out of Tiffanys and walked towards me. As he approached the middle of the street (this was lunch hour), I suddenly walked up to him, pulled a gun out of my authentic New York Police Western Costume, and shot Fred in the stomach. Fred grabs his stomach, hits the blood bag, and blood spurts all over the street. So the crowd is going crazy, looking at me shooting Fred Williamson who is now staggering across Fifth Avenue with blood spurting out of him. I disappear into the crowd, and chaos ensues. But, of course, out of a second-story window is Larry Cohen shooting the whole scene with a camera. This was the first shot in *Black Caesar*. For the next three weeks, we shot in a similar fashion all over New York. We had two taxicabs. One contained equipment. The other was for Fred Williamson, myself, and whoever else was in the scene. We went around New York, virtually stealing every scene. We just set up the camera and started shooting. Williamson was terrific. He never complained and often changed, like the rest of us, in a cab.

Another time, we shot the scene of Fred Williamson getting away in a cab while I was chasing it. It was going down the street. I had my gun out when a real New York police car appeared around the corner. When the real cops saw this, our cab driver panicked and stopped. The policemen jumped out of their car, with guns drawn. I didn't know if they were going to shoot. Nor did I realize I had my rented policeman's uniform on. So I dived into the cab and Fred Williamson is in there trying to get underneath me because he knew they were not going to shoot me. They're going to shoot Fred Williamson! When this happened, everybody on the crew (there were not too many) scattered, except for Larry Cohen. He was screaming at the cameraman, trying to make him capture the action — "Get it! Shoot it! Shoot it! Did you get it?"

TW: You never worked on *Bone*?

JD: *Bone* was shot before *Black Caesar*. At the time, I was in New York. I used to continually travel back and forth from California, doing a lot of commercials. *Black Caesar* was really the first film I made with Larry Cohen. I also worked behind the scenes in every film I did with him. Whatever was to be done was done. We worked very closely together on things like finding actors and locations.

TW: Did you find it difficult combining the roles of associate producer and actor in the films?

JD: No. On every Larry Cohen film I worked on, I never thought of doing anything else but being an actor and working behind the scenes, and doing whatever had to be done. So we'd go to one location, and if we couldn't work, that is, if anybody stopped us, we would just go on to another. Larry always used to be thinking things out as we went along, changing the scene if we had to. He loved it. He couldn't stand the fact of just being stuck in one location for more than two days. He wants to roam around with the camera. That's what he does. He loves New York. That's why so many of his pictures are shot there. He has a thorough knowledge of New York. He knows the city very well. Larry just wants to keep going and going and moving on to the next location.

TW: Was footage from *Black Caesar* used in the credit sequences of *Hell Up in Harlem*?

JD: There were some additional scenes shot, also. I was very inexperienced at the time. I didn't know that you should really not die in a Larry Cohen film, especially when there's always the possibility of a sequel! Fred Williamson killed me in *Black Caesar*.

But I couldn't stay dead because Larry needed me for the next film. He put flashbacks in *Hell Up in Harlem*, so I lived again! One of the scenes was shot in the same style as *Black Caesar*. I was sitting in the little park in Times Square. I think it's called Father Duffy Park — that little triangular park in the middle of Times Square. Fred Williamson comes up behind and kills me. The crowd, thinking it's real, goes crazy again. Nobody knows what's going on. So I did more work in the sequel.

TW: Janelle told me you shot *Hell Up in Harlem* about the same time you worked on *It's Alive*.

JD: We used to shoot on the same day. I appeared in both films. Some days we'd shoot *It's Alive* in the morning and *Hell Up in Harlem* in the afternoon. I remember we used a location in North Hollywood, which was a little hospital off of Victory Boulevard. But it wasn't functioning as a hospital anymore. It operated as a drying-out place, an alcoholic recovery unit. We'd run right through the wards. All these people would be lying in bed with D.T.'s. They'd see us running through in the morning, filming *It's Alive*, and, the next thing they knew, we'd be running through shooting *Hell Up in Harlem*. I'd be in my New York police uniform with all these black guys chasing me or me chasing them. The drunks in their beds didn't know what the hell was going on, especially when, later on, I would be back, this time in my Lt. Perkins outfit, chasing the baby monster from *It's Alive*.

TW: Larry usually casts you as a cop in his films.

JD: Well, who looks more like a cop, especially an Irish cop, than me? So, I was always the cop in these pictures. In *God Told Me To*, all the cops marched in the St. Patrick's Day Parade in New York. I was running through all these cops, chasing Andy Kaufman who played the police assassin in the film. I grew up in New York and knew many of the cops marching in the parade that day. They'd stop, look, and start yelling at me, "Hey Dixon! What the hell are you doing here?" I'd been in high school with many of these guys, so I'd stop, talk to them, and bring them over to me as if they were actually working as extras in the movie. And, of course, there was Larry Cohen shooting the whole damn thing. So we had same great cop crowd scenes in *God Told Me To*.

TW: Michael Moriarty describes this as "guerrilla film making."

JD: Yeah. That's exactly what we did, taking advantage of locations and events, especially cops marching in the St. Patrick Day's Parade.

TW: Did you also work behind the scenes on this film?

JD: Yeah. That was another example of the things we did. Larry found Andy Kaufman doing a standup routine at the Improv in New York. Andy was very nervous at the time, during the scene. But he was quite good. He was always telling those terrible jokes, which he made up as we went along.

TW: You appear as Riley in *The Private Files of J. Edgar Hoover* in one scene.
JD: I wasn't around for that picture. The scenes I appeared in were shot later on. They were shooting in Washington, D.C., but I was in New York at the time, doing commercials. Later, Larry shot some scenes which were supposed to take place in 1920s Washington in downtown L.A.

TW: Do you think Larry was ahead of his time in making this film, especially in the light of recent revelations about Hoover?

JD: Larry was always fascinated by J. Edgar Hoover and that period of history, especially the McCarthy era. Larry always went around doing imitations of the McCarthy hearings. I guess many of us were kids at the time in New York when they televised it. This was one of the first live television broadcasts. Joseph N. Welch presided over the hearings. Larry would do impersonations of McCarthy and Welch. He was always talking about "J. Edgar Hoover" (imitation drawl). A lot of the things in *The Private Files of J. Edgar Hoover* are now acknowledged, so it was ahead of its time. If that picture were made now, it would resemble something like Oliver Stone's *JFK*, particularly in its parallels of what actually happened at that time, why Nixon did what he did in Watergate, and how Hoover had tapes on everybody, especially Nixon, and Nixon knew it. This was probably the reason why Nixon did not destroy his tapes.

TW: In *It Lives Again*, you reappear as Lt. Perkins. Why did Larry decide to make a sequel?

JD: *It's Alive* was a big hit for Warner Bros., so they were very happy to do a sequel. We shot most of it in L.A., with a few scenes in Arizona.

TW: You then worked on *Full Moon High*.

JD: We shot much of it in an old house in Burbank during one of the hottest summers that year. Ed McMahon was in it, young Arkin, and Alan Arkin. We also shot quite a lot of the picture in New Jersey. It was one of Larry's rare attempts at making a full-blooded comedy. *Full Moon High* was a very funny picture. Bill Kirchenbauer was also in it. He had his own television show after that.

TW: Michael Moriarty told me Larry should do a straightforward comedy.

JD: Well, of course, he should. But Larry does comedy all the time. He should do as many comedies as he can.

TW: Would you describe the making of *Q* as being one example of Larry's "guerrilla filmmaking" activities?

JD: Yes, absolutely! We had planes flying over New York City, with people shooting at them from the tower of the Chrysler Building. The New York police were called in. They were informed that a terrorist situation was happening on top of the Chrysler Building and shut us down. But we were back shooting the next day, so there was no problem and everything was fine.

TW: I see you are credited as acting and co-producing on *The Stuff*.

JD: Yes. *The Stuff* was shot in a little town, Kingston, about a hundred miles north of New York City. We also shot that during a very hot summer. I remember that it was so hot during the daytime that we had to change scenes from day to night. We took over the entire town, using them as extras for the big scenes in the picture, and closed down all the streets. We also shot some of it in Manhattan, using Danny Aiello in some of those scenes. Paul Sorvino and Garrett Morris also acted in the film.

TW: You appeared for the third time as Lt. Perkins in *It's Alive III: Island of the Alive*. What do you remember most about this film?

JD: It was mostly shot in Hawaii. In one scene, we shot in a rain forest on Kauai. It was entirely in the middle of nowhere. We had Art Lund, who played Joey in the original production of *The Most Happy Fella*. He also appeared in *Black Caesar*. He played a professor, and we had to tie him up in a tree. All of a sudden, there was a flash flood in the little valley we were shooting in. Everybody forgot about Art Lund. We all took off, leaving Art Lund up on the tree. After the flash flood, we returned and got Art Lund down. Everything cleared up and we started shooting again. Then, all of a sudden, a wild boar entered the scene. So everybody takes off, except for Larry, of course, who's screaming at the cameraman, "Did you get it? Did you get it?" Naturally, the cameraman is long gone, hiding in the forest somewhere and, of course, nobody knew if there were any more boars around, so that shut us down for a little bit. Then we started shooting again.

TW: Michael Moriarty told me an amusing story about the boat sequence.

JD: We didn't know anything about boats, and the one we hired had a cement bottom. So it was rolling around, going all over the place. Everybody was throwing up over the sides, and Larry was running around, giving lines to everybody because they were too sick to read their scripts and learn the lines. This was shot off the coast of Hawaii. Michael Moriarty was great in the scene. I don't know how far we were from the shore, but it seemed like we were in the middle of nowhere. So what does Michael do? Just like the script calls for—he jumps off the boat, right into the middle of the ocean. He's swimming around out there like he's in a backyard pool.

TW: I see you worked on the script of *A Return to Salem's Lot*. Did you use Larry's original screenplay for *Salem's Lot*?

JD: No. It was an original story by Larry Cohen. Since I used to live in New England, I worked on the screenplay. We were familiar with Stephen King's book, but *A Return to Salem's Lot* had nothing to do with it, except for using the same town and the theme of a vampire community.

TW: What was it like working with Samuel Fuller?

JD: He's a great guy. He had more energy than the rest of the entire cast. Fuller was unbelievable, running around with those cigars. I didn't think he could have been as good as he was. He's a damn good actor. I'd don't know if he started as one, but he certainly knew what he was doing.

TW: You appear as a policeman, Clancy, in *Maniac Cop*. Was Larry going to direct this film?

JD: No. It was directed by Bill Lustig. It was a deal that was set up a long time before I knew anything about it. I was only around for a couple of days, filming my scenes. Clancy returns as a different cop in *Maniac Cop 2*. Larry wasn't there on the days I was present. I think he left Lustig to his own devices.

TW: You appear as "Jughead" in *The Ambulance*. I think it is one of Larry's best films.

JD: It's actually a very good film. The problem had to do with the company behind it. They didn't do enough to really release it properly. But it's out now. *The Ambulance* is a really good picture. Eric Roberts is terrific in it.

TW: You've known Larry a long time. How would you sum up his place in American cinema?

JD: Every time you see Larry Cohen, he's got a new idea. He really should run his own studio. He has so many ideas that, if he ever got into that position, he could be making his kind of movies all the time.

# Cohen on
# Guerrilla Filmmaking

"Guerrilla filmmaking" is a term used by Michael Moriarty and other Larco collaborators to describe Larry Cohen's method of making films. As a low-budget independent director, Cohen's style and manner of production is certainly different from that of mainstream Hollywood and most examples of independent cinema. His practices are full of the radical, iconoclastic risk-taking features present in his completed films. During the seventies, the Canadian journal *Take One* published an influential article about a low-budget independent horror film, *Cannibal Girls*, made entirely on credit. When the actual film made the distribution circuits in both American and Britain, the disappointing final product certainly contradicted the enthusiastic feature applauding its production merits. The methods used to finance and make *Cannibal Girls* appeared unique — at least until Larry Cohen furnished the following information. This interview examines a particular mode of independent filmmaking practice associated with a group of films far more exciting and innovative than *Cannibal Girls*.

The following material was supplied by Larry Cohen during November 1994:

The majority of films made by Larco productions did not follow the usual techniques of picture making. Since I was in total control of the film, I was in the unique position of doing what I pleased without consulting production managers or studio executives. Many of my films were financed on a negative pickup basis. American International or any other backer usually advanced me a small proportion of the film's budget. I then obtained credit from laboratories, film equipment houses such as Panavision, and other vendors with contracts which did not require payment for seven months. This would give me time to make the picture, deliver it, receive payment from the distributor, and pay my bills. Therefore I did not require a completion guarantee. A completion guarantor usually has to check every element of the budget because he guarantees to pay the difference if the film goes over budget. In my case, I was responsible for overages. So, in effect, I was only responsible to myself.

Usually a film has a production board listing every day of the shoot, the actors appearing in the scenes, props, and other items. But I didn't make any of these production boards on my first dozen movies. I carried all that information around in my head. I'd written the script, knew the story, and the changes I intended to make. If any different factors came up, I'd be able to work them into the script somehow, and keep on shooting. For example, if it rained, I wouldn't go home. I would simply improvise the story around the rain so it would work for us rather than against us. For some reason, I was very secretive about when I was going to shoot. The director of photography and other key personnel were always asking me to plan ahead. But, somehow, I wanted to keep the control in my own pocket and the best way to do this was to have nobody else know what was going to happen next. Making these movies was almost a mystical experience because everything could have gone wrong, but nothing ever did. Fate always worked to my advantage.

When we were shooting *God Told Me To*, I wrote a sniper sequence in which a young man fired a rifle from the top of a water tower in downtown Manhattan. We hauled the camera up and hoisted the actor into place. Everything was set to go, when the prop person arrived and told me he'd been unable to get a telescopic rifle. Without the rifle there was no scene. We were on a rooftop and many of the tenants in the building had come upstairs to watch the filming process. I turned to this crowd of people and said, "Who's got a telescopic rifle?" Unbelievable as it seems, one man raised his hand. He rushed downstairs to his apartment and returned with the rifle. Then I proceeded to shoot the scene. The stunt double who was going to take a dive off the water tower had never actually done a fall before. He wanted to be a stunt man and I gave him the chance. I even made him do the stunt twice. I suppose it could have been a disaster, but we did have professional stunt men setting up the cardboard cartons which would break his fall. So everything went off without a hitch. A few days later, I filmed down on the streets of Third Avenue, in front of Bloomingdales Department Store where people were supposed to be shot and fall to the sidewalk as victims of the sniper. I started out with a few principals and a couple of extras, even doing one of the falls to the sidewalk myself. But as more and more people gathered to watch, I suddenly got the idea that they might like to participate. I asked, "Who wants to fall down?" I soon had quite a number of volunteers. There were hundreds of spectators now, and those who didn't want to fall certainly wanted to run away from the sniper's bullets. So I organized them into different groups, depending on whether they fell or ran away from the barrage of bullets. I sent one of the cameramen up to the roof to get an overhead shot of this organized chaos. An attractive young woman showed up and identified herself as being from the Department of Labor. She told me that I could not use all those people on my movie without paying them. So I took her to lunch and we continued filming. The guy who played the sniper was Sammy Williams. He won the Tony Award for the Best Actor in Broadway for his role in *A Chorus Line*. To my knowledge this was his only motion picture appearance. He was a courageous fellow, going up on that water tower. Tony Lo Bianco was much more frightened up there.

In all of my pictures, I always try to enhance what was already in the script and make the picture bigger and better. If I cut out something, I always replaced it with a more spectacular scene. When I wrote the script for *Q— The Winged Serpent*, I did not write it especially for the Chrysler Building because I was afraid that I might not be able to deliver this particular location. In fact, the Chrysler Building management refused us four or five times. I kept sending my production assistant back, and finally paid them about eighteen thousand, five hundred dollars to use the building in the movie, because it was a perfect location since its feathered structure is bird-like. It also had gargoyles of birds jutting out on all sides. The Chrysler Building was an ideal spot for a giant "Q" to choose for its nest. We could never have afforded to build the pinnacle of the Chrysler Building, so we had to shoot in the actual location. That meant hoisting all the cameras, equipment, and lights, etc., straight up the tower. The actors had to climb up a very precarious series of metal ladders. But the Chrysler Building management thought we were going to shoot on a lower level. When they discovered that we were climbing higher into the needle of the building, they demanded additional insurance. Fortunately, our insurance agent rushed to the location and wrote the policy on the set, so we could continue filming. David Carradine actually climbed into the very tip of the needle. It was only wide enough for one person to navigate. He fired his machine gun off from there and the helicopter cameras came as close as possible to get shots of him in action. Apparently, hundreds of people down below in the streets heard the machine-gun fire, and some of them thought an assassination was actually taking place. The *New York Daily News* is only a few blocks away, and they sent over reporters. They featured us in a front-page story with the headline, "Hollywood Movie Company Terrorizes New York." But the fact was that nobody down in the street reacted in terror. I know that for certain, because I sent a cameraman down there to film any interesting crowd reactions that I might be able to reincorporate into the film. But New Yorkers are so blasé, so they just continued on their way, even though they heard machine-gun fire and saw a helicopter circling the pinnacle. The story was completely exaggerated in the press. Other newspapers printed it and, finally, the Commissioner of Motion Pictures for New York had to issue a public apology. Of course, we did have a permit to do all this, and the people firing machine guns were off-duty New York police officers. But I kept my mouth shut and let the Film Commission lay the blame on me, because I needed their cooperation to complete the film. Actually, the shells from the automatic weapons fired off the top of the building were falling down towards the street. But construction was in progress and there were protective canopies built so the shells fell into them and never came near anyone on the sidewalks below.

Shooting up on top of the Chrysler Building was a precarious situation, to say the least. I had a stunt man whose job it was to follow me around all day and make sure I did not fall off the Chrysler Building. He always stood directly behind me. There were no guardrails up there. It was like a platform with huge V-shaped vents perched some eighty-five floors above the street. If I stepped back too far, I'd simply fall off the building. One night when we were shooting late, the set was suddenly plunged into darkness. The power failed before we could evacuate anyone. Michael Moriarty, myself, and the entire crew were trapped there in pitch blackness. The city looked absolutely dazzling all around us. I shouted that everyone should remain frozen in their positions until the lights came back. So we all stood there for about fifteen minutes. Mercifully, the lights came on and we were able to descend.

I believe we even had a pigeon wrangler with us that day. Since we needed pigeons in the film, we had to hire a professional pigeon man to bring his birds to the top of the building. The needle in the Chrysler Building was too narrow to accommodate the giant bird's nest and egg, so that part of the film was shot in the dome of the abandoned old New York Police Headquarters in Lower Manhattan's Little Italy. After we concluded filming, I told everybody to strike the set. They removed all the lights, cables, other equipment, and the egg. But I suppose someone was too lazy to remove the nest itself. It had to be built by hand and it was probably too unwieldy to get down. At the time, the building was empty except for rats and a few guard dogs. Some years later, they began a renovation project to turn it into expensive condominiums. A story then appeared on the front page of the *New York Times* about anthropologists flying to New York to examine a huge nest that had been discovered on top of the old police headquarters building. It was assumed that some large animal had built this nest. Apparently, the nest had been there for years, and nobody had ventured up and discovered it until workmen came upon it and freaked out. I couldn't have written a more amazing coda to the making of the film.

Once again, I never used a production schedule or board during the making of *Q*. I simply carried ideas around in my pocket every day and told the crew where we would shoot tomorrow. In order to carry something off like this, you have to have the complete confidence of the actors. If they are supportive, you don't have to worry because the crew usually follows suit. They assume you know what you are doing. You have to assume that yourself.

When I made *The Private Files of J. Edgar Hoover*, I arrived in Washington, D.C., with little hope of getting official cooperation. At first, everyone turned me down. I knew I would have to revise the schedule in my head every day to accommodate whatever locations might become available. The entire crew for the film was probably less than a dozen people. Sometimes we would put the actors into a huge limousine and form a procession of cars, with the camera equipment truck and other cast members following behind. We would drive around until we could find some place where we could shoot. I went to Clyde Tolson's apartment building, buzzed the people who were now living there, and asked if we could come up and shoot. A few moments later, we were actually there shooting the film. Later, we arrived at J. Edgar Hoover's home and startled the maid. She never asked if we had permission. Since Broderick Crawford, Dan Dailey, José

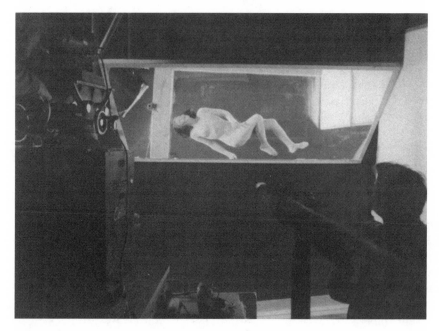

This studio shot from *God Told Me To* reveals behind-the-scenes information showing how a female becomes suspended in air by the invisible rays from the alien spaceship.

Ferrer, and Rip Torn accompanied us, people assumed we had permission to
shoot and did not question us. The day we shot outside Hoover's home. Broderick Crawford and Dan Dailey came out the door and paused on the lawn while
delivering their dialogue. The neighbor from across the street, who had just
recovered from a heart attack, came out and saw two dead men alive again standing in front of Hoover's house. From where he stood, it looked like Hoover and
Tolson had returned from the grave. The poor gentleman suffered a mild heart
seizure and an ambulance was called.

When Betty Ford invited Broderick Crawford and Dan Dailey to dinner, I
used this opportunity to call government agencies and ask for permission to shoot
that week. I dropped the fact that the stars of my film were dining at the White
House that day with President Gerald Ford. This resulted in allowing me permission to shoot in the courtyard of the Justice Building over a holiday weekend. Originally, we were only permitted to shoot entrances and exits to and from
the building. But nobody was around that weekend. The FBI agent who super-
vised us was a very pleasant chap named T. Carson. He was one of the few black
FBI agents at the time. The bureau had been receiving constant criticisms for not
having any black agents, so, I suppose, they put this gentleman in a very visible
position for public relations reasons. T. Carson was also a very accomplished jazz
pianist who often sat in with Count Basie's orchestra and often took over for him

when Basie became ill. Soon after my acquaintance with him began, T. Carson resigned from the FBI. But his presence on that day was a blessing. Since the instructions from the FBI supervisors were vague, we soon found ourselves shooting in the FBI corridors. Eventually, we filmed in what used to be Hoover's office. We began moving deeper and deeper into the FBI headquarters. Finally, we filmed inside the Attorney General's private conference room. When the Attorney General, Levi, returned on the following Tuesday and found out where I'd filmed, he had a fit. He sent me a letter forbidding me to use the material filmed in his office. But he relented and mailed me a second letter giving me permission. Fortunately, his second letter arrived first.

In *The Private Files of J. Edgar Hoover*, I covered fifty years in a man's life without using a production schedule or board. Janelle did a fabulous job in providing support and got me everything I needed. I'd brought down a truckload of costumes, but she augmented them with garments she picked up at thrift shops and antique stores. Some we bought. Others we borrowed. I couldn't afford to hire vintage cars and many extras, so I contacted antique automobile clubs in Maryland. Huge numbers showed up in full costume, driving their period cars. They even brought their families along, all outfitted in the period of the antique cars they were driving. I must have had forty old cars going down Pennsylvania Avenue, simulating the late 1920s. Again, I never obtained permission to shoot this. I found some wooden barricades on the street corners of Pennsylvania Avenue, which the police used to hold back crowds whenever dignitaries were passing by. I instructed the crew members to use them to close down the street. I simply decided to close down Pennsylvania Avenue to all traffic other than my antique vehicles. Police came by and waved to us. They must have assumed I had permission to do all this. Who else would do something as insane as close down a public thoroughfare in the nation's capital? I even had people pull down the no parking signs and remove them from the sidewalks. They wouldn't have been appropriate for the period. Later, I ordered people to go into the Justice Department Building and remove air conditioners from the first floor windows. There were no air conditioners in the old days. It was the middle of summer and stiflingly hot. I saw the air conditioners suddenly disappear. For no apparent reason, everyone complied with my wishes. I find that when you are making a movie, people will do almost anything you ask them or *tell* them to.

When I made *A Return to Salem's Lot* in Peachum, Vermont, the inhabitants virtually gave us the entire town. I disrupted normal activities for several weeks. Since the film was about vampires, I shot late into the night and recruited the townspeople to be extras and their children to play young vampires. Parents had to keep their children up all night long, and we generally served dinner at five or six in the morning. Everything was topsy turvy. We felt like vampires ourselves. The townspeople later said, "We were very happy when you came and we will be very happy when you leave!" I shot the schoolroom sequence, where the vampire children learn about vampire history and philosophy, at four A.M. All the children slept in sleeping bags on the floor of an abandoned church. Then the parents

woke them up and brought them into the schoolhouse for the scene. The children were all bleary-eyed and appropriately vampire-like for that sequence.

Samuel Fuller played the old vampire hunter in the film. During certain of
his sequences, I fired several sound technicians, blaming them for crackling sounds
on our radio microphones. Then I discovered the real reason. Sam had cellophane-
wrapped cigars inside his coat pockets! He did not want to leave them in his hotel
room so brought them with him. I couldn't believe that the man who had directed
some twenty films could be so absent-minded.

In most of my films, I've been required to climb to the top of something.
Like many people, I have a fear of heights. Yet as far back as *Daddy's Gone A-Hunting*, I had to climb to the top of the Mark Hopkins Hotel in San Francisco and
scale the roof above the Top of the Mark restaurant, scouting the location for a
climactic chase scene. When I wrote *El Condor*, I had to climb to the top of a
half-constructed fortress built in Almeria, Spain. In *God Told Me To*, I climbed
up a water tower, and, of course, in *Q*, I had to scale the heights of the Chrysler
Building. When you are directing a picture, you can show no fear. When I asked
Fred Williamson to climb a narrow metal ladder to the top of the Sony sign over
Times Square, with a high-powered rifle slung over his shoulder, it was no surprise when Fred turned to me and said, "Cohen, *You* do it first!" So I climbed to
the top of the sign high above Times Square. Once I'd done it, Fred could hardly
refuse. Next, a stalwart young cameraman, James Signorelli (who had an amazing amount of physical strength), scaled the ladder. When he was halfway up, a
lens slipped, but Jim pushed his body against it, holding it against the ladder so
it wouldn't fall. He cried for help, so I had to climb up again until I could reach
him and pluck the lens to safety. This was a very valuable lens, and if it had fallen
it would have cost me a thousand dollars deductible from the insurance. So it
was worth the climb.

Perching above Times Square with a high-powered rifle in his hands was
dangerous for Fred, since a police helicopter patrol could certainly have mistaken
him for a real-life sniper. Fortunately, no police helicopters came along. When
Fred ran down the streets of New York, wounded and bloody, during the climactic
scenes of *Black Caesar*, he was chased by a policeman. We were tracking him with
a hand-held camera. Fred was running. The cop was running. And I was running, waving my arms and screaming, "It's only a movie!"

When I shot a scene in a coal yard for *Hell Up in Harlem*, I noticed a huge
piece of equipment used to scoop up coal, and suggested that we use it to attack
Fred, scoop him up, and bury him in a huge pile of coal. Once again Fred said,
"*You* do it first." So I allowed myself to be scooped up and buried. Once I managed to climb up from under the coal, I was as black as Fred Williamson. We
took a picture together.

My movies involve taking all kinds of chances. When I directed *The Private
Files of J. Edgar Hoover*, the cast insurance company refused to supply coverage
for Dan Dailey. I realized that if Dan was refused insurance, we would never be
able to work in this or any other film. So I went back to the insurance company

After rehearsing a scene for Fred Williamson's benefit on the set of *Hell Up in Harlem*, Larry Cohen emerges from a coal tip with a darker complexion than his leading actor! Williamson appears not pleased at the fact that he will now have to perform the same scene (courtesy of Larry Cohen).

and canceled cast insurance for *everybody*. That way, Dan's application would be torn up and there would be no record of his having been refused insurance. But in so doing, I exposed myself to risks, since we had so many old actors in the film. If Broderick Crawford, Dan Dailey, Lloyd Nolan, or any of the other elderly actors had died or become incapacitated, I could have been in a great deal of trouble. But, as it was, one of the younger members of the cast died tragically. Jack Cassidy, who played Damon Runyon, completed his scenes at the Copacabana nightclub in New York, which was supposed to be the Stork Club. We had purchased a number of ashtrays marked with the Stork Club insignia and placed them on tables. Jack returned after finishing his day's shooting and asked me if he could possibly have one of those Stork Club ashtrays as a souvenir. I ran and got one for him. That was the last I saw of him. A few days later, he burned to death in his Los Angeles apartment. Apparently, a cigarette fell on the couch where he slept. I couldn't help but think about that ashtray... In making *Perfect Strangers*, I staged a scene on Delancey Street in New York, in which the husband runs off with the child and Anne Carlisle pursues him. She's screaming at him to give her child back. Naturally, the cameras were hidden. A huge mob formed around the poor actor. People actually wanted to beat him up. I was mixed in the crowd with them — to protect the actor. But things were looking nasty. Finally, I shoved the actor myself, and he returned the kid to Anne — and the crowd dispersed. It looked real because it was.

Making my films involved an act of *supreme willpower* because often they were not fully financed before I started shooting. I'd just make up my mind that the picture would be shot and go into production, laying out my own money. I recall that I shot the St. Patrick's Day Parade before I raised the money to make *God Told Me To.* I'd seen Andy Kaufman appear at the Improvisation Club in New York and thought he had a brilliant talent. I told him I wanted to be the first to put him in a movie and that he should report for duty at the St. Patrick's Day Parade. I also asked him for his sizes for the police uniform he'd wear. Andy didn't know what size shirt, jacket, or pants he wore. I couldn't believe that an adult person didn't know his clothing sizes, but Andy assured me he always wore his father's old "hand me downs." I also asked what he did all day. He replied he slept and only awoke in time to go down to the comedy club and do his act. I didn't have any sound recording equipment available during the St. Patrick's Day's Parade, so Andy never really spoke the lines "God told me to." I dubbed my voice in later. But, for many years afterwards, Andy claimed it was his voice. I told him we didn't have any sound equipment that day, and he knew it. However, Andy still insisted it had to be his voice because he recognized it. I had the same situation with Tony Lo Bianco who claimed he appeared in many of the scenes that were actually filmed with his double. To this day, Tony will swear he recalls shooting the sequence himself. I guess that's the best tribute any film director could get, when his own actors have been fooled into believing something happened, which never did.

I think that's the greatest thrill in being a director, of taking a few strips of film and linking them together in such a way that you create an event that never actually occurred. It's perfectly all right to blow up a building. All that costs is money and technicians who are familiar with explosives. Anybody can do that. But to create a complex sequence out of nothing is an achievement. We shot the St. Patrick's Day Parade as it was actually taking place. The parade was not going to stop for us, so three camera units had to move along with the marchers on Fifth Avenue, and keep ahead of the parade. They would stop, shoot the parade as it went past, and would have to double time it ahead to be in front of the parade for the next shot. Andy Kaufman had infiltrated the parade, dressed as a policeman. We had a few other extras posing as cops, and some of our principal actors playing detectives running through the parade, looking for the assassin who was going to open fire any minute. We shot the sequence within the actual parade itself, without any police or city permit, surrounded by cops. The person on the grandstand who gets shot in the head at the beginning of the burst of gunfire is me. The police were rather good-natured about us running around doing our scene in their midst.

But, of course, to make it really work, we had to restage the St. Patrick's Day Parade in downtown Los Angeles some months later. I did this by contacting

"Back to where we both started from!" Larry Cohen and James Earl Jones share a joke when both lie in the gutter while filming *The Ambulance* (courtesy of Larry Cohen).

various Irish-American organizations with marching bands, drum and bugle corps, etc. All of these people loved to march, but they only got to do it on St. Patrick's Day. I gave them the opportunity to live St. Patrick's Day all over again. They all showed up in buses at their own expense, with musical instruments, costumes, and bringing their families along as free extras. Then we re-created the parade, complete with all the blood squibs, blanks being fired, and stunt men doing falls. We cut the New York and Los Angeles footage together, creating the effect of one continuous sequence. If I had made a big-budget picture, I suppose I could have shot the entire scene once by using hundreds and hundreds of extras. But it was more of an achievement for me to have finessed the entire sequence for virtually no money in two different places that appear to be the same location.

Many years later, when I shot *The Ambulance*, I edited the film together and decided the villain was not good enough. He was played by Wesley Addy, a very competent character actor but an elderly man without sufficient menace. I prevailed upon the production company to grant me one day of additional photography to replace the villain of the piece. My mother is an avid soap-opera fan and she recommended Eric Braeden who is a big daytime soap star and a very fine actor. He was hired to play the diabolical doctor who performs the surgeries

Whenever the right circumstances arise, Larry Cohen is eager both to direct as well as write his next film.

and appears in many scenes throughout the picture. The trick was to shoot all the sequences in that one day. We put Braeden inside the ambulance as the driver. Instead of just an ambulance with some phantom driving inside was now a villainous identifiable person, someone to hate. We re-shot the scene between Red Buttons and the villain, and created a new scene with Janine Turner and Braeden. A number of insert shots were added. By the end of a ten-hour day, we had completed our task and created the illusion that Eric Braeden is present throughout the entire film. The picture previewed much better once we'd done this trick. It's an important lesson that a movie is only as good as the villain. I had made a mistake in this regard when I directed *The Stuff*. I took a youngster to see the picture. He was sitting on my lap and, halfway through, he turned and said to me, "Who's the bad guy?" It was only then I realized that I had neglected to give the audience an identifiable villain to fear and hate. The reviews for *The Stuff* were excellent, but it never performed as well at the box office as it should have.

Incidentally, in directing *The Stuff*, I'd searched for a long time for the proper material to make the stuff from. It was supposed to be a yogurt-like dessert which has run amok. I had to fill an entire room with this substance, and shot in upstate New York in the heat of the summer. We all wore bandannas soaked in ice water around our foreheads to keep from passing out. I'd taken over an old factory, which was going to be flooded with the type of white foam utilized by fire departments to put out blazes. It was made from ground up fish bones. You can imagine the smell. We were near the upper reaches of the Hudson River. When the actors emerged covered with this goo, they were nearly overcome by the heat, so ran out and threw themselves into the river.

Paul Sorvino was a delight in this picture. He sang opera for us every day during meal breaks. Danny Aiello consented to play a brief role in the film and reported for work the next day, only to find he had eight pages of dialogue to learn. I convinced him he could do it with no trouble and, lo and behold, Danny did his lines properly on the first take, and I got the master shot with no problem at all. Then Danny became convinced he needed cue cards for the close-ups. But, once we put them up, he became distracted and couldn't remember anything. I should never have allowed him to use cue cards, because I find that professional actors have a remarkable ability to learn lines quickly, particularly when you write them out by hand. I often take a pen or magic marker, write several pages of new dialogue, and hand them to the actor before he does the take. Usually, actors can't believe this is happening to them but, invariably, they know the lines perfectly and do a marvelous job. When you give actors new lines to do, it distracts them. They probably have worked out everything for themselves and, suddenly, they have to deal with a new dimension to the scene or a new piece of business. By adapting to it, a freshness is evident in their performance.

Often, during the middle of a scene, I'll yell something for an actor to say that I've just thought of. In *The Ambulance*, Eric Roberts would come over to me and say, "Give me a Larry Cohen line for this" or "Give me a Larry Cohen line for that." He loved the way I'd come up with some new dialogue or new joke. Red Buttons also thrived in this kind of situation. Most of the actors I've worked with have appeared in hundreds of films and television plays. Very often they are cast in similar roles, such as cop, authority figure, or villain. They could play these parts with their eyes closed. The trick is to get them to do something different. Otherwise they will simply give you an adequate performance. I love it when Michael Moriarty and Yaphet Kotto tell me they have done their best acting work for me. I also enjoy it when actors drop in to see what is happening on the set on days they're not scheduled to work. It's gratifying to see an actor show up, because he's so interested in what's going on that he'll come by on his day off to be part of the proceedings. Naturally, I'm grateful to all the actors who work hard and long hours, and don't put in for their overtime. Rip Torn returned to *The Private Files of J. Edgar Hoover* to do additional work just for taxi fare and meals. Rip Torn and I started off badly on that film. We had a fight on the first day and nearly came to blows. I fired Rip and asked him to check out of the hotel in Washington. He walked away cursing me, only to come back a few minutes later and say, "Let's just make a movie." We shook hands. After that, we were buddies. The night Geraldine Page won an Oscar for *The Trip to Bountiful*, I ran into Rip and Geraldine entering the Academy Governor's Ball Party at the Hilton Hotel. She had her Oscar in her hands, but Rip, characteristically, couldn't find the tickets to the ball, and the security people would not let them in. I protested, "Look, The woman is holding an Academy Award in her hands!" But they wouldn't listen. So I ran inside and got Warren Cowan, a famous publicist, who managed to straighten things out. Rip and Gerry Page were about to go home.

With some actors it's necessary to have a fight, to stand up to them and let them know what the ground rules are. When Eric Roberts and I began *The Ambulance,* we had a terrific fight prior to filming. I told him, "Either you're out of this picture or I am." He cursed me and slammed the door as he exited. I began to empty my desk, figuring that the producers would probably remove me before they replaced him. A moment later, he returned, apologized, and we shook hands. After that Eric would come to me and say, "What do you want me to do today, Boss?" At the end of the day, he'd say, "Thanks for a great day," and give me a kiss on the cheek. Whenever I'd give him a bit of direction, he'd quickly say, "Got it!" and do what I asked. It was a fun working relationship and I think he did an unusually fine job in that picture. My task was to make him more human and likable. Eric Roberts is usually distant. He appears a bit frightening and cold to audiences. I had to warm him up. Finally, he told me, "I'm doing you!" In playing the role, Eric was doing an imitation of me. He was also instrumental in getting me James Earl Jones, who is a wonderful guy. I had the nerve to ask Jones to die, chewing gum. He immediately jumped at it with enthusiasm. "Let's try it!" he exclaimed. James Earl Jones is the kind of actor who'd rather try something than talk about it. He couldn't get over the fact that I had my ex-wife, Janelle,v working on the picture and that we were good friends.

As you can see, I've had a great deal of enjoyment out of making these films. There's always a sense of danger of the unknown. And, yet, you have to proceed with the absolute belief that everything will work out fine — and it has. Isn't that what life is all about?

# Appendix A:
# The Television and
# Film Credits of
# Larry Cohen

The following entries list the screenplay, directing, and story credits of Larry Cohen. They are generally based upon material available for viewing. Inaccessible items and story credits appear in abbreviated form. Due to Cohen's prolific diversity, a complete listing of all his credits presents a difficult bibliographical challenge. Although his work as director is important, it is also fitting that his contributions to television as writer and creator are noted. Asterisks denote video availability.

**"Kraft Mystery Theatre: '87th Precinct'"** (June 25, 1958)
**Credits:** *Director:* Paul Bogart; *Producer:* Alex March; *Writer:* Larry Cohen; based on characters created by Evan Hunter; a Talent Associates Production; *Network:* NBC; *Running Time:* 50 minutes. **Cast:** Robert Bray (Steve Carella), Martin Rudy (Meyer Meyer), Joseph Sullivan (Captain Byrnes), Joan Copeland (Louise Carella), Pat Henning (Keetso), Salome Jens (Rita), Henderson Forsythe (Clavin), William Larson (Austin Ranny), Ellen Ray (Mrs Faye).

**"Kraft Mystery Theatre: 'Night Cry'"** (August 13, 1958)
**Credits:** *Director:* Michael Dreyfuss; *Producer:* Alex March; *Writer:* Larry Cohen; story adapted from the novel by William A. Stuart; broadcast in color; *Network:* NBC; *Running time:* 50 minutes. **Cast:** Jack Klugman (Mark Deglan), Diana Van der Vlis (Morgan Taylor), Martin Roberts (Redfield), Peter Falk (Izzy), Roy Poole (Captain), John McQuade (Riley).

**"United States Steel Hour: 'The Golden Thirty'"** (August 9, 1961)
**Credits:** *Director:* Tom Donovan; *Producer:* the Theatre Guild; *Executive producer:* George Kondolf; *Writer:* Larry Cohen; *Running time:* 50 minutes. **Cast:** Henny Youngman (Buddy Parker), Keir Dullea (David March), Nancy Kovack (Fran Loring), Bibi Osterwald (Mrs. Ross), Don Di Leo (Harry Brock).

**"Way Out: 'False Face'"** (May 26, 1961)
**Credits:** *Director:* Henry Kaplan; *Producer:* Jacqueline Sassin; *Writer:* Larry Cohen; *Running time:* 25 minutes. **Cast:** Alfred Ryder (Michael Drake), Martin Brooks (The Face), Jerry Jedi (Rita Singer), Dana Elcar (Flop House Proprietor).

**"Checkmate: 'Nice Guys Finish Last'"** (December 13, 1961)
**Credits:** *Director:* Alan Crosland, Jr.; *Producer:* Dick Berg; *Writer:* Larry Cohen; *Network:* CBS; alternative version of "Night Cry" modified to fit requirements of a series format; *Running time:* 50 minutes. **Cast:** Anthony George (Don Corey), Sebastian Cabot (Dr. Carl Hyatt), Doug McClure (Jed Sills), James Whitmore (Lt. Dave Harker), Diana Van Der Vlis (Hope Riordan), Dennis Patrick (Nick Culley).

**"The Defenders: 'Kill or Be Killed'"** (January 5, 1963)
**Credits:** *Director:* Sydney Pollack; *Producer:* Robert Markell; *Executive Producer:* Herbert Brodkin; *Writer:* Larry Cohen; *Story Editor:* David Shaw; *Network:* CBS; *Runnign time:* 50 minutes. **Cast:** E. G. Marshall (Lawrence Preston), Robert Reed (Kenneth Preston), Gerald S. O'Laughlin (Bernard Jackman), Joanne Linville (Vera Jackman), Simon Oakland (District Attorney), Joanna Roos (Elsa Lundee).

**"The Nurses: 'Night Sounds'"** (January 24, 1963)
**Credits:** *Director:* Don Richardson; *Producer:* Arthur Lewis; *Executive Producer:* Herbert Brodkin; *Writer:* Larry Cohen; *Story Editor:* Earl Booth; *Network:* CBS; *Running time:* 50 minutes. **Cast:** Shirl Conway (Liz Thorpe), Zina Bethune (Gail Lucas), Donald Davis (Norman Ruskin), Noah Keen (Dr. Furst), Patricia Benoit (Edith Ruskin), Alan Alda (Dr. John Griffin).

**"The Defenders: 'The Traitor'"** (February 16, 1963)
**Credits:** *Director:* David Greene; *Producer:* Robert Markell; *Executive Producer:* Herbert Brodkin; *Writer:* Larry Cohen; *Story Editor:* David Shaw; *Network:* CBS; *Running time:* 50 minutes. **Cast:** E. G. Marshall (Lawrence Preston), Robert Reed (Kenneth Preston), Fritz Weaver (Vincent Kayle), Tom Clancy (Merv Erwin), Howard Weirum (Malcolm Standish), George Hall (Lew Bartlett).

**"Sam Benedict: 'Accomplice'"** (March 9, 1963)
**Credits:** *Director:* Richard Donner; *Producer:* William Froug; *Writer:* Larry Cohen; *Network:* NBC; *Running time:* 50 minutes. **Cast:** Edmond O'Brien (Sam Benedict), Richard Rust (Henry Tabor), Eddie Albert (Lew Wiley), Brock Peters (Frank Elton), Roger Perry (Leonard Pitman), Phillip Pine (District Attorney), Ellen Holly (Melissa Ryan).

**"The Nurses: 'Party Girl'"** (March 28, 1963)
**Credits:** *Director:* Stuart Rosenberg; *Producer:* Herbert Brodkin; *Writer:* Larry Cohen, from a story by Jay Roberts; *Script Editor:* Earl Booth; *Network:* CBS; *Running time:* 50 minutes. **Cast:** Shirl Conway (Liz Thorpe), Zina Bethune (Gail Lucas), Inger Stevens (Clarissa Robin), Inga Swenson (Sandra Leonard), James Broderick (Dr. Tom Milford), Robert Gerringer (Hal Leonard), Tim O'Connor (Bert Handell), Vincent Gardenia (Mervyn Fowler), Arlene Golonka (Ronnie).

**"The Defenders: 'The Colossus'"** (April 13, 1963)
**Credits:** *Director:* Paul Bogart; *Producer:* Robert Markell; *Executive Producer:* Herbert Brodkin; *Writer:* Larry Cohen; *Script Consultant:* William Woolforth; *Network:* CBS; *Running time:* 50 minutes. **Cast:** E. G. Marshall (Lawrence Preston), Robert Reed (Kenneth Preston), Leo Genn (Dr. Morton Cheyney), Joe Mantell (District Attorney), Donald Moffat (Dr. Leo Elm), Frances Reid (Mary Cheyney), Tonio Selwart (Dr. Von Ecker), Jon Voight (Alan Link).

**"The Defenders: 'The Noose'"** (April 27, 1963)
**Credits:** *Director:* Stuart Rosenberg; *Producer:* Robert Markell; *Executive Producer:* Herbert Brodkin; *Writer:* Larry Cohen; *Script Consultant:* William Woolforth; *Network:* CBS; *Running time:* 50 minutes. **Cast:** E. G. Marshall (Lawrence Preston), Robert Reed (Kenneth Preston), Milton Seltzer (Constable Raymond Kimball), Bruce Gordon (Bennet Fletcher), Roy Poole (Lee Sanderson), Rochelle Oliver (Jean Lowell), Larry Hagman (Jim Lewton).

**"The Defenders: 'The Captive'"** (October 12, 1963)
**Credits:** *Director:* Charles S. Dubin; *Producer:* Robert Markell; *Executive Producer:* Herbert Brodkin; *Writer:* Larry Cohen; *Story Editor:* David Shaw; *Network:* CBS; *Running time:* 50 minutes. **Cast:** E. G. Marshall (Lawrence Preston), Robert Reed (Kenneth Preston), Ludwig Donath (I. Vorchek), Andrew Duggan (Franklin Rawlins), Mary Fickett (Joanne Rawlins), Robert Ellenstein (Anton Lazlov), Tim O'Connor (U.S. District Attorney Jim Evans), Dana Elcar (Rankin).

**"Arrest and Trial: 'My Name Is Martin Burnham'"** (October 13, 1963)
**Credits:** *Director:* Ralph Senensky; *Executive Producer:* Frank P. Rosenberg; *Writer:* Larry Cohen; *Network:* NBC; *Running time:* 80 minutes. **Cast:** Ben Gazzara (Sergeant Nick Anderson), Chuck Connors (John Egan), John Larch (Deputy District Attorney Miller), James Whitmore (Martin Burnham), Nina Foch (Ellen Burnham), Richard Eyer (Jerry Burnham), John Kerr (Barry Pine), Kenneth Tobey (Bill Latham), Noah Keen (Lt. Carl Bone), Don Galloway (Mitchell Harris).

**"The Nurses 'The Gift'"** (October 17, 1963)
**Credits:** *Director:* Alex March; *Producer:* Herbert Brodkin; *Writer:* Larry Cohen; *Story Editor:* Earl Booth; *Network:* CBS; *Running time:* 50 minutes. **Cast:** Shirl Conway (Liz Thorpe), Lee Grant (Doris Kelly), Robert Webber (Arthur Luskin), Edward Asner (Phil Granger), Robert Gerringer (Dr. Thorsen), Anne Meacham (Claire Luskin).

**"Espionage: 'Medal for a Turned Coat'"** (January 15, 1964)
**Credits:** *Director:* David Greene; *Producer:* Herbert Brodkin; *Writer:* Larry Cohen; *Network:* NBC; *Running time:* 50 minutes. **Cast:** Fritz Weaver (Richard Keller), Joseph Furst (Von Elm), Nigel Stock (Harry Forbes), Rosemary Rogers (Ilsa), Catherine Lacey (Mother), Richard Carpenter (Luber), Michael Wolf (Ernst), Sylvia Kay (Ellen), Gerard Heinz (Doctor).

**"The Defenders: 'The Secret'"** (February 8, 1964)
**Credits:** *Director:* Paul Bogart; *Producer:* Robert Markell; *Executive Producer:* Herbert

Brodkin; *Writer:* Larry Cohen; *Story Editor:* David Shaw; *Network:* CBS; *Running time:* 50 minutes. **Cast:** E. G. Marshall (Lawrence Preston), Robert Reed (Kenneth Preston), Martin Landau (Daniel Orren), Georgann Johnson (Phyllis Orren), George Voskovec (Dr. Ladzlaw), Tim O'Connor (U.S. District Attorney Evans), Cec Linder (Dr. Bell).

**"The Defenders: 'Mayday! Mayday!'"** (April 18, 1964)
**Credits:** *Director:* Stuart Rosenberg; *Producer:* Robert Markell; *Executive Producer:* Herbert Brodkin; *Writer:* Larry Cohen; *Story Editor:* David Shaw; *Network:* CBS; *Running time:* 50 minutes. **Cast:** E. G. Marshall (Lawrence Preston), Robert Reed (Kenneth Preston), Torin Thatcher (Admiral Lucas J. Kiley), Skip Homeir (Commander Randall Kiley), Frances Sternhagen (Louise Kiley), Tim O'Connor (U.S. District Attorney Evans).

**"The Defenders: 'Go-Between'"** (October 15, 1964)
**Credits:** *Director:* Paul Sylbert; *Producer:* Robert Markell; *Executive Producer:* Herbert Brodkin; *Writer:* Larry Cohen; *Story Editor:* David Shaw; *Network:* CBS; *Running time:* 50 minutes. **Cast:** E. G. Marshall (Lawrence Preston), Robert Reed (Kenneth Preston), Arthur Hill (Matthew T. Ryder), Phyllis Thaxter (Dolores Ryder), Addison Powell (Harrison Alder), John Randolph (FBI Agent Slattery), Sally Gracie (Carolyn Harkness), Roberts Blossom (Riggs).

**"The Fugitive: 'Escape into Black'"** (November 17, 1964)
**Credits:** *Director:* Jerry Hopper; *Producer:* Alan A. Armer; *Executive Producer:* Quinn Martin; *Writer:* Larry Cohen; *Network:* ABC; *Running time:* 50 minutes. **Cast:** David Janssen (Dr. Richard Kimble), Barry Morse (Lt. Gerard), Ivan Dixon (Dr. Towne), Betty Garrett (Margaret Ruskin), Paul Birch (Captain Carpenter), Bill Raisch (One-Armed Man).

**"Branded: 'Survival'"** (January 24, 1965)
**Credits:** *Director:* Richard Whorf; *Producer:* Cecil Barker; *Executive Producer:* Harris Kattleman; *Creator and Writer:* Larry Cohen; *Network:* CBS; *Running time:* 22 minutes. **Cast:** Chuck Connors (Jason McCord), Alex Cord (Jim Colbee), Robert Carricart (Indian), Sally (Janet DeGore), Jessy (Valerie Szabo).

**"Branded: 'The Vindicator'"** (January 31, 1965)
**Credits:** *Director:* Joseph H. Lewis; *Producer:* Cecil Barker; *Executive Producer:* Harris Kattleman; *Creator and Writer:* Larry Cohen; *Network:* CBS; *Running time:* 22 minutes. **Cast:** Chuck Connors (Jason McCord), June Lockhart (Mrs. Pritchett), Claude Akins (Ned Travis), Harry Carey, Jr. (Lt. John Pritchett), John Litel (General James Reid), Johnny Jensen (Johnny Pritchett), John Pickard (Sergeant).

**"The Defenders: 'The Unwritten Law'"** (February 4, 1965)
**Credits:** *Director:* Robert Stevens; *Producer:* Robert Markell; *Executive Producer:* Herbert Brodkin; *Writer:* Larry Cohen; *Story Editor:* David Shaw; *Network:* CBS; *Running time:* 50 minutes. **Cast:** E. G. Marshall (Lawrence Preston), Robert Reed (Kenneth Preston), David Opatoshu (Leo Rolf), Kim Hunter (Eileen Rolf), Jessica Walter (Sharon Ruskin).

**"Branded: 'Rules of Game'"** (February 14, 1965)
**Credits:** *Director:* Lawrence Dobkin; *Creator and Writer:* Larry Cohen; *Network:* CBS; *Running time:* 22 minutes. **Cast:** Chuck Connors (Jason McCord); Jeanne Cooper (Else Brown), Russ Conway (Sheriff Pollard), Brad Weston (Vance).

**"Branded: The Bounty'"** (February 21, 1965)
**Credits:** *Director:* Harry Harris; *Writers:* Richard Carr, Jerry Ziegman, and John Wilder; *Story:* Larry Cohen; *Network:* CBS; *Running time:* 22 minutes. **Cast:** Chuck Connors (Jason McCord), Pat Conway (Johnny Dolan), Gene Evans (Paxton), Michael Ansara (Thomas Frye).

**"Branded: Coward Step Aside'"** (March 7, 1965)
**Credits:** *Director:* Harry Harris; *Writers:* John Wilder and Jerry Ziegman; *Story:* Larry Cohen; *Network:* CBS; *Running time:* 22 minutes. **Cast:** Chuck Connors (Jason McCord). Johnny Crawford (Clay Holden), Richard Arlen (Hatton), G. V. Homeier (Garrett).

**"Branded: 'The Mission'; Parts I, II and III"** (March 14, 21, 28, 1965)
**Credits:** *Director:* Bernard McEveety; *Writer:* Jameson Brewer; *Story:* Larry Cohen; *Network:* CBS; *Running time:* 22 minutes each. Color. Released theatrically in Britain under the title, *Broken Sabre.* **Cast:** Chuck Connors (Jason McCord), Kamala Devi (Laurette Lansing), McDonald Carey (Senator Lansing), Peter Breck (Crispo), John Carradine (General McCord), Wendell Corey (Major Whitcomb), Rochelle Hudson (Mrs. Whitcomb), Cesar Romero (General Arriola), H. M. Wynant (Brissac), Patrick Wayne (Corporal Dewey).

**"Branded: 'Taste of Poison'"** (May 2, 1965)
**Credits:** *Director:* Ron Winston; *Writers:* William Putnam and Nicholas Rowe; *Story:* Larry Cohen; *Network:* CBS; *Running time:* 22 minutes. **Cast:** Chuck Connors (Jason McCord), Carol Rossen (Dr. Cole), Walter Burke (Luke), Clarke Gordon (Howard), Stuart Margolin (Taeger).

**"Branded: 'Price of a Name'"** (May 23, 1965)
**Credits:** *Director:* Leonard Horn; *Writer:* Nicholas Rowe; *Story:* Larry Cohen; *Network:* CBS; *Running time:* 22 minutes. **Cast:** Chuck Connors (Jason McCord), Marilyn Maxwell (Lucy Benson), Keith Andes (Roy Harris), Don Megowan (Carruthers), Jess Kirkpatrick (Pete), Don Douglas (Banker), Charles Frederick (Boss).

**"Blue Light: 'The Last Man'"** (January 12, 1966)
**Credits:** *Director:* Walter Grauman; *Producer:* Buck Houghton; *Executive Producer:* Walter Grauman; *Creators:* Walter Grauman and Larry Cohen; *Writer and Executive Script Consultant:* Larry Cohen; *Network:* ABC; *Running time:* 25 minutes. **Cast:** Robert Goulet (David March), Christine Carére (Suzanne Duchard), John van Dreelen (von Lindendorf), Donald Harron (Spaulding), Werner Peters (Elm), Christiane Schmidtmer (Erika von Lindendorf), John Alderson (Gorlek).

**"Blue Light: 'Target — David March'"** (January 19, 1966)
**Credits:** *Director:* Walter Grauman; *Producer:* Buck Houghton; *Executive Producer:*

Walter Grauman; *Creators:* Walter Grauman and Larry Cohen; *Writer and Executive Script Consultant:* Larry Cohen; *Network:* ABC; *Running time:* 25 minutes; Color. **Cast:** Robert Goulet (David March), Christine Carére (Suzanne Duchard), Edward Binns (Major Traynor), Alan Cuthbertson (Colonel Dennison), Geoffrey Frederick (Eddie Fry), Hans Reiser (Colonel Richter), Margit Saad (the Baroness), John Alderson (Gorlek).

**"Blue Light: 'The Fortress Below'"** ( January 26, 1966)
**Credits:** *Director:* Walter Grauman; *Producer:* Buck Houghton; *Executive Producer:* Walter Grauman; *Creators:* Walter Grauman and Larry Cohen; *Writer and Executive Script Consultant:* Larry Cohen; *Network:* ABC; *Running time:* 25 minutes; Color. **Cast:** Robert Goulet (David March), Christine Carére (Suzanne Duchard), John van Dreelen (von Lindendorf), Eva Pflug (Gretchen Hoffmann), Peter Capell (Professor Felix Eckhardt), Horst Frank (Luber), Osman Ragheb (Dr.Brunner), Dieter Eppler (Dr. Stolnitz), Manfred Andrea (Dr. Zimmer), Alexander Allerson (Kraus).

**"Blue Light: 'The Weapon Within'"** (February 2, 1966)
**Credits:** *Director:* Walter Grauman; *Producer:* Buck Houghton; *Executive Producer:* Walter Grauman; *Creators:* Walter Graumann and Larry Cohen; *Writer and Executive Script Consultant:* Larry Cohen; *Network:* ABC; *Running time:* 25 minutes; Color. **Cast:** Robert Goulet (David March), Christine Carére (Suzanne Duchard), John van Dreelen (von Lindendorf), Eva Pflug (Gretchen Hoffmann), Horst Frank (Luber), Osman Ragheb (Dr. Brunner), Dieter Eppler (Dr. Stolnitz), Manfred Andrea (Dr. Zimmer).

**"Blue Light: 'Traitor's Blood'"** (February 9, 1966)
**Credits:** *Director:* Walter Grauman; *Producer:* Buck Houghton; *Executive Producer:* Walter Grauman; *Creators:* Walter Grauman and Larry Cohen; *Writer and Executive Script Consultant:* Larry Cohen; *Network:* ABC; *Running time:* 25 minutes; Color. **Cast:** Robert Goulet (David March), Christine Carére (Suzanne Duchard), Lyle Bettger (Colonel), Henry Beckman (Schreiber), David Macklin (Brian March), William Wintersole (von Clausitz), Jerry Ayres (Hodges), James Dixon (Kelly).

**"Blue Light: 'Agent of the East'"** (February 16, 1966)
**Credits:** *Director:* James Goldstone; *Producer:* Buck Houghton; *Executive Producer:* Walter Grauman; *Creators:* Walter Grauman and Larry Cohen; *Writer:* Donald S. Sanford; *Story and Executive Script Consultant:* Larry Cohen; *Network:* ABC; *Running time:* 25 minutes; Color. **Cast:** Robert Goulet (David March), Christine Carére (Suzanne Duchard), Jan Malmsjo (E. W. Vorchek), James Mitchell (Colonel Freidank), Dick Davalos (Captain Hegner).

**"Blue Light: 'Sacrifice!'"** (February 23, 1966)
**Credits:** *Director:* William Graham; *Producer:* Buck Houghton; *Executive Producer:* Walter Grauman; *Creators:* Walter Grauman and Larry Cohen; *Writer:* Dick Carr; *Story and Executive Script Consultant:* Larry Cohen; *Network:* ABC; *Running time:* 25 minutes; Color. **Cast:** Robert Goulet (David March), Christine Carére (Suzanne Duchard), Larry Pennell (Nick Brady), John Ragin (Major Zimmer), Barry Ford (Captain Klauss), Harry Davis (Frenchman), James Brolin (American Pilot), Barry Cahill (American Intelligence Officer).

*I Deal in Danger* (Twentieth Century–Fox, 1966)
**Credits:** *Director:* Walter Grauman; *Producer:* Buck Houghton; *Screenplay:* Larry Cohen; *Photography:* Sam Leavitt, Kurt Grigoleit; *Editors:* Jason Bernie, Dolf Rudeen; *Music:* Lalo Schifrin and Joseph Mullendore; *Running time:* 89 minutes. **Cast:** Robert Goulet (David March), Christine Carére (Suzanne Duchard), Donald Harron (Spauling), Horst Frank (Luber), Werner Peters (Elm), Eva Pflug (Gretchen Hoffmann), Christine Schmidtmer (Erika von Lindendorf), John Van Dreelen (von Lindendorf), Hans Reiser (Richter), Margit Saad (the Baroness), Peter Capell (Eckhardt), Osman Ragheb (Brunner), John Alderson (Gorlek), Manfred Andrea (Dr. Zimmer).

*I Deal in Danger* is a feature film compilation of the first, second, third and fourth episodes of "Blue Light": "The Last Man," "The Fortress Below" (Part I), and "The Weapon Within" (Part II). Released on September 21, 1966, four months after the final (17th) episode of the series was televised, it ran theatrically in America and Britain. It is currently unavailable for viewing. For further information, see the *American Film Institute Catalog: Feature Films 1961–1970*, ed. Richard P. Krafsur (New York: R. R. Bowker, 1976), 514–15.

Cohen also rewrote several "Blue Light" teleplays in his role of executive script consultant, but gave credit to the original writers.

*Sedgewick Hawk-Styles: Prince of Danger* (Ashmont Productions, 1966)
**Credits:** *Executive Producer:* William Asher; *Writers:* Larry Cohen and Bud Freeman; *Running time:* 30 minutes; Unsold television comedy pilot. **Cast:** Paul Lynde (Sedgewick Hawk- Styles), Hermione Baddeley, Liam Redmond, Maurice Ballimore.

*Return of the Seven*\* (United Artists, 1966)
**Credits:** *Director:* Burt Kennedy; *Producer:* Ted Richmond; *Screenplay:* Larry Cohen; *Photography:* Paul Vogel; *Editor:* Bert Bates; *Music:* Elmer Bernstein; *Running time:* 96 minutes; Color. **Cast:** Yul Brynner (Chris), Robert Fuller (Vin), Warren Oates (Colbee), Claude Akins (Frank), Julien Mateos (Chico), Jordan Christopher (Manuel), Emilio Fernandez (Francisco Lorca), Fernando Rey (Priest), Virgilio Texeira (Luis Delgado), Rudolfo Acosta (Lopez).

**"The Rat Patrol: 'The Blind Man's Bluff Raid'"** (October 24, 1966)
**Credits:** *Director:* Lee H. Katzin; *Producer:* Stanley Shpetner; *Writer:* Larry Cohen; *Creator:* Tom Gries; *Network:* ABC. *Running time:* 25 minutes; **Cast:** Christopher George (Sgt. Sam Troy), Larry Casey (Mark Hitchcock), Gary Raymond (Sgt. Jack Moffit), Justin Tarr (Private Tully Pettigrew), Hans Gudegast (Captain Hans Dietrich), Salome Jens (Patricia Bauer), James Philbrook (Doctor Keller).

*Daddy's Gone A-Hunting*\* (Warner Bros. 1969)
**Credits:** *Director and Producer:* Mark Robson; *Screenplay:* Larry Cohen and Lorenzo Semple, Jr.; *Photography:* Ernest Lazslo; *Editor:* Dorothy Spencer; *Music:* John Williams; *Running time:* 108 minutes; Color. **Cast:** Carol White (Cathy Palmer), Paul Burke (Jack Byrnes), Scott Hylands (Kenneth Daley), Mala Powers (Meg Stone), James Sikking (Joe Menchell), Walter Burke (Jerry Wolfe), Dennis Patrick (Doctor Parkington).

*El Condor*\* (National General Pictures, 1970)
**Credits:** *Director:* John Guillermin; *Producer:* Andre DeToth; *Screenplay:* Steven Carabatsos and Larry Cohen, from a story by Steven Carabatros; *Photography:* Henri Persin; *Editors:* William M. Ziegler and Walter Hanamann; *Music:* Maurice Jarre; *Running time:* 102 minutes. **Cast:** Jim Brown (Luke), Lee Van Cleef (Jaroo), Patrick O'Neal (Chavez), Mariana Hill (Claudine), Iron Eyes Cody (Santana), Elisha Cook (Old Convict), Imogen Hassel (Dolores) Gustavo Rojo (Colonel Aguinaldo).

**"In Broad Daylight"** (September 16, 1971)
**Credits:** *Director:* Robert Day; *Producer:* Robert Mirisch; *Writer:* Larry Cohen; *Photography:* Arch R. Dalzell; *Editor:* Edward Mann; *Music:* Leonard Rosenman; *Network:* ABC; Aaron Spelling Productions; *Running time:* 90 minutes. **Cast:** Richard Boone (Tony Chappel), Suzanne Pleshette (Kate Todd), Stella Stevens (Elizabeth Chappel), John Marley (Lt. Bergman), Fred Beir (Alex Crawford), Whit Bissell (Captain Moss), Paul Smith (Charles the Doorman).

**"Cool Million"** (aka **"Mask of Marcella"**) (September 16, 1972)
**Credits:** *Director:* Gene Levitt; *Producer:* David J. O'Connell; *Writer:* Larry Cohen; *Photography:* Gabor Pogany; *Editor:* Michael Economou; *Music:* Robert Prince; *Network:* NBC; Universal; *Running time:* 120 minutes. **Cast:** James Farentino (Jefferson Keyes), John Vernon (Inspector Duprez), Barbara Bouchet (Carla Miles), Christine Belford (Adrienne/Marcella Pascal), Jackie Coogan (Merrill Cossack), Lila Kedrova (Mme. Martine), Patrick O'Neal (Dr. Emile Snow), Guido Alberti (Tomlin).

**"Call Holme"** (April 24, 1972)
**Credits:** *Director:* Gary Nelson; *Producer:* William Baumes; *Writer:* Gerald Gardner; *Creator:* William Baumes; developed by Larry Cohen and Fred Freeman; *Network:* NBC; Screen Gems; First aired as a segment of NBC's "Triple Play '72" and later rebroadcast in 1984 on CBS; *Running time:* 30 minutes. **Cast:** Arte Johnson (Holme), Arlene Golonka (Miss Musky), Jim Hutton (Lt. Frank Hayward), Linda Crystal (Phadera Hayes), Helmut Dantine (Freidrich Von Klug).

***Bone*** (aka ***Housewife, Beverly Hills Nightmare, Dial Rat for Terror*)** (Larry Cohen Productions, 1972)
**Credits:** *Writer, Producer and Director:* Larry Cohen; *Executive Producer:* Peter Sabiston; *Co-Producer:* Janelle Cohen; *Associate Producer:* Peter Vizer; *Photography:* George Folsey Sr.; *Editor:* George Folsey, Jr.; *Music:* Gil Melle; *Running time:* 93 minutes. **Cast:** Yaphet Kotto (Bone), Andrew Duggan (Bill Lennick), Joyce Van Patten (Bernadette Lennick), Jeannie Berlin (Girl), Casey King, Brett Somers (X-Ray Lady), James Lee, Ida Berlin (Old Lady on Bus).

***Black Caesar*** (aka ***Godfather of Harlem*)**\* (American International, 1973)
**Credits:** *Writer, Producer and Director:* Larry Cohen; *Executive Producer:* Peter Sabiston; *Co-Producer:* Janelle Cohen; *Associate Producer:* James Dixon; *Photography:* Fenton Hamilton, (Harlem) James Signorelli; *Editor:* George Folsey, Jr.; *Music:* James Brown; Larco Productions; *Running time:* 94 minutes. **Cast:** Fred Williamson (Tommy Gibbs), D'Urville Martin (Reverend Rufus), Gloria Hendry (Helen), Art Lund (John McKinney), Val Avery (Cardoza), Minnie Gentry (Mrs. Gibbs), Julius

W. Harris (Mr. Gibbs), Phillip Roye (Joe Washington), William Wellman, Jr. (Alfred Coleman), Myrna Hansen (Virginia Coleman), Omar Jeffrey (Young Tommy), James Dixon (Bryant), Don Pedro Colley (Crawdaddy), Michael Jeffrey (Young Joe).

*Hell Up in Harlem** (American International, 1973)
**Credits:** *Writer, Producer and Director:* Larry Cohen; *Co-Producer:* Janelle Cohen; *Executive Producer:* Peter Sabiston; *Photography:* Fenton Hamilton; *Editor:* Peter Honess; *Music:* Fonce Mizell and Freddie Perren; Larco Productions; *Running time:* 98 minutes. **Cast:** Fred Williamson (Tommy Gibbs), Julius W. Harris (Mr. Gibbs), Gloria Hendry (Helen), Margaret Avery (Sister Jennifer), D'Urville Martin (Reverend Rufus), Tony King (Zack) Gerald Gordon (Di Angelo).

*It's Alive** (Warner Bros., 1973)
**Credits:** *Writer, Producer and Director:* Larry Cohen; *Executive Producer:* Peter Sabiston; *Co-Producer:* Janelle Cohen; *Photography:* Fenton Hamilton; *Editor:* Peter Honess; Music: Bernard Herrmann; *Makeup:* Rick Baker; Larco Productions; *Running time:* 91 minutes. **Cast:** John Ryan (Frank Davies), Sharon Farrell (Lenore Davies), Andrew Duggan (Professor), Guy Stockwell (Clayton), James Dixon (Lt. Perkins), Michael Ansara (Captain), Robert Emhardt (Executive), William Wellman, Jr. (Charley), Shamus Locke (Doctor Norton), Daniel Holzman (Chris Davies), Mary Nancy Burnett (Nurse), Patrick Macalister, Gerald York, Jerry Taft, Gwil Richards, and W. Allen York (Expectant Fathers).

**"Shoot Out in a One-Dog Town"** (January 9, 1974)
**Credits:** *Director:* Burt Kennedy; *Producer:* Richard E. Lyons; *Writers:* Dick Nelson, Larry Cohen; *Photography:* Robert B. Hauser; *Editor:* Warner E. Leighton; *Music:* Hoyt Curtin; *Network:* ABC; Hanna-Barbera Productions; *Running time:* 90 minutes. **Cast:** Richard Crenna (Zack Wells), Stefanie Powers (Letty Crandell), Jack Elam (Handy), Arthur O'Connell (Henry Gills), Michael Ansara (Reynolds), Dub Taylor (Halsey), Gene Evans (Gabe), Michael Anderson Jr. (Billy Boy); Richard Egan (Petry), John Pickard (Preston).

**"Man on the Outside"** (June 19, 1975)
**Credits:** *Director:* Boris Sagal; *Producer:* George Eckstein; *Writer:* Larry Cohen; *Photography:* Mario Tosi; *Editors:* Bud Hoffman, Douglas Stewart; *Music:* Elliot Kaplan; *Network:* ABC; Universal; *Running time:* 120 minutes. **Cast:** Lorne Greene (Wade Griffin), James Olsen (Gerald Griffin), Lee H. Montgomery (Mark Griffin), Lorraine Gary (Nora Griffin), Brooke Bundy (Sandra Ames), Ken Swofford (Lt. Matthews), William Watson (Ames), Bruce Kirby (Scully), Charles Knox Robinson (Mr. Arnold).

*God Told Me To* (aka *Demon*) (New World Pictures, 1976)
**Credits:** *Writer, Producer and Director:* Larry Cohen; *Photography:* Paul Glickman; *Editors:* Arthur Mandelberg, William J. Walters; *Music:* Frank Cordell; Larco Productions; *Running time:* 89 minutes. **Cast:** Tony Lo Bianco (Peter J. Nicholas), Deborah Raffin (Casey Forster), Sandy Dennis (Martha Nicholas), Sylvia Sidney (Elizabeth Mullin), Sam Levene (Everett Lukas), Robert Drivas (David Morten), Mike Kellin (Deputy Commissioner), Richard Lynch (Bernard Phillips), Sammy Williams

(Harold Gorman), Jo Flores Chase (Mrs. Gorman), Harry Bellaver (Cookie), Lester Rawlins (Board Chairman), William Roerick (Richards), George Patterson (Zero), Walter Steele (Junkie), John Heffernan (Bramwell), Alan Caudwell (Bramwell as a Youth), Robert Nichols (Fletcher), Andy Kaufman (Police Assassin), James Dixon (Sgt. Duff), Al Fann, Bobby Ramsen, Peter Hock, Alex Stevens, Harry Madsen, Randy Jurgensen (Detective Squad), Sherry Steiner (Mrs. Phillips), Vida Taylor (Miss Mullin as a Girl), Mason Adams (Obstetrician).

*The Private Files of J. Edgar Hoover** (Larco Productions, 1977)
**Credits:** *Writer, Producer and Director:* Larry Cohen; *Co-Producer:* Janelle Cohen; *Executive Producer:* Peter Sabiston; *Photography:* Paul Glickman; *Editor:* Christopher Lebenzon; *Music:* Miklos Rozsa; *Running time:* 111 minutes; **Cast:** Broderick Crawford (J. Edgar Hoover), José Ferrer (Lionel McCoy), Michael Parks (Robert F. Kennedy), Ronee Blakely (Carrie DeWitt), Rip Torn (Dwight Webb, Jr.), Celeste Holm (Florence Hollister), Michael Sacks (Melvin Purvis), Dan Dailey (Clyde Tolson), Raymond St. Jacques (Martin Luther King, Jr.), Andrew Duggan (Lyndon B. Johnson), John Marley (Dave Hindley), Howard Da Silva (Franklin D. Roosevelt), June Havoc (Mrs. Hoover), James Wainwright (Young Hoover), Lloyd Nolan (Attorney General Stone), Lloyd Gough (Walter Winchell), Brad Dexter (Alvin Karpis), George Plimpton (Quentin Reynolds), Jack Cassidy (Damon Runyon), Henderson Forstyhe (Harry Suydam), Lloyd Gough (Walter Winchell), George D. Wallace (Senator Joseph McCarthy), William Wellman, Jr. (Dwight Webb, Sr.), Art Lund (Benchley), James Dixon (Reilly), Brooks Morton (Earl Warren), Richard Dixon (President Nixon), James Dukas (Frank the Waiter).

*It Lives Again** (Warner Bros., 1978)
**Credits:** *Writer, Producer and Director:* Larry Cohen; Associate Producer: William Wellman, Jr.; *Executive Producer:* Peter Sabiston; *Photography:* Fenton Hamilton; *Editors:* Curt Burch, Louis Friedman, Carol O'Blath; *Music:* Bernard Herrmann; *Additional Music:* Laurie Johnson; Larco Productions, *Running time:* 91 minutes. **Cast:** Frederic Forrest (Eugene Scott), Kathleen Lloyd (Jody Scott), John P. Ryan (Frank Davis), John Marley (Mallory), Andrew Duggan (Dr. Perry), Eddie Constantine (Dr. Forrest), James Dixon (Lt. Perkins), Dennis O'Flaherty (Dr. Peters), Melissa Inger Cohen (Valerie), Victoria Jill Cohen (Cindy), Bobby Ramsen (Dr. Santo De Silva), Glenda Young (Lydia), Lynn Wood (Jody's Mother).

*I Do, I Don't* (Joe Hamilton Productions, 1979)
**Credits:** *Producers:* Larry Freeman and Larry Cohen; *Writers:* Larry Freeman and Larry Cohen; Unsold Television Pilot (Marital Comedy); *Running time:* 30 minutes. **Cast:** John Considine, Jo Ann Pflug, David Elliot, Jennifer Perito.

*Me on the Radio* (Warner Bros. Television, 1980)
**Credits:** *Director and Producer:* William Asher; *Writers:* Fred Freeman and Larry Cohen; Unsold Television Pilot (World War II Soap Opera Comedy); purchased by CBS but never produced as a series; *Running time:* 30 minutes. **Cast:** Sally Struthers, Judy Kaye.

*The American Success Company* (Columbia, 1980)
**Credits:** *Directors:* William Richert and Larry Cohen; *Producers:* Daniel H. Blatt and Edgar J. Sherick; *Screenplay:* Larry Cohen; *Photography:* Anthony Richmond; *Editor:* Ralph E. Winters; *Music:* Maurice Jarre; *Running time:* 94 minutes. **Cast:** Jeff Bridges (Harry), Belinda Bauer (Sarah), Ned Beatty (Mr. Elliot), Steven Keats (Rick Duprez), Bianca Jagger (Corinne), John Glover (Ernst), Mascha Gonska (Greta), Michael Durrell (Herman).

*Full Moon High* (Filmways Pictures, 1981)
**Credits:** *Writer, Producer and Director:* Larry Cohen; *Production Coordinator:* Pamela Cohen; *Photography:* Daniel Pearl; *Editor:* Armond Leibowitz; *Music:* Gary William Friedman, with songs by Janelle Cohen; Larco Productions; *Running time:* 93 minutes. **Cast:** Adam Arkin (Tony Walker), Ed McMahon (Mr. Walker), Roz Kelly (Jane), Alan Arkin (Dr. Jacob Brand), Tom Aldredge (Jailer), Pat Morita (Silversmith), Bill Kirchenbauer (Jack Flynn), Joanne Nail (Ricky), Kenneth Mars (Coach), Elizabeth Hartman (Miss Montgomery), James Dixon (Deputy), Louis Nye (Reverend), Desmond Wilson (Cabbie Busdriver), Jim Bullock (Eddie), Tom Clancy (Priest), Bob Saget (Sportscaster), Melissa Inger Cohen, Victoria Jill Cohen and Anthony Dana Arkin (Youngsters at Game).

"Momma the Detective" (November 12, 1981)
**Credits:** *Director, Writer, and Creator:* Larry Cohen; *Producers:* Larry Cohen and Hal Schaffel; *Photography:* Paul Glickman; *Music:* Joey Levine and Chris Palmaro; *Network:* CBS; Big Hit Productions; *Running time:* 60 minutes. **Cast:** Esther Rolle (Momma Sykes), Kene Holliday (Sgt. Alvin Sykes), Paul Dooley (Ames Prescott), Andrew Duggan (Edward Forbes), Jean Marsh (Sally Hackman), Frank Converse (Tom Hackman), Laurence Luckinbill (Dr. Glickman), Fritz Weaver (Mr. Foster), Claude Brooks (Jessie Sykes), William Walker, II (Andy Sykes), James Dixon (Sweeney).

This pilot became the basis for a series. Cohen added 30 additional minutes to the opening episode, giving it the new title, "See China and Die."

*I, the Jury** (American Cinema, 1981)
**Credits:** *Director:* Richard T. Heffron; *Producer:* Robert Solo; *Screenplay:* Larry Cohen, based on the novel by Mickey Spillane; *Photography:* Andrew Lazlo; *Editor:* Garth Craven; *Music:* Bill Conti; *Running time:* 111 minutes. **Cast:** Armand Assante (Mike Hammer), Barbara Carrera (Dr. Charlotte Bennett), Laurene Landon (Velda), Alan King (Charles Kalecki), Geoffrey Lewis (Joe Butler), Paul Sorvino (Det. Pat Chambers), Judson Scott (Kendricks), Barry Snider (Romero), Julia Barr (Norma Childs), Jessica James (Hilda Kendricks), Frederick Downs (Jack Williams), Mary Margaret Amato (Myrna Williams), Lee Ann Harris and Annette Harris (Twins).

*Q— The Winged Serpent** (United Film Distribution Company, 1982)
**Credits:** *Writer, Producer and Director:* Larry Cohen; *Executive Producer:* Peter Sabiston; *Photography:* Fred Murphy; *Editor:* Armond Lebowitz; *Music:* Robert O. Ragland, with songs written by Andy Goldmark, Janelle Webb Cohen, and Michael Moriarty; Larco Productions; *Running time:* 92 minutes. **Cast:** Michael Moriarty (Jimmy Quinn), Candy Clark (Joan), David Carradine (Det. Shepard), Richard Roundtree

(Sgt. Powell), James Dixon (Lt. Murray), Malachy McCourt (Commissioner), Fred J. Scollay (Captain Fletcher), Peter Hock (Det. Clifford), Ron Cey (Det. Hoberman), Mary Louise Weller (Mrs. Pauley), Bruce Carradine (Victim), John Capodice (Doyle), Larkin Ford (Curator), Larry Pine (Professor), Tony Page (Webb), Shelly Desai (Kahsa), Lee Louis (Officer Banyon), Fred Morsell (1st Robber), Ed Kovens (2nd Robber).

**"Women of San Quentin"** (October 23, 1983)
**Credits:** *Director:* William A. Graham; *Producers:* R.W. Goodwin and Stephen Cragg; *Executive Producer:* David Gerber; *Teleplay:* Mark Rodgers, from a story by Larry Cohen and Mark Rodgers; *Photography:* Robert Steadman; *Editor:* Ronald J. Fagan; *Music:* John Cacavas; *Network:* NBC; David Gerber Company/MGM Television; *Running time:* 120 minutes. **Cast:** Stella Stevens (Lt. Janet Alexander), Debbie Allen (Carol Freeman), Hector Elizondo (Captain Mike Reyes), Amy Steel (Liz Larson), Rosana De Soto (Adela Reynosa), Williams (Gregg Henry), William Allen Young (Larry Jennings), Yaphet Kotto (Sergeant Therman Patterson).

**Scandalous** (Orion, 1984)
**Credits:** *Directors:* Rob Cohen and John Byrum; *Producers:* Arlene Sellers and Alex Winitsky; *Screenplay:* Rob Cohen and John Byrum, based upon a story by Larry Cohen; *Photography:* Jack Cardiff; *Editor:* Michael Bradsell; *Music:* Dave Grusin; *Running time:* 92 minutes. **Cast:** Robert Hays (Frank Swedlin), Pamela Stephenson (Fiona Maxwell Sayle), Ron Travis (Porno Director), M. Emmet Walsh (Simon Reynolds), John Gielgud (Uncle Willie), Ed Dolan (Purser).

One of the worst travesties ever made out of a Cohen original story, the film is based on the stage play *Motive* (aka *Trick*), but distorted from its more innovative theatrical original. It is included here as a major example of the type of distortion Cohen's writing often undergoes in the hands of lesser talents.

**Perfect Strangers** (aka **Blind Alley**) (Hemdale Film Corporation, 1984)
**Credits:** *Director and Writer:* Larry Cohen; *Producer:* Paul Kurta; *Photography:* Paul Glickman; *Editor:* Armond Lebowitz; *Music:* Dwight Dixon; Larco Productions; *Running Time:* 87 minutes. **Cast:** Anne Carlisle (Sally), Brad Rijn (Johnny Ross), John Woehrle (Fred), Matthew Stockley (Matthew), Stephen Lack (Lt. Burns), Anne Magnuson (Maida), Zachary Hains (Meletti), Otto von Wernherr (Private Detective), Kitty Summerall (Joanna), Steven Pudenz (Man in Cemetery).

**Special Effects\*** (Hemdale Film Corporation, 1984)
**Credits:** *Director and Writer:* Larry Cohen; *Producer:* Paul Kurta; *Photography:* Paul Glickman; *Editor:* Armond Lebowitz; *Music:* Michael Minard; Larco Productions; *Running time:* 103 minutes. **Cast:** Zoe Tamerlis (Andrea Wilcox/Elaine Bernstein), Eric Bogosian (Chris Neville), Brad Rijn (Keefe Waterman), Kevin O'Connor (Lt. Phillip Delroy), Bill Oland (Det. Vickers), Richard Greene (Leon Gruskin), Steven Pudenz (Wiesanthal), Heidi Bassett (Neville's Assistant Director), John Woehrle (Studio Executive), Kitty Summerall (Andrea's Roommate), Kris Evans (Cosmetician), Mike Alpert (Taxi Driver).

***The Stuff**** (New World Pictures, 1985)
**Credits:** *Director, Producer and Writer:* Larry Cohen; *Photography:* Paul Glickman; *Editor:* Armond Lebowitz; *Music:* Anthony Gueffen; *Running time:* 87 minutes. **Cast:** Michael Moriarty (David "Mo" Rutherford), Andrea Marcovicci (Nicole), Garrett Morris ("Chocolate Chip" Charlie), Paul Sorvino (Colonel Spears), Scott Bloom (Jason), Danny Aiello (Vickers), Patrick O'Neal (Fletcher), James Dixon (Postman), Alexander Scourby (Evans), Russell Nye (Richards), Gene O'Neill (Scientist), Colette Blonigan (Jason's Mother), Frank Telfer (Jason's Father), Brian Bloom (Jason's Brother), Harry Bellaver (Old Miner), Rutanya Alda (Psychologist), Brooke Adams, Laurene Landon, Tammy Grimes, Abe Vigoda, Clara Peller (Special Guest Stars in "Stuff" Commercials)

***It's Alive III: Island of the Alive**** (Warner Home Video, 1986)
**Credits:** *Director and Writer:* Larry Cohen; *Producer:* Paul Stader; *Photography:* Daniel Pearl; *Editor:* David Kern; *Music:* Laurie Johnson; *Original Theme Music:* Bernard Herrmann; Larco Productions; *Running time:* 91 minutes. **Cast:** Michael Moriarty (Stephen Jarvis), Karen Black (Ellen Jarvis), Laurene Landon (Sally), James Dixon (Lt. Perkins), Gerrit Graham (Ralston), MacDonald Carey (Judge Watson), Neal Israel (Dr. Brewster), Art Lund (Dr. Swenson), Ann Dane (Dr. Morrell), William Watson (Cabot), C. J. Sussex (Hunter), Patch McKenzie (Robbins), Bobby Ramsen (TV Host), Kevin O'Connor (Cab Driver), John Woehrle (1st Cop).

***A Return to Salem's Lot**** (Warner Home Video, 1987)
**Credits:** *Director:* Larry Cohen; *Producer:* Paul Kurta; *Writers:* Larry Cohen, James Dixon; *Photography:* Daniel Pearl; *Editor:* Armond Lebowitz; *Music:* Michael Minard; Larco Productions; *Running time:* 96 minutes. **Cast:** Michael Moriarty (Joe Weber), Ricky Addison Reed (Jeremy Weber), Samuel Fuller (Dr. Van Meer), Andrew Duggan (Judge Axel), Evelyn Keyes (Mrs. Axel), Jill Gatsby (Sherry), June Havoc (Aunt Clara), Ronee Blakely (Sally), James Dixon (Rains), David Holbrook (Deputy), Katja Crosby (Cathy), Tara Reid (Amanda), Brad Rijn (Clarence), Georgia Janelle Webb (Sarah), Robert Burr (Dr. Fenton), Bobby Ramsen (Jungle Guide).

***Best Seller*** (Orion, 1987)
**Credits:** *Director:* John Flynn; *Producer:* Carter De Haven; *Writer:* Larry Cohen; *Photography:* Fred Murphy; *Editor:* David Rosenbloom; *Music:* Jay Ferguson; *Running time:* 95 minutes. **Cast:** James Woods (Cleve), Brian Dennehy (Dennis Meachum), Victoria Tennant (Roberta Gillian), Allison Balson (Holly Meachum), Paul Shenar (David Madlock), George Coe (Graham), Mary Carver (Cleve's Mother), Kathleen Lloyd (Cleve's Sister), Sully Boyar (Munks), Jeffrey Josephson (Pearlman).

***Deadly Illusion**** (Columbia, 1987)
**Credits:** *Directors:* Larry Cohen, William Tannen; *Producer:* Irwin Meyer; *Writer:* Larry Cohen; *Photography:* Daniel Pearl; *Editors:* Steve Mirkovich, Ronald Spang; *Music:* Patrick Gleason; *Running time:* 92 minutes. **Cast:** Billy Dee Williams (Hamberger), Vanity (Rina), Morgan Fairchild (Jane/Sharon), John Beck (Alex Burton), Joe Cortese (Det. Lafferty), Dennis Hallahan (Fake Alex Burton), Michael Wilding, Jr. (Castillion), Allison Woodward (Nancy Castillion), Joe Spinell (Man with Gun), Michael Emil (Medical Examiner), George Loros (Levante), John Woehrle (Boardroom Executive).

**"Desperado: Avalanche at Devil's Ridge"** (May 24, 1988)
**Credits:** *Director:* Richard Compton; *Producer:* Charles E. Sellier, Jr.; *Writer:* Larry Cohen; *Creator:* Elmore Leonard; *Network:* NBC (Movie of the Week); Walter Mirisch Productions and Charles E. Seiler, Jr., Productions. **Cast:** Alex McArthur (Duell McCall), Hoyt Axton (Sheriff Ben Tree), Alice Adair (Rachel Slaten), Lise Cutter (Nora), Rod Steiger (Silas Slaten).

This program was the third attempt at a pilot for a proposed series that never materialized.

***Wicked Stepmother**** (MGM Home Video, 1988)
**Credits:** *Director and Writer:* Larry Cohen; *Producer:* Robert Littman; *Executive Producer:* Larry Cohen; *Photography:* Bryan Englund; *Editor:* David Kern; *Music:* Robert Folk; Larco Productions, *Running time:* 90 minutes. **Cast:** Bette Davis (Miranda), Barbara Carrera (Priscilla), Colleen Camp (Jenny Miller), Lionel Stander (Sam Fisher), David Raische (Steve Miller), Tom Bosley (Lt. McIntosh), Richard Moll (Nat Pringle) Evelyn Keyes (Witch Tutor), Seymour Cassel (Feldshine), Mike Shawn (Donahue), Susie Garrett (Mandy), Laurene Landon (Vanilla), James Dixon (Det. Flynn), Cynthia Costas (Receptionist).

***Maniac Cop**** (Shapiro Glickenhaus Entertainment Corporation, 1988)
**Credits:** *Director:* William Lustig; *Producer and Writer:* Larry Cohen; *Photography:* Vincent J. Rabe; *Editor:* David Kern; *Music:* Jay Chattaway; *Running time:* 85 minutes. **Cast:** Tom Atkins (Frank McCrae), Bruce Campbell (Jack Forrest), Laurene Landon (Theresa Mallory), Richard Roundtree (Police Commissioner Pike), William Smith (Captain Ripley), Robert Z'Dar (Officer Matt Cordell), Sheree North (Sally Nolan), Nina Averson (Regina Shepard), Lou Bonacki (Det. Lovejoy), Victoria Catlin (Ellen Forrest), Jim Dixon (Clancy), Jill Gatsby (Cassie Phillips), Jake LaMotta (Detective), William Lustig (Hotel Manager), Sam Raimi (Parade Reporter).

***Maniac Cop 2**** (Movie Sales Company Ltd/Fadd Enterprises, 1990)
**Credits:** *Director:* William Lustig; *Producer and Writer:* Larry Cohen; *Photography:* James Lemmo; *Editor:* David Kern; *Music:* Jay Chattaway; *Running time:* 88 minutes. **Cast:** Robert Davi (Det. Sean McKinney), Claudia Christian (Susan Riley), Michael Lerner (Edward Doyle), Bruce Campbell (Jack Forrest), Laurene Landon (Theresa Mallory), Robert Z'Dar (Matt Cordell), Clarence Williams III (Blum), Leo Rossi (Turkell), Lou Bonacki (Det. Lovejoy), Paula Trickey (Cheryl), Charles Napier (Lew Brady), Santos Morales (Store Clerk), James Dixon (Range Officer), Sam Raimi (Newscaster).

***The Ambulance**** (Epic Productions, 1990)
**Credits:** *Director and Writer:* Larry Cohen; *Producers:* Moctesuma Esparza and Robert Katz; *Photography:* Jacques Haitkin; *Editors:* Armond Leibowitz and Claudia Finkle; *Music:* Jay Chattaway; 1993 American Video Release; *Running time:* 95 minutes. **Cast:** Eric Roberts (Josh Baker), Megan Gallagher (Officer Sandy Malloy), James Earl Jones (Det. Lt. Spencer), Red Buttons (Elias Zacharias), Janine Turner (Cheryl), Eric Braeden (Doctor), Richard Bright (Det. Lt. McCloskey), Nicholas Chinland (Hugo), Stan Lee (Marvel Comics Editor), Jill Gatsby (Jerilyn), James Dixon (Det. "Jughead" Ryan), Deborah Headwell (Nurse Feinstein), Cynthia Costas (Cynthia from Chicago), Peter Sabiston (Man in Disco #1), Janelle Webb (Nurse Carter).

***Maniac Cop 3: Badge of Silence**\** (New Motion and First Work Pictures, 1992)
**Credits:** *Directors:* William Lustig and Joel Soisson; *Producers:* Michael Leahy and Joel Soisson; *Co-Producer and Writer:* Larry Cohen; *Photography:* Jacques Haitkin; *Additional Scenes:* Joel Soisson; *Editor:* David Kern; *Music:* Joel Goldsmith; *Additional Music:* Joel Soisson; *Running time:* 85 minutes. **Cast:** Robert Davi (Det. Sean McKinney), Caitlin Dulany (Dr. Susan Fowler), Gretchen Becker (Officer Katie Sullivan), Paul Gleason (Hank Cooney), Jackie Earle Haley (Jessop), Julius Harris (Houngan) Grand Bush (Willie), Doug Savant (Dr. Peter Myserson), Robert Forster (Dr. Powell), Bobby Di Cicco (Bishop), Frank Pesce (Tribble), Lou Diaz (Leon), Vanessa Marquez (Terry), Ted Raimi (Reporter), Jeffrey Hamilton (Teen Witness).

***Guilty as Sin**\** (Buena Vista, 1993)
**Credits:** *Director:* Sidney Lumet; *Producer:* Martin Ransohoff; *Writer:* Larry Cohen; *Photography:* Andrzej Bartkowiak; *Editor:* Evan Lottman; *Music:* Howard Shore; *Running time:* 107 minutes. **Cast:** Rebecca De Mornay (Jennifer Haines), Don Johnson (David Greenhill), Stephen Lang (Phil Garson), Jack Warden (Moe Plimpton), Dana Ivey (Judge Tompkins), Ron White (DiAngelo), Norma Dell'Agnese (Emily), Luis Guzman (Lt. Bernard Martinez), Robert Kennedy (Caniff), James Blendick (McMartin), Tom Butler (Heath), Brigit Wilson (Rita Greenhill).

***Bodysnatchers*** (Warner Bros., 1994)
**Credits:** *Director:* Abel Ferrera; *Producer:* Robert H. Solo; *Screenplay:* Stuart Gordon, Dennis Paoli, and Nicholas St. John; *Story:* Raymond Cistheri and Larry Cohen; *Photography:* Bojan Bazelli; *Editor:* Anthony Reidman; *Music:* Joe Delia; *Running time:* 87 minutes. **Cast:** Gabrielle Anwar (Marti Malone), Terry Kinney (Malone), Billy Wirth (Tim), Forest Whitaker (Major Collins), Meg Tilley Carol) Christine Elise (Jenn), Lee Ermey (Colonel).

**"NYPD Blue"** (March 22, 1995)
**Credits:** *Director:* Eddie Leone; *Producer:* Ted Mann; *Writer:* Larry Cohen; *Creators:* David Milch and Steven Bochco; *Photography:* Brian J. Reynolds; *Editor:* Stanford Allen; *Music:* Mike Post; *Network:* ABC; *Running time:* 50 minutes. **Cast:** Jimmy Smits (Det. Simone), Dennis Franz (Det. Sipowicz), James McDaniel (Lt. Lou Fancy), Gail O'Grady (Donna), Gordon Clapp (Det. Medavoy), Sharon Lawrence (Costas), Nicholas Turturro (James), Susanna Thompson (Joyce Novak), Bill Brochtrup (John Irvin), Bill Macy (Mo Neiberg), Murray Rubenstein (Ernie Neiberg), Steve Antin Det. Savino), John Finn (Jimmy "Socks" Matlow), Ken Lerner (David Neiberg).

**"As Good as Dead"** (May 10, 1995)
**Credits:** *Director, Producer, Writer:* Larry Cohen; *Photography:* Billy Dickson; *Editor:* Neil Mandelberg; *Music:* Patrick O'Hearn; *Network:* USA Cable Movie; *Running time:* 87 minutes. **Cast:** Judge Reinhold (Ron), Crystal Bernard (Susan Warfield), Traci Lords (Nicole Grace), Carlos Carrosco (Eddie Garcia), George Dickerson (Edgar), Jerry Borders (Funeral Director), Cynthia Costas (Ms. Webb).

**"Ice"** (February 18, 1996)
**Credits:** *Director:* Bradford May; *Producer:* Diana Kerew; *Teleplay:* Larry Cohen; *Photography:* Bradford May; *Editor:* Budd Hayes; *Music:* Joseph Contan; *Network:*

NBC/Hearst Entertainment; *Running time:* 100 minutes. **Cast:** Dale Midkiff (Steve Carella), Joe Pantoliano (Meyer Meyer), Paul Johansson (Kling), Andrea Parker (Eileen), Dean McDermott (Brother Anthony), Andrea Ferrell (Emma Forbes), Diana Douglas (Teddy), Nicholas Bennett (Tim), Michael Cross (Lt. Byrnes), Lenore Zann (Angie).

***Original Gangstas*** (Orion, 1996)
**Credits:** *Director:* Larry Cohen; *Producer:* Fred Williamson; *Screenplay:* Aubrey Rattan; *Photography:* Carlos Gonzalez; *Editors:* David Kern and Peter B. Ellis; *Music:* Vladimir Horunzhy; *Running time:* 99 minutes. **Cast:** Fred Williamson (John Bookman), Jim Brown (Jake Trevor), Pam Grier (Laurie Thompson), Paul Winfield (Reverend Dorsey), Isabel Sanford (Gracie Bookman), Oscar Brown, Jr. (Marvin Bookman), Richard Roundtree (Slick), Christopher B. Duncan (Spyro), Eddie Bo Smith, Jr. (Damien), Dru Down (Kayo), Shyheim Franklin (Dink), Robert Forster (Detective Slatten), Charles Napier (Mayor Ritter), Wings Hauser (Michael Casey), Tim Rhoze (Blood).

**Other Productions:**
Cohen also acted as advisor for the "Columbo" series, and wrote seven episodes including "Any Old Port in a Storm" (1973) and "A Matter of Honor" (1976).

**"Any Old Port in a Storm"** (October 7, 1973) features Peter Falk, Donald Pleasance, Dana Elcar, Julie Harris, Joyce Jillson, Gary Conway, Robert Ellenstein, Robert Waldon, and Reid Smith.

**"An Exercise in Fatality"** (September 15, 1974) features Peter Falk, Robert Conrad, Phil Burns, Collin Wilcox, Jude Farese, Gretchen Corbett, Pat Harrington.

**"A Matter of Honor"** (February 1, 1976) features Peter Falk, Ricardo Montalban, Pedro Armendariz, Robert Carricart, A. Martinez, Mario Grimm, and Evita Munoz.

**Spies Like Us** (1985)
This was a gimmicky comedy whose main feature is the appearance of film directors such as Costa Gavras, Michael Apted, Sam Raimi, and Larry Cohen in brief acting roles. Larry Cohen also created the series "Cop Talk" (featuring Sonny Grosso) for Tribune Syndication in 1990.

# Appendix B:
# The Theatrical
# Work of Larry Cohen

*Nature of the Crime* (March 23, 1970–April 26, 1970; 41 performances) Bouwerie
Lane Theatre, New York
**Credits:** *Writer:* Larry Cohen. **Cast:** Tony Lo Bianco (Daniel Aronoff), James Antonio (James Garrett), Samuel Ullman (Robert F. Simon), Adam Keefe (Kirsch), Gerald Gordon (Theodore Benjamin), Barbara Badcock (Ruth Aronoff), John Benson (Judge).

*Motive* (1976) Guildford Theatre, England, and subsequent tour
**Credits:** *Writer:* Larry Cohen. **Cast:** Honor Blackman (Paula Cramer), George Cole (Andrew Creed), Ian Hendry (Wallace Barrows).
Carroll Baker replaced Honor Blackman on tour.

*Trick* (February 4, 1979–February 11, 1979; nine performances and 19 previews) Playhouse Theatre, New York
**Credits:** *Presenter:* Joshua Logan; *Writer and Director:* Larry Cohen. **Cast:** Tammy Grimes (Paula Cramer), Donald Maddern (Wallace Barrows), Lee Richardson (Andrew Creed).

*Washington Heights* (1987-1988 Season) Performed by the Jewish Repertory Theatre, New York
**Credits:** *Director:* David Saint; *Writer:* Larry Cohen; *Set Design:* Chris Pickart; *Costume:* Edi Giguere; *Lighting:* Douglas O'Flaherty; **Cast:** Robert Hitt (Dan), Zachariah Overton (Danny), Jeff Brooks (Al), Leah Doyle (Marcia), Martha Greenhouse (Grandma).

# Appendix C:
# The Strange Case
# of "Coronet Blue"

Larry Cohen wrote many screenplays and teleplays throughout his career. It is natural that he does not remember everything he has written, especially works altered by the producers. Cohen claims he never wrote the "Coronet Blue" episode, "A Dozen Demons." However, this appendix lists certain details about this episode, available at the Museum of Television and Broadcasting, as a subject for future research. Even if the teleplay is not Cohen's work, it may derive from a story he actually wrote. In any case, the story is far more interesting than other surviving ones in this short-lived series.

**"Coronet Blue: 'A Dozen Demons'"** First aired on CBS, March 7, 1967.
**Credits:** *Director:* David Greene; *Writer:* Robert Crean(?); *Creator:* Larry Cohen; *Executive Producer:* Herbert Brodkin. Plautus Productions.

    **Synopsis**: Michael Alden (Frank Converse) walks through Central Park. He stops and looks at an attractive dark-haired girl (resembling Eileen in the later memory scenes) playing basketball. The mysterious dark-suited assassin (tracking him throughout the series) sees Alden and shoots him with a silencer. The wounded Alden falls over a small bridge. A group of dark-suited men pass by him. One man (Brian Bedford) recognizes him and comes to his aid. As Alden recovers from his wounds, a montage of shots reveals a number of monks looking at him, commenting on his resemblance to Saint Anthony. Alden owes his life to Brother Anthony (Brian Bedford), an unorthodox novice in the monastery. Like Alden, Brother Anthony has another identity he never reveals in this episode. He has many similarities to Alden. While Alden cannot reveal his real identity, due to amnesia, Brother Anthony conceals his former identity, wishing to take on a new personality in the peaceful world of the monastery. At one point, he nearly reveals it to Alden before hastily suppressing his "slip of the tongue." Both men seek refuge from hostile forces. Alden faces unknown pursuers. Anthony wishes to reject an alienating modern world.

    Another parallel between Alden and Anthony involves both having unorthodox

424

personalities. The Father Superior (Donald Moffatt) comments on Anthony, "I don't know whether he's going to be a monk or a secret agent."

The community give Alden a monk's robes to wear while he remains with them. Passing a statue of the Virgin Mary, Alden notes she has a blue coronet on her head. (This is interesting, since this episode does attempt to give one solution to the enigmatic term "coronet blue.") Brother Anthony also shows Alden a stained glass window depicting Saint Anthony pursued by a dozen demons, all with human faces. Alden finds out the artist's name is Matthew Straight. He attempts to leave the monastery but faces attack by some unidentified assailants before returning to safety. Intrigued and caring about his new friend, Brother Anthony decides to help Alden in the outside world. Both leave the monastery by another exit.

Alden and Anthony find work in "The Seeing Eye" cafe run by Joe (Max Silver). Both men find Matthew Straight's studio. But his daughter, Jenny (Lynda Day), tells them her father is dead. She does not recognize Alden. Resenting Alden's aggressive questioning, but attracted by Anthony's gentle nature, she shows them a photograph her father used for the "dozen demons." The edge is missing. Alden believes he was in the photo depicting a group known as "The Shooting Club." While Alden visits the last surviving member of the group, Jenny and Anthony become attracted to each other.

By uttering the words "Shooting Club," Alden manages to bypass a protective, muscular, male servant and gain admission to see Manitee (House Jameson). Aged, infirm, and speaking with gay vocal undertones, Manitee wishes to purchase the photo from Alden, believing him to be a blackmailer. He denies that Alden was ever in the missing portion of the photo: "No one, except the young man." The absent figure was "a nasty boy" who died in a "cowardly" manner. He collected photographs for the Shooting Club, a group of male decadents dealing in certain types of "photographs," produced for "pleasure" for those "who could afford the product." Manitee is the remaining survivor of the original group, all of whom have long died of "various excesses." The Shooting Club was a private organization for those who "enjoyed the better things in life," dealing in "books and pictures." Realizing that Manitee cannot help him, Alden leaves him the photograph.

Returning to Straight's studio, Alden finds that Matthew Straight (John Beal) is alive. Jenny tells him that her father had a mental breakdown and has been in a mental asylum. Straight has returned, since he cannot stand incarceration. Jenny describes her father as "a tired old man pursued by demons": "His demons are his own. Every artist has them." Straight tells Alden that he drew his image when he saw him in a park one day.

They all return to Central Park, to the place where Straight first saw Alden. Straight tells Alden that he never actually spoke to him, but saw him attempting to say farewell to a dark-haired girl. Straight remembers Alden's distress: "It seemed as if all the demons on earth were trying to drag you down to hell." He noticed Alden appeared "tormented" in trying to explain things to the girl. Alden's memory returns to the incident. The image of the woman appears in dissolves, a woman Alden calls "Eileen." Before he can remember anything further, the assassin takes a shot at the group. His bullet penetrates the sketch of Alden's face that Straight began drawing to aid the memory process.

Alden and Anthony then return to the monastery to return their robes. Anthony decides to remain in the world with Jenny. Alden now has some more information to continue deciphering the enigma of "Coronet Blue" as a means to recovering his identity.

**Comments:** The credits list a "Robert Crean" as the writer. It is difficult to believe that this episode does not have some relationship to Cohen's ideas. Like other late '60s screenplays (*Return of the Seven, Daddy's Gone A-Hunting*) the execution of ideas is botched, but some "Cohen touches" seem to be there.

*Dualities:* Alden/Anthony; "Dozen Demons" of the "Shooting Club"/Twelve Disciples; Saint Anthony as religious martyr/Michael Alden as Soviet agent wishing to reject the demonic realms of the Evil Empire to become a convert to American democracy. Alden and Anthony are also dual figures, a common Cohen theme. Jenny is attracted to the more gentle Anthony and alienated by an aggressive Alden.

*The Seeing Eye* cafe may be an indirect Hitchcock reference. Do the dozen demons anticipate the twelve-disciple, Wall Street stockbrokers in *God Told Me To*?

"A Dozen Demons" may be an original Cohen story. It contains several familiar themes, such as duality, gayness, and the amnesia motif Cohen used in "Escape into Black." Until further evidence emerges, and unless Larry Cohen remembers involvement in this episode, the verdict remains "not proven."

# Notes

## Introduction

1. See Robin Wood, *Hitchcock's Films Revisited* (New York: Columbia University Press, 1989); Tania Modleski, *The Women Who Knew Too Much: Hitchcock and Feminist Theory* (New York: Methuen, 1988). Subscribing to a "belief in human agency, however restricted," Sumiko Higashi speaks of Cecil B. DeMille "not only as a figure who was shaped and influenced by the forces of his era but as a filmmaker who has left his own signature on the culture industry." See *Cecil B. DeMille and American Culture: The Silent Era* (Berkeley: University of California Press, 1994), 5. This parallels my attitude toward Larry Cohen. Although his influence is not as great as DeMille's, Cohen's significance lies more in the fact that he articulates concerns that the culture industry should express. His very marginalized status speaks more for his refusal to compromise than any supposed creative limitations assigned to him by critics who need to investigate his work far more closely.

## Chapter 1

1. Richard Corliss, *Talking Pictures: Screenwriters in the American Cinema 1927–1973* (Woodstock, New York: The Overlook Press, 1974), xvii–xxviii.
2. Raymond Williams, *Keywords: A Vocabulary of Culture and Society*, revised edition (New York: Oxford University Press, 1985), 252.
3. See Henry Cecil Wyld and Eric H. Partridge, eds. *The Little and Ives Webster Dictionary and Home Reference Library*, International Edition (New York: J.J. Little & Ives Co., Inc., 1957), 48.
4. David Desser and Lester D. Friedman, *American-Jewish Filmmakers: Traditions and Trends* (Urbana: University of Illinois Press, 1993).
5. Patricia Erens, "You Could Die Laughing: Jewish Humor and Film," *East-West Film Journal*, 2.1 (1987), 52.
6. Desser and Friedman, 296. See also Sarah Blacher Cohen, "Introduction: The Varieties of Jewish Humor," *Jewish Wry: Essays on Jewish Humor*, Ed. Sarah Blacher Cohen (Bloomington, Indiana University Press, 1987), 14; Maurice Chaney, "Stanley Elkin and Jewish Black Humor," *Jewish Wry*, 178; and Mark Shechner, "Dear Mr. Einstein: Jewish Comedy and the Contradictions of Culture," *From Hester Street to Hollywood*, ed. Sarah Blacher Cohen (Indiana University Press, 1983), 142–43. I wish to express my gratitude to David Desser for suggesting these references.

7. Andre Bazin, "La politique des auteurs," *The New Wave*, ed. Peter Graham (New York: Viking, 1968), 137–55.

8. John Caughie, ed., *Theories of Authorship* (London: Routledge & Kegan Paul, 1981), 206.

9. J. Hoberman, "Calling all Cohen heads (*Q*)," *Village Voice*, 27 (October 19, 1982), 56; "God Told Him To," *Village Voice*, 31 (August 5, 1986), 58.

10. Op. cit.

11. Robin Wood, *Hollywood from Vietnam to Reagan* (New York: Columbia University Press, 1986), 95.

12. Op. cit.

13. Wood, *Hollywood*, 95–108; Andrew Britton, Richard Lippe, Tony Williams, and Robin Wood, eds. *The American Nightmare: Essays on the Horror Film* (Toronto Festival of Festivals, 1979), 75–86.

14. Wood, *Hollywood*, 102.

15. Fred Camper, "Reel Life: the low budget genius of American film," *Chicago Reader* (June 12, 1987), 7.

16. See Amy Taubin, "Shooting script: the lion sleeps tonight," *Village Voice*, 34 (May 9, 1989), 76.

17. Camper, op. cit.

18. William Beard and Piers Handling, "The Interview," *The Shape of Rage: The Films of David Cronenberg*, ed. Piers Handling (New York: Zoetrope, 1983), 192; see also the rebuttal by Robin Wood, "Cronenberg: A Dissenting View," *The Shape of Rage*, 119, with the concluding sentence, "If I continue to prefer *It's Alive* to *The Brood* it is because it seems to me so much more complex: so many things are going on in it, so that it becomes the site of a genuinely rich and disturbing intersection of ideological conflicts."

19. Wood, *Hollywood*, 98.

20. Donald Rignalda, *Fighting and Writing the Vietnam War* (Jackson, Mississippi: University of Mississippi Press, 1994), 182.

21. SCREEN, 15.2 (1974).

22. Rignalda, 185.

23. See Brian Henderson, "Cartoon and Narrative in the Films of Frank Tashlin and Preston Sturges," *Comedy/Cinema/Theory*, ed. Andrew Horton (Berkeley: University of California Press, 1991), 153–73.

24. See Andrew Horton, *Comedy/Cinema/Theory*, 8–9. Horton quotes from Kenneth McLeish, *The Theatre of Aristophanes* (New York: Taplinger, 1980). Horton also cites Jacques Derrida's subversive use of irony as a strategy of using language to expose language similar to Godard's cinematic exploration of film language. He sees Derrida's writings as involving a mingling of play with the serious necessitating the active involvement of the reader in a textual process: "To be *Homo ludens* is to be aware: to be alert to others and to alternatives, probabilities, possibilities, and chance (that major factor in games of every sort). Thus, play and discipline go together. Not to be aware is to be a victim, a fool, a braggart, a dictator." (8)

This raises several interesting possibilities for further explorations of Cohen's work, a director who spontaneously uses a comic-strip visual style to interrogate both cinema and ideology. Derrida's recent emphasis of Marx's relevance in a post–Communist, postmodernist era also suggests some fertile directions.

25. See Grigoris Daskalogrigorakis, "Routine Work, Routine Gorin," *The Spectator*, 8.2 (1988), 94–95.

26. Julio Garcia Espinosa, "For an Imperfect Cinema," *25 Years of the New Latin Cinema*, ed. Michael Chanan (London: British Film Institute & Channel 4 Television, 1983), 33.

27. Henderson, 171.

28. See Henderson, 162, who quotes from E.M. Forster, Aspects of the Novel (New York: Harcourt, Brace, 1927), 71–72.

29. Scott McCloud, *Understanding Comics* (Massachusetts: The Kitchen Sink Press, 1993); see also Will Eisner, *Comics and Sequential Art* (Princeton, Wi.: The Kitchen Sink Press, 1992). These two works are essential introductions for anyone seriously interested in understanding the comic strip as an art form.

30. McCloud, 16–17.

31. Op. cit., 18.

32. Op. cit., 30–31.

33. Wood, 106.

34. McCloud, 41.

35. Op. cit., 45.

36. Op. cit., 49. McCloud also quotes a statement Rudolphe Topffer made in 1845 involving historical recognition of both the limitless potential of the comic strip as an art form as well as the attitudes hindering its reception as such: "...the picture story, which critics disregard and scholars scarcely notice, has had great influence at all times, perhaps even more than written literature...in addition, the picture-story appeals mainly to children and the lower classes..." For the above references to comedy technique, see Steve Neale and Frank Krutnik, *Popular Film and Television Comedy* (London: Routledge, 1990), 18, 79–80, 90.

37. Robin Wood, *Hitchcock's Films Revisited* (New York: Columbia University Press, 1989).

38. Bazin, 142.

39. Harlan Ellison, *The Glass Teat* (Manchester, England: Savoy Books, 1978), 200.

40. See Mikhail Bakhtin, *The Dialogic Imagination* (Austin: University of Texas Press, 1985), 324, 276.

41. J. Hoberman, "Frank Tashlin: vulgar modernist," *Frank Tashlin*, ed. Roger Garcia (London: British Film Institute, 1994), 92.

42. See Ruth Perlmutter, "Zelig According to Bakhtin," *Quarterly Review of Film and Video*, 12.1–2 (1989), 42–43.

43. Perlmutter, 45, n.1. She cites Bakhtin's *The Dialogic Imagination* in this context.

44. Linda Hutcheon, "An Epilogue: Postmodern Parody: History, Subjectivity, and Ideology," *Quarterly Review of Film and Video*, 12.1–2 (1989), 129.

45. Elayne B. Graham Chaplin, *Monstrous Masculinity? Boys, Men, and Monsters in the Films of Larry Cohen* (University of Sunderland, England, doctoral dissertation, 1993).

# *Chapter 2*

1. For Brodkin's significance, see Desser and Friedman, 166. As they also note, "Much scholarly work remains to be done on television, especially the golden age, a subject of much nostalgia but little analysis of actual programs. The work of Herbert Brodkin remains fascinating *terra incognita* from the perspective of Jewish contributions to American television" (220, n.3). Although certain episodes of "The Defenders," "The Nurses," "Espionage," and "Coronet Blue" are available in archives such as the Museum of Television and Radio in New York, Brodkin's productions are rarely (if ever) screened on television. However, for those remembering the original transmissions (in America and Great Britain) and investigating the archives, the individual episodes do support claims

made for their relevant social concerns. These series represent the best of American television, showing what the medium is really capable of.

2. See Desser and Friedman, 160–223.

3. See Cohen's comments on the script alterations below.

4. Meticulous in dating events throughout the course of *Schindler's List*, Spielberg hypocritically never supplies 1944 as a date influencing Schindler's major efforts to save his Jews. The film also avoids interrogating Schindler's actual personal and historical reasons for acting as he did. Cohen's "Medal for a Turned Coat" is far more mature and analytic. It deserves rediscovery and recognition.

## Chapter 4

1. See Richard Drinnon, *Facing West: The Metaphysics of Indian-Hating and Empire Building* (New York: New American Library, 1980).

2. See Richard Slotkin, *Regeneration Through Violence: The Mythology of the American Frontier, 1600-1860* (Middletown, Connecticut: Wesleyan University Press, 1973), 510–15; and Leslie A. Fiedler, *Love and Death in the American Novel* (New York: Criterion Books, 1960).

3. Robin Wood, *Hollywood from Vietnam to Reagan* (New York: Columbia University Press, 1986), 141.

4. Wood, 97, 141.

5. Further criticisms of DePalma's cinema appear in my *Hearths of Darkness: The Family in the American Horror Film* (New Jersey: Fairleigh Dickinson Press, 1996).

6. See Wood, Hitchcock's Films Revisited (New York: Columbia University Press, 1989), 336–57.

7. Roland Barthes, *Camera Lucida: Reflections on Photography*, Tr. Richard Howard (New York: Hill and Wang, 1981), 92.

8. Barthes, 110.

9. Barthes, 79.

10. Other problems occur in Robson's direction. While a fly wallows on the kitchen floor after imbibing some of the poisoned milk Cathy has spilled, Meg drinks an entire glass without any ill effects. Also, it is unclear how the police trace the rendezvous between Cathy and Kenneth, despite the repeated flashback of the snowball hitting her. Presumably, they must somehow have assumed that the snow on the car windscreen meant that the vehicle must have traveled from the Sierras to the air terminal station.

11. Jaroo's discovery and killing of two gay soldiers sleeping together during a night attack on a military unit exercising "lord of the manor" rights on helpless, attractive, female Mexican villagers is one possible reference. But it is thrown away in a sequence notable only for its manufactured cleverness.

## Chapter 5

1. See Donald Crafton, *Emile Cohl, Caricature and Film* (New Jersey: Princeton University Press, 1990), 10, 46.

2. See Raymond Carney, *American Dreaming: The Films of John Cassavetes and the American Experience* (Berkeley: University of California Press, 1985); and *The Films of John Cassavetes: Pragmatism, Modernism, and the Movies* (New York: Cambridge University Press, 1994).

3. Carney, *American Dreaming*, 6.

4. Carney, *The Films of John Cassavetes*, 24–25.

5. Donald Crafton, *Before Mickey: The Animated Film 1898–1928* (Cambridge, Massachusetts: The MIT Press, 1982), 348.

6. Crafton, *Emile Cohl*, 307.

7. Crafton, 80.

8. See Ernst Scheyer, *Lyonel Feininger: Caricature and Fantasy* (Detroit, Michigan: Wayne State University Press, 1964), 63, 69. Caricature and political commentary also have historical precedents. See Syd Hoff, *Editorial and Political Cartooning* (New York: Stravon Educational Press, 1976), 16–31. For a concise definition of a political cartoon having both a serious and lasting significance, see Charles Press, *The Political Cartoon* (Rutherford, New Jersey: Fairleigh Dickinson University Press, 1981), 23–26.

9. For Neal Adams, Dick Briefer, and John Buscema, see Ron Goulart, *The Great Comic Book Artists* (New York: St. Martin's Press, 1986), 2–3, 14–15, 16–17. According to Buscema, Stan Lee of Marvel Comics recommended that he think in terms of camera angles when drawing his comic strips. It is more than coincidental that Cohen's last feature to date, *The Ambulance* (1990), stars Eric Roberts as a comic-strip artist working for Marvel Comics in a film featuring Stan Lee in a cameo role. For Mike Kaluta and Ogden Whitney, see Ron Goulart, *The Great Comic Book Artists, Volume 2* (New York: St. Martin's Press, 1989), 64–65, 110–111.

10. When talking to Larry Cohen about his method of obtaining good performances from African-American actors, he commented that race never entered into his mind, only acting ability. Raymond Carney's comments concerning critical over-emphasis on racial angles in the films of John Cassavetes also apply to Larry Cohen. Regarding Cassavetes as being "among the most colorblind of filmmakers," Carney notes the following: "In recent American film, only the work of Charles Burnett seems equally free from racial stereotyping. While, for example, in Spike Lee's work, a person's race is the most important fact about him, in Cassavetes and Burnett we are all absolutely equal under the skin." See Carney, *The Films of John Cassavetes*, 286, n.5. The same is equally true for Larry Cohen.

11. See, for example, the Ed Rimer commercial at the end of *The Defenders* episode "Kill or Be Killed." It begins with Rimer addressing the television audience with a microphone as he walks through a desolate junkyard of abandoned cars.

12. The association of better clothing with the gangster's rise to power is a key iconographical feature of the genre, as various examples including *Little Caesar* (1930), *Public Enemy* (1931), *Scarface* (1932), *House of Bamboo* (1955) and *A Better Tomorrow* (1986) show.

13. *Black Caesar* also contains another example of Cohen's interest in radical montage that is worthy of some mention. As Tommy strangles his police assassin, "Irish" (James Dixon), Cohen cuts to repeated shots of a huge digital clock ticking away the last moments of the victim's life. This remains in the footage reused in the opening scenes of *Hell Up in Harlem*. Several cuts to smoke emerging from the mouth of a billboard advertising cigarettes (breath dying away?) is not retained. Although these shots may be dismissed as trivial, they do belong to Cohen's vision of the New York landscape acting as a character in the film and, possibly, ironically commenting on the surrounding scenes.

14. Relatively few contemporary reviews actually discerned the unique nature of *Black Caesar* in relation to what was commonly termed "blaxploitation." However, Brandon Wander noted that "*Black Caesar* exploits blacks without a word of criticism. His empire of drugs and prostitutes is no different from the Mafia before him." (7). Furthermore, in both *Superfly* and *Black Caesar*, "we witness an ebony Horatio Alger story, whose scenario is the ghetto jungle of Social Darwinism."(9) See his interesting article "Black

Dreams: The Fantasy and Ritual of Black Films," *Film* Quarterly, 29 (1975), 2–11. Furthermore, Thomas Doherty also noted the relationship of *Black Caesar* to the "psychological realm of the family drama. Gibbs is defined and determined not by what he does — the consolidation of a nationwide, black criminal empire — but by his familial relationships. Even as he constructs his underground network, his mother dies, his father rejects a reconciliation at her graveside, and his wife runs off with his best friend. McKinney, his childhood nemesis, is now a commissioner on the mob's payroll. He forces Gibb's ex-wife to set him up for a hit." (38) However, although there is no evidence that Tommy actually married his girlfriend, the family relationships are certainly there. Finally, Doherty notes another significant aspect of Tommy's final avenging humiliation of McKinney that supports the family dynamics structuring *Black Caesar*: "But if McKinney's transformation into a black man before he finally succumbs to Gibbs' blows is meant to add irony to the complete revenge, it allows the character to enact the oedipal wish and kill an (equally resented) black patriarch at the same time he is dispatching a white one." (39) In other words, Tommy's revenge is no real victory. He wishes to become a complete white man by killing a surrogate victim for the black father who created him, gave him his non-white identity, and whom he wishes to secretly destroy as his final barrier, denying him entry into capitalist white society. See Thomas Doherty, "The Black Exploitation Picture: *Superfly* and *Black Caesar*," *Ball State University Forum* 24.2 (1983), 30–39.

15. Due to the hasty rewriting of *Black Caesar*'s relationship to *Hell Up in Harlem*, some uncertainty results over whose children they actually are. In the previous film, they are Joe and Helen's children. Since Joe drops out of the picture in the sequel, they appear to be Tommy's children. At least this is what Mr. Gibbs' comment to Helen suggests: "I'm trying not to let them know what their mother did to their father." In his last encounter with Helen, Tommy comments, "She left me for my best friend, Joe. She had two kids." Who the father actually was remains unclear in this film.

16. Tony Williams, "Cohen on Cohen," *Sight and Sound*, 53.1 (1983/84), 23.

17. See Stephen Neale, "Melodrama and Tears," *Screen*, 16 (1986), 21–22.

18. These features are examined in my *Hearths of Darkness: The Family in the American Horror Film* (New Jersey: Fairleigh Dickinson University Press, 1996).

19. Robin Wood, *Hitchcock's Films Revisited* (New York: Columbia University Press, 1989), 321–26.

20. On this device, see François Truffaut, *Hitchcock* (London: Secker and Warburg, 1967), 157–58.

21. On the significance of this term, see Richard Slotkin, *Regeneration Through Violence: The Mythology of the American Frontier, 1600–1860* (Middletown, Connecticut: Wesleyan University Press, 1973).

## Chapter 6

1. I am grateful to Ms. Janelle Webb Cohen for emphasizing this fact during a conversation in New York on March 3, 1995.

2. See Robin Wood, *Hitchcock's Films Revisited*, 301; and Paul Gordon, "Sometimes a Cigar is Not Just a Cigar," *Literature Film Quarterly* 19.4 (1991), 271.

3. See Raymond Bellour, "Hitchcock, The Enunciator," *Camera Obscura* 2 (1977), 66–91.

4. See variously Tania Modleski, *The Women Who Knew Too Much*, 43–56; Wood, 231–32, 240–44; Rhona J. Berenstein, "'I'm Not the Sort of Person Men Marry': Monsters, Queers and Hitchcock's *Rebecca*," *cineACTION* 29 (1992), 82–97; Wood, "Rebecca

Reclaimed for Daphne du Maurier," op. cit., 97–100; and Karen Hollinger, "The Female Oedipal Drama of *Rebecca* from Novel to Film," *Quarterly Review of Film and Video* 14.4 (1993), 17–30.

    5. See *Hollywood*, 105.

    6. See Elayne B. Graham Chaplin, *Monstrous Masculinity? Boys, Men, and Monsters in the Films of Larry Cohen*. Ph.D. dissertation. University of Sunderland (England), 1992, 203–04. To be fair, Wood also notes that if the god of the film "was ever pure, his purity has been corrupted through incarnation in human flesh and the agents he is forced to use (the disciples are businessmen and bureaucrats, the possessed executants are merely destructive)" (106). But Chaplin emphasizes more significant aspects, such as the murderous father's "chillingly detailed confession of trickery and betrayal" (203) when he speaks to Peter, which overwhelms any positive associations suggested in this scene.

    7. For the nature of this concept, see Robin Wood, *Hollywood*, 46–69, 105.

    8. Cosimo Urbano, "A Question of Narrative: Notes on a Radical Horror Parody," *cineACTION*, 37 (1995), 37.

    9. Chaplin, 209.

    10. Wood, 106.

    11. Mikhail Bakhtin, *Problems of Dostoevsky's Poetics* (Minneapolis: University of Minnesota Press, 1984), 193. See also Urbano, 36.

    12. Wood, 98.

    13. Richard Combs, "*The Private Files of J. Edgar Hoover*," *Sight and Sound* 48.3 (1979), 193.

    14. Coombs, 194.

    15. "World of Gods and Monsters," *The American Nightmare*, eds. Richard Lippe and Robin Wood, (Toronto: Festival of Festivals, 1979), 84–85.

    16. See respectively, John A. Lent, *The Asian Film Industry* (Austin, University of Texas Press, 1990), 114, 116; and Tony Williams, "To Live and Die in Hong Kong: The Crisis Cinema of John Woo," *cineACTION* 36 (1995), 44–45.

    17. Wood, *Hollywood*, 113.

## *Chapter 7*

    1. Wood, *Hollywood*, 94.

    2. Wood, 133.

    3. Wood, 94.

    4. See Andrew Britton, "Blissing Out: The Politics of Reaganite Entertainment," *Movie* 31/32 (1986), 1–42; and Douglas Kellner, "Film, Politics, and Ideology: Reflections on Hollywood Film in the Age of Reagan," *The Velvet Light Trap* 27 (1991), 9–24.

    5. I wish to thank David Desser for suggesting this book to me.

    6. Henry Jenkins, *What Made Pistachio Nuts? Early Sound Comedy and the Vaudeville Aesthetic* (New York: University of Columbia Press, 1992), 4.

    7. Jenkins, 5.

    8. Jenkins, 6.

    9. Jenkins, 13. See also *Frank Tashlin*, ed. Roger Garcia (London: British Film Institute, 1994). Tashlin began as a comic-strip artist and worked for Max Fleischer before he entered film, directing Bob Hope, Dean Martin and Jerry Lewis in his many pictures. Michael Selig has drawn attention to the American cultural influences affecting Lewis' films, such as modernist strategies of reflection, "schizophrenic doubling," and parodies of other film genres, as common elements in Hollywood cinema rather than being uniquely

identified with the director. See Selig's highly informative "*The Nutty Professor*: A 'Problem' in Film Scholarship," *The Velvet Light Trap* 26 (1990), 42–56.

    10. Jenkins, 98.

    11. Jenkins, 102.

    12. Mary Douglas, "The Social Control of Cognition: Some Factors of Perception," *Man* (new series) 3(3), 1968, 365.

    13. Stephen Bissette, in conversation with Neil Gaiman and Tom Vietch, "Change or Die," *The One*, ed. Rick Veitch (West Townsend, VT.: King Hell Press), 202. Bissette acclaims Cohen for his "most original ideas" concerning the Superman legend in the *ReSearch* interview. I am grateful to Brad Moore for drawing my attention to this reference.

    14. Frank Krutnik, "The Clown-Prints of Comedy," *Screen* 25. 4–5 (1984), 52–53.

    15. Jenkins, 217.

    16. Jenkins, 241–42.

    17. Jenkins 151.

    18. Kim Newman, "Full Moon High," *Monthly Film Bulletin*, 387.

    19. Wood, 102.

    20. Newman, op. cit.

    21. This was the subject of one of the most interesting *Sam Benedict* episodes, "Read No Evil," featuring Robert Lansing, first broadcast on May 16, 1963.

    22. Wood, 188.

    23. Chaplin, 236.

    24. Fred Camper, "Larry Cohen," *International Directory of Films and Filmmakers*, 160.

    25. See Janet Bergstrom, "Enunciation and Sexual Difference (Part I)," *Camera Obscura* 3/4 (1979), 47–48.

    26. *Classical Hollywood Comedy*, eds. Kristine Brunovska Karnick and Henry Jenkins (New York: Routledge, 1995), 158.

    27. Chaplin quotes Wood's comments on *The Birds* from *Hitchcock's Films Revisited* in her chapter on *Q— The Winged Serpent*. See p. 247.

    28. For this and other references see Chaplin, 250.

    29. Paul Taylor, "*The Stuff*," *Monthly Film Bulletin*, 53 (April 1986), 121.

    30. See Andrew Britton, "Blissing Out: The Politics of Reaganite Entertainment," *Movie*, 31/32 (1986), 1–42.

    31. Dennis Fischer, "Directed, Written, & Produced by Larry Cohen: From Monster Babies to Homicidal Maniacs," *Midnight Marquee*, 34 (Fall 1985), 25. Cohen's targets also included the fast food industry, as the following comment shows: "One of the great moments in this film is where we blow up the Stuff franchise, and on one side there's a Kentucky Fried Chicken and on the other there's a McDonald's. I think that's everybody's subliminal wish — to see a fast food franchise blown to smithereens." See Maitland McDonagh, "Larry Cohen: Thriving Outside the Mainstream," *Film Journal*, 88 ( July 1985), 7.

## Chapter 8

    1. Ephraim Katz, *The International Film Encyclopedia* (New York: Macmillan, 1979), 216. For further information on the cinema of John Cassavetes, see Raymond Carney's two works, *American Dreaming: The films of John Cassavetes and the American Experience* (Berkeley: University of California Press, 1985) and *The Films of John Cassavetes: Pragmatism, Modernism, and the Movies* (New York: Cambridge University Press, 1994).

2. Although the films are never mentioned in the dialogue, *Tomorrow Is Forever* (1946) and *Carousel* (1956) are Fred's main references here.

3. William Rothman, *Hitchcock: The Murderous Gaze* (Cambridge, Massachusetts: Harvard University Press, 1982), 364.

4. See Rothman, 8–9, 292–307.

5. On Sir John's hubris in Hitchcock's *Murder!*, see Rothman, 97–107. It is not accidental that Sir John's theatrical qualities become associated with later Hitchcock villains such as Vandamm in *North by Northwest* (1959).

6. For the significance of this theme, see Raymond Bellour, "Hitchcock, the Enunciator", *Camera Obscura*, 2 (1977), 66–91.

7. Richard Combs, "*Special Effects*," *Monthly Film Bulletin* 53, 627 (April 1986), 158.

# Chapter 9

1. See the review in *Variety*, 329.2 (November 4, 1987), 11, 18. The anonymous reviewer also notes evidence of Cohen's familiar style in scenes using "hidden camera techniques and other evidence of guerrilla filmmaking." For a *New York Times* film reviewer's amazingly inaccurate perceptions, see Vincent Canby, "*Deadly Illusion*," *New York Times*, 137 (October 31, 1987), 10.

2. For an interesting analysis distinguishing between cinematic, critical modernist practices and conservatively oriented pastiche tendencies in film noir, see Leighton Grist, "Moving Targets and Black Widows: Film Noir in Modern Hollywood," *The Book of Film Noir*, Ed. Ian Cameron (New York: Continuum, 1992), 267–85.

3. Raymond Williams, *The Politics of Modernism and Other Essays* (London: Verso, 1989).

4. Elayne B. Graham Chaplin, *Monstrous Masculinity*, 50.

5. This becomes explicit in Stephen's question to prosecutor Ralston (Gerrit Graham): "Do you deny you have execution squads roaming the country to kill the infants on sight?"

6. Chaplin, 49.

7. Chaplin, 60.

8. For the significance of Van Meer as an alternative father figure, see Chaplin, 190–94.

9. According to a letter by Max Allan Collins published in *Psychotronic* 12 (1992), 5, *Deadly Illusion* is based on a script by Cohen, which he derived from the Mickey Spillane novel *Vengeance Is Mine*. Had *I, the Jury* not encountered problems, this would have been Cohen's second Mickey Spillane movie. Collins notes, "Cohen merely changed the detective from white to black, and the name Hammer to Hamberger!" Furthermore, *Deadly Illusion* uses an incident derived from the original *I, the Jury* screenplay: "the leap out of the window of the RCA building with the hero's fall broken by the giant Christmas tree at Rockefeller Center." However, although Collins is correct in his research, Hamberger now bears very little relationship to his Spillane prototype. Furthermore, although Collins criticizes Cohen for complaining about *I, the Jury*'s sex and violence scenes that derive from the original screenplay, he ignores the different way Cohen would have treated them had he remained as director. A Mickey Spillane movie without sex and violence would be a very curious product. But the actual screenplay does reveal several instances of Cohen attempting to use these aspects as a means of subverting the Mike Hammer character. Richard Heffron's direction merely dwells on their gratuitous aspects.

10. See Whitney Stine, *Conversations with Bette Davis* (New York: Pocket Books, 1990), 264–67; Barbara Leaming, *Bette Davis* (New York: Simon and Schuster, 1992), 348–53; and Randall Reise, *Bette Davis: Her Life from A to Z* (Chicago: Contemporary Books, 1993), 460–69. Despite Bette Davis's comments on talk shows about Cohen's abilities as a director, the evidence clearly shows that the star, not the director, was at fault. See the sworn statement by Bette Davis, taken by a lawyer for an insurance company, held at the offices of Gottlieb, Schiff, Bomser and Sendroff, P.C., June 14, 1988, p. 4, where Davis admits that she began the film with full knowledge of the dental problems that caused her to abandon the production. On pages 10 and 14, Davis admits that she did not feel well enough to return to the film after Cohen generously allowed her to "go east" and have the problems fixed.

11. See Henry Jenkins, *What Made Pistachio Nuts: Early Sound Comedy and the Vaudeville Aesthetic* (New York: Columbia University Press, 1992), 245–76; and Kathleen K. Rowe, *The Unruly Woman: Gender and the Genres of Laughter* (Austin: University of Texas Press, 1995).

12. See *Wicked Stepmother*, original story and screenplay by Larry Cohen (undated), 1.

13. *Wicked Stepmother*, 85.

14. *Wicked Stepmother*, 22.

15. The Maltese Falcon on his desk does not appear in the original screenplay. See *Wicked Stepmother*, 41–43.

## Chapter 10

1. Paul Taylor, "*I, the Jury*," *Monthly Film Bulletin*, 49, 279 (April 1982), 63.

2. *I, the Jury*, original screenplay by Larry Cohen, 117–8.

3. For information on Steranko's "psychedelic ... bigger than life" comic style, see Ron Goulart, *The Great Comic Book Artists* (New York: St. Martin's Press, 1986), 102. Taylor notes that Cohen originally offered the role of Mike Hammer to Clint Eastwood.

4. *I, the Jury*, 84.

5. For similar associations in Scorsese's *Raging Bull*, see Robin Wood, *Hollywood from Vietnam to Reagan* (New York: Columbia University Press, 1986), 245–58.

6. In the current film, an overhead shot shows Mike reading the file. He then tears it up. The original screenplay contains these lines spoken by Dr. Bennett: She tells Mike that Jack "would have done anything for you ... followed you around, dogging your tracks, trying his best to act like you, to play the part. Myrna knew. Any wife would know. She came here with him. She tried her best. But he had to face himself before he could be helped, and that's something he wasn't prepared to do." (55).

7. The device of robbers wearing rubber masks depicting the president also appeared some years later in Kathryn Bigelow's *Point Break* (1991). But, in this instance, the robbers wear masks depicting other American presidents such as Kennedy, Johnson, Carter, and Reagan—in addition to Richard M. Nixon!

8. Again, Cohen's Hitchcock appropriations mirror ideas contained in William Rothman, *Hitchcock: The Murderous Gaze* (Cambridge, Massachusetts: Harvard University Press, 1982) concerning theater, performance, and murder.

9. For the significance of this system of exchange, see Eve Kosofsky Sedgwick, *Between Men: English Literature and Homosocial Desire* (New York: Columbia University Press, 1985).

10. See *Cordell*, original story and screenplay by Larry Cohen, (1987).

11. Paul Taylor, "Maniac Cop," *Monthly Film Bulletin*, 56 (1989).

12. The screenplay emphasizes this point ,showing Cohen's utilization of another Hitchcock plot device. We had not expected to see McCrae die. He is our hero and yet he is being killed" (62).

13. For relevant details, see the chapter "Cohen on Cohen," and Steve Voce,"William Lustig," *Psychotronic*, 20 (1995), 58–59.

14. See Philip Strick, "Guilty as Sin," *Sight and Sound*, 45–46: "Left to his own devices, Cohen could have been expected to film all this with a vibrant delirium, but with Sidney Lumet at the helm the production becomes, despite itself, a class act. Curiously uncritical of the story's absurdities ... Lumet is as always more interested in immediacy than in anticipation."

15. Strick, 46.

## Chapter 11

1. I wish to thank Larry Cohen for generously allowing me access to these three plays.

2. According to Larry Cohen, (in a telephone conversation on June 20, 1995) Chapman directed the opening night performance and then left the production, leaving Cohen in charge.

3. See *Motive*, act one, scene one, pages one and two. The abbreviations in parenthesis refer to acts, scenes, and pages in the script.

4. The reference is actually in the script. See 2-2-14.

5. See Terry Curtis Fox, "*Trick*," *Variety*, 24.8 (Feb. 19, 1979), 85. Fox faults the play for the climax's failure to "achieve the glee or horror that would make the assumption threatening to the audience." However, Cohen's meanings are implicit, leaving his audience to work out the implications for themselves.

6. I wish to thank Janelle Webb Cohen for allowing me access to a copy of the 1986 version.

## Chapter 12

1. See Franco Minganti, "Gods and Demons: I Film Di Larry Cohen," *Cinema e Cinema*, 47 (Dec. 1986), 17.

2. Donald Liebensen, "Good Films That Go Straight to Video," *Chicago Tribune*, September 28 (1993). I am grateful to Mike Robbins for this clipping.

3. Five years before making *The Ambulance*, Cohen spoke about filming a comic-strip adaptation: "I recently did an adaptation involving the comic-book character Dr. Strange for Kings Row pictures because I was interested in working with Stan Lee, who created Spiderman." See Maitland McDonagh, "Larry Cohen: Thriving Outside the Mainstream," *Film Journal*, 88 (July 1985), 7.

# Selected Bibliography

Bakhtin, Mikhail. *The Dialogic Imagination*. Austin: University of Texas Press, 1985.

Barthes, Roland. *Camera Lucida: Reflections on Photography*. Tr. Richard Howard. New York: Hill & Wang, 1981.

Bazin, Andre. "La politique des auteurs," *The New Wave*. Ed. Peter Graham. New York: Viking, 1968.

Beard, William, and Piers Handling. "The Interview," *The Shape of Rage: The Films of David Cronenberg*. Ed. Piers Handling. New York: Zoetrope, 1983.

Beaupre, Lee. "*Hell Up in Harlem*," *Variety*, 273 (Jan. 2, 1974).

Berenstein, Rhona J. "'I'm Not the Sort of Person Men Marry': Monsters, Queers, and Hitchcock's *Rebecca*," *cineACTION*, 29 (1992).

Bergstrom, Janet. "Enunciation and Sexual Difference, Part I," *Camera Obscura*, 3/4 (1979).

Bellour, Raymond. "Hitchcock, the Enunciator," *Camera Obscura*, 2 (1977).

Bruce, Bryan. "It's Alive," *Movie*, 31/32 (1986).

Camper, Fred. "Reel Life: The Low Budget Genius of American Film," *Chicago Reader* (June 12, 1987).

_____. "Larry Cohen," *International Directory of Films and Filmmakers*. New York: Macmillan, 1991.

Canby, Vincent. "*Deadly Illusion*," *New York Times*, 137 (October 31, 1987).

Carney, Raymond. *American Dreaming: The Films of John Cassavetes and the American Experience*. Berkeley: University of California Press, 1985.

_____. *The Films of John Cassavetes: Pragmatism, Modernism, and the Movies*. New York: Cambridge University Press, 1994.

Caughie, John. Ed. *Theories of Authorship*. London: Routledge & Kegan Paul, 1981.

Chaplin, Elayne. "*Demon, aka God Told Me To*," *Movie*, 34/35 (1990).

_____ B. Graham. *Monstrous Masculinity? Boys, Men, and Monsters in the Films of Larry Cohen*. Ph.D. dissertation. University of Sunderland (UK), 1992.

Cohen, Sarah Blacher, ed. *Jewish Wry: Essays in Jewish Humor*. Bloomington: Indiana University Press, 1987.

Cohn, Lawrence. "Cohen's first big buck pic: *I, the Jury*," *Variety* (April 15, 1981).

Coleman, John. "Inside the Tent," *New Statesman*, 97 (May 25, 1979).

Combs, Richard. "*The Private Files of J. Edgar Hoover*," *Sight and Sound*, 48.3 (1979).

_____. "*Special Effects*," *Monthly Film Bulletin*, 53.627 (April 1986).

Corliss, Richard. *Talking Pictures: Screenwriters in the American Cinema, 1927–1973.* Woodstock, New York: The Overlook Press, 1974.

Crafton, Donald. *Before Mickey: The Animated Film, 1898–1928.* Cambridge, Massachusetts: The MIT Press, 1982.

_____. *Emile Cohl, Caricature and Film.* Princeton, New Jersey: Princeton University Press, 1990.

Crane, Margaret. "*God Told Me To,*" *Research #10: Incredibly Strange Films,* 1986.

Crist, Judith. "Bewitched, Bothered, and Therefore Bewildered," *New York,* 7 (Jan. 21, 1974).

Daskalogrigorakis, Grigoris. "Routine Work, Routine Gorin," *The Spectator,* 8.2 (1988).

Desser, David, and Lester D. Friedman. *American Jewish Filmmakers: Traditions and Trends.* Chicago: University of Illinois Press, 1993.

Doherty, Thomas. "The Black Exploitation Picture: *Superfly* and *Black Caesar,*" *Ball State University Forum,* 24.2 (1983).

Douglas, Mary. "The Social Control of Cognition: Some Factors in Joke Perception," *Man,* (new series) 3(3), 1968.

Drinnon, Richard. *Facing West: The Metaphysics of Indian-Hating and Empire-Building.* New York: New American Library, 1980.

Eisenberg, Adam. "Year of the Werewolf: *Full Moon High,*" *Cinefantastique,* 10.3 (1980).

Eisner, Will. *Comics and Sequential Art.* Princeton, Wisconsin: The Kitchen Sink Press, 1992.

Ellison, Harlan. *The Glass Teat.* Manchester, England: Savoy Books, 1978.

Erens, Patricia. "You Could Die Laughing: Jewish Humor and Film," *East-West Film Journal,* 2.1 (1987).

Espinosa, Julio Garcia. "For an Imperfect Cinema," *25 Years of the New Latin Cinema.* Ed. Michael Chanan. London: British Film Institute and Channel 4 Television, 1983.

Everitt, David. "The Arresting Saga of *Maniac Cop 2,*" *Fangoria,* 96 (1990).

Fiedler, Leslie. *Love and Death in the American Novel.* New York: Criterion Books, 1960.

Fischer, Dennis. "Directed, Written, & Produced by Larry Cohen: From Monster Babies to Homicidal Messiahs," *Midnight Marquee,* 34 (Fall 1985).

_____. "*The Ambulance,*" *Cinefantastique,* 21.5 (1991).

_____. *Horror Film Directors, 1931–1990.* Jefferson, North Carolina: McFarland & Co., 1991.

_____. "Bernard Herrmann: Director Larry Cohen Talks," *Soundtrack: The Collector's Quarterly,* 11 (September 1992).

Fox, Terry Curtis. "*Trick,*" *Variety,* 24.8 (Feb. 19, 1979).

Gaiman, Neil, Tom Veitch, and Stephen Bissette, "Change or Die," *The One.* Ed. Rick Veitch. West Townsend, VT: King Hell Press, 1989.

Garcia, Roger, ed. *Frank Tashlin.* London: British Film Institute, 1994.

Gordon, Paul. "Sometimes a Cigar is Not Just a Cigar," *Literature Film Quarterly* 19.4 (1991).

Goulart, Ron. *The Great Comic Book Artists.* New York: St. Martin's Press, 1986.

_____. *The Great Comic Book Artists, Volume 2.* New York: St. Martin's Press, 1989.

Grist, Leighton. "Moving Targets and Black Widows: Film Noir in Modern Hollywood," *The Book of Film Noir*. Ed. Ian Cameron. New York: Continuum, 1992.

Hege. "*The Private Files of J. Edgar Hoover*," *Variety*, 294 (Feb. 7, 1979).

Henderson Brian. "Cartoon and Narrative in the Films of Frank Tashlin and Preston Sturges," *Comedy/Cinema/Theory*. Ed. Andrew Horton. Berkeley: University of California Press, 1991.

Higashi, Sumiko. *Cecil B. DeMille and American Culture: The Silent Era*. Berkeley, University of California Press, 1994.

Hoberman, J. "God Told Him To," *Village Voice*, 31 (August 5, 1986).

_____. "Calling all Cohen heads (Q)," *Village Voice*, 27 (Oct. 19, 1982).

_____. "Frank Tashlin: vulgar modernist," *Frank Tashlin*. Ed. Roger Garcia. London: British Film Institute, 1994.

Hoff, Syd. *Editorial and Political Cartooning*. New York: Stravon Educational Press, 1976.

Hollinger, Karen. "The Female Oedipal Drama of *Rebecca* from Novel to Film," *Quarterly Review of Film and Video*, 14.4 (1993).

Horton, Andrew, ed. *Comedy/Cinema/Theory*. Berkeley: University of California Press, 1991.

Hutcheon, Linda. *A Theory of Parody: The Teachings of Twentieth-Century Art Forms*. New York: Methuen, 1985.

_____. *A Poetics of Postmodernism: History, Theory, Fiction*. New York: Routledge, 1988.

_____. *The Politics of Postmodernism*. New York: Methuen, 1990.

_____. "An Epilogue: Postmodern Parody: History, Subjectivity, and Ideology," *Quarterly Review of Film and Video*, 12.1–2 (1989).

Jenkins, Henry. *What Made Pistachio Nuts? Early Sound Comedy and the Vaudeville Aesthetic*. New York: Columbia University Press, 1992.

Juno, Andrea and Vale. "Interview: Larry Cohen," *Research #10: Incredibly Strange Films* (1986).

Kael, Pauline. "Bone," *New Yorker*, 49 (Jan. 21, 1974).

Karnick, Kristine Brunovska, and Henry Jenkins. *Classical Hollywood Comedy*. New York: Routledge, 1995.

Karp, Alan. "It Came from the Refrigerator: Larry Cohen Talks About '*The Stuff*,'" *Box Office*, 121 (July 7, 1985).

Kellner, Douglas. "Film, Politics, and Ideology: Reflections on Hollywood Film in the Age of Reagan," *The Velvet Light Trap*, 27 (1991).

Krutnik, Frank. "The Clown Prints of Comedy," *Screen*, 25.4–5 (1984).

Leaming, Barbara. *Bette Davis*. New York: Simon and Schuster, 1992.

Lent, John. *The Asian Film Industry*. Austin, University of Texas Press, 1990.

Liebenson, Donald. "Good Films That Go Straight to Video," *Chicago Tribune*, October 28, 1993.

McCloud, Scott. *Understanding Comics*. Massachusetts: The Kitchen Sink Press, 1983.

McDonagh, Maitland. "Larry Cohen: Thriving Outside the Mainstream," *Film Journal* 88 (July 1985).

_____. "Dispatches from the Cohen Zone," *Psychotronic*, 11 (Fall 1991).

McGillivray, David. "*Godfather of Harlem*," *Monthly Film Bulletin*, 41. 484 (May 1974).

Mack, "*It's Alive*," *Variety*, 276 (October 16, 1974).
Maslin, Janet. "*The Private Files of J. Edgar Hoover*," *New York Times*, 129 (March 11, 1980).
Milne, Tom. "*It Lives Again*," *Monthly Film Bulletin* 45.539 (December 1978).
Minganti, Franco. "Gods and Demons: I Film di Larry Cohen," *Cinema e Cinema*, 47 (December 1986).
Modleski, Tania. *The Women Who Knew Too Much: Hitchcock and Feminist Theory*. New York: Methuen, 1988.
Neale, Stephen. "Melodrama and Tears," *Screen*, 27 (1986).
_____ and Frank Krutnik, *Popular Film and Television Comedy*. London: Routledge, 1990.
Nebane, Mary F. "Blacks don't want to see losers," *New York Times*, 122, section 2 (May 6, 1973).
Newman, Kim. "*Full Moon High*," *Monthly Film Bulletin*, 53.635 (December 1986).
_____. "*Maniac Cop 2*," *Monthly Film Bulletin*, 58.683 (Jan. 1991).
Perlmutter, Ruth. "*Zelig* According to Bakhtin," *Quarterly Review of Film and Video*, 12.1–2 (1989).
Press, Charles. *The Political Cartoon*. Rutherford, New Jersey: Fairleigh Dickinson University Press, 1981.
Riese, Randall. *Bette Davis: Her Life from A to Z*. Chicago: Contemporary Books, 1993.
Rignalda, Donald. *Fighting and Writing the Vietnam War*. Jackson, Mississippi: University of Mississippi Press, 1994.
Rothman, William. *Hitchcock—The Murderous Gaze*, Cambridge, Massachusetts: Harvard University Press, 1982.
Rowe, Kathleen K. *The Unruly Woman: Gender and the Genres of Laughter*. Austin: University of Texas Press, 1995.
Scheyer, Ernst. *Lyonel Feininger: Caricature and Fantasy*. Detroit, Michigan: Wayne State University Press, 1964.
Schlesinger Jr., Arthur M. "A Phantasmagoric J. Edgar Hoover," *Saturday Review*, 5 (Feb. 18, 1978).
Sedgwick, Eve Kosofsky. *Between Men: English Literature and Homosocial Desire*. New York: Columbia University Press, 1985.
Selig, Michael. "*The Nutty Professor*: A 'Problem' in Film Scholarship," *The Velvet Light Trap*, 26 (1990).
Shapiro, Marc. "On the Beat with *Maniac Cop*," *Fangoria*, 72.8 (1988).
Shechner, Mark. "Dear Mr. Einstein: Jewish Comedy and the Contradictions of Culture," *From Hester Street to Hollywood*. Ed. Sarah Blacher Cohen. Bloomington: Indiana University Press, 1983.
Slotkin, Richard. *Regeneration Through Violence: The Mythology of the American Frontier, 1600–1860*. Middletown, Connecticut: Wesleyan University Press, 1973.
Stine, Whitney. *Conversations with Bette Davis*. New York: Pocket Books, 1990.
Strick, Philip. "*Q—The Winged Serpent*," *Monthly Film Bulletin*, 50 (March 1983).
_____. "*Guilty as Sin*," *Sight and Sound*, 4.1 (New Series) (Jan. 1994).
Swires, Steve. "The Mutant Master Cometh: Part One," *Fangoria*, 67.7 (1987).
_____. "The Private Files of Larry Cohen: Part Two," *Fangoria*, 68.7 (1987).
Taubin, Amy. "Shooting script: the lion sleeps tonight," *Village Voice*, 34 (May 9, 1989).

Taylor, Paul. "*The Private Files of J. Edgar Hoover*," *Monthly Film Bulletin*, 46.541 (1979).

———. "*I, the Jury*," *Monthly Film Bulletin*, 49.279 (April 1982).

———. "*The Stuff*," *Monthly Film Bulletin*, 53.627 (April 1986).

———. "Hitchcock, humor and sit-com, *Monthly Film Bulletin*, 53 (April 1986).

———. "*Maniac Cop*", *Monthly Film Bulletin*, 65 (Feb. 1989).

Taylor, Paul, Christopher Wicking, and Tise Vahimagi, "Checklist 117 — Larry Cohen," *Monthly Film Bulletin*, 46 (April 1979).

Truffaut, François. *Hitchcock*. London: Secker & Warburg, 1967.

Urbano, Cosimo. "A Question of Narrative: Notes on a Radical Horror Parody," *cine-ACTION*, 37 (1995).

Vahimagi, Tise, and Paul Taylor. "Checklist 131— Larry Cohen (Part II)," *Monthly Film Bulletin*, 50 (March 1983).

van Gelder, Laurence. "At the Movies — Larry Cohen Incognito," *New York Times*, 136 (September 25, 1987).

Verrill, Addison. "Says under $8 million films bore majors," *Variety*, 279 ( July 30 1975).

Voce, Steve. "William Lustig Interview," *Psychotronic*, 20 (1995).

Wander, Brandon. "Black Dreams: The Fantasy and Ritual of Black Films," *Film Quarterly*, 29 (1975).

Wells, Jeffrey. "Larry Cohen: from hip pocket movies to ACP's *I, the Jury*," *The Film Journal*, 84.18 (May 4, 1981).

———. "Larry Cohen, Like A Cat: The Writer/Director of UFD's *Q* on Life in the Jungle," *The Film Journal*, 85 (Oct. 20, 1982).

Williams, Raymond. *Keywords: A Vocabulary of Culture and Society*. Revised edition. New York: Oxford University Press, 1986.

———. *The Politics of Modernism and Other Essays*. London: Verso, 1989.

Williams, Tony. "Cohen on Cohen," *Sight and Sound*, 53.1 (1983/1984).

———. "To Live and Die in Hong Kong: The Crisis Cinema of John Woo," *cine-ACTION*, 36 (1995).

———. *Hearths of Darkness: The Family in the American Horror Film*. Rutherford, New Jersey: Fairleigh Dickinson University Press, 1996.

Wood, Robin. "Gods and Monsters," *Film Comment*, 14 (1978).

———. "World of Gods and Monsters," *The American Nightmare*. Ed. Robin Wood and Richard Lippe. Toronto: Festival of Festivals, 1979.

———. "Cronenberg: A Dissenting View," *The Shape of Rage: The Films of David Cronenberg*. Ed. Piers Handling. New York: Zoetrope, 1983.

———. *Hollywood from Vietnam to Reagan*. New York: Columbia University Press, 1986.

———. *Hitchcock's Films Revisited*. New York: Columbia University Press, 1989.

———. "*Rebecca* Reclaimed for Daphne du Maurier," *cineACTION*, 29 (1992).

———, and Richard Lippe. "Larry Cohen Interview," *Movie* 31/32 (1986).

# Index